THE WOLVES OF HEAVEN

THE CIVILIZATION OF THE AMERICAN INDIAN SERIES

Blue, blue light far away
Blue, blue light far away
Blue, blue light far away
Downward the spirit came
Downward the spirit came
Downward the spirit came
Spinning, spinning, spinning
Spinning, spinning, spinning
Spinning, spinning, spinning
Earth, beautiful earth.

—EVENK SHAMAN'S SONG, IKENIPKE
CEREMONY, NORTHERN SIBERIA

BY KARL H. SCHLESIER

Stilgeschichtliche Einordnung der Nazca Vasenmalereien: Beitrag zur Geschichte der Hochkulturen des vorkolumbischen Peru (Rome, 1959)
(coauthor) *The Rights of the Indians of the Americas* (Amsterdam, 1980)
Die Wölfe des Himmels (Cologne, 1985)
The Wolves of Heaven: Cheyenne Shamanism, Ceremonies, and Prehistoric Origins (Norman, 1987)

LIBRARY OF CONGRESS CATALOGING-IN-PUBLICATION DATA

Schlesier, Karl H.
    The wolves of heaven.

    (The Civilization of the American Indian series; #183)
    Translation of: Die Wölfe des Himmels.
    Bibliography: p. 193
    Includes index.
    1. Cheyenne Indians—Religion and mythology. 2. Cheyenne Indians—Rites and ceremonies. 3. Cheyenne Indians—Antiquities. 4. Shamanism. 5. Indians of North America—Antiquities. I. Title. II. Series: Civilization of the American Indian series; v. 183.

E99.C53S23   1987   299'.78   86-27252
ISBN 0—8061—2057—6 (alk. paper)

"Nanēhov meohotoxc" ("I am the star of dawn")

THE WOLVES
OF HEAVEN

*Cheyenne Shamanism, Ceremonies,
and Prehistoric Origins*

By Karl H. Schlesier

Drawings by Wah-pah-nah-yah, Dick West

UNIVERSITY OF OKLAHOMA PRESS : NORMAN AND LONDON

For *vonoom*. For my parents who are part of it, Karl and Maria Schlesier, Edward and Minnie Red Hat. "Haho naheve." For the Tsistsistas, who have been there for a very long time and who should be there in the future.

Contents

Illustrations

MAPS

Preface

THIS BOOK deals with the early Tsistsistas (Cheyenne) times in the Plains. Tsistsistas is the name the Cheyennes use to denote themselves as a people separate from other peoples and as participants in a unique cultural tradition. The word Tsistsistas derives from the root *zes* (pronounced like *ts* in *colts*), meaning "something extended, pointing forward, drawn out" (Petter 1915:228). In contrast, the term Cheyenne, by which the tribe generally is addressed, stems from the Sioux name given to them, in Lakota Shahi-yena, Shai-ena, or Shai-ela, meaning "people of alien speech" (Mooney 1907:362). Although the term Cheyenne includes all members of this tribe on tribal rolls in Oklahoma and Montana, the term Tsistsistas excludes the Suhtai branch of Northern Cheyennes. The Suhtais, originally an independent tribe, associated themselves with the Tsistsistas during the eighteenth century. They did not become Tsistsistas, however. Descendants of this branch perform in Tsistsistas ceremonies to the present as Suhtais, not as Tsistsistas. Because of the time period under consideration here, the term Tsistsistas is used in this book.

This book focuses on the transition period of people becoming Tsistsistas from an earlier population (Proto-Tsistsistas). This transition took place in the Dakotas, after, linguistically speaking, bands of Western Algonquian taiga hunters arrived in the northeastern portion of the Plains from the north. Whether they were a people with shared ethnic boundaries upon their arrival cannot be deduced. They became Tsistsistas through the gift of an earth-giving ceremony, the Massaum, which required the formation of an ethnic entity closed to outsiders, an entity that had to be maintained over time. This event took place sometime between 500 and 300 B.C.

The definition of the Massaum as an earth-giving ceremony, of its importance for the development of the Tsistsistas as a people, and of the time and place of the transition expounded in this book contradicts *all* of the extant literature on the Cheyennes. That literature assumes that Tsistsistas institutions emphasized by ethnographers during reservation-period fieldwork were initiated by the tribe after its removal from the Minnesota River area to the Missouri River and the Black Hills during the eighteenth century, thus preceding the beginning of reservation time by little more than a century. The flat historical perspective extolled in the literature denies Tsistsistas cultural depth and perseverance over a span of time comparable to that of nation-states.

The question what Tsistsistas culture might have been before the year 1700 had never been seriously raised by anthropologists or historians until I began research for this book. The literature sees them as a cluster of bands, not yet a people, coming out of empty space, apparently without a culture, and then, during the course of the eighteenth century, achieving ethnic unity and a Plains-adapted culture by pragmatically assembling parts and pieces learned from Indian groups already present in the region. These fallacious speculations are taught in Oklahoma classrooms and elsewhere as scientific facts. Thus Cheyenne children have been forced to believe that their ancestors came into the grasslands late, after Europeans had already made their appearance there, that they were recent immigrants from elsewhere, that the Tsistsistas never possessed sovereignty and therefore should not claim special rights to parts of their former range.

This book deals not with the factual Tsistsistas' reentry into the mixed-grass prairie during the eighteenth century or with the episode of their absence but with the Tsistsistas' presence in the same region at a much earlier time. It reconstructs the Massaum, thereby allowing a reinterpretation of Tsistsistas culture acceptable to the Tsistsistas, and a delineation of much older pre-Massaum (Proto-Tsistsistas) cultural elements as well as of those that came into being with the Massaum.

It also places the Tsistsistas' world understanding in the context of Algonquian thought and traces the history of this language family through the archaeological record to its first manifestations in North America around 8000 B.C. In a concise comparison of the Tsistsistas world view (here representing Algonquian groups) with that of northern Siberian groups, in which 134 religious and philosophical categories are listed, it is documented that they shared in a common heritage that survived in both North America and northern Siberia through the European invasions and in significant aspects to the present.

This book superimposes Tsistsistas cultural categories, many of which are defined and explained here for a first time, on archaeological remains in the northern Plains, thus establishing the Tsistsistas presence there during the period from about 500 B.C. to A.D. 800. It is hoped that this effort furthers the understanding by students of the cultural history of the Middle Missouri and northern Plains region during the Late Archaic, or Late Early Woodland and subsequent periods, because early Tsistsistas ceremonialism influenced other early cultures that entered the area from the east and southeast.

The Massaum (derived from the word *massa'ne,* "crazy" or acting contrary to normal; see Grinnell 1923, 2:285; Petter 1915:300, 313–14) is the most elusive of Tsistsistas tribal ceremonies. There are a number of reasons for this.

One is that the ceremony disappeared over fifty years ago. The last performance was held in Montana in 1911 and in Oklahoma in 1927. The second reason is that from the beginning of the Tsistsistas reservation period in the 1870s to the final performances the ceremony was conducted only a very few times both in Oklahoma and in Montana. Petter (1915:335–36), writing in 1914, says that it had not been held "for over 22 years among the Southern Cheyenne." Curtis (1911:115), commenting on the Montana situation, mentions that it had been "long obsolete until reenacted in the summer of 1909" (the next-to-last performance there). A third reason is that during the hard decades preceding reservation time, from the 1830s to the 1870s, because of incessant warfare and the destruction of human life by epidemics of smallpox, measles, cholera, and the like, the ceremony was held only sporadically. A fourth reason is that throughout this time period, that is, for nearly a full century, the ceremony was perhaps never conducted according to its full requirements.

After 1934, when external pressure on the Tsistsistas subsided somewhat and religious freedom of Indian tribes was recognized through the Indian Reorganization Act, the Massaum did not return. Its complexity and the extermination by whites of Plains animals that had to be participants in the ceremony are factors leading to its termination.

Considering the facts given here, ethnographers had little opportunity to observe a Massaum, and none at all to record a complete one. Grinnell's (1923, 2:285–336) account of the 1911 Montana Massaum is the only careful description of the ceremony published until now. His work, as is usual for him, is excellent. The ceremony, however, was seriously flawed by mistakes and omissions, and the priests explained nothing to him.

This book makes use of all written sources on the Tsistsistas and of information from the great volume of works on Middle Missouri and northern Plains ethnology, ethnohistory, prehistory, and linguistics. In addition, Tsistsistas ceremonial men and women provided important testimony.

This book would not have been possible without my action anthropology engagement with the Tsistsistas, which began in 1969 and continues (Schlesier 1974, 1980b, 1981). I began it in the tradition of the Chicago school, where I had been a student of Sol Tax and an eyewitness to the end of the Fox Project, but it appears that I have gone beyond it. This is not the place to elaborate on it especially, because my action anthropology "project" has been discussed relatively widely elsewhere. It is, perhaps, the place to thank Sol for what he taught me and for the strength that he passed on to me. In this book I have combined action anthropology with the best principles of the cultural anthropological method—those of cognitive anthropology. This approach uses language itself, here the Tsistsistas language, as the datum of the description and bases interpretation on cognitive categories and mental structures inherent in the language.

As a consequence, and to verify the authenticity of my challenging reinterpretation of Tsistsistas world perception and cultural features, it was essential to use Tsistsistas terms here as key elements of the data. Most are not of common Tsistsistas language but belong to the hidden language of *ononeovätaneo,* the esoteric group of old that comprised the shamans (*zemaheonevesso*) and persons working for the sacred (*maheonhetaneo*). Petter long ago collected and published many of them in his dictionary. I have invoked them not without hesitation. They are, however, the undeniable messengers of truth. Without their protection I would have been seen as standing on shaky ground. Their being revealed here, in another positive way, will return them for discussion and reflection to a wide Tsistsistas audience, including those Cheyennes who have forgotten much.

This book could not have been written without the compassion and support of Edward Red Hat and his family. Keeper of *nimā-henan,* the sacred arrows, he instructed me in Tsistsistas religion from his first visit to my house in Wichita on October 15, 1971, to his death on February 24, 1982. My work on the Massaum and Tsistsistas beginnings started when he placed me in the Massaum position in a ceremony held at the Tsistsistas sacred mountain, Nowah'wus (Bear Butte, South Dakota), on September 24, 1979. He guided my search into the past with a keen, unflinching interest. To him and to my wife, Claire, I owe more than I can say. Our daughters, Sedna and Sibylle, and my mothers were with us in Tsistsistas country at important occasions.

I am grateful to Bill Red Hat, Jr., Ted J. Brasser, Gordon M. Day, L. Adrien Hannus, E. Leigh Syms, and James V. Wright, who commented on the manuscript with knowledge and vigor. James H. Howard had agreed to read the manuscript, but he passed away before he could do so.

At Wichita State University, I thank Martin Reif, Frederick Sudermann, John Breazeale, Lloyd Benningfield, and Paul Magelli, who trusted me and who gave me the time I needed and some financial help when it was urgent. I am grateful to the Stiftung Volkswagenwerk for a grant that made possible basic research on the issues explored. At the University of Oklahoma, John H. Moore was helpful whenever I called upon him.

The lot of making visible in drawings crucial moments of his people's past fell to Dick West, my friend, who had seen a Massaum in Oklahoma when he was a boy. It is one of the many strange occurrences related to this book that he had already painted for me the sacred runners of the great ceremony before we ever met.

KARL H. SCHLESIER

Wichita, Kansas

Pronunciation Guide

RODOLPHE PETTER's *English-Cheyenne Dictionary* (1915) and *Cheyenne Grammar* (1952) are the classic reference works on these subjects because they achieved a high degree of accuracy. Because of this I have generally followed his spelling of Tsistsistas words. Where I added some which he had not included, I used his rules of transcription. Each letter written is pronounced.

That Petter was a native speaker of German may have been an advantage because the Tsistsistas sound system is much closer to German than to English; vowels have the same sound as those in German. Petter's tendency to capitalize some Tsistsistas nouns is perhaps due to his own language background. I found it useful to do the same in certain instances to emphasize the special quality of a specific term. Moore (1974:iv) observed in a tongue-in-cheek statement that if a non-Tsistsistas speaks Tsistsistas according to Petter's instructions he will have a slight German accent.

The following is a key to the Tsistsistas alphabet as written by Petter (1915:vi).

a, as in *papa; -â-* = *a* + *o,* pronounced like *ou* in *house; -ä-* = *a* + *e,* pronounced like *I; -ā-* is a long *a; -á-* (hiatus) is *a* followed by a short gasp; *-à-* is *a* spoken with expiring breath.

b, as in *babe.*

c, is used to express the combined sound of *c* and *h,* as in *church,* but softer.

d, as in *dad.*

e, as in *prey; -ē-* is long *e,* similar to *a* in *ate; -é-* is *e* followed by a short gasp (hiatus).

g, as in *go.*

h, as in *hate,* with strong aspirate sound.

i, as in *pit.*

k, as in *key.*

m, as in *moment.*

n, as in *none.*

o, as in *obey;* -ō- is long like *o* in *home;* -ô- = *o* + *e,* pronounced like *oy* in
      decoy; -ó- is *o* with hiatus; -ò- is *o* with expired breath.
p, as in *paper.*
q, similar to *coo* in *coop,* but expired.
s, as in *sense;* -s'- like *ss* but separated by a hiatus; -ŝ- as *sh* in *she.*
t, as in *table.*
v, like *f* in *of.*
x, as *ch* in the German *ach.*
y, as in *year.*
z, as *ts* or German *z.*

THE WOLVES OF HEAVEN

1. Tsistsistas World Description and Shamanism[1]

> *Wolf I am.*
> *In darkness*
> *in light*
> *wherever I search*
> *wherever I run*
> *wherever I stand*
> *everything*
> *will be good*
> *because Maheo*
> *protects us.*
> *Ea ea ea ho.*
>
> —SONG OF A TSISTSISTAS SCOUT
> TRAVELING IN ENEMY TERRITORY.

A SEARCH leading to the Massaum must start with a recognition of Tsistsistas shamanism and the philosophical principles upon which it is based. The Massaum, initiated by a shaman, is irrevocably derived from the shamanistic world interpretation. The same is true for tribal ceremonies that came in later, such as the Maxhoetonstov (Ceremony of the Sacred Arrows) and the Oxheheom (New Life Lodge, "Sun Dance"). Unfortunately, ethnographers who have worked with the Tsistsistas have failed to produce a study of Tsistsistas shamanism and have generally ignored the phenomenon altogether.

[1] A note of advice to the readers. This book has a story to tell, the story of the early Tsistsistas in the grasslands, where they came from, how they became Tsistsistas, and how their presence can be recognized in the archaeological record. Like a good play, it develops the story slowly from scene to scene to end. And, again, like a good play, it does not explain everything in the first scenes; rather, each chapter is a functional part of the whole. Although the preface sets the stage and shows the direction, and the table of contents the internal structure, some readers might be puzzled about some engrossing early matter-of-fact statements given without immediate verification. The

3

This chapter addresses itself to the issue and provides a description of the old—and in many ways continuing—Tsistsistas view of life and the universe that existed already during the initiation of the Massaum. It must be assumed that its roots were founded far back in the Proto-Tsistsistas past.

Tsistsistas World View as Shamanistic World Interpretation

Hestanov is the Tsistsistas term for the universe. Standing on the grass surface of the earth, a viewer is located in *votostoom*, the middle zone that bridges *heamahestanov*, the world above, and *atonoom*, the world below. *Votostoom* ends a few yards under the viewer's feet where the roots of trees and grasses end. Below lies *nsthoaman*, the deep earth, which provides the substance of physical life on earth.

To the realm of the deep earth belong the *maheonoxsz*, the sacred caves, where human seekers of knowledge may be received and in-structed by the *maiyun*, powerful spirits. The *maheonoxsz* serve as models for the Tsistsistas institution of spirit lodges where shamans conduct seances. The ceremonial structures of the great Tsistsistas ceremonies—the wolf tipi of the Massaum, the world lodge of the Oxheheom, and Motseyoef's tipi of the Maxhoetonstov—are images of the *maheonoxsz* where the original granting of the ceremonies took place. The most prominent sacred cave of the Tsistsistas tradition is located inside Nowah'wus (The Sacred Mountain Where People Are Taught), Bear Butte, at the northeast edge of the Black Hills.

To the realm of the deep earth belong also the *heszevoxsz*, the ani-mal caverns, where the spirits, *hematasoomao* (or *matasoomao*), of ani-mals of all species are gathered. From there they may be released to join physical form, that is, become available as animals once again, or they may be kept there, that is, refused rebirth. The present world-wide skrinking of animal populations and the accelerating extinction of species in Tsistsistas interpretation represents a conscious with-holding of animal *hematasoomao* by their *maiyun* protectors to ex-clude the original animals from the destruction of the earth waged by the industrial nations. After the self-destruction of the global

---

evidence is forthcoming, but, as in a good play, it appears at the proper place. Because of my singular rewriting of Tsistsistas world understanding and primary cultural fea-tures, any other approach would have rendered the book unreadable. It is possible to read it as though nothing had ever been published about the Tsistsistas before. In fact, even some professionals steeped in extant works on the Tsistsistas might not recognize the culture described but for some familiar terms.

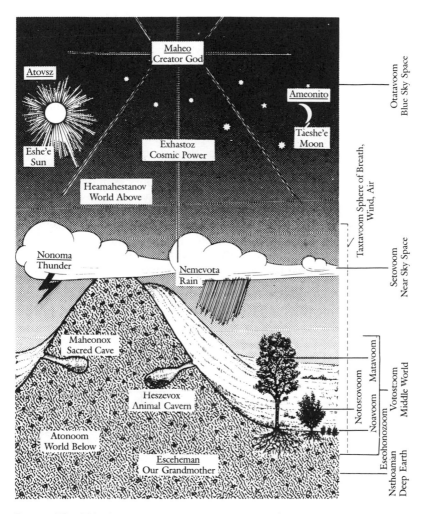

FIG. I. The Tsistsistas universe, *hestanov*. *Hestanov*, the generally visible world includes *matasoomhestanov*, the generally invisible world of spirits. Underlined words denote the personal ceremonial names of spirits *(maiyun)* who represent powerful potencies in the world. *Nsthoaman*, the deep earth, begins below the region of roots but includes surface areas free of vegetation such as high mountains. Mountain peaks are especially sacred places because there the deep earth and the near sky space come into direct contact.

mass of human population, the *maiyun* are to rehabilitate physical conditions on earth and reopen the *heszevoxsz*.

During Tsistsistas ceremonies, when sod is excavated to provide sacred space to enact ritual, performers operate directly on the deep earth. Thus they are in contact with the powerful substance of *nsthoaman* and in the proximity of the *maheonoxsz* and *heszevoxsz*. The painted buffalo skull imbedded in excavated ground in the Massaum and Oxheheom ceremonies represents the *maiyun* of the deep earth, who, resting on *nsthoaman,* participates in the sacred drama. Trees are powerful beings because their roots penetrate into *nsthoaman.* The deep earth is directly accessible where it is not blanketed with vegetation, for example, in pebbles and rocks, mountain peaks, sandbars, desert stretches, the interior of caves, and so forth. These are considered powerful manifestations.

The region where the roots of trees and grasses end marks both the surface of *atonoom,* the world below, and the lowest part of *votostoom,* the transition zone of *heamahestanov,* the world above. The lowest region of *votostoom* is *eseohonozoom,* the region of roots, where badgers and rodents have their homes, where bears often hibernate and wolves and coyotes den. Above the surface of the ground, *votostoom* includes three more regions: *noavoom,* the region of short grasses, sedges, low-growing plants and small animals; *notostovoom,* the region of tall grasses, bushes, humans, and large animals; and *matavoom,* the region of trees and forests. In the Massaum the sacred food prepared by the Hohnuhka Society to feed the *maiyun* included three plants that represented the lower three of the four growth regions of *votostoom.* These stood symbolically for all edible wild fruits and for all of plant life in general.

The four regions of *votostoom* are connected with the next region of the world above, *setovoom,* the near sky space, through *taxtavoom,* the sphere of breath, wind, and air. It is *taxtavoom* that makes physical life possible through its power of *omotomhestoz,* the gift or quality of breath. *Taxtavoom* ends above the clouds and the peaks of high mountains.

Setovoom, the near sky space, is the region of mountains and clouds and bends upward into *otatavoom,* the blue sky. Mountains are sacred places because their bare peaks, parts of the deep earth, reach directly into the sky space. Thunderstorms, tornadoes, and the high-flying formations of migratory birds in spring and fall, all move in the region of *setovoom.*

The most sacred region of the Tsistsistas universe is *otatavoom*, (literally "blue sky lodge," from *otatav*, "blue sky," and *om*, "lodge"), the blue sky space. Its color blue visually represents Maheo, the Supreme Being. He created *emämanstoon*, "all the world," and gave it the order, *vonoom*, to which the Tsistsistas world description is adapted. From him emanates the cosmic power, *exhastoz*, that permeates and maintains the world. The world descriptions of other small ethnic societies are seen by the Tsistsistas as meaningful variations of their own world experience. The annual Tsistsistas tribal ceremonies, held in the presence of Maheo and the spiritual powers of the universe, depict the ancient order, *vonoom*, of the creation and serve its preservation. Today the Tsistsistas, forced to live in an environment destroyed by others, view the physical destruction of the world as an episode nearing its frightful end.

In the Massaum ceremony the creation of the world and its order was ritually reenacted. The ceremony began with nonexistence before existence, the time before all time. On the second day of the secret part of the ceremony, in the seclusion of the wolf tipi, the priest knelt on the ground west of the center pole. Because the center of the tipi had been cleared from sod, he knelt on the deep earth. He gently pressed the thumb of his right hand into the smooth earth. He marked four more spots about five inches from the central one, on the northeast, southeast, southwest, and northwest.

The universe was created from the center. The priest who represented Maheo in this action, opened the ground with a digging stick at the location of his first thumbprint (the cosmological singularity). He broke earth from the opening four times and placed it on the markers of the four ceremonial directions. The round opening, now about three inches wide and deep, was in the center of four small mounds. Between these, extending from the opening, he painted on the ground a white cross whose arms extended in the cardinal directions. The cross and the four mounds of the corners delineated *hestanov*, the universe. He covered the southeastern and southwestern mounds with red powder and the other two with black. These represented the mountains of the *maheyuno*, the four sacred guardians at the corners of the universe.

Then the priest made the *maiyun* (the spirits who work in the seven regions of the universe) and the *hematasoomao*, the immortal spiritual forms of plants, animals, and human beings.

Stars, *hotoxceo*, belong to *otatavoom*, the blue sky. Like all other manifestations in the Tsistsistas universe, they possess spiritual and physical forms. Tsistsistas language differentiates the two, using separate words in referring to one category or the other. The sun as daylight, for instance, is called *eshe'e;* his name as a *maiyun* (perceived in Tsistsistas as male) is Atovsz. The moon as a body of light is called *taeshe'e* (night sun); as a *maiyun* (also perceived as male) his name is Ameonito.

Physical and spiritual life in the universe comes from Maheo; the *maiyun* work according to his plan. Physical forms of plants, animals, and human beings are made possible through the potencies of the *maiyun* Atovsz (Sun), Nonoma (Thunder, who directs the clouds), Nemevota (Rain, assisting Thunder) and Escheman (Our Grandmother), the female spirit of the deep earth. In Tsistsistas ceremonials or prayers, the *maiyun* are addressed only by their personal spirit names.

Because of their sacredness the *maheyuno* have personal spirit names only. The keeper of the southeast is Hesenota; he of the Southwest is Sovota; Onxsovota guards the northwest, and Notamota the northeast. *Maheyuno* and *maiyun,* for special reasons, may reveal themselves to a Tsistsistas in physical form. The appearance they select for this purpose uses a symbolism with which Tsistsistas are familiar.

The *maiyun* most responsible for physical life on earth belong either to the deep earth or to the sky spaces. In Tsistsistas ceremonies they are celebrated especially and represented through plant and animal forms. Animals close to Escheman, the *maiyun* of the deep earth, are the badger, buffalo, bear, and wolf. Animals close to the *maiyun* of the near sky space are the wolf, raven, red-headed woodpecker, dragonfly, whooping crane, and so forth. The golden eagle, the gyrfalcon ("white eagle"), and magpie belong to the blue sky and Maheo. In Tsistsistas ceremonies plant and animal forms signifying the *maiyun* or aspects of the *maiyun* are entwined with plant and animal forms that represent the seven levels of the Tsistsistas universe.

In accordance with the long Tsistsistas hunting tradition the ceremonies generally feature predatory animals over game animals. Among the exceptions is the buffalo, which is regarded both as a game animal and as a powerful spiritual being.

Each animal species has its species-specific protector (*Artgeist*) who is also a *maiyun* but serves under the *maiyun* of the deep earth and the sky spaces. He is considered male and may make himself

visible on important occasions as an animal of great size. He is erroneously sometimes called "father" of a species. He punishes hunters
for abuse of animals under his protection by withholding game or by
inflicting injury on the offender(s). Conversely, he may grant special
privileges.

The bear *maiyun,* Voxpenako, for example, appears as an enormous white bear in Tsistsistas seances and visionary experiences. It
is interesting that he exhibits the physical characteristics not of the
modern North American bears but of the North Asian brown bear
(*Ursus arctos*). The wolf *maiyun,* Maheone'honehe, is a very large red
wolf; Moore (1974 : 176, 239) reports that the rare solitary red wolf of
the Plains, Xaenone, was considered to be one of his manifestations.

The dark side of existence is reflected through owls, who are considered *mista,* spooks, or close to *mista. Mista* have come into the
world through the misuse of shamanistic power.

Plant, animal, and human physical forms originate from the repro-
duction process as given in each species. The initiation of new life,
however, is not solely the result of the biological fusion of parental
particles but requires, for procreation, the infusion of spiritual forms
that remain with the organism until death.

The spiritual forms of every living being under the laws of Maheo's
order (*vonoom*) consist of *omotome,* the immortal gift of breath essentially derived from *exhastoz,* cosmic power, and the immortal *hematasooma* (see also Moore 1974 : 166; Straus 1976, 1978), the spiritual potential consisting of four separate forces. This concept is basic to an
understanding of Tsistsistas religious as well as everyday life.

Upon physical death the *hematasooma* of a Tsistsistas becomes
free; after killing an animal the hunter is obligated to free ceremonially its *hematasooma.* The *omotome* of both become localized in
those body remains that resist decay longest (teeth, bones, claws,
feathers, etc.) that they eventually depart to rejoin their *hematasoomao* to become spirit selves in the spirit world. The *hematasooma* of
an animal returns to the *heszevoxsz* and the protection of the *maiyun*
Escheman (female spirit of the deep earth) and Nonoma (Thunder), the animal keepers. The *hematasoomao* of the Tsistsistas may
travel through the sky spaces of the world above, may join once
again a new *omotome* for reincarnation as a Tsistsistas in physical
form, or may remain near Tsistsistas living in physical form and participate in the continuing expressions of Tsistsistas culture as guardians and helpers.

It appears that Proto-Tsistsistas and early Tsistsistas may have observed two phases of the freeing of the spirit from the body that would have been reflected in burial custom: a preliminary first burial to start the process of disengaging the *omotome* and a secondary burial to free the *omotome* for joining it with the *hematasooma* already free. The secondary burial would have concluded with the sending away of the spirit self or by its temporary formal retention in an object ("keeping the soul") by a shaman. It seems that similar burial customs were practiced for animals also.

Parts of animals kept for ceremonial purposes (claws, teeth, bones, feathers, etc.) with permission of the animal spirits provided the human practitioner with a part of the *omotome* of a guardian animal into which its *hematasooma* could be called for action or assistance.

The *hematasooma* of an animal or the *hematasoomao* of animals of different species might choose to associate with the *hematasooma* of a human for the time of his physical existence and grant him spiritual influence on one or more species. A specially qualified person, a shaman, might project one or two parts of his or her *hematasooma* into game animals with the assistance of the *hematasoomao* of his or her guardian animals belonging to the species and call them near hunters or into prearranged structures, such as pounds. Every human distinguished by tutelary animals accepted personal responsibilities in regard to the species involved which had been defined by the animals.

In the past the temporary, conscious detachment of parts of one's *hematasooma* could be achieved by nearly all Tsistsistas. This allowed for phenomena interpreted as paranormal in the European literature; their culmination was reached in Tsistsistas shamanism. The unconscious separation of three of the four parts of one's *hematasooma* led to sickness and eventually to physical death.

The original order of the universe as created by Maheo requires ethnic entities that occupy life zones—as animal species do—that they are charged to protect. This responsibility, for instance, is exemplified in Tsistsistas ceremonies that were originally taught by the *maiyun* and are held annually in their presence.

As each animal species, each ethnic entity was endowed by the creator with a limited number of *hematasoomao;* the total of all *hematasoomao* expresses the plan of life of the cosmos as instituted by Maheo. Plants and animals domesticated by humans remain outside the primal order and because they have no access to *hematasoomao* are only physical. They are nonexistent in terms of this order. The same applies to the great mass of global human population today. In Tsis-

tsistas thought, the self-domestication of ethnic groups to civilizations and to a condition of exploiting the world has led to a withdrawal of *hematasoomao*.

World Experience and Tsistsistas Shamanism

In Tsistsistas thought the differences between all forms of life as
granted in the original order were minimal.

Plants, excluding the domesticated forms, have both a physical and
a spiritual component. The only domesticated plant granted original
status is corn, which entered the Tsistsistas realm late in history. The
tradition describes the consecration of corn by the *maiyun* Esceche-
man, who gave the plant ceremoniously to the Tsistsistas for use.
Edible plants were regarded as powerful beings because they allowed
animal and human physical life. Without the use of plant physical
forms in artifacts and a wide range of cultural activities, human life
would not have been possible. Plants could not be abused, and plants
physically killed had to be propitiated.

The ingestion of plant food made animals and humans part of the
plant community. Plants sought by Tsistsistas shamans and herbalists
could not be used without the consent of their *hematasoomao*. Often
plants revealed themselves to a specific person and disclosed their
healing properties. The Tsistsistas tradition retains examples where
the *hematasoomao* of shamans identified with specific plant species. In
their plant manifestations, some are celebrated in Tsistsistas ceremonies to the present.

Because of their solidarity with plants, Tsistsistas shamans used
their spiritual power to heal plant diseases or to change weather conditions harmful to vegetation growth.

Because game animals sustain themselves with the original, powerful potency of plants, the Tsistsistas regard their flesh as sacred. The
ingestion of animal flesh made the human a part of the animal community also. Because of the transience of physical form and the trans-
mutability of *hematasoomao,* occasionally a Tsistsistas hunter might
kill a buffalo into whom a Tsistsistas *hematasooma* had entered. Or, a
hunter who had been joined by the *hematasooma* of a buffalo might
kill a buffalo endowed with either a buffalo or a Tsistsistas spirit, or
with both. What was slain, however, was physical form alone, not a
hematasooma, either buffalo or Tsistsistas. The dark fear of the Iglulik
shaman Aua—"We, hunting animals as we do, live by slaying other
souls" (Halifax 1979, 164–65)—does not pertain to the Tsistsistas.
The formal releasing of the *hematasooma* after taking an animal and

the respectful treatment of all physical parts including those that retained the *omotome* (especially, skulls) were founded in Tsistsistas hunting laws controlled by the *maiyun*.

In Tsistsistas thought, the human body, after the *hematasooma* had separated, first became animal food, of maggots, birds, coyotes, and so forth. After the *omotome* had departed, the body became plant food and so an inseparable participant in plant and animal existence according to the eternal cycle of transformation. This cycle meant that all participants in the exchange—plants, animals, and the human hunters—were parts of each other in a kinship as deep as the mystery of life.

It follows that Tsistsistas hunting was a sacred ritual ruled by the game, not by the hunter. Without their and their *maiyun* protectors' assent, animals could not be taken. Animals were celebrated as beautiful, mysterious, powerful, dangerous, and benevolent. In Tsistsistas memories, animals talked with humans, took pity on them, protected and taught them, gave to them special power and knowledge, healed them from wounds and sicknesses, kept them alive with self-sacrifice and, finally, became human themselves to help them in great need. This is the story of Ehyophstah, the yellow-haired buffalo maiden of the Massaum ceremony.

The early Tsistsistas material—and ceremonial—culture derived largely from the bodies and spirits of animals. The Tsistsistas dressed as animals because their clothing consisted of skins and furs. The Tsistsistas fashioned themselves after animals of their chosing, or rather, after animals that had chosen them. The person who was selected by wolves, for example, became a wolf without changing physical form, although some could do so according to Tsistsistas experiences. He or she certainly dreamed wolf dreams, possessed wolf skills and power, acted like a wolf, immersed himself or herself in wolf lore, talked with wolves, hunted with wolves, was taught by wolves, protected wolves, painted himself or herself as a wolf and wore wolf *omotome* on his or her body and in a bundle. Here the border between a human and a wolf had been cracked in the physical world. In *matasoomhestanov*, the world of spirits, human being and wolf had become the same.

Because of their solidarity with animals Tsistsistas shamans used their spiritual power to heal animals and animal diseases and to protect species against hunters of their own human community.

In Tsistsistas thought each Tsistsistas was also a powerful being, as were people in Tsistsistas-like original human communities. Each

Tsistsistas had had personal experiences that confirmed the reality of the Tsistsistas world understanding. The so-called vision quest, about which much has been written, was not really what the term indicates. It rather represented a formal submission by the individual to the spiritual powers of the universe, a readiness to accept the solidarity of life and the solidarity of physical death, an opening of the self to *exhastoz*, cosmic power, and to the entering of out-of-body spirit selves, *hematasoomao*. The latter act was considered a real event, not a vision. It also meant self-purification, not as suppression of the individual but as a freeing of the individual from materialistic and immature restraints initiating a sharing in the mysterious and beautiful physical and spiritual workings of the world.

Whenever the spirit selves of plants, animals, or Tsistsistas, or the *maiyun* associated themselves with a human, during a quest or at any other time, the selection was made by them; the human was "adopted." This organization of relationships was available to every Tsistsistas and determined the direction of his or her life.

This organic Tsistsistas world description, in which all parts of the universe were interrelated, saw life as wondrous. Physical form meant only a temporary constraint; spiritual form was immortal and free in space and time. This is perhaps the greatest achievement of shamanism since its development during, perhaps, the Middle Paleolithic: to interpret the world with all its manifestations as a place of miracles, transformations, and immortality where fear has no reason.

Some Tsistsistas, because of unusual sensitivity, great creative talent, and propensity for physical ordeal were distinguished by *hematasoomao* and the *maiyun* more highly, or more severely, than others. These were the intellectual leaders of Tsistsistas culture who introduced new institutions when it was necessary. Generally, they were called by the *maheyuno* and *maiyun* and were instructed in the *maheonoxsz*, the sacred caves, or from the *heszevoxsz*, the animal caverns. Because of these relationships and because of obedience to their strenuous vocation, they were sometimes considered to be of the *maiyun* world when still in physical form. In Tsistsistas memories, these persons had power over physical form and physical death, including their own.

This is mentioned in the Motseyoef stories (Curtis 1930:117; Grinnell 1908:271–72, 282–83; 1923, 2:345–47) where the prophet, as a boy, kills himself during a shamans' meeting and brings himself back to life. It is the feat of the androgyne shaman (for a discussion of this phenomenon, see Eliade 1965:78–124).

Zemaheonevsz ("the mysterious one," plural, *zemaheonevesso*) and *maheonhetan* (someone who serves the sacred, plural *maheonhetaneo*) are the Tsistsistas terms for shaman; the latter term refers to one who has also served as priest in one of the great ceremonies. The term for shamanism is *ehōneheonevestoz*. Physicians and healers, *náetan* or *náe* (plural *náo*), who often work without the assistance of a helping spirit or a *maiyun*, are not considered shamans. A personal spirit helper, or guardian spirit (sometimes called "familiar" in the literature), who represents the *hematasooma* of a human or an animal, is called *nisimōn*. *Maiyun-ef* is the term for someone who was granted spiritual power by the *maiyun;* the suffix *ef* (*iv*) attached to a person's name denotes the same condition.

Originally shamans formed an esoteric, closed group, *ononeovätaneo,* which used language hidden to outsiders. In a much-reduced form, the *ononeovätaneo* and its special language persist to the present; the terms here used belong to it.

To resist the call of the *maiyun* was not possible for shamans. For the interpretation of details of the vocation the neonate might turn to an experienced shaman. The *ononeovätaneo* was composed of men and women. Because shamanistic power was granted by the *maheyuno, maiyun,* and *hematasoomao* alone, no one could purchase or obtain shamanistic knowledge from other shamans. After the *maiyun* introduced, through shamans, tribal ceremonies such as the Massaum, Maxhoetonstov, and Oxheheom, a group of priests developed, *zevonhäevesso* (*vonhätaneo,* male priests; *vonhäe,* priestesses), who remained responsible for their maintenance. All of these, well into the reservation period, were shamans also. Up to the present, priests and priestesses need *maiyun* permission and support for their service; that is, they submit to the old shamanistic rules.

As a group, Tsistsistas shamans represented the spiritual powers of the seven regions of the universe. Within the *ononeovätaneo,* shamans associated with the sky spaces were separate. They were androgyne shamans, that is, concerned with primordial time and the creation of the universe—the dissolution of opposites. They represented, some of them within themselves, the *coincidentia oppositorum,* the mystery of totality (Schlesier 1982). Their separateness, their quest for the reconciliation of contraries, was expressed in appearance and behavior.

The *hemaneh* ("half-man, half-woman") were transvestite shamans associated with the blue sky space. Because of their ritual bisexuality, they were barred from sexual acts. They symbolically represented the union of the blue sky with the deep earth; they were famous physicians.

Tsistsistas memory dimly retains knowledge of another group of shamans also associated with the blue sky space. These appear to have represented cosmic fire including, perhaps, the *maiyun* of the sun, Atovsz. During special performances, they ate burning coals, drank boiling soup, and walked through fires with naked feet. It seems that these shamans joined in the Hohnuhka contrary society with the introduction of the Massaum. This ritual secret society performed during the Massaum as the spiritual assistants of the *maiyun*. At these occasions, they acted through their contrary behavior as sacred clowns. They healed sicknesses or wounds with contrary techniques, for example, with fire or throwing patients high into the air or jumping over people. During these demonstrations, they were capable of extraordinary physical and mental feats.

A third group of persons associated with the blue sky space was mentioned by Petter (1915 : 1009) in 1914. He wrote that "an old informant said that the Cheyenne used to have experts who knew the stars and the names of all their different groups, but this knowledge had been gradually neglected and forgotten." For the correct performance of the Massaum, as will be seen in chapter 5, the knowledge of these specialists of celestial forms was essential. Their passing contributed to the demise of the ceremony. No one today knows if these were shamans. Because star constellations provided signals at certain times for Tsistsistas actions on earth and because some star clusters are considered Tsistsistas spirits, relatives in the sky, it would be surprising if they had not been shamans.

Associated with the near sky space were shamans who were also called Hohnuhka because of their contrary behavior; they used inverted speech. They never joined the Hohnuhka secret society, however. Members of this group had received their vocation from Nonoma, the *maiyun* of Thunder, and served as keepers of a *Hohnuhkawo'*, a spirit lance in contrary form ("bow lance"). These shamans were capable of calling *nonoma hemahe*, Nonoma's arrow, lightning, into the spirit lance and of unleashing its striking power over distance. Because of this great power, they were isolated from other Tsistsistas and committed to a life of privation and meditation; it was required that they remain celibate. Shamans representing *votostoom*, the middle or transition zone, and the deep earth were called by the *maiyun* Esceheman, by the species-specific protector *maiyun*, or by the *hematasoomao* of animals and Tsistsistas.

Shamans who were associated with Escheman possessed influence over game species, held ceremonies concerning the protection of animals and the propitiation of animal spirits, and directed medicine hunts in which they led animals into Tsistsistas camps or into prepared structures, such as pounds. Medicine hunts (see chapter 4) were preceded by spirit lodge (*nisimàtozom*) or sweat lodge (*vonhäom*) ceremonies in which shamans of this group called on the *hematasoomao* of their spirit allies to bring the animals in. Following medicine hunts, a second ceremony was held in which the *hematasoomao* of the slain animals were ritually freed, propitiated, and released to the *heszevoxsz*. Another ceremony, also held in a sweat lodge, dealt with healing sick and disabled persons, or revived a person already physically dead; the power of Escheman and the shaman's spirit helpers assisted him or her.

Shamans associated with *votostoom* were distinguished by plant, animal, and Tsistsistas spirit helpers. They also conducted spirit lodge seances (Schlesier 1983; see also chapter 4) in which the *hematasoomao* of the Tsistsistas, or even the *maiyun,* were called to provide advice and information concerning questions of the past, present, and future. Phenomena defined by modern parapsychology as out-of-body experiences and psychokinesis were integral parts of these seances.

E'ehyo'm is the Tsistsistas term for shamans who were able to do harm over long distances. This group included the Hohnuhka keepers of a *hohnuhkawo'* and other shamans who had control over an *oxzem,* a spirit lance (see fig. 2). Attached to its shaft near the point was a small braided wheel into which a specific spirit could be called who moved the *oxzem* physically. To this category of shamans, up to the present time, belongs the keeper of *nimãhenan,* the sacred arrows.

After the arrival of *nimãhenan,* the male keeper assumed the highest position among the *maheonhetaneo* (persons serving the sacred). Through *nimãhenan,* he belongs most intimately to the blue sky space; he nevertheless represents all seven levels of the Tsistsistas universe. He serves under the mandate of Motseyoef and in his succession. Because of this, he is qualified to make the Tsistsistas earth drawing that was originally granted to Motseyoef in the presence of Maheo, the *maheyuno,* and the *maiyun* to mark the earth region given to his people (see chapter 5). Therefore, this earth drawing is acknowledged by all spiritual powers of the universe. The keeper of *nimãhenan* bears great responsibility concerning the internal unity of the Tsistsistas world and its boundary delineation to the outside.

FIG. 2. *Oxzem*, spirit lance, also called wheel lance. Its length is about five feet. The shaft of this particular weapon is carved and arranged to present symbolically a humanlike physical image that either housed a shaman's spirit helper permanently or on special occasions. The right side of its body is painted black, the left side red. A single eagle feather is attached to the head. The braided spirit wheel features a black hoop on the outside, a red hoop on the inside; eleven eagle feathers are attached. The stone lance point is painted blue.

During the time in Tsistsistas history when spirit lances were prominent, no *oxzem* was like any other in detail because each exemplified secret knowledge and power and was made according to the instructions of the spirits. Each represented a dangerous gift from the spirit world to its shaman keeper who alone mastered the required ritual and care. As with the *hohnuhkawo'*, negligence or disobedience to the rules imposed by the spirits turned the *oxzem* against its keeper. Upon his death, the weapon was either buried with him or deposited at a hidden place, that is, returned to the spirit world.

Earth drawings left open, that is, not ritually erased at the conclusion of ceremonies, hold forever the attention and protection of cosmic powers for Tsistsistas lands.

When the Evenks of Siberia described, to Anisimov (1963a:106–11), "mythical fences," *marylya,* consisting of spirit helpers called up by shamans to protect "clan" territories, they expressed very similar thoughts.

The power of Tsistsistas shamans was inescapably linked to the obligation demanded by *maheyuno* and *maiyun* that it be used within the order of Maheo's design. Witchcraft, *ehōnestoz,* was possible, especially through *ovahoamazistoz,* magical shooting, because the power necessary for its execution was available. Tsistsistas ethics, however, demanded that any unjust harm caused innocents struck back at the person who had abused power and punished members of his or her own family. This law is understood to prevail to the present and is known to every Tsistsistas. It has certainly not prevented witchcraft but has curbed it.

Tsistsistas shamans acted on the highest level of achievement possible to humans in the frame of a world description that they originally formulated a very long time ago. Each shaman used complex "techniques" through which, for example, during seances he or she made spiritual potencies available in invisible or physically recognizable form. He or she assessed the primary source of power ("energy"), *exhastoz* (see chapter 9), which produced his or her verified feats, as located essentially outside of himself or herself, that is, granted through the intrusion of spirits who responded to his or her call. Calling techniques had been taught by those who let themselves be called.

"Possession phenomena," so called by Western authors, generally associated with shamanistic performances, did not exist in Tsistsistas shamanism. To each Tsistsistas, the *Viereinigkeit* (unity of four fissionable parts) of his or her *hematasooma* was an empirical certainty that allowed for a wide range of interesting possibilities. The entering of a free *hematasooma* or the appearance of a *maiyun* in the mental process of a person was understood as a distinction (Schlesier 1981). When a *maiyun* spoke directly through the mind and the vocal cords of a person, it resulted, as I have observed, neither in ventriloquism nor in ecstatic stammering but in intelligent speech.

2. Northern Siberian World Description and Shamanism

This ceremony for successful hunting—
Mother of Animals
in olden times
you have made it so.
You must predict the catch.
Show me the game
that you will give to us.
In early times
it was so decided
when everything was given life.
After the earth was made
it was always this way.
For shingken, *your woolen threads,*
your animal spirits,
I am asking you.
Speak to me!
At the campfire I will call you.
To the center of the earth
I will follow you,
Mother of Morning,
on this search for your animals.
Show yourself to me!
Show me the place
which I should reach.
Ancestors, you who are circling around me,
do also speak to me!
Come quietly
hargi *spirits*
mälkän *spirits*
fly before me.
Whatever you say
all around
all around.

—EVENK SHAMAN'S SONG, SHINGKELEVUN CEREMONY, SYM RIVER,
RECORDED BY N.P. NIKULSHIN

I HAVE SUGGESTED that the Tsistsistas world description and institutions as outlined in chapter 1 were essentially in existence during the time of the Proto-Tsistsistas' arrival in the northeastern Plains and that their roots reached back far beyond. The evidence for this assessment derives from a close look at cultures in northern Siberia. A comparison of the principles and cultural features of their world understanding with those of the Tsistsistas shows, beside interesting differences, signifcant similarities. Both sets of phenomena must be taken into account.

It is concluded here that groups ancestral to northern Siberian cultures once shared a common heritage with groups ancestral to the North American Algonquian language family, including Tsistsistas. Because they were physically separated from each other for an unknown number of millennia and because no linguistic relationships remained, the time of the development of their common heritage must significantly precede their separation.

Northern Siberian World View as Shamanistic World Interpretation

The universe of northern Siberian tribes consists of three layers: the world above, the middle world, and the world below. Some groups separate the sky space into three, seven, or nine regions and view the world below as having an equal number. Perhaps observation of the seeming annual circular movement of the sky led to the concept, nearly universal in northern Siberia, that the universe turns around a world axis, a cosmic pole or tree that connects the three major parts. In northern Siberia special poles set outside structures or in a central position within structures, including tents, represent the cosmic tree. These poles are usually carved with seven indentations that symbolize the seven layers of the world above through which a shaman's spirit potential may travel. A young tree, birch or larch, with seven branches left at the top, jutting from the smoke hole of a circular lodge, the trunk wedged firmly in the center of the ground, is called the "shaman's tree." It represents the world tree and serves as a ladder for the shaman's ascent during seances.

The Kets of the Yenisey River view the world below as an immense cavern with seven successive layers sealed by the ceiling of the middle world. A Khant shaman, when visiting the Earth Mother, traveled along the seven underground marks of the cosmic tree (Paulson 1962:31). The Nanays of the Lower Amur perceive of three world trees, one for every region of the universe, and of a cosmic mountain that arises from an earth navel located in the center of the deep earth.

In northern Siberia the vault of heaven is often interpreted as an immense tent roof with the North Star as sky navel. In Dolgan, Nanay, and Evenk thought, the Supreme Being rests at the apex of the cosmic tree, in the uppermost sky region. There shamans take the spirit selves of deceased humans to reside as little birds in high branches near the Supreme Being. And from there they are brought back by shamans for reincarnation in their original human community.

The Evenks, in all dialects, call the three-layered universe *buga* or *dunne* (Vasilevich 1963a : 48−83). Both terms refer also to all the world outside the *chum*, the circular living tent, or to "locality," "original land," "place of birth," or "grave" because ancestral graves marked ethnic territorial boundaries. Evenks of the Podkamenaya Tunguska sometimes called the vault in heaven *kalan* (kettle), expressing the poetic idea that the sky is a kettle turned upside down. It is interesting that a kettle tied to the sacred arrows' pole during one part of the Tsistsistas Maxhoetonstov ceremony is based on identical thought. Vasilevich states, however, that the oldest Evenk idea of the heavens is that of a skin thrown over the earth, with the North Star as an opening, a passage to the world above.

Anisimov (1963a : 108) gives the term *ugu dunne* for the world above, which the Evenks believed to consist of several heavens. The uppermost is the region of Amaka Sheveki, the Supreme Being; the second is the region of Eksheri Sheveki, protector of birds, animals, fishes, and plants. In the rest of the heavens are the other spiritual beings of the upper world: Delyacha, Sun; Bega, Moon; Agdy, Thunder; *asiktal*, stars; *tukse*, clouds, and so on. "The light-blue canopy of heaven is the taiga of the upper world, the Milky Way the tracks of the heavenly people's skis, the constellation Ursa Major is the scene of the heavenly people's collective hunt" (Anisimov 1963a : 108).

Among Evenks of the Yenisey Basin existed a shamanistic concept of three worlds located outside the original three (Vasilevich 1963a : 56−57). According to this cosmogony, the principal river of shamans, *engdekit* (literally "place of prohibition"), connects the three levels, flowing from the upper world, *tymanitki*, toward the east, eventually falling into *bukit*, the world below. *Tymanitki* lies to the east, where the sun rises, above the sources of *engdekit*. Some shamans could travel along *engdekit* into the world above after passing through seven layers, or clouds. The world below could only be entered by a specific category of shamans (Vasilevich 1963a:57). During the Evenk Earth Renewal Ceremony, Ikenipke, the sky shaman, assisted by his spirit helpers, penetrated the highest level of the world above. Beings living in the middle world were invisible to beings of the other two worlds, and vice versa, a condition that was important, for example, in Evenk spirit lodge ceremonies.

Evenks of the Podkamenaya Tunguska place animal spirits free of physical form in the deep earth under the protection of Bugady Mushun, or Dunne Enin, the Earth Mother, also called Eneke, Grandmother, spirit of the earth and keeper of animals. She resides in the deep earth with her husband but can be reached by shamans who undertake the arduous journey.

In the annual ceremony called Shingkelevun (Anisimov 1963b: 175–78; Rudy 1963:67–75), an Evenk ethnic entity (perhaps erroneously called a "clan" by Soviet scholars) camped in the fall, before the hunting season, at a *bugady*, a sacred place, in this instance a sacred mountain, that served as entrance to the realm of Dunne Enin.

During the first part of the complex Shingkelevun, the earth shaman, assisted by his or her spirit helpers, sent parts of his or her spiritual potential through the *bugady* to Dunne Enin to request from her the number of game animals needed for the survival of his or her people. After the earth spirit granted a specific number of *shingken*, animal spirits contained in woolen threads, he or she was permitted a spirit hunt among Dunne Enin's spirit herds, catching the precise number of animals allowed. Upon return to the middle world, *dulugu buga*, he or she distributed the *shingken* in the taiga where they turned into live animals.

The following parts of the ceremony featured (1) dances in which the animals were invited to join—which they did, represented by human participants dressed lavishly in animal costumes; (2) the construction of an artificial taiga made from young trees into which the game was called; (3) a ritual hunt concluded with the propitiation of the slain animals; and (4) purification of the hunters.

Another Evenk ceremony, Girkumki, also featured an elaborate pantomime of drawing game released by the Earth Mother into the hunters' range.

The Kets say that Tomam, mother of animals, "whose eyes are like the sky and whose cheeks resemble dawn," comes to the middle world in spring. Standing on a high cliff above the Yenisey, she shakes her sleeves over the river. The falling-down feathers transform into ducks, geese, swans, and other migratory birds that are thus once more released for their journey north (Anisimov 1963b:188).

Ceremonies similar to the Shingkelevun, Girkumki, and Kamlanye (see following text) were practiced in northern Siberia as far east as among the Itelmens on Kamchatka (Rudy 1962:73) and among the Koryaks of the Kolyma Range (Rudy 1962:78). Soviet scholars, following Okladnikov (1964:54–57), generally identify Neolithic populations of the Upper Amur and Upper and Middle Lena rivers, and of the Lake Baikal region, as ancestral to Evenk and Yukagir. These are considered to be Paleo-Siberian, suggesting an even earlier presence. Early Neolithic rock engravings on the Upper (e.g., Shishkino) and Middle Lena are viewed as representing powerful shamanistic animal spirit helpers in the tradition of the Evenk ceremonies mentioned (Rudy 1963:73–78). Okladnikov (1970:92–100) has interpreted drawings on the cliff of Suruk-taakh-kaya, on the Markha River near the Middle Lena, in terms of the Shingkelevun ceremony, and has found, through the artifacts recovered that were deposited there as offerings, that the site was used continuously from the Late Neolithic to the nineteenth century.

The Evenk spirit lodge ceremony, Kamlanye (Anisimov 1963a), was interpreted as originating from instruction by spirits of the world below. The structure of the circular conical *shevenchedek*, the shaman's lodge raised for this occasion, was an enlarged *chum* to accommodate many observers. The entrance was to the east. Prior to the ceremony, the shaman fasted for an extended period of time, during which he sent his *khargi*, one of his spiritual forms transformed into an animal, to the world below. The *khargi* sought instruction relative to the precise organization and emphasis of the Kamlanye.

The large lodge symbolized a *bugady*, a sacred mountain, as well as all of the middle world. The shamanistic cosmic tree, *turu*, was drawn through the smoke hole; the butt was dug into the center of the lodge next to the fire. The shaman sat on a small platform on the west side. Two galleries were raised outside. One, the *darpe*, was placed east of the lodge, consisting of a long row of young trees. Wooden carvings representing spirits in human and animal physical forms were put between the tree trunks. The *darpe* represented the world above, place of origin of the river *engdekit* with which the spirits were associated. Behind the lodge (the middle world), the second gallery, *onang*, was sent up on the western side. Because it represented the world below, the region where the *engdekit* ends, it was built from wind-fallen, dead trees. Here also stood numerous images in anthropomorphic and animal form, spirits of the lower world.

A *turu* pole was raised southeast of the *darpe* and covered with gifts for the most sacred spirits of the universe: red or white cloth for the Supreme Being, black cloth for the earth spirit, and additional cloth for others. A sacrificial animal hide hung from a crosspiece fastened to the top of the pole. Sun circle and moon sickle were carved on wood and suspended, along with other images called *khomokor* (cf. *khomoty,* "bear"). All around the lodge, the galleries, and the *turu* pole was placed a circle of young larches to form an unbroken wall.

Within it the whole universe and all its spiritual powers were represented. Before the ceremony of calling the spirits began, *darpe* (the world above), and *onang* (the world below) were ritually closed, and the observers of Kamlanye were locked with the shaman in the middle world of the *shevenchedek* and the enfolding drama of the struggle of spirits.

The Evenk term *nimngakavun* (Vasilevich 1963a:46) refers to the beginning of the universe, when everything was formed. Perhaps it is the equivalent of Tsistsistas *vonoom,* the original order given by the Supreme Being. *Nimngakavun* also means "legend, origin story": *nimngakan,* "to put on a shamanistic performance"; *nimngamat,* "to induce spirit helpers to enter one's body"; and *nimngangki,* "shaman's drum." The creation of the universe is interpreted as a shamanistic performance, the first one, by the Supreme Being when spirits were called—brought into the world.

That the northern Siberian middle world sank beneath waters and was rescued by bird helpers of the Supreme Being represents a secondary event. Among Evenks, Nenets, Yuraks, and Mansis, the bird that dives below and brings the earth back to the surface is the loon or the goldeneye; among the Ilimpeya Evenks, the helper is a crow (Vasilevich 1963a:74). Once the earth had partly risen above the waters the mammoth, *sheli,* decided to help humans. He put his tusks under the water and drew out so much *nyangnya* ("dirt", "mud") (Anisimov 1963b:166) that the earth became complete again. The giant serpent, *dyabdar,* helped the mammoth to smooth the clods pulled up. Both recreated the earth's surface. When this work was done, the mammoth returned to the world below with all his offspring. Regarding this great service in Yenisey Evenk art, the mythical mammoth helper is crowned with moose antlers, whereas the tail of a fish is attached to his body.

According to Vasilevich (1963a:73), the stories of the rescue of the earth from a watery waste originated at the end of the last glaciation when vast areas of northern Siberia were covered with glacial lakes and melt waters of retreating ice masses: "The fact that analogous concepts are present among certain North American Indian tribes further suggests that they arose before various groups had ceased moving from Asia to America."

Generally, the Supreme Being of northern Siberian tribes is a distant creator of the universe (*deus otiosus*) who is not represented in art and rarely addressed directly in ceremonies. Although He provided the spiritual and physical forms of life in the universe, He rarely interferes in his creation. The existence of the three worlds of the universe is guarded and controlled by powerful mediator spirits who act according to the given cosmic order. Evenks and Koryaks sacrificed white (albino) reindeer to the Supreme Being—those present faced east during the ritual (Paulson 1962:41, 51). Shirokogoroff (Paulson 1962:40), however, insisted that no attempt was made to influence the Supreme Being; apparently, as among Plains Indians generally, an albino, because of its color, was considered a rare visitor not to be used by humans as common game (see chapter 4).

The Ket term for the Supreme Being is Es, Yukagir Pon, Itelmen Kutkhu, Koryak Naininen, Samoyed Num, Khant Num-turam, Mansi Numi-taram (Paulson 1962:41–61), and Nivkhi (Gilyak) Kurn (Sternberg 1905:244).

For some northern Siberian groups, the stars represented openings to the higher levels of the world above. In one story a woman, after arriving in the upper world, looks down through a hole. Out of longing for her native land she weeps tears, and the people on earth think that it is rain (Anisimov 1963b:217).

For others, the constellations of the night sky provided signals for events on earth. Sternberg (1905) observed the Nivkhis followed "heavenly bodies during certain periods of the year because the migratory fish come with astronomic precision in specific months, on a specific day."

Generally the universe was conceived of as a living being and was often identified with images of animals. Most of the Evenk tribes called the constellation Ursa Major *kheglun*, moose. The cosmic bear, *mangi*, was viewed as the constellations Boötes and Arcturus hunting *kheglun* across the skies and killing him. *Mangi* is half-animal, half-human: He is a bear but pursues the great moose on skis. In Evenk shamanism, *mangi* represents the mythical first ancestor, closely linked to the shaman's vocation and to the transformations of the shaman's spiritual powers (Anisimov 1963b:164).

On shamans' drums of northern Siberia, beside the sun and moon, Venus and the Pleiades are often depicted, suggesting special atten-

tion by shamans. Unfortunately, ethnographers have failed to establish their meaning (see Mandoki 1963, for critique). Evenks called
Venus rising in the morning *tymani typkenin* (literally "wedge of
morning").

In Evenk thought, two spirits of the world above played an important role in the annual cycle, both benevolently. Dylacha, Sun, the
spirit of heat and light, stored the heat in the fall and released it again
with full power in spring. Upon the first signs of warmth returning
to the middle world, Agdy, Thunder, the old man of the heavens,
struck his flint causing rumbling, the sparks turning into lightning
that destroyed evil forces (Anisimov 1963b:161). It was at that time
that Evenks held the *ikenipke* (literally "revivals") earth renewal ceremony that featured a cosmic hunt in pantomime during which the
sacred heavenly animal was slain, came to life again, and with it all of
nature: The river ice broke up, the snows melted, fresh green covered
the earth, and young animals were born (Anisimov 1963b:163).

Some animals were associated in northern Siberia with specifically
sacred regions of the universe and treated with awe. Holmberg (1922:
28) reported that among Yakuts, Dolgans, and Evenks birds such as
the "diver, the goose, the swan, the eagle enjoyed so great a respect
that even their names are never mentioned and it is regarded as
wrong to point at them with the finger." When a hunter found one of
these birds dead, he placed the body with ceremony on a burial platform. They were never hunted. A Buryat shaman's song also mentions animals as important to regions: "The grey hare is our runner,
the grey wolf our messenger, the bird *Khon* our *khubilgan*, the eagle
Khoto our emissary" (Holmberg 1922:29).

The concept that powerful spirits protected all animals was universal in northern Siberia. They held the threads of animal physical life
and were keepers of the immortal animal spiritual forms. These protector spirits were grouped in several categories in a hierarchical
order to which every northern Siberian group directed constant concern. These spirits were revered, celebrated, and placated. Without
their permission, no game became available. Animals themselves
were also objects of veneration; without their consent, they would
not be taken either.

Because hunting and fishing had been the only means of human
survival in northern Siberia since the first arrival of humans there,
the adaptation of human cultures to the region had to be as perfect as, for example, that of the wolf. Shirokogoroff (1929, 1935) has
eloquently testified to the intelligence of Evenk understanding of

human–animal relationships and to the functional quality of their hunting customs. The relatively recent aboriginal introduction of reindeer breeding in some areas of northern Siberia did not significantly change the old order or question its meaning. The cultures of the people of the North were altered dramatically as a result of Tsarist and Soviet invasions, and first the Christian, then the Soviet ideological persecutions of shamanism.

The highest spirits were those who protected all of animal life of the northern Siberian world. Some were female, for example, Yanebya, the Earth Mother of the Nentsys (Levin and Potapov 1964: 564), Dunne Enin of the Evenks, and Tomam of the Kets, both already mentioned, or Ylyunda Kotta of the Selkups (Anisimov 1963b: 191–92). Some were male, for example, Eksheri Sheveki of some Evenk groups (Anisimov 1963b:160–61), and Bua of the Udegeys and Orochis (Levin and Potapov 1964:743, 757). Kalgama of the Nanays was androgynous (Paulson 1961:88).

Next came spirits of regions: of taiga or tundra, and, for coastal tribes, of the sea. Again, as in all Siberian categories of spirits, some were female ("mothers"), some male ("fathers"). The Yukagirs distinguished a spirit of the earth, Lebie-po'gil, a spirit of freshwater, O'jin-po'gil, and a spirit of the sea, Cobun-po'gil (Paulson 1961:55). The Koryaks knew a spirit of the land, Picvu'cin, and a female spirit of the sea, Anqa'ken-etinvilan (Paulson 1961: 67–68). A similar recognition of a protector spirit of land animal and one for sea creatures (including sea mammals) existed among the Chukchis (Levin and Potapov 1964: 822; Paulson 1961: 60–65), Itelmens (Paulson 1961: 69), Yakuts (Paulson 1961: 90–92), Khants (Paulson 1961: 107–12), Nivkhis (Paulson 1961:74), and others. Some tribes of the Amur River area identified the taiga spirit with the tiger, for example, the Udegeys and Orochis (Levin and Potapov 1964: 743, 757).

Below these spirits were spirits of specific localities: of a mountain or a river, a valley, a lake, a point on the coast, a cove, or a jutting rock.

Each animal species had its species-specific protector spirit (*Artgeist*) who was viewed as serving under the earth spirits and the spirits of land and sea. An *Artgeist* was also either female (e.g., the Chukchi "mother of walrus") or male (e.g., Nivkhi Tlangi-ys'n, "master of wild reindeer," from *ys'*, "master"). *Artgeister* might make themselves visible to human beings as animals of extraordinary, sometimes miniature, size. Like the higher spirits, they also would punish game abuse, refuse or bless hunters.

Throughout northern Siberia the physical form of every living being was understood to possess reincarnate spiritual form. Because, without the infusion of reincarnate spiritual form, new life was not possible, spiritual as well as physical forms were limited in total numbers following the original intent of the creation. Belief in multiple souls, including one reincarnate soul, remained universal well into the Russian occupation.

Chernetsov (1963) describes a concept of four souls from the Khants and Mansis. The first one, called *is,* "soul shadow," is also called "big soul" or "grave soul." It is a material soul and connected with the visible shadow cast by every object. It remains with physical form but continues only as long as something remains of the body. With the decay of flesh and bone, the *is* transforms itself into a water beetle. As long as the *is* exists in a grave, the person interred is not considered dead.

The second soul is called *lonxal'minne is,* "the soul that goes down the river," and it appears primarily only after a person's death. It leaves a person regularly during sleep, traveling widely. Shamans, during a Kamlaniye (shamanistic performance, Chernetsov's spelling), detach their second soul for special assignments. This soul lives on the surface of a person. Khants and Mansis tattooed birds on person's shoulders for this soul to enter, attempting to hold it close. After a person's death, the second soul becomes *urt,* traveling to the afterworld in the form of a bird, swallow, magpie, or cuckoo. But it does not set out on its journey immediately. "In the course of the period during which the body lies at home, it wanders over the whole earth. It goes to those places where it used to be. Only afterward does it go down forever [that is, in the direction of the Lower Ob] (Chernetsov 1963:25). During group ceremonies sacrificial food was placed on sticks around the camp to feed passing soul birds.

The third soul lives outside a person and comes to him or her only during sleep. Therefore it is called *ulem is,* "the dreaming soul." It is an external taiga soul in the form of a wood grouse. If it perishes, and if a shaman with his or her spirit helpers' assistance cannot catch it in time, the person dies.

The fourth soul is the reincarnation soul, *man is,* "little soul," which stays with a person most of the time but moves with the speed of the mind, traveling during sleep. Its dwelling place is the head, particularly the hair. Chernetsov (1963:24) interprets the former Khant and Mansi custom of scalping as an attempt to keep the main soul of an enemy and hence prevent his rebirth. The "little soul" often appears as a soul bird on a person's head in aid and defense of his or her "master." The "little soul" is inherited from generation to generation in persons of the same descent group. Because each child represents the reincarnation of a past ancestor, the correct ancestral name is bestowed on the child after a long and probing search. Names are limited in numbers, matching the original grant of "little souls."

Khants and Mansis perceive of three stages of death. When the second soul leaves a person permanently, he is an "inwardly living dead man." The second stage of death occurs when his fourth soul abandons him. Final death takes place when the body decays and the "soul shadow" leaves. Because of these concepts, the Khants and Mansis practiced a first platform burial followed later by a secondary burial of the nearly decomposed bones. Oftentimes the reincarnate soul of the deceased was kept by attaching a lock of his hair to a small wooden figurine (*agan,* "doll"). This doll was treated as the original live person until it was freed (buried or burned) a few years later.

The Kets believed in seven souls, the Yukagirs in three, and the Koryaks in two (Paulson 1962:118–23).

The Nanays (Anisimov 1963b:206–207) recognized three souls: *omia; uksuki,* identified with *ergeni,* "breathing"; and *fanya,* identified with shadow. The first stage of death occurs when the *omia* leaves a person's body to return to the ancestral place of *omia,* whereas the breath soul remains with the body. The second stage occurs after the first funeral when the shaman settles the shadow soul in a wooden doll. The third stage is represented by the last funeral when the shaman removes the shadow soul from its figurine container and joins it with the *omia* already free. After the two have merged into one, the *omia* is once more available for reincarnation.

Evenks also believed in three souls (Anisimov 1963b:203–205). In the Evenk Anan Ceremony, the shaman escorted the *omi,* the reincarnate soul of the deceased, safely to the ancestral place in the world above. In the Omilattan Ceremony, he journeyed there to obtain an *omi* for a future child upon request of a woman who wished to become pregnant. Holmberg (1926:40) mentions that Evenks in the past scalped enemies for apparently the same reasons the Khants and Mansis did.

Because of the general belief in northern Siberia that a body soul survived in bones and skulls for many years, burial customs, though varied, were elaborate everywhere. Because the same concept was extended to animals, these were included in the burial complex also.

The only difference between human and animal burials was in degree; the former was somewhat more complex.

The one animal treated nearly everywhere with the same elaboration as a deceased human was the bear. A number of Siberian groups buried the whole bear skeleton (Holmberg 1926:39–40; Obayashi and Paproth 1966:224–28). Where a special treatment of human skulls (as depositories of reincarnate souls) was emphasized, bear— and wolf and tiger—skulls were specially treated also. Where tree or platform burial was practiced, bears and some other animals, already mentioned, were buried the same way.

Generally in northern Siberia, animal skulls and bones were handled with great care and were deposited undamaged (Holmberg 1926; Paulson 1963). Where it was customary to keep bones or skulls of a deceased relative (e.g., among the Yukagirs), bones, teeth, claws, feathers, and skulls of animals were kept for the same reason. Actually, from the Samis of the northern Scandinavia to Kamchatka, bear claws and teeth as well as teeth, beaks, and claws of many predators were kept for the protection of humans by the animals' spirits. Surviving physical parts of many nonpredatory animals were included in this complex also.

Animal reincarnate souls, once freed from physical form by the hunters, returned, as human souls did, into the custody of spirit protectors in the spirit world.

Small animal figurines in bone, stone, and ivory were important in many areas of Siberia until recently and may have served as "soul catchers" similar to the human dolls of the Khants, Mansis, Nanays, and others. Animal and human figurines found at the Paleolithic campsite Mal'ta, on the Belaya River northwest of Lake Baikal (Gerasimov 1964), document the great antiquity of the northern Siberian world description.

World Experience and Northern Siberian Shamanism

Thinking this world description to conclusion, one could say that the middle world constitutes a meeting ground where the same spirits meet again and again since time began. Reborn to physical form through the chains of generations, the same hunters may always hunt the same animals. Or, because of openness to transformation, an animal spirit may choose reimbodiment in human physical form and, for a time, become a hunter of his former species, adding new spiritual properties to a human descent group. Transformation into objects other than animal and human was possible also. In a Chukchi story (Anisimov 1963b: 216–17) a girl, fleeing from the physical advances of the Moon spirit, changes herself into a hillock and a lamp, but may, judging by the text, turn also into a hammer, a stone block, a pole, a sack, a particle of earth, and so forth.

Spirits are the only enduring, indestructible entities who act out a dreamlike drama on the stage of the middle world. However intricate the play, offense is possible only against temporary physical form. Still, future physical form can be denied by the spirits' withholding of themselves or through their retention by keeper spirits. This, in the interpretation of the old world of northern Siberia, is the reason for the disappearance of species and of human ethnic groups. Because their spirits are immortal, they reside as, for example, the mammoth spirits (see *sheli*, previously mentioned), in the spirit world whence they might rejoin physical form in the future.

In the "creativity of life," as Anisimov (1963b: 217) calls it, "every material object can act according to its own will (*gekulilin*, as the Chukchis say, i.e., 'it has its own voice')." This concept naturally included plants and trees also; vegetation and animals were created before humans. Some Siberian groups traced their descent from trees. The Chumikan and Upper Zeya Evenks related that "man was born from a tree. There was a tree, it split in two. Two people came out. One was a man, the other a woman. Until a child was born they were covered with hair. The first child was born without hair" (Vasilevich 1963a: 68). Among the Negidals, persons came from a larch. Among Sym Evenks, the mythical reindeer *epkachan* splits a pine tree, and in the center appears a woman who sings.

In Evenk origin stories, all animals received their names and had their place and the purpose of their existence defined upon their creation by the Supreme Being, Amaka Sheveki (Vasilevich 1963a: 69). They were given the characteristics of physical form at the same time. The goldeneye duck, for example, that assisted in rescuing the earth from submergence in waters, was kissed on its head by the creator and carries a white mark there since. Each species was given its territory to be respected by others. For each species, laws were made as it had to be hunted (for Yakuts, Paulson 1961: 90) by predators later, including humans. Sometimes the hunting weapons were presented to the spirit keepers of game before the hunt (for Chukchis, see Levin and Potapov 1964: 822). These relations, according to Shirokogoroff (1929: 43), writing about Manchurian Evenks (Tungus), "compel the Tungus, first of all, to know every valley thoroughly, and also to know which animals inhabit it. He must know where he may travel without annoying other animals, just as he does in reference to other ethnical groups."

Throughout northern Siberia, animals were regarded as sacred (for Nentsys, see Paulson 1961:94–95), their death as sacrifice (Holmberg 1926:43–44). The hunting laws imposed by the spirits, including the animal spirits, demanded that no animal should suffer when slain (Holmberg 1926:20). The use of all physical parts of an animal was subject to stringent rules. Greatest care was exercised in the freeing, propitiation, and the Iomante (in Ainu, "sending off") of the spirit.

Regarding the taking of game, Shirokogoroff (1935:89) lists these Evenk rules:

(1) no animals must be killed if the hunter cannot carry the spoil; (2) animals which are not needed by hunter must not be killed; (3) the animals especially cervines of certain age and sex must not be killed at certain periods; (4) the animal wounded must be followed by the hunter until it is killed.

Some animals were considered to have been human. The Selkups said that "the bear was once a man, and that man also now lives in the bear" (Prokofyeva 1963:145). The Eastern Evenks recounted that the wolf at one time had been an Evenk, and "when meeting him one had to step aside, having asked him to leave one alone" (Vasilevich 1963a:71). The Podkamenaya Tunguska Evenks had the same attitude toward the eelpout because they felt that his face looked like an Evenk face; they also had a story about how an eelpout once had fed an abandoned boy with his liver. The Chukchis (Levin and Potapov 1964:824) considered the wolf a changeling and never hunted him.

Many Siberian groups traced their descent from animals. The Sym and Baykit Evenks told about their origin as coming from the bear:

A girl, *Kheladan,* was walking on and on until at last she came to the bear. The bear said: "Kill me and cut me up. Place my heart to sleep beside you, put my kidneys in the place of honor (*malu*) behind the hearth, my duodenum and rectum place opposite you, spread out my fur in a dry ditch, hang my small intestine on a dry, bent-over tree, and put my head to sleep near *malu.*" *Kheladan* killed the bear and did all as he had ordered. In the morning she awoke and looked. At the place of honor there were two children (the kidneys) playing, an old man (the head) was sleeping near them, while opposite him were sleeping an old man and an old woman (the intestines). She glanced outside—there were some reindeer (the fur) walking about and the little valley was full of reindeer. She ran out of the yurt, and there were some halters (the small intestines) hanging on the slanting tree. [Vasilevich 1963a:68]

Some Sakhalin and Okhotsk Evenks had a story about the descent of some Evenks from a girl whose husbands were a man and a bear. "This girl lived at a time when there was no bow and arrow, and when people hunted wild animals with a pointed stone held in the hand" (Vasilevich 1963a:68). The Udegeys and other groups of the Lower Amur also attributed their origin to the marriage of a girl with a bear (Levin and Potapov 1964:743). Some Amur peoples traced their descent from a tiger (Holmberg 1922:26).

In Siberian thought, the bear, a visitor in the middle world especially beneficial to humans, is associated with both the world above and the world below. He is the cosmic hunter visible in the night skies, mentioned before, and the powerful being released in the Iomante bear festivals of the Amur, Sakhalin, and Hokkaido tribes to his homeland in the sacred high mountains (Paproth 1976:13–14; Slawik 1952). But because the sacred mountains are entrances to the world below, in the symbolism of shamans' costumes, he represents this region of the universe more deeply than any other animal spirit. The underground dwellings of the Selkup Earth Mother, *Ylyunda kotta*, for example, are guarded by her two protectors, half-bear, half-man (Prokofyeva 1963:145). Other animal spirits generally associated with the world below are the otter and the loon.

The sacred birds of the world above are swan, crane, magpie, and eagle. The eagle was considered the chief intermediary between humans and the Supreme Being. Enets, for example, called the eagle *minley* "son of god," "sovereign of the wind," who "could take the shape of a man" (Prokofyeva 1963:133). To the Buryats, the eagle was an emissary sent by the Supreme Being to protect humans from disease. He was the first shaman made by the creator, but people did not understand him. Finally, he approached a woman sleeping under a tree and left her with a child that grew up to become the first Buryat shaman (Holmberg 1922:26). Among some groups, the children of a swan woman became the first shamans (Findeisen 1957:28).

Throughout northern Siberia (as among early Tsistsistas) "the ancient hunters strove to make themselves resemble beasts: They disguised themselves in their skins and later for the same purpose wore special costumes resembling the animal in form—special caps with horns, jackets made of wild-reindeer skins, and others" (Anisimov 1963a:109). Lavish animal costumes were integral parts of fall game-bringing ceremonies of Shingkelevun and Girkumki types, and of releasing, "sending-off" (Iomante) ceremonies. The animal impersonators in such ceremonies identified with the "social groups" (Slawik 1952:194) of species as members.

The most intensively studied of Iomante ceremonies are those concerning the bear. Bear festivals culminating in the "sending off" of the slain bear's spirit retained a wide distribution until the beginning of this century. Hallowell (1926) and Paproth (1976) have traced bear festivals in a number of variations from northern Scandinavia across Eurasia to the northern half of North America and the Greenland Eskimos. With shamanistic performances and ceremonies concerning animals, bear ceremonialism seems to have been practiced at least as early as the European Upper Palaeolithic, as Narr (1959, 1961, 1966), Lommel (1967), and Zotz (1958) have concluded from the evidence extant in the art and archaeological remains of the period.

Although bear ceremonialism rarely retained in North America (Munsee-Mahicans, chapter 8) the complexity with which it had survived in vast regions of northern Siberia, significant traces are found among Eskimos, many Athapaskan groups, on the Northwest Coast, among some Siouan tribes (Assiniboines, Santees) and, especially, northern, central, and eastern Algonquian groups (Montagnais-Naskapis, Crees, Ojibwas, Ottawas, Algonquins, Menominis, Sauks, Foxes, Micmacs, Malecites, Penobscots, Abnakis, Delawares) (Hallowell 1926). If the proto-Tsistsistas had participated in bear ceremonialism in the past, they may have lost it as a result of their removal into the Plains.

Bear ceremonialism, however, should not be treated as an isolated phenomenon. Although the bear Iomante does justice to a specific— and magnificent—animal, the laws of the early northern Siberian and North American world descriptions required that justice was done to *all* animals. These laws were obeyed in "sending-off" ceremonies everywhere that, although often overlooked by ethnographers, existed side by side with the bear Iomante, and also existed where a complex bear ceremonialism was not practiced.

In northern Siberia each person not only participated in the expressions characteristic of the world experience of his or her specific group but also played an active part as an individual—much as in early Tsistsistas culture described in chapter 1. That human beings as groups and as individuals, were also considered powerful beings has already been shown in this chapter and requries no further evidence.

Perhaps the *gekulilin* concept of the Chukchis should be remembered: *everything* "has its own voice."

The power of the individual's perseverence and creative drive, inherent in all original stories collected among northern Siberian groups, has nevertheless been largely ignored by ethnographers because observation has always been tilted toward group expressions ("cults") and the shamans—although, in regard to both, much of the literature is corrupted by either Western scientific bias or by Christian religious or Marxist materialist superstitions (see also Golowin 1981 on this issue). In aboriginal times, the human condition in northern Siberia, as that of the Tsistsistas, required that each individual was a finely tuned entity by himself or herself. That cooperation with others was equally important was the second law. Both laws were taught by the one animal that peoples of northern Siberia and the Tsistsistas regarded as the master hunter par excellence—the wolf. (Note that Lopez 1978 has suggested that more could be learned about the origins of humans as social animals by studying the social structure of wolf packs than could be learned by studying primates.)

In many types of group expressions, shaman leadership was not required. Among the Evenks (Anisimov 1963a : 99), each family owned a bundle containing ancestor guardian spirits that was used first when a family member had fallen ill. Only if the case proved to need extraordinary measures was a shaman called in. Among the Nivkhis (Taksami 1963 : 437–44), after a band had moved to a new location, each family fed the spirits of the locality and the river spirits at the ice fishing hole with specially prepared food. When a person went away for a visit, a family member fed the earth spirit, depositing a spoonful of food at a nearby tree, asking for a safe journey. Upon return, the person himself or herself made a gift of thanksgiving at the same place. Nivkhi band ceremonies held at the closing of the Amur with ice, at the time of the thawing of the river, and the Festival of the Sky in winter were directed by the oldest male of the group. Similar rules were observed throughout northern Siberia.

Shamans were individuals—male and female—singled out by the spirits as unusually gifted to serve as mediators between the spiritual forces in the regions of the universe and spirits temporarily embodied in physical form in the middle world. Vasilevich (1963a : 75) believes that shamanism was originally a woman's prerogative. Anisimov (1963a : 97) mentions that the robe of an Evenk shaman is always cut in the characteristic design of a woman's garment.

An Evenk shaman was not permitted to accept payments for his or her services (Vasilevich 1963b : 379). Even the gifts placed on a *turu* at the beginning of a spirit lodge ceremony (Kamlanye), during which the shaman was strained to the limits of his or her physical and mental endurance, were afterward not granted him or her but were distributed among ailing members of the group (Vasilevich 1963a : 379), perhaps because they had been touched by cosmic power during the performance. Because of their constant attention to information coming from the spirit world, Evenk shamans lived largely a secluded life.

In Evenk, member of the Tungus language family, there are four terms for shaman. *Saman* (*šaman*) is the least complex of these. It is this term, introduced through Russian into the literature, that has become the technical term for the phenomenon of the shaman worldwide. The word *saman* appears in all Tungusic languages, and in Turkic and Mongolian.

According to Vasilevich (1963b : 369–72), three other Evenk terms are considerably older in origin. One derives from the stem *seven* (sheven), meaning "spirit," "spirit helper" of the shaman; *sevenche*, "to shamanize" or "to be in the condition of *seven*," that is, "inhaling helping spirits," "to reach for the soul of a sick person." Another stems from *nimngakan*, or *nimngan*, "to put on a shamanistic performance"; *nimngamat*, "to induce spirit helpers to enter one's body"; *nimngangki*, "shaman's drum"; and *nimngavka*, "to ask to shamanize." The last, and the oldest of all, is *yayan*, "shaman"; *yaya*, "to perform by the campfire," "to shamanize." *Yaya* also designates the shaman's drum. Among non-Tungusic Paleo-Asiatic groups such as the Chukchis and Koryaks, the Evenk term *yaya* occurs in derivation: Chukchi *jarar* and Koryak *jajaj* mean both "drum" and the "shamanistic performance."

The eastern Algonquian Penobscots called the shaman *medo'olinu*, "drum sound person," derived from the stem *mede*, "sound of drumming." For Penobscots and their linguistic relatives, the Abnakis, Wavenocks, Malecites, Passamaquoddys, and Micmacs, the shaman's power was thought partly to lie in his drum (Speck 1919 : 240–41).

Throughout northern Siberia, individuals who were to become shamans were elected by the spirits and forced by them to accept the vocation (see also Kalweit 1984 : 146). Refusal led to mental illness and death.

Oftentimes the office was inherited. In extensive genealogies that Vasilevich (1963b : 374–75) has recorded among Evenk groups, she found forty-eight cases in which it was remembered that shamans had inherited the helping spirits of shaman ancestors. In forty of these, they came from a grandfather or father/mother who had been shamans.

Anisimov (1963a:115–16) calls this process the "passive means of obtaining the shamanistic gift." As "active means," he describes a quest that would lead a person into the forest where he or she would "reproduce all the features characteristic of the shamanistic choosing, acquire by long fasting and physical exhaustion an appropriate patron spirit and then be considered capable of shamanistic service. The patron spirit . . . [most frequently an animal or a bird] . . . taught the person all the particulars of the shamanistic ritual and provided the requisite number of spirit helpers." Vasilevich (1963b: 375) was told that spirit helpers of deceased shamans who did not elect a successor among members of the descent group traveled in the taiga until they met and entered a person of their choice.

Among Manchurian Evenks, Anisimov's two categories are the basis for two classes of "great shamans"—those who inherit through the descent group and those who are independent of it (Shirokogoroff 1935:344). Among Buryats, shamanism also is either inherited or brought about by intervention of the sky spirits, for example, by striking a person with lightning or showing him or her stones dropping from the sky (Eliade 1974:19).

Generally, election by the spirits had dramatic consequences. The neophyte suffered a severe initiatory illness followed by his or her experience of death, resurrection, and transformation (see also Kalweit 1984:101–16).

Lying in a comalike trance, he or she was forced into out-of-body experiences in which he or she was drawn into the spirit world where he or she became a passive witness of his or her own dismemberment: the limbs and organs were removed, the flesh scraped from the bones to be exposed, cooked, and eaten. Among tribes that practiced bear festivals, such as Yakuts, Evenks, and Buryats, the neophyte's body was dissected and consumed by the spirits as that of the bear by humans in the Iomante feast (Lehtisalo 1937:19–20).

After having seen themselves reduced to a skeleton, stripped utterly of their former physical appearance, they also observed their reconstitution by the spirits. They were rebuilt from their bones to a new life and a mystical condition that permitted them direct association with the spirit world.

Which spirits elected the neophytes decided their capabilities as shamans. Because they themselves could not choose, they had no control over the process. The spirits' attachment did not lead to "pseudo-possession," "possession," or a split personality. Rather, as Paulson (1962:129) has concluded, based on information from throughout northern Eurasia, shamans remained themselves but gained another dimension.

Three categories of spirits can be distinguished with whom a shaman might be associated. The first comprised the powerful beings of sky and earth spaces, of celestial bodies, or regions, localities and *Artgeister* (species-specific protector spirits). One of these might call on a shaman for special services or might be agreeable to provide guidance, even respond to a shaman's call and speak in a seance.

Most intimately, however, a shaman was connected with a being of the second category—a tutelary spirit. This spirit, also called in the literature guardian or patron spirit or "a familiar" because of his familiarity with the shaman, was usually an animal spirit who had adopted the shaman for life. Here a fusion took place: the tutelary spirit became the shaman's alter ego, his or her double into which, in many cases, he or she could transform himself or herself physically and become a bear, a wolf, a crane, a deer, and so forth. Where shaman's robes were used in northern Siberia, the robe itself was conceived as a visual, material expression of the tutelary spirit.

Helping spirits formed the third category. They might be enlisted by the tutelary spirit, could be inherited (i.e., join a neophyte along the descent line) as a group or could choose a person singly in succession over time. Helping spirits were added as physical representations to the shaman's robe in the form of pendants, dolls, small figurines, masks, and the like. Shamans were capable of joining a part of their soul with a helping spirit who performed tasks in the spirit world. They responded to his call in seances, assisted in healing and in the safe conduct of human souls to the spirit world, and provided information on matters of the past, present, and future. They also served as guardians—as a magical fence—around the territory of the shaman's human social group.

Among the Nanays, according to Sternberg (Eliade 1974:71–73), the tutelary spirit was called *ayami,* the helping spirit, *syven.* In one Nanay shaman's confession, he revealed that his *ayami* was a beautiful, small woman with one half of her face painted red, the other half black. She could appear in the guise of an old woman, a wolf, or a winged tiger. She had provided him with three spirit helpers: *jarga,* (leopard), *doonto* (bear) and *amba* (tiger). "When I am shamaning, the *ayami* and the assistant spirits . . . penetrate me, as smoke or vapor would. When the *ayami* is within me, it is she who speaks through my mouth, and she does everything herself."

Generally, because spirits were not visible to humans alive in the middle world, shamans, because they could see, were in condition of a living dead person.

After the initiatory experience of death and resurrection, the spirits taught the neophyte their special knowledge including songs, terms, and ritual signs with which to call them: a secret language not to be used by others who were not in the shaman's condition. A non-shaman using a shaman's equipment and spirit songs might be able to call the spirits up but would suffer death or permanent injury because he was unprepared for their power.

Generally, in northern Siberia, after the first teachings of the spirits the new shaman received additional training from an experienced shaman that included the preparation of paraphernalia and objects necessary for his specific performance of the craft. Among the Evenks (Anisimov 1963a:116–17), the whole group participated in their making; once they were completed each person of the group was expected to handle them before they were turned over to the new shaman. He or she then vivified the equipment, settling the spirits in their symbolic physical lodgings; afterward, because of the spirits' presence in it, the equipment, with the exception of the drum, could not be used by anyone but him or her. Upon his or her death, his equipment was either deposited at the grave or placed on a tree in the taiga (Paulson 1962:132).

Most important of the shaman's equipment were the robe (often consisting of two pieces), headdress, face mask, boots, gloves, drum, drumstick and staff. Generally the costume was most elaborate in the central and northwestern regions of northern Siberia, rather simple in the northeast (Chukchis, Koryaks) and southeast (on the Amur).

Holmberg (1922:14–18) distinguished three categories of shaman costumes: the reindeer, bear, and bird types. Findeisen (1957:81) added one more: the deer costume. Each costume represented the total physical form of the animal guardian spirit, including its skeleton, in elaborate ornamentation. In the case of the three mammals, the legs of the shaman (including his boots) were the animal's hind legs, the arms (including the gloves) were the animal's front legs. Of the headdresses most conspicuous were those of bird and reindeer costumes. The first often featured a feather bonnet (Diószegi 1963, figs. 2, 3, 48, 49, 59, 63, 70, 74) with feathers of the tutelary spirit bird (eagle, owl, crane, etc.), the second reindeer antlers on a crownlike frame (Holmberg 1922, fig. 6; Prokofyeva 1963, fig. 19). Among the spirit helper representations added to the costume as pendants were often actual physical parts of these animal spirits, including wolf- or foxtails, bear paws, claw necklaces, and so forth. It appears that among the earliest artistic descriptions of a masked reindeer shaman preserved is a wall painting in Trois Frères Cave, in southern France, of the Magdalenian period of the Upper Paleolithic (Miyakawa and Kollautz 1966:162–64, 185). One of the best preserved Evenk costumes was published in detail by Lommel (1967:figs. 17–21, 24).

In regard to the regions of the universe, the bird shaman generally was associated with the sky space, the bear shaman with the deep earth, whereas reindeer and deer shamans could be associated with either region or the middle world.

The shaman's drum was considered a living being once its owner spirit ("master") had been called into it. In Enets' shamanism, the drum was regarded as a symbol of the universe (Prokofyeva 1963:150), the iconography of its painting, done in red and black colors, expressing the spirits of the regions. Everywhere in northern Siberia the drum was the chief instrument of the shaman when he communicated with the spirits. The drum also served as vehicle of his or her magical flights. The drum of a male shaman was covered with the skin of a buck; that of a female shaman with the skin of a doe. Occasionally, during seances a shaman's assistant might work the drum for him or her when he or she was hung from a pole. On drumsticks, often a face was carved; among the Enets it represented *kua kaza,* the "birch man," spirit of the drumstick made of birch (Prokefyeva 1963: 150–52) and was "greased," that is, fed, before a performance.

Among some groups, for example, Enets, Selkups, Nenets, shamans of the highest order (sky shamans) also had a staff or wand that was used for protection when traveling in the spirit world. A face cut into the upper end of the staff depicted its owner spirit; the lower end was fashioned as a deer hoof. It appears that the animal spirit of this staff was also fed at times.

As the northern Siberian universe consisted of different regions, each protected by spirits of different categories and power, there were also different categories of shamans. The vast literature reveals this only indirectly; ethnographers who worked there generally did not ask such questions and therefore received no answers. There are exceptions, however. Using her husband's excellent field notes, Prokofyeva (1963:124, 149) was able to discover three categories of shamans among the Enets and related groups on the Yenisey that pertain to regions: (1) *budtode*, "having power to contact celestial spirits"; (2) *dyano*, "defending people from malicious spirits"; and (3) *savode*, "communicating with the world of the dead." *Budtode* shamans had two drums: "one for shamanizing to the upper world, the other for the lower world." The first drum was called *nano peddi*, "the sky drum," the second, *dyano peddi*, "the earth drum." *Dyano* shamans possessed only one drum, the *dyano peddi*, because they were tied to the world below.

Androgyne shamans of transvestite type have been reported from northeastern Siberia among Chukchis, Koryaks, Asiatic Eskimos, and groups on Kamchatka (Findeisen 1957:140–47). If their vocation represented a symbolical union of sky and earth spaces (as among the Tsistsistas) has been left unexplored in the literature. It is interesting, however, that among Koryaks the transvestite shaman was considered the most powerful of all shamans (Halifax 1979:24, after Jochelson).

North Siberian shamans served as protectors of their ethnic groups with respect to any danger. They played a key role in intergroup warfare where they used their spirit allies against enemies, killing over a distance. Evenk shaman leadership on a dangerous trail is expressed in the following lines written by the Evenk poet Aleksey Salatkin (Anisimov 1963a:118):

> And on their journey they were led by
> The shaman himself, the clan's eldest,
> Making signs upon tree trunks,
> That they might go unimpeded.

In summary, the main tasks of northern Siberian shamans were these: (1) to maintain harmony among all physical and spiritual forms within a territory identified with their ethnic group; (2) to protect this territory against outside abuse (repel foreign intrusion) and remedy abuse from within it (by members of one's own group); (3) to assist annually in the spring the regeneration of life by directing earth renewal ceremonies (Evenk, Ikenipke) in which the solidarity of all living forms according to the original purpose of the creation was acted out in sacred play; (4) to provide annually in the fall the game animals required over the year for the physical survival of their ethnic group by directing ceremonies (Evenk, Girkumki, Shingkelevun) at the sacred place where they could reach the Earth Spirit and achieve her assent; (5) to heal illness of members of the ethnic group; and (6) to guard the dying, lead their souls safely to their places in the spirit world, and return from there souls for reincarnation to maintain equilibrium in the ethnic group and territory.

In concordance with the old northern Siberian world experience, I might ask: Who needed the shaman most? The answer is: the spirits themselves. They made the shaman; they acted, and they explained the world through the shaman.

The Khanty tale *pro sovu* ("for the owl") (Chernetsov 1963 : 40) has a lesson that rings into our time. The spirit master of the world above asks the owl: "Of whom are there more on earth, the living or the dead?" The owl answers that there are more dead. "Since when," says the spirit in surprise, "was it a success to die?"

3. Concepts and Expressions of World Description and Shamanism Among Northern Siberian Groups and Tsistsistas: A Comparison

My black mountains
where I have walked
are deserted now—
my land
of golden grasses
where I have walked.
My black mountains are left behind.
My white mountain peaks are left behind.
All my strength is left behind.
Of my large tribe
I alone am still alive.
My lakes
where I have fished
are left behind.
I cannot see them any more.
My tent is rotting
and my bark clothing hangs in shreds.
It is over.

—LAMENT OF A SAMOYED SHAMAN, RECORDED BY KAI DONNER

AROUND 500 B.C., bands of Proto-Tsistsistas taiga hunters entered the northeastern edge of the Plains. That their distant ancestors once had been there may have been beyond their memory. They came as strangers into territory unknown to them. They came from the north where, for a very long time, they had hunted the subarctic woodland and the transitional zone between woodland and tundra of the southern Keewatin and southeastern Mackenzie districts (see chapter 8). Their main game animals had been caribou and moose. They had largely depended upon the forest but had used the barrens seasonally.

Their withdrawal southward appears to have occurred around 1000 B.C., after climatic changes, beginning in 1500 B.C., resulted in the southward retreat of the tree line up to distances of two hundred miles. At around 1000 B.C., the tundra reached south well into northern Manitoba and northeastern Saskatchewan. Added to the pressure of a changing environment may have been population pressure as a result of crowding and the advance of Pre-Dorset Eskimo hunters who, already established in the barrens, followed the expanding tundra south.

Proto-Tsistsistas bands did not move south alone. They were part of a general migration of northern Algonquian hunters that would eventually lead some into the Plains, others into southern Ontario, the Great Lakes region, and beyond.

In the north, in the region west of Hudson Bay (southeastern Mackenzie and southern Keewatin districts, northern Manitoba, northern Saskatchewan and northwestern Ontario), they had all been participants in what Wright (1972b) calls the Shield Archaic way of life. It is suggested here that at the time of their withdrawal they had shared in concepts described for Tsistsistas in chapter 1. The re-evaluation of the ethnographies of historic western and central Algonquian groups, cutting through the familiar pictures passed on through the literature would, I believe, reveal the ancient common base. To extend the investigation to all historic Algonquian groups would be illuminating and requires attention but reaches beyond the scope of this book.

It is not proposed that Proto-Tsistsistas culture remained the same after the arrival in the Dakotas. On the contrary, the Massaum ceremony and some of its associated features represent a significant cultural change leading to a perfect adaptation to the northern Plains. The principal structures of the Proto-Tsistsistas world description, nevertheless, remained intact and, over 2000 years later, were carried into the reservation period.

The facts presented in chapter 2 force the conclusion that northern Siberian cultures once shared with the Algonquians a common heritage. Because of the time span of the separation, it follows that the principles of the Tsistsistas world description and shamanism as outlined in chapter 1 existed far back in the Proto-Tsistsistas past.

The strength of these statements rests on the following comparison that excludes functional categories and material traits.

The last three units of data in table 1 appear both in the Evenk *shevenchedek* of the Kamlanye ceremony and in the wolf lodge of the Massaum (see chapter 6).

Table 1. Selected Comparative Data

Concept	Northern Siberia	Tsistsistas
The universe is multilayered	x	x
Each layer possesses powerful spirits	x	x
Deep earth	x	x
Earth spirit as keeper of animals	x	x
Animal spirits are underground	x	x
Cosmic tree	x	x
Vault of heaven as skin thrown over earth	x	—
Vault of heaven as a kettle	x	x
North Star as sky navel	x	—
Several sky regions	x	x
Supreme Being in uppermost sky region	x	x
Supreme Being as creator of universe	x	x
Creation of universe as shamanistic act	x	x
Four sacred guardians at four corners of universe	—	x
Shamanistic concept of a second universe outside the first	x	x
Sacred mountain as entrance to deep earth and earth spirit	x	x
Ceremony in which game is obtained from earth spirit	x	x
Animal impersonators in ceremony	x	x
Center pole of ceremonial lodge represents Supreme Being	x	x
Earth renewal ceremony in spring	x	x
Spirit lodge ceremonies for healing and the propitiation of game spirits	x	x
Spirit lodge as sacred mountain	x	x
Sweat lodge	—	x
Story about the earth rescued from waters with bird assistance	x	x
Mammoth as helper in retrieving earth from beneath waters	x	—
Giant serpent	x	x
Supreme Being as *deus otiosus*	x	?
Sacrifices to Supreme Being	x	x
Sacrifices to Supreme Being of white (albino) animals	x	x

Concept	Northern Siberia	Tsistsistas
Cosmic order guarded by powerful mediator spirits	x	x
Stars as opening to higher levels of the world above	x	?
Star constellations as relatives or mythical ancestors	x	x
Stars providing signals for actions below	x	x
Importance of number 7	x	x
Importance of number 4	—	x
Sky spirits cause seasonal changes on earth	x	x
Specific animals sacred to different regions of universe	x	x
Powerful spirit protectors of animals	x	x
Animals are objects of veneration	x	x
Animals themselves grant slaying	x	x
Earth spirit female	x	x
Earth spirit male	x	—
Spirits of regions (taiga, tundra, etc.)	x	?
Spirits of localities	x	x
Species-specific protector spirits (*Artgeister*)	x	x
All physical form alive is endowed with reincarnate spirit (soul)	x	x
Concept of multiple souls, or spirit with multiple parts including one reincarnate one	x	x
Original grant of spirits limited for humans and animals	x	x
Spirits are indestructable	x	x
Transmutability of spirits	x	x
Spirits inherited in descent group or species	x	x
Concept of death as long process of separation of souls	x	x
This is true for humans and animals	x	x
During first stage of death, a person's spirit travels far	x	x
One part of spirit remains in skeleton until decay of bones	x	x

Concept	Northern Siberia	Tsistsistas
Temporary retention of body soul of humans and animals	x	x
First and secondary burial of humans	x	x
Embodying spirit of deceased in figurine or object	x	x
Special laws regarding treatment of animal bones	x	x
Burial of animal remains	x	x
Embodying animal spirits in figurines	x	x
Animals can be withheld from reincarnation by spirit keepers	x	x
Human spirits can refuse reincarnation	x	x
Spirits travel with the speed of thought	x	x
"Everything has its own voice"	x	x
Trees and plants have spirits also	x	x
Animal species have territories as human groups have	x	x
Animals are regarded as sacred	x	x
Hunting as sacred ritual designed by game and spirit keepers	x	x
Abuse of animals punished by spirits	x	x
Sometimes humans descended from animals	x	x
Bear associated with the world below	x	x
The bear as celestial hunter	x	?
Iomante (sending-off) rituals	x	x
Bear iomante	x	—
Eagle as sacred bird of world above	x	x
Crane as sacred bird of world above	x	x
Magpie as sacred bird of world above	x	x
Swan as sacred bird of world above	x	—
Humans fashion themselves after animals	x	x
Wolf as master hunter; special rules concerning wolves	x	x
Bundles containing spirits	x	x
Feeding spirits for special reasons	x	x
Conscious detachment of parts of one's spirit possible to most people	—	x
Conscious detachment of parts of one's spirit exercised by shamans	x	x

Concept	Northern Siberia	Tsistsistas
Almost every person has a tutelary spirit	—	x
Each shaman has a tutelary spirit	x	x
Each shaman has helping spirits	x	x
A shaman may inherit a tutelary spirit	x	—
A shaman may seek or is sought by a spirit	x	x
A shaman is capable of "paranormal" demonstrations	x	x
A shaman is elected by spirits	x	x
During his or her initiation, a shaman is dismembered and resurrected	x	—
During his or her initiation, the shaman experiences a transformation	x	x
The power of the spirits decides the shaman's capabilities	x	x
Spirits may use a shaman's speech apparatus directly to express themselves	x	x
A shaman is taught first by the spirits	x	x
Later he or she receives additional training from an experienced shaman	x	x
A shaman's equipment is vivified	x	x
A shaman's equipment cannot be used by others	x	x
A shaman's equipment is abandoned after his or her death	x	x
Shaman's mask	x	—
Shaman's face painting	?	x
Shaman's robe	x	x
Shaman's belt	x	x
Shaman's gloves and boots	x	—
Shaman's headdress	x	x
Shaman's drum	x	x
Shaman's rattle	—	x
Shaman's use of eagle, magpie, crane feathers	x	x
Sky shamans	x	x
Some shamans are specialists on stars	x	x
Earth shamans	x	x
The shaman has a sky bow	x	x

Concept	Northern Siberia	Tsistsistas
On shaman's staffs a spirit face may be carved	x	x
Oxzem (spirit wheel)	—	x
Spirit catchers (animal figurines)	x	x
Shaman's dolls	x	x
Shamans represent every region of universe	x	x
Shamans use a secret language	x	x
Shamans form an esoteric group	?	x
Contrary shamans	x	x
Transvestite shamans	x	x
Shamans kill over distance	x	x
Shamans protect territory with spirit help	x	x
Shamans take the souls of the dead to the afterworld	x	—
Shamans bring souls from the afterworld for reincarnation	x	—
Shamans may control death, including their own	x	x
Shamans direct ceremonies	x	x
Medicine hunts	?	x
Sacred poles	x	x
During one type of spirit lodge performance, the lodge has a center tree	x	x
The tree has seven markings	x	x
The tree is the world tree	x	x

4. The Coming of Strangers

There used to be a children's game called nakonistoz., *bear play. One player represented a she bear in a den. The others approached with a pole featuring a sharpened, split end. They poked cautiously into the den and, touching the she-bear player, twisted the jagged point into the animal's fur before attempting to pull it out. While they were preparing to do this, they would comment loudly what kind of game was hidden there, listing names of other animals, although they knew it was a bear. They were not allowed to use bear terms, for example,* nako, *"bear,"* nakoová, *"bear hairy," and so forth. The game prescribed that finally one of the players would speak one of the forbidden words. The she bear, upon hearing her name would charge from the den and chase and overpower the hunters. This game recapitulated Proto-Tsistsistas bear hunting rules as they had been practiced in the old north country.*

In the story of the Pleiades, the celestial she bear, maheonhovàn, *Nako, came to earth to punish those who had insulted bears by calling their name. It happened near the Black Hills, and of the Tsistsistas camp destroyed by the giant bear spirit, only a girl survived. On her flight before* maheonhovàn *a powerful spirit tried to help by throwing obstacles behind her to stop the pursuer, but still she came. Then Manohotoxceo, the Seven Brothers (Pleiades), came from the sky to help her but they fought the bear without success.*

Finally, in answer to the girl's prayers, a great mountain grew up under their feet, so steep and smooth that the she bear could not climb it. She tried and tried but always slid back, tearing deep grooves into the mountain's sides with her claws. She went to the river and painted her face with red clay. She came back and called: "Give me the girl. If you do not, I shall hug this mountain and throw it down."

But they refused. Four times she called up, but still the brothers refused. The bear rose on her hind legs and reached her forepaws around the mountain. She hugged hard, twisting and pushing, so that it began to lean.

Some say the youngest of the brothers killed her then. Others say that he tried but could not and that they fled to the sky taking the girl with them as their sister. The bear followed, they say, and is still chasing them across the dome of the night sky.

Others say that it was Motseyoef who, using his shamanistic power, made the mountain open up, bring Nako in, and close behind her. According to this tra-

dition, she is still there, alive, waiting to be unleashed from her confinement to take revenge on those who are destroying the wild animal world.

The mountain that rose to protect the girl and the Seven Brothers is just to the Northwest of the Black Hills. Tsistsistas call it Nakoevē, Bear Peak. On road maps it is listed as Devil's Tower.

ONE OF THE EARLIEST Tsistsistas stories, generally misunderstood because some of its features are assumed by ethnographers to have biblical connotations, places the Proto-Tsistsistas in the far north. Their withdrawal from the region as told in the story is seen here as the one leading to their eventual arrival in the Dakotas. The story describes the beginning of their movement, in which a shaman played a crucial role, with these words:

Many thousands of years ago the Cheyenne inhabited a country in the far north, across a great body of water. For two or three years they had been overpowered by an enemy that outnumbered them . . . and they were filled with sorrow. Among their number was a great medicine-man who possessed a wooden hoop like those used in the games of to-day. On one side of the hoop were tied magpie feathers, while opposite them, on the other side of the hoop, was a flint spear head, with the point projecting toward the center of the hoop. One night . . . he told the people to come to a certain place. When they were assembled he led them away. He kept in advance of them all the time, and in his left hand he held a long staff, and in his right hand he held his hoop horizontally in front of him with the spear head of the hoop pointing forward. No one was allowed to go in front of him. [Dorsey 1905, 1:37]

From the analyses provided in Chapters 1 and 2 it is obvious that he carried a shaman' staff and an *oxzem*, a spirit wheel, whose spirit guided the trek to a new territory. There are great bodies of water around the location pinpointed in the last chapter.

Regarding the social and political organization of the Proto-Tsistsistas, very little is known. Callendar (1962:73–75) sees Proto-Central Algonquians, with whom the Proto-Tsistsistas were related during these times, as small nomadic hunting groups. Proto-Tsistsistas bands may have been relatively independent but would have cooperated seasonally with others in activities requiring concentration, for example, ceremonies, collective hunts and trading; perhaps marriages were formed at such times. The story quoted here may suggest that bands saw themselves as a people with ethnic boundaries. The term "tribe" does not seem applicable (see Fried 1975) because systems of tribal chiefs and soldier societies, with which Tsistsistas entered the late historic period, were not necessary yet and had not yet been developed.

It is most likely that Proto-Tsistsistas and related groups brought from the North an annual fall ceremony through which game was obtained from the Earth Mother, similar to the Evenk Shingkelevun and Girkumki, and an annual earth renewal ceremony held in spring, similar to the Ikenipke. The Massaum would have built on the first, whereas the Oxheheom (New Life Lodge, "Sun Dance"), introduced later, would have developed out of the second. Both the Massaum and the Oxheheom have a "northern cast," especially the latter because the annual spring ice breakup and the earth regeneration is nowhere experienced more intensely than in arctic and subarctic regions. It is therefore not surprising that the Plains "Sun Dance" of historic times had achieved its deepest and most complex expressions among formerly Northern Algonquian hunters: Suhtais, Tsistsistas, Arapahos, and Atsinas.

Some Proto-Tsistsistas institutions were incorporated in the Massaum, although they also continued a powerful presence outside of it. Without explaining these, the Massaum cannot be understood. They have already been mentioned briefly in chapter 1. The following descriptions discuss these in more detail.

Medicine Hunts

The Tsistsistas used the term *medicine hunt* for a collective hunt in which members of one band or a number of bands acted under shaman directorship abiding by strict rules. Proto-Tsistsistas bands carried a full-blown medicine hunt complex into the Dakotas; medicine hunts were continued to the late 1860s. After that date, ceaseless armed conflict with White intrusion, coupled with the beginning destruction of the great herds, made them impossible.

The adoption of maize horticulture before 1700 and the acquisition of horses after 1700 never jeopardized the Tsistsistas medicine hunt complex because it was deeply embedded in the Massaum. Horses, as "new" and "foreign" animals, were kept outside the Massaum and therefore were never given a significant role in medicine hunts either.

In medicine hunts, a Tsistsistas antelope shaman used his antelope spirit helper to call antelopes into pits, and a buffalo shaman used his buffalo spirit helper to call a buffalo herd into camp or pound. Whatever the technique that was employed, the treatment of animal bodies and spirits necessarily obeyed the laws formulated by the animals themselves. This is why the Proto-Tsistsistas and the Tsistsistas, un-like other peoples of the northern Plains, refused the cruel method of driving game herds over cliffs but called them into camps and pounds instead. The driving of antelopes over cliffs in the 1870s, reported from the Northern Cheyennes (e.g., Wooden Leg, in Marquis 1967: 88), represents an aberration and an offense against the Massaum law.

The Tsistsistas used three types of buffalo medicine hunts: (1) the surround; (2) bringing a herd into the camp circle; (3) bringing a herd into a pound. What particular type was used in a specific situa-tion may have been determined by seasonal game conditions in a given region besides the shaman's personal power and preference. Each of the three types of buffalo procurement was put into action and controlled by a shaman or, rarely, by shamans working together.

The medicine hunt was preceded by the shaman's performance in a spirit lodge or sweat lodge culminating in the sending out of his buffalo spirit helper to bring a herd in. Often during the ceremony, physical parts containing buffalo *omotome* (e.g., skulls, hooves) were used in addition to special equipment from the shaman's sacred bundle, the *nisimōnevehaneo*. *Naoetaevoan* is the Tsistsistas term for a shaman who had the power to call buffalo. The end of the medi-cine hunt took place once again in the closed lodge where the sha-man propitiated the slain animals, released their spirits, and fed and thanked his spirit helper before letting him return to the spirit world.

If four successive attempts to bring a herd in had failed, the sha-man, or members of his family, stood to suffer personal injury in-flicted by the spirits. The same happened if the bodies and spirits of animals were not treated properly after a hunt by either the shaman or the hunters; he alone was held responsible for misconduct. If a shaman either abused the secret formulas guiding his relationship to his spirit helpers, or erred in the application, the spirits might kill him (see the fate of Listening-to-the-Ground, in Grinnell 1926:170).

When the surround was used, the shaman caused a herd to be brought near the camp or, if a herd was already close, caused it to remain there. The hunters, led by the shaman, walked to the herd, preferably numbering from twenty to forty buffalo (Grinnell 1923, 1:265). They surrounded it, closed in on the animals, and forced them to run in a circle within the "human pound" (an appropriate phrase used by Kehoe 1973:179), where they were killed. According to a description published by Grinnell (1907, 182–83), the first buf-falo killed might receive special attention: He was smoked; his head was turned to the four directions and the sun; and his meat was used for the ceremonial feast concluding the hunt and was finally shared as sacred food by all people in camp. Perhaps this was the lead animal whose actions to a considerable degree determined success or failure of the hunt. Among some northern Plains tribes (e.g., the Plains Ojibwas), the "bison leader" was allowed to escape, whereas among others (e.g., some Blackfoot bands), he was killed and ritualized (Kehoe 1973 : 185).

Motseyoef called buffalo herds to a surround near camp (Grinnell 1923, 2 : 366–67) during a four-day spirit lodge performance long before he brought *nimāhenan,* the sacred arrows, to the Tsistsistas. After he had introduced *nimāhenan* and the Ceremony of the Sacred Arrows, buffalo used to appear at the end of the ceremony and allowed themselves to be taken outside the camp (Dorsey 1905, 1 : 46). Keepers of *nimāhenan* used two of the sacred arrows to cause buffalo to run in a circle until the number of animals needed was killed. "When they did this the rule was to take everything except the head, and to leave the horns on, and to leave the backbone attached to the head and the tail. Every animal killed with the medicine-arrows had to be treated in that way" (Dorsey 1905, 1 : 2).

In the story of Mukije (Short Woman), collected by Hoebel (1978 : 45–49), the woman shaman introduces a medicine hunt ritual focusing on a holy woman using a buffalo stone for bringing game. This is reminiscent of the Blackfoot concept in which a holy woman serves as drive ritualist with the assistance of the *iniskim* buffalo stone (Grinnell 1962 : 125–26; Kehoe 1973 : 180–81; Schaeffer 1962 : 30–31). Mukije belongs in the Suhtai tradition; contrary to Hoebel's belief, she had no influence on Tsistsistas culture. The woman celebrated in Tsistsistas religion and hunting tradition is Ehyophstah, the buffalo spirit of the Massaum.

When a herd was brought into the camp circle, the camp itself served as a pound.

In one of the Motseyoef stories, the camp was located west of Nowah'wus, Bear Butte; the opening faced the sacred mountain and sunrise. Before he held a buffalo-calling ceremony in a spirit lodge set in the camp's center, he advised the people "to take the dog-travois and to fill up all the gaps in the circle between the lodges; and the people did so. This work occupied four days" (Grinnell 1908 : 316). During the first night of Motseyoef's performance, the buffalo surrounded the camp. During the second night the buffalo "began to run against the travois in the gaps between the lodges." During the third night, they entered the camp circle "and followed it around," and "they were killed from the doors of the lodges as they passed." The spirit-releasing part of the ritual took place the following morning. Part of the ceremonial feast is described as follows:

The next morning they took all the tongues into the lodge in the center of the village, and cooked them by digging a hole in the center of the lodge, and putting into it green hide for a lining, and putting in water and tongues, and throwing hot stones into the water, and so boiling the tongues. [Grinnell 1908:317]

During the fourth night, Motseyoef brought buffalo again into the camp circle. "There were so many of them that the young calves and cows rubbed against the lodges, and caused the poles to bend and squeak." Motseyoef ordered the killing stopped when an adequate number of buffalo had been taken.

The presence of young calves in the herd indicates that this event took place in the fall. Informants told this story reverently to Grinnell and with astonishing detail because it is part of the account of Motseyoef's return from Nowah'wus with *nimāhenan*.

It is likely, although not mentioned in Grinnell's report, that all lodges in camp were closed during the buffalo-calling ritual, including the smoke holes, and that all fires were extinguished. Grinnell's (1907:182) informants described this in another medicine hunt account. It is to be expected that the dogs were taken inside the lodges and were muzzled before and during the arrival of the buffalo.

The impounding of buffalo in a camp circle was a common type of Tsistsistas buffalo hunting. In another account published by Grinnell (1923, 1:264–69), two shamans walked to a herd and, using eagle wing fans, lead it through the entrance into camp.

When a herd was brought into a pound, the location and construction of the feature was determined by the shaman who conducted the buffalo-calling ceremony. As the impounding portion of the Massaum ceremony (chapter 6) indicates, the spirit lodge was built in the center of the camp, the corral next to it; ideally, the lodges were arranged in a half circle behind both. Because Tsistsistas corrals were usually built in an arroyo or "under a cutbank or bluff, which formed one or more walls of the pen" (Grinnell 1923, 1:264), an arrangement of the camp in a clean half-circle was sometimes made impossible by dissected terrain. Nevertheless, semblance to it was required.

Usually, a Tsistsistas enclosure was "a large pen out of wood and

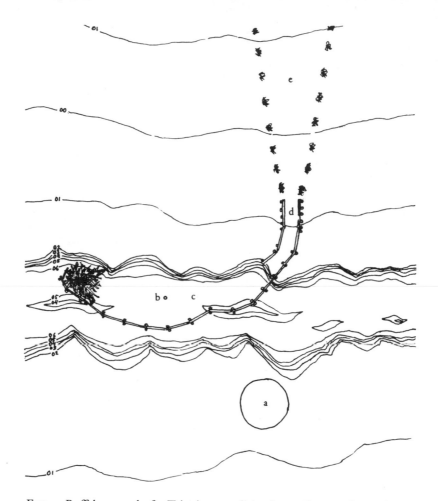

FIG. 3. Buffalo pound of a Tsistsistas medicine hunt. Contour intervals in meters. A corral such as the one shown needed only one restraining wall downslope because the cutbank of the arroyo formed a natural second wall too steep for the trapped animals to breach. The lower end of the corral was closed with driftwood and tree branches. The restraining wall started at the chute and consisted of heavy timber stacked between paired posts. The structure was sturdy enough to withstand and deflect the weight of the herd on its downhill rush. The brush wings of the drive lane extended well beyond the crest of the hill, thus masking the trap waiting below. Once the herd had passed the crest of the hill, its own speed and mass made an escape, from the chute looming up, impossible. (a) Spirit lodge; (b) medicine lance or medicine pole; (c) corral; (d) chute; and (e) brush wings of drive lane.

FIG. 4. The sketch of the buffalo pound is made from the perspective of the spirit lodge.

brush, with a gap in one side, and a chute with diverging wings running far out on the prairie, fences which shall hide the people from the buffalo" (Grinnell 1923, 1:266).

Variations in the construction were due to the individual shaman's, the "poundmaker's," demands. He himself was instructed concerning the pound in a dream, or his design was confirmed in a dream.

Generally the entrance to the corral was formed by two tight fences eight to ten feet high—the chute—behind which trenches were dug where guards hid until the buffalo were passing. From these parallel fences the wings, consisting of spaced branches and young trees, extended perhaps 500 yards out. Rock piles, reported from buffalo drive features of many northern Plains tribes (e.g., Kehoe 1973; Malouf and Conner 1962), are neither reported nor remembered as having been used in Tsistsistas wing composition.

To bring a herd into a pound, a shaman used the ritual already described. In one case mentioned by Grinnell (1923, 1:266–68), two shamans walked to a herd and led it into the wings and the corral using eagle wing fans and singing their spirit songs.

Sometimes two buffalo lances, later, arrows, were made by the shaman and were used as ritual emblems by two messengers who went out, circled a buffalo herd, and coached it with the shafts to walk into the wings and into the corral from where the shaman was calling. For antelope medicine hunts, antelope arrows were used (see drawing,

Grinnell 1923, 1:284). Sometimes, and even in the Late Historic period, such an arrow, which bore no semblance to an arrow or dart released from a weapon, consisted of

a long upright, with a short cross-piece tied to it near the upper end. The upright and the cross-piece were wound with a strip of wolf fur, and to the top of the upright was tied a magpie feather. [Grinnell 1923, 1:290]

Planted in the corral itself, this Tsistsistas medicine lance resembles the "medicine pole" observed as a feature of Plains Cree and Assiniboine pounds (see Kehoe 1973:174–75) and may serve to explain the latter. The medicine lance of the Massaum ceremony (chapter 6) is used in the corral.

The decoration of the medicine lance described previously in Tsistsistas religious symbolism signifies two animals important in the medicine hunt complex: the magpie, who helped the Tsistsistas runner in the Great Race near the Black Hills, and who won it with him, and the wolves, gamekeepers of the spirit herds, assistants of Ehyophstah and messengers of the Massaum.

The two men using buffalo lances, or arrows, should be called messengers, not runners, because they neither ran nor pulled a herd in. In the Tsistsistas interpretation, the animal spirit helpers of the shaman were placed in the ceremonial weapons for the duration of the hunt; their power stirred the herd into movement and gave it direction. Runners achieved great ritual and technical importance in Blackfoot buffalo drives (Grinnell 1926:230; Kehoe 1973; Schaeffer 1962). In Tsistsistas medicine hunts, runners were not used because the animals were not "driven" but were called.

The Tsistsistas took elk in medicine hunts featuring ritual and pounds similar to buffalo hunts. Antelope were called into surrounds or into pits.

It is suggested here that virtually every Proto-Tsistsistas and, perhaps, until the eighteenth century, every Tsistsistas collective hunt was a medicine hunt under shaman leadership. After this date, the Tsistsistas dispersions coupled with the acquisition of horses initiated collective buffalo "runs" on horseback outside the continuing medicine hunt complex.

The Spirit Lodge

The Proto-Tsistsistas spirit lodge ritual, as expressed in Tsistsistas time, was of four types: (1) the lodge where spirits were called for information or advice regarding important matters; (2) the lodge where spirit allies were called before medicine hunts and from which they were released after the slain animals' spirits had been formally freed and sent away; (3) the lodge from which the *omotome* of the deceased were released after the conclusion of the secondary burial or where a *hematasooma* might be joined with an *omotome* to be kept temporarily by a person or persons of the family of the deceased; and (4) the lodge where a sick person was healed or where a person physically "dead" was revived by calling his *hematasooma,* already free, back into his body.

The wolf lodge of the Massaum must also be seen as a spirit lodge where the *maheyuno* and *maiyun* were called and where some spirits were joined with the physical forms of impersonators who played roles in the sacred drama.

The old Proto-Tsistsistas and Tsistsistas concept of the spirit lodge derives from the configuration of the sacred mountain (e.g., No-wah'wus, Bear Butte) that itself is a spirit lodge and that is associated with *maheonoxsz,* the sacred caves, and *heszevoxsz,* the underground caverns where the animal spirits reside.

Two Tsistsistas terms for the spirit lodge ritual are *nisimàtozom* (from *nisimàtoz,* "bringing a spirit ally," or "conjuring" a spirit helper, and *om,* "lodge") and *mxeeom* (from *mxee,* "apparition," "manifestation from the spirit world," and *om,* "lodge").

The first of the four types of spirit lodge performances listed has survived to the present. It is related, as is to be expected, to the "shaking tent rite" of other Algonquian groups (e.g., see Burgesse 1944; Cooper 1944; Flannery 1944), indicating a common origin.

In this *mxeeom,* the shaman causes spirits to come to the lodge and to express themselves there. In its most dramatic form, sketched later, the shaman places himself at the mercy of the spirits; without their swift intervention, he would not survive the ordeal. He neither becomes "possessed" nor ecstatic. He does not perform tricks and does not speak in voices, although his speech apparatus might be used by the spirits directly at other times. He does not send out from the spirit lodge forces of his *hematasooma,* as he would during game-calling ceremonies.

This ritual was conducted by a shaman following a request by a member or members of his group or, on the last day of the Max-hoetonstov, the Ceremony of the Sacred Arrows, as a regular feature integrated with the ceremony. There were many variations of this performance, all dependent on a specific shaman's style that in turn was dependent on the spirits' tolerance. Reduced to essentials, the main events were the following:

A large lodge, the *mxeeom*, consisting of two or three regular tipi covers, was raised in the evening facing east. Behind it a bundle of tall willows or saplings was tied to a pole on which offerings of cloth were exposed (compare the Evenk's *kamlanye* and *turu* pole with gifts of cloth outside the spirit lodge). Near dawn, at the end of the ritual, these offerings were distributed in camp. Because they had been touched by the spirits during the night they had acquired protective power.

Inside the lodge a fire was started after nightfall, and many witnesses assembled, sitting in a tight circle along the inner wall of the lodge. On the west side of the fireplace, a small buffalo-skin tipi was erected; sometimes, instead, a small sweat lodge was built there. A line of coals extended from the entrance of the buffalo tipi across the fire to the east entrance of the large lodge; on these, sweetgrass was burned all night. The shaman entered wearing a breechclout and moccasins; he was usually painted red.

He was tied barefoot within the packed circle of witnesses. He was tied with four bowstrings: each finger of each hand separately to the next finger, both hands tied together behind his back; each toe of each foot separately to the next toe; both feet tied together and tied securely to his bound hands. This operation was executed by sceptics who were called up and charged to tie the shaman as hard as their strength permitted. Their efforts were closely watched by the people present.

In a bent, inextricable position he was placed inside the buffalo tipi; sometimes, when no interior lodge was used he was tied to a tipi pole (Grinnell 1923, 2:113). A rope was tied around his neck and, extending through the pole frame of the buffalo tipi, was held by either four or eight men sitting next to it on opposite sides. A painted rattle and an eagle-bone whistle were placed near the shaman before the buffalo tipi was closed.

The fires had died down. The shaman sang one summoning song to call one of his spirit helpers. When he had ended, the assistants raised him inside the buffalo tipi by pulling hard on the rope. When the men dropped him he lay dead.

The helping spirit, traveling with the speed of thought, entered at the top of the *mxeeom* and rushed down to free and revive his shaman associate. The rope slackened. He came with the force of a whirlwind and caused the large lodge to vibrate violently. The whistle sounded, the rattle bounced among the lodge poles, and lightning flashes lit the dark.

Then the spirit helper spoke. He identified himself by name. If he was the spirit self of a person who had died within the memory of persons present, he was recognized by voice. He answered questions and informed on missing persons or objects and predicted future events.

Some spirits who came were *maiyun;* some were celestial spirits. All of a shaman's spirit helpers could come one after another. All arrived with a terrifying display of power. Animal voices approached from below ground and from the night sky. The spirits left after the shaman, who sometimes had remained silent after the inviting songs, released them with a parting song. Their departure was as impressive as their arrival had been. The fire was started again, and the shaman left the buffalo tipi. The bowstrings with which he had been tied were found knotted into a ball, sometimes in an observer's clothing.

During the spirit lodge ritual of the 1908 Maxhoetonstov, as outlined by William Somers, a participant, to Truman Michelson (in Powell 1969, 2 : 889−90), four inviting songs were sung not by the shaman, Bull Thigh, but by "medicine people, both men and women." The spirits who were called were not Bull Thigh's spirit helpers but seven celestial spirits. They advised on tribal affairs and prophesied the Tsistsistas future. Bull Thigh, in this performance not permitted to call on his personal spirit allies, faced certain death by hanging in the small tipi if the first of the spirits had not responded quickly to the summoning calls of the medicine people.

The spirit lodge has remained an integral part of the Maxhoctonstov from Motseyoef's original instruction of this ceremony to the present. Motseyoef, who was prominent in Proto-Tsistsistas and Tsistsistas history, was a famous spirit lodge conductor.

Some shamans, during a spirit lodge ritual or at other occasions, were able, with the aid of *maiyun* helpers, to dissolve physical form temporarily, thus making themselves invisible and, after moving their *hematasooma* to another location, to reconnect the two there. Castaneda (1979 : 301−10) surprised readers by describing an action with a similar outcome in which he says he participated. Tsistsistas memory retains the names of persons who could perform such feats. Grinnell (1923, 2 : 114−17) mentions Stone Forehead and Ice in this context, and publishes Ice's personal account and interpretation in full (see also Curtis 1911 : 123−24).

Tsistsistas lore also recounts many instances in which shamans

called on their spirit allies in emergencies in broad daylight, in view
of many witnesses, and caused them to move objects, cover the Tsistsistas against enemies, or change weather conditions to hide people
in flight.

The Sweat Lodge

The Proto-Tsistsistas pre-Massaum sweat lodge is mentioned in the
Ehyophstah accounts (Grinnell 1907 : 173−78; Kroeber 1900 : 179−81)
in which the spirits heal the injured young man in a sweat lodge set
inside a mountain (see chapter 5 for a detailed interpretation). That
the healing performance centered on four successive applications of
water to hot stones is listed there; the physical structure of the sweat
lodge, however, is not described.

It appears that originally the Proto-Tsistsistas' sweat lodge was a
special kind of spirit lodge in which heat and steam were used for purification so that participants could receive the unadulterated power
of the spirits unharmed directly. Its physical structure did not symbolize a sacred mountain as that of the spirit lodge described in the
preceding section but the skeletal form of a sacred animal. During
Plains times, the Tsistsistas sweat lodge, with its oval form, its north-
to-south organized willow frame, and its single willow shaft extending from the east entrance to the western end, binding the feature as
a backbone, may, as Curtis (1911 : 116−17) suggests, have symbolized a
buffalo who in turn symbolized the earth. Previously, in northern
Canada, the frame may have symbolized a caribou or a moose.

During early Tsistsistas times the sweat lodge served the following
purposes: (1) to heal a sick person or revive a person already physically dead; (2) to place participants in a purified condition before
major ceremonies or a war expedition and to change them to normal
condition afterwards; and (3) to call spirit helpers before and after
medicine hunts, including in this sequence the sending away of the
spirits of the slain animals.

Apparently, either a spirit lodge or a sweat lodge could be used at
the time of the secondary burial of humans when the *omotome* of the
deceased were joined with their *hematasoomao* in a special ceremony.
Animals, whole or in part interred with the bundles containing the
human remains, received a similar treatment.

According to information collected by Curtis (1911 : 117) among the
Northern Cheyennes, the origin of the sweat lodge was ascribed by
them to the buffalo, thus giving the Suhtai version. It is interesting
that other northern Plains tribes (e.g., Mandans, see Bowers 1950 :

221–23) also traced the origin of the sweat lodge to instruction by animal spirits.

After Motseyoef had used shamanistic power to clear the Black Hills from the mortal enemies of the Tsistsistas, the mysterious Two Faces (chapter 5), he collected the skulls and bones of slain members of his people and brought them back to life in a sweat-lodge ceremony. The miraculous boy, Stone (Grinnell 1926 : 180–81), performed the same feat in a sweat lodge for his seven murdered uncles, and Falling Star (Grinnell 1926 : 182–83) used the sweat lodge to heal the severely injured victims of powerful sorcerers.

Two Tsistsistas terms for the sweat lodge are *emaom* (from *ema*, "concealed," and *om*, "lodge") and *vonhäom* (from *vonä* or *vonhä*, "to lose by heat," and *om*, "lodge"). The first, the "concealed lodge," refers to a small sweat lodge taken by a single person or a number of persons with or without elaborate ritual. The second designates a ceremonial sweat lodge, a "lodge of purification by heat." Petter (1915 : 1029, 1035) was told by a priest, Lefthandbull, that the *vonhäom* observed during reservation time, with its emphasis on curing, was a rather recent derivation. Curtis (1911 : 118–19) published a sweat lodge prayer in which the shaman conductor called "my sweat lodge" *naimaomé;* either the rendition should have been *naemaom*, or Curtis recorded a valid dialect variation based on the term *emaom*.

Grinnell (1923, 1 : 272–73) quoted an account dated 1867 in which a sweat lodge was used for purification prior to sacrificing the skin of a freshly killed white buffalo to the Supreme Being:

> The next day a pole was set in the ground to which the white hide was to be tied. Before this was done a very large sweat-house was built, and many of the old men went in to take a sweat and pray. Before they went in, women came in crowds, bringing their children, and various offerings—calico, beads, moccasins, and other gifts—which were to be tied to the pole. . . . Before it was folded up to be tied to the pole, the hide was painted on the hair side with blue paint. The folded hide was tied to the pole by an old man who was naked, and was painted. While he was tying the hide to the pole he was constantly praying, and as each child was brought to him with an offering he prayed, passing his hands over its head, arms, and sides, and asking for good luck for it, long life, health, and abundance of everything. Other old men stood about the man who was tying the hide, praying fervently.

The Buffalo Ceremony of the sweat lodge, which was observed in part by Grinnell (1919) in 1906 and interpreted by Anderson (1956), is a Suhtai derivation emphasizing health and healing built upon old

Tsistsistas and Suhtai concepts. It is significant that the ceremonial bundle associated with this ceremony was sheltered in the Suhtai Sacred Hat Tipi (Anderson 1956:95). The sweat lodge frame of this ceremony did not use a single east-to-west willow ridge pole to bind the other poles but used two (Grinnell 1919: 367−69), thus altering the original structure.

A *vonhäom* was held by a shaman on his own cognizance or following a request made by a pledger and his wife. In the latter case, both had important roles in the ceremony. Often, four to eight persons participated; at special occasions many more took part. Each performance varied in detail, according to the shaman's personal approach. Because of this, sometimes young trees were implanted in the ground around the sweat lodge. Each detail of the ceremony had symbolic significance. After preparations, the ceremony might last one day or one day and one night. When a sweat lodge was conducted on a war expedition (Grinnell 1923, 2:10, 196−97), it was of necessity of shorter duration. From World War I to the Vietnam War, Tsistsistas serving in the U.S. Army underwent a secret purification ritual related to the sweat lodge before going into combat. With this ritual they also submitted themselves to the ancient law of Tsistsistas tribal soldiers to protect war prisoners and noncombatants, if necessary with their own lives.

The principal element groupings of the sweat lodge might be outlined as follows (see Curtis 1911:116−23; 1930:140−42; Grinnell 1919; 1923, 2:133):

A circular hole about eighteen inches in diameter and twelve inches deep was cut. The sod removed was shaped into a low mound about thirty-five feet slightly northeast of the hole, and a buffalo bull skull was placed on it. Over the hole the sweat lodge frame was raised, consisting of willow shoots placed in the ground on the south and north sides. These were bent and tied together in the center in north-south pairs. Because of the east-west orientation of the lodge, a single willow ridge pole tied the frame securely from east to west. The central hole was sometimes covered with sand in which an earth painting was outlined in red. The ground inside the lodge was laid out with sage. The willow poles were painted red on the south side, black on the north side. The frame was closed with five buffalo robes; four were attached from the four ceremonial directions; one was placed on top. Then a tipi cover was put over the structure.

An earth indentation was made on smoothed ground before the buffalo skull, which had been painted and faced the lodge entrance.

Later the ashes from the ceremonial smoking of the sacred pipe were deposited on the earth indentation. On the east side of the lodge below the buffalo skull a log-and-boulder pyramid a few feet high was raised to heat the stones.

The first five stones brought into the sweat lodge were painted by the pledger's wife: two red, two black, one red and black. They were placed in the earth hole in their ceremonial positions. Two fire sticks were used to carry the stones: One was painted red; the other was painted black. Cedar and other herbs were placed on the heated painted stones for purification. More hot stones were carried in, and the lodge was closed tightly.

Four cycles of four spirit songs each were sung. After each song, water was poured on the stones. Each person present received a drink of water before steam filled the lodge. After each cycle of four parts, the lodge covers were raised on the west and east side to clear the lodge of steam. A sacred pipe was passed before each cycle, was smoked out, and the ashes were deposited carefully on the earth indentation before the buffalo skull. The ceremony was concluded with final prayers and a ceremonial smoke; the participants sat in a row to the east of the sweat lodge facing the rising sun.

Curtis (1911:116) stated:

With the Cheyenne the sweat bath is one of the most essential religious observances. Through its agency their purified minds and bodies are brought into accord with the supernatural powers. Even when it is employed in healing disease the thought is that the power of the spirits, not the steam, will expel the sickness.

By the time the sweat lodge descriptions extant in the literature were collected by ethnographers, a shift had taken place in the use of the sweat lodge, emphasizing healing. The important spirit lodge aspect of the sweat lodge, as the spirit lodge itself, along with the mystical orientation of Tsistsistas shamanism outlawed by missionaries and reservation officials, had declined. What was left had gone underground. With the game herds gone, animals could no longer be brought by a shaman's animal spirit ally—or perhaps both had agreed to leave it be. With the rise of Christianized and acculturated Cheyenne factions promoted by all segments of White society, eventually the last of the Tsistsistas *zemaheonevesso*—the shaman group—formed a circle around the Sacred Arrow tipi that was invisible to outsiders.

The Tsistsistas sweat lodge as a purification and healing institution has endured to the present.

The *Coincidentia Oppositorum*

When Proto-Tsistsistas bands entered the Dakota grasslands, they brought with them institutionalized contrary behavior patterns expressed through individuals.

In his study of the various aspects of this behavior, Ray (1945), although omitting the ceremonial clowns of the Pueblos, sees the center of development among Algonquian groups of the Great Lakes area and the diffusion of traits from there into the Plains. He agrees that the Tsistsistas achieved the greatest elaboration of contrary themes of any North American group but believes that "the Cheyenne were essentially borrowers" (Ray 1945:105), adopting traits from Assiniboines, Dakotas, Pawnees, and others.

Ray's interpretation of Tsistsistas borrowing is based solely on the assumption maintained in the literature on Plains archaeology, ethnohistory, and ethnology that these tribes preceded Tsistsistas into the grasslands. This assumption is false; the Proto-Tsistsistas, in my view, arrived in the Dakotas nearly 1,500 years earlier than the groups mentioned. If borrowing of contrary behavior took place in the Plains, there is no question that the Tsistsistas were the chief donors. Contrary and noncontrary thoughts and actions are essential to the Massaum, which features the ceremonial union of both and, therefore, the dissolution of opposites.

In Proto-Tsistsistas time, there were two types of contrary shamans—*hemaneh* and *hohnuhka*—both representing achievement in symbolic androgynization while each pursued and realized it on different levels (see chapter 1). Although they provided one of the intellectual and ethical foundations that made the Massaum possible, they remained outside it after they had assisted in the formulation of the Massaum Hohnuhka society. In the literature on the Cheyenne all three have been thoroughly misunderstood.

Eliade (1965) wrote a lucid book, which was a conclusive set of statements on the great volume of ancient and modern literature concerning the *coincidentia oppositorum,* or, the mystery of the totality, and androgyny, the union of opposites preceding the creation of the universe.

This vast literature, built on ancient universal beliefs, sees, according to Eliade, creation as a divine intervention dissecting the compact and homogeneous primal mass, or the "chaos" of undifferentiated unity, into form in order that the universe could exist. With creation, division into parts and into sets of opposites, such as light and dark, earth and sky, male and female sexuality, physical and spiritual form, and so forth took place. Androgyny describes a return to the plentitude and totality of potentialities before separation, a search for the oneness of all things.

The Proto-Tsistsistas might perhaps not have said it exactly in this way, but they must have thought it. *Hemaneh* and *hohnuhka* are both travelers in the androgynal quest.

Hemaneh in Tsistsistas means "half-man, half-woman" (chapter 1). Hoebel (1978 : 83–85), speaking of the nineteenth century, describes them as highly respected doctors and officiators at the "scalp dance" and social dances. His interpretation of the *hemaneh* phenomenon, however, is flawed because of his injection of psychological notions inadequate for the understanding of Tsistsistas concepts. He sees the *hemaneh* as "neurotically anxious about sex relations and their own virility" and as finding "their refuge in total rejection of male sexuality" (Hoebel 1978 : 102).

The opposite is true. A *hemaneh* united in himself both male and female sexuality. His own person constituted a sacred marriage. Grinnell (1923, 2 : 39) reports that a *hemaneh* had both a man and a woman's name. According to Eliade (1965 : 116), the transvestite shaman "symbolically restores the unity of Sky and Earth, and consequently assures communication between Gods and men. This bisexuality is lived ritually and ecstatically; it is assumed as an indispensible condition for transcending the condition of profane man."

This ritual bisexuality was sometimes triggered by the demands of a shaman's spirit helper (e.g., among Chukchis, see Eliade 1974 : 125) or by a "celestial spouse" (Eliade 1974 : 168) or followed selection by supernatural powers (e.g., among Ngadju Dayaks of Borneo, see Eliade 1974 : 352–53). As a specific feature, it was generally found wherever shamanism existed.

Tsistsistas *hemaneh* wore women's clothes to make visible the "other," the contrary condition of struggle for the termination of opposites in physical and spiritual appearances. Their struggle was life-long; because of their ritual bisexuality, they were barred from sexual behavior. They did not have to use inverted speech because they were inverted by costume already.

The last two *hemaneh* shamans died in 1868 (Pipe–Pipe Woman) and 1879 (Good Road–Good Road Woman) (Grinnell 1923, 2 : 39–40). During the bitter White wars of these decades, they had been forced to hide their identity to outsiders behind dressing up "as old men."

Hohnuhka in Tsistsistas refers to doing the opposite of what is said (chapter I). They used inverted speech; others addressing them had to apply the same pattern.

Dorsey (1905, 1:24−26) described them as inverted warriors forming a society apart from other warrior societies; they were regarded as pure; they were philosophers. Hoebel (1978:102−103) maligned these contraries by asserting that they "seek validation in an exaggerated male rejection of heterosexuality." He adds that "the Contrary, then, is the Cheyenne warrior male with a monomania for what might be called military virility." About their main symbol, Hoebel has remarked: "Symbolically, the Thunder Bow suggests the male sex organ tied and restrained."

Grinnell (1923, 2:79−86), however, like Dorsey, treated the *hohnuhka* with respect. He saw them as individuals set apart from other men. He reported that at any time there was only a handful of them; they were not a society. A man became *hohnuhka* because he feared Thunder. He carried "a peculiar lance which was the especial property of Thunder" and that protected him. Originally, he said, they were single men living alone, but during the 1860s a few married men carried Thunder Bows. A man remained a *hohnuhka* until another man requested the lance after incurring overwhelming fear of Thunder. They and their few possessions were painted red because they were imbued with the power of Thunder. They could not be touched by anyone.

I see the *hohnuhka* of the middle of the nineteenth century as keepers of a *hohnuhkawo'*, a lightning lance, which was passed from keeper to keeper through time. The lance itself was reinterpreted as bow lance with an unstrung bowstring after the Tsistsistas adopted the bow and arrow, perhaps sometime during the fifth century A.D. Although it was topped with a projectile point painted blue, it was a shamanistic spirit weapon, not a physical weapon comparable to other lances. In form, the *hohnuhkawo'* itself was inverted: It was a lance shaped like a bow five feet long. The inversion of this ritual weapon was based on its meaning: It was capable of containing the spiritual and the striking power of lightning.

Originally, the *hohnuhka* shamans appear to have played a key role in the defense of Proto-Tsistsistas and Tsistsistas territory against intrusion by outsiders. Late in Tsistsistas history, after the formation of soldier societies, their services were no longer crucial for survival.

During the nineteenth century, *hohnuhka* rarely participated in raiding. In defensive warfare, they fought with extreme bravery, off

FIG. 5. *Hohnuhkawo'*, the awesome lightning lance in the form of a double-curved thunder bow. The sketch attempts to depict the weapon that, according to Tsistsistas tradition, was once carried by Motseyoef himself. It was nearly six feet long, with a white wooden shaft and a white bowstring. The handle was wrapped with white "male" sage tied in two places with white bear intestines, the ends of which hung down loosely. Three bundles of five eagle feathers each were tied to the handle and both arms of the weapon. Whether or not the stone projectile point was painted is not known today.

Instead of eagle feathers, Thunder bows sometimes featured owl, hawk, or magpie feathers. Occasionally, the complete body of a bird was tied near the tip. Usually the shaft was painted red, the projectile point blue.

by themselves, carrying only their mysterious weapon. These lances were repaired and renewed at the time of the Ceremony of the Sacred Arrows.

In Proto-Tsistsistas and early Tsistsistas times, when lances and darts were used in hunting and warfare, the lightning lance must have featured an inverted "crooked" shaft.

Ultimately, the *hohnuhkawo'* was a special type of spirit lance reserved for *nonoma hemāhe,* the spirit of lightning as the messenger and dart of Nonoma, the *maiyun* of Thunder. He was called into the *hohnuhkawo'* by the shaman keeper at special instances under the power granted to him by Nonoma.

Perhaps the *hohnuhka* of the middle nineteenth century were no longer shamans and were no longer capable of using the spirit lance for its original purpose—the unleashing of the *tremendum* of lightning from the *hohnuhkawo'*. Perhaps they had become mere keepers who reverently maintained the sacred object. Still, the initiatory terror of selection by Nonoma remained the prerequisite for becoming a *hohnuhkawo'* keeper.

The significance of the *huhnuhkawo'* and the *hohnuhka* shaman in Proto-Tsistsistas and early Tsistsistas times can be deduced from analogy. Among the Enets (or Khantys) of the Yenisey River of northern Siberia, for instance, the highest of three categories of shamans, the *budtode,* had the power to contact the sky spirits (Prokofyeva 1963:124). They were shamans who used a "sky drum" and a "sky bow" (Prokofyeva 1963:153, fig. 31) in their association with the "upper world and the sky god." The *budtode,* as separate from the other categories of Enet shamans, also possessed an "earth drum" for their work with the spirits of the world below. They comprised both opposites within their own person. Therefore, according to the terms discussed earlier, the *budtode* were acting in the realm of the *coincidentia oppositorum* and were travelers in the androgynal quest.

Proto-Tsistsistas and early Tsistsistas *hohnuhka* shamans transcended opposition through obedience to the sacred, through solitude, meditation, asexuality, and a contrary behavior denoting the fearsome, irrevocable selection by Nonoma and the presence of the *hohnuhkawo'*.

The third Tsistsistas contrary institution, the Hohnuhka Society, was created with the Massaum as essential element in the ceremony. The society was based on concepts already expressed in *hemaneh* and *hohnuhka;* It carried Tsistsistas contrary philosophy to a logical conclusion. The name Massaum derives from the performance of the

Hohnuhka Society in the ceremony, *massa'ne* meaning "crazy," or more precisely, "acting contrary to normal."

The *hemaneh* and *hohnuhka* in possession of a *hohnukawo'* remained outside the Hohnuhka Society. Members of this society were shamans, both men and women, and they conducted initiation ceremonies for new members once every few years. Grinnell (1923, 2: 204–10) observed the public part of one from outside the ceremonial contrary lodge in which the main events took place. The main task of the Hohnuhka Society was its performance in the Massaum. Its members expressed contrary behavior clearly during (1) the initiation ceremony; (2) in the contrary lodge set up inside the Massaum camp circle; and (3) in the actions of members during the Massaum.

Curtis (1911:115), who saw the society perform in Oklahoma and Montana, says that it claimed

the ability to perform remarkable if not supernatural feats, such as lifting great weights, jumping extraordinary distances, throwing their fellow men about as though they were without weight, taking objects from the bottom of kettles filled with boiling soup, and dancing barefoot on hot coals. The Indians state that they used internally some herb to make it possible for them to perform these superhuman feats of strength.

Petter (1915:699–700) gives the Tsistsistas term for this herb as *hestamōkan.*

Their astounding feats are mentioned also by Mooney (1907:415) and are corroborated by Tsistsistas participants and observers of the last Massaum ceremonies held in Oklahoma (in 1926 and 1927). When in a contrary condition, Hohnuhka Society members accomplished great feats in healing the sick and disabled, applying inverted techniques that included jumping high over people or tossing people through the air.

Membership in the Hohnuhka Society derived from—and may have been limited to—the group of shamans that represented cosmic fire (see Chapter 1). They are clearly related to the *wabeno* shamans of the Central Algonquians (Grim 1983:67, 129, 144–49) and shared with them a common heritage.

The *wabeno* phenomenon is not clearly understood; it is well known, however, that shamans of this category opposed European intrusion as well as the rise of the Midewiwin Medicine Society. This society developed among Central Algonquians during the seventeenth century (Müller 1954) as a reaction to European encroachment (Keesing 1939:48–49) and fearful population losses as result of smallpox epidemics introduced by Europeans (Schlesier 1975, 1976). Hickerson (1963) has demonstrated that the Midewiwin was not aboriginal. Ethnographers who investigated the Midewiwin generally adopted the opinion of practitioners of this society who were in conflict with the *wabeno* and therefore put them in an unfavorable light.

In his recent study of the *wabeno*, Krusche (1981) has summarized the existing knowledge. The term *wabeno* (*wabano*) means "it dawns," "it is day." *Wabanowiwin* refers to "men to the dawn"; some sources describe them as associated with the star of dawn, or the morning star. The ceremonial object most characteristic of *wabeno* shamans was a flat tambourine drum painted with the image of the tutelary spirit; some *wabeno* were capable of shooting tiny, "magic" arrows from it. Wooden spirit figurines were set on the east side of a *wabeno* shaman's lodge. They were said to be capable of transforming themselves into various animals, and at night one might "be seen flying rapidly along in the shape of a ball of fire, or a pair of fiery sparks, like the eyes of some monstrous beast" (Krusche 1981:83, after Hoffman). Most significant are reports about their control of heat, including the "mouthing" of red-hot stones, boiling water, bubbling maple syrup, and gunpowder set afire in their mouths. Predicting a cosmic crisis because of the European destruction of the Central Algonquian world, the *wabeno* said the world would be consumed by flames, that a *wabeno*, however, would be "standing in flames, but not to be burnt."

The Central Algonquian *wabeno* represented an ancient Northern Algonquian shamanistic tradition from which also Proto-Tsistsistas shamans of cosmic fire and contrary shamans are derived. The Hot Dances of the Hidatsas, Mandans, Arikaras, Pawnees, and others clearly originated from these Algonquian sources.

In the Massaum ceremony, Hohnuhka Society members served as the physical and spiritual doubles of spirits who assist Nonoma in the fertilization and regeneration of the earth and who ride and direct the thunder clouds bearing a *hohnuhkawo'* in their left hand.

Because the Massaum is an earth-giving ceremony, it is a ceremony of totalization performed in order that the success of a beginning (the beginning of Tsistsistas as a ceremonial and cultural unit in the realm of time and physical space with all its things) is assured.

Because of the requirement of totality, the Hohnuhka Society performed in the ceremony the "other"—the position of the opposite. The sacred animals of the Massaum could not be hunted by human hunters or by the spirit selves of shamans assisted by animal spirits, as animals were hunted at other times.

In the Massaum, they were hunted by the doubles of the thunder spirits dressed as sacred clowns—contraries—using sacred miniature sky bows with four types of miniature arrows: one sharp, one blunt, one softened by chewing at the point, and one with a hardened rawhide point. These were ritual arrows used by ritual hunters on ritual game. Before the time or arrows, they were miniature sky lances. They killed ritually (using the herb *vanovan* that caused profuse bleeding) and brought the dead game back to life immediately. Ritually, at the same time, those killed, the sacred animals, also healed humans and themselves. One of the messages of the Massaum is that all is dead while alive, and alive while dead: Life and death have meaning only in regard to physical form but no meaning in the spirit world.

5. The Rise of the Tsistsistas

When the boy was about ten years old he desired to go and take part in one of the magic dances given by the great medicine-men. He insisted that his grandmother go to the chief of the medicine-men and gain for him admission to the dance. His grandmother told one of the medicine-men of the boy's desire, and so they let him enter the lodge. When the boy went into the lodge the chief said to him, "Where do you want to live?" Without ceremony the boy took his seat beside the chief. He wore his robe, and had the man who brought him in paint his body red, with black rings around his face, and around each wrist and ankle. The performance began at one end of the circle. When the boy's turn to perform came he told the people what he was going to do. With sweet grass he burned incense. Through the incense he passed his buffalo sinew bow-string east, south, west, and north. Then he asked two men to assist him while he performed. First he had them tie his bow-string around his neck, then cover his body with his robe, then pull at the ends of the string. They pulled with all their might, but could not move him. He told them to pull harder, and as they pulled at the string again his head was cut off and rolled from under his robe, and his body was left under the robe. They took his head and placed it under the robe with his body. Next they removed the robe, and there sat a very old man in place of the boy. They covered the old man with the robe, and when they removed the robe again, there was a pile of human bones with a skull. They spread the robe over the bones, and when it was removed there was nothing there. Again they spread the robe, and when they removed it, there was the boy again.

He arose with a smile. He did this once to show the people what he was. A long time afterward he grew up.

—A PART OF THE MOTSEYOEF STORY AS RECORDED BY GEORGE A. DORSEY AND EDWARD S. CURTIS

WHEN GROUPS with a world description and a shamanistic world interpretation related to those discussed in chapters 1 and 2 broke away from their old territories and searched for new ones, they were vulnerable not only to resistance by other groups already there but to the land itself. They were strangers to its physical features, the impact of its seasonal changes, the animal and plant species and their specific ways, and so forth. Especially, they were ignorant of its spiritual life and therefore in danger of offending all spirits there. To overcome "spirit fences" set against them by shamans of other groups, they were forced to find and to plead with the major spirits of the region to receive permission to stay and the permission to hunt from the spirit gamekeepers and the animals themselves.

This quest was shaman's work and dangerous; if it was successful, the new arrivals could stay; if not, they would depart. If permission to stay was granted along the hierarchy of spiritual powers, the new-comers entered a phase of instruction that eventually led to their inte-gration with all forms of physical and spiritual life in the region. This achievement was always evidenced through solemn explanation in ceremonies granted by the spirits and acted out formally in their presence. The covenant that bound together all participants included a definition of the relationship between the new groups and older groups in or near the area. These understandings may underlie many, perhaps most, "movements" of North American Indian groups from prehistoric times to at least the early part of the European era.

When Northern Athapaskan groups ancestral to Navajos, for ex-ample, arrived in the Southwest before A.D. 1500, they passed through the stages outlined previously. Their shamans located the sacred mountain, Rim Hill (on maps often identified as Yale Point, north-west of Chinle), where Black God, who travels by lightning, keeps animal spirits under his protection. The Navajo Deer Huntingway (Luckert 1975:22–59) describes the granting of hunting rights and hunting laws to Navajos by four sacred deer, the deer's journey north and south from Black God's home to mark Navajo territorial bounda-ries, and their naming of prominent locations within with Navajo words. Thus these northern hunters became Navajo. For centuries after, however, the spirits of the dead were thought to return to the north country—the "ancestral ghostland" (Luckert 1975:199).

And Dhegiha Sioux groups passed through these stages when they arrived in the prairie country of northwestern Iowa between A.D. 1650 and 1660. Refugees and survivors of the smallpox epidemics that had decimated their people in Indiana during the 1640s and earlier, they meandered through portions of southeastern South Dakota and southwestern Minnesota (Schlesier 1975:186–88). Eventually, per-haps coached by Iowa–Oto groups, they attempted to build their first permanent settlement since leaving the Ohio near the pipestone quarries. Their sorrows were not over. Because the Tsistsistas consid-ered this area as part of their territory at that time, they struck the

newcomers hard, leaving so many Dhegiha Sioux dead that a great
mound was raised over their bodies (Fletcher and LaFlesche 1972,
1:73). Additional years of wandering in country still hostile to them
followed. Eventually the land accepted them and so did the Tsistsistas.

When negotiating a binding peace with the Tsistsistas, they received the sacred pole made from a mysterious tree as a gift from
Thunder. "The Thunder birds come and go upon this tree, making a
trail of fire that leaves four paths on the burnt grass that stretch toward the Four Winds. When the Thunder birds alight upon the tree
it bursts into flame and the fire mounts to the top" (Fletcher and
LaFlesche 1972, 1:218). The sacred pole became their symbol of identity. At the location of their peace meeting with the Tsistsistas (on
the loop of the Big Sioux River; Schlesier 1980a:27–28, 146–47),
they organized themselves into tribal divisions, formulated their political organization bound together with two sacred tribal pipes, and
made three sacred tents: one to contain the sacred pole imbued with
the power of Thunder, one to hold the white buffalo hide that
allowed them to hunt buffalo, one to receive the war bundle to defend them against enemies. Thus they became Omaha.

The Origin of the Massaum

The earliest stories about the Proto-Tsistsistas, collected in Oklahoma by George Bent, son of William Bent and Owl Woman, from
1905 to his death in 1918, mention the ancient homeland "on the shore
of great lakes in the far north" of a time "before the Cheyenne had
bows and arrows" (Hyde 1968:4). From there they moved south,
stopping at a number of places for some time. Eventually they reached
the prairie of northeastern North Dakota: "There was no wood,
nothing but the tall grass. . . . In this country there were no buffalo,
but deer abounded" (Hyde 1968:6). Upon their arrival they were in
the situation already discussed in regard to Navajos and Omahas. The
stories, however, do not indicate that there were other groups in the
region at that time.

The Ehyophstah account, in rudimentary versions published by
Kroeber (1900:179–81) and Grinnell (1907:173–78; 1926:244–52),
represents "the story of the beginning of the people, way up on the
other side of the Missouri River" (Grinnell 1907:173). It is a sacred
story because it describes the first stage in the initiation of the Massaum. It is presented in the following version in its essential elements
using both published and unpublished sources:

They were camped in the foreign tall grass country. They were confused, and they were starving because animals were withheld from them. The country was empty and hostile. Two young men, the elder of whom was a shaman, were sent out as ceremonial scouts "to find something for the whole tribe, and bring back good news." The two traveled many days until, near death, they reached a blue mountain with a body of water at its base. They decided to die together on the mountain. When they crossed the water, the younger one was caught by a great horned water serpent, *ax-xea*, that slowly pulled him under. He said, "Tell my people what has happened to me. Tell them not to cry for me. Some mysterious power holds me." They parted crying, and the shaman continued walking toward the mountain. There a man appeared wearing a red wolf skin on his head and back, and he rushed in and killed the serpent. He told the shaman, "Go to the peak. You will see there a big rock, which is a door. There you will find an old woman. Tell her that grandfather has killed the serpent he has so long been trying to get."

When the shaman reached the rock, it opened like a door, and an old, old woman came out. He reported what had happened, and she followed him to the water. The Wolf Man and the shaman pulled the injured young man and the serpent out; the Old Woman butchered the *ax-xea*. Together they carried the young man and the serpent's meat to the mountain door. Inside was a large lodge, the *maheonox*, with a sweat lodge on one side. It was the lodge of the Wolf Man and the Old Woman. These two *maiyun* held a sweat lodge ritual for the dying young man and healed him. Then the Old Woman gave each of them a white flint knife and fed them from stone bowls that were white as snow. She asked them about the purpose of their visit, and they explained the condition of their people.

The two spirits took pity on them. A very handsome young woman, Ehyophstah, was brought into the lodge, and the Wolf Man asked, "Do you want to take this woman for your sister, or do either of you wish to marry her?" The shaman answered, "My friend here is poorer than I [in regard to shamanistic knowledge]; let him take her for his wife." So it was agreed.

Then the Wolf Man let them see animals in the four directions, and said, "Now you shall go to your home. Take our daughter with you to your camp. It is very fortunate that one of you took her for his wife. She is to be a great helping power to your people. She will take everything that I have shown you to your people. Everything will follow her."

Before the three left, the Wolf Man instructed his daughter, "I send you there for a special purpose. Those poor people have only fish and a few birds to eat, but now that you are there, there will be plenty of game of all kinds; the skins of all these animals will also be useful for wearing."

When they stepped from the *maheonox* they faced south, standing in

this order: The Old Woman was on the east side; at her right side the
Wolf Man, next to him Ehyophstah, then her husband, then the shaman.
When they parted, the Wolf Man said, "My daughter, rest four times on
your way." He meant four stops, not four nights, because he had given
her the power to travel fast. When the three reached the camp of their
people, the hidden animals of the Plains had followed them and let
themselves be killed. The buffalo came up to the lodge in which Ehyophstah lived and rubbed against it, and she sat and laughed. She was loved,
but she was not like other women; she would hardly ever speak.

Thus the strangers were admitted to the grasslands and were given the
right to slay animals that lived there.

But the Wolf Man had given Ehyophstah one other instruction: If
ever a buffalo calf was brought into camp, she should not express pity.
After she had lived with her husband for eight years she disobeyed this
rule one day and had to leave the people for her parent's lodge in the
mountain. Her husband went with her, and never returned.

The Wolf Man of the story is Nonoma; the Old Woman is Escheman; both are the keepers of animal spirits of the Plains. Ehyophstah,
Yellow-haired Woman, is a buffalo spirit turned into a human to assist
the Tsistsistas: Her parents placed her in the position of master spirit
of animals and therefore gave her the power to bring game (among
Selkups of northern Siberia it was also the daughter of the forest spirit
who gave the animals to the hunters, Anisimov 1963b:189).

Of the two young men, the elder is Motseyoef, the prophet and
immortal androgyne shaman who, in Tsistsistas religious tradition,
has played a crucial role from the first organization of Tsistsistas culture through later innovations to the present time. According to this
tradition, he has been with the Tsistsistas a number of times, always
returning when the survival of his people was seriously threatened.
The *maheonox,* lodge of the *maiyun,* where Ehyophstah was given to
Motseyoef's companion, is Nowah'wus—Bear Butte.

The healing ritual conducted in the sacred mountain reaffirmed
the power of the sweat lodge as demonstrated by the *maiyun* themselves. It was again given by them to Motseyoef and Ehyophstah's
husband because they had participated, that is, had been instructed
in it. The ritual held inside Nowah'wus brought about the revivifica-
tion of the young man who thereby was brought into a special condition that allowed him to eat of the spirit food served by Escheman
and to be with the holy woman, Ehyophstah. Motseyoef, because he
was a shaman, already was in the condition of the initiated.

The giving of the Ehyophstah established a kin relationship between the *maiyun* and the Tsistsistas and a kin relationship between the Tsistsistas and the animals under the tutelage of the *maiyun* and Ehyophstah.

Because Ehyophstah had represented in her person the center of this relationship, her leaving put everything in question. And so the second stage in the intitation of the Massaum began.

Motseyoef returned alone to Nowah'wus where the *maiyun* made him the spiritual representative of the Tsistsistas. Nonoma and Esceheman taught him, for the Tsistsistas, the circular earth drawing, which is maintained to this day, that marks the earth region given to his people. This drawing is recognized by all spiritual powers of the universe and, when executed, calls for their attention and protection.

The earth giving to the Tsistsistas at Bear Butte was embedded in a larger frame of instruction by the *maiyun*—the Massaum. The ceremony, as taught to Motseyoef by Nonoma and Esceheman, explains the giving of the earth in the four directions around Nowah'wus. It commemorates the relationship of the Tsistsistas to the spirit world of the grasslands, the sacred relationship with animals as expressed through Ehyophstah's continuing spiritual presence, and the proper approach of hunting Plains herd animals by calling them into camps and pounds.

Motseyoef went back and led those who wanted to participate across the Missouri to Moxtavhohona—the Black Hills. He conducted the first Massaum ceremony at the foot of Nowah'wus. All of Tsistsistas tradition agrees that the Massaum was brought by Motseyoef and that the place, where the "wonderful dance" (Curtis 1930: 135) was begun, is at Bear Butte.

The gift of the Massaum required the existence of a cultural entity to which earth could be given and that served as protector of the realm over time under the laws annually explained in the performance of the ceremony. Thus formerly Northern Algonquian bands were forged into the Tsistsistas.

According to Tsistsistas tradition, they encountered the first resistance in the grasslands after they had moved to the Black Hills. These enemies are still called *haztova hotoxceo* (from *haztova*, "both," in the sense of "on either side different," and *hotoxceo*, "stars")—two face star people. They preyed on Tsistsistas camps, killed people, and ate their flesh. They appeared invincible until Motseyoef, using shaman power, and acting under the grant of the spirits of the region, found their hideout in a cave in the southern part of the Black Hills and entirely destroyed them. He restored the remains of slaughtered

Tsistsistas to life in a sweat lodge ceremony which he conducted at the cave.

The Black Hills became the first and the permanent Tsistsistas homeland in the Plains. Nowah'wus has remained the very center of their world because the *maiyun* still speak there to those who go there on pilgrimages today.

But their movements after the granting of the Massaum were not restricted to the Black Hills and the adjacent region. Because the Massaum was an earth-giving ceremony, it granted to the Tsistsistas the right to hunt in the four directions from the wolf lodge—the ritual counterpart of Nowah'wus—wherever the ceremony was held. Therefore, any shifts of Tsistsistas hunting ranges were presaged by the staging of the Massaum. Once a Massaum was held in new territory in the grasslands for whatever reasons, including climatic changes and shifts in animal populations, the region accepted Tsistsistas guardianship.

This state of affairs had consequences concerning the relations of the Tsistsistas with other groups in the northern Plains. In a move of northern Tsistsistas and Suhtai against the Crows as late as either 1872 or 1873, for example, as Wooden Leg reported (Marquis 1967: 18–19), two abbreviated Massaums were held on two locations on the Little Bighorn River in the month of June on lands then hunted by the Crows. With the two performances, the Tsistsistas laid claim to this area versus Crow "ownership" or, perhaps, reconfirmed aboriginal rights to this area because they had hunted there a millennium before groups ancestral to the Crows arrived from the east.

The Massaum Camp and the Maheonox—the Wolf Lodge

Because of the nature of the Massaum, it had to be performed annually, and in midsummer (see the following section). For the duration of the ceremony, the Massaum camp, in which attendance of all Tsistsistas bands was required, represented the universe of the grasslands. Outside of it the world stood still. Ultimately, the Massaum camp was a spirit camp in which all spirits were present, from the Supreme Being, Maheo, through the *maheyuno* to the *maiyun*, to the spirits of animals and plants and to the spirits of the Tsistsistas. Each Massaum performance was a renewal of the covenant granted by the *maiyun* through the medium of the Tsistsistas: Here humans served as impersonators of the spirits.

Some spirits were too powerful to associate with humans directly. Maheo was venerated in the tree of the wolf lodge; the *maheyuno* were represented in sacred bundles attached to the four major lodge poles.

The *maiyun* instructors of the Massaum—Nonoma and Esceheman—were impersonated by shaman actors after a purification ritual. This was also required of the other main performers including Hohnuhka Society members and the many who represented animal spirits.

The physical arrangement of the Massaum camp circle followed the demands of the ceremony. The Massaum camp circle consisted basically of three camps organized in relationship to the wolf lodge.

Because the wolf lodge was the ritual expression of the Maheonox, lodge of the *maiyun,* Bear Butte, it stood in the center of the camp circle. During the ceremony, it represented the center of the universe.

It was surrounded in a wide horseshoe circle by the lodges of the Tsistsistas camp representing the Tsistsistas. Within this was a second circle of lodges, the animal camp, whose spirits were impersonated by Tsistsistas performers. The camp of the Thunder spirits consisted of the single contrary lodge of the Hohnuhka Society raised to the southwest of the wolf lodge in front of animal lodges. After *nimāhenan,* the sacred arrows, had come to the Tsistsistas, their tipi stood to the southeast of the wolf lodge in front of the animal lodges.

The opening of the camp circle had to be directed toward Nowah'wus, Bear Butte, wherever the ceremony was held, to allow the extension of an unimpeded line connecting the lodge of the *maiyun* with its ritual counterpart in the Massaum camp. Furthermore, because on the fifth day of the ceremony (see chapter 6) the animals were called into the sacred pound constructed next to the wolf lodge, it was necessary that they enter from the direction of the sacred mountain and the *heszevoxsz,* the underground animal caverns, from where they had been released. A sizable source of water, preferably a running stream, was needed about half a mile beyond the opening of the camp circle for the cleansing ritual at the end of the ceremony.

Because the Massaum camp represented the universe of the grasslands, everything in it participated in the ceremony. From the sky derived the water used; from the ground the many paints applied by the performers. All species of vegetation were either directly or symbolically contained in the huge artifact inventory of the ceremony. Furthermore, the tree of the wolf lodge stood for the universe itself. All animal species were directly or symbolically represented by impersonators.

Each animal lodge represented a specific species or symbolically a large number of species through one. Each animal lodge was under the direction of a shaman or a person whose tutelary spirit belonged to the species of that lodge.

Animal lodges were preparatory lodges in which participants were ritually transformed into animals before they responded to Ehyophstah's call (see chapter 6). In the context of the ceremony, animal lodges were the ritual equivalent of the *heszevoxsz,* the underground caverns in which Escheheman retained the animal spirits and from which she and Nonoma granted adequate numbers to maintain balance in the physical world of the grasslands.

The exception was a pair of sacred wolves and a kit fox who were not associated with the lodges of their species. The two wolves, one red, one white, belonged to the maheonox, the center lodge of the Massaum that was named "wolf lodge" in the ceremony because of their service. These and the kit fox were directly connected with the sacred mountain.

The male red wolf—*Maheone honehe*—is the wolf *maiyun,* the species-specific protector spirit, or *Artgeist,* of wolves. His female companion, the white wolf, is *Eveŝev honehe*—the Horned Wolf. They are the master animals of all wolves and are the guardians of the sacred mountain and the messengers of the *maiyun.* They were also the master hunters of the grasslands and, with their species, the protectors of animals. Nonoma wore the red wolf skin in the Ehyophstah story; sometimes he appeared as a red wolf in the physical world. In the Massaum, the red wolf was the messenger during the day; the white wolf was the messenger during the night.

After the Proto-Tsistsistas had become the Tsistsistas through adoption of the Massaum ceremony and the Massaum law, the two sacred wolves had been instructed by the *maiyun* to teach the newcomers the hunting way of the grasslands.

The wolves became—if they had not been already—the benefactors of the Tsistsistas, animal hunters emulated by human hunters. As the "invitation song" of wolves called raven, coyote, and fox to share in their kill, so did Tsistsistas hunters call wolves to their kill or set meat aside for their use.

Because the Massaum law emphasized the calling of game into camp or pound, the pound structure including the brush wings of the "drive lane" was built by women organized in a Young Wolf Society who acted as assistants to Ehyophstah and the sacred wolves (see chapter 6). This appears to have been the first society initiated by the Tsistsistas. Wolf songs addressed to wolf spirit helpers as messengers were often used by shamans in game-calling ceremonies in the spirit lodge or sweat lodge. According to Bent (Hyde 1968 : 9–11), Tsistsistas dogs, and well into the late historic period, were nearly pure wolf.

In the Massaum observed by Grinnell (1923, 2 : 285–336) in Montana in 1911, the skin of a yellow wolf (photograph in Powell 1969, 2 : 455) was used instead of that of a red wolf, suggesting either error or a Suhtai modification because that performance was directed by White Frog, a Suhtai, and the bundle of the Suhtai priest Box Elder served in a prominent role (on Box Elder's wolf helpers, see Grinnell 1923, 2 : 112). Throssel (Curtis 1911 : 115–16) failed to mention the two special wolves in his two-page remarks about the Massaum he saw in Montana in 1909. During the last performances in Oklahoma, the single gray wolves of the 1926 (Curtis 1930 : 128–31) and 1927 ceremonies were unpainted.

Voh'kis, the female kit fox, also belonged to the *maheonox,* the wolf lodge of the Massaum, and was prepared, that is, brought to life there. She served under the two wolves; the symbolism concerning this animal spirit is discussed later and described in detail in chapter 6.

The Blue Star, Spirit Wheels of Stone

The main persons of the Ehyophstah account were also the main performers in the Massaum. The instructors in the ceremony represented Nonoma and Esceheman. The female and male pledgers represented Ehyophstah and her husband. The ceremonial man who sat on the southeast side in the wolf lodge behind the Tsistsistas earth drawing, who served as witness throughout the ceremony and who formally concluded it on the fifth day, represented Motscyoef. Grinnell (1923, 2 : 290), who did not understand the Massaum, called this priest "the master of ceremonies" (Bobtail Horse served in this position in 1911).

The annual ceremonial period recognized by the Tsistsistas before the adoption of the Oxheheom (the New Life Lodge) was begun and ended by signals from the sky. After the Suhtais were admitted, the Oxheheom was held at the time of the summer solstice; it was preceded on the camp site by the Maxhoetonstov (Ceremony of the Sacred Arrows) and was followed directly by the Massaum. This arrangement was a compromise resulting from intratribal and external demands; it altered the original requirements of the Massaum.

The early Tsistsistas ceremonial period consisted of fifty-six days. It started with the heliacal rising of the red star—Aldebaran (∞ Tau), around June 22, on the same day or one day before summer solstice. This star flashed briefly in early dawn above the northeastern horizon. It ended fifty-six days later when the white star—Sirius (∞ CMa)—rose heliacally in the southeast. The Massaum was annually held in the middle of this period. The fifth, public day of the ceremony was tied to the heliacal rising of the blue star of summer dawn—Rigel (β Ori)—that flashed across the horizon from the Southeast. Rigel appeared for the first time exactly twenty-eight days after Aldebaran's first rising and was in turn followed by the rising of Sirius twenty-eight days later.

Bound between the brilliant beacons of Aldebaran and Sirius, the Massaum focused on Rigel. When the five main persons of the Ehyophstah account stepped outside the maheonox of Bear Butte, they stood facing south, observing the blue flash of Rigel in the early dawn. When the five main performers of the Massaum stepped from the wolf lodge in the dawn of the fifth day of the ceremony, they waited for Rigel's signal before they walked to the corral to start the sacred hunt.

In the Massaum, the blue star design in the traditional form of the German iron cross was painted on the buffalo skull placed on the deep earth on the west side of the wolf lodge and on the faces of Ehyophstah, her husband, and the seven women of the Young Wolf Society (chapter 6). Voh'kis, the kit fox, was also painted with blue lines. Instead of a kit fox, a blue fox could be used who would not require the ceremonial blue paint.

On the deepest levels of Massaum symbolism, Aldebaran represented Maheone Honehe, the Red Wolf *maiyun* (also a manifestation of Nonoma); Sirius represented Evevŝev Honehe, Horned Wolf (also a manifestation of Escheman); and Rigel represented Voh'kis (also a manifestation of Ehyophstah).

Most likely, scattered bands of Tsistsistas began moving toward the designated Massaum camp site following Aldebaran's rising, which would have allowed for a twenty-three day period prior to the first day of the ceremony. Experts able to accurately predict the day of Aldebaran's first appearance at dawn were available (Chapter 1).

Among surviving boulder configurations in the northern Plains, two, because of the complexity of their features and their structural alignments, have caused considerable attention. One is the Bighorn Mountain Medicine Wheel, located near the summit of Medicine Mountain of the Bighorn Mountains in northern Wyoming, at an altitude of about 10,000 feet. The other is the Moose Mountain Medicine Wheel, situated atop Moose Mountain in the rolling prairie of southeastern Saskatchewan.

The Bighorn wheel consists of an irregular circle of large stones with a diameter of about ninety feet. In the center of this circle is an inner circle of large stones about twelve feet in outside diameter and about seven feet inside (Grinnell 1922 : 300). From the wall of this hub twenty-eight lines of small stones (spokes) radiate to the outer circle, leaving a small opening on the southeast side. At intervals along the periphery of the wheel are six cairns of rocks. One is inside the circle on the west side; the others are either attached to the outside of the circle or are entirely away from it. Grinnell (1922 : 304) recorded six additional cairns from between 71 and 277 feet outside the hub of the wheel; these apparently no longer exist today.

The Moose Mountain wheel consists of a large stone pile (totaling about eighty tons; Eddy 1981 : 20) as the center from which six lines of stones radiate, each with a cairn at the end. The total configuration is nearly twice as large as the Bighorn wheel if the original outlying cairns of the latter are discounted.

The astronomer John Eddy investigated the Bighorn wheel first; he later cooperated with archaeologists Alice and Thomas Kehoe on the Moose Mountain feature. He noted that the twenty-eight spokes of the Bighorn wheel were close to the number of days in a lunar month and that the positions of the cairns might be related to astronomical phenomena. As a result of his investigation, he concluded (Eddy 1974 : 1981) that the cairn alignments were oriented toward the heliacal risings of Aldebaran (and summer solstice), Rigel, and Sirius. Based on a computation of the exact locations where the three stars appeared briefly above the horizon in the past, he suggested that the Bighorn wheel was built between A.D. 1600 and 1700.

At the Moose Mountain wheel, Eddy found cairn alignments also pointing to Aldebaran, Rigel, and Sirius's risings. Here, however, he arrived at a date somewhere between A.D. 100 and 500 for the deposition of the structure. Excavation of portions of the feature by the Kehoes (1979) in 1976 led to one radiocarbon date of 2650 ± 245 years on charcoal fragments interpreted as resulting from burning off the grass before construction. Although the radiocarbon date appears to be too early, it supports Eddy's contention based on careful mathematical computation that the structure is of considerable antiquity.

The three investigators have no answer concerning the purpose

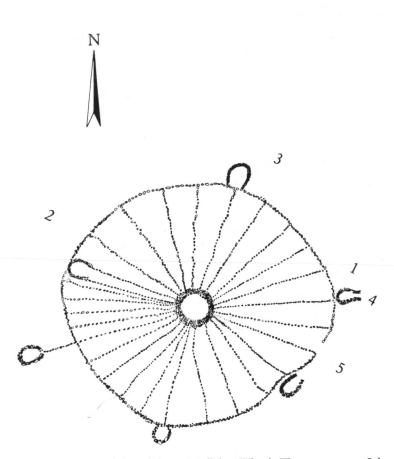

N

FIG. 6. Diagram of the Bighorn Medicine Wheel. The astronomer John Eddy discovered that the arrangement of peripheral cairns with the central cairn of the feature is directed toward celestial events in the summer sky. Most important of these are the heliacal risings of three stars that follow one another consecutively in the predawn: Aldebaran, the brightest star in the constellation Taurus; Rigel, the brightest star in Orion; and Sirius, the brightest star in the sky. (1) Sunrise at summer solstice; (2) sundown at summer solstice; (3) Aldebaran rises; (4) Rigel rises; and (5) Sirius rises.

of both structures. Grinnell (1922 : 307–308) suggested long ago that the Bighorn wheel represents the ground plan of the Tsistsistas Oxheheom lodge.

If the Bighorn wheel represents the structure of a Tsistsistas ceremonial lodge on a horizontal plane oriented toward Aldebaran, Rigel, and Sirius, this would be not an Oxheheom lodge but a Massaum wolf lodge built on a twenty-eight pole frame with a center tree. When Grinnell (1922 : 307) asked Cheyenne informants about the wheel, Elk River told him that the cairn within the circle on the west side was "the place from which thunder came." In the wolf lodge of the Massaum, both Nonoma and Esceheman are positioned on the west side, and Nonoma, in addition, is painted on the inside lodge cover in this location (chapter 6). In the Oxheheom ceremony, the summer solstice is significant; Aldebaran, Rigel, and Sirius are not.

I suggest that the Bighorn and Moose Mountain structures were indeed built by the Tsistsistas after the initiation of the Massaum because the alignments are in agreement with the heliacal risings of the three stars. It follows that they are not solstice aligned. I further suggest that they do not represent observation points. It is significant that Stands in Timber (1972 : 124) saw the Bighorn wheel as a Tsistsistas boundary mark; "there were rocks placed in a few places."

I believe that the Bighorn and Moose Mountain structures represent surviving Tsistsistas *oxzemeo,* spirit wheels of stone, marking the Tsistsistas presence in the region as granted through the Earth-giving Ceremony (Massaum). Because they are located on mountaintops and not visible from below, they are directed to the sky—toward the spirits of the world above.

If this is correct, they also may represent territorial "fences" (chapter 1) into which spirits could be called by shamans for protection. Their locations and the time frame of their construction are clearly within Tsistsistas time and distribution ranges (chapter 7).

Because of their unique religious significance, the state of Wyoming and the province of Saskatchewan should undertake serious measures for their protection.

6. The Massaum Ceremony

The original prophet of the Cheyenne [Motseyoef] foretold all that has come to pass. Everything that he foretold has taken place in exactly the way he said it would. He told the following about the coming of the white man: "A person who has long hair on chin and on legs, and carries with him sickness of all kinds, is coming to you in the future. With him he will bring an animal that has flashing eyes, and a tail that touches the ground, and one hoof on each foot. This animal will be restless, and the hairy person will also be restless. Do not try to be like them. This hairy person will also bring a spotted animal with horns, big eyes. This animal will live on dirt, and will eat anything. If you take after it and eat it, you will eat almost anything else." He prophesied of the future of the Cheyenne in this language: "My brothers and children, and all my people of this earth! Listen and remember my words, for they are as sharp as the points of the great sacred arrows, and keep my prophecies of the future in your minds as long as your people and the earth last, and then the Cheyenne as a people will never become extinct as long as the blue heavens, the sun, moon, and earth last. Do not forget your sacred arrows. Remember them always, and no other. You will renew your sacred arrow shafts four times."

—PART OF THE MOTSEYOEF STORY AS RECORDED BY GEORGE A. DORSEY

THE FOLLOWING DESCRIPTION of the Massaum represents a reconstruction of the core of the ceremony. Because the ceremony has an inherent logical structure, the essential sequences and events can be recaptured. Any omission of these would distort the ceremony. Although the Massaum was intruded by new features in the course of centuries, these were nonessential because the core could not be jeopardized without damaging its meaning and purpose.

Because the existence of the Tsistsistas as a people of hunters in the grasslands was founded upon the Massaum covenant, Tsistsistas violations of it in Tsistsistas world understanding meant self-destruction.

They did not violate it. They maintained the ceremony for over two millennia. They tried tenaciously to keep it alive long after they had been confined to reservations; half a century after their sacred animals had been slaughtered by the Whites, they were forced to let it go.

Details of the following description are defined as parts of the core of the ceremony and therefore as ancient. Details that are omitted here, although contained in the four Massaum reports in the literature or in the recollection of participants, are considered as nonessential additions of later times.

A critical review of the literature on the Massaum is not necessary; there is so little of it. Ethnographers who have written about the Cheyennes either omit the ceremony altogether (Dorsey 1905; Mooney 1907; Moore 1974; Powell 1969) or base brief descriptions (Anderson 1970:152–55; Hoebel 1978:23–24) on Grinnell's (1923, 2: 285–336) account of the 1911 ceremony. Of the four eyewitness reports, Throssel's account (Curtis 1911:115–16) of the 1909 Massaum, and Curtis's (1930:128–31) description of the 1926 ceremony are too brief and too random to be of assistance. Medicine Elk, who served as male pledger of the last, shortened performance in 1927 (Edelmann 1970, appendix A) was never told what he was doing. The participants never received, perhaps never sought, interpretations of what they saw, or, in Medicine Elk's case, acted out. Grinnell, a veteran interpreter of Indian thought, might have arrived at an understanding if the priests had not denied him access.

In my description, I do not distinguish between conflicting sources, published or unpublished, because it is meaningless to the presentation. Some information was kept secret by the Tsistsistas until used here. Therefore, it was necessary to publish it so that the truth about the Massaum order and Tsistsistas rights in the grasslands could be established.

To hold the Massaum required a pledger who accepted the serious responsibility voluntarily. Because Ehyophstah was the focal point of the ceremony, the pledger was a woman. If she was married, her husband could serve as Ehyophstah's ritual husband in the ceremony; if not, another man had to pledge himself to take this position.

The Ehyophstah pledger could be a member of the Young Wolf Society bud did not have to be. After completion of the ceremony, she was qualified to serve as instructor of woman pledgers in Massaum performances in later years.

The Ehyophstah pledger had to secure the instructors who would assume the positions of Nonoma and Escheman; both had to have been pledgers before. Together, they chose the ceremonial man to serve in the position of Motseyoef. It was the pledger's responsibility to determine the location where the ceremony was to be held. Because of the implications of this decision, already discussed, it is most likely that it was made in agreement with Tsistsistas ceremonial leaders.

After the location had been decided, messengers were sent to dispersed Tsistsistas bands. When they assembled for the ceremony after the middle of July, the camp circle opening faced the direction of Bear Butte. When the lodges had been raised, the main performers went through sweat lodge purification ceremonies, thereby undergoing transformation into a condition in which they could act unharmed as receptacles of sacred power.

The main events of the five days described next were accompanied by complex ritual, which are not recaptured here, that included prayer, cycles of songs, ceremonial sign language, ceremonial painting, ceremonial smoking, and combinations of these. The pipes used were of the ancient "straight" type, made from shank bones of deer or antelope. The five main performers and additional assistants or singers who came into the ceremony at specific times were painted with the sacred color, red. The important transformational paints of Ehyophstah and her husband are mentioned separately.

First Day (the Maheonox)

There were four main actions on this day.

Bringing the Sacred Tree

The tree was selected in a grove near camp by the male instructor. With him were the woman instructor, the pledgers, and the man who played the role of Motseyoef. The tree generally chosen was a straight, young cottonwood, perhaps twenty-five feet high and five to seven inches at the base. After a pipe had been smoked with the tree spirit, the purpose of the people's coming was explained. Then the tree was felled; all branches were removed except for seven at the top. The pledger and her instructor moved the tree to the center of the camp circle.

After a hole had been excavated by the male pledger, the tree was raised with lodge poles because it could no longer be touched with hands. This work was done by seven women of the Young Wolf Society.

Raising the Lodge

The four-post frame of the wolf lodge consisted of four tipi poles lashed together in pairs and lifted by Young Wolves over the standing tree. These poles were pulled in the four ceremonial directions: southeast, southwest, northwest, northeast. Next, the remaining twenty-four lodge poles were leaned against the forks, and two lodge covers were put up. The lodge had no door; it was entered by raising the lodge cover. The tree stood in the center of the lodge, and its trunk extended through the smoke hole above which the top branches formed a rustling canopy.

Smoothing the Earth

Inside the wolf lodge, the living grass was removed. A large circular space was excavated through the sod to the surface of the deep earth around the base of the tree, leaving a strip of ground six feet wide between the lodge poles and the edge of the circle. The sod removed was taken outside the lodge. The shallow bench around the circle was covered with a bed of white sage, except on the east side where a narrow strip of cleared surface was left untouched. The floor of the excavated circle was carefully smoothened.

The Fireplace

On the east side of the tree base a fire was started within the circle. In this lodge, any wood could be used for firewood except cedar and pine because these two trees represent an association with Nonoma that were not to be invoked in the Massaum.

At the end of the first day, the wolf lodge represents the universe before creation. It is built from the center, and it represents the shell of the universe with its central creative force, the Supreme Being Maheo, who is visualized in the symbol of the tree. The tree is the world tree, the world pillar, or the navel from which the universe is born. The wolf lodge returns to the primordial totality before time when Maheo was everything.

The "tree that becomes a cult object is not worshipped as a *tree,* but as a *hierophany,* a manifestation of the sacred" (Eliade 1965: 199). In the created universe, the world tree is also an *axis mundi*—a world axis—that connects the lower, middle, and upper worlds.

In the northern Siberian world description, the tree protruding through the smoke hole of the circular lodge became a road to the sky (chapter 2). In Evenk ceremonialism, the *turu,* the shaman's tree, was an essential part of the shaman's tent in a number of ceremonies. The *turu* was a "tall young larch . . . placed in the center of the shaman's tent, with its top drawn through the smoke hole" (Anisimov 1963a : 85–86, also figs. 4, 8, 9). It became the shaman's ladder for his journey into the upper world; his spirit helpers rested on its branches. "In the shaman's concept, the *turu* larch symbolized the shamanistic world tree."

Among Ngadju Dayaks, the world tree, represented with seven branches, also served as the shaman's ladder "by which he climbs to the sky to bring back the patient's fugitive soul" (Eliade 1974 : 285).

Among the Tsistsistas, the Massaum world tree with seven branches represents the seven levels of the universe. It precedes the sacred pole of the Maxhoetonstov Ceremony to which, with the sacred arrows, seven branches (six chokecherry, one plum) are tied. Thus the arrows' pole ritually becomes the world tree.

The number 7 is important in both ceremonies. Seven refers especially to the celestial spirits of the Seven Brothers prominent in Tsistsistas thought (Curtis 1930 : 143–48; Grinnell 1926 : 178–82, 216–31). In the night sky, they are identified as *manohotaxceo,* with the Pleiades.

The fire lit in the wolf lodge during the first night represents the power of life inherent in the universe due to Maheo's will. From the second day of the Massaum on, it also symbolizes the presence of Atovsz, the spirit of the sun, or is its ritual counterpart.

Second Day (the Creation of the Universe, the Lodge of the *Maiyun,* the Tsistsistas Earth)

There were four main actions on this day.

The Universe and the Maheyuno

Early in the morning the male instructor made a sand painting on the west side of the circle halfway between the world tree and the edge of the sage-covered bench. In this performance, he did not represent Nonoma, and the other main actors of the ritual play did not assume their Massaum positions. All did not exist yet in time, for time did not yet exist. They were eyewitnesses to the ritual creation of the universe.

The male instructor acted in the following movements in the role of the Supreme Being, Maheo, and near the world tree in His presence. He touched the ground firmly with his thumb, then made four more indentations about five inches to the southeast, southwest, northwest, and northeast. The universe was about to be created from its center. With a digging stick, he excavated a circular hole (the cosmological singularity) about three inches wide, three inches deep, in the spot he had marked first. The earth was removed four times and placed on the four directional indentations in the order used earlier. Four little mounds had arisen. He covered the two to the south with a red color, the two to the north with a black color. These represented the four sacred mountains of the *maheyuno*—the guardians placed by Maheo at the four corners of the universe.

Starting from the opening in the center, the male instructor marked, on the ground in white powdered gypsum, a line to the south about five inches long, one to the north, one to the west, and one to the east. Thus the opening in the ground became the center of a white cross that extended to the four cardinal points. With the four mounds, the sand painting became the symbol of the universe after creation with Maheo at the center.

Next, four bundles of white sage were tied to the four main poles of the wolf lodge about seven feet above ground. In their positions, the posts and bundles were directly in line with the four small mounds on the ground. A fifth bundle was tied to the westernmost pole of the lodge frame. The bundles represented Maheo and the *maheyuno;* the wolf lodge itself had become the universe after the act of creation.

The Maiyun

In this action, the *maiyun* and the lodge of the *maiyun*, Nowah'wus, were created. The male instructor, still in his sacred role of Maheo, went outside the lodge and painted a red disk on the lodge cover on the east side at the height of a man's head. This represented the spirit of the sun, Atovsz. On the west side, he painted a blue-black crescent, the spirit of the moon, Ameonito. Thus with their guardian spirits, day and night were made. Returning inside, he painted on the wall next to the bundle of Sovota, the *maheyuno* of the southwest, the figure of a man wearing horns, with eagle talons as feet, and a body spotted with black dots. This painting represented Nonoma.

Next Esceheman was made. The woman pledger left the lodge and returned carrying a buffalo skull, placing it on the west side of the sage-covered bench facing the world tree. The skull was painted by the male instructor after the eye sockets and the nasal cavity had been filled with round bundles of grass. The male instructor drew a black line from the back of the skull down its center to the nasal opening, then traced, along both sides of the black line, two lines with white

color. The remainder of the skull, including the horn cores, was covered with dry red paint. The three lines represented day and night;
the red paint of the skull the earth. Next the three grass plugs were
painted red; they represented all the vegetation that grows from
the earth.

On the top of the skull, between the horn cores and the eyes,
a drawing in solid blue was executed, resembling in form a German iron cross; this represented the blue star of midsummer dawn
(Rigel). When a solid red disk (the sun) was painted on her right jaw
and a black crescent (the moon) on the left, Esceheman had been
made and was ritually present.

Next she was put in the location that represented her home. The
painted skull was moved, and in the exact place on the west side of
the bench an opening was excavated to the bottom of the sod layer,
to the deep earth, starting again from the center, then removing sections of sod around it from the southeast, southwest, northwest,
northeast. The sod removed was placed in a little mound on the
southwestern side next to the tent cover. The painted buffalo skull
was set in the earth opening. A bundle of white sage was placed in
front of its nose (east), a buffalo chip behind the skull (west).

From this point in the ceremony on, the male instructor represented Nonoma, the female instructor, Esceheman. The wolf lodge
had turned into the lodge of the *maiyun,* the sacred mountain (see
fig. 7 for more information regarding this entire ceremony).

The Tsistsistas Earth

The seating order in the wolf lodge during the next action was the
following: on the sage cover to the south of the buffalo skull sat Esceheman, to her right Nonoma, who was followed by the woman
pledger and the male pledger. This line of performers, therefore, was
representative of the ritual southwestern direction, from which, in
Tsistsistas world perception, Nonoma brings the life-giving thunderstorms and rain clouds in the spring.

The man who would represent Motseyoef sat on the southeastern
side of the bench in front of the bundle of Hesenota, the *maheyuno* of
the southeastern corner of the universe. After receiving instruction
from Nonoma, the man bent forward and drew, with the thumb of
his right hand, a small spiraling circle about two inches in diameter
in the smooth, powdered surface of the interior circle of the lodge.

This act represented the creation of the Tsistsistas as a people in
the lodge of the *maiyun* through Nonoma and Esceheman, in the
presence of the *maheyuno,* with the power granted by Maheo.

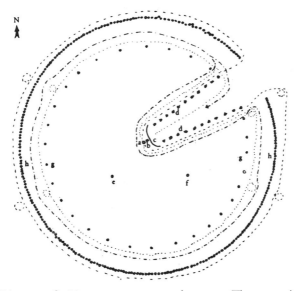

N

Fig. 7. Diagram of a Massaum camp around 700 A.D. The camp circle opens to the northeast, that is, the camp is located southwest of Bear Butte. The Tsistsistas camp circle consists here of 260 tipis; because six persons should be considered as average per tipi, approximately 1560 people are present. The total Tsistsistas population around 700 A.D. may have numbered at least three times this figure, perhaps considerably more. Features include (a) wolf lodge *(maheonox)*; (b) frames on which the two wolves and the kit fox were exhibited late in the afternoon of the fourth day; (c) corral; (d) wings of the drive lane; (e) lodge of the hohnuhka society; (f) lodge of the sacred arrows; (g) animal lodges *(heszevoxsz)*; (h) the Tsistsistas camp.

- - - - Trail of the red wolf on the evening of the fourth day. When he calls from the four sacred directions he marks a small circle.
· · · · Trail of the white she-wolf on the evening of the fourth day. She also calls four times and marks circles in the sacred directions.
· · · · Trail of the female kit fox at early dawn on the fifth day. From the wolf lodge, she follows the trail of the white wolf to the last animal lodge in the northeast. She had also called from the four sacred directions. She continues her run by entering the drive lane, thus approaching the corral from the direction of Bear Butte. When she reaches the corral, because she represents Ehyophstah, the blue star, Ehyophstah has symbolically and physically returned to the Tsistsistas.
- · - · Animals execute a full circle around the animal camp before they enter the drive lane. While completing the circle, they are not allowed to cross the opening of the camp circle; if they would stray into it they would block the invisible line connecting Bear Butte with the spirit performers present in the corral. On its trail, the mass of animals, therefore, moves around the pound and the wolf lodge. When they finally enter the drive lane in response to Ehyophstah's call, they enter from the direction of Bear Butte.

Through this act, Moseyoef was made the spiritual representative of the Tsistsistas. For this people, he was given a ritual position in the world of spirits, the southeast. This is also the direction of the blue star's heliacal rising.

The circular earth drawing represents the Tsistsistas earth, the Tsistsistas physical place in the universe, and documents their right to live in this world as Tsistsistas as formulated by the spirits.

Motseyoef remained seated in the southeastern position behind the Tsistsistas earth throughout the remainder of the ceremony conducted in the wolf lodge.

Teaching the Tsistsistas

The impeccable skins of a male red wolf, a female white wolf, and a female kit fox were brought into the lodge and placed on the sage north of the buffalo skull, in the northwestern position. Painted rattles were taken to the soutwestern side. Additional people came into the lodge, both men and women.

When night had fallen, the lodge of the *maiyun* revealed itself as a spirit lodge. From the eastern arm of the white cross to the base of the world tree eight coals were placed in intervals, and sweet grass was burned on these for a number of hours. The two Tsistsistas present in the lodge of the *maiyun* (Motseyoef and his companion who would become Ehyophstah's husband) were taught spirit songs, *maheonenootoz,* and were instructed in the calling of spirits of animals of the world of the grasslands and in the rules regarding their use.

Third Day (Ehyophstah and the Master Hunters)

There were four main actions on this day.

The Giving of Ehyophstah

Early in the morning, Ehyophstah was ritually created and given to the Tsistsistas companion of Motseyoef. All five main performers were present in the wolf lodge. Escheman painted black rings around Ehyophstah's ankles and wrists, a black sun between her breasts, a black crescent moon on her right shoulder blade, and black vertical lines on her face: one reaching from the hair across the forehead to the end of the nose, three on each cheek. This was her father's paint.

Nonoma lit a pipe and passed it to Ehyophstah. She smoked alone. Thus she had ritually accepted the obligation of service to the Tsistsistas as requested by Nonoma and Escheman.

Next a pipe was offered by the male pledger. After it had been passed in smoking among the five persons, Ehyophstah had been ritually joined with a Tsistsistas husband in the presence of her parents and the keeper of the Tsistsistas earth—Motseyoef.

When Ehyophstah later assisted Nonoma in the preparation of the red wolf, Esceheman had painted her daughter's face with green color in the same design that she had followed earlier. This was Ehyophstah's mother's paint. In Tsistsistas color symbolism, green represents new life, the fresh growth of spring emerging from the earth; it also represents hailstones derived from thunder clouds that accompany Nonoma's gift of moisture.

The Master Hunters

After the giving of Ehyophstah, a woman of the Young Wolf Society was called into the wolf lodge and instructed to bring the two men who had been selected to prepare the white wolf and the kit fox. She was painted with the design of her society: a red line extending from the hair down the forehead to the root of the nose; the lower half of her face was solidly painted red. She served as a messenger during the remainder of the ceremony held in the lodge.

She returned with the two men who took their places next to the animal hides on the northwestern side. Seven white stone bowls were brought in containing clear water in one and paint in the other six— blue, black, white, yellow, light red, dark red. Assisted by Ehyophstah, Nonoma began to work on the red male wolf hide while the two men prepared the female white wolf and the female kit fox.

They needed most of the day for this work. When they were done, the three animal skins rested in a line on the sage of the northwestern side of the wolf lodge. The red wolf was next to the buffalo skull followed by the white wolf and the kit fox.

Maheone honehe, the sacred red wolf, was carefully stretched and combed and was painted on both the head and body. His head was modeled by sewing together the skin of muzzle and throat and inserted grass bundles. From the nose to ears, his face was first painted blue-black. On this base, numerous lines were drawn horizontally, using the four directional colors: white (southeast), red (southwest), yellow (northwest), black (northeast), and the ceremonial color of the star of midsummer dawn—blue.

The lines of alternating colors numbered fifty five. Starting from the wolf's nose, the eleventh (blue), twenty-second (red), thirty-third (yellow), forty-fourth (black), and fifty-fifth (white) lines were executed larger than the others. The last line (white) reached the top of the wolf's head just behind the ears.

The body painting of the wolf was done in blue-black color. On the back of his head a face was drawn in abstract design; the wolf's ears stood like horns attached to it. The body of a man was indicated by two parallel lines extending from the face across the wolf's back to his tail. The center of this man drawing, which represented Nonoma, was marked with a round spot—the heart. On both sides of the skin, two parallel crescent-shaped lines indicated rainbows. In the rainbow of the animal's right side was the symbol of the sun; on the left side appeared the moon sickle. Four small wheels, *oxzemeo,* were painted red, representing the *maheyuno;* they were sewed to the hide at the shoulders and hips. A larger wheel representing Maheo was fastened to the middle of the back above the heart of the man figure. The flesh side of the hide was painted white.

Evevŝev honehe, the white wolf, wore a long strip of buffalo fur attached to the carefully modeled head. It extended along the female's back beyond her tail, actually trailing on the ground when the wolf was worn by a runner the following day. Two polished buffalo-horn tips were tied to the sides of the buffalo skin directly behind the wolf's ears. The immaculate white fur of Evevŝev honehe was not painted. The flesh side of her skin was painted white.

Voh'kis, the kit fox, was painted with a blue line across her glossy yellow fur from the tip of her nose to the tip of her tail. Blue lines ran up her black feet and joined the line along her back. On her right side was a blue sun disk; on her left was the blue moon crescent. The head of the kit fox had also been shaped to give a lifelike appearance. The flesh side of her hide was painted yellow.

This part of the Massaum was concluded when the *maiyun* present ritually made the three animals come alive.

Maheone honehe, the wolf *maiyun* and male master wolf, was also a manifestation of Nonoma; Evevŝev honehe, the female master wolf, was a manifestation of Esceheman. In appearances and range of obligations regarding animals, they also represented the sky and earth, day and night. Together they were the game keepers of animals released from the *heszevoxsz* and controlled hunting by predators, including the Tsistsistas. They were instructed by the *maiyun* to teach the Tsistsistas the right hunting way once the Tsistsistas had been granted the earth in the grasslands.

Voh'kis was the servant of the master wolves because she is associated with the blue star. Tsistsistas hunting time, as it was with the wolf packs of the Plains, began formally each day with the rise of the morning star (including *võ*, Venus), heralding the end of night and the coming of the sun.

Sharing Food with the Spirits

At noon, while work on the three hides was still in progress, food was brought into the wolf lodge by women of the Hohnuhka Society. It consisted of four categories: meat and food from plants that grow underground, from the ground, and above ground (chokecherries).

The meat was dog meat (puppy), which was flesh from an animal as distant from a wolf as could be obtained during times before domesticated animals were available because in the lodge of the *maiyun* the flesh of animals spiritually and physically related to Escheman and Nonoma was not admitted. The original food of the *maiyun* was the flesh of the *ax-xea,* the great horned water serpent hunted by Nonoma (chapter 5)—a monster outside Escheman's care. In the Massaum, dog meat served as a substitute for the flesh of the *ax-xea* because it was "contrary" to other animal flesh.

The more domesticated dogs became the farther they were removed from Escheman's guardianship. The Tsistsistas used dog meat only as sacred food in ceremonies that demanded "nonnatural" meat. For this reason, dog meat played a role in the meetings and initiation rituals of the Hohnuhka Society. It was also used in spirit lodge performances when the spirits were ritually fed. In Tsistsistas culture, dogs were highy regarded; to profane dogs constituted an offense against the spirits.

At noon in the wolf lodge five small portions of each of the four types of food brought in were deposited at the base of the world tree and under each of the *maheyuno* bundles. The remainder was passed reverently among all present in the lodge and consumed.

The Teaching of the Tsistsistas

When night had fallen, the wolf lodge again turned into a spirit lodge. Another line of eight coals was placed next to the ashes of the first row. Sweet grass was burned. The spirit songs taught during this night included *honehe nenootoz*—songs of the wolf spirits who were present.

Fourth Day (the Camp Is the Universe)

The five main performers had not eaten again after they had shared the food of the spirits on the day before. They would break their fast after the conclusion of the ceremony on the fifth day. On the evening of the fourth day, they were joined in their fast by everyone in camp, an exception made only for very small children. There were six main actions on this day.

The Animal Lodges

Early in the morning, a second camp circle was raised within the first camp circle of Tsistsistas lodges, perhaps a hundred yards apart from it. This inner ring of lodges symbolized the animal dens below the sacred mountain. Together the lodges represented all animal life of the grasslands. The opening of this camp circle was also oriented toward Nowah'wus. After the lodges were in place, each was joined by those who would, on the next day, impersonate the animals that belonged to it. Because of the great number of species, nearly a sixth of the Tsistsistas population had to take the part of animals. Both sexes and all age groups were needed, including children.

Considerable amounts of equipment and materials were moved to the animal camp to be worked into the elaborate costumes worn on the next day. In the early afternoon, the lodges were closed. In each lodge, instructors prepared participants for their sacred roles with a purification ritual followed by instruction and, finally, ritual transformation into animals.

The Hohnuhka lodge had already been set up the day before in the open space halfway between the wolf lodge and the other animal lodges, to the southwest. After *nimāhenan* had come to the Tsistsistas, the tipi of the sacred arrows stood southeast of the wolf lodge. True to the contrary principle, the appearance of the Hohnuhka lodge was different from all other lodges in camp: The tipi poles were on the outside; the lodge cover was turned inside out; the smoke flaps were turned the wrong way. Hohnuhka Society members had already assembled and passed their secret transformation ceremony before they had cooked the sacred food for the wolf lodge.

Preparing to Come Out into the World

In the wolf lodge on this morning were the five main performers and the two men who had prepared Evevŝev honehe and Voh'kis.

Four freshly cut, straight shafts of cottonwood were shortened to a length of about thirty inches to serve as walking sticks. Five bundles of white sage were attached to the top of each stick. Because the walking sticks were used by the wolf runners of the Massaum as the front legs of the animals, Maheone honehe and Evevŝev honehe were symbolically endowed with the power of the center (the Supreme Being) and the power of the four sacred directions (*maheyuno*) and therefore controlled animals in the four directions of the universe. The walking sticks of the red wolf were painted red; those of the white wolf were peeled and painted white. After they had been finished, they were placed along the sides of the animals resting on the sage.

Next, the pipe to be used in the animal-calling part of the Massaum was prepared. This was a sinew-wrapped deer-bone pipe rubbed with red paint. Nonoma instructed Ehyophstah's husband how to handle it correctly. First, the bottom of the pipe was closed with a ball of sinew. Four portions of smoking material (herbs mixed with buffalo kidney fat) were put in; when the pipe was formally smoked on the next day, all of plant and animal life was symbolically present in it. The pipe opening was sealed with a piece of animal fat.

Ehyophstah moved a coal from the fire with a fire stick and placed sweet grass on it. After the pipe had been purified in it, it was made alive; it was placed in front of the buffalo skull along with a pipe stick.

Seven women, Young Wolves, were called into the lodge. They wore the face painting of their society, which has already been described. They represented the human doubles of wolf spirit helpers and were charged with constructing the pound. Now they were purified by Nonoma and formally instructed where the pound should be built; they left to do their work.

Three men were called into the wolf lodge who had been selected to impersonate the three animal spirits. They were purified and taught regarding their roles.

The Sacred Pound

The seven Young Wolves erected a high, crescent-shaped shade about twenty feet away from the wolf lodge; the opening faced the opening in the camp circle and Nowah'wus. About a dozen lodge poles and four lodge coverings were used. Next, freshly cut cottonwood trees and branches from ten to fifteen feet high were planted in prepared holes in the ground extending from near the horns of the shade (the corral) in two long, expanding lines to points just behind the circle of animal lodges but in front of the opening in the Tsistsistas camp circle. These were the wings of the "drive lane" of the sacred pound (see fig. 7). A chute, oftentimes a feature of Tsistsistas buffalo pounds (see chapter 4) was not built here because it was not needed. The work was completed in the middle of the afternoon. Next, the Young Wolves raised three low three-pole frames in the narrow space between the rear of the corral and the wolf lodge.

Maheone honehe, Evevŝev honehe, and Voh'kis Are Coming Out

During this time in the wolf lodge, the two men who would wear the wolves' attire were painted with the ceremonial designs of their position. They had stripped to breechclout and moccasins. The body of the man who would represent the red wolf was painted red; the body of the man who would wear the white wolf attire was painted white. A black sun was marked on their chests, and a black moon was drawn on their right shoulder blades. The white wolf runner was painted with short, vertical black lines under the eyes.

Next, Ehyophstah and her husband were ritually brought into the condition to conduct the sacred animals from the sacred mountain out into the world. They undressed to breechclout and moccasins and were painted red over their body and hair, with black rings around their ankles and wrists, and black suns and moons on their chest and shoulder blade. They dressed again. All waited.

A Young Wolf came and reported that the pound had been completed. Then Nonoma sent a crier to announce to the Tsistsistas camp that the sacred animals were coming out. After a while, Ehyophstah and her husband were instructed how to proceed in taking the animals out. Maheone honehe came first. With their hands together, they stood over the wolf; they motioned three times, and with a fourth motion placed their hands firmly on his back. With four motions they lifted him, and three times they moved him with his head outside beneath the raised lodge cover before they carried him out. With four motions, they placed him on the first frame. Evevŝev honehe came next, then Voh'kis. They were handled the same way and placed on the remaining frames. Ehyophstah and her husband returned to the closed lodge.

Now came the first public part of the ceremony. From the Tsistsistas camp, many people came to stand and look at the three animals from a distance. They stood silently, observing closely and confirming the details. No one came from the animal lodges because the Tsistsistas there were ritually animals then. When they had dispersed, Ehyophstah and her husband brought the three animals back into the wolf lodge.

Making the World Holy

It was evening, and all the lodges in the camp were closed, the fires extinguished. All camp dogs had been taken inside the Tsistsistas lodges. No one was allowed to move outside the camp circle or within.

When the first runner was prepared, Nonoma put the red wolf on the man's back and tied him securely; the wolf's head projected over the man's forehead. Nonoma placed the walking sticks in his hands. The rattles began, and wolf songs were sung when Maheone honehe left the wolf lodge and ran beside the right wing of the "drive lane" and beyond the Tsistsistas lodges. He ran into the prairie and turned to his right.

When he reached the first of the sacred directions outside the camp, he howled the calling song of the hunting master wolf. He continued, running around the Tsistsistas camp, calling from the three remaining positions. Thus he had stopped at the southeast, southwest, northwest and northeast, marking a small circle at each location. He reentered the camp at the opening and ran outside the left wing of the brush line, passed the corral, and slipped back into the wolf lodge.

Nonoma put the white she-wolf on her runner's back, secured the hide, and handed the man the walking sticks. Again the rattles and wolf songs resounded as Evevŝev honehe left the lodge and ran along the right wing of the brush lane. She ran beyond the animal lodge camp circle but turned right before reaching the Tsistsistas circle. She ran between the two rings of lodges, stopping at the four sacred places to make the calling songs of the master wolf. She entered beside the left brush line and returned running to the wolf lodge.

The whole camp had become the universe. Everything had been made holy inside and outside the wolf lodge. Outside the camp circle, time stood still. The animal lodges had become *heszevoxsz*, the dens of the animal spirits in the deep earth of Esceheman's realm.

The Teaching of the Tsistsistas

With the dark, the wolf lodge became a spirit lodge again. Another line of eight coals was placed beside the ashes of the lines of the preceding nights. The smell of sweet grass arose once more. This was the last night of teaching the Tsistsistas the calling songs of the animal spirits.

Fifth Day (the Coming of Ehyophstah, the Sacred Hunt)

There were six clusters of actions on this day.

The Coming of the Spirits

Very early in the morning, when it was still dark outside, the main performers in the wolf lodge prepared their coming out. Present were the five spirits, the two painters (instructors) of Evevŝev honehe and Voh'kis, and three men who impersonated the master wolves and the kit fox. The body and facial paints worn on the previous day were put on again. The Voh'kis runner was painted yellow by his instructor, with vertical black lines under his eyes, and blue dots running along his sides from ankles to shoulders—from there along the outside of his arms to his wrists.

Esceheman painted a blue cross on Ehyophstah's face; its four branches encased the forehead, eyes, and nose. The painter of Voh'kis painted Ehyophstah's husband the same way. The seven Young Wolves entered the lodge; they were also painted with the blue star design by Esceheman.

Ehyophstah's husband left the wolf lodge, lifted an unpainted, bleached buffalo skull lying south of the lodge, and carried it into the enclosure of the pound where he put it on the ground halfway between the horns, facing the open space between the brush wings of the "drive lane." He returned to the ceremonial lodge.

The Blue Star

All waited until it was nearly morning. The five spirits left the wolf lodge first. They stood and faced southeast in the order used when they had stepped from Nowah'wus upon the leaving of Ehyophstah with the two Tsistsistas (chapter 5): Esceheman on the left, Nonoma to her right, Ehyophstah, her husband, and Motseyoef following in line.

They stood and waited for the signal from the sky. Finally, the blue beacon of Rigel blazed above the dark horizon. They stood and watched. For a few minutes the star shone intensely, then dimmed and quickly disappeared.

They walked into the enclosure and sat in a line on both sides of the buffalo skull, Esceheman and Ehyophstah on the left, Nonoma, Ehyophstah's husband, and Motseyoef on the right. Behind this group sat the seven women of the Young Wolf Society. The Voh'kis instructor sat next to Ehyophstah, with the two wolves and the second instructor to his left. The sacred straight pipe was placed in front of the buffalo skull on a bundle of white sage. Inside the left horn of the enclosure, a medicine lance and a sheet of dried buffalo meat were placed on the ground. The medicine lance, or "medicine pole," (for a description, see chapter 4) had been prepared by a shaman in one of the animal lodges.

The ceremonial hunt had formally begun. People waited silently in the early dawn everywhere in camp. Voh'kis emerged from the wolf lodge and ran her sacred circle around the *heszevoxsz* on the trail of the white wolf of the evening before.

She called the eagerly awaited signals from the four sacred directions. She entered the "drive lane" and the enclosure. Nonoma removed the kit fox from the runner and placed her, fleshside down, on the buffalo skull, facing the opening of the wings and Nowah'wus.

The Sacred Hunt

Now the great public display of the Massaum began. The lodge covers of the tipis of the Tsistsistas camp circle were pulled up; the people looked out. The costumed, masked, painted impersonators of many animal species spilled from the animal dens.

Herd animals and animals that lived in small groups emerged in bands from their dens: buffalos, elks, deer, antelopes, otters, wolves, and birds, such as cranes. Solitary animals appeared with single representatives: coyote, badger, grizzly bear, black bear, cougar, different kinds of foxes, eagles, hawks, raven, magpie, and so forth. Actors imitated the behavior of the species they represented. The colorful mass of animals walked, circled, or ran in the space between the Tsistsistas camp circle and the ring of animal lodges, drifting in clockwise fashion.

In the enclosure, Esceheman lifted the sacred pipe up and placed it in Ehyophstah's hand. These two, followed by the seven Young Wolves, walked into the wings of the pound. They stood there quietly, praying. Ehyophstah, holding the pipe with both hands, offered it toward the opening and Nowah'wus, thus calling the animals. "*Nanēhov meohotoxc*," "I am the star of dawn."

The act confirmed that Ehyophstah had been granted the position of master spirit of animals in the realm of the grasslands given to Tsistsistas guardianship.

Maheone honehe, Evevŝev honehe, and Voh'kis left the enclosure and ran along the stream of animals, forcing it to complete a full circle around the animal camp before entering the drive lane. While making the circle, the animals did not cross the opening of the brush wings but passed behind the wings, the enclosure, and the wolf lodge. Calling songs were sung when the animals finally came in and surrounded the nine women.

From the Hohnuhka lodge seven contraries (Thunder spirits) ran up, dressed only in breechclout, with their body and hair painted white. The hair that was tied in a knot over the forehead was decorated with a single eagle feather. They carried miniature sky lances painted red. After the bow and arrow had been adopted (chapter 4), they used miniature sky bows and four types of miniature arrows. Here they acted as sacred hunters, *emhoniu,* and because they were ritually in a contrary condition, as sacred clowns.

They passed along the sacred animals milling around in the pound, ritually killing with stabbing motions. Animals who were struck staggered and fell, spurting blood, but raised themselves again. The mimicry in the display of injured and bleeding animals was extraordinary.

After the animals had completed a dance around Esceheman, Ehyophstah, and the Young Wolves, they filed out of the brush lane and returned to the dens. While they were moving back, the doctoring portion of the Massaum began. Those in the Tsistsistas camp who were ill or disabled or who wanted a blessing directly from the animal spirits sat motionless in front of the lodges. When passing them, the animals performed brief shamanistic healing or cleansing rituals. Hohnuhka who were asked to doctor treated patients in their mysterious contrary way at this time.

Esceheman, Ehyophstah, and the Young Wolves had returned to their places in the enclosure when the animals were leaving the pound. They waited. When the *heszevoxsz* were closed once again, the second hunt began.

Esceheman placed Maheonẹ honehe on Ehyophstah, tying the wolf securely to the woman's neck and shoulders; the wolf's head projected over her forehead. Both, followed by the Young Wolves, again went midway between the wings, this time walking there in a circle. By wearing the wolf *maiyun,* Nonoma's red master wolf was shown as the servant of Ehyophstah to the Tsistsistas and animal witnesses who were present. It also testified that the power of her father, Nonoma, was with her.

Again the animals streamed from their lodges, and the actions of the peceding hunt were repeated. The third hunt followed the second hunt in detail; Ehyophstah again wore the wolf *maiyun*. The fourth hunt repeated the first hunt, and Ehyophstah once more stood with the pipe.

This time the group of women again stood silently in the dancing, colorful mass of animals that was prodded by Hohnuhka hunters. Ehyophstah offered the pipe to the animal spirits a last time. At the conclusion of this last impounding, the animals did not return to their dens. They stood watching the last acts performed in the enclosure. It was midday.

The Medicine Lance and the Sacred Food

Escheman, Ehyophstah, and the Young Wolves had returned to the enclosure. The sacred pipe rested again in its special place. Nonoma placed the sheet of dried buffalo meat on the grass in front of the buffalo skull. He handed the medicine lance to Ehyophstah and her husband and instructed them how to proceed. With four motions they thrust the tip of the ceremonial weapon through the meat, raised the shaft, and stuck it in an opening in the ground near the buffalo skull. Nonoma placed four buffalo chips on the grass a few yards away from the medicine pole, marking the four sacred directions.

The Maheone honehe runner walked up with the red wolf hide attached to his head and back. He placed his hands and feet on the four buffalo chips, facing the medicine lance, the buffalo skull, and the five spirits. The act demonstrated the power of the master wolf over the hunting of game to the southeast, southwest, northwest, and northeast.

The coyote came running, and with three faints, crawled through under Maheone honehe with the fourth motion. This act symbolized the power of the red wolf over all other predators. It also commissioned the coyote to perform the servant's role in the next event.

When the coyote had passed under the Maheone honehe, Voh'kis, after three feints, ripped the dried meat from the medicine lance with a fourth jump. Because she had signaled the arrival of hunting time, she also signaled the end of four successful hunts by making the food of the sacred animals available for distribution.

Immediately, the *hohnuhka* snatched the meat from the kit fox and tore it into seven portions. They ran out in seven directions to the Tsistsistas camp, and they distributed tiny fractions of the meat to every person, to share in the animal food blessed by the spirits.

The Coyote Leader and the Animal Race

Coyote placed himself at the head of the animal groups when they moved out of the wings and into the prairie in the direction of No-wah'wus. On both sides the Tsistsistas people followed them from the distance. The coyote caused the joyful mass of animals to stop four times before they reached the stream. A Massaum song was sung at each stop. After the fourth song, a race took place that carried all to the water's edge. Everyone took a drink, thus ritually ending the fast. This act also made the stream holy because the sacred animals had blessed it by their drinking.

On returning, the animals stopped again four times to sing a Massaum song; they dispersed immediately after reaching the "drive lane." The *hohnuhka,* who had accompanied them to the stream, returned to their own lodge for the "brushing-off" ritual that ended their contrary condition. All through the camp, Tsistsistas and animal impersonators ended the ceremony by using white sage for the "brushing" that returned them to their ordinary condition.

The Lodge of the Maiyun

The main performers, with the two wolves, the kit fox, and their instructors had returned to the wolf lodge. Once again the five spirits took the seating order that had been established on the second day of the ceremony when the Tsistsistas earth had been made. On the sage cover south of the buffalo skull sat Esceheman, followed on her right by Nonoma, Ehyophstah, and her husband. Motseyoef sat on the southeastern side alone, behind the Tsistsistas earth. The wolf and the kit fox hides were removed from the runners and displayed on the northwestern side of the lodge. Behind, and next to them, sat the instructors.

Ehyophstah took the sacred pipe to Motseyoef, who broke the seal and lit it. The pipe passed from Motseyoef along the line to the Voh'kis instructor who was sitting in the northernmost position and directly back from him to Motseyoef. When the pipe was smoked completely, it was passed to him again. He placed the ashes in four motions upon the Tsistsistas earth in front of him. He used the pipe stick to brush ashes and the earth symbol to the fireplace, leaving no trace on the clean, smooth ground.

Now Nonoma erased the sand painting of the universe on the western side of the world tree. One by one the performers stood in front of him. He brushed them with a small bundle of white sage, touching them lightly along both sides of their bodies from their heads to the earth. The Massaum had ended.

They left the lodge, taking the animal hides, rattles, pipe, and other articles with them. They would go to the sweat lodges later. The Young Wolves removed the cover of the wolf lodge on the next day. Because it had served as the sacred mountain, it belonged to the spirits. They took it to the stream and placed it gently in the waters.

The world tree and the twenty-eight pole frame were left standing. During the following days, the large camp broke up. The various bands went away to their fall locations where the impounding of real game in accordance with the Massaum law would begin later.

7. Early Tsistsistas in the Northern Plains

The object of the ceremony [Oxheheom, New Life Lodge, "Sun Dance"] *is to make the whole world over again, and from the time the Lodge-Maker makes his vow everything is supposed to begin to take on new life, for the Medicine-Spirit, having heard the prayer of the pledger, begins at once to answer it. When the man makes the vow, he does it not so much for himself or his family, as for the whole tribe. Attending upon his vow and its fulfillment is an abundance of good water and good breath of the wind, which is the same as the breath of the Medicine-Spirit who regards all things. At the time of the Lone Tipi, when the earth is first created, it is just beginning to grow. As the ceremony progresses, this earth increases in size, and when the lodge itself is erected we build a fire which represents the heat of the sun, and we place the lodge to face the east that the heavenly bodies may pass over it and fertilize it.*

—EXPLANATION OF THE MEANING OF THE OXHEHEOM CEREMONY
AS TOLD TO GEORGE A. DORSEY

THERE IS ONE Tsistsistas sacred story that goes beyond the Ehyophstah accounts published by Grinnell and Kroeber. On October 15, 1971, the keeper of the *nimāhenan*, the sacred arrows, Edward Red Hat, came to my house for a serious visit. He was accompanied by two arrow priests as eyewitnesses (Schlesier 1974:279–80; 1980b:55). Events leading to this visit, and the results of it, have been discussed elsewhere (1974, 1980b) and will not be repeated here.

During this visit it was considered as necessary by the arrow keeper that I should be informed about Tsistsistas origins in order to comprehend their unrelenting struggle for survival and their long journey through time. The visitors had come prepared with a tape recorder. When they switched it on, we listened to an instructor's voice telling carefully in English the sacred story of the creation of the Tsistsistas as a people of the grasslands. It is a spirit story and had never been told outside a small circle of persons within the *ononeovätaneo* and perhaps never will be told again.

In my presentation in this book of the Massaum and its significance for the formation of Tsistsistas, I have not disclosed the sacred
story but have assembled external facts and internal Tsistsistas perceptions that are in agreement with it. I am permitted to give the
location and date of the creation of the Tsistsistas; both have already
been mentioned in this text—North Dakota, around 500 B.C. This is
the information I started with when I described the time and place of
the Proto-Tsistsistas—Tsistsistas transition.

The place and date do not invalidate Tsistsistas stories about the
ancient homeland in the far north but complement them. The Tsistsistas themselves draw a line between the Tsistsistas and their distant ancestors. They see themselves as having been the same people
in the far north, but then something special happened to them in the
grasslands.

Some readers might argue that it is impossible to base a reconstruction of Tsistsistas beginnings and early times on "oral tradition,"
even though two facts come from a sacred story that demands that it
be preserved unaltered over time. This is perhaps true in many cases,
but regarding the Tsistsistas I disagree. Over the many years of my
close relationship with Tsistsistas ceremonial people, I have found
them to be astonishingly accurate concerning events of the near and
distant past. In contrast, I have found the ethnological literature
about Cheyennes oftentimes woefully inept and erroneous. Generally—and there are good exceptions—errors once printed become
embedded in later publications because anthropologists sometimes
tend to perpetuate errors from each other's works instead of asking
their informants directly.

The following section may decide if the Tsistsistas and I are right
when I identify the early Tsistsistas with archaeological remains in
the northern Plains. For this effort, the preceding chapters are essential because the Tsistsistas world description and specific features and
behavior derived from it must be superimposed on archaeological
material to distinguish the early Tsistsistas presence from the presence of other groups.

Groups Coexisting with the Tsistsistas

Groups of the Pelican Lake Phase

"Pelican Lake" is the type name for a distinctive projectile point (Pelican Lake Corner Notched) found in all components of what Reeves
(1970:68) defines as a phase. He assigned "some 90 archaeological

components" to this phase and divided it into 8 regional subphases that he sees as corresponding in varying degrees to distinctive environmental areas of the northern Plains (1970:68–72). It should be noted that Foor (1982:25–29, 81) defined Pelican Lake as a culture. Because I believe that groups participating in Pelican Lake are of different cultural backgrounds and represent a number of different language stocks, I cannot agree with the use of this term. This essay will use Reeves's terms and categories.

Sites of the Pelican Lake Phase extend from the northern half of Colorado through western Nebraska, Wyoming, South Dakota, and Montana to Alberta, southern Saskatchewan, and southwestern Manitoba (Reeves 1970, fig. 3). The heaviest concentrations are in Wyoming and Montana.

The time period of this phase extends in the High Plains from at least 1000 B.C. to A.D. 250. Temporal and spatial distributions of sites signal a withdrawal of Pelican Lake Phase groups westward from the eastern portions of the region (southern Manitoba, South Dakota, and Nebraska) around A.D. 100 and from the Saskatchewan Basin, northern Montana and eastern Wyoming between A.D. 200 and 250 (Reeves 1970, fig. 7). In the Rocky Mountains of Alberta and Montana, in southern Montana, and in the Bighorn Basin, sites continue until about A.D. 700; Foor (1982:84–89) has suggested that they lasted there until A.D. 1000.

Reeves (1970:142–49) interprets the Pelican Lake phase as a serial component of a cultural tradition he calls TUNAXA, which is divided into three temporal phases—McKean, Hanna, and Pelican Lake.

The McKean Phase, named after the diagnostic lanceolate projectile point found at the McKean site in northeastern Wyoming, appeared in the western High Plains around 3600 B.C. (G. Wright 1982:150). The earliest dates come from the Bighorn Mountains and southern Montana. Although sites of this phase occur from western Nebraska to Manitoba and from Wyoming to Alberta, the heaviest concentration is in Wyoming (Reeves 1973, fig. 6). Two other projectile points are often associated with McKean points in sites of this phase—Duncan and Hanna. A gradual transition from the McKean Phase to the Hanna Phase apparently began around 2000 B.C. The last dates for McKean, so far, range from about 1500 B.C. (Brumley 1978:176; G. Wright 1982:150) to 1230 B.C. (Greiser 1985:121). Development from the Hanna Phase to the Pelican Lake Phase began around 1300 B.C., as is evidenced by the low incidence of Pelican Lake points

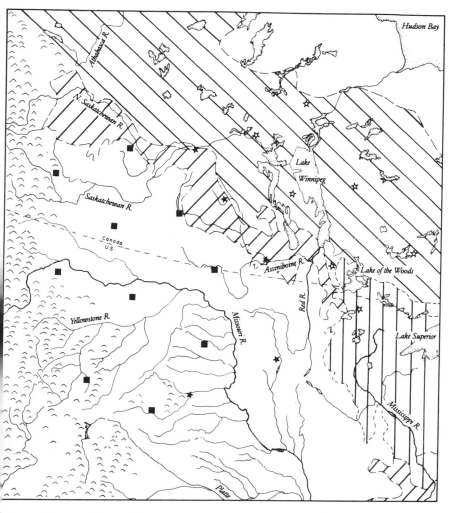

MAP I. The northern plains and adjacent regions, 200 B.C.

Vegetation zones

Grassland; tundra and taiga north of the boreal forest

Conifer-hardwood and deciduous forest

Parkland

Boreal forest

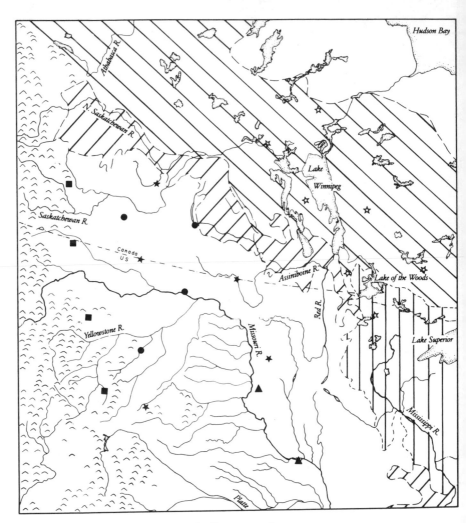

MAP 2. The northern plains and adjacent regions, A.D. 300

Archaeological entities and their linguistic affiliations

■ Pelican Lake (Aztec-Tanoan)

● Avonlea (Athapaskan)

▲ Valley (Caddoan)

★ Besant (Algonquian)

☆ Laurel (Algonquian)

✪ Blackduck (Algonquian)

▼ Proto-Mandan (Hokan-Siouan)

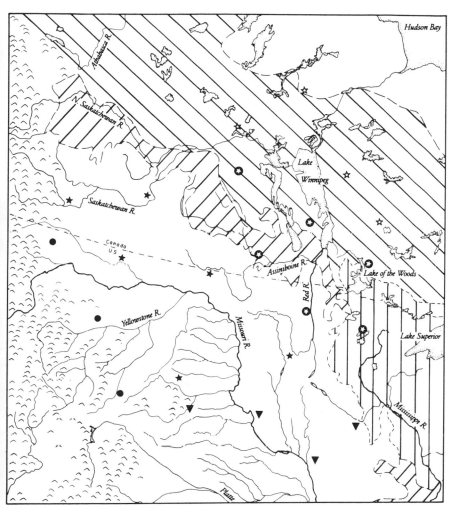

MAP 3. The northern plains and adjacent regions, A.D. 800

FIG. 8. A shaman leads the migration from the far north. When the Proto-Tsistsistas started on their long journey, they were led by a shaman who walked ahead of the people with an *axzem*, a spirit wheel, in his right hand. The shaman's spirit helper in the *axzem* showed him the trail to be taken. Drawing by Dick West.

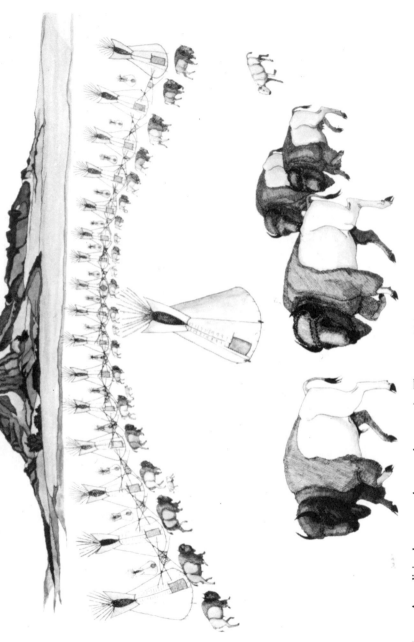

Fig. 9. A medicine hunt near the sacred mountain. The proto-Tsistsistas arrived in the Plains with a fully developed medicine hunt system. A medicine hunt was a communal hunt in which an animal herd was brought into camp or constructed pound by a shaman's spirit helper. The medicine hunt here depicted took place near the Tsistsistas sacred mountain—Bear Butte, South Dakota, which rises in the background. Drawing by Dick West.

FIG. 10. The giving of Ehyophstah in the spirit lodge of the sacred mountain. The two spirits *(maiyun)* who are the keepers of animal spirits of the Plains, Nonoma, the spirit of Thunder, and Esceheman, "Our Grandmother," the Earth spirit, gave their daughter Ehyophstah to Tsistsistas. Ehyophstah, "Yellow-haired Woman," was a young female buffalo transformed by her *maiyun* parents into a beautiful girl to help the Tsistsistas. Her parents placed her in the position of master spirit of animals and therefore gave her the power to bring game. She was given as a wife to one of two Tsistsistas ceremonial scouts who on their visionary, death-defying search had found the spirit lodge of the *maiyun*—Bear Butte. The white bear represents Voxpenako, servant and protector of Esceheman. Drawing by Dick West.

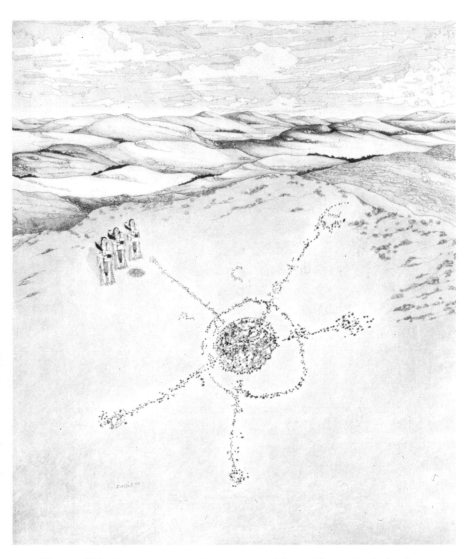

Fig. 11. Tsistsistas shamans at the *oxzem* on Moose Mountain, Saskatchewan. In the northern Plains, the Tsistsistas built large stone features on high elevations. They were regarded as *oxzemeo,* spirit wheels of stone, and were directed to the spirits of the world above. They served as evidence of the Tsistsistas presence and called on the spirits for protection. They also served as boundary markers. The alignments of spokes and cairns were oriented in the direction of the heliacal risings of three stars of summer dawn important in Tsistsistas religious philosophy: Aldebaran, Rigel, and Sirius. Drawing by Dick West.

Fig. 12. The creation of the universe ritually reenacted and explained, Massaum, second day. In the seclusion of the ceremonial lodge, the priest knelt on the ground west of the center pole. In this action, he represented Maheo, the Supreme Being. The universe was created from a cosmological singularity. The singularity is at the very center of the earth painting that the priest is shown finishing. The small mounds in the ceremonial directions and the white cross extending in the cardinal directions represent *hestanov*, the universe, in the process of expansion immediately following on the event of the cosmological singularity. Drawing by Dick West.

FIG. 13. Motseyoef and the Tsistsistas earth, Massaum, second day. The Massaum is here revealed as an earth-giving ceremony. Four of the five main performers sit in the southwestern position. Next to the painted buffalo skull is Esceheman, followed by Nonoma, Ehyophstah, and her husband, Motseyoef sits alone on the southeastern side. Nonoma has instructed him to execute a small circular earth drawing on the bare ground in front of him. This represents the earth given to Motseyoef as the spiritual representative of the Tsistsistas and grants to his people the right to the grasslands. The location where the Tsistsistas earth was given by Nonoma and Esceheman is the spirit lodge of Bear Butte, here represented by the Massaum wolf lodge. The artist's drawing shows this specific event as it is commemorated in the ceremony. Drawing by Dick West.

FIG. 14. The blue star, Voh'kis, descends from the sky to conduct the sacred hunt, Massaum, fifth day. In the predawn of the fifth day of the ceremony, after the actual heliacal rising and the quickly following disappearance of Voh'kis (the star Rigel) in the southeastern sky, the yellow kit fox, painted with blue lines, appears and runs her circle around the wide arc of the animal camp. She enters the drive lane and the corral. She represents

both the star and Ehyophstah who has once again returned to the Tsistsistas. The major performers of the ceremony are waiting for her in the corral. Of these the woman pledger who plays the sacred role of Ehyophstah, her ritual husband, and the seven women of the Young Wolf Society are painted with the blue star design, the symbol of Voh'kis. Drawing by Dick West.

Fig. 15. Ehyophstah directs the sacred hunt, Massaum, fifth day. Ehyophstah calls the animals from the drive land near the corral. She stands silently, offering the sacred straight pipe to Bear Butte and the animals that are beginning to arrive and to dance around her.

Next to her stands her mother, Escheman; behind her are the seven wolf helpers. Coyote, in the foreground, is watching the antics of two Hohnuhka Society members who perform as ritual hunters and sacred clowns. Drawing by Dick West.

FIG. 16. Red wolf, white wolf walking, Massaum, fifth day. The male red wolf is Maheone honehe, the wolf *maiyun* and species-specific protector spirit of wolves, or Artgeist. The white wolf is Evevŝev honehe, the horned wolf, the female counterpart of the red wolf. Both are the master hunters of all grassland predatory animals, the guardians of the sacred mountain, and the messengers of the spirit world. As game protectors, they taught the Tsistsistas the hunting etiquette of the grasslands. As spirits, they represent both the earth and the sky regions. In the Massaum symbolism, the red wolf also represents Nonoma, the Thunder spirit, and the red star Aldebaran. The white she-wolf represents Esceheman, the earth spirit, and the white star Sirius. On the fifth day of the Massaum, both wolves assist Ehyophstah in bringing the game into the drive lane and the corral. The carefully prepared and decorated skins of the two wolves are worn by painted runners. Drawing by Dick West.

associated with Hanna points after this date. Around 1000 B.C., Pelican Lake points dominate assemblages, signaling phase transition (Brumley 1978:176). A few Hanna corner-notched points are present in early Pelican Lake Phase sites.

According to Reeves (1970:87), the available data indicate that the Pelican Lake Phase economy was based primarily on the communal hunting of buffalo where buffalo populations were dense. In other areas, a more generalized hunting pattern existed, with the grinding of wild plants for food. North of Wyoming, grinding slabs and handstones are lacking. Riverine and lacustrine resources were utilized where they were advantageous. The Bighorn Basin and the Alberta and Montana Rocky Mountains were seasonally used by groups of this phase for hunting elk, deer, and sheep (Reeves 1970:84). Ceramics are extremely rare; Reeves (1970:80–81) considers this phase to be preceramic or aceramic. The main hunting weapon was the atlatl (spear thrower).

The bow and arrow were not adopted by groups of this phase although in southern Saskatchewan and eastern Montana, they lived for at least a century in close proximity to groups of the Avonlea Complex who had brought the bow and arrow with them into the region.

Buffalo kill sites, which are more prevalent in the northern area used by the people of the Pelican Lake Phase, include jumps and pounds. Post molds and logs representing holding corrals are occasionally preserved (Reeves 1970:83). Ceremonial structures have not been found.

According to the most recent investigations (Brink and Baldwin 1985), the burial system of Pelican Lake during the early stages and at least in some regions (Alberta, Saskatchewan, Montana) includes the following: placement of the burial site on a high, prominent spot usually with a commanding view and with interment in shallow subsurface pits. Rock cairns are often placed over the infilled pits, and burials are almost always secondary burials, and more than one individual is usually represented. Red ocher covers nearly all the bones and appears to have been placed in the pit infill as well. There are always other grave goods, often in large numbers, and these typically include Pelican Lake projectile points, native copper, clam shell and clam shell beads, dentalia shells, and the like. Reeves (1970:88), however, reports primary flexed pit interments with few associated grave goods for the relatively late Glendo subphase of Pelican Lake in Wyoming.

Applying culture-specific categories to the Pelican Lake Phase archaeological evidence, it can be stated conclusively that this phase does not represent the Tsistsistas people. The beginning and ending dates of Pelican Lake and its location within the TUNAXA tradition further strengthen this conclusion.

The TUNAXA tradition entered the High Plains from the Rocky Mountain west (Benedict and Olson 1973; Husted 1969:91) and from the Great Basin (see, e.g., Brumley 1978:188). Linguistically, as Husted has suggested, at least a part of Pelican Lake should be identified with Aztec-Tanoan speakers. I would include the ancestors of the Kiowas and believe that groups ancestral to the Kutenais and Nez Perces participated in it also.

Groups of the Avonlea Phase

The Avonlea Phase is characterized by a distinctive triangular side-notched arrow point with frequent, finely serrated edges. The name derives from the Avonlea type site located southwest of Regina in south-central Saskatchewan. Reeves (1970, table 4) assigned thirty-six components to this phase.

Avonlea sites extend from southwestern Manitoba (where they are rare) through Saskatchewan to Alberta, south through Montana into northeastern Wyoming and western South Dakota (1970, fig. 5). The largest concentrations are in Saskatchewan, Alberta, Montana, and northeastern Wyoming. Avonlea artifacts occur quite often in association with Besant Phase material, indicating a high degree of contact between two different traditions sharing the same region.

Initial dates mark the arrival of groups of this phase in the Alberta and Saskatchewan Plains at the beginning of the Christian era. Their expansion southward is evidenced by sites in the Black Hills and Northeastern Wyoming dated around A.D. 400 (Reeves 1970, fig. 7). Coexistence with Besant groups in much of this area began well before this time. After A.D. 600, Avonlea groups concentrated in the western portions of the High Plains from Alberta to Wyoming. They may have been partly responsible for the withdrawal of Pelican Lake Phase groups into the Rocky Mountains and the Bighorn Basin. By A.D. 700 Avonlea groups had abandoned the Saskatchewan Basin, and the region was used almost exclusively by Besant Phase hunters. In southern Montana and adjacent areas in Wyoming, Avonlea sites continued until A.D. 1000 (Husted 1969:92–95; Reeves 1970, fig. 7).

At the Head-Smashed-In buffalo jump in southern Alberta

(Reeves 1978), Avonlea follows Pelican Lake in time; at the Gull Lake buffalo drive site in southwestern Saskatchewan, the terminal Avonlea presence is dated at A.D. 660 (Kehoe 1973:77).

The economy of the Avonlea Phase was based on highly efficient buffalo hunting in the regions of dense buffalo populations. Communal hunts were of considerable importance; jumps, pounds and traps were used. Avonlea is best known from kill sites. Habitation sites are located on stream terraces and in caves, and settlement features are still generally unknown. Smaller game formed only a minimal part of the diet (Reeves 1970:106). Collecting activities included fowling, fishing, and plant gathering.

Although no ceremonial structures associated with Avonlea buffalo drives have been found, two investigators (Kehoe and Kehoe 1968:28) believe that game-calling ceremonies played an important role. Ceramics existed throughout much of the Avonlea temporal range (Syms 1977:92−93). The Avonlea burial system featured a primary flexed or extended pit burial (Reeves 1970:106).

The Avonlea Phase must be credited with having introduced the bow and arrow into the northern Plains. It is interesting that Besant groups, generally on friendly terms with Avonlea people, continued use of the atlatl (spear thrower) for centuries after they knew about the bow-and-arrow performance. The Besant transition from atlatl to bow and arrow took place after A.D. 400 (Reeves 1970:89).

Applying culture-specific categories to the Avonlea archaeological evidence, it can be conclusively stated that this phase does not represent the historic Tsistsistas people.

Kehoe (1973:76−78, 192), against the unfounded objections of other investigators, has suggested that the Avonlea groups were Athapaskan speakers who entered the Alberta and Saskatchewan parks and grasslands from the north where they had hunted woodland buffalo earlier. He sees the Avonlea groups on the Montana-Wyoming border of the period around A.D. 1000 as the vanguard of historical Athapaskans of the central Plains and of Navajo and Apache groups in the Southwest. No evidence contradicts this interpretation.

It might also be suggested that Avonlea groups in Alberta became the historical Sarcee whose relationships with the historic Blackfoot were close and of long standing. It is therefore not surprising that Apache languages of the Southwest have their closest linguistic ties in the north with Sarcee (Krauss and Golla 1981:68). Both researchers have postulated, on the basis of Athapaskan language differentiation, that an Athapaskan expansion occurred out of the upper drainages of the Yukon River and northern British Columbia in two directions. One was eastward into the Mackenzie River drainage, eventually reaching Hudson Bay. The other was south along the eastern Rockies (Krauss and Golla 1981:68). The latter appears to be reflected in the Avonlea arrival.

Archaelogical evidence from the Great Slave Lake region documents the first expansion. Noble (1981:102–3) has defined the Taltheilei Shale Tradition as a major Athapaskan tradition. Its earliest manifestation, the Hennessey Complex, entered from the west and occupied territory from the Great Slave Lake to Lake Athabasca and eastward to Keewatin from 500 to 200 B.C. Avonlea was probably not part of this complex because the bow and arrow were not present in it.

The bow and arrow, however, were available in North British Columbia for the second Athapaskan expansion south into the Alberta Plains. In the Frazer Canyon, for example, stemmed arrow points appear around 1000 B.C., corner-notched arrow points about 350 B.C. (Reeves 1970:178).

Groups of the Laurel Tradition

The term *Laurel* was first applied to burial mounds in northern Minnesota and southwestern Ontario, located on both sides of the Rainy River. J. Wright (1967:2) calls Laurel a tradition because of the "perpetuation of a common archaeological material culture through time which lacks major discontinuities in either sequential change or regional variation." Syms (1977:80) uses the term Laurel Composite because Laurel regional expressions "share a common core of traits: toggle head harpoons, overlapping projectile point typologies and conical ceramic vessels with varying frequencies of pseudoscallop shell stamping, linear stamping and stab-and-drag stamping decorative techniques applied to the upper part of the vessel."

Laurel Tradition sites range from east-central Saskatchewan through most of Manitoba and Ontario to Northwestern Quebec. In the South, sites extend into Northern Minnesota and Michigan. J. Wright (1972:59; 1981:89–90) describes Laurel groups as Archaic peoples of the Canadian Shield who adopted pottery. Related groups in Quebec and Labrador did not accept pottery and thereby retained a Shield Archaic identification. J. Wright has revised the initial dates for Laurel from 300 B.C. (1981:90) to 600 B.C. (personal communication). According to Syms (1977:81, table 5), dates continue to A.D. 1030 with no evidence of clustering.

In the western portion of the region, the Laurel Tradition overlaps, beginning during the latter part of the eighth century A.D., with the Blackduck Tradition (Syms 1977:101, fig. 18). This tradition ended in Minnesota perhaps during the fifteenth century. In western Ontario, north and west of Lake Superior, it extended into historic times. The southern boundaries of Blackduck include the boreal forest portions of northern Minnesota, the aspen parkland of the Lower Red River Valley, the Pembina Valley, the Assiniboine River valley, and the grasslands of southwestern Manitoba (Syms 1977:103, fig. 18). Differences in the material culture of the two traditions are minimal, probably indicating a common economic base and a common heritage.

Laurel—and Blackduck—groups continued a way of life basically indistinguishable from that of their Shield Archaic ancestors. The only additions are ceramics and burial mounds for secondary interment. Both are believed to be the result of stimulus diffusion from regions further south. Because there are no similarities between Laurel pottery and ceramic complexes from which the stimulus should have come, J. Wright (1967:132–33) initially contemplated the possibility of a Siberian origin. All investigators are confident that burial mounds were first built by these groups in the southwestern portion of their range and that the concept was introduced to them by others. Perhaps so, but because these groups were culturally related to the Proto-Tsistsistas and the Tsistsistas and shared a very similar world description, they must have practiced a secondary burial system for a very long time before they used mounds in this region. Chernetsov (1963:41), after explaining the Ob Ugrian concepts of the soul (chapter 2), reminds us that

among the nomads of the steppes, and seminomadic hunters, the leaving of the dead in the dwelling, or in a structure imitating it, was most widespread. Such is the disposition of corpses in burial mounds, the leaving of the dead in the tent among the Nenets, or in houses with all the property belonging to them among the Yakuts, the Kamchadals, and some of the Ugrians.

Laurel sites are most often located on lake shores or river systems. Syms (1977:83) has defined at least three different subsistence economies based on hunting, fishing, and collecting: (1) seasonally intensive utilization of fish on the Great Lakes, followed by diffuse hunting; (2) seasonal shifts across mixed conifer–hardwood and parkland biomes in Minnesota; and (3) scattered distribution of sites depending on diffuse resources in eastern and northern Manitoba and adjacent Ontario. Sedentary settlements were not advantageous.

The best information comes from the village debris used in the construction of the burial mounds. Most of the mounds are over fifty feet in diameter and six feet tall, and may contain up to 100 secondary burials. These usually consist of bones wrapped in bundles indicating that the dead had been allowed to decompose, perhaps on a platform or scaffold, prior to reburial (J. Wright 1972a:61). A range of artifacts made of hammered native copper includes awls, barbs, chisels, and beads. The occasional occurrence of Wyoming obsidian in Laurel sites suggests trade relations with Plains groups, perhaps with both Avonlea and Besant peoples.

In my opinion, Laurel groups were not Tsistsistas. They were marginal to the northern Plains during the time period under consideration. But I believe that both groups (or clusters of groups) derived from a common origin and that they must have had contact with each other over an extended period of time.

Linguistically, Laurel and Blackduck groups—as those of the later Selkirk Horizon in the area—were Algonquian speakers as J. Wright's (1972b, 1981) studies of Canadian Shield populations have clearly demonstrated. Differences between the three are insignificant in archaeological terms, although the cultural expressions of ethnic groups that composed these traditions (or horizons) must have shown interesting variations.

I believe that Laurel–Blackduck groups were directly ancestral to Central Algonquians. I am convinced that they were also ancestral to such Western Algonquians (chapter 7) as the historic Arapahos-Atsinas, and Suhtais. Further, in my opinion, Selkirk groups are direct ancestors of historic Algonquian tribes in the northwestern boreal forest portion of the Algonquian range.

Groups of the Valley Phase

Sites of the Valley Phase are characterized by a ceramic ware called Valley Cord-Roughened. It features vertical or spiral cord-roughening, a bulge at midpoint on the vessel, a straight rim lacking a shoulder, a single row of interior punctates below the lip, and occasionally incised lines; bases are tapered and rounded (Syms 1977:88). Reeves (1970:107, table 4) assigned eighteen components to this phase.

Valley sites are distributed from eastern Kansas through eastern Nebraska, following the Missouri upriver as far west as Havre, Montana. Neuman (1975:84) observed that Valley Phase ceramic traits are related to some pottery of his Sonota Complex. He also sees a close general resemblance between the side-notched projectile points, atlatl weights, bone tubes, and awls of the Valley Phase and Sonota. This is not surprising because Sonota is part of the Besant Phase. Although Besant and Valley each utilized a different subsistence system, groups of both phases were contemporaneous for a time in Montana, North Dakota, and the northern part of South Dakota. Syms (1977:88) views the Central Plains and South Dakota as the core area of the Valley Phase and regards its extension north of the Missouri River as secondary. Southwestern Manitoba was peripheral to these groups.

According to Reeves (1970:108–9), this phase developed during the first century A.D.; phase transition to the Loseke Phase occurred at A.D. 500–600. The distribution of Loseke Phase sites in northeastern Nebraska, southeastern South Dakota, and northwestern Iowa appears to signal a retreat of Valley groups from the Missouri River valley lying to the north. Syms (1977:88) describes the Valley Phase as at least contemporaneous with, and possibly later than, Kansas City Hopewell, which is dated from about 100 B.C. to 900 A.D.

Valley subsistence activities concentrated on diffuse, riverine resources. The taking of small game such as deer, antelope, water birds, turtles, and rabbits was important, as was shellfish collecting. Buffalo hunting was insignificant. Reeves (1970:111) believes that corn horticulture can be inferred from the abundance of ceramics and permanent habitations; he interprets Valley groups as semisedentary hunter-gatherer-horticulturists. It is curious that handstones and grinding slabs are absent. Habitation sites are located on creek and river terraces. Ceremonial structures have not been found. The burial system consisted of secondary burial in a pit with no overlying mound or secondary burial in a pit basin or on the mound floor below a mound (Reeves 1970:111).

Applying culture-specific categories to the Valley Phase archaeological remains, it can be stated conclusively that they do not represent the Tsistsistas.

The Valley Phase marks the intrusion of groups into the northern Plains from the central Plains and regions lying to the east. Linguistically, they may be identified as Caddoan speakers.

The Tsistsistas in the Northern Plains, 500 B.C. to A.D. 800

Tsistsistas are here identified, in archaeological terms, with the eastern regional subphase of the Besant Phase. Both Reeves (1970) and Syms (1977) include Neuman's (1975) Sonota Complex in Besant. Sonota is here considered as part of eastern Besant.

The Besant Phase: The Archaeological Evidence

The name Besant comes from the Besant Valley, in Saskatchewan. It designates the characteristic atlatl (spear thrower) projectile-point type (Besant Side-Notched) that was first described and named by Boyd Wettlaufer at the Mortlach site. Prairie Side-Notched (or Samantha in some areas) is the type designation for the corresponding arrow point. According to Reeves (1970:89), the technological transition in Besant from atlatl to arrow took place after A.D. 420.

Reeves (1970:89) originally assigned fifty-one components to this phase; more have been added since the time of his writing. No regional subphases have been defined until now.

Besant sites extend from southwestern Manitoba through Saskatchewan to Alberta, south into Montana and eastern Wyoming, and eastward into South Dakota (apparently excluding the southeastern portion of the state) and most of North Dakota. Besant is absent from the Bighorn and Shoshoni basins of Wyoming and from the central Plains, although Besant points appear there occasionally.

The earliest Besant sites are in the eastern part of the region. Boundary Mound 3, on the Missouri River in south-central North Dakota, provided a date of 250 B.C., which is considered to be too early by the investigator (Neuman 1975:88). Syms (1977:90) expects beginning dates for Besant in southwestern Manitoba around 100 B.C. Reeves (1970:91), agreeing that the Besant Phase initiation varies from east to west, views a beginning in the North Dakota–Missouri River area between A.D. 1–100, at A.D. 100–200 in the Belle Fourche and western Montana area, and at A.D. 150–250 in the Saskatchewan Basin. I believe that the early date in North Dakota (250 B.C.) is in agreement with the proposed time period of the Proto-Tsistsistas arrival in the prairies of Manitoba and Saskatchewan and with the Tsistsistas movement southwest toward the Black Hills (chapter 5). If this is correct, dates preceding that for Boundary Mound 3 should eventually come from the northeastern Plains edge.

In Manitoba, Besant boundaries are marked by Laurel people; in Minnesota, by Malmo groups. Some aspects of the burial systems of

Laurel and Malmo are similar to Besant. In Saskatchewan, Besant groups shared the region with Avonlea people after the latter's arrival. The location of the Tsistsistas stone spirit wheel, on Moose Mountain (chapter 5), nevertheless, suggests that they were careful to document their special rights there. Because the withdrawal of Pelican Lake groups westward coincides with the direction of the Besant and Avonlea penetration of the northern Plains, it appears reasonable to consider both the latter responsible for it. If the *haztova hotoxceo* enemies of Tsistsistas tradition, encountered in the Black Hills and removed from there, were actually people who resisted intrusion, as is most likely, I believe they would have been Pelican Lake groups. The termination of Besant, or its transformations, remain a puzzle in the archaeological literature.

In Alberta and the Saskatchewan Basin, the western Besant subphase is replaced by the Old Women's Phase around A.D. 750 (Reeves 1970:92, fig. 7), which lasted into the nineteenth century (Reeves 1978:165–66; Davis and Zeier 1978:227). Because the archaeological record shows a gradual transition from one phase to the next and no changes in the way of life are indicated, it may be assumed that both phases represent the same ethnic groups. Therefore, I suggest that western Besant represents Western Algonquian groups ancestral to the various Blackfoot divisions of the late Old Women's Phase and historic times.

Eastern Besant groups Tsistsistas appear to have abandoned the southwestern portion of their range (west and south of the Black Hills) after A.D. 600, slowly shifting back toward the region of their entrance a thousand years earlier.

Because their next withdrawal from the eastern portion of their range and the Black Hills coincides with the arrival there of Proto-Mandans (Mandans *before* the initiation of the Okipa ceremony; see chapter 8) of the Initial Middle Missouri Tradition, it seems reasonable to consider the latter responsible for it.

Wood (1967:119–66) has traced the evolving Mandan tradition on the Missouri River from the Thomas Riggs Focus (A.D. 1100–1400) through the Huff Focus (A.D. 1400–1600) and the Heart River Focus (A.D. 1600–1797) to Historic Mandan (A.D. 1797–1886). The Okipa ceremony, which required a permanent ceremonial lodge fronting a village plaza, was initiated at the beginning of the Thomas Riggs Focus, around A.D. 1100, because these features are an integral part of settlements of this focus (Wood 1967:156–57). From A.D. 1100 to the beginning of reservation time these features remained the center of every Mandan village, although plaza location and the structure of the Okipa lodge itself changed over time. At the beginning of the Thomas Riggs Focus, Mandan settlements were distributed on the Missouri from the mouth of the White River, South Dakota, to the mouth of the Little Missouri in North Dakota, over a stretch of about 350 miles (Wood 1967:130).

Directly ancestral to the Thomas Riggs Focus and early Mandans is the Initial Middle Missouri Tradition that includes such archaeological entities as Cambria, Mill Creek, and Great Oasis and is dated from about A.D. 800–1300 (Syms 1977:112; Ludwickson et al. 1981: 133–54). Archaeological sites range from southwestern Minnesota (Cambria, see Watrall 1974) to northwestern Iowa (Mill Creek, see Baerreis and Alex 1974), the upper Big Sioux and lower James rivers, and along the Missouri in South Dakota from the White to the Cheyenne River (Ludwickson et al. 1981:136, 142). The Proto-Mandan arrival, as documented archaeologically in Cambria, Great Oasis, and Mill Creek assemblages, introduced to the region sedentary villages with mixed horticultural and hunting subsistence activities.

Archaeology has essentially corroborated the Mandan traditions that describe a general migration from the southeast upriver on the Mississippi and the movement of separated bands into the mixed-grass prairie from the grassland edges in Minnesota and Iowa (Maximilian, n.d., 2:93–103; Bowers 1950:25–26, 156–63). The traditions also mention that some Proto-Mandan bands ranged west as far as the Black Hills and north into southwestern Manitoba before they began congregating on the Missouri River shortly before A.D. 1100; they nevertheless continued to use the area from the Black Hills northward seasonally.

The band specified by the tradition as having moved to the Black Hills from the first settlements of Proto-Mandans near the mouth of White River are the Awigaxa (Bowers 1950:160) who were led by the shaman Good Furred Robe whose skull has been kept in one of the major Mandan ceremonial bundles (Maximilian, n.d. 2:100; Bowers 1950:160, 196). According to Wolf Chief's narrative (Bowers 1950:162), one group of Awigaxa "was lost while making sinews near the Black Hills."

Perhaps the reason for their disappearance is to be found in the Awigaxa tradition collected by Maximilian at Fort Clark in the winter of 1833–34; it certainly mentions the first enemies of this band. Arriving near the Black Hills, Good Furred Robe's people "at that time knew nothing of enemies. Then, when a Mandan woman was scraping a hide, a Cheyenne came and killed her" (Maximilian, n.d., 2:100). Following this incident, long-lasting warfare developed with the Cheyennes (Maximilian, n.d., 2:100–103) who obviously defended their territory against the new arrivals. This condition led to the creation by Good Furred Robe of Awigaxa soldier societies (Maximilian, n.d., 2:101) that eventually defeated the Cheyennes in a great battle. The tradition continues in describing that the Awigaxa were later joined by a Hidatsa band that also suffered from Cheyenne raiding (Maximilian, n.d., 2:102). The combined strength of the two groups successfully resisted Cheyenne hostilities; this happened after the Awigaxa had moved to the Missouri River in North Dakota (2:102).

Because the early warfare near the Black Hills, according to Maximilian's and Bowers's informants, took place *before* the formulation of the Okipa, it belongs to a time period preceding the Thomas Riggs Focus, and therefore I believe must be located in the Initial Middle Missouri Tradition time, around and after A.D. 800. Because the first Hidatsa band settled near the Mandans after the extension of the Thomas Riggs Focus to the Little Missouri, that is after A.D. 1100, the traditions suggest a time span of nearly three hundred years of Tsistsistas-Mandan warfare. Archaeologically, the early Hidatsas appear to be represented by the entity called tentatively the Devil's Lake–Sourisford Burial Complex, with sites distributed from eastern North Dakota to Southwestern Manitoba and southeastern Saskatchewan (Syms 1977:122–24, fig. 18; 1979:294–97, fig. 8). Syms's (1979:301–302) proposed dates for this complex, A.D. 900–1400, are in agreement with my interpretation.

The Awigaxa presence near the Black Hills has recently been documented by archaeology. Adrien Hannus (personal communication) has found Initial Middle Missouri Tradition sites in the Fog Creek drainage in the South Dakota Badlands. Initial Middle Missouri Tradition village sites have been recorded at the southeastern edge of the Black Hills (site 39FA23), on the eastern slope (the Phelps site), and on the Belle Fourche River (site 39BU2) to the north. Dates for these sites, so far, cluster between A.D. 950 and 1300 (Adrien Hannus, personal communication). The latter site, called the Fortified Smiley Evans site by the excavators, Lynn and Bob Alex, with C^{14} dates around A.D. 1000, is only a few miles north of Bear Butte. Haug et al. (1980:31, 298) have found sites of the tradition in the southern part of the Black Hills, mainly as rockshelter occupations. They believe that these groups made extensive use of the Black Hills as a resource base.

In southeastern Saskatchewan and southern Manitoba, eastern Besant terminal dates are around A.D. 1000 (Reeves 1970, fig. 7; Syms 1977:90). It appears that before that date the first of their bands went south into the Red River–Minnesota River area, where I see them in the archaeological record as the entity called the Arvilla Complex. Ossenberg (1974:38–39), in her analysis of discrete traits in cranial samples from Minnesota and the adjacent plains of the time period 200 B.C. to A.D. 1700, appears to support this view. She has identified Arvilla skeletal material as ancestral Cheyenne. Syms (1981:37–38), after reviewing the evidence, at least agrees that "Arvilla includes a predominance of an Algonquian population spread throughout eastern and central Minnesota with the Red River as a western boundary." Populations east of Arvilla were ancestral Dakota; Moore (1986a: 97–117, 145–54) has emphasized the long-standing and intimate Cheyenne-Dakota relationship in the region. In the 1680s their vanguard had abandoned the Minnesota River–Lake Traverse region to return to the Missouri, once again facing the Black Hills and Bear Butte. According to Tsistsistas tradition, the sacred mountain had been visited regularly, at least by ceremonial people, throughout the time periods mentioned.

Reeves (1970:176) views Besant as representative of a Plains cultural tradition separate from both the TUNAXA and the Plains Horticultural traditions. He named this tradition NAPIKWAN and believes that it resulted from the movement of groups into the northern Plains from the outside.

Frison (1978:223), after excavating two eastern Besant sites (Ruby, Muddy Creek), has this to say:

The Besant cultural incursion into the Northwestern Plains brought with it, or else developed there, the most sophisticated bison procurement methods the area had seen. Hunters were able to incorporate sophisticated artificial structures into certain features of the natural topography and produce highly efficient buffalo corrals or pounds. As a result, these hunters were less dependent upon the arroyo trap and the jump and consequently could set up operations in a wider variety of favorable bison habitat areas. Of particular interest is the effort expended on the construction of the two corrals [a reference to the Ruby and Muddy Creek sites] and the Ruby site religious structure. The latter indicates that the shaman's role in communal bison procurement was of considerable importance by at least about 1800 years ago. The corrals, the weaponry, and the drive lane complexes reflect a high level of competence in handling bison and careful attention to various details that helped ensure success.

I believe that Besant groups arriving in the northern plains from the boreal forest brought with them a world description common to all. After their entry, some clusters of bands underwent special developments (such as the elaboration of the Tsistsistas Massaum) that over a period of time, differentiated them culturally from others. Contemporaneous with these factors were movements of these band clusters in different directions where they adapted to specific environments and to new cultural influences. Once Besant groups were distributed from eastern North Dakota to Alberta, regional differences became more significant, although all would continue to share in a common, prevailing world-description base. Differences between them should, relatively speaking, be more pronounced at both ends of the spatial spectrum. Western and eastern groups would overlap and exchange with each other most in the middle of the Besant range. To differentiate one cluster of bands from the others in the archaeological record would be most difficult there.

Generally, the eastern subphase is here viewed as moving largely within southwestern Manitoba, southeastern Saskatchewan, the Dakotas, and northeastern Wyoming, living in different, specific regions over time. The western subphase is viewed as moving largely within western Saskatchewan, Alberta, and the High Plains of Montana, also favoring specific regions over time. It is to be expected that groups of both subphases made long-range visits and excursions into each other's territories. The eminence of Knife River flint in the artifact inventories of both eastern and western groups attests to this.

The archaeological evidence shows that ceremonial structures such as burial mounds and stone spirit wheels occur only in the eastern Besant culture and are lacking in western Besant sites. Spirit lodges were almost certainly used by both groups; as archaeological features, the evidence, so far, comes from eastern Besant (Ruby). Excavated basin-shaped, earth-filled hearths associated with the piles of fired rocks appear to occur among all groups (Reeves 1970:96) and may represent sweat lodge features (chapter 4). Heated rocks were, of course, also used for cooking in skin containers, a technique that made ceramics unimportant. Ceramics do occur and are more frequent in the eastern rather than in western Besant sites; the pottery consists of simple corded or punctated conoidal vessels. Ceremonial hunts by eastern Besant groups emphasized carefully constructed pounds according to the Massaum description; jumps were rejected. Western groups used jumps, arroyo traps, and pounds.

Knife River flint from southwest-central North Dakota and from deposits such as West Horse quarry (site 39SH37, investigated by Adrien Hannus, personal communication) in southwestern South Dakota was the preferred material of eastern Besant knappers but occurs often also in western Besant sites. In addition, western groups in southern Montana used local materials such as basalt and obsidian (Davis and Zeier 1978:227–30), whereas in Alberta local Avon chert is significant (Reeves 1970:95).

Winter and summer habitation sites of both subphases may have been nearly identical due to the similar social organizations, the band system, and the nomadic way of life. Eastern Besant summer campsites, however, are occasionally associated with burial mounds (e.g., the Stelzer site; Neuman 1975:3–37). The western Besant Rose Glen winter campsite in southeastern Alberta, investigated by Quigg (1981), features eighteen stone circles (indicating tipis of up to eight meters in diameter) grouped in two adjacent clusters. Sites such as this continued throughout the northern Plains into the early historic period. Quigg (1981:13–15) thinks that at Rose Glen two bands comprising about 100 people camped together for a few weeks in the early fall around A.D 500. Of two eastern Besant sites, the Main Muddy Creek Village in southeastern Wyoming (Frison 1983:87–88; Reher 1983:202–203) contains an estimated seventy-three stone circle features located directly southeast of the bison pound, whereas the Sprenger site, in central North Dakota (Schneider 1983:94–96), had eighty-one tipi rings.

The Besant Phase economy of all regions concentrated on the communal hunting of buffalo. Collecting activities included both fowling and fishing and some shell collecting. The general lack of grinding implements indicates little reliance on seed grinding. Throughout Besant, "bone uprights" (bones stuck vertically in the ground with articular surfaces upward) may have been used as "anvils" in the manufacture of stone tools, a technique already applied in the eastern European Upper Paleolithic, for example, in Kostenki I on the Don River (Klein 1969:120, 127–29; Semenov 1964:174).

Eastern Besant: Important Archaeological Features

If the assessment of Sonota by its main investigator, Neuman (1975: 79–95), is correct, and if Syms's (1977:89–90) discussion of south-central Manitoba is considered, the archaeological record at present shows five probable centers of eastern Besant ceremonial structures—burial mounds.

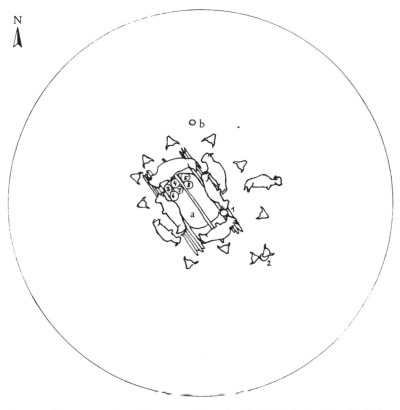

FIG. 17. Reconstruction of features, Mound 2, Swift Bird site. The site is located on a terrace above the western edge of the Missouri River floodplain,
seven and a half miles across the river and downstream from Mobridge,
South Dakota. Features include (a) subfloor burial pit; (3–8) bundles with
multiple secondary interments. They contained skeletal remains of thirty-
two individuals of all ages and both sexes; (1, 2) bundles with multiple secondary interments located on the mound floor. They contained remains of
six persons. Burial 2 was partially covered by two bison skulls; and (b) a
small, circular depression, 2.15 feet in diameter, stained with red ocher. Seven
nearly complete skeletons of buffalo calves and yearlings and eleven skulls
of mature bison surrounded the burial pit on the mound floor. Wood from
a log lying along the edge of the burial pit has been dated at A.D. 350
±100 years.

One is situated on the west side of the Missouri River about eight miles below the mouth of Grand River, in South Dakota. Within an area of two and a half miles are nine burial mounds: two at the Swift Bird site, four at Grover Hand, and three at Arpan. Associated with the Grover Hand burial mounds is the Stelzer habitation site, which is a Besant summer camp.

A second center is situated upstream on the same side of the river just across the North Dakota boundary line. Within an area of two miles there are five burial mounds, four at the Boundary Mound site, one at Alkire.

A third center consists of the eight burial mounds at the Schmidt site, located upriver southwest of Bismarck, North Dakota, once again on the west side of the Missouri.

A fourth center has two burial mounds at the Baldhill site on the east, situated on the east bank of the upper Sheyenne River.

And a fifth center lies to the north, in the Killarney locality of the Pembina Valley in south-central Manitoba, where an area within a two-mile radius features eastern Besant kill sites, habitation sites, and burial mounds.

It is curious that no similar clustering of burial mounds has been found in or around the Black Hills. This is perhaps due only to the fact that this area has not been sufficiently investigated archaeologically.

The burial mounds average about 70 feet in diameter and 2½ to 3 feet tall. The burial pits that underlie the mounds range in shape from ovoid to rectangular, with flat bottoms and vertical walls. In size, they range from about 12 feet by 6 feet, to 8 feet by 6 feet, with depths ranging from 4 to 2 feet below the mound floor. On the mound floor, they are usually lined with timber on the long sides. Neuman (1975:94) believes that portions of the pits had been lined with matting. Secondary bundle burials in pits range from eight to fifty individuals of both sexes and of all ages. Bundles usually include the bones of a number of persons, with many parts of the skeletal remains missing. Often, bones show incision marks indicating that parts of the skeleton structure had been dissected and cleaned before final burial.

Bones and bundles had been rubbed with red ocher. Among the many grave offerings, artifacts of more exotic nature are made of marine shell (olivella and dentalium) that were part of a trade network that reached the Pacific coast.

Associated with the burial pits are buffalo burials of whole carcasses, often of calves and yearlings, that line the pits on the mound

FIG. 18. Mound 2, Swift Bird site, in cross section. The tumulus measured 75 feet in diameter and had a maximum apical height of 3.1 feet above the surrounding ground surface. Before the burial pit was dug, sod was excavated from the mound floor later to be used as the mound surface. The pit measured 10.4 feet northwest-southeast, 6.4 feet northeast-southwest, and it extended 2.5 feet below the original ground surface. Before bundle interment, the burial pit has been laid out with sage. Before it was filled in and the mound raised, the bundles with human remains and the buffalo remains had been covered with red ocher.

floor. These are mixed with the skulls of mature animals. At Mound 2 of the Swift Bird site, for example, eighteen buffalos are represented, at Arpan Mound 1 no less than forty-eight.

The investigations have determined that prior to burial pit excavation, eastern Besant people removed the sod from the whole area that was later covered by the mound.

The Ruby site, located in the extreme southeastern part of the Powder River Basin, is a single-component Besant site consisting of three main cultural features. One of these is a buffalo pound, the second is a ceremonial structure, and the third is a processing area or a campsite. Frison (1971; 1978:213–23) excavated the first two areas and tested the third. The site has been dated A.D. 280. According to Frison, the presence in the bone beds of calves from five to eight months old suggests that the pound was used throughout the autumn.

The corral of the pound was built in the meander bend of an arroyo; its steep bank partly formed one side of the restraining wall. In its location, it was not visible from the flat terrain above. The chute, the final part of the drive lane leading to the corral, was built downslope with a sharp bend that obscured the corral from view of the animals until they were committed to the final rush into it. Those portions of the chute (the wall facing the arroyo) where the heavy bodies of the buffalos exerted the greatest pressure were the most solidly constructed. There heavy timber was stacked between a system of paired posts forming a wall capable of deflecting the animals. Besant projectile points (from lances and dart shafts) begin to appear where the corral entrance first became visible from the chute. Almost certainly the pound originally featured brush wings on the terrain above, leading to the chute entrance, but these have disappeared. Frison

(1978:222) estimates that the pound was designed to take a nursery herd of about twenty-five animals, or a few more.

Another buffalo pound excavated by Frison near Muddy Creek located 100 miles southwest of Ruby in southeastern Wyoming has very similar features. Frison (1978:221) views it as closely related culturally to the one at the Ruby site. He also believes that a religious structure may have been present next to this pound but that it was destroyed by recent gullying.

What Frison (1971:85–86) calls the ceremonial structure at the Ruby site is a feature six feet east of the chute of the pound. Postholes outlined a structure thirty-nine feet long and fifteen feet wide (Frison 1978, fig. 1). It was ovoid in form, pointed at both the northern and southern ends. Additional postholes bridged the structure at its widest section. Inside the southern half were three small holes, each containing either the third or fourth bison thoracic vertebrae with the dorsal spines in the ground. Eight buffalo skulls were arranged around the southern ring of postholes. Two holes were located on the west side between the structure and the chute. One contained four thoracic vertebrae with the dorsal spines in the hole, the other the articulated cervical vertebrae excluding the axis and atlas (Frison 1971, fig. 3).

Postholes were perpendicular to the ground surface; the structure, therefore, should have had straight sides. Because of the positions and sizes of decomposed logs present, Frison believes that the southern half of the structure might have been roofed. There was no fire hearth. A posthole in the corral, surrounded by bone deposits (Frison 1971, fig. 3), suggests that a sturdy pole had been implanted before buffalo were impounded.

Cultural Interpretation of Eastern Besant Archaeological Features

The following Tsistsistas categories are shared with the burial mound and Ruby pound features.

Hohanenō is the Tsistsistas term for small mounds raised in ceremonial lodges during religious observances. *Vós* (plural *vósoz*) designates a sacred mound or mountain that arises from *nsthoaman*, the deep earth, and may be associated with a cave or den. A Besant burial mound represents a *vós* because it is built on *nsthoaman* that was laid open by sod removal before mound construction. The burial pit should be understood as an artificial sacred cave—*vox*.

For primary burials, platforms on trees or scaffolds were used near where a person died in order to start the process of decomposition,

FIG. 19. Hypothetical reconstruction of the spirit lodge feature above mound floor and burial pit of the Swift Bird site before interment of human and buffalo remains. Because of the northwestern-southeastern orientation of the burial chamber, the four center posts must also have been oriented in these directions. Considering the size and shape of the burial mound and the Tsistsistas numerical symbol system it appears logical to assume that a circular structure based on sixteen forked peripheral posts was used. This would allow the placement of rafters from the four ceremonial—southeast, southwest, northwest, northeast—and the cardinal directions, a total of eight. The skeleton frame of this spirit lodge clearly resembles the traditional structure of the Tsistsistas "Sun Dance" lodge, although the latter features one center pole instead of the four-post arrangement. Because the spirit lodge was here raised over a burial pit, a center post was not feasible. The sketch shows the excavated mound floor and the burial chamber; at the conclusion of the ceremony the mound was raised above both. During the ceremony, the lodge must have been closed above with saplings and branches that were supported by the rafters and beams.

that is, the disengagement of the *omotome* of the deceased (chapter 1). After a number of years the remains were collected, apparently cleaned, bundled, and brought to a prearranged location for secondary burial. This took place in the late summer or fall, as shown by the presence of calves among the buffalo burials. Also, frozen ground would not have permitted the excavation of the burial pit.

The ceremony to free the *omotome* of all those whose remains had been brought began with the construction of a large spirit lodge. Its size was determined by the buffalo burials associated with the burial pit. Because of its size the lodge apparently was a vertical structure not unlike the circular Oxheheom (New Life Lodge, "Sun Dance") lodge but without a center pole. Instead, it seems to have featured a four-post center frame joined by rafters with the exterior posts.

After the frame had been built and covered, sod was removed from the whole interior of the lodge and taken outside. Between the four center poles the burial pit was excavated and laid out with sage. On this bed the bundles containing the human bones and skulls were placed. Buffalo skulls, probably painted, were arranged near the pit. Probably the bodies of buffalo killed in the immediate vicinity of the spirit lodge were carried in before the ceremony began.

During the ceremony the bundles in the pit and perhaps the buffalo burials were sprinkled with red ochre—sacred paint. Probably sweetgrass was burned. In the ceremony, conducted by a shaman, the *omotome* of the deceased were formally released to join their *hematasooma* (chapter 1), already free, to become spirit beings in the spirit world. Also, the spirits of the slain animals were separated from physical form; the floor of the lodge became a *heszevox*—an animal den in the realm of the *maiyun* of the deep earth.

After the conclusion of the ceremony the burial pit was filled in. To permit construction of the mound, the center frame and the rafters of the lodge were removed and placed on the lodge floor alongside the pit. A mound was raised high enough to cover the bison carcasses (up to three feet). The sod excavated from the lodge floor was packed tightly across the mound surface. When this was finished, everything under the sod had become part of the deep earth and could never be opened again by a Tsistsistas.

What happened to the exterior poles of the lodge is uncertain. Perhaps they were left standing for some time, turned into a spirit fence by the shaman to protect the burial place. Or they were pulled out to make the burial place invisible from a distance in the rolling grass country.

Given the Tsistsistas intention to bury buffalo carcasses with human remains and to leave them undisturbed by predators, the concept of an earthen mound responds well to religious demands and proves highly functional. Locked in under a tightly packed, if shallow mound, the smell of rotting buffalo flesh would not escape and trigger predator scavenging.

It is highly probable that the Proto-Tsistsistas had a similar burial custom in the far north before their entering the Plains. Animal burials would have featured different species. What structure of enclosing human and animal remains would have been used is an open question, but a certain degree of permanence would have been necessary. If the concept of burial mounds reached the Proto-Tsistsistas, or Tsistsistas, through stimulus diffusion at the northeastern edge of the plains, it could be argued that their much later adoption of circular earth lodges in the Red River—Minnesota River area was less the result of foreign influence than a logical development derived from the burial mound feature. A circular earth lodge, after all, was an artificial mound raised over an excavated floor, secured by an interior four-post frame connected by rafters with peripheral posts secured in place by beams. And it had a certain degree of permanence. Atonoomhetaneo, Mound People (from *atonoom*, the world below, and *hetaneo*, people), is the Tsistsistas term for people who lived in the ground.

Naoetaevoan is the Tsistsistas term for a shaman who had the power to call buffalo; *vohaenohonistoz* means the impounding of buffalo. *Vohaeátoz* is the word for the chute leading to the corral. These are ceremonial terms. The arrangement of structures at the Ruby bison pound reveals the features of the classic Tsistsistas medicine hunt as prescribed in the Massaum ceremony. I know of no other Plains people where the impounding of game *and* the pound structure itself were integral parts of a major tribal religious ceremony. The sacred hunt of the Massaum was the model for all Tsistsistas medicine hunts.

A camp of the size of the Besant Ross Glen site, consisting of eighteen lodges and, with an average of six people to a lodge, a population of slightly over one hundred, would have been sufficient to build the Ruby pound in a week to ten days. Frison (1978:216) estimated that a hunting group consisting of twenty males mobilizing the group effort might have required a period of ten days to two weeks to do the work. It should be remembered that in Tsistsistas pound construction women (the Young Wolves) played ceremonially and physically an important role, as is evidenced in the Massaum.

Another factor, generally neglected in the literature, requires consideration. The relatively high mobility of early Tsistsistas bands was made possible by the use of large, wolf like dogs for transporting lodge and camp equipment. George Bent (Hyde 1968:9), referring to Tsistsistas prehorse times based on testimony he collected in 1910, stated that

the tribe had a great number of large dogs, and these animals were employed to pack or drag burdens. When the people were moving about in the buffalo plains these dogs transported the little lodges and lodgepoles, all the camp equipage and baggage. The dogs were used just as horses were in later times. Some of the dogs had little pack-saddles or saddlebags and carried loads on their backs; others were fitted up with little travois made of two small poles the ends of which dragged on the ground behind the dog. The load was fastened to the poles on short crosspieces. These dogs of the olden times were not like Indian dogs of today. They were just like wolves, they never barked but howled like wolves, and were half-wild animals. The old people say that every morning just as day was breaking, the dogs of the camp, several hundred of them, would collect in one band and all howl together, waking the whole camp.

It could be assumed that a camp of eighteen lodges, with a population of slightly over one hundred people, would require about the same number of adult dogs able to move loads. Including pups and younger animals, the dog population of a camp of this size might easily reach 150 and require a considerable meat supply consistently. The relatively high mobility of Besant groups, as demonstrated by the wide distribution of sites, was built on efficient dog traction that in turn was built on consistent hunting success.

At the Ruby site the pound was probably built after the location of the spirit lodge had been determined. Because both the pound organization and the spirit lodge structure were determined by the *naoetaevoan*, variations in impounding sites are due to his personal preferences in response to the demands of his spirit helpers (chapter 1). At the Ruby site, the spirit lodge featured buffalo parts (skulls and vertebrae) that still contained buffalo *omotome*.

It is significant that at the Ruby bison site, vertebrae were placed in exactly the same location where the sacred animals of the Massaum, the two wolves and the kit fox, were moved on the evening before the sacred hunt—in the narrow space between the spirit lodge (wolf lodge) and the corral (see chapter 6).

In Siberia, the vertebrae of sacrificed animals were treated with special attention, for example, among Evenks. Shirokogoroff (1935: 200) mentions that "in certain cases some parts are considered especially preferred by the spirits, as a mark of sacrifice, as for instance, vertebrae of sacrificed animals fixed to a post erected on the spot; skulls of sheep, bears or horses mounted on a special platform."

The ovoid structure of the spirit lodge is reminiscent of Tsistsistas sweat lodges that were also used for game-calling ceremonies. Tsistsistas sweat lodges, with their oval frame and with a single pole binding the feature as a backbone, appear to have symbolized a buffalo. This concept may also underlie the Ruby lodge. Frison (1971:85) interprets one of the poles excavated at the site as a ridge pole that may have extended from the southern end to the center of the structure. Perhaps a second ridge pole originally connected the center with the northern end. Because of the size of the structure, two ridge poles would have been needed if indeed a "backbone" was being expressed.

The vertical frame of the Ruby lodge may have been preferred over a tipi setting in order to accommodate a larger number of people in the ceremony. Cooper (1944:79), reporting on the spirit lodge structure of sixteen Central Algonquian groups, mentions considerable variations: "In all 16 cases this tent was cylindrical or barrel-shaped or 'vertical'—not beehive or low-domed shaped as sweat lodges usually are, nor strictly conical like tipis."

In this lodge, both the game-calling and the "sending-off" ceremonies were held. According to the Massaum prescription, wolf runners may have gone out after the game-calling performance to call a buffalo herd up. As discussed in chapter 4, the Tsistsistas preferred to corral small herds numbering from twenty to forty animals. During this part of the medicine hunt the dogs would have been taken into the lodges of the camp or tied.

There is an element in Tsistsistas medicine hunts that is difficult to perceive and acknowledge by anyone educated in the Western scientific world description. Joseph Medicine Crow, a participant in a panel discussion on buffalo jumps held in 1962 (Malouf and Conner 1962:41), mentioned it, but it was ignored by the non-Indian members of the conference. Regarding the Tsistsistas corralling of game, Medicine Crow had this to say:

They would dig at the foot of a hill, not necessarily a cliff, but a little hill. The medicine man would stand at the pit and go through his routine, and as the runners drove the herd near, the medicine man's medicine would begin to stir out all the animals in this area and they couldn't leave the area, they would come down the hill, and even birds couldn't fly out of the area. There is something about it that we don't know, it just drives them to the pit with little human effort. That's why I think the medicine man had a very important part in the buffalo drive.

After the herd had been brought in, killed and butchered, and a portion of the meat taken to the camp on the stripped hides, the sending-off ceremonies would formally be held in the spirit lodge. The corral had been opened before butchering; after the ceremony, the dogs were released to feed on the carcasses and clean the corral. If predators such as wolves, coyotes, foxes, raven, and the like had been drawn by the kill, they were let in unmolested. There were exceptions. In the story of Black Wolf (Grinnell 1926:112) this man used the spiritual power granted to him by wolves to heal two wolves who had been shot by the Tsistsistas after they "had been into a buffalo pound where people were."

By applying Tsistsistas medicine hunt concepts, it is likely that the Ruby pound was used four times over a period of perhaps two and a half months.

8. Through a Looking Glass; Origins; Of Space and Time

We have lived with these things
a long time.
These things we have in this Tipi,
we are going to live a long time
with these things.

We have come a long way with this truth;
no one can say anything different—
on the side of us, in the front of us,
in the back of us.
We are not here to talk about anyone else.
This is what we should know;
we will go a long ways from now.

Look back and respect our law and religion;
be happy and know the truth,
do what is right.
People should look to what is
truth only.
Judge yourself what is good.
That is what Maheo taught us.

—MESSAGE FROM THE TSISTSISTAS ARROW KEEPER,
EDWARD RED HAT, NOVEMBER 10, 1978

MUCH IN THIS BOOK is concerned with locating events in time. The first section of this chapter steps back very far, attempting to sketch some of the decisive events in the history of the Algonquian language family. These occurred over a period of about 9000 years. The most distant images of hunting bands belonging to this language family appear before the drama of colossal late and postglacial environmental changes, changes that were among the most profound the northern half of the continent had ever experienced. Here the images of these bands are traced over time through crucial migrations and cultural transformations. Within this frame, the origin and the position of the Proto-Tsistsistas become understandable.

The second section allows a glimpse of the diversity and the astounding continuity of expressions of the ancient Algonquian world
perception. They remained close to Siberian thought despite the vast
spatial separation. Two Algonquian world-renewal ceremonies are
singled out as examples, located at the opposite ends of the distribution range of the language family. One was formulated by the
Yuroks of the northwest California coast, the other, clear across the
continent, by the Munsee-Mahicans who, at the time of the European arrival (the early sixteenth century), occupied the area comprising the present states of Vermont and New York. Both ceremonies
presuppose the concept of an original earth giving at their locations
by the spiritual powers of the universe. Both cultures, adapted to different environments and to different pre-European influences, nevertheless operated from the basis of a common world view that they
shared with the Tsistsistas, far away in the middle of the continent.
The carriers of the three cultures would have understood the ceremonies of the others if they had been given a chance to see them.

The Okipa ceremony of the Mandans, outlined in section three of
this chapter, stands apart. It was necessary to look at this ceremony
because many ethnohistorians and ethnographers believe that the
Okipa influenced the Massaum. No evidence has ever been given to
explain this interpretation. Here a concise comparison is made, and
the question, in my opinion, is resolved.

The Long Walk, 8000 to 500 B.C.

Using archaeological, ethnohistorical, and linguistic evidence, J.
Wright (1972a, 1972b, 1981) has concluded that the Algonquian language family, as it existed at the time of the European arrival, was
spoken by people of the archaeological entity he has termed the
Shield Archaic. The pattern of culture of this tradition, as a perfect
adaptation to the harsh environment of the Canadian Shield, began
well before 4000 B.C. and continued in some areas west, south, and
east of Hudson Bay into historic times.

The Canadian Shield covers nearly one-half of Canada, including
the Labrador coast and all of Quebec, all of Ontario but its south-
ernmost portion, adjacent areas in Wisconsin and Minnesota, three-
fourths of Manitoba, the northern half of Saskatchewan, the eastern
half of the Northwest Territories, and most of Baffin Island in the
North. The center of the shield is Hudson Bay. Most of this vast region
is boreal forest, but its northernmost portions (in northern Labrador,
Quebec, and in the Northwest Territories) consist of tundra.

The shield represents the newest land surface on the continent because it was one of the regions covered by the inland ice of the glaciation of the Wisconsin period. The Laurentide ice sheet originated from highland growth centers in Greenland, on Ellesmere and Baffin islands, in Labrador and Quebec. Before 18,000 B.C. it had joined with the Cordilleran ice coming out of the Rocky Mountains. By 18,000 B.C. a great sheet of ice covered nearly all of the northern half of the continent; its southern border formed a wall that extended from the Washington coast to New York, through Idaho, Montana, the Dakotas, Iowa, Illinois, Indiana, Ohio, and Pennsylvania. Ice-free areas in Alaska were connected with northeast Asia by the Bering land bridge—a land mass a thousand miles wide during its maximum.

When deglaciation became significant, around 13,000 B.C., the ice retreated toward its centers of origin. By 10,500 B.C. the Laurentide and Cordilleran ice masses had separated, opening a slowly widening corridor that reached from Alberta north to the mouth of the Mackenzie River on the Arctic coast. Vegetation regions moved with the retreating ice. Around 18,000 B.C. the Plains had been a boreal and mixed forest except for a narrow north-south band at about 99W, from 35N to the Gulf Coast (Ross 1970:235; Wendland 1978:277). Around 13,000 B.C. the southern limit of the boreal forest was in Kansas; by 10,000 B.C., in South Dakota; and by 9000 B.C., in North Dakota.

Ice shrinkage in the northern half of the continent was not uniform. The Great Lakes had emerged after 7500 B.C., the Saint Lawrence and Labrador coasts after 6500 B.C., and much of the Northwest Territories by 5500 B.C. (Wendland 1978, figs. 2–5). The ultimate disappearance of the ice in mainland Canada occurred around 2500 B.C. in the mountains of north-central Quebec.

The retreat of the ice created changes nearly as drastic as its advance had. The earth's crust, relieved from the weight of the inland ice, rose, in some areas more than 500 feet. The rebound was unequal, depending on differences in the thickness of the erstwhile ice sheet. As a result, lake basins that collected melt waters were canted and found new drainages. Giant glacial lakes southwest (Lake Agassiz) and southeast (Lake Barlow–Ojibway) of Hudson Bay finally shrank back after 4500 B.C. The Canadian Shield reached essentially its present physiographic features west of Hudson Bay by 3500 B.C., south of James Bay around 4000 B.C., and in north-central Quebec after 2500 B.C.

Following in step with deglaciation, tundra, with boreal forest be-

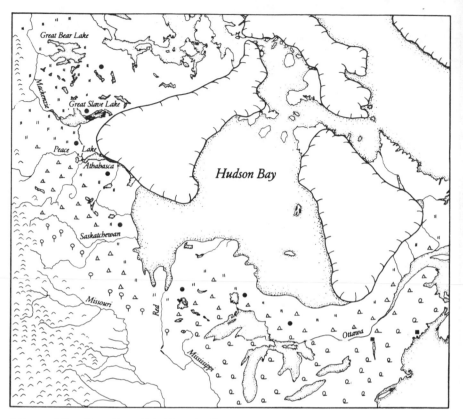

MAP 4. The Canadian Shield and adjacent regions, 5000 B.C.

 Groups of the western Paleo-Indian tradition (Plano) ancestral to
the Algonquian language stock, adapting to the emerging Canadian
Shield

■ Groups of the eastern Paleo-Indian tradition in transition to the
Maritime and Laurentian Archaic

Vegetation zones

Tundra and grassland		Conifer-hardwood and deciduous forest
Tundra and taiga		Parkland
Boreal forest		Border of ice shield

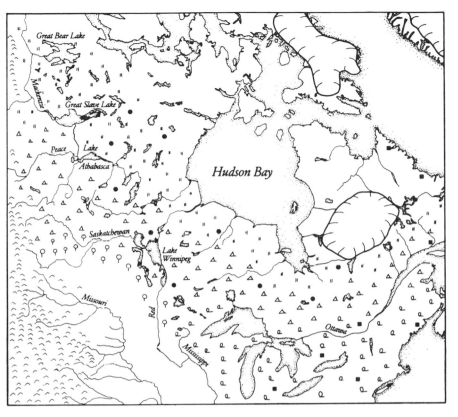

MAP 5. The Canadian Shield and adjacent regions, 3000 B.C.

● Shield Archaic groups ancestral to the Algonquian language stock
■ Groups of the Maritime and Laurentian Archaic

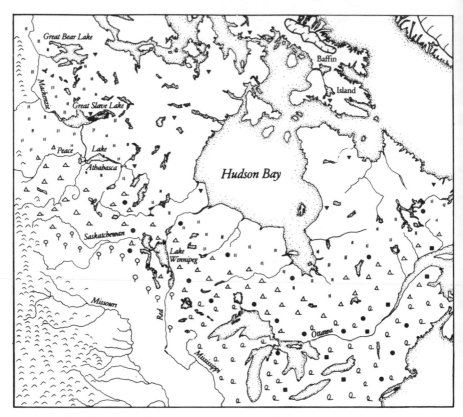

MAP 6. The Canadian Shield and adjacent regions, 1000 B.C.

● Proto-Algonquian groups
■ Late Archaic–Early Woodland groups, probably Proto-Iroquoian
▼ Pre-Dorset Eskimo groups

156

hind, expanded into newly liberated landscapes, and various faunal species were then drawn by their shifting ecosystems. Many species, however, suffered extinction during these times. Within the short period from 8000 to 6000 B.C., the North American megafauna, comprising such animals as mammoth, mastodon, camel, horse, giant bisons, four-horned antelope, tapir, and so forth, disappeared. Only three of these—mammoth, mastodon, and giant bisons—had been hunted significantly by human groups. Hester (1967:170) has argued cogently that early hunters could not have caused the extinction of the megafauna until after natural causes had greatly reduced the population of each species. He sees as an alternative explanation that changes in ecological niches resulting from the disappearance of the late Wisconsin ice sheet had subjected animal species to selective pressures. Hester's position is supported by evidence concerning the Pleistocene extinction of the megafauna in the Soviet Union (Vereshchagin 1967).

Animal species that survived the extinction, such as caribou, musk ox, moose, bear, beaver, wolf, and so on, occupied shield regions after the decline of the glaciation, wherever possible. The response of human populations came last and was delayed in some areas for another thousand years due to giant glacial lakes and the marine submergence of the Hudson Bay lowland.

During the period of the emergence of the shield, human penetration occurred from three directions. One followed its eastern periphery. It consisted of Archaic cultural groups derived ultimately from eastern Paleo-Indian big-game hunters who had used Clovis projectile points. Adjusted to the great changes that were occurring in the region, they expanded from Nova Scotia and parts of New Brunswick to the Gulf of Saint Lawrence coasts, Newfoundland, and the coast of Labrador. Tuck (1978, fig. 1) has called this archaeological entity the Maritime Archaic because the faunal resources of the sea played a key role in it. The habitation sites along the coast existed at a time when the vast interior of Quebec was still covered by an ice shield. These people built burial mounds on the Labrador coast beginning before 5000 B.C.: Ultimately, their burial ceremonialism gave rise to the Early Woodland ceremonial developments further south, eventually leading to the spectacular features of the Adena culture (Tuck 1978:43). Grave goods in Maritime Archaic cemeteries have shown a tool inventory with strong emphasis on sea-mammal hunting, especially seal and small whales (Harp 1978:108–11). This way of life centered on the coast; incursions into the interior of the shield were sporadic at best, even after the decline of the Quebec ice shield.

J. Wright (1972b) has subsumed the Maritime Archaic into a larger entity he calls the Laurentian Archaic, of which the Maritime Archaic is the northeastern branch. The western branch appeared about 4000 B.C. in southern Ontario (J. Wright 1972a:27–33), extending eastward through the lower Ottawa River area to the Gulf of Saint Lawrence. Populations used the resources of the Great Lakes–St. Lawrence forest zone, depending primarily on larger game (deer, elk, bear, beaver) and on fish. In a comparison of the Laurentian and Shield Archaic artifact classes, J. Wright (1972b, table 25) has demonstrated the significant differences between the two.

Laurentian populations, according to the archaeological evidence, were considerably larger than those of the shield to the North. Apparently they had settled comfortably into the hemlock-pine-hardwood forests and refused expansion into the boreal forest. Because, in portions of Ontario and Quebec, the dividing line between the two physiographic areas is quite sharp, Shield and Laurentian Archaic sites are often situated quite close to one another. J. Wright (1972b: 78) views the relationship between groups of both traditions to have been quite similar to the historic relationship between northern Algonquian and Iroquoian speakers in the same area.

The penetration of the fringe of the Canadian Shield by eastern Laurentian groups had no influence on the development of the Shield Archaic. This tradition was formed by groups entering the shield from two directions: from the northwest (the Northwest Territories) and the south (from around Lake Superior). These groups had a common origin in a big-game hunting tradition in which groups ancestral to the Laurentian had *not* participated—the Plano.

The Plano Tradition represents a Paleo-Indian tradition that had specialized in buffalo hunting in the Plains. Its beginnings are around 8000 B.C. in the northern Plains, near the corridor that had opened north to south between the retreating Cordilleran and Laurentide ice shields. Because the corridor had opened 2500 years before Plano emerged it may be assumed that populations who developed the tradition in Montana and Wyoming had entered from the north. Who their antecedents in the far north may have been is unclear; Müller (1982:201) sees them as "the people behind the ice" (north of the Wisconsin glaciation), as sea mammal and caribou hunters around the shores of the Arctic Ocean. That they developed their specific tool inventory favoring elegant lanceolate parallel-flaked projectile points in the northern Plains is unquestionable; earlier in the north they may have used bone and ivory projectile points.

Readapting to the changing environment south of the retreating Laurentide ice shield, they became the most efficient buffalo hunters the Plains had ever seen. Their communal hunts had a medicine hunt aspect as is indicated by Dennis Stanford's excavations at the Jones-Miller site, where he found evidence of a medicine pole in a buffalo pound associated with artifacts that he interprets as ceremonial objects. He concludes that "if our assumptions about the post-mold, offerings, and ceremonial lodge are correct, one must postulate 10,000 years of socio-religious continuity in the Northern Plains" (Stanford 1978:97). Frison (1978:149–77), who has excavated Plano sites in Wyoming featuring Agate Basin and Hell Gap projectile points, has commented on the efficient hunting techniques used by these groups; generally, small herds were impounded or killed in arroyo or sand dune traps.

While some Plano groups, after 8000 B.C., expanded into the southern Plains, others remained in the northern Plains, following game that followed the cold weather vegetation in the back of the retreating ice. One reason for this northward movement was the demise of the herds of giant bison.

Fronting the southwestern lobe of the ice shield were some Plano groups that favored Agate Basin lanceolate projectile points.

Some of these groups, perhaps around 6500 B.C., worked their way around the western edge of Lake Superior and entered the pocket to the north that was bounded in the west (Lake Agassiz) and east (Lake Barlow-Ojibway) by glacial inland seas, in the north by the wall of the ice sheet still south of Hudson Bay. The presence of these eastern Agate Basin hunters is documented by finds of their characteristic projectile points in Manitoba and the southwestern portion of northern Ontario (J. Wright 1972b:73; 1981:88). They also worked quarry sites along the north shore of the Great Lakes (J. Wright 1972a, map 2).

It is this area of the emerging Canadian Shield where the gradual transformation of these eastern Agate Basin groups from Plano to a Shield Archaic culture took place. They remained the same people; only their tool kit changed slowly through time. When passage through the boreal forest eastward had become possible, they expanded in that direction. In the Mistassini region of western Quebec, they appear with the tool inventory of the Shield Archaic in the Wenopsk Complex, dated around 4000 B.C. The investigators of the

Mistassini territory, Charles Martijn and Edward Rogers (J. Wright 1981:95–96), view the hunters of the Wenopsk Complex as having arrived from the boreal forest to the west. At 4000 B.C. and for another 1,500 years, when they were hunting caribou in the region, the diminishing ice shield of the Laurentide stood immediately to the east and northeast.

I identify these first groups of Shield Archaic hunters of the regions south and east of Hudson Bay with Algonquians who already were, or became those whom Goddard (1978b), in his linguistic classification, lists as Proto-Eastern Algonquian (PEA) speakers.

Some other Agate Basin groups, beginning also around 6500 B.C., worked their way northward along the west shore of Lake Agassiz that stood from east-central Saskatchewan southeasternward through Manitoba into northeastern North Dakota (Wendland 1978: figs. 4, 5, 6). Above this inland sea, which had temporarily separated eastern and western Agate Basin groups, was the slowly moving ice shield; its western wall still covered the northern half of Saskatchewan and the southeastern part of the Northwest Territories.

These western Agate Basin groups passed beyond the edge of the grassland into the boreal forest. In the north, McConnell glacial lake halted their further movement until about 5000 B.C., when it had shrunk into three discrete bodies of water: Lakes Athabasca, Great Slave, and Great Bear. Although a few Agate Basin groups may have stayed in the boreal forest east of Lake Athabasca, their vanguard moved into the developing spruce parkland and the tundra in the region extending from the north shore of Great Slave Lake northward to within seventy miles of the Arctic coast, below Coronation Gulf.

In this area, over a stretch of 350 miles north to south, consisting west to east of parkland and tundra, their presence, in archaeological terms, is designated the Acasta Lake Complex; its beginnings are dated at 5000 B.C. (Noble 1981:97–98). The tool inventory of these northern groups of western Agate Basin hunters includes artifacts for spearing and skinning game and for working bone, antlers, and wood. Noble (1981:97–98), who has investigated this region, found classic Agate Basin lanceolates as the most popular weapon point in addition to stemmed and incipient-stemmed varieties. There are also leaf-shaped side-notched projectile points, reflecting a direction in projectile point change that led directly to the Shield Archaic a thousand years later. Noble's (1981:98) archaeological fieldwork has shown, from the evidence of animal remains in roasting hearths, that these people lived in the boreal forest and parklands and used the tundra seasonally. They were the first caribou hunters behind the retreating Laurentide ice.

Other Plano groups from the northern Plains, carrying different sets of projectile points, also participated in the Agate Basin move north but passed on their western flank and continued their movement into Alaska. Their presence is noted in a number of archaeological assemblages there (Tolstoy 1958:65–69; MacNeish 1962:140–41; 1964, fig. 82, 345), but few archaeologists would see them penetrate farther. It is a curious fact, however, that parallel-flaked Planolike projectile points of Plainview, Angostura, and Scottsbluff types appear in the Lena River basin and Lake Baikal regions in northern Siberia around 4000 B.C., where they last until 2000 B.C. (Tolstoy 1975:177). These characteristic projectile points are accompanied by other typical Plano artifacts such as paired sandstone shaft smootheners and tci-tho scrapers (Tolstoy 1958:65–69).

Perhaps it should be remembered that Franz Boas, Waldemar Bogoras, and Waldemar Jochelson, the chief investigators of the Jesup Expedition of 1897–1900, traced definite cultural similarities between groups in northern Siberia and some North American Indian groups to a postglacial movement of peoples from Alaska to northeastern Siberia (Boas 1910:15). They postulated that this "American" element in northern Siberia was boxed in and sealed off later by a Paleo-Eskimo intrusion. Müller (1982:10–33) has brought attention to this issue again.

Archaeological sites of the Acasta Lake Complex, deposited by the northern groups of western Agate Basin hunters, disappear from the first area of their concentration (from Great Slave to Great Bear lakes) after 4500 B.C. (Noble 1981:98–99). Apparently, they had followed the expanding tree line eastward into the southeastern areas of the Mackenzie District and southern Keewatin.

This is where J. Wright (1972b, fig. 1) has located their descendants; their transition to the Shield Archaic culture was concluded by 4000 B.C. Like their relatives in western Quebec, they continued to operate out of the boreal forest, hunting caribou around the southern lobe of the diminishing Keewatin ice center, which still covered the central and northern parts of the district. This inland ice mass dissolved completely after 3500 B.C. (Wendland 1978, figs. 6–8), opening central Keewatin to penetration by the northernmost of the Shield Archaic (formerly Agate Basin) groups by 3000 B.C.

Around 4000 B.C. culturally and linguistically related groups of common origin were living in two large areas of the Canadian Shield:

in western Quebec and west of Hudson Bay; in the latter area they extended from southeastern Mackenzie and southern Keewatin southward into Manitoba. The most common Plano points in Manitoba are of the Agate Basin type (J. Wright 1981:88) Transformation to the Shield Archaic appears to have been contemporaneous there with developments to the north. Around 4000 B.C. contact between western and eastern groups through the boreal forest may not have been intensive, as is suggested by the linguistic evidence. Tool inventories, however, were very similar, indicating that no cluster of groups was completely isolated from the other.

I identify the western groups of the Shield Archaic hunters with Algonquians who became those whom Goddard (1978b), in his linguistic classification, lists as Plains and Central-Algonquian speakers, both derived from the ancestral Proto-Algonquian (PA).

The tool kit of Shield Archaic groups, according to J. Wright (1981: 88–89), was dominated by three artifact classes: scrapers, bifacial blades (knives), and projectile points. Generally, during the early period, scrapers constitute 40 percent, bifacial blades 25 percent, and projectile points 15 percent of the stone-tool assemblage. It must be assumed that bone figured prominently in artifact manufacture, but the acid soils of the boreal forest destroyed all evidence. Through time the frequencies of scrapers and projectile points increased, whereas the frequency of bifacial blades decreased. Within the projectile point varieties, the most important single trend is the decrease through time of lanceolate points with a corresponding increase in smaller side-notched points. J. Wright (1981:89) lists as a significant negative trend the nearly complete absence of stone grinding in tool manufacture, posing a sharp contrast to Laurentian Archaic preferences.

Griffin (1978:237) has called the great arc of the Canadian Shield around Hudson Bay the "infertile crescent." J. Wright (1981:86–87), in contrast, has emphasized the cultural continuity in the region, partly owing to the boreal environment, which lasted in many areas for the extraordinary time span of around 7,000 years. He has discovered the reasons for the homogeneity of both prehistoric and historic Algonquians over the enormous tracts of the shield in a number of inseparably related physical and cultural phenomena:

1. Food resources were closely linked with the lake and river networks that also provided the most effective routes of travel and communication, by birch-bark canoe in summer, in winter by snowshoes on the wind-packed snow atop the ice.

2. Two major food resources, caribou and fish, dominated the region, although other game, such as moose and beaver, with migrating waterfowl, were also important in some areas. Without caribou and fish, however, humans could not have occupied the total area on a permanent basis.

3. Enormous forest fires not only displaced all animals including the hunters but also caused a sequence of plant and animal reclamation of burned areas (sometimes more than 10,000 square miles wide) that led to forced shifts in hunting territories.

4. Small hunting groups and regional bands of Algonquians featured flexible residence and marriage patterns, and much individual freedom, while maintaining far-flung social connections. Under this system, women appear to have been very mobile.

5. The limitations imposed by the harsh environment on subsistence patterns and social organization inhibited culturally disruptive incursions of peoples and concepts inadequate to the region from the outside.

Noble (1981:99−100) has traced four incursions from the northern Plains into the eastern Great Slave Lake area, at the edge of the shield, between 3000 B.C. and A.D. 200 (in sequence, Artillery Lake, Oxbow, Caribou Island-Duncan, and Pelican Lake complexes). None penetrated to the barren grounds, and no exchange of ideas with the Shield Archaic appears to have taken place.

In his discussion of the origins of the Besant Phase, Reeves (1970: 173−76) has pointed to the occurrence of Besant or Besantlike points in the Lockhart River area northeast of Great Slave Lake, which was first noted by MacNeish (1964:404−405, fig. 87). MacNeish (1964, fig. 82) provided a tentative date of 1400 B.C. for the Lockhart River Complex; the date has been revised by Noble (1981:104) to the period A.D. 1100−1300. Perhaps both dates are in need of revision, especially because Noble agrees that corner and side-notched points make their first appearance in the area with this archaeological complex and that "the origin of this concept requires future clarification." Because the Lockhart River area lies at the border of the northernmost Shield Archaic groups, it would be interesting to know if the proto-Tsistsistas people used Besant projectile points already in the far north before their removal toward the northern Plains.

Two events had great consequences for the Algonquians of the Shield Archaic: the arrival of Pre-Dorset Eskimos and the deterioration of the weather leading to a southward retreat of the boreal forest west and east of Hudson Bay, beginning around 1500 B.C.

After 3000 B.C., Pre-Dorset Eskimo groups expanded eastward along the Arctic coast from Alaska. Their movement developed rapidly, and within a few centuries they had passed through the islands of the Canadian archipelago into northern Greenland and to Baffin Island. The earliest sites, so far, are on the south coast of Baffin Island, dating to ca. 2400 B.C.; the Pre-Dorset Independence I Complex of northeastern Greenland is dated around 2000 B.C. (Harp 1978:116). They were firmly established around northern Hudson Bay by 2000 B.C.

Their arrival on the northern coast of Labrador coincided with the southward removal of the Maritime branch of the Laurentian Archaic. Tuck (1978:34) has investigated the time sequence of this removal; the north-to-south time slope leads from 1940 B.C. at Saglek Bay in northern Labrador to 1800 B.C. at Hamilton Inlet and to 1280 B.C. at Port au Choix on the west coast of the island of Newfoundland. Within a period of about seven hundred years, 700 miles of Labrador coast had been given up by Laurentian groups. In their wake the area was occupied by Pre-Dorset hunters equipped with short, recurved, composite bows, who had come farther south in Labrador and Newfoundland than any Eskimos had ever gone (Harp 1978:122). The Beothuk of the island of Newfoundland appear to have been linear descendants of the old Maritime Archaic of the Labrador coast. Their linguistic affiliation is an unresolved question because these groups were the first victims of the European intrusion in the early sixteenth century; they perished without a record.

Around 1500 B.C., when climatic changes began to force the tree line south to distances of about 200 miles, pre-Dorset hunters followed the expanding tundra along the west and east coasts of Hudson Bay (Harp 1978:116–117). They also entered the barren grounds of central Keewatin, where they adapted to the tundra-taiga as a distinctive culture emphasizing caribou hunting.

Between 1500 B.C. and 1000 B.C., Algonquian groups abandoned the southeastern Mackenzie and central Keewatin districts, pulling south (J. Wright 1972b:4–5; 1981:88–89). When the tree line had retreated into northeastern Saskatchewan and northern Manitoba, Pre-Dorset or related Eskimo groups expanded as far south as Lake Athabasca and Black Lake in Saskatchewan and to northeastern Manitoba (Noble 1981:100–101). The archaeological evidence indicates that they had adapted to the forest border by 1200 B.C. (Noble 1981:100). They were then either in direct competition with Algonquian groups of the Shield Archaic or, most likely, the latter had already completely withdrawn into the boreal forest.

It appears that the northernmost Algonquian groups left first. I believe that they passed other groups and, going south, eventually arrived in the northern plains, where they adapted to a different environment, which is known archaeologically as the Besant Phase. My identification of western Besant with groups ancestral to the various historic Blackfoot divisions and of eastern Besant with the Tsistsistas is in agreement with the linguistic data that gives both Blackfoot and Cheyenne, speakers of Plains or Western Algonquian, the greatest linguistic distance from the parental Proto-Algonquian core (Pentland 1978, figs. 1, 2).

Other Algonquian groups from west of Hudson Bay removed eastward through the boreal forest below Hudson Bay, where their presence may be reflected archaeologically in the Laurel and succeeding traditions. Perhaps again the northernmost groups, after the removal of those to become Plains Algonquians, may have passed others, who eventually became linguistically Central Algonquians, and whose future took them south of the Great Lakes: the Potawatomis, Menomini, Foxes and their congeners (Sauks and Kickapoos), Miami-Illinois, and Shawnees.

Taking the distribution of subarctic Algonquian languages of early historic times into account (Rhodes and Todd 1981, figs. 1, 2), groups comprising the various dialects of Ojibwa may have gone next and eventually occupied the regions north of the Great Lakes, from western Quebec (Algonquin) to Minnesota.

Perhaps last to shift eastward were groups speaking the various dialects of Cree who occupied the area to the north of Ojibwa speakers. They were to form an arc around the southern shores of Hudson and James bays, reaching from Labrador through Quebec and Ontario to Manitoba.

The arrival of Eastern Cree speakers (East Crees, Naskapis, Montagnais) in Quebec coincided with both the retreat of the taiga and the Pre-Dorset, or Dorset, advance along the Labrador and Hudson Bay coasts. These factors together may have triggered the final removal of eastern Shield Archaic groups (Proto-Eastern Algonquians) east and south across the Saint Lawrence, where they took up positions on the Atlantic coast, eventually extending from New Brunswick to North Carolina. Snow (1978:60) has emphasized the cultural continuity of Eastern Algonquian occupation in this area, from pre-

historic to historic times. Tuck (1978:34) has dated the beginning of
the Proto-Eastern Algonquian movement across the Saint Lawrence
around 1000 B.C. Goddard (1978a, 1978b) essentially concurs with this
interpretation on the basis of an analysis of Algonquian linguistic
developments.

There remains the question concerning the whereabouts, during
these times of considerable change, of groups ancestral to Plains
Algonquian-speakers such as Arapahos-Atsinas and Suhtai. Because
these Arapahos-Atsinas are linguistically closer to Proto-Algonquians
than Blackfeet and Cheyennes, or even Plains Crees, and Montagnais
(Pentland 1978, figs. 1, 2), they must have separated from the Proto-
Algonquian core later than the previously mentioned groups. I suspect that groups ancestral to the Arapahos-Atsinas may be represented archaeologically in the western depositions of the Blackduck
Tradition (Syms 1977, fig. 18), reaching into the parkland and prairie
zone of Manitoba around A.D. 800.

The Suhtais remain a puzzle. The general belief of plains ethnolo-
gists that the Tsistsistas and Suhtai languages were closely related is
contradicted by the facts presented by Goddard (1978). The linguistic
distance between the two is confirmed by the ethnographic evidence
that states clearly that the Tsistsistas and Suhtais came in contact
with each other only at the beginning of the historic period.

Relatives Through Space and Time

Yurok: Making the World Holy
for the Deer Coming Through the Saltwater Sea

The Yuroks (from the Karok term *yuruk*, "downriver") are a small
tribe on the northwestern coast of California (Pilling 1978). With
their immediate neighbors on the south, the Wiyots (Elsasser 1978b),
they are linguistically classed together under the name Ritwan. The
controversy regarding the genetic relationship of Ritwan, completely
isolated in California, has been resolved by Haas (1958:159), who has
demonstrated that it belongs within the Algonquian language family.
Archaeological evidence suggests that the Yuroks and the Wiyots arrived in the area of their historic occupation perhaps a thousand
years ago. Elsasser (1978a:50) gives the earliest date on the coast for
either group, or for both groups, as around A.D. 900. From what direction these Algonquian speakers penetrated to northwestern California is unknown.

At the time of Waterman's (1920) fieldwork, the Yuroks consisted of two distinct dialect and regional divisions. One, the "river people," occupied the lower thirty-six miles of the Klamath River. The other, the "coast people," occupied the seashore from a few miles north of the mouth of the Klamath south to Trinidad Bay, over a distance of forty-two miles. Because of the wealth of food resources of the mountains, the river, and the sea coast, they lived in small sedentary villages.

Every summer the river people engaged in a series of ceremonies in which a medicine hunt (corralling of salmon) played an important role. The corrals *(tse'tsin,* "corral"), ten in number, were traps built into a fish dam annually constructed to span the river at two locations: at Kepel and farther upstream at Lo'olego (Waterman and Kroeber 1938:50). Although Erikson (1943:277) gives 1906 as the last year of fish-dam ceremonies at Kepel, Pilling (1978:149) places this event in 1913. The following is a reconstruction of the essential elements of Yurok summer ceremonies at Kepel for which the previously mentioned literature provided the initial information.

The Supreme Being (We'sona-me'getol, World Maker), after he had made the universe, the earth, sea, mountains, rivers, and immortal spirits, created the blue sky at qe'nek, on the Klamath, a few miles upstream from Kepel. He made a giant net, took hold of it, and threw it upward. As it sailed high, it became solid and stretches above us as the blue sky. Above it is an upper sky country, *wo'noiyik,* which extends to the ends of the universe. Later, when animals and people were created by the spirit Wohpekumeu, the upper sky country became the place where the spirits of children and deer reside, close to the Supreme Being. This is also where the geese fly on their annual migration to the northwest. In the blue sky is a sky hole through which geese fly to wo'noiyik and through which spirits and shamans are able to pass. Just above Kepel (at Qe'nek-pul, Downstream from Qe'nek) is an invisible ladder, that leads to the upper sky country. The Supreme Being, in northern Siberian fashion (see chapter 2), remained a *deus otiosus*—a distant god.

The Klamath River country, with its vegetation, animals, and the Yuroks, was made by the spirit Wohpekumeu, who had come across the sea. He established a binding boundary line between the saltwater sea and the river, placed the deer in the mountains, and initiated the salmon runs. He presides over the spirits in any physical form: in rock, deer, acorns, salmon, sea lion, Yurok, and so forth.

He keeps the salmon across the ocean at "salmon house," *kowe'tsik,* under the guardianship of the salmon chief (Artgeist) Nepêwoi and annually releases enough salmon for the Yuroks to catch. During his creation activity he was assisted by Thunder, Earthquake, and other spirits, including a giant horned serpent that made some of the physical features of Yurok country (such as creeks) with the weight of its body. The "old woman who lives in the earth," the earth spirit, is the protector of things that come from the ground but not of salmon.

At the end of his creation activity any of the immortal spirits who were in existence before Wohpekumeu's work had become animals, trees, and rocks. They remained teachers of the Yuroks in many ceremonial activities after Wohpekumeu's leaving for his home on the other side of the world, due west from the mouth of the Klamath. These spirits, *woge,* are those who force a woman to become a shaman "doctor." Male shamans belonged to a different shaman group associated with animals (sea lion skull depositories), sky spaces (deer and "jumping" ceremonies), and the salmon.

The annual Yurok "river people" summer ceremonies featured the return of Wohpekumeu to the place of his creation, reestablishing for another year the order that he had given this part of the world. In this he required the Yuroks to reenact the events of the original time of his creation. The sacred salmon, the deer of the saltwater sea, accompanied him from salmon house as proof of his continuing benevolence.

Salmon caught at the Kepel fish dam (or salmon-deer pound) during the medicine hunt were called "deer." In Yurok there were no stories about salmon because they were too sacred to be talked about.

The summer ceremonies began in the spring at the river mouth. A shaman of the coast Yuroks, ceremonially responsible for the border between the saltwater and the river, of the village of Welkwä, held a secret ceremony in which he ritually removed the barrier for the time of the salmon runs to allow salmon to cross and swim upriver. This concept is reminiscent of Samoyeds of northern Siberia (Paulson 1961:99) where the shaman held a similar ceremony at the mouth of the Ob River.

Word was passed upriver when the ceremony was completed. Until the beginning of the ceremonial hunt at Kepel, it was prohibited to catch salmon; breaking this taboo meant death for the offender inflicted by the salmon.

Upriver the ceremonies were initiated and conducted throughout by the *wi-lo-hego* shaman ("dam maker"; this term was usually shortened to *lo)*. He set out on a ceremonial journey dressed in a deer-hide blanket wrapped with a deerskin belt; on his forehead he wore a piece of eel net, which symbolized the original form of the blue sky during creation. He carried his medicine bundle and was accompanied by an assistant who paddled the dugout on the river. Their faces were painted black, Wohpekumeu's ceremonial color.

At the town of Sa'a, adjacent to Kepel, they moved into a specially raised sweat house. It represented the world house; its sacred center pole was the world pillar. With his assistant the shaman went through secret calling ceremonies; the people in both settlements were confined to their houses. Wind blowing from downriver into the rear door of the sweat house provided this signal: "When I blow in there, I am calling you."

Fresh oak twigs were placed on the sweat house roof, and four crescent-shaped rocks, later to be used for pounding in the stakes of the dam, were put on top. Now bright new fires were lit in the closed village houses with everyone listening. The shaman, unseen, stood on the four stones atop the sweat house (ritually he stood on the four corners of the universe). Burning sacred angelica root, he purified the Klamath world for the return of Wohpekumeu. He shouted the sacred formulas downriver and upriver.

With Wohpekumeu arrived other spirits as well, and the spirits of deceased Yuroks assembled on the opposite (north) side of the river to be present. Lo stayed during ten days in the sweat house during daytime. At night, leaving through the sacred (downriver) door, he traveled the landmarks set by Wohpekumeu in river Yurok lands, following the sacred route of the creator, speaking the sacred words of creation at the spirit places. He traveled for ten nights, with his assistant; he was allowed one meager meal after sundown and no water. No one was allowed to see him. After ten days he began timber cutting in the mountains. Perhaps two thousand people assembled, living in temporary camps on the south side of the Klamath.

Now the shaman journeyed to the mountains to take the first three stakes from the tree spirits: one for the center, two as the flanking stakes of the dam. This work was done ritually, after praying with the trees, with stone tools. The shaman returned to the sweat house for a four-day period of secret ceremonies and set the date for the beginning of dam construction. All over Yurok lands, trees were cut by selected teams with stone tools and elkhorn wedges, so that all of the different kinds of tree spirits were present in the dam.

The building of the dam required ten full days. The shaman supervised the placing of the first three stakes, only speaking the ceremonial language. All people went into a ten-day fast that allowed, despite the hard labor, one small meal a day. Men working in cutting and construction slept in sweat houses during this time. During the day, the shaman sat silently on a small mound raised for him on the north shore—the spirit side. Because the dam was built across the river from both shores simultaneously, workers operating on the north shore were under the most severe restrictions.

The ten days of fasting were imposed in honor of the salmon pushing up from the sea. Salmon needed about ten days to reach Kepel; they had begun their migrational fast after leaving the saltwater.

Waterman (1920:179) has called the Kepel dam "the largest mechanical enterprise undertaken by the Yurok, or for that matter by any northwest California Indian." The completed wooden structure spanned a fast river and featured ten pens, or corrals, also called "salmon houses." The first corral gate, in the center of the dam, was built by the shaman. When he started it, he sang the sacred song to the salmon chief across the sea, calling salmon up. Then he put up the gate, working under water. When he came up, he was allowed to speak in everyday language to everyone.

After construction was completed, deer and "jumping" dances were held, featuring, among much elaborate regalia, the skins of white deer, headbands of wolf fur and others to which the scalps of red-headed woodpeckers were attached. This obviously represented the spirits of the upper sky country who had come down the sky ladder at qe'nekpul, performing the sky ceremonies that they held everyday at Rkrgr, in Wohpekumeu's spirit country across the ocean. White hides and wolf fur, in northern Siberian and in Algonquian thought, clearly represented the upper sky region; in Algonquian world renewal ceremonies (e.g., Suhtai and Tsistsistas Oxheheom, New Life Lodge, and "Sun Dance"), the red-headed woodpecker symbolizes the spirit of the sun.

After the ceremonies had been held, for a period of ten days only, salmon were "impounded," trapped in the pens, taken out, split, and dried for winter use. This was only done in the afternoons; the shaman controlled the handling of the salmon. The first salmon, or deer, was treated with great ceremony. In the mornings and at night three floodgates in the structure were opened to allow the salmon passage upriver.

After ten days the killing was stopped. Propitiation or Iomante ceremonies are not reported in the sketchy literature about the Kepel ceremonies, perhaps only because anthropologists failed to ask the right question. But they must have been held, perhaps by the shaman and his assistant—and alone in the confinement of the sweat house.

Concluding ceremonies featured a feeding of the spirits including children participants who seem to have represented the spirit children of the upper sky world. All participants were free of restrictions after the concluding ceremonies, but the shaman stayed at the Kepel dam another month until it was washed away by the river. Then the holy period initiating another year was over.

Yurok summer ceremonies at Kepel were an adaptation of ancient Algonquian world renewal concepts to the specific condition of the Klamath River country in northwestern California. In another place the Tsistsistas developed the Massaum based on these concepts; both are variations in form of a common world perception.

Erikson (1943:282) asked the following question:

The creator is said to have liberated the salmon; *is* he the salmon? If so, he lives unharmed through the magic battle at Kepel, for the salmon says: "I shall not be taken. I shall travel as far as the river extends. I shall leave my scales on nets and they will turn into salmon, but *I myself shall go by and not be killed.*"

Munsee-Mahican: Sky Bear, Earth Bear

Munsee and Unami are two closely related Eastern Algonquian languages. Groups speaking dialects of either language were included by early European settlers on the East Coast in the tribal designation Delaware. Although Munsee and Unami speakers were culturally similar, they had never formed a single political unit. Mahican is Eastern Algonquian but is sharply distinct linguistically from Munsee (Goddard 1978d:213); culturally Mahican and Munsee groups were very similar. At the beginning of the European invasion the Mahicans were in the Upper Hudson River Valley and in western Vermont (Brasser 1978:198); the Munsees lived directly to the south, on the Lower Hudson and Upper Delaware rivers, whereas the Unamis were farther south, on the lower Delaware and on both sides of Delaware Bay (Goddard 1978d:214−15). They had occupied these regions since perhaps 1000 B.C. (see above).

Neighbors northwest and west of the Muncees and Mahicans were the Iroquois. Falling back step by step before the European advance across the continent, drastically reduced in population by epidemics and warfare, Unami survivors and some Munsees eventually reached Kansas (1835) and Indian Territory (Oklahoma, 1876). Some Munsee groups and affiliated Mahicans settled on the Fox River in Wisconsin

FIG. 20. The celestial bear has come to earth and goes to his sacrifice in the Munsee–Mahican Big House. The Munsee–Mahican world renewal ceremony featured a bear sacrifice in which a bear of the forest became ritually the representative of the celestial bear. During the ceremony, the Big House represented the world house, or universe. Two large smoke openings in the roof allowed the celestial bear to gaze down upon the sacrifice of his counterpart and the correct performance of the ceremony. The sacrificial bear was selected in a dream by a woman dreamer. Thirteen hunters were sent out to locate the bear's den hidden in deep snows, raise him from hibernation, and explain to him his role

in the ceremony. The animal had to be male; sows were giving birth to cubs in their dens at about the time the ceremony was held or a little later. During the twelve nights of the ceremony, the bear's flesh served as sacred food. With undamaged skull and skin tied to the center pole of the Big House, the bear was an eyewitness to the ceremony. His spirit was later formally released as messenger to the Supreme Being and the spirit world. This Munsee–Mahican ceremony is very closely related to Siberian, especially Evenk, bear ceremonialism. Drawing by Dick West.

in 1828; others had crossed with the Iroquois into Canada (Ontario) following the Revolutionary War. One band, termed Musee-Mahican by Speck (1945:7–16), joined the Iroquois on Six Nations reserve.

The most important religious event in the annual ceremonial cycle of Mahicans, Munsees, and Unamis was a world renewal ceremony. The Mahicans' ceremony featured a midwinter bear sacrifice (Brasser 1978:199); the Munsees and Unamis' ceremony consisted of the twelve-night fall ceremony of the Big House. Both ceremonies are ancient. Two variations of the world-renewal concepts of the three linguistic groups survived into the reservation period. Of these, the Oklahoma Big House ceremony, utilized largely by Unami descendants, has received the most attention by ethnographers (summaries in Speck 1945:18–20; Miller 1980:110–11), perhaps because it survived as a complete ceremony to 1924. After that date it was suspended because of "friction, the lack of new visionaries, and the related growth of evil and impurity in the world" (Miller 1980:109); three brief Big House meetings, however, were held during World War II to "pray for the World and the safe return of servicemen."

The Munsee-Mahican ceremony, participated in by the most traditionally oriented segments of these groups, represented a unique creation because it blended the core of Mahican bear sacrifice and Munsee Big House theology into one overarching structure. Unfortunately, it was last held on Six Nations reserve in 1850. It was reconstructed in Speck's (1945) single account based on testimony provided by the Munsee ceremonial man Nekatcit during fieldwork done between 1932 and 1938. About Nekatcit and his collaboration, Speck (1945:xiii) has written this:

Without riches to leave behind, without heroic deeds to be recited by his descendants, without a career or accomplishment in leadership, his mission was to leave behind an epic of the poetical philosophy and religious drama of his people. It was destined to be written down by one who came into his life only within its last decade. That was my privilege, and it was not the first time that such fell to my lot.

Some Munsee Big House elements in the joint Munsee-Mahican ceremony reflected old concepts that were used by Miller (1980) in his structural analysis of the Oklahoma Unami ceremony for the interpretation of specific features of the latter. The infusion of the Mahican bear sacrifice ritual into the Munsee-Mahican ceremony added a dimension that had not been foreign to Munsees and Unamis.

One of the important ceremonial officials of the Unami Big House

was the *misingw* (mask spirit) impersonator who supervised the ceremonial deer hunt. His costume consisted of a bearskin body suit
(Speck 1931:39–44, fig. 9) and a mask painted red on the right half
of the face, black on the left half. He carried a turtle-shell rattle and
a shaman's staff. Harrington (1921:32–33) wrote that this was the
"most remarkable deity" who was "made guardian by the creator of
all the wild animals of the forest, and was sometimes seen riding on
the back of a buck, herding the deer." Speck (1931:44) felt that the
misingw "is fraught with the possibilities of an archaic northern background, into which fits a series of beliefs and practices extending
across boreal North America through northeastern Asia. The game
owner concept, in short, stands forth in high relief among the far
northern Algonkian."

In the Munsee-Mahican ceremony no game-owner spirit appear-
ing as a bear was featured. Instead, the celestial bear itself, come to
earth for his sacrifice in the physical form of a bear of the forest, was
the focal point of the ceremony.

Munsee-Mahican tradition does not seem to explain when the
ceremony began. It does, however, describe that during a time in the
past, when still in their old country on the Hudson River, they failed
to practice it because "they were still under a spiritual ban" (Speck
1945:41). The Supreme Being, Pa'tama'was (literally Being Prayed
To), interfered and showed himself as a giant stone face on a mountain side. They reinitiated the ceremony and carved his face, as they
had seen it, on the center pole and the doorposts of the Big House.

The ceremony was celebrated in the presence of the Supreme Being
and the spirits, the eternal unity of all creation and the continuing
relationship between sky beings and earth beings. It was held in January at the appearance of the first phase of the moon, lasted originally
twelve nights, and started a new year *(withke'katen)*. The medium
through which the order of the universe, as given by the Supreme
Being, was expressed was the bear who also served as messenger between earth and sky beings.

The date for the ceremony was set by annual signals from the
sky. Mahicans, Munsees, Unamis, many other Eastern Algonquian
groups, and some Central Algonquian groups viewed the constellation Ursa Major as a celestial bear hunt (Müller 1956:291–95). In their
interpretation the four stars of Ursa Major, that form an irregular
rectangle mark the body of the cosmic bear, and the three stars that
form the handle of the "Dipper" represent three hunters accompanied by a dog (the star Alcor). Revolving around the North Star,

the cosmic bear leaves his den (Corona Borealis) in spring followed by seven hunters—the three of the "Dipper" handle and the four consisting of Arcturus and the three stars of the constellation Boötis. They trail the bear through the summer and slay him in the fall. The Abenakis attribute

the autumnal reddening of the forest foliage to the tinting of the leaves by the blood of the celestial bear slain at this turn of the season by the star hunters, and the white mantle of early winter snow on earth to the coating of white bear's grease falling upon earth when the sky hunters try out the fat of the slain bear. [Speck 1945:57]

But the celestial bear comes to life again, remaining dormant during the winter and once again emerging from his den in spring to reenact the eternal drama of the hunt in the sky.

It is significant in this context that in northern Siberian (Evenks) thought, the constellations Ursa Major, Boötis, and Arcturus also represent a celestial hunt. Here, however, Ursa Major is the cosmic moose, *kheglun,* who is hunted by the bear *mangi* who is visible in the constellations Boötis and Arcturus (see chapter 2). Perhaps this Evenk concept explains the position of the *misingw* as the spirit controlling the ceremonial deer hunt in the Unami Big House ceremony—a reenactment of a celestial hunt. This, then, is based on ideas that have their closest counterpart in northern Siberia (see Ikenipke, chapter 2).

If my interpretation is correct, Munsee-Mahicans and Unamis practiced *two* versions of a sky hunt in their renewal ceremonies: In the first version the bear was the prey of spirit hunters; in the second the bear was the spirit hunter himself. It is remarkable that both existed side by side within three closely affiliated Eastern Algonquian groups.

Speck (1945:32) has written this about the symbolism of the Munsee–Mahican ceremony:

The Munsee–Mahican Big House is a sky projection upon earth, specifically the constellation Ursa Major projected upon the floor of the Big House sanctuary. The interior furnishings of the sanctuary and the stations formally occupied by the ceremonial officials correspond to the position of the stars forming the constellation. The acts and movements of the ritual performers parallel the movements of Ursa Major as the events of the annual life cycle of the earth bear sacrificed in the ceremony is conceived as a fragment of the celestial bear, and everything done during the ritual is a transcendental reference to him.

The ceremony was held in the Big House, Xwate'k'an, a rectangular wooden building (fifty by thirty feet) with its long axis running east to west. The structure represented the universe: its bare floor the earth, its four walls the four directions, its ceiling, the sky spaces thought to consist of twelve layers atop which the Supreme Being resides. The center pole, a tree trunk, symbolized the world tree *(axis mundi)*. There were an east door and a west door. Halfway between the doors and the center pole were two fires; there were two smoke holes in the roof above them. A carved wooden mask above each door faced the center pole; the one on the east side was white; the one on the west side was red. Two more masks, suspended on the center pole, faced east and west. The one on the east side was red; the one on the west side white. Thus two red masks faced east, two white masks faced west, indicating the colors of the two directions and the inherent dualism in the universe (earth-sky, life-death, male-female). This concept was also expressed in the arrangement of participants: Women were located in the eastern half of the structure, men in the western half. (Perhaps it should be recalled that, of the sacred wolves of the Massaum, the male wolf was red, the female wolf, white.)

The skin of the sacrificed bear was tied around the center pole beneath the red and white face masks, thus ceremonially unifying both opposites on the world tree.

During the ceremony four male drummers were stationed on the men's (west) side. During the second part of the ceremony they used a deerskin stitched into a rectangular cushion, with the hair side in, serving as a drum (Speck 1945, fig. 3). One half of this unique drum was painted red, the other white. A bear painted black was superimposed on the red, facing a black crescent moon in the white field. Four drum beaters were paddle-shaped, painted white and red, with a star in the white field. Howard (1980:153), commenting on the Oklahoma Unami ceremony, observed that the deerskin drum represented a "very ancient and unique type of drum in North America . . . of probable Asiatic origin." In one Tsistsistas ceremony a buffalo hide is used as a drum.

Another important object in the ceremony was a turtle-shell rattle that was used exclusively by visionaries when they recited their visions in the Big House. In Munsee-Mahican and in Unami thought the earth region rested symbolically on the back of a great turtle, placed there by the creator after the separation of sea and land. Because the shield structure of the turtle is organized in recurrent numbers of twelve, the turtle carried the mark of the twelve layers of the sky space. In Munsee-Mahican directional interpretations, the turtle represented also the west-to-east transition, therefore repeating the orientation of the world house—the Big House of the ceremony.

The ceremony required that a woman dreamed the bear to be sacrificed, or rather, the bear spirit selected a woman dreamer, revealing himself and his location, thus initiating the ceremony. The dreamer of the 1850 ceremony was Twenyucis (Speck 1945:50, 61), a woman of Munsee and Tutelo tribal descent. The dreamer described the details to the chief who apparently played the role of the Supreme Being in the ceremony. He selected twelve ceremonial men and the *maxkok*—the leader of the sacred hunt. The thirteen men left at dark to reach, at daybreak, the bear's hibernation place seen by the dreamer, sometimes traveling many miles. They stayed a day and a night around the den, in silence. At daybreak the *maxkok* struck the den, telling the bear: "You we have found" (Speck 1945:61). And: "The chief wants you. Now you go and take the lead." With the bear leading, the group walked through the forest to the Big House, entering through the eastern door. He was killed with blow to his head at the center pole by the chief.

The chief addressed the animal, "telling him that they would later all meet above [in the sky]. He admonished him to go in advance of his slayers and to inform the spirits in the sky that everything was right on earth, that men were faithful to their obligations to each other and to the spirits of the deceased" (Speck 1945:65).

The *maxkok* skinned the animal ceremonially, that is, reversing the cutting of animals killed for food or fur. He removed from the center pole the bear hide of the last ceremony and tied the fresh hide in its place, just beneath the red and white masks. The bear's body was removed to the cookhouse at the east side of the Big House where it was entrusted to a number of selected women and a male helper. Through the twelve nights of the ceremony, all participants shared in the sacred food at the conclusion of each night's performance. The bear's head was used as were all other parts of his body. The bones were carefully collected and burned in the eastern fire of the Big House close to the end of the ceremony. The bear's flesh alone was the sacred food; neither salt nor plant matter was added.

The Big House night portions of the ceremony began on the night of the bear's death. No ethnographer appears to have asked why the performances were held only at night, and therefore no answer was given. Asking the question now, the answer is obvious to me: Only at night was the celestial counterpart of the sacrificial bear of the ceremony visible, gazing down into the Big House from the northern sky.

The ceremony was apparently separated into three equal parts. For the first four nights, for short periods only that were ended by the rising moon, the leader of the ceremony explained the purpose of the ceremony and gave thanks to all forces and spiritual and physical forms of the universe. For four nights, the ritual of spirit experiences, *alo'man,* followed, in which the performers were accompanied by four singers using the deerskin drum. This section of the ceremony was concluded by a men's dance, a mixed dance, and a women's dance. After these, the ceremonial objects (deerskin drum and drum beaters, turtle-shell rattle) were removed. The last four nights were devoted to dances that featured animal representations and masked performers as well as social dances, the latter "to afford social relaxation to the people" (Speck 1945:73). These were accompanied with a water drum painted red with the four directions. The ceremony was ended before daybreak following the twelfth night. At that time the moon had reached its full phase.

The main reason Speck gives for the disappearance of this ceremony after 1850 is the conversion of the Munsee-Mahican band to Christianity. Perhaps so. In a world emptied of old symbolism and old physical form, an earth bear, acting under the instruction of a celestial bear, no longer reached a dreamer open to the dream. Perhaps the disappearance of the dreamer initiated the physical disappearance of the bear.

Close Enemies of Long Ago: The Okipa and the Massaum

Mandans: Suffering for the Buffalo

The Mandans are a Hokan–Siouan-speaking tribe residing on the Fort Berthold Reservation in North Dakota. Before 1780 they consisted of five divisions: Is'topa, Nuptadi, Manana're, Awigaxa, and Nuitadi (Bowers 1950:24–25), each with a number of permanent villages. These were located along the Missouri River, extending from the Heart River upstream to the Painted Woods. They lost 80 percent of their population in the smallpox epidemic of 1780; the survivors joined in two earth-lodge villages below Knife River (Wedel 1961:202). In 1837 another smallpox epidemic took four-fifths of their remaining people (Schlesier 1968:43). In 1862, the shattered bands of survivors of the sedentary tribes of the Missouri River region—Mandans, Hidatsas, and Arikaras, who together had numbered close to a hundred thousand people before 1780—assembled in a single village near Fort Berthold (Schlesier 1968:43).

As the Proto-Tsistsistas became the Tsistsistas through the introduction of the Massaum ceremony, Proto-Mandans became Mandans through the introduction of the Okipa ceremony. With the Okipa a permanent ceremonial lodge that faced a village plaza was built. Because these features are an integral part of the Thomas Riggs Focus, which begins around A.D. 1100, Wood (1967:156–57) has concluded that the Okipa was developed at the initiation of this archaeological entity (for Mandan prehistory and protohistory, see chapter 7).

The ceremony required that it was performed annually. It was last held in 1890; after that date it was prohibited by the army officer in charge of the reservation (Bowers 1950:119). When the Collier administration, in response to the Indian Reorganization Act of 1934, lifted the ban, the Okipa did not return. The annihilation of the bison had made it unnecessary; the death of a whole generation of priests and knowledgeable participants during the intervening years had made it impossible.

Curtis (1930:128) believed that "certain features" of the Massaum "suggest borrowings from the Mandan Okipé." Hoebel (1978:23) also thought it "highly probable that the Cheyennes borrowed . . . from the Mandan Okeepa ceremony, which they would have had occasion to see during the period of their stay on the Missouri River," referring to the time after 1700. Both argue the case on the notion that the Tsistsistas were latecomers to the region occupied by the Mandans already for nearly a thousand years, a notion that is rebuked by Mandan tradition itself (chapter 7).

What the Tsistsistas are supposed to have borrowed Curtis and Hoebel did not say. If their logic that the people in place passed knowledge to those who came later applies, the Tsistsistas contributed to the Mandan ceremony, not vice versa. Tsistsistas warfare with Proto-Mandans before and during the period in which the Okipa developed may not have given the latter a chance to observe a Massaum directly, although they could have learned about it through a third party. A solution to the question depends on a comparison of the two ceremonies.

According to Mandan tradition, Proto-Mandan bands arrived in the northeastern Plains from the Mississippi River and entered the grasslands separately from different points (southwestern Minnesota, northwestern Iowa, see chapter 7). The Awigaxa tradition states that they arrived with a Corn Medicine Ceremony (Bowers 1950, 158–60). Expanding to the Black Hills, the Awigaxa found the land itself and the people they encountered (the Tsistsistas) hostile: "In the mountains they planted corn out there, but the seasons were too short, and the yields were small" (Bowers 1950:163). They were visited by the Supreme Being (First Creator) and Lone Man, his son, who became the spiritual representative of the Mandans. Mandan tradition explains that he has been with them a number of times during their long history in the grasslands. First, Creator and Lone Man together taught them the first version of the Buffalo Dance, which was elaborated over many following years and eventually incorporated in the Okipa ceremony.

While Proto-Mandan bands still ranged over a wide region, extending from southwestern Manitoba to the White River in South Dakota, First Creator and Lone Man, the tradition says, prepared their final homeland in North Dakota; First Creator restructured the land west of the Missouri River, Lone Man the country lying east (Maximilian, n.d., 2:94–95). When eventually Proto-Mandans concentrated in sedentary villages along the Missouri, Lone Man caused himself to be born into the Nuptadi division. He organized the Nuptadis and other northern Proto-Mandan bands into the buffalo moiety, adding a number of matriclans. At a time when buffalo and all other game were confined to a mountain (Dog Den Butte) by Hoita, the eagle spirit of the people above, Lone Man brought about the animals' release by introducing the Okipa.

Because the ceremony was held annually thereafter, each Mandan village was reorganized to feature a plaza fronting the permanent Okipa lodge. The traditions state that Lone Man protected his people during a great flood (caused by the spirits after Mandans had abused buffalo calves) by erecting a fence that the waters did not overcome. A symbol of this spirit fence was erected afterward on each Mandan plaza. When the Awigaxa and southern Mandan bands (the Corn People) joined their upriver relatives (the Buffalo People), they became the corn moiety. In the seating arrangement of the Okipa lodge, the matriclans of the buffalo moiety sat on the west side, those of the corn moiety on the east side (Bowers 1950:113). The total number of clans was sixteen; they were called out by name on the fourth day of the ceremony (Bowers 1950:147–48).

The Okipa commemorated the freeing of animals from Dog Den Butte where Hoita had held them captive after a quarrel over a white buffalo hide (Bowers 1950:349–51, 356–59). Because his people were starving, Lone Man went into Dog Den Butte disguised as a rabbit and observed the Buffalo Dance there. He learned the songs and dance steps, and after his return advised the Mandans to hold a ceremony modeled after the animal dance in the mountain. This was the first Okipa held. Hoita came over and watched it, then released the animals. "He sent the black-tail deer to the badlands, the white-tail deer to the timber, the bears to the points in the river, the buffalo to the flat, and the antelope to the hills" (Bowers 1950:351).

The word Okipa means "to look alike," referring to the bull dancers who were dressed and painted as the animal dancers in Dog Den Butte. The songs and prayers of the ceremony were in the Nuptadi dialect. The main Okipa ceremonial bundle was inherited through the WaxikEna clan that Lone Man had established after he had been born into the Nuptadis (Bowers 1950:113, 118).

The ceremony was held in the summer in each Mandan village; often there were two performances in each village (Bowers 1950:122). The Okipa lodge with its six central posts and rectangular form was a replica of Dog Den Butte. In front of it, on the plaza, stood the small circular structure of cottonwood planks that symbolized the spirit fence erected by Lone Man during the great flood (Catlin 1976, plate 2). A red-painted cedar post inside the enclosure "represents Lone Man and all the people," as White Calf told Bowers (1950:352). During the Okipa performance the Hoita impersonator directed the activities inside the ceremonial lodge, the Lone Man impersonator those held outside. Women were not allowed to participate in the ceremony or to enter the Okipa lodge during the performance. Some women fasted on top of the structure from the morning of the first day to sunset on the third day (Bowers 1950:147), perhaps for the benefit of sons or husbands who were undergoing torture features.

The main performers in the Okipa were Lone Man (Numakmax-Ena), the Speckled Eagle (Hoita), and the pledger, or Okipa maker (Koni'saka); it was required that the latter had dreamed of the ceremony and had heard buffalo singing Okipa songs (Bowers 1950:121). The Lone Man impersonator had to be a member of the WaxikEna clan; the priest taking the Hoita position belonged either to the WaxikEna or Tamisik clans (Bowers 1950:120). After the dates had been set, the Okipa lodge was cleaned, and sage was placed on the bare earth. The three eastern posts were painted with red bands a few inches wide, the western posts with black bands. The crier went through the village before daylight announcing that Lone Man would open the lodge at sunrise on the following morning.

On this morning Lone Man approached from the prairie to the south. He was dressed in a wolf robe; his body and face were painted white. He wore a headdress of jackrabbit fur and porcupine hair to which a raven was tied. In his left hand he carried a pipe, in his right hand a flat ash club with a moon and thunderbird design on one side, morning star and sun on the other (Bowers 1950:125). At the village entrance, he was stopped by members of a soldier society. He explained who he was and the purpose of his return. He was taken directly to the Okipa lodge. There he told the sacred story of his relationship with the Mandans, including the origin story of the ceremony. Then he passed through the village from lodge to lodge, addressing the people directly.

The ceremony began in the evening. After the participants had assembled in the Okipa lodge, Hoita and the Okipa maker sat on the north side, and Lone Man sat on the west side in front of a dry buffalo hide rolled up like a cylinder to serve as a drum (Bowers 1950:126). Many male fasters sat along the walls, according to clan and moiety membership. An altar was set up between the northeast and northwest posts of the lodge, consisting of a four-post frame symbolic of the four posts of the universe (Bowers 1950:128). The knives and splints for the torture features were placed beneath the altar. The altar was flanked on the west and east sides by two pairs of human skulls and two pairs of buffalo skulls (Bowers 1950:127; Catlin 1976, plate 3).

On this evening, Lone Man transferred his pipe to the Okipa maker, thus placing him in charge of the ceremony. Then he called on Hoita to supervise the performance and to see that every detail of the dance was done correctly (Bowers 1950:128). The dance began at once and lasted until midnight; the drummers used the hide drum.

On the morning of the first day, the Okipa maker left the lodge and stood at the spirit fence on the plaza, touching the wooden planks with both hands, his forehead against the wood. Standing on a buffalo skull, he prayed to the original Lone Man "to hear him . . . and to bring the buffaloes near the villages, and to keep all bad luck away" (Bowers 1950:129). While he was standing there, the fasters came out covered with buffalo robes, with the hair on the outside. Accompanied by the drummers, they danced toward the sacred cedar, imitating a buffalo herd. During the first day this performance was repeated four times: at sunrise, before noon, midafternoon, and before sunset. At sunset the Lone Man impersonator went out to collect from their keepers three water-filled hide drums called "turtle drums," which replaced the cylinder-shaped hide drum used previously. Dances in the Okipa lodge lasted until midnight.

On the second day eight elaborately dressed buffalo bull dancers (Catlin 1976: plate 4) performed eight times on the plaze while the Okipa maker stood praying at the spirit fence. The fasters imitating a buffalo herd danced once.

On this day the torture feature began (Catlin 1976, plates 10, 11). Fasters presented themselves to clan "fathers" who took knives from the altar and cut holes through muscle and flesh for the skewers:

Two skewers were inserted through the skin on the back or the breast by which the candidate was suspended in midair by a lariat fastened over a pole in the Okipa lodge. Other skewers were inserted through the skin of the legs to which buffalo skulls were attached [Bowers 1950:135].

The fasters thus suspended were violently turned until they lost consciousness; then they were lowered down but left untouched on the ground until they came to.

The third day was called "Everything Comes Back." The bull dancers performed twelve times on the plaza. They were joined by new dancers representing spirits featured in sacred bundles of other Mandan ceremonies and had been selected by bundle owners. The spiritual powers of these bundles were joined with the Okipa; this demonstrated the primary position of the Okipa in Mandan religious life. In this display of spirits, performers in elaborate costumes represented day and night (Catlin 1976, plate 7), bald eagles, holy women (impersonated by male dancers), swans, snakes (Catlin 1976, plate 8), calumet eagle, hawk, grizzly bears, black bears, beavers, wolves, coyote, meadowlark, and antelopes.

The torture feature continued. After the first dance of the day was completed, the Foolish One (OxinhEde) arrived from the prairie, running up painted black with white circles on his body and white teeth painted around his mouth (Catlin 1976, plate 9). He carried a staff with a symbolic human head attached; he "wore a rod and two small pumpkins representing male genitals" (Bowers 1950:145). He represented a spirit hostile to the ceremony. In attempting to mate with the dancing bulls and running at women in the crowd of onlookers, he acted in contrary fashion (Catlin 1976; plate 4). Eventually, he was arrested by the Okipa maker. Stripped of headdress and necklace, his staff broken, he was evicted from the village. Perhaps he also symbolized former enemies of the Mandans.

The fourth day was called the "Hunting Day." Only four bull dancers performed on the plaza on this day. They appeared sixteen times, one time for each of the original Mandan clans, which were recited by name. The Okipa maker and the remaining fasters were tortured before the "freeing of the animals" and the "animal hunt" took place, that is, after the last dance. Hoita emerged from the Okipa lodge carrying Lone Man's pipe. Now the bulls came out, four times and each time hunters, standing in line and using poles as lances, charged them, inflicting painful wounds.

After the hunt the bulls stood at the four cardinal points, calling. The north buffalo represented winter buffalo, the east, spring buffalo, the south, summer buffalo, and the west, fall buffalo. The ceremony neared its end when the last fasters, with heavy buffalo skulls attached to their flesh, were dragged around the plaza in a frantic, painful race until they fainted (Catlin 1976, plate 12).

George Catlin (1976:67), who observed the ceremony in 1832, remarked about this scene:

In this pitiable condition each sufferer was left, his life again entrusted to the keeping of the Great Spirit, the sacredness of which privilege no one had a right to infringe upon by offering a helping hand. Each one in turn lay in this condition until the Great Spirit gave him strength to rise upon his feet.

For the permission to take animal life, humans voluntarily suffered for the animals as these had suffered for humans so often. Those who had offered severe pain all had experienced ritual death and transformation. The tools used in the sacrifices (knives, skewers, ropes) were dropped into the Missouri, as gifts to the river, along with other gifts. A sweat lodge ceremony for all participants closed the Okipa.

The comparison of the essential concepts and features of the two ceremonies indicates that both are incompatible as are the world descriptions of the two cultures. The Tsistsistas ceremony takes one to deep levels, beyond the act of creation by the Supreme Being to the perceived undifferentiated unity of form, and carries in logical sequence existence through time to the gift of the grassland earth that was received from the spirits. In contrast, the Mandan ceremony refers to one event described by the tradition as having occurred relatively recently. Where similarities between the two ceremonies are visually the most striking, for example, in the extensive use of animal impersonators, they are incongruous in meaning.

Table 2. Selected Comparative Data

Concept	Massaum	Okipa
The ceremonial lodge is the universe	x	—
The ceremonial lodge has a center pole	x	—
The ceremonial lodge is a permanent structure	—	x
The creation of the universe is reenacted	x	—
The guardians of the four corners are made	x	—
The spirits are made	x	—
The ceremonial lodge is a spirit lodge	x	x
The ceremonial lodge is an animal den	x	x
The ceremony is held in the summer	x	x
The ceremony is an earth-giving ceremony	x	—
The ceremony describes a specific event	x	x
This event focuses on buffalo	x	x
The earth spirit is the keeper of animals	x	—
Two important spirits are donors of the ceremony	x	—
The animals are the donors	—	x
A buffalo maiden is given to a human	x	—
Two important shamans are in the ceremony	x	x
One shaman is the spiritual representative of the people and returns in dangerous times	x	x
In the ceremony hunting rules are taught	x	—
Two master wolves are the master hunters	x	—
Women perform in the ceremony	x	—
The ceremony features a ceremonial hunt	x	x
The ceremonial hunt describes a specific hunting technique	x	—
All animal species are represented	x	—
Animals are ritually killed	x	x
They are killed by spirit hunters (contraries)	x	—
They are killed by ordinary human hunters	—	x
A contrary society is important in the ceremony	x	—
One contrary acts in a prominent role	—	x
Impersonators represent spirits who have initiated other ceremonies and sacred bundles	—	x
Night and day are represented	x	x
Night and day are represented by impersonators	—	x
Torture features (suffering for the animals)	—	x
Healing features (the animals are the healers)	x	—
Membership in a special group, or clan, decides selection of chief performers	—	x

The Tsistsistas, when they had an opportunity to observe an Okipa, had nothing to learn from a ceremony that was initiated over a thousand years after the Massaum, and was alien to their world perception. Conversely, the Massaum must have been alien to Mandan observers if they were ever told its meaning. On its own terms each ceremony was complete and needed no additions from alien sources. It is unlikely that either influenced the other.

9. Conclusion

We need another and a wiser and perhaps a more mystical concept of animals. Remote from universal nature, and living by complicated artifice, man in civilization surveys the creature through the glass of his knowledge and sees thereby a feather magnified and the whole image in distortion. We patronize them for their incompleteness, for their tragic fate of having taken form so far below ourselves. And therein we err, and greatly err. For the animal shall not be measured by man. In a world older and more complete than ours they move finished and complete, gifted with extensions of the senses we have lost or never attained, living by voices we shall never hear. They are not brethren, they are not underlings; they are other nations caught with ourselves in the net of life and time, fellow prisoners of the splendour and travail of the earth.

—HENRY BESTON, *THE OUTERMOST HOUSE*

The English philosopher Alfred North Whitehead, writing about human inquiry into the nature of the universe, said that in simply discussing the issues, the merest hint of dogmatic certainty is an exhibition of folly. This tolerance for mystery invigorates the imagination; and it is the imagination that gives shape to the universe.

—BARRY LOPEZ, *OF WOLVES AND MEN*

"Reality" means "everything you can think about." This is not "that-which-is." No idea can capture "truth" in the sense of that-which-is.

—DAVID BOHM, IN A LECTURE GIVEN AT BERKELEY, APRIL, 1977

THE FOUNDATION of Tsistsistas and Proto-Tsistsistas cultures is a shamanistic world interpretation originally shared with all fellow members of the Algonquian language family.

This shamanistic world interpretation persisted through historic times into the reservation period and in important aspects has survived to the present as is evidenced by the continuing annual performance of the Maxhoetonstov and Oxheheom ceremonies.

It was carried by groups ancestral to the Algonquians from the

188

Arctic into regions south of the retreating Wisconsin glaciation ice shield, at least 12,000 years ago.

It was shared earlier in common by groups ancestral to the Algonquians with groups ancestral to early populations in northern Siberia. In intricate variations of its themes and in many identical and near-identical features, it continued in both regions for millennia after the groups were separated on two separate continents.

The Tsistsistas Massaum ceremony has its closest relative not in North America but in the Shingkelevun of the Evenks of northern Siberia. Next in order are concepts underlying New Year ceremonies such as those of the Yuroks and Munsee-Mahicans, expressed at opposite ends of the Algonquian spatial distribution. Both these, through space and time, have independently closely related expressions in northern Siberia also (see chapter 2).

The major ceremonies described in this book, in northern Siberia as well as in North America, have perished due to centuries of oppression of native groups by materialist civilizations in both regions and the destruction of their environments waged.

In terms of cultural evolution, the old Tsistsistas world description, like that of the Yuroks, Evenks, Yukagirs, Orochis, and so forth must be defined as culturally successful because the principles upon which it is built are at least one thousand, perhaps two thousand generations old. Without the European conquests it would not have been in jeopardy.

It is obvious, therefore, that the world interpretation as explained in Tsistsistas shamanism is not rejected by a universe viewed as unexplicable by modern physics. That it is rejected by a scientific rationalism that developed in the seventeenth and eighteenth centuries is irrelevant because the latter constitutes nothing but another world description in Europe. Thus two different world descriptions oppose each other.

Of the two, that of the Tsistsistas—and of the Yuroks, Evenks, Yukagirs, Orochis, and so on—objectively is the superior because it allows recognition of the other. The rationalistic world description, in contrast, has excluded the experience of the other because of its anthropocentric and mechanistic orientation and its ethnocentric discrimination.

The development of a sophisticated technology made possible by the rationalistic concept of science appears, viewed from the Tsistsistas world description, as a fetishism of physical existence and a trivial manipulation of particles and potencies. An artificial intercontinental flight vehicle does not impress someone whose *hematasooma* is capable of superluminal intergalactic space travel. The new scientific paradigm initiated by physics and astronomy during the last decades has not only overthrown the rationalistic description that has dominated science for merely four centuries but is testing concepts regarded as factual in the Tsistsistas world description.

The Tsistsistas world description understands power ("energy") in the universe, following on the cosmological singularity, as cosmic power, *exhastoz*. *Exhastoz* conglobates in spiritual potencies: *maiyun, hematasoomao,* which have unrestrained access to *exhastoz*. They are not limited by time or space. Both may join with physical form. Both are generally invisible to the human diagnostic senses but may enter human cognition visually and audibly and execute tasks that can be measured physically; that is, they have control over quantum phenomena.

In Tsistsistas understanding, they are causal (they can be brought about by specific Tsistsistas behavior) and noncausal (they may manifest themselves without a trigger). They are nonlocal (i.e., they are everywhere) and local (i.e., they may appear in a specific locality or in a specific physical form). They are fissionable: They may be local at a number of places at the same time. They are outside, or, outside *and* within the construct of time and therefore represent universal "information."

The old Tsistsistas culture, as the others mentioned, concentrated its attention on spiritual forces, those residing in physical form and those that were free. To be a Tsistsistas meant to know the interplay of spiritual and physical forms and to participate in it. The power of the *maiyun* and *hematasoomao* over a wide range of manifestations in the universe was empirical knowledge to each Tsistsistas. If this had not been so, this world description would neither have developed nor would it have existed through an enormous number of generations. To observe and experience the metamorphosis of forces was considered normal in Tsistsistas culture. What would have been paranormal cannot now be known.

Epilogue: To the Tsistsistas

WHEN HIS, our Old Man's, the Arrow Keeper's eyes failed, I became his eyes as an eagle's, looking deep. He took me into his heart, made me dream with him of eagle men, of spirit circles standing wide, of the white bear, of hide turning heavy as a buffalo bull. They were sitting there with us, *maheyuno*. He did not apologize, just explained, and they looked way into my bones. He asked them or rather told. He wanted me to tell about the long, long time, about what was, and what still is. For the Tsistsistas, most of all. For the Tsistsistas to come back. Silently they watched, *maheyuno*. So they and he watched me while I was doing this book, keeping me straight. This was the most severe test of all; to get the evidence, however dissected in literature and life, was nothing, compared.

So I say I did us something, a favor perhaps, but I didn't do it alone. Many there are who have been with me. Perhaps it is not too late. But judge for yourself and think about it when you are reading it. Words are difficult and a gift. To bring it all together in a sequence, on paper, to sit there squarely, in black, well, spirits are indestructible, and they can dream it in colors different and still be right. But I use what I must, and I tried to be perfect. Remember that the badger still lives underground, the red-headed woodpecker still flies, and wolves still roam somewhere.

So do we.

Bibliography

Anderson, R.
    1956   The Buffalo Men: A Cheyenne Ceremony of Petition Deriving from the Sutaio. *Southwestern Journal of Anthropology* 12:92–104.
    1970   A Study of Cheyenne Culture History, with Special Reference to the Northern Cheyenne. Ph.D. dissertation. Ann Arbor, Mich.: University Microfilms International.

Anisimov, A. F.
    1963a The Shaman's Tent of the Evenks and the Origin of the Shamanistic Rite. In Henry N. Michael, ed. *Studies in Siberian Shamanism,* pp. 84–123. Toronto: University of Toronto Press.
    1963b Cosmological Concepts of the Peoples of the North. In Henry N. Michael, ed., *Studies in Siberian Shamanism,* pp. 157–229. Toronto: University of Toronto Press.

Baerreis, David A., and Robert A. Alex
    1974   An Interpretation of Midden Formation—The Mill Creek Example. In Elden Johnson, ed., *Aspects of Upper Great Lakes Anthropology,* pp. 143–48. St. Paul: Minnesota Historical Society.

Benedict, James B., and Byron L. Olson
    1973   Origin of the McKean Complex: Evidence from Timberline. *Plains Anthropologist* 18:323–27.

Boas, Franz
    1910   Die Resultate der Jesup-Expedition. *Verhandlungen des 16 Internationalen Amerikanisten-Kongresses* 1:3–18. Vienna.

Bowers, Alfred W.
    1950   *Mandan Social and Ceremonial Organization.* Chicago: University of Chicago Press.

Brasser, T. J.
    1978   Mahican. In Bruce Trigger, ed., *Northeast,* pp. 198–212. *Handbook of North American Indians,* vol. 15. Washington, D.C.: Smithsonian Institution.

Brink, Jack, and Stuart J. Baldwin
    1985   Thoughts on a Human Burial System During Pelican Lake Times. Paper presented at the 43d Plains Conference, Iowa City.

Brumley, John H.
   1978   McKean Complex Subsistence and Hunting Strategies in the
          Southern Alberta Plains. In Leslie B. Davis and Michael Wil-
          son, ed., *Bison Procurement and Utilization: A Symposium,*
          pp. 175– 93. *Plains Anthropologist* 23, Memoir 14.
Burgesse, J. Allan
   1944   The Spirit Wigwam as Described by Tommie Moar, Pointe
          Bleue. *Primitive Man* 17:50–53.
Callendar, Charles
   1962   *Social Organization of the Central Algonkian Indians.* Milwaukee
          Public Museum Publications in Anthropology no. 7.
Castaneda, Carlos
   1979   *The Second Ring of Power.* New York: Simon & Schuster.
Catlin, George
   1976   *O-Kee-Pa: A Religious Ceremony and Other Customs of the Man-
          dans.* Lincoln: University of Nebraska Press.
Chernetsov, V. N.
   1963   Concepts of the Soul Among the Ob Ugrians. In Henry N.
          Michael, ed., *Studies in Siberian Shamanism,* pp. 3–45. Toronto:
          University of Toronto Press.
Cooper, John M.
   1944   The Shaking Tent Rite Among Plains and Forest Algonquians.
          Primitive Man 17:60–84.
Curtis, E. S.
   1911   *The Cheyenne. The North American Indian,* 6:87–135, 155–58.
          Norwood, Mass.
   1930   *The Southern Cheyenne. The North American Indian,* 19:107–48.
          Norwood, Mass.
Davis, Leslie B., and Charles D. Zeier
   1978   Multi-Phase Late Period Bison Procurement at the Antonsen
          Site, Southwestern Montana. In Leslie B. Davis and Michael
          Wilson, eds., *Bison Procurement and Utilization: A Symposium,*
          pp. 222–35. *Plains Anthropologist* 23, Memoir 14.
Diószegi, V.
   1963   Zum Problem der ethnischen Homogenität des tofischen (ka-
          ragassischen) Schamanismus. In V. Diószegi, ed., *Glaubenswelt
          und Folklore der Sibirischen Völker,* pp. 261–357. Budapest: Akade-
          miai Kiado.
Dorsey, G. A.
   1905   *The Cheyenne: I, Ceremonial Organization.* Field Columbian
          Museum Publication 99, Anthropological Series 9, no. 1.
          Chicago.
Eddy, John A.
   1974   Astronomical Alignment of the Big Horn Medicine Wheel. *Sci-
          ence* 184:1035–43.

1981   Medicine Wheels and Plains Indian Astronomy. In K. Brecher and M. Feirtag, eds., *Astronomy of the Ancients,* pp. 1–24. Cambridge, Mass.: MIT Press.

Edelmann, Sylvia S.
1970   Medicine Elk: Die Autobiographie des Hüters der Heiligen Pfeile der Cheyennes. Ph.D. thesis, Universität Wien.

Eliade, M.
1965   *The Two and the One.* Chicago: University of Chicago Press.
1974   *Shamanism.* Bollingen Series, vol. 76. Princeton, N.J.: Princeton University Press.

Elsasser, Albert B.
1978a Development of Regional Prehistoric Cultures. In Robert F. Heizer, ed., *California,* pp. 37–57. *Handbook of North American Indians,* vol. 8. Washington, D.C.: Smithsonian Institution.
1978b Wiyot. In Robert F. Heizer, ed., *California,* pp. 155–63. *Handbook of North American Indians,* vol. 8. Washington, D.C.: Smithsonian Institution.

Erikson, Erik H.
1943   *Observation on the Yurok: Childhood and World Image.* University of California Publications in American Archaeology and Ethnology 35(10):257–301.

Findeisen, Hans
1957   *Schamanentum.* Stuttgart: W. Kohlhammer Verlag.

Flannery, Regina
1944   The Gros Ventre Shaking Tent. *Primitive Man* 17:54–59.

Fletcher, Alice C., and Francis LaFlesche
1972   *The Omaha Tribe.* 2 vols. Lincoln: University of Nebraska Press.

Foor, Thomas Allyn
1982   Cultural Continuity on the Northwestern Great Plains, 1300 B.C. to A.D. 200: The Pelican Lake Culture. Ph.D. dissertation. Ann Arbor, Mich.: University of Microfilms International.

Fried, Morton H.
1975   *The Notion of Tribe.* Menlo Park, Calif.: Cummings Publishing Co.

Frison, George C.
1971   The Buffalo Pound in Northwestern Plains Prehistory: Site 48 CA 302, Wyoming. *American Antiquity* 36:77–91.
1978   *Prehistoric Hunters of the High Plains.* New York: Academic Press.
1983   Stone Circles, Stone-filled Firepits, Grinding Stones, and High Plains Archaeology. In Leslie B. Davis, ed., *From Microcosm to Macrocosm: Advances in Tipi Ring Investigation and Interpretation,* pp. 81–91. *Plains Anthropologist* 28, Memoir 19.

Gerasimov, M. M.
1964   The Palaeolithic Site Malta: Excavations of 1956–1957. In Henry

N. Michael, ed., *The Archaeology and Geomorphology of Northern Asia: Selected Works,* pp. 3–32. Toronto: University of Toronto Press.

Goddard, Ives

1978a Central Algonquian Languages. In Bruce Trigger, ed., *Northeast,* pp. 583–87. *Handbook of North American Indians,* vol. 15. Washington, D.C.: Smithsonian Institution.

1978b Eastern Algonquian Languages. In Bruce Trigger, ed., *Northeast,* pp. 70–77. *Handbook of North American Indians,* vol. 15. Washington, D.C.: Smithsonian Institution.

1978c The Sutaio Dialect of Cheyenne: A Discussion of the Evidence. In William Cowan, ed., *Papers of the Ninth Algonquian Conference,* pp. 68–80. Ottawa: Carleton University.

1978d Delaware. In Bruce Trigger, ed., *Northeast,* pp. 213–39. *Handbook of North American Indians,* vol. 15. Washington, D.C.: Smithsonian Institution.

Golowin, Sergius

1981 Zwischen Sachlichkeit und ideologischem Aberglauben: Dargestellt an der Erforschung des eurasischen Schamanismus im 19. 20. Jahrhundert. In H. P. Duerr, ed., *Der Wissenschaftler und das Irrationale,* 1:175–83. Frankfurt: Syndikat.

Greiser, Sally Thompson

1985 Predictive Models of Hunter-Gatherer Subsistence and Settlement Strategies on the Central High Plains. *Plains Anthropologist* 30, Memoir 20.

Griffin, James B.

1978 The Midlands and Northeastern United States. In Jesse D. Jennings, ed., *Ancient Native Americans,* pp. 221–79. San Francisco: W. H. Freeman.

Grim, John A.

1983 *The Shaman.* Norman: University of Oklahoma Press.

Grinnell, George B.

1907 Some Early Cheyenne Tales. *Journal of American Folklore* 20: 169–94.

1908 Some Early Cheyenne Tales, 2. *Journal of American Folklore* 21:269–320.

1918 Early Cheyenne Villages. *American Anthropologist* 20:359–80.

1919 A Buffalo Sweatlodge. *American Anthropologist* 21:361–75.

1922 The Medicine Wheel. *American Anthropologist* 24:299–310.

1923 *The Cheyenne Indians.* 2 vols. New Haven, Conn.: Yale University Press.

1926 *By Cheyenne Campfires.* New Haven, Conn.: Yale University Press.

1962 *Blackfoot Lodge Tales.* Lincoln: University of Nebraska Press.

Haas, Mary R.
1958   Algonkian-Ritwan: The End of a Controversy. *International Journal of American Linguistics* 24:159–73.
Halifax, Joan
1979   *Shamanic Voices*. New York: E. P. Dutton.
Hallowell, I.
1926   Bear Ceremonialism in the Northern Hemisphere. *American Anthropologist* 28:1–175.
Harp, Elmer, Jr.
1978   Pioneer Cultures of the Sub-Arctic and the Arctic. In Jesse D. Jennings, ed., *Ancient Native Americans*, pp. 95–129. San Francisco: W. H. Freeman.
Harrington, Mark R.
1921   *Religion and Ceremonies of the Lenape*. Indian Notes and Monographs, no. 19. New York: Museum of the American Indian, Heye Foundation.
Haug, James K., Jeanette E. Buehrig, John A. Moore, and James A. Sartain
1980   *Archaeological Excavations in the Highway 18 Right-of-Way, Fall River County, South Dakota, 1978–1979*. Fort Meade: South Dakota Archaeological Research Center.
Hester, James J.
1967   The Agency of Man in Animal Extinctions. In P. S. Martin and H. E. Wright, Jr., eds., *Pleistocene Extinctions*, pp. 169–92. New Haven, Conn.: Yale University Press.
Hickerson, Harold
1963   The Sociohistorical Significance of Two Chippewa Ceremonials. *American Anthropologist* 65:67–85.
Hoebel, E. A.
1978   *The Cheyennes*. New York: Holt, Rinehart & Winston.
Holmberg, Uno
1922   The Shaman Costume and Its Significance. *Annales Universitatis Fennicae Aboensis*, series B, 1(2):3–36.
1926   Über die Jagdriten der Nördlichen Völker Asiens und Europas. *Journal de la Société Finno-Ougrienne* 151:2–53.
Howard, James H.
1980   Discussion: Social Context of Late 19th and Early 20th Century Delaware Religion. In John H. Moore, ed., *Ethnology in Oklahoma*, pp. 153–61. Papers in Anthropology, vol. 21, no. 2.
Husted, Wilfred M.
1969   *Bighorn Canyon Archaeology*. Publications in Salvage Archaeology, no. 12. Lincoln: Smithsonian Institution River Basin Surveys.

Hyde, George E.
  1968   *Life of George Bent Written from His Letters.* Norman: University of Oklahoma Press.
Kalweit, Holger
  1984   *Traumzeit und Innerer Raum.* Bern: Scherz Verlag.
Keesing, F. M.
  1939   *The Menomini Indians of Wisconsin: A Study of Three Centuries of Cultural Contact and Change.* Memoirs of the American Philosophical Society, vol. 10. Philadelphia.
Kehoe, Thomas F.
  1973   *The Gull Lake Site: A Prehistoric Bison Drive Site in Southwestern Saskatchewan.* Milwaukee Public Museum Publications in Anthropology and History, no. 1.
Kehoe, Thomas F., and Alice B. Kehoe
  1968   Saskatchewan. In Warren W. Caldwell, ed., *The Northern Plains: A Symposium,* pp. 21–35. Center for Indian Studies, Rocky Mountain College, Occasional Papers, no. 1. Billings, Mont.
  1979   *Solstice-Aligned Boulder Configurations in Saskatchewan.* National Museum of Man, Mercury Series, Canadian Ethnology Service Paper no. 48. Ottawa: National Museum of Canada.
Klein, Richard
  1969   *Man and Culture in the Late Pleistocene. A Case Study.* San Francisco: Chandler Publishing Co.
Krauss, Michael E., and Victor K. Golla
  1981   Northern Athapaskan Languages. In June Helm, ed., *Subarctic,* pp. 67–85. *Handbook of North American Indians,* vol. 6. Washington, D.C.: Smithsonian Institution.
Kroeber, A. L.
  1900   Cheyenne Tales. *Journal of American Folklore* 13:161–90.
Krusche, Rolf
  1981   The Wabeno Cult as an Adversary of the Midewiwin. In Pieter Hovens, ed., *North American Indian Studies: European Contributions,* pp. 77–98. Göttingen: Edition Herodot.
Lehtisalo, T.
  1937   Der Tod und die Wiedergeburt des künftigen Schamanen. *Journal de la Société Finno-Ougrienne* 48:3–34.
Levin, M. G., and Potapov, L. B., eds.
  1964   *The Peoples of Siberia.* Chicago: University of Chicago Press.
Lommel, A.
  1967   *The World of the Early Hunters.* London: Evelyn, Adams & Mackay.
Lopez, Barry H.
  1978   *Of Wolves and Men.* New York: Charles Scribner's Sons.

Luckert, Karl W.
1975   *The Navajo Hunter Tradition.* Tucson: University of Arizona Press.

Ludwickson, John, Don Blakeslee, and John O'Shea
1981   *Missouri National Recreational River: Native American Cultural Resources.* Lincoln: Nebraska State Historical Society.

MacNeish, Richard S.
1962   The Great Lakes to the Barren Lands. In John M. Campbell, ed., *Prehistoric Cultural Relations Between the Arctic and Temperate Zones of North America,* pp. 140–42. Technical Paper no. 11. Montreal: Arctic Institute of North America.
1964   Investigations in Southwest Yukon: Archaeological Excavation, Comparisons and Speculations. In *Investigations in Southwest Yukon.* Papers of the Robert S. Peabody Foundation for Archaeology, vol. 6, no. 2. Andover, Mass.

Malouf, Carling, and Stuart Conner, eds.
1962   Panel Discussion on Buffalo Jumps. In *Symposium on Buffalo Jumps,* pp. 40–56. Montana Archaeological Society, Memoir no. 1. Missoula.

Mandoki, L.
1963   Asiatische Sternnamen. In V. Diószegi, ed., *Glaubenswelt und Folklore der Sibirischen Völker,* pp. 519–32. Budapest: Akademiai Kiado.

Marquis, T. B.
1967   *Wooden Leg.* Lincoln: University of Nebraska Press.

Maximilian, Prinz zu Wied
N.d.   *Reise in das Innere Nordamerika.* 2 vols. Munich: Lothar Borowsky.

Miller, Jay
1980   A Structural Analysis of the Delaware Big House Rite. In John H. Moore, ed., *Ethnology in Oklahoma,* pp. 107–33. Papers in Anthropology, vol. 21, no. 2. Norman.

Miyakawa, H. and A. Kollautz
1966   Zur Ur- und Vorgeschichte des Schamanismus. *Zeitschrift für Ethnologie* 91:161–93.

Mooney, J.
1907   The Cheyenne Indians. *Memoirs of the American Anthropological Association,* vol. 1, pt. 6:357–442.

Moore, John H.
1974   A Study of Religious Symbolism Among the Cheyenne Indians. Ph.D. dissertation. Ann Arbor, Mich.: University Microfilms International.
1984   Cheyenne Names and Cosmology. *American Ethnologist* 11: 291–312.

1986a *The Cheyenne Nation. A Social and Demographic History.* Lincoln: University of Nebraska Press, in press.

1986b The Ornithology of Cheyenne Religionists. *Plains Anthropologist* 31:177–92.

Müller, Werner
  1954 *Die Blaue Hütte.* Wiesbaden: Franz Steiner Verlag.
  1956 *Die Religionen der Waldlandindianer Nordamerikas.* Berlin: Dietrich Reimer Verlag.
  1982 *Amerika—Die Neue oder die Alte Welt?* Berlin: Dietrich Reimer Verlag.

Narr, K. J.
  1959 Bärenzeremoniell und Schamanismus in der Älteren Steinzeit Europas. *Saeculum,* pp. 233–72.
  1961 *Urgeschichte der Kultur.* Stuttgart: Alfred Kröner Verlag.
  1966 Geistiges Leben in der frühen und mittleren Altsteinzeit. In Karl J. Narr, ed., *Handbuch der Urgeschichte,* pp. 158–68. Berlin: Francke Verlag.

Neuman, Robert W.
  1975 *The Sonota Complex and Associated Sites on the Northern Great Plains.* Nebraska State Historical Society, Publications in Anthropology, no. 6. Lincoln.

Noble, William C.
  1981 Prehistory of the Great Slave Lake and Great Bear Lake Region. In June Helm, ed., *Subarctic,* pp. 97–106. *Handbook of North American Indians,* vol. 6. Washington, D.C.: Smithsonian Institution.

Obayashi, Taryo, and Ruediger Paproth
  1966 Das Bärenfest der Oroken auf Sachalin. *Zeitschrift für Ethnologie* 91:211–36.

Okladnikov, A. P.
  1964 Ancient Population of Siberia and its Culture. In M. G. Levin and L. P. Potapov, eds., *The Peoples of Siberia,* pp. 13–98. Chicago: University of Chicago Press.
  1970 *Yakutia.* Edited by Henry N. Michael. Montreal and London: McGill-Queens University Press.

Ossenberg, Nancy S.
  1974 Origins and Relationships of Woodland Peoples: The Evidence of Cranial Morphology. In Elden Johnson, ed., *Aspects of Upper Great Lakes Anthropology,* pp. 15–39. Saint Paul: Minnesota Historical Society.

Paproth, Hans Joachim
  1976 *Studien über das Bärenzeremoniell: I. Bärenjagdriten und Bärenfeste bei den tungusischen Völkern.* Uppsala: Tofters Tryckeri AB.

Paulson, Ivar
  1961   *Schutzgeister und Gottheiten des Wildes (der Jagdtiere und Fische) in Nordeurasien.* Uppsala: Almquist & Wiksell.
  1962   Die Religionen der Nordasiatischen (Sibirischen) Völker. In Ivar Paulson, Ake Hultkrantz and Karl Jettmar, eds., *Die Religionen Nordeurasiens und der Amerikanischen Arktis,* pp. 1–144. Stuttgart: W. Kohlhammer Verlag.
  1963   Zur Aufbewahrung der Tierknochen im Jagdritual der nordeurasischen Völker. In V. Diószegi, ed., *Glaubenswelt und Folklore der sibirischen Völker,* pp. 483–90. Budapest: Akademiai Kiado.
Pentland, David H.
  1978   A Historical Overview of Cree Dialects. In William Cowan, cd., *Papers of the Ninth Algonquian Conference,* pp. 104–26. Ottawa: Carleton University.
Petter, Rodolphe
  1915   *English-Cheyenne Dictionary.* Kettle Falls [Mont.].
  1952   *Cheyenne Grammar.* Newton: Mennonite Publication Office.
Pilling, Arnold R.
  1978   Yurok. In Robert F. Heizer, ed., *California,* pp. 137–54. *Handbook of North American Indians,* vol. 8. Washington, D.C.: Smithsonian Institution.
Powell, P. J.
  1969   *Sweet Medicine.* 2 vols. Norman: University of Oklahoma Press.
Prokofyeva, Y. D.
  1963   The Costume of the Enets Shaman. In Henry N. Michael, ed., *Studies in Siberian Shamanism,* pp. 124–56. Toronto: University of Toronto Press.
Quigg, Michael
  1981   *Social Structure at the Ross Glen Tipi Ring Site.* Medicine Hat, Ala.: Ethos Consultants.
Ray, Verne F.
  1945   The Contrary Behavior Pattern in American Indian Ceremonialism. *Southwestern Journal of Anthropology* 1:75–113.
Reeves, Brian O. K.
  1970   Culture Change in the Northern Plains, 1000 B.C.–A.D. 1000. 2 vols. Ph.D. thesis, University of Calgary.
  1973   The Concept of an Altithermal Cultural Hiatus in Northern Plains Prehistory. *American Anthropologist* 75:1221–53.
  1978   Head-Smashed-in: 5500 Years of Bison Jumping in the Alberta Plains. In Leslie B. Davis and Michael Wilson, eds., *Bison Procurement and Utilization: A Symposium,* pp. 151–74. *Plains Anthropologist* 23, Memoir 14.
Reher, Charles A.
  1983   Analysis of Spatial Structure in Stone Circle Sites. In Leslie B.

Davis, ed., *From Microcosm to Macrocosm: Advances in Tipi Ring Investigation and Interpretation,* pp. 193–222. *Plains Anthropologist* 28, Memoir 19.

Rhodes, Richard A., and Evelyn M. Todd
  1981   Subarctic Algonquian Languages. In June Helm, ed., *Subarctic,* pp. 52–66. *Handbook of North American Indians,* vol. 6. Washington, D.C.: Smithsonian Institution.

Ross, Herbert H.
  1970   The Ecological History of the Great Plains: Evidence from Grassland Insects. In Wakefield Dort, Jr., and J. Knox Jones, Jr., eds., *Pleistocene and Recent Environments of the Central Great Plains,* pp. 225–40. Lawrence: University of Kansas Press.

Rudy, Z.
  1962   *Ethnosoziologie sowjetischer Völker.* Bern: Francke Verlag.

Schaeffer, Claude E.
  1962   The Bison Drive of the Blackfoot Indians. In C. Malouf and S. Conner, eds., *Symposium on Buffalo Jumps,* pp. 28–34. Montana Archaeological Society, Memoir no. 1. Missoula.

Schlesier, Karl H.
  1968   Migration und Kulturwandel am Mittleren Missouri, 1550–1850. *Zeitschrift für Ethnologie* 93:23–48.

  1974   Action Anthropology and the Southern Cheyenne. *Current Anthropology* 15:277–83, 298–99.

  1975   Die Irokesenkriege und die Grosse Vertreibung, 1609–1656. *Zeitschrift für Ethnologie* 100:157–94.

  1976   Epidemics and Indian Middlemen: Rethinking the Wars of the Iroquois, 1609–1653. *Ethnohistory* 23:129–45.

  1980a   *The Blue Vision: Indians of the Central North American Grasslands,* Unfinished manuscript.

  1980b   Zum Weltbild einer neuen Kulturanthropologie. Erkenntnis und Praxis: Die Rolle der Action Anthropology. *Zeitschrift für Ethnologie* 105:32–66.

  1981   Tsistsistas-Praxis im Tsistsistas-Universum, 1969–1980. In H. P. Duerr, ed., *Der Wissenschaftler und das Irrationale,* 1:143–53. Frankfurt: Syndikat.

  1982   Gedanken ueber den Tsistsistas (Cheyenne) Schamanismus— Eine Reinterpretation. In Rolf Gehlen und Bernd Wolf, eds., *Festschrift Werner Müller,* pp. 121–36. Berlin: Karin Kramer Verlag.

  1983   Anmerkungen ueber Tsistsistas (Cheyenne) Hemaneh und Hohnuhka oder die Coincidentia Oppositorum. In. H. P. Duerr, ed., *Sehnsucht nach dem Ursprung,* pp. 239–49. Frankfurt: Syndikat.

Schneider, Fred A.
1983   Artifact Distribution at Tipi Ring Sites: A Cautionary Tale. In
        Leslie B. Davis, ed., *From Microcosm to Macrocosm: Advances in
        Tipi Ring Investigation and Interpretation*, pp. 93–100. *Plains
        Anthropologist* 28, Memoir 19.
Semenov, S. A.
1964   *Prehistoric Technology*. London: Cory, Adams and Mackay.
Shirokogoroff, S. M.
1929   *Social Organization of the Northern Tungus*. Shanghai: Commer-
        cial Press
1935   *Psychomental Complex of the Tungus*. London: Kegan Paul,
        Trench, Trübner.
Slawik, A.
1952   Zum Problem des Bärenfestes bei den Ainu und Giljaken:
        Kultur und Sprache. *Wiener Beitraege zur Kulturgeschichte und
        Linguistik* 9:189–203.
Snow, Dean R.
1978   Late Prehistory of the East Coast. In Bruce Trigger, ed., *North-
        east*, pp. 58–69. *Handbook of North American Indians*, vol. 15.
        Washington, D.C.: Smithsonian Institution.
Speck, Frank G.
1919   Penobscot Shamanism. *Memoirs of the American Anthropological
        Association* 6:236–98.
1931   *A Study of the Delaware Indian Big House Ceremony*. Publications
        of the Pennsylvania Historical Commission, vol. 2. Harrisburg.
1945   *The Celestial Bear Comes Down to Earth*. Scientific Publications,
        no. 7. Reading, Pa.: Reading Public Museum and Art Gallery.
Stanford, Dennis J.
1978   The Jones-Miller Site: An Example of Hell Gap Bison Procure-
        ment. In Leslie B. Davis and Michael Wilson, eds., *Bison Pro-
        curement and Utilization: A Symposium*, pp. 90–97. *Plains An-
        thropologist* 23, Memoir 14.
Stands in Timber, J., and M. Liberty
1972   *Cheyenne Memoirs*. Lincoln: University of Nebraska Press.
Sternberg, Leo
1905   Die Religion der Giljaken. *Archiv für Religionswissenschaft* 8:
        244–74, 456–73.
Straus, Anne S.
1976   *Being Human in the Cheyenne Way*. Ph.D. dissertation. Ann Ar-
        bor, Mich.: University Microfilms International.
1978   The Meaning of Death in Northern Cheyenne Culture. *Plains
        Anthropologist* 23:1–6.
Syms, E. Leigh
1977   Cultural Ecology and Ecological Dynamics of the Ceramic Pe-

riod in Southwestern Manitoba. *Plains Anthropologist* 22, Memoir 12.

1979   The Devil's Lake-Sourisford Burial Complex on the Northeastern Plains. *Plains Anthropologist* 24:283–308.

1981   The Arvilla Burial Complex: A Re-Assessment. Paper presented at the 39th Plains Anthropological Conference, Bismarck, N. Dak.

Taksami, T. M.

1963   Zu den alten religiösen Riten und Verboten der Nivchen (Giljaken). In V. Diószegi, ed., *Glaubenswelt und Folklore der Sibirischen Völker*, pp. 437–52. Budapest: Akademiai Kiado.

Tolstoy, Paul

1958   The Archaeology of the Lena Basin and Its New World Relationships. Parts 1 and 2. *American Antiquity* 23:397–418; 24: 63–81.

1975   From the Old World to the New World via Bering Strait. In Shirley Gorenstein, ed., *North America*, pp. 165–85. New York: St. Martin's Press.

Tuck, James A.

1978   Regional Cultural Development, 3000–300 B.C. In Bruce Trigger, ed., *Northeast*, pp. 28–43. *Handbook of North American Indians*, vol. 15. Washington, D.C.: Smithsonian Institution.

Vasilevich, G. M.

1963a   Early Concepts About the Universe Among Evenks. In Henry N. Michael, ed., *Studies in Siberian Shamanism*, pp. 46–83. Toronto: University of Toronto Press.

1963b   Erwerbung der Schamanenfähigkeiten bei den Ewenken (Tungusen). In V. Diószegi, ed., *Glaubenswelt und Folklore der Sibirischen Völker*, pp. 369–80. Budapest: Akademiai Kiado.

1963c   Schamanengesänge der Ewenken (Tungusen). In V. Diószegi, ed., *Glaubenswelt und Folklore der Sibirischen Völker*, pp. 381–404. Budapest: Akademiai Kiado.

Vereshchagin, N. K.

1967   Primitive Hunters and Pleistocene Extinction in the Soviet Union. In P. S. Martin and H. E. Wright, eds., *Pleistocene Extinctions*, pp. 365–98. New Haven, Conn.: Yale University Press.

Waterman, T. T.

1920   Yurok Geography. *University of California Publications in American Archaeology and Ethnology* 16(5):177–315.

Waterman, T. T., and A. L. Kroeber

1938   The Kepel Fish Dam. *University of California Publications in American Archaeology and Ethnology* 35(6):49–80.

Watrall, Charles R.

1974   Subsistence Pattern Change at the Cambria Site: A Review and

Hypothesis. In Elden Johnson, ed., *Aspects of Upper Great Lakes Anthropology*, pp. 138–42. St. Paul: Minnesota Historical Society.

Wedel, Waldo R.
1961 *Prehistorical Man on the Great Plains*. Norman: University of Oklahoma Press.

Wendland, Wayne M.
1978 Holocene Man in North America: The Ecological Setting and Climatic Background. *Plains Anthropologist* 23:273–87.

Wissler, Clark
1917 *The American Indian*. New York: Macmillan.

Wood, Raymond W.
1967 *An Interpretation of Mandan Culture History*. Bulletin 198, Bureau of American Ethnology, Smithsonian Institution.

Wright, Gary A.
1982 Notes on Chronological Problems on the Northwestern Plains and Adjacent High Country. *Plains Anthropologist* 27:145–60.

Wright, James V.
1967 *The Laurel Tradition and the Middle Woodland Period*. National Museums of Canada Bulletin 217, Anthropological Series 79. Ottawa.

1972a *Ontario Prehistory*. Ottawa: National Museums of Canada, Archaeological Survey of Canada, National Museum of Man.

1972b *The Shield Archaic*. National Museums of Canada, National Museum of Man, Publications in Archaeology, no. 3. Ottawa.

1981 Prehistory of the Canadian Shield. In June Helm, ed., *Subarctic*, pp. 86–96. *Handbook of North American Indians*, vol. 6. Washington, D.C.: Smithsonian Institution.

Zotz, L. F.
1958 Die Altsteinzeitliche Besiedlung der Alpen und deren geistige und wirtschaftliche Hintergründe. *Sitzungsberichte der Physikalisch-Medizinischen Sozietät zu Erlangen* 78:76–101.

Index

Abnaki: 34, 36, 176
Action anthropology: xvi
Agan (Khant, Mansi, "doll," used to keep soul of deceased): 29
Agdy (Evenk term for thunder spirit): 21, 26
Ainu: 32
Algonquian: 20, 34, 44, 51, 52, 59, 72, 79, 132, 138, 151, 152, 160, 162, 164–66, 170, 171, 188, 189; Proto-, 51, 162, 165, 166; Proto-Eastern, 160, 165–66; Eastern, 165–66, 171; Central, 71, 132, 149, 162, 165, 175; Plains, 132, 162, 165–66
Algonquin: 34, 165
Amaka sheveki (Evenk term for Supreme Being): 21, 31
Anan (Evenk shaman's journey with soul of deceased): 29
Androgyny: 14–15, 27, 41, 66–73, 78
Anqa'ken-etinvilan (Koryak spirit of sea): 27
Apache: 129
Arapaho: 52, 132, 166
Archaic: Laurentian, 158, 164; Maritime, 157, 158, 164; Shield, 44, 152, 155–56, 158–63, 165
Arikara: 180
Artgeist: 8, 27, 38; of bear, 9, 118; of wolf, 9, 82, 126; of salmon, 167
Arvilla complex: 138
Asiktal (Evenk term for stars): 21
Assiniboin: 34, 58, 66
Athapaskan: 34, 75, 129–30
Atonoom (Tsis. term for world below): 4–6; *atonoomhetaneo* (lit. "world below people"), 147
Atsina: 52, 132, 166
Avonlea phase: 113–15, 127, 128–30, 132, 135; as Athapaskan speakers, 129; intro-

duction into Plains of bow and arrow, 129–30
Ax-xea (Tsis. term for giant serpent): 77; food of *maiyun*, 99
Ayami (Nanay term for tutelary spirit): 38–39; *syven* (helping spirit), 38

Bear: as ancestor, 25, 32–33; burial, 30; ceremonialism, 34, 172–79; cosmic, 25, 33, 50, 175–79; selecting dreamer, 178; protector of earth spirit, 33, 118; festival, 33, 34, 37, 174–79; as game owner, 175, 176; as messenger, 175; as spirit helper of shaman, 38–39; associated with world below, 8, 33, 118
Bega (Evenk term for the spirit of the moon): 21; represented in ceremony, 24
Beothuk: 164
Besant phase: 113–15, 128, 129, 132–40, 163, 165; Eastern subphase (Tsistsistas), 135–44, 165; Western subphase (Blackfeet), 135, 139–40, 165; as Algonquian speakers, 135; cultural interpretation, 144–50; transition atlatl to arrow, 129, 134
Black: associated with earth spirit, 23, 93–94, 118, 121; used in Massaum ceremony, 93–109; in Okipa ceremony, 184; in design on shaman's drum, 40, 177; in sweat-lodge symbolism, 65; in thunder-spirit painting, 93, 121; in Unami and Munsee-Mahican big-house ceremony, 177–79; representing part of the universe, 7, 93, 120, 121; associated with Yurok culture hero, 169
Blackduck tradition: 114–15, 131–32, 166; as Algonquian speakers, 132
Blackfeet: 54, 58, 166; origin in western Besant subphase, 135, 139–40, 165

208   THE WOLVES OF HEAVEN

Blue: representing Supreme Being, 7;
representing upper sky region, 21, 167;
star, 84, 104–105; star design in Massaum ceremony, 84, 94, 104–109,
121–24
Bua (Udegey and Orochi term for the
spirit who protects animals): 27
Budtode (Enet term for sky shaman): 41,
70; dyano, savode, other categories of
shamans, 41
Buga (or dunne, Evenk term for universe, or "original land"): 21
Bugady mushun (Evenk term for earth
spirit, also eneke, "grandmother"): 22;
Dunne enin, 22, 27
Bukit (Evenk term for world below): 21
Burial: of animals, 10, 26, 29, 142, 143,
145–48; sites marking ethnic boundaries, 21; in stages, 10, 29, 62
Buryat: 26, 33, 37

Chukchi: 27, 30–32, 36, 39, 41, 67
Chum (Evenk term for circular tent): 21,
23
Cobun-po'gil (Yukagir spirit of the sea):
27
Cognitive anthropology: xvi
Coincidentia oppositorum: 14, 66–73
Corn: 11
Cosmic pole or tree: as axis mundi, 20,
21, 91–92, 177; in central position
within lodge, 20, 23–24, 90–92; in
Massaum ceremony, 80, 90–92; in
Munsee-Mahican big-house cere-
mony, 177–78; as sacred arrows' pole,
21, 92; as shaman's ladder, 20, 21, 92;
as symbolic representation of Supreme
Being, 80, 91
Cosmological singularity: 7, 93, 120, 190
Cree: 34, 58, 165, 166
Crow: 80

Dakota: 66, 138
Darpe (Evenk term for a gallery during
a ceremony): 23–24
Death, as long process: 9–10, 28–29
Delaware: 34, 171; see also Munsee-
Mahican, Unami
Delyacha, or dylacha (Evenk term for

spirit of the sun): 21, 26; represented
in ceremony, 24
Devil's Lake–Sourisford complex: 137
Dhegiha Sioux: 75–76
Dolgan: 21, 26
Domestication, self-domestication: 10–11
Duluga buga (Evenk term for middle
world): 22
Dyabdar (Evenk term for giant serpent):
24

Eagle: bone whistle, 60; as messenger,
26, 33; in Mandan Okipa ceremony,
181–87; as first shaman, 33; associated
with Supreme Being, 8, 33; as tutelary
spirit, 40; associated with world
above, 8, 33
E'ehyo'm (Tsis. term for shamans who
were able to kill over distance): 16
Ehōneheonevestoz (Tsis. term for shamanism): 14
Ehōnestoz (Tsis. term for witchcraft): 18
Ehyophstah (Tsis. "yellow hair on top
woman," daughter of thunder and
earth spirits): 12, 54, 62, 82, 83; account of, 76–79; in Massaum ceremony, 83–84, 89–109; as master of
animals, 78, 104–109; as blue star, 84,
104–109, 121–25
Eksheri sheveki (Evenk term for spirit of
lower sky region): 21, 27
Emämanstoon (Tsis. "He [the Supreme
Being] created everything"): 7; reenacted in Massaum ceremony, 7,
92–94, 120
Emaom (Tsis. term for small sweat
lodge, from ema, "concealed," and
om, lodge): 63
Enet: 33, 40, 41, 70
Engdekit (Evenk "place of prohibition,"
river of shamans): 21, 33
Epkachan (Evenk term for mythical reindeer): 31
Esceheman (Tsis. "our grandmother,"
spirit of deep earth): 5, 8, 82; associated with animals, 8; protector of animal spirits, 9; represented in painted
buffalo skull, 6, 93–94, 121; consecrat-
ing corn plant, 11; as instructor in

214

THE WOLVES OF HEAVEN

Valley Phase: 132–33; as Caddoan speakers, 133
Vanován (Tsis. term for herb used by *hohnuhka* society): 73
Vision quest: 13
Vō (Tsis. term for Venus): 99
Voh'kis (Tsis. term for kit fox): 83, 84; as manifestation of blue star, 84, 98; as manifestation of Ehyophstah, 84; in Massaum ceremony, 97–109
Vonhäom (Tsis. term for sweat lodge, from *vonhä*, "to lose by heat"): 16, 63–65; used by *maiyun* (spirits), 77; ending Massaum ceremony, 109
Vonoom (Tsis. term for the original order of universe): 7, 9, 24; excludes domesticated life forms, 10–11
Vós (Tsis. term for sacred mound): 144; as Besant burial mound, 141–47
Votostoom (Tsis. term for four-layered middle zone, or middle world): 4–6; represented by shamans, 15–16
Voxpenako (Tsis. "white bear," term for *Artgeist* of bear species): 9, 118

Wabeno (category of central Algonquian shamans): 71–72; *wabeno* ("it dawns"), *wabanowiwin* ("men of the dawn"), 72
Wavenock: 36
We'sona-me'getol (Yurok term for Supreme Being): 167
White: color associated with Supreme Being, 23; buffalo sacrificed to Supreme Being, 63; buffalo hide of Omaha, 76; bear as *Artgeist*, 9, 118; deer hides of Yurok, 170; color of equipment used by earth spirit, 77; paint used in Massaum ceremony, 93–109; sage used in Massaum, 91–109; reindeer sacrificed to Supreme Being, 25; star, 84–87; color of Tsis. master wolf (female), 82, 95–109; paint used in Okipa ceremony, 183; color used in Unami and Munsee-Mahican bighouse ceremonies, 177–79; color representing part of the universe, 7, 120, 121, 177

Wiyot: 166; linguistically Ritwan, 166
Wohpekumeu: Yurok name for culture hero, 167–71; initiated salmon runs, 167
Wolf: as ancestor, 32; as representation of Tsis. earth spirit, 84, 98; associated with near sky space, 8; as changeling, 32; *omotome*, 12; fur on head band, 170; fur on medicine lance, 58; as messenger, 26, 77, 82; as instructor in hunting way, 82, 98; gamekeeper of spirit herds, 82, 98; as master hunter, 35, 82, 97–109; in Massaum ceremony, 97–109; robe worn by Mandan Lone Man performer, 183; as representation of Tsis. thunder spirit, 84, 98; songs, 3, 82–83, 96, 99, 103; as tutelary spirit, 12, 38, 40; treatment of skull, 30

Xaenone (Tsis. term for rare solitary red Plains wolf, also considered to be wolf *maiyun* or *Artgeist*): 9

Yakut: 26, 27, 31, 37, 131
Ya-nebya (Nentsy term for earth spirit): 27
Yayan (Evenk term for shaman, *yaya*, "to perform by the campfire," also referring to drum): 36
Ylunda kotta (Selkup term for earth spirit): 27, 33
Young Wolves (Tsis. woman's society assisting in Massaum): 82, 84, 89–109, 147
Yukagir: 23, 27, 29, 30, 40, 189
Yurak: 24
Yurok: 152, 166–71; linguistically Ritwan, 166; Kepel ceremonies, 167–71, 189

Zemaheonevsz (Tsis. "mysterious one," term for shaman): 14; *zemaheonevesso* (pl., shamans as group), 14, 65
Zevonhäevesso (Tsis. term for priests as group): 14

HOMOSEXUALITY
BIBLIOGRAPHY:

Second Supplement, 1976-1982

by
WILLIAM PARKER

The Scarecrow Press, Inc.
Metuchen, N.J., & London
1985

Library of Congress Cataloging in Publication Data

Parker, William, 1921-
    Homosexuality bibliography. Second supplement,
1976-1982.

    Includes index.
    1. Homosexuality--Bibliography. I. Title.
Z7164.S42P34   1985   [HQ76.25]   016.3067'66 84-20299
ISBN 0-8108-1753-5

CONTENTS

PREFACE

With this second supplement, covering the years 1976 through 1982, my bibliography on homosexuality now consists of three volumes listing over 10,000 items. All items refer to works written in English or translated into English.

This volume employs the same format that was used in the earlier works. Most of its sections are as comprehensive and complete as I have been able to make them. However, because several thousand items could have been listed for each of the sections on newspaper articles and articles in gay publications, these categories are highly selective. The articles included were chosen, on the one hand, because they contain information, deal with problems and issues, or reflect ideas and attitudes that are of interest and importance to both the general public and the gay community; and, on the other hand, because of the availability of the publications in which they appear. Where the titles of articles in these two sections did not sufficiently indicate their content, summary statements, noted by the absence of quotation marks, have been substituted.

The section on "Literary Works" found in the two earlier volumes has been omitted here. The Scarecrow Press publication in 1982 of the second edition of Ian Young's comprehensive bibliography entitled The Male Homosexual in Literature (see item no. 377) and the 1981 release by Naiad Press of the third edition of The Lesbian in Literature (no. 223) made the inclusion of such a section unnecessary.

The amount of material published on the subject of homosexuality has increased with each passing year. In general, the quality of that material has also improved. Still, there is a need to remain cautious and critical in the use and evaluation of this material.

It is hoped that this latest supplement will prove useful and timely for all those who use it, whether they be general readers or research specialists.

BOOKS (NON-FICTION)

ANTHOLOGIES

1) Batchelor, Edward Jr. (ed.). Homosexuality and Ethics. New York: Pilgrim Press, 1980. 261 pp. (See nos. 472, 668, 672, 674, 675, 713, 743, 764, 772, 807, 865, 869, 927, 935, 949, 952, 977, 1014, 1025, 1031, 1057, 1058, 1067, and 1092.)

2) Beck, Evelyn T. (ed.). Nice Jewish Girls: A Lesbian Anthology. Watertown, Mass.: Persephone Press, 1982. 286 pp. (See nos. 677, 688, 746, 786, 877, 890, 920, 979, 993, and 1091.)

3) Berzon, Betty, and Robert Leighton (eds.). Positively Gay. Millbrae, Cal.: Celestial Arts Press, 1979. 219 pp. (See nos. 660, 685, 698, 725, 751, 754, 775, 859, 866, 891, 905, 914, 926, 933, 1005, and 1060.)

4) Boldt, Steven (comp.). While Aggressively Waiting: A Sequel to Static Creation. Ithaca, N.Y.: Cornell University Press, 1978. 145 pp.

5) Cedar and Nelly (eds.). A Woman's Touch: An Anthology of Lesbian Eroticism and Sensuality for Women Only. Eugene, Ore.: WomanShare Books, 1979. 157 pp.

6) Chesebro, James W. (ed.). Gayspeak: Gay Male and Lesbian Communication. New York: Pilgrim Press, 1981. 367 pp. (See nos. 703, 716, 722-24, 745, 750, 759, 769, 780, 797, 804, 820, 821, 860, 874, 945, 953, 956, 965, 967, 1004, 1034, and 1036.)

7) Crew, Louie (ed.). The Gay Academic. Palm Springs, Cal.: ETC Publications, 1978. 444 pp. (See nos. 673, 699, 738, 740, 753, 762, 767, 781, 783, 787, 789, 802, 862, 868, 896, 902, 903, 976, 999, 1008, 1045, 1047, and 1053.)

8)   Cruikshank, Margaret (ed.). The Lesbian Path: 37
      Lesbian Writers Share Their Personal Experiences,
      Viewpoints, Traumas, and Joys. Monterey, Cal.: An-
      gel Press, 1980. 248 pp.

9)   _____ (ed.). Lesbian Studies: Present and Future.
      Old Westbury, N.Y.: Feminist Press, 1982. 286 pp.
      (See nos. 678, 684, 705, 728, 747, 748, 763, 773, 777,
      785, 790, 826, 843, 919, 921, 932, 944, 982, 985,
      1003, 1040, and 1099.)

10)   Dyer, Richard (ed.). Gays and Films. London: Brit-
      ish Film Institute, 1977. 73 pp. (See nos. 765 and
      1027.)

11)   Faderman, Lillian, and Brigitte Eriksson (eds. and
      trans.). Lesbian-Feminism in Turn-of-the-Century
      Germany. Tallahassee, Fla.: Naiad Press, 1980.
      97 pp. (See no. 1013.)

12)   Fone, Byrne R. S. (ed.). Hidden Heritage: History
      and the Gay Imagination: An Anthology. New York:
      Irvington Publications, 1979. 323 pp. (See no. 1055.)

13)   Gay Left Collective (eds.). Homosexuality: Power and
      Politics. London: Allison and Busby, 1980. 223 pp.
      (See nos. 666, 687, 715, 718, 731, 737, 757, 798,
      822, 824, 834, 858, 925, 947, 1030, 1075, and 1076.)

14)   Gonsiorek, John C. (ed.). Homosexuality and Psycho-
      therapy: A Practitioner's Handbook of Affirmative Mod-
      els. New York: Haworth Press, 1982. 212 pp. (Sep-
      arate printing of vol. 7, nos. 2 and 3, of the Journal
      of Homosexuality, 1981-82. See nos. 2643, 2644, 2645,
      2710, 2711, 2713, 2779, 2818-20, 2853, 2909, 2943,
      2954, 2968, 2978, 3003, 3011, 3056, 3057, and 3074.)

15)   Grier, Barbara, and Coletta Reid (eds.). The Lavender
      Herring: Lesbian Essays from "The Ladder." Balti-
      more: Diana Press, 1976. 357 pp. (See nos. 702,
      721, 735, 899, 973, 1028, and 1087.)

16)   Harry, Joseph, and Man Singh Das (eds.). Homosex-
      uality in International Perspective. New Delhi: Vikas
      Publishing House, 1980. 134 pp. (See nos. 696, 707,
      758, 850, 898, 907, 950, 974, and 1082.)

17) Jackson, Ed, and Stan Persky (eds.). Flaunting It! A Decade of Gay Journalism from "The Body Politic." Toronto: Pink Triangle Press, 1982. 320 pp. (See nos. 676, 693, 755, 817, 830, 855, 917, 998, 1050, 1062, and 1066.)

18) Jay, Karla, and Allen Young (eds.). Lavender Culture. New York: Jove Publications, 1979. 493 pp. (See nos. 671, 681, 710, 727, 736, 760, 774, 792, 816, 852, 857, 863, 882, 893, 915, 941, 1023, 1029, 1033, 1048, 1086, 1094, and 1096.)

19) Keysor, Charles W. (ed.). What You Should Know About Homosexuality. Grand Rapids, Mich.: Zondervan Publishing House, 1979. 254 pp.

20) Knutson, Donald C. (ed.). Homosexuality and the Law. New York: Haworth Press, 1980. 160 pp. (Separate printing of vol. 5, nos. 1 and 2, of the Journal of Homosexuality, Fall-Winter 1979-80. See nos. 2660, 2844, 2859, 2900, 2959, 3026, 3060, 3064, 3118, and 3160.)

21) Koertge, Noretta (ed.). The Nature and Causes of Homosexuality: A Philosophic and Scientific Inquiry. New York: Haworth Press, 1981. 150 pp. (Separate printing of vol. 6, no. 4, of the Journal of Homosexuality, 1980-81. See nos. 2673, 2738, 2741, 3083, and 3135.)

22) Levine, Martin P. (ed.). Gay Men: The Sociology of Male Homosexuality. New York: Harper and Row, 1979. 346 pp. (See nos. 662, 744, 809, 810, 832, 839, 908, 909, 936, 954, 989, 997, 1006, 1016, 1017, 1043, 1073, 1079, 1093, 1100, 2891, and 2918.)

23) Licata, Salvatore J., and Robert P. Peterson (eds.). Historical Perspectives on Homosexuality. New York: Haworth Press, 1981. 224 pp. (Separate printing of vol. 6, nos. 1 and 2, of the Journal of Homosexuality, 1980-81. See nos. 2691, 2727, 2757, 2767, 2809, 2832, 2893, 2911, 2924, 2991, 3025, 3035, and 3170.)

24) Marmor, Judd (ed.). Homosexual Behavior: A Modern Reappraisal. New York: Basic Books, 1980. 416 pp. (See nos. 689, 717, 756, 811, 827, 840, 872, 880, 888,

923, 942, 955, 964, 981, 996, 1018, 1020, 1021, 1038, 1063, and 1072.)

25) Mitchell, Pam (ed.). Pink Triangle: Radical Perspectives on Gay Liberation. Boston: Alyson Publications, 1980. 192 pp. (See nos. 690, 779, 795, 796, 808, 885, 913, 939, 994, 1032, and 1088.)

26) Paul, William, and James D. Weinrich (eds.). Homosexuality: Social, Psychological, and Biological Issues: Final Report of the Society for the Psychological Study of Social Issues' Task Force on Sexual Orientation. Beverly Hills, Cal. : Sage Publications, 1982. 416 pp. (See nos. 734, 749, 752, 793, 805, 823, 837, 889, 900, 910, 969-71, 975, 1001, 1052, 1059, and 1081.)

27) Plummer, Kenneth (ed.). The Making of the Modern Homosexual. Totowa, N. J. : Barnes and Noble, 1981. 280 pp. (See nos. 691, 778, 887, 924, 931, 980, and 1077.)

28) Richmond, Len, and Gary Noguera (eds.). The New Gay Liberation Book: Writings and Photographs About Gay (Men's) Liberation. Palo Alto, Cal. : Ramparts Press, 1979. 224 pp. (See nos. 665, 776, 851, 901, 948, 954, 988, 1000, 1035, and 1078.)

29) Samois Collective (eds.). Coming to Power: Writings and Graphics on Lesbian S /M. Rev. ed. Boston: Alyson Publications, 1982. 240 pp.

30) Stambolian, George, and Elaine Marks (eds.). Homosexualities and French Literature: Cultural Contexts, Critical Texts. Ithaca, N. Y. : Cornell University Press, 1979. 387 pp. (See no. 695.)

31) Tsang, Dan (ed.). The Age Taboo: Gay Male Sexuality, Power, and Consent, Boston: Alyson Publications, 1981. 278 pp. (See nos. 664, 692, 714, 795, 808, 867, 940, 943, 958, 987, 990, 1012, 1065, and 1098.)

32) Twiss, Harold L. (ed.). Homosexuality and the Christian Faith: A Symposium. Valley Forge, Pa. : Judson Press, 1978. 110 pp. (See nos. 680, 949, 1621, 1622, 1684, and 1705.)

33) Vida, Ginny (ed.). Our Right to Love: A Lesbian Resource Book. Englewood Cliffs, N. J. : Prentice-

Hall, 1976. 319 pp. (See nos. 661, 669, 686, 742,
803, 812, 818, 854, 861, 897, 918, 937, 957, 962, 966,
986, 995, 1019, 1022, 1051, 1061, and 1069.)

34) Walter, Aubrey (ed.). Come Together: The Years of
Gay Liberation. New York: Gay Men's Press, 1980.
224 pp.

35) Warren, Carol A. B. (ed.). Sexualities: Encounters,
Identities and Relationships. Beverly Hills, Cal.:
Sage Publications, 1976. 136 pp.

36) Wolfe, Susan J., and Julia P. Stanley (eds.). The
Coming Out Stories. Watertown, Mass.: Persephone
Press, 1980. 251 pp. (See no. 741.)

37) Ziebold, Thomas O., and John E. Mongeon (eds.).
Alcoholism and Homosexuality. New York: Haworth
Press, 1982. 128 pp. (Separate printing of vol. 7,
no. 4, of the Journal of Homosexuality, 1981-82. See
nos. 2674, 2709, 2754, 2966, 2990, 3007, 3114, 3183,
3194, and 3195.)

BIOGRAPHICAL AND AUTOBIOGRAPHICAL WORKS

38) Adair, Casey, and Nancy Adair (eds.). Word Is Out. New
York: Dell Publishing Co., 1978. 337 pp. (See also
Appendix II, PBS.)

39) Agnos, Peter. The Queer Dutchman. Translated from
the Dutch by Michael Jelstra. New York: Green Eagle
Press, 1979. 138 pp.

40) Arce, Hector. The Secret Life of Tyrone Power: The
Drama of a Bisexual in the Spotlight. New York: William Morrow, 1979. 317 pp.

41) Arthurs, Peter. With Brendan Behan: A Personal
Memoir. New York: St. Martin's, 1981. 320 pp.

42) Ashton, Dore, and Denise B. Hare. Rosa Bonheur: A
Life and a Legend. New York: Viking Press, 1981.
206 pp.

43) Baetz, Ruth. Lesbian Crossroads: Personal Stories of
Lesbians' Struggles and Triumphs. New York: William
Morrow, 1980. 273 pp.

44) Baskett, Edward E. Entrapped: An Accused Homosexual Looks at American Justice. Westport, Conn.:
   Lawrence Hill and Co., 1976. 151 pp.

45) Basse, Laura (pseud.). An Uncertain Memory: The
   True Story of an Uncommon Marriage. New York:
   William Morrow, 1982. 262 pp.

46) Bell, Arthur. Kings Don't Mean a Thing: The John
   Knight Murder Case. New York: William Morrow,
   1978. 228 pp.

47) Birkin, Andrew. J. M. Barrie and the Lost Boys: The
   Love Story That Gave Birth to Peter Pan. New York:
   Clarkson Potter, 1979. 323 pp.

48) Boldt, Steven. Static Creation: A Metaphor of Meta-
   morphosing Lust. Ithaca, N. Y.: Static Creation Press,
   1978. 289 pp.

49) Borhek, Mary V. My Son Eric. New York: Pilgrim
   Press, 1979. 160 pp.

50) Bosworth, Patricia. Montgomery Clift. New York:
   Harcourt Brace Jovanovich, 1978. 438 pp.

51) Boyd, Malcolm. Take Off the Masks. Garden City,
   N. Y.: Doubleday, 1978. 160 pp.

52) Brogan, Jim. Jack and Jim: A Personal Journal of
   the '70s. Bolinas, Cal.: Equanimity Press, 1982.
   174 pp.

53) Brome, Vincent. Havelock Ellis: Philosopher of Sex.
   London: Routledge and Kegan Paul, 1979. 271 pp.

54) Brown, Howard. Familiar Faces, Hidden Lives: The
   Story of Homosexual Men in America Today. New York:
   Harcourt Brace Jovanovich, 1976. 246 pp.

55) Carpenter, Humphrey. W. H. Auden: A Biography.
   Boston: Houghton Mifflin, 1981. 496 pp.

56) Cassidy, Jules, and Angela Stewart-Park. We're Here:
   Conversations with Lesbian Women. New York: Quartet Books, 1977. 152 pp.

57) Chalon, Jean. Portrait of a Seductress: The World of Natalie Barney. Translated from the French by Carol Barko. New York: Crown Publishers, 1979. 248 pp.

58) Chapman, A. H. Harry Stack Sullivan: His Life and His Work. New York: Putnam's, 1976. 280 pp.

59) Chapman, Graham. A Liar's Autobiography. New York: Methuen, 1981. 240 pp.

60) Crisp, Quentin. How to Become a Virgin. New York: St Martin's, 1982. 192 pp.

61) Curtis, Anthony. Somerset Maugham. New York: Macmillan, 1977. 216 pp.

62) Dawson, Terry. My Heaven to Hell. New York: Vantage Press, 1979.

63) Deford Frank. Big Bill Tilden. New York: Simon and Schuster, 1976. 286 pp.

64) Denneny, Michael. Lovers: The Story of Two Men. New York: Avon Books, 1979. 159 pp.

65) Dobkin, Alix. Alix Dobkin's Adventures in Women's Music. Preston Hollow, N.Y.: Tomato Publications, 1979.

66) Douglas, Alfred B. Oscar Wilde and Myself. New York: AMS Press, 1979. (Reprint of work published in 1914.)

67) Driberg, Tom. Ruling Passions. New York: Stein and Day, 1977. 271 pp.

68) Ebert, Alan. The Homosexuals. New York: Macmillan, 1977. 332 pp.

69) Faber, Doris. The Life of Lorena Hickok: E. R.'s [Eleanor Roosevelt's] Friend. New York: William Morrow, 1980. 384 pp.

70) Finney, Brian. Christopher Isherwood: A Critical Biography. New York: Oxford University Press, 1979. 336 pp.

71) Fricke, Aaron. Reflections of a Rock Lobster: A
    Story About Growing Up Gay. Boston: Alyson Publica-
    tions, 1981. 116 pp.

72) Fryer, Jonathan. Isherwood: A Biography. Garden
    City, N. Y.: Doubleday, 1977. 304 pp.

73) Furbank, Philip N. E. M. Forster: A Life. New
    York: Harcourt Brace Jovanovich, 1978. 359 pp.

74) Galana, Laurel, and Gina Covina. The New Lesbians:
    Interviews with [21] Women Across the United States
    and Canada. Berkeley, Cal.: Moon Books, 1977.
    223 pp.

75) Gibson, Clifford G., and Mary J. Risher. By Her Own
    Admission: A Lesbian Mother's Fight to Keep Her Son.
    Garden City, N. Y.: Doubleday, 1977. 276 pp.

76) Gibson, E. Lawrence. Get Off My Ship: Ensign Ver-
    non E. Berg III and the United States Navy. New York:
    Avon Books, 1978. 385 pp.

77) Ginsberg, Allen. Journals: Early Fifties -- Early
    Sixties. Edited by Gordon Ball. New York: Grove
    Press, 1977. 302 pp.

78) Graves, Richard. A. E. Housman: The Scholar Poet.
    New York: Scribner's, 1980. 304 pp.

79) Greif, Martin. The Gay Book of Days. Secaucus,
    N. J.: Lyle Stuart, 1982. 217 pp.

80) Grier, Barbara, and Coletta Reid (eds.). Lesbian
    Lives: Biographies of Women from "The Ladder."
    Oakland, Cal.: Diana Press, 1976. 432 pp.

81) Grosskurth, Phyllis. Havelock Ellis: A Biography.
    New York: Knopf, 1980. 492 pp.

82) Higham, Charles. Charles Laughton: An Intimate
    Biography. Garden City, N. Y.: Doubleday, 1976.
    239 pp.

83) _____. Errol Flynn: The Untold Story. Garden
    City, N. Y.: Doubleday, 1980. 370 pp.

84) Holland, Vyvyan. Oscar Wilde and His World. New
York: Scribner's, 1978. 144 pp. (Reprint of work
published in 1960.)

85) Hunt, Nancy. Mirror Image: The Odyssey of a Male-
to-Female Transsexual. New York: Holt, Rinehart,
and Winston, 1978. 263 pp.

86) Hyde, Louis (ed.). Rat and the Devil: Journal Letters
of F. O. Matthiessen and Russell Cheney. Hamden,
Conn. : Archon Books, 1978. 408 pp.

87) Hyde, Mary (ed.). Bernard Shaw and Alfred Douglas,
A Correspondence. London: Ticknor and Fields,
1982. 237 pp.

88) Isherwood, Christopher. Christopher and His Kind.
1929-39. New York: Farrar, Straus, and Giroux,
1976. 339 pp.

89) _____ . My Guru and His Disciple. New York:
Farrar, Straus, and Giroux, 1980. 338 pp.

90) Jussim, Estelle. Slave to Beauty: The Eccentric Life
and Controversial Career of F. Holland Day. Boston:
David R. Godine Publishers, 1981. 310 pp.

91) Kantrowitz, Arnie. Under the Rainbow: Growing Up
Gay. New York: William Morrow, 1977. 255 pp.

92) Kaplan, Justin. Walt Whitman: A Life. New York:
Simon and Schuster, 1980. 432 pp.

93) King, Billie Jean, and Frank Deford. Billie Jean.
New York: Viking Press, 1982. 220 pp.

94) King, Francis H. E. M. Forster and His World.
New York: Scribner's, 1978. 128 pp.

95) Kohn, Barry, and Alice Matusow. Barry and Alice:
Portrait of a Bisexual Marriage. Englewood Cliffs,
N.J. : Prentice-Hall, 1980. 217 pp.

96) Kopay, David, and Perry D. Young. The David
Kopay Story. New York: Arbor House, 1977. 247 pp.

97) Kronenberger, Louis. Oscar Wilde. Boston: Little,
Brown, 1976. 236 pp.

98)   LaGuardia, Robert. Monty: A Biography of Mont-
       gomery Clift. New York: Arbor House, 1977. 304
       pp.

99)   Lahr, John. Prick Up Your Ears: The Biography of
       Joe Orton. New York: Knopf, 1978. 302 pp.

100)   Lane, Erskine. Game Texts: A Guatemalan Journal.
       San Francisco: Gay Sunshine Press, 1978. 156 pp.

101)   Langguth, A. J. Saki: A Life of Hector Hugh Mon-
       roe. New York: Simon and Schuster, 1981. 366 pp.

102)   Lees-Milne, James. Harold Nicolson: A Biography.
       2 vols. Hamden, Conn. : Archon Books, 1980-81.
       429 and 403 pp.

103)   Lehmann, John. In the Purely Pagan Sense. London:
       Blond and Briggs, 1976. 255 pp.

104)   Levey, Michael. The Case of Walter Pater. London:
       Thames and Hudson, 1978. 232 pp.

105)   Leyland, Winston (ed.). Gay Sunshine Interviews.
       2 vols. San Francisco: Gay Sunshine Press, 1978-
       82. 327 and 288 pp. (Includes: William Burroughs,
       Charles Henri Ford, Jean Genet, Allen Ginsberg,
       John Giorno, Christopher Isherwood, John Rechy, Gore
       Vidal, Tennessee Williams, and 19 others.)

106)   _____ (ed.). Straight Hearts' Delight: Love Poems
       and Selected Letters. 1947-80: Allen Ginsberg and
       Peter Orlovsky. San Francisco: Gay Sunshine Press,
       1980. 239 pp.

107)   Liddell, Robert. Cavafy: A Critical Biography. New
       York: Schocken Books, 1977. 222 pp.

108)   Lineham, Kevin. Such Were Some of You: The
       Spiritual Odyssey of an Ex-Gay Christian. Scottsdale,
       Pa. : Herald Press, 1979. 231 pp.

109)   Marotta, Toby. Sons of Harvard: Gay Men from the
       Class of 1967. New York; William Morrow, 1982.
       288 pp.

110)   Maugham, Robin. Conversations with Willie: Rec-
       ollections of W. Somerset Maugham. New York:

Simon and Schuster, 1978.   188 pp.

111)   Meigs, Mary. Lily Briscoe: A Self-Portrait. Van-
       couver: Talon Books, 1982.

112)   Mendelson, Edward. Early Auden. New York: Viking
       Press, 1981.   407 pp.

113)   Millett, Kate. Sita. New York: Farrar, Straus,
       and Giroux, 1977.   321 pp.

114)   Mitzel, John. John Horne Burns: An Appreciative
       Biography. Dorchester, Mass.: Manifest Destiny,
       1976.   135 pp.

115)   Moore, Paul. Take a Bishop Like Me. New York:
       Harper and Row, 1979.   200 pp.

116)   Morgan, Ted. Maugham. New York: Simon and
       Schuster, 1980.   711 pp.

117)   Nicholls, Mark. The Importance of Being Oscar:
       The Life and Wit of Oscar Wilde. New York: St.
       Martin's, 1980.   238 pp.

118)   Olson, Stanley (ed.). Harold Nicolson: Diaries and
       Letters, 1930-1964. New York: Atheneum, 1980.
       436 pp.

119)   Osborne, Charles. W. H. Auden: The Life of a
       Poet. New York: Harcourt Brace Jovanovich, 1979.
       336 pp.

120)   Pinchin, Jane L. Alexandria Still: Forster, Durrell,
       and Cavafy. Princeton, N.J.: Princeton University
       Press, 1977. 245 pp.

121)   Raphael, Frederic. W. Somerset Maugham and His
       World. New York: Scribner's, 1977.   128 pp.

122)   Rayfield, Donald. The Dreams of Lhasa: The Life of
       Nikolai Przhevalsky, Explorer of Central Asia.
       Athens: Ohio University Press, 1982.   221 pp.

123)   Rechy, John. The Sexual Outlaw: A Documentary.
       New York: Grove Press, 1978.   307 pp.

124)   Reich, Charles.   The Sorcerer of Bolinas Reef.   New
       York: Random House, 1976.   266 pp.

125)   Richardson, Frank M.   Mars Without Venus: A Study
       of Some Homosexual Generals.   Edinburgh: Black-
       wood and Sons, 1981.   188 pp.

126)   Rignall, Jeff, and Ron Wilder.   Twenty-Nine Below.
       Chicago: Wellington Press, 1980.   257 pp.   (Story
       of boys murdered by John Gacy.)

127)   Royle, Trevor.   Death Before Dishonor: The True
       Story of Fighting Mac [Sir Hector MacDonald].   New
       York: St. Martin's, 1982.   176 pp.

128)   Rumaker, Michael.   A Day and Night at the Baths.
       Bolinas, Cal.:   Grey Fox Press, 1978.   81 pp.

129)   _____.   My First Saturnalia.   Bolinas, Cal.:
       Grey Fox Press, 1981.   180 pp.

130)   Schwartz, Charles.   Cole Porter.   New York: Dial
       Press, 1978.   365 pp.

131)   Seabrook, Jeremy.   Mother and Son.   New York:
       Pantheon Books, 1980.   189 pp.

132)   Shilts, Randy.   The Mayor of Castro Street: The
       Life and Times of Harvey Milk.   New York: St. Mar-
       tin's, 1982.   388 pp.

133)   Siciliano, Enzo.   Pasolini: A Biography.   Translated
       from the Italian by John Shepley.   New York: Ran-
       dom House, 1982.   435 pp.

134)   Simon, Linda.   The Biography of Alice B. Toklas.
       Garden City, N.Y.:   Doubleday, 1977.   324 pp.

135)   _____.   Thorton Wilder, His World.   Garden City,
       N.Y.:   Doubleday, 1980.   298 pp.

136)   Smith, Jane S.   Elsie de Wolfe: A Life in the High
       Style.   New York: Atheneum, 1982.   366 pp.

137)   Steward, Samuel M.   Chapters from an Autobiography.
       San Francisco: Grey Fox Books, 1981.   147 pp.

138)   _____ (ed.). Dear Sammy: Letters from Gertrude
        Stein and Alice B. Toklas. Boston: Houghton Mifflin,
        1977.   260 pp.

139)   Summers, Claude J. Christopher Isherwood. New
        York: Frederick Ungar Publishing Co. , 1980.   182 pp.

140)   Valentine, John (pseud.). Puppies. Glen Ellen,
        Cal. : Entwhistle Books, 1979.   173 pp.

141)   Vining, Donald. A Gay Diary, 1933-1967. 3 vols.
        New York: Pepys Press, 1979-81.   483, 493, and
        485 pp.

142)   Wells, Anna M. Miss Marks and Miss Woolley. Bos-
        ton: Houghton Mifflin, 1978.   268 pp.

143)   White, Edmund. States of Desire: Travels in Gay
        America. New York: E. P. Dutton, 1980.   336 pp.

144)   White, T(erence) H. Letters to a Friend: The Cor-
        respondence Between T. H. White and L. J. Potts.
        Edited by François Gallix. New York: Putnam's,
        1982.   393 pp.

145)   Whitmore, George. The Confessions of Danny Slocum:
        Or Gay Life in the Big City. New York: St. Mar-
        tin's, 1980.   215 pp.

146)   Wickes, George. The Amazon Letters: The Life and
        Loves of Natalie Clifford Barney. New York: Put-
        nam's, 1976,   286 pp.

147)   Windham, Donald (ed.). Tennessee Williams' Letters
        to Donald Windham, 1940-1965. New York: Holt,
        Rinehart, and Winston, 1978.   333 pp.

148)   Winston, Richard. Thomas Mann: The Making of an
        Artist. New York: Knopf, 1981.   352 pp.

149)   Wolff, Charlotte. Hindsight. London: Quartet Books,
        1982.   308 pp.

150)   "Y. " The Autobiography of an Englishman. New
        York: State Mutual Books, 1980.   176 pp.

151)   Youth Liberation. Growing Up Gay. 2d ed. Brook-
        lyn, N. Y. : Youth Liberation, 1978.

GENERAL AND SPECIALIZED WORKS

152)   Adams, Stephen D. The Homosexual as Hero in Con-
        temporary Fiction. Totowa, N.J.: Barnes and
        Noble, 1980. 208 pp.

153)   Altman, Dennis. Coming Out in the Seventies. Bos-
        ton: Alyson Publications, 1981. 312 pp.

154)   _____. The Homosexualization of America, the
        Americanization of the Homosexual. New York: St.
        Martin's, 1982. 242 pp.

155)   Alyson, Sasha (ed.). Young, Gay, and Proud. Rev.
        ed. Boston: Alyson Publications, 1980. 96 pp.

156)   Atkinson, David J. Homosexuals in the Christian
        Fellowship. Grand Rapids, Mich.: Eerdmans, 1981.
        127 pp.

157)   Austen, Roger. Playing the Game: The Homosexual
        Novel in America. Indianapolis: Bobbs-Merrill, 1977.
        240 pp.

158)   Babuscio, Jack. We Speak for Ourselves: Experiences
        in Homosexual Counseling. Philadelphia: Fortress
        Press, 1977. 146 pp.

159)   Bach, Gerard. Homosexualities: Expression, Repres-
        sion. Paris: Edition Sycamore, 1982. 119 pp.

160)   Bahnsen, Greg L. Homosexuality: A Biblical View.
        Grand Rapids, Mich.: Baker Books House, 1978.
        152 pp.

161)   Barnhouse, Ruth T. Homosexuality: A Symbolic Con-
        fusion. New York: Seabury Press, 1977. 190 pp.

162)   Bayer, Ronald. Homosexuality and American Psychia-
        try: The Politics of Diagnosis. New York: Basic
        Books, 1981. 216 pp.

163)   Bell, Alan P., and Martin S. Weinberg. Homosexual-
        ities: A Study of Diversity Among Men and Women.
        New York: Simon and Schuster, 1978. 505 pp.

164)   _____; _____; and Sue K. Hammersmith. Sexual

Preference: Its Development in Men and Women.
Bloomington: Indiana University Press 1981. 242 pp.

165)   _____; _____; and _____. Sexual Preference:
Statistical Appendix. Bloomington: Indiana University
Press, 1981. 321 pp.

166)   Berger, Raymond M. Gay and Gray: The Older
Homosexual Man. Urbana: University of Illinois
Press, 1982. 233 pp.

167)   Berkson, Bill, and Joe LeSeuer (eds.). Homage to
Frank O'Hara. Berkeley, Cal.: Creative Arts Book
Co., 1982. 224 pp.

168)   Bessell, Peter. Cover Up: The Jeremy Thorpe Affair. Oceanside, Cal.: Simons Books, 1981. 574 pp.

169)   Bode, Janet. View from Another Closet: Exploring
Bisexuality in Women. New York: Hawthorn, 1976.
252 pp.

170)   Boswell, John. Christianity, Social Tolerance, and
Homosexuality: Gay People in Western Europe from
the Beginning of the Christian Era to the Fourteenth
Century. Chicago: University of Chicago Press, 1980.
448 pp.

171)   Boyd, Malcolm. Look Back in Joy: The Celebration
of Gay Lovers. San Francisco: Gay Sunshine Press,
1981. 127 pp.

172)   Boyle, Andrew. The Fourth Man: The Definitive Account of Kim Philby, Guy Burgess, and Donald Mac-
Lean and Who [Sir Anthony Blunt] Recruited Them to
Spy for Russia. New York: Dial Press, 1980. 504
pp.

173)   Bray, Alan. Homosexuality in Renaissance England.
London: Gay Men's Press, 1982. 149 pp.

174)   Brooks, Virginia R. Minority Stress and Lesbian
Women. Lexington, Mass.: Lexington Books, 1981.
219 pp.

175)   Brown, Rita M. A Plain Brown Wrapper. Baltimore:
Diana Press, 1976. 236 pp.

176)   Bryant, Anita. The Anita Bryant Story: The Survival
       of our Nation's Families and the Threat of Militant
       Homosexuality. Old Tappan, N. J. : Fleming Revell
       Co. , 1977. 156 pp.

177)   _____, and Bob Green. At Any Cost. Old Tappan,
       N. J. : Fleming Revell Co. , 1978. 154 pp.

178)   _____, and _____. Running the Good Race.
       Boston: G. K. Hall and Co. , 1977. 215 pp.

179)   Bullough, Vern L. Homosexuality: A History. New
       York: New American Library, 1979. 196 pp.

180)   _____. Sexual Variance in History. New York:
       John Wiley and Sons, 1976. 715 pp. (Reprinted by
       University of Chicago Press, 1980.)

181)   _____; W. Door Legg; and W. Elcano Barrett
       (comps.). An Annotated Bibliography of Homosexual-
       ity. 3 vols. New York: Garland Publishing Co. ,
       1976. 843 pp.

182)   Califia, Pat. Sapphistry: The Book of Lesbian Sexu-
       ality. Tallahassee, Fla. : Naiad Press, 1980. 180
       pp.

183)   Cavanagh, John R. , and John F. Harvey. Counseling
       the Homosexual. Huntingdon, Ind. : Our Sunday
       Visitor, 1977. 352 pp. (Revision of work published
       in 1965).

184)   Clanton, Gordon, and Chris Downing. Face to Face:
       An Experiment in Intimacy. New York: Ballantine
       Books, 1976. 256 pp.

185)   Clark, Donald H. Living Gay. Millbrae, Cal. : Ce-
       lestial Arts, 1979. 192 pp.

186)   _____. Loving Someone Gay. Millbrae, Cal. : Ce-
       lestial Arts, 1977. 192 pp.

187)   Clark, Mason. A Nation of Gay Babies: Causing and
       Curing Homosexuality. Los Altos, Cal. : Frontal Lobe,
       1978.

188)   Coleman, James, Jr. The International Homophilics

Institute: A History on Its Fifteenth Anniversary.
Boston: International Homophilics Institute Press,
1977.

189)   Coleman, Peter E.   Christian Attitudes to Homosex-
         uality.   London: Society for the Promotion of Chris-
         tian Knowledge Press, 1980.   310 pp.

190)   Corsaro, Maria, and Carole Korzeniowsky STD: A
         Commonsense Guide to Sexually Transmitted Diseases.
         New York: Holt, Rinehart, and Winston, 1982.   104
         pp.

191)   Cummings, John.   Homophilics: A Doctor's View.
         Boston: International Homophilics Institute Press,
         1977.

192)   Curry, Hayden, and Denis Clifford.   A Legal Guide
         for Lesbian and Gay Couples.   Reading, Mass. :
         Addison-Wesley Publishing Co. , 1980.   254 pp.

193)   Curzon, Daniel.   The Joyful Blue Book of Gracious
         Gay Etiquette.   San Francisco: D. Brown Books,
         1982.   115 pp.

194)   Damiani, Peter.   Book of Gomorrah: An Eleventh
         Century Treatise Against Clerical Homosexual Prac-
         tices.   Translated from the Latin by Pierre J. Payer.
         Waterloo, Ontario: Wilfrid Laurier University Press,
         1982.   108 pp.

195)   Damon, Gene (pseud.).   Lesbiana: Book Reviews from
         'The Ladder. "   Reno, Nev. : Naiad Press, 1976.
         309 pp.

196)   Dannecker, Martin.   Theories of Homosexuality.   New
         York: Gay Men's Press, 1981.   128 pp.

197)   Davis, Nancy, and Jeff Graubert.   Heterosexual.   New
         York: Vantage Press, 1976.   143 pp.

198)   Delph, Edward W.   The Silent Community: Public
         Homosexual Encounters.   Beverly Hills, Cal. : Sage
         Publications, 1978.   186 pp.

199)   Devi, Shakuntala.   The World of Homosexuals.   New
         Delhi, India: Vikas Publishing House, 1977.   160 pp.

200)   Dey, Richard. A General Ontology of Homophilia.
        Boston: International Homophilics Institute Press,
        1977.

201)   _____. An Introduction to Arcadian Theory. Bos-
        ton: International Homophilics Institute Press, 1977.

202)   _____. An Introduction to Uranian Theory. Bos-
        ton: International Homophilics Institute Press, 1977.

203)   _____, and others (eds.). A Homophilics Work-
        book. Boston: International Homophilics Institute
        Press, 1977.

204)   Dover Kenneth J. Greek Homosexuality. Cambridge,
        Mass. : Harvard University Press, 1978. 244 pp.

205)   Drakeford, John W. A Christian View of Homosexual-
        ity. Nashville, Tenn. : Broadman Press, 1977. 140
        pp.

206)   DuMas, Frank. Gay Is Not Good. Nashville, Tenn. :
        Thomas Nelson, 1979. 331 pp.

207)   Emory, Michael (ed.). The Gay Picture Book. Chica-
        go: Contemporary Books, 1978. 125 pp.

208)   Ettore, E(lizabeth) M. Lesbians, Women, and Society.
        London: Routledge and Kegan Paul, 1980. 208 pp.

209)   Evans, Arthur. Witchcraft and the Gay Counter Cul-
        ture: A Radical View of Western Civilization and Some
        of the People It Has Tried to Destroy. Boston: Fag
        Rag, 1978. 180 pp.

210)   Faderman, Lillian. Surpassing the Love of Men:
        Romantic Friendship and Love Between Women from
        the Renaissance to the Present. New York: William
        Morrow, 1981. 496 pp.

211)   Fairchild, Betty, and Nancy Hayward. Now That You
        Know: What Every Parent Should Know About Homo-
        sexuality. New York: Harcourt Brace Jovanovich,
        1979. 228 pp.

212)   Fenwick, R. D. , and Nathan Fain. The Advocate
        Guide to Gay Health. Rev. ed. New York; E. P.
        Dutton, 1982. 236 pp.

213)   Fernbach, David. The Spiral Path: A Gay Contribu-
        tion to Human Survival. Boston: Alyson Publications,
        1981. 240 pp.

214)   Fortunato, John E. Embracing the Exile: Healing
        Journeys of Gay Christians. New York: Seabury
        Press, 1982. 137 pp.

215)   French, Joel and Jane. Straight Is the Way. Minne-
        apolis: Bethany Fellowship, 1979. 159 pp.

216)   Gangel, Kenneth O. The Gospel and the Gay. Nash-
        ville, Tenn.: T. Nelson, 1978. 202 pp.

217)   Gay, A. Nolder (pseud.). The View from the Closet:
        Essays on Gay Life and Liberation, 1973-77. Bos-
        ton: Union Park Press, 1978. 108 pp.

218)   Goldstein, Philip. Magic Men. Boston: International
        Homophilics Institute Press, 1977.

219)   Goode, Lacey. The Lesbian Handbook: Or, What
        You May Not Know About the Girl Next Door. New
        York: Carlyle Communications, 1976. 204 pp.

220)   Goodich, Michael. The Unmentionable Vice: Homo-
        sexuality in the Later Medieval Period. Santa Bar-
        bara, Cal.: ABC-Clio Press, 1979. 164 pp.

221)   Gottlieb, David I. The Gay Tapes: A Candid Dis-
        cussion About Homosexuality. New York: Stein and
        Day, 1977. 178 pp.

222)   Greene, Michael; David Holloway; and David Watson
        The Church and Homosexuality: A Positive Answer
        to Current Questions. London: Hodder and Stoughton,
        1980.

223)   Grier, Barbara. The Lesbian in Literature. 3d ed.
        Tallahassee, Fla.: Naiad Press, 1981. 168 pp.

224)   Halloran, Joe. Understanding Homosexual Persons:
        Straight Answers from Gays. Hicksville, N.Y.: Ex-
        position Press, 1979. 81 pp.

225)   Hanckel, Frances, and John Cunningham A Way of
        Love, a Way of Life: A Young Person's Introduction
        to What It Means to Be Gay. New York: Lothrop,

Lee and Shepard Books, 1979. 189 pp.

226)   _____, and Susan Windle (eds.). Lesbian Writer:
Collected Works of Claudia Scott. Tallahassee, Fla. :
Naiad Press, 1981. 114 pp.

227)   Hanscombe, Gillian E. Rocking the Cradle: Lesbian
Mothers: A Challenge to Family Living. Boston:
Alyson Publications, 1982. 172 pp.

228)   Harry, Joseph. Gay Children Grown Up: Gender Culture and Gender Deviance. New York: Praeger Books,
1982. 288 pp.

229)   _____, and William B. DeVall. The Social Organization of Gay Males. New York: Praeger Books,
1978. 223 pp.

230)   Hart, John, and Diane Richardson The Theory and
Practice of Homosexuality. Boston: Routledge and
Kegan Paul, 1981. 212 pp.

231)   Heger, Heinz. The Men with the Pink Trinagle.
Translated from the German by David Fernbach. Boston: Alyson Publications, 1980. 117 pp.

232)   Helbing, Terry (comp. and ed.). Gay Theater Alliance Directory of Gay Plays. New York: J. H.
Press, 1980. 122 pp.

233)   Herdt, Gilbert H. Guardians of the Flutes: Idioms
of Masculinity. New York: McGraw-Hill, 1981. 382
pp.

234)   Hjorth, Neils, and Henning Schmidt. Venereology in
Practice: The Sexually Committed Diseases. Chicago:
Year Book Medical Publishers, 1980. 100 pp.

235)   Hocquenghem, Guy. Homosexual Desire. Translated
from the French by Dangoor Daniella. New York:
Shocken Books, 1980. 144 pp.

236)   Horner, Tom. Homosexuality and the Judeo-Christian
Tradition. Metuchen, N.J. : Scarecrow Press, 1981.
141 pp. (A bibliography)

237)   _____. Jonathan Loved David: Homosexuality in
Biblical Times. Philadelphia: Westminster Press,

1978.   163 pp.

238)   Human Rights Foundation.   Demystifying Homosexuality:
       A Teacher's Source Book About Lesbians and Gay Men.
       New York: Irvington Publishers, 1982.   150 pp.

239)   Hunt, Morton M.   Gay: What You Should Know About
       Homosexuality.   New York: Farrar, Straus, and
       Giroux, 1977.   210 pp.

240)   Hyde, H. Montgomery.   The Cleveland Street Scandal.
       New York: Coward, McCann and Geoghegan, 1976.
       266 pp.

241)   International Homophilics Institute Staff.   Who Was
       Gay?   Boston: International Homophilics Institute
       Press, 1977.

242)   Jackman, Abraham L.   The Paranoid Homosexual Ba-
       sis of Anti-Semitism.   New York: Vantage Press,
       1979.   191 pp.

243)   Jay, Karla, and Allen Young.   The Gay Report: Les-
       bians and Gay Men Speak Out About Sexual Experiences
       and Lifestyles.   New York: Summit Books, 1979.
       816 pp.

244)   Jay, Michael.   Gay Love Signs.   New York: Ballan-
       tine Books, 1980.   387 pp.

245)   Johnson, Barbara E.   Where Does a Mother Go to
       Resign?   Minneapolis: Bethany Fellowship, 1979.
       154 pp.

246)   Johnson, Paul R., and Thomas F. Eaves, Sr.   Gays
       and the New Right: A Debate.   Los Angeles: Marco
       and Johnson, 1982.   144 pp.

247)   Johnston, Gordon.   Which Way Out of the Men's Room?
       Options for a Male Homosexual.   South Brunswick,
       N.J.: A. S. Barnes, 1979.   330 pp.

248)   Jones, Clinton R.   Understanding Gay Relatives and
       Friends.   New York: Seabury Press, 1978.   133 pp.

249)   Karlinsky, Simon.   The Sexual Labyrinth of Nikolai
       Gogol.   Cambridge, Mass.: Harvard University Press,
       1976.   333 pp.

250)   Katz, Jonathan. Gay American History: Lesbians
        and Gay Men in the U. S. A. New York: Thomas Y.
        Crowell, 1976. 690 pp. (See nos. 771, 800, 801, 825,
        835, 845-49, 906, 951, 1071, and 1089.)

251)   Keeley, Edmund. Cavafy's Alexandria: Study of a
        Myth in Progress. Cambridge, Mass. : Harvard Uni-
        versity Press, 1976. 196 pp.

252)   Keith, Louis, and Jan Brittain. Sexually Transmitted
        Diseases. New York: Irvington Publishers, 1978.
        100 pp.

253)   Kirk, Jerry R. The Homosexual Crisis in the Main-
        line Church: A Presbyterian Minister Speaks Out.
        Nashville, Tenn. : Thomas Nelson, 1978. 191 pp.

254)   Klein, Fred. The Bisexual Option. New York: Ar-
        bor House, 1978. 221 pp.

255)   Kleinberg, Seymour. Alienated Affections: Being Gay
        in America. New York: St. Martin's, 1981. 256 pp.

256)   Kronemeyer, Robert. Overcoming Homosexuality.
        New York: Macmillan, 1980. 220 pp.

257)   LaHaye, Tim F. The Unhappy Gays: What Everyone
        Should Know About Homosexuality. Wheaton, Ill. :
        Tyndale House Publishers, 1978. 207 pp.

258)   Larkin, Purusha. The Divine Androgyne. San Diego:
        Sanctuary Publications, 1982. 200 pp.

259)   Larzelere, Bob. The Harmony of Love. San Fran-
        cisco: Context Publications, 1982. 137 pp.

260)   Lee, John A. Getting Sex, A New Approach, More
        Fun, Less Guilt. Don Mills, Ontario: Musson Book
        Co. , 1978. 318 pp.

261)   Lesbian and Gay Media Associates. Talk Back! Bos-
        ton: Alyson Publications, 1982. 116 pp.

262)   Levin, James. The Gay Novel: The Male Homosexual
        Image in America. New York: Irvington Publishers,
        1982. 250 pp.

263) Lewis, Sasha G. Sunday's Woman, A Report on Lesbian Life Today. Boston: Beacon Press, 1979. 217
pp.

264) Linedecker, Clifford L. [Wayne Gacy] The Man Who
Killed Boys. New York: St. Martin's, 1980. 222 pp.

265) Lloyd, Robin. For Money or Love: Boy Prostitution
in America. New York: Vanguard Press, 1976. 326
pp.

266) Loovis, David. Straight Answers About Homosexuality
for Straight Readers. Englewood Cliffs, N.J.:
Prentice-Hall, 1977. 190 pp.

267) Lovelace, Richard F. Homosexuality and the Church.
Old Tappan, N.J.: Fleming Revell Co., 1978. 158
pp.

268) Macauley, E. V., and J. Frederick Smith. Sappho:
The Art of Loving Woman. New York: Chelsea
House, 1980 160 pp.

269) Macourt, Malcolm (ed.). Towards a Theology of
Gay Liberation. London: Student Christian Movement
Press, 1977. 113 pp.

270) Maddox, Brenda. Married and Gay: An Intimate Look
at a Different Relationship. New York: Harcourt
Brace Jovanovich, 1982. 220 pp.

271) Magee, Bryan. The Gays Among Us. New York:
Stein and Day, 1978. 181 pp. (Revision of One in
Twenty published in 1966.)

272) Malloy, Edward A. Homosexuality and the Christian
Way of Life. Lanham, Md.: University Presses of
America, 1981. 382 pp.

273) Malone, John W. Straight Women/Gay Men: A Special Relationship. New York: Dial Press, 1980.
207 pp.

274) Marotta, Toby. The Politics of Homosexuality. Boston: Houghton Mifflin, 1981. 369 pp. (See no. 582.)

275) Martin, Robert K. The Homosexual Tradition in

American Poetry. Austin: University of Texas
Press, 1980. 259 pp.

276) Masters, William H. , and Virginia Johnson. Homosexuality in Perspective. Boston: Little, Brown,
1979. 450 pp.

277) McElfresh, Adeline. Wives Who Love Women. New
York: Walker and Co. , 1978. 183 pp.

278) McNaught, Brain. A Disturbed Peace: Selected Writings of an Irish Catholic Homosexual. Washington,
D. C. : Dignity, Inc. , 1981. 125 pp.

279) McNeill, John J. The Church and the Homosexual.
Kansas City, Kans. : Sheed, Andrews, and McMeel,
1976. 211 pp.

280) Mendola, Mary. The Mendola Report: A New Look
at Gay Couples. New York: Crown Publishers, 1980.
269 pp.

281) Messer, Alfred. When You Are Concerned with Homosexuality. St. Meinrad, Ind. : Abbey Press, 1980.
96 pp.

282) Meyers, Jeffrey. Homosexuality and Literature, 1890-
1930. Montreal: McGill-Queens University Press,
1977. 183 pp.

283) Mieli, Mario. Homosexuality and Liberation: Elements of a Gay Critique. Translated from the Italian
by David Fernbach. London: Gay Men's Press, 1980.
247 pp.

284) Miller, James E. T. S. Eliot's Personal Waste Land:
Exorcism of Demons. University Park: Pennsylvania
State University Press, 1977. 176 pp.

285) Mitzel, John. The Boston Sex Scandal. Boston: Glad
Day Books, 1980. 149 pp.

286) Morin, Jack. Men Loving Themselves: Images of
Male Self-Sexuality. Burlingame, Cal. : There Press,
1980. 104 pp.

287) Morris, Paul. The Shadow of Sodom: Facing the

Facts of Homosexuality. Wheaton, Ill.: Tyndale House Publishers, 1978. 164 pp.

288)   Moses, Alice E. Identity Management in Lesbian Women. New York: Praeger Books, 1978. 118 pp.

289)   _____, and Robert O. Hawkins, Jr. Counseling Lesbian Women and Gay Men: A Life-Issues Approach. St. Louis: C. V. Mosby Co., 1982. 263 pp.

290)   Muchmore, Wes, and William Hanson. Coming Out Right: A Handbook for the Gay Male. Boston: Alyson Publications, 1982. 204 pp.

291)   Munger, Michael S. Out of the Closet into the Light. Santa Barbara, Cal.: Pacific Press, 1980. 144 pp.

292)   Nahas, Rebecca, and Myra Turley. The New Couple: Women and Gay Men. New York: Seaview Books, 1979. 291 pp.

293)   Nichols, D. W. Toward a Perspective for Boy-Lovers. Lansing, Mich.: Editorial Creative Projects, 1976. 99 pp.

294)   Nichols, Jack. Welcome to Fire Island. New York: St Martin's, 1976. 148 pp.

295)   Nicosia, Gerald, and Richard Roff. Bughouse Blues: An Intimate Portrait of Gay Hustling. Chicago: Vantage Press, 1977. 207 pp.

296)   Noble, Robert C. Sexually Transmitted Diseases: Guide to Diagnosis and Therapy. New York: Medical Examination Publishing Co., 1979. 166 pp.

297)   O'Carroll, Tom. Paedophilia: The Radical Case. London: Peter Brown, 1980. 280 pp.

298)   Odin, Eric. The Secret Sex Men Never Talk About. Beverly Hills, Cal.: Firestar Publishing Co., 1978. 220 pp.

299)   O'Donnell, Mary, and others. Lesbian Health Matters. Santa Cruz, Cal.: Women's Health Center, 1979. 101 pp.

300)   Oraison, Marc. The Homosexual Question. Translated

from the French by Jane Z. Flinn. New York: Harper and Row, 1977. 132 pp.

301)   Parker, William (comp.). Homosexuality Bibliography: Supplement, 1970-1975. Metuchen, N.J. :
Scarecrow Press, 1977. 337 pp.

302)   Payne, Leanne. The Broken Image: Restoring Personal Wholeness Through Healing Prayer. West-
chester, Ill. : Good News, 1981. 188 pp.

303)   Pennington, Sylvia. But Lord, They're Gay. Haw-
thorne, Cal. : Lambda Christian Fellowship, 1982.
171 pp.

304)   Perrin, Elula. So Long As There Are Women.
Translated from the French by Harold J. Salemson.
New York: William Morrow, 1980. 215 pp.

305)   _____. Women Prefer Women: A Sexual Memoir.
Translated from the French by Harold J. Salemson.
New York: William Morrow, 1978. 239 pp.

306)   Phillips, Mike, and Barry Shapiro. Forbidden Fantasies: Men Who Dare to Dress in Drag. New York:
Macmillan, 1980. 121 pp.

307)   Philpott, Kent. The Gay Theology. Plainfield, N.J. :
Logos International, 1977. 194 pp.

308)   Pittenger, W. Norman. Time for Consent: A Christian's Approach to Homosexuality. 3d ed. rev. and enlarged. London: Student Christian Movement Press,
1976. 104 pp.

309)   Ponse, Barbara. Identities in the Lesbian World: The
Social Construction of Self. Westport, Conn. : Greenwood Press, 1978. 228 pp.

310)   Praunheim, Rosa von. Army of Lovers. London:
Gay Men's Press, 1980. 207 pp.

311)   Propper, Alice M. Prison Homosexuality: Myth and
Reality. San Diego: Lexington Book Co. , 1981.
256 pp.

312)   Raile, Arthur L. (pseud.). A Defense of Uranian

Love. New York: AMS Press, 1979. (Reprint of
work published in 1928.)

313)   Raymond, Janice G. The Transsexual Empire: The
Making of the She-Male. Boston: Beacon Press,
1979. 220 pp.

314)   Read, Kenneth E. Other Voices: The Style of a Male
Homosexual Tavern. Novato, Cal. : Chandler and
Sharp Publishers, 1980. 212 pp.

315)   Rector, Frank. The Nazi Extermination of Homosexuals. New York: Stein and Day, 1981. 189 pp.

316)   Reinhardt, Madge. The Year of Silence. St. Paul,
Minn. : Back Row Press, 1978. 177 pp.

317)   Rekers, George A. Growing Up Straight: What
Families Should Know About Homosexuality. Chicago:
Moody Press, 1982. 158 pp.

318)   Reynols, Robert. The Homophile Aristos. Boston:
International Homophilics Institute Press, 1977.

319)   Richter, Rosalyn. Anti-Gay Legislation: An Attempt
to Sanction Inequality? New York: Lambda Legal
Defense and Education Fund, 1982. 210 pp.

320)   Rivers, Julius E. Proust and the Art of Love: The
Aesthetics of Sexuality in the Life, Times and Art of
Marcel Proust. New York: Columbia University
Press, 1980. 440 pp.

321)   Roberts, J. R. (comp.). Black Lesbians: An Annotated Bibliography. Tallahassee, Fla. : Naiad
Press, 1981. 93 pp.

322)   Rodgers, Bruce. Gay Talk: A (Sometimes Outrageous) Dictionary of Gay Slang. New York: Putnam's,
1979. 265 pp.

323)   Rodgers, William D. The Gay Invasion: A Christian Look at the Spreading Homosexual Myth. Denver,
Colo. : Accent Books, 1977. 160 pp.

324)   Rofes, Eric. "I Thought People Like That Killed
Themselves": Lesbians, Gay Men, and Suicide. San
Francisco: Grey Fox Press, 1982. 162 pp.

325) Rossman, Parker. Sexual Experience Between Men and Boys: Exploring the Pederast Underground. New York: Association Press, 1976. 247 pp.

326) Rowan, Robert L., and Paul J. Gillette. The Gay Health Guide: A Complete Medical Reference for Homosexually Active Men and Women. Boston: Little, Brown, 1978. 239 pp.

327) Rowbotham, Sheila, and Jeffrey Weeks. Socialism and the New Life: The Personal and Sexual Politics of Edward Carpenter and Havelock Ellis. New York: Pluto Press, 1980. 200 pp.

328) Rowse, Alfred L. Homosexuals in History: Ambivalence in Society, Literature, and the Arts. New York: Macmillan, 1977. 346 pp.

329) Rubinstein, Ronald A., and Patricia B. Fry. Of a Homosexual Teacher: Beneath the Mainstream of Constitutional Equalities. Tarrytown, N.Y.: Associated Faculties Press, 1981. 98 pp.

330) Rueda, Enrique T. The Homosexual Network: Private Lives and Public Policy. Old Greenwich, Conn.: Devin Adair Co., 1982. 680 pp.

331) Russo, Vito. The Celluloid Closet: Homosexuality in the Movies. New York; Harper and Row, 1981. 256 pp.

332) Sanders, Dennis. Gay Source: A Catalog for Men. New York: Coward, McCann and Geoghegan, 1977. 288 pp.

333) Sandfort, Theo. The Sexual Aspect of Paedophile Relations: The Experience of Twenty-five Boys. Amsterdam: Pan/Spartacus, 1982. 136 pp.

334) Sarotte, Georges-Michel. Like a Brother, Like a Lover: Male Homosexuality in the American Novel and Theater from Herman Melville to James Baldwin. Garden City, N.Y.: Doubleday, 1978. 339 pp.

335) Savage, John. The Gay Astrologer. Port Washington, N.Y.: Ashley Books, 1982. 119 pp.

336)   Scanzoni, Letha, and Virginia R. Mollenkott. Is the
         Homosexual My Neighbor? Another Christian View.
         New York: Harper and Row, 1980. 176 pp.

337)   Schonauer, Betty, and others. Healing for the Homo-
         sexual. Oklahoma City: Presbyterian Charismatic
         Communion, 1978.

338)   Scott, Jane (pseud.). Wives Who Love Women. New
         York: Walker and Co. , 1978. 183 pp.

339)   Seabrook, Jeremy. A Lasting Relationship: Homo-
         sexuals and Society. London: Allen Lane, 1976,
         231 pp.

340)   Silverstein, Charles. A Family Matter: A Parents'
         Guide to Homosexuality. New York: McGraw-Hill,
         1978. 214 pp.

341)   _____. Man to Man: Gay Couples in America.
         New York: William Morrow, 1981. 347 pp.

342)   _____, and Edmund White. The Joy of Gay Sex:
         An Intimate Guide for Gay Men to the Pleasures of a
         Gay Lifestyle. New York: Crown Publishers, 1977.
         239 pp.

343)   Simpson, Colin; Lewis Chester; and David Leitch. The
         Cleveland Street Affair. Boston: Little, Brown, 1976.
         236 pp.

344)   Simpson, Ruth. From the Closet to the Courts: The
         Lesbian Transition. New York: Viking Press, 1976.
         180 pp.

345)   Sisley, Emily L. , and Bertha Harris. The Joy of
         Lesbian Sex: A Tender and Liberated Guide to the
         Problems and Pleasures of a Lesbian Lifestyle. New
         York: Crown Publishers, 1977. 223 pp.

346)   Smith, Don. Why Are There "Gays" at All? Why
         Hasn't Evolution Eliminated "Gayness" Millions of
         Years Ago? London: Quantum Jump Publications,
         1978. 96 pp.

347)   Smith, Herbert F. , and Joseph A. Dilenno. Sexual
         Inversion: The Questions with Catholic Answers.
         Boston: Daughters of St. Paul, 1979. 177 pp.

348)   Socarides, Charles W. Homosexuality. New York:
        J. Aronson, 1978. 642 pp.

349)   Spada, James. The Spada Report: The Newest Sur-
        vey of Gay Male Sexuality. New York: New American
        Library, 1979. 339 pp.

350)   Spence, Alex (comp.). Homosexuality in Canada: A
        Bibliography. Toronto: Pink Triangle Press, 1979.
        85 pp.

351)   Stewart-Park, Angela, and Jules Cassidy. We're
        Here: Conversations with Lesbian Women. New York:
        Quartet Books, 1977. 152 pp.

352)   Switzer, David K. and Shirley A. Parents of the
        Homosexual. Philadelphia: Westminster, 1980. 118
        pp.

353)   Tanner, Donna M. The Lesbian Couple. Lexington,
        Mass. : Lexington Books, 1978. 142 pp.

354)   Tarnovskii, Veniamin M. Anthropological, Legal,
        and Medical Studies on Pederasty in Europe. New
        York: AMS Press, 1978. 233 pp. (Reprint of work
        published in 1933.)

355)   Trump, Barbara. Forgiven Love. Edina, Minn. :
        Jeremy Books, 1979.

356)   Vojir, Dan. The Sunny Side of Castro Street. San
        Francisco: Strawberry Hill Press, 1982. 144 pp.

357)   Walker, Mitch. Men Loving Men: A Gay Sex Guide
        and Consciousness Book. San Francisco: Gay Sun-
        shine Press, 1981. 160 pp.

358)   _____. Visionary Love: A Spirit Book of Gay
        Mythology and Transmutational Faerie. Berkeley,
        Cal. : Tree Roots, 1980. 102 pp.

359)   Waugh, Auberon. The Last Word: An Eyewitness
        Account of the Trial of Jeremy Thorpe. Boston:
        Little, Brown, 1980. 240 pp.

360)   Weeks, Jeffrey. Coming Out: Homosexual Politics in
        Britain from the Nineteenth Century to the Present.

New York: Horizon Press, 1977. 278 pp.

361) West, Donald J. Homosexuality Re-examined. Rev.
      ed. Minneapolis: University of Minnesota Press,
      1977. 359 pp.

362) White, John. Eros Defiled. Downers Grove, Ill. :
      Inter-Varsity, 1977. 169 pp.

363) Williams, Don. The Bond That Breaks: Will Homo-
      sexuality Split the Church? Los Angeles: BIM Pub-
      lishing Co. , 1978. 176 pp.

364) Winter, Alan D. The Gay Press: A History of the
      Gay Community and Its Publications. Austin, Tex. :
      Privately Printed, 1977. 114 pp. (Mimeographed)

365) Wittig, Monique, and Sande Zeig. Lesbian People:
      Material for a Dictionary. New York: Avon Books,
      1979. 170 pp.

366) Wolf, Deborah G. The Lesbian Community. Berkeley:
      University of California Press, 1979. 196 pp. (See
      no. 656.)

367) Wolfenden, John, and others. Report of the Committee
      on Homosexual Offences and Prostitution. Westport,
      Conn. : Greenwood Press, 1976. 154 pp. (Reprint
      of work published in 1957.)

368) Wolff, Charlotte. Bisexuality: A Study. London:
      Quartet Books, 1977. 245 pp.

369) WomanShare Collective. Country Lesbians: The Story
      of the WomanShare Collective. Grants Pass, Ore. :
      WomanShare Books, 1976. 196 pp.

370) Wooden, Wayne S. , and Jay Parker. Men Behind
      Bars: Sexual Exploitation in Prison. New York:
      Plenum Press, 1982. 264 pp.

371) Woodman, Natalie J. , and Harry R. Lenna. Coun-
      seling with Gay Men and Women: A Guide for Facili-
      tating Positive Life-styles. San Francisco: Jossey-
      Bass Publishers, 1980. 144 pp.

372) Woods, Richard. Another Kind of Love: Homosexuality

and Spirituality. Rev. ed. Garden City, N. Y. :
Doubleday, 1978. 155 pp.

373) Woodward, Nancy. Pleasures: The Secret Garden
of Sexual Love Between Women. New York: Warner
Books, 1978.

374) Wright, Ezekiel, and Daniel Inesse. God Is Gay: An
Evolutional Spiritual Work. San Francisco: Tayu
Institute Press, 1979.

375) Wright, Stephen. A Brief Encyclopedia of Homosexuality. New York: Stephen Wright Press, 1978. 144 pp.

376) Young, Allen. Gays Under the Cuban Revolution. San
Francisco: Grey Fox Press, 1982. 112 pp.

377) Young, Ian (comp.). The Male Homosexual in Literature: A Bibliography with Essays. 2d ed. Metuchen, N. J. : Scarecrow Press, 1982. 350 pp.
(4,285 items, plus 5 essays. See nos. 856, 959,
and 1095.)

378) Young, Tracy. Women Who Love Women. New York:
Pocket Books, 1977. 222 pp.

379) Zane, David. Oh! Downtrodden: Sexual Inversion and
the Multiple Roots of Homosexuality. Roslyn Heights,
N. Y. : Libra Publishers, 1976. 774 pp.

PAMPHLETS AND DOCUMENTS

380)   American Library Association, Gay Task Force. A
        Gay Bibliography. 6th ed. Philadelphia: Gay Task
        Force, 1980. 16 pp. (563 items)

381)   American Psychological Association, Task Force on
        the Status of Lesbian and Gay Male Psychologists.
        Removing the Stigma: Final Report of the Board of
        Social and Ethical Responsibility. Washington, D.C.:
        American Psychological Association, 1980. Manuscript
        No. 2121. 151 pp. (Summarized in Catalog of Selected
        Documents in Psychology, 10:84-85, 1980.)

382)   Archdiocese of San Francisco, Commission on Social
        Justice. Homosexuality and Social Justice: Report of
        the Task Force on Gay/Lesbian Issues. San Fran-
        cisco: Commission on Social Justice, 1982. 155 pp.

383)   Arthur, L. Robert. Homosexuality and the Conserva-
        tive Christian. Los Angeles: Samaritan Theological
        Institute, 1982. 56 pp.

384)   Baars, Conrad W. The Homosexual's Search for Hap-
        piness. Chicago: Franciscan Herald Press, 1977.
        34 pp.

385)   Balliet, Bev, and Patti Patton. Graphic Details.
        Phoenix, Ariz.: Starr Publications, 1981. 44 pp.

386)   Barnett, Walter. Homosexuality and the Bible: An
        Interpretation. Wallingford, Pa.: Pendle Hill Publi-
        cations, 1979. 32 pp.

387)   Beer, Chris, and others. Gay Workers: Trade Unions
        and the Law. New York: State Mutual Book and Peri-
        odical Service, 1981.

33

388)   Bernstein, Edward. Bernstein on Homosexuality: Articles from "Die Neue Zeit," 1895 and 1898. Translated from the German by Angela Clifford. Belfast, Ireland: Anthol Books, 1977. 40 pp.

389)   Biren, Joan E. Eye to Eye: Portraits of Lesbians: Photographs. Washington, D. C. : Glad Hag Books, 1979. 72 pp.

390)   Blair, Ralph. Ex-Gay. New York: Homosexual Community Counseling Center, 1982. 50 pp.

391)   _____. Holier-Than-Thou Hocus-Pocus and Homosexuality. New York: Privately Printed, 1977. 48 pp.

392)   _____. Homophobia in the Church. New York: Privately Printed, 1979. 25 pp.

393)   Boswell, John. Rediscovering Gay History. London: Gay Christian Movement, 1982.

394)   Burns, Richard, and others. Gay Jubilee: A Guide to Gay Boston--Its History and Resources. Boston: Lesbian and Gay Task Force, 1980. 64 pp.

395)   Carson, Paul. Socialism and the Fight for Lesbian and Gay Rights. New York; Grassroots Press, 1982. 47 pp.

396)   Catholic Council (of the Netherlands) for Church and Society. Homosexual People in Society. Translated from the Dutch by Bernard A. Nachbar. Mt. Rainer, Md. : New Ways Ministry, 1980. 21 pp.

397)   Catholic Social and Welfare Commission of the Bishops of England and Wales. An Introduction to the Pastoral Care of Homosexual People. Mt. Rainer, Md. : New Ways Ministry, 1981. 15 pp.

398)   Chambers, Chester V. Some Questions for Christians About Homosexuality. Toledo, Ohio: Privately Printed, 1980.

399)   Christenson, Susan, and others. Lesbians, Gay Men and Their Alcohol and Other Drug Use Resources. Madison, Wis. : Clearinghouse for Alcohol and Other Drug Use Information, 1980. 17 pp.

400) Church of England General Synod, Board for Social
     Responsibility. Homosexual Relationships: A Con-
     tribution to the Discussion. London: Church Infor-
     mation Office, 1979. 94 pp.

401) Coggin, Sara. Sexual Expression and Moral Chaos.
     Cambridge, England: Gay Christian Movement, 1976.
     11 pp.

402) Coleman, Gerald. Homosexuality--An Appraisal.
     Chicago: Franciscan Herald Press, 1978. 88 pp.

403) Colwell, Mollie. Sexual Politics in Britain During
     1976: A Bibliographic Guide. Brighton, England:
     Harvester Press, 1979. 28 pp.

404) Community Attitudes on Homosexuality and About
     Homosexuals: A Report on the Environment in
     Norman, Oklahoma. Norman, Okla.: Human Rights
     Commission, 1978.

405) Dade County Bible: The Holy Bible: Containing Some
     Old Things Translated by Wagging Tongues, Being a
     Version Set Forth A.D. 1977 by Anita Bryant, Dale
     Evans, and John Briggs, Gadfly. Healdsburg, Cal.:
     Hermes Free Press, 1977. 14 pp.

406) Department of the Attorney General and of Justice.
     Homosexual Offences. Sydney, Australia: New South
     Wales Bureau of Crime Statistics and Research, 1977.
     43 pp.

407) Diamond, Liz. The Lesbian Primer. Salem, Mass.:
     Women's Educational Media, 1979. 83 pp.

408) England, Michael E. The Bible and Homosexuality.
     San Francisco: Metropolitan Community Church, 1980.
     44 pp.

409) European Court of Human Rights. The Dudgeon Case,
     October 22, 1982, in Publications of the European
     Court of Human Rights, Series A, Vol. 45, 1982.
     48 pp.

410) Fairchild, Betty. The Church's Ministry to Gay Peo-
     ple and Their Families. Denver, Colo.: Parents of
     Gays, 1976.

411) _____ . Parents of Gays. Washington, D. C. :
      Lambda Rising, 1976. 27 pp.

412) Ferris, Dave. Homosexuality and the Social Services:
      The Report of a National Council for Civil Liberties
      Survey of Local Authority Social Service Committees.
      London: National Council for Civil Liberties, 1977.
      89 pp.

413) Field, David. The Homosexual Way--A Christian
      Option? Rev. ed. Downers Grove, Ill. : Inter-
      Varsity Press, 1979. 50 pp.

414) Final Report of the Task Force on Sexual Preference.
      Portland, Ore. : Department of Human Resources,
      1978.

415) Fischer, Hal. Gay Semiotics: A Photographic Study
      of Visual Coding Among Homosexual Men. San Fran-
      cisco: NFS Press, 1977. 56 pp.

416) Forgione, Steve and Kurt T. Hill. (eds.). No Apol-
      ogies: The Unauthorized Publication of Internal Dis-
      cussion Documents of the Socialist Workers Party
      (SWP) Concerning Lesbian /Gay Male Liberation. Part
      II: 1975-79. New York: Lesbian and Gay Monitoring
      Group, 1980. 149 pp.

417) Furnish, Victor P. , and others (eds.). Homosexuality,
      In Search of Christian Understanding: Biblical,
      Theological-Ethical, and Pastoral Care Perspectives.
      Nashville, Tenn. : Discipleship Resources, 1981. 55
      pp.

418) Gay Athletic Games I [Summer 1982]. San Francisco:
      Gay Athletic Games, 1982. 64 pp.

419) Gay Christian Movement. The Bible and Homosexual-
      ity. 2d ed. London: Gay Christian Movement, 1977.
      18 pp.

420) Gay Civil Rights: Support Statements and Resolutions
      Packet. New York: National Gay Task Force, 1976.
      50 pp.

421) Gay Council on Drinking Behavior. The Way Back:
      The Stories of Gay and Lesbian Alcoholics. Washing-
      ton, D. C. : Whitman-Walker Clinic, 1982. 90 pp.

422)   Gay Fathers: Some of Their Stories, Experience and
       Advice. Toronto, Ont.: Gay Fathers of Toronto,
       1982. 74 pp.

423)   Gay/Lesbian Media Directory Worldwide. Chicago:
       Vox Populi Publications, 1981.

424)   Gay Military Counselor's Manual. San Diego: Gay
       Center for Social Services, 1976.

425)   A Gay Parents' Legal Guide to Child Custody. San
       Francisco: National Lawyers Guild, 1980. 44 pp.

426)   Gay Parents' Support Packet. New York: National
       Gay Task Force, n. d.

427)   Gay Rights Writers' Group. It Could Happen to You--
       An Account of the Gay Civil Rights Campaign in
       Eugene, Oregon. Boston: Alyson Publications, 1982.
       90 pp.

428)   Gay Teachers' Group. Out and Positive: An Account
       of How John Warburton Came Out at School and the
       Consequences. London: Gay Teachers' Group, 1978.
       70 pp.

429)   Geyer, Marcia. Human Rights or Homophobia: The
       Rising Tide. Los Angeles: Universal Fellowship,
       1977.

430)   Gidlow, Elsa. Ask No Man Pardon: The Philosophical
       Significance of Being Lesbian. Mill Valley, Cal.:
       Druid Heights Books, 1976.

431)   Gonsiorek, John C. Psychological Adjustment and
       Homosexuality. Washington, D. C.: American Psy-
       chological Association, 1977. Manuscript No. 1478.
       49 pp. (Summarized in Catalog of Selected Documents
       in Psychology, 7;45, 1977.)

432)   Goodman, Bernice. The Lesbian: A Celebration of
       Difference. Brooklyn, N. Y.: Out and Out Press,
       1977. 69 pp.

433)   Haas, Harold I. Homosexuality. St. Louis: Privately
       Printed, 1978. 24 pp.

434)   Harris, Connie (ed.). In the Spirit of Stonewall.

New York: World View Publications, 1979. 85 pp.

435) Illinois Legislative Investigating Commission. The
Sexual Exploitation of Children. Chicago, 1980. 317
pp.

436) Lambda Rising Bookstore. The Whole Gay Catalog:
Books for Gay Men and Lesbians, Their Families and
Friends. Washington, D. C. : Lambda Rising, 1982.
112 pp.

437) A Legislative Guide to Gay Rights. Portland, Ore. :
Portland Town Council, 1977. 80 pp.

438) Leopold, Kathleen, and Thomas Orians. Theological
Pastoral Resources: A Collection of Articles on Ho-
mosexuality from a Pastoral Perspective. 6th ed.
Washington, D. C. : Dignity, 1981. 88 pp.

439) Lesbians and Gay Men: The Law in Pennsylvania.
Philadelphia: American Civil Liberties Union of
Pennsylvania, 1981. 59 pp.

440) Lipshitz, Susan. Sexual Politics in Britain: A
Bibliographical Guide with Historical Notes. Hassocks,
England: Harvester Press, 1977. 41 pp.

441) Mannion, Kristiann. Female Homosexuality: A Comprehensive Review of Theory and Research. Washington, D. C. : American Psychological Association, 1976.
Manuscript No. 1247. 95 pp. (Summarized in Catalog
of Selected Documents in Psychology, 6:44, 1976.)

442) McCubbin, Bob. The Gay Question: A Marxist Appraisal. New York: World View Publishers, 1976.
83 pp.

443) McDonald, A. P. , Jr. An Annotated Subject Indexed
Bibliography of Research on Bisexuality, Lesbianism,
and Male Homosexuality (1975-1978). Washington,
D. C. : American Psychological Association, 1981.
Manuscript No. 2206. 38 pp. (Summarized in Catalog
of Selected Documents in Psychology, 11:16, 1981.)

444) McLean, Duncan (ed.). Gay Liberation in Canada: A
Socialist Perspective. Toronto, Ont. : Pathfinder
Press, 1977. 34 pp.

445) Michael, John. The Gay Drinking Problem--There Is a Solution. Minneapolis: CompCare Publications, 1976. 15 pp.

446) _____. Sober, Clean, and Gay. Minneapolis: CompCare Publications, 1978. 19 pp.

447) Michaels, Kevin. The Gay Book of Etiquette. New York: MLP Enterprises, 1982. 72 pp.

448) Mickley, Richard R. Christian Sexuality: A Reflection on Being Christian and Sexual. Los Angeles: Universal Fellowship, 1976.

449) _____. Prison Ministry Handbook. 3d ed. Los Angeles: Metropolitan Community Church, 1980.

450) Miller, Alan V. (comp.). Homosexuality and Employment: A Selected Bibliography. Toronto: Ontario Ministry of Labour Library, 1978. 111 pp.

451) _____. Homosexuality and Human Rights: A Selected Bibliography. Toronto: Ontario Ministry of Labour Library, 1978. 67 pp.

452) _____. Homosexuality in Specific Fields: The Arts, the Military, the Ministry, Prisons, Sports, Teaching, and Transsexuals: A Selected Bibliography. Toronto: Ontario Ministry of Labour Library, 1978. 58 pp.

453) Mitzel, John. Sports and the Macho Male. Boston: Fag Rag Books, n.d. 31 pp.

454) Moody, Roger. Indecent Assault. London: Word Is Out/Peace News, 1980. 80 pp.

455) Morin, Stephen F. Annotated Bibliography of Research on Lesbianism and Male Homosexuality, 1967-1974. Washington, D.C.: American Pyschological Association, 1976. Manuscript No. 1191. 58 pp. (Summarized in Catalog of Selected Documents in Psychology, 6: 15, 1976.)

456) Moss, Roger. Christians and Homosexuality. Exeter, England: Paternoster Press, 1977. 48 pp.

457)   Myers, Victoria. Sexual Preference Study. Tulsa,
        Okla.: Community Relations Commission, 1976. 93
        pp.

458)   National Commission on the Observance of the Inter-
        national Women's Year. Sexual Preference. Washing-
        ton, D. C.: Government Printing Office, 1977. 65
        pp.

459)   National Gay Health Directory. 2d ed. New York:
        National Lesbian and Gay Health Conference, 1980.
        52 pp.

460)   Nomadic Sisters. Loving Women. 2d ed. rev.
        Sonora, Cal.: Nomadic Sisters, 1976. 55 pp.

461)   Nugent, C. Robert, and Jeannine Gramick (eds.).
        Homosexual Catholics: A New Primer for Discussion.
        Washington, D. C.: Dignity, 1982. 28 pp.

462)   _____, and _____ (eds.). A Time to Speak:
        A Collection of Contemporary Statements from United
        States Catholic Sources on Homosexuality, Gay Minis-
        try, and Social Justice. 2d ed. Mt. Rainer, Md.:
        New Ways Ministry, 1982. 21 pp. (67 Statements)

463)   Ogg, Elizabeth. Changing Views of Homosexuality.
        New York: Public Affairs Information Service, 1978.
        Public Affairs Pamphlet No. 563. 28 pp.

464)   _____. Homosexuality in Our Society. New York:
        Public Affairs Information Service, 1977. Public
        Affairs Pamphlet No. 484. 28 pp.

465)   Pedophilia and Public Morals. London: Campaign
        Against Public Morals, 1980. 95 pp.

466)   Peron, Jim. The Christian Counselor and the Ho-
        mosexual Client. Glen Ellyn, Ill.: Privately Printed,
        1979. 10 pp.

467)   _____. Homosexuality and the Miracle Makers.
        Glen Ellyn, Ill.: Privately Printed, 1978. 20 pp.

468)   Pittenger, W. Norman. Gay Lifestyles: A Christian
        Interpretation of Homosexuality and the Homosexual.
        Los Angeles: Universal Fellowship, 1977.

469) Presbyterian Church in the United States, Council on
      Theology and Culture. The Church and Homosexuality:
      A Preliminary Study. Atlanta: Office of the Stated
      Clerk, 1977. 37 pp.

470) Prologue: An Examination of the Mormon Attitude
      Towards Homosexuality. Salt Lake City: Prometheus
      Enterprises, 1978. 58 pp.

471) Quinn, John R. Pastoral Letter on Homosexuality.
      Boston: Daughters of St. Paul, 1980.

472) Report of the Task Force on Homosexuality of the
      Episcopal Diocese of Michigan. Detroit: Episcopal
      Diocese, 1973. (Reprinted in Batchelor, entry no. 1,
      pp. 127-34.)

473) Richter, Rosalyn. Gays and the Law: A Guide for
      Lay People. New York: Lambda Defense and Educa-
      tion Fund, 1982.

474) Rivers, Walter C. Walt Whitman's Anomaly. Fol-
      croft, Pa.: Folcroft Library Editions, 1977. 70 pp.

475) Schuman, Joseph. The Draft: Gay Questions, Serious
      Answers. San Diego: Military Task Force, n.d.

476) Sexual Orientation Report. Lansing, Mich.: Depart-
      ment of Civil Rights, 1977.

477) Slater, Don, and Ursula E. Copely. (eds.). Directory
      of Homosexual Organizations and Publications. 6th ed.
      Los Angeles: Homosexual Information Center, 1982.
      62 pp.

478) Stanley, Julia P. Sexist Slang and the Gay Commu-
      nity--Are You One Too? Ann Arbor; University of
      Michigan Press, 1979. 18 pp.

479) Thorstad, David (ed.). Gay Liberation and Socialism:
      Documents from the Discussion on Gay Liberation In-
      side the Socialist Workers Party (1970-1973). New
      York: Privately Printed, 1976. 142 pp.

480) Ulrichs, Karl H. Raging Sword. Translated from
      the German by Michael A. Lombardi. Los Angeles:
      Century Typographics, 1979. 50 pp.

481) United States Congress, House of Representatives.
      Committee on Education and Labor.   Subcommittee on
      Employment Opportunities.   Civil Rights Amendments
      Act of 1979:   Hearing October 10, 1980 on HR 2074 to
      Prohibit Discrimination on the Basis of Affectional or
      Sexual Orientation, and for Other Purposes.   96th
      Congress, 2d Session.   Washington, D. C. :   Govern-
      ment Printing Office, 1980.   161 pp.

482) _____ . _____ . _____ . Civil Rights Amend-
      ments Act of 1981:   Hearing January 27, 1982 on HR
      1454 to Prohibit Discrimination on the Basis of Af-
      fectional or Sexual Orientation, and for Other Pur-
      poses.   97th Congress, 2d Session.   Washington,
      D. C. :   Government Printing Office, 1982.   89 pp.

483) _____ . _____ .   Subcommittee on Select Edu-
      cation.   Sexual Exploitation of Children.   95th Con-
      gress, 1st Session.   Washington, D. C. :   Government
      Printing Office, 1977.   451 pp.

484) _____ .   Committee on the Judiciary.   Subcommittee
      on Crime.   Sexual Exploitation of Children.   95th Con-
      gress, 1st Session.   Washington, D. C. :   Government
      Printing Office, 1977.   477 pp.

485) United States Congress, Senate.   Committee on the
      Judiciary.   Subcommittee to Investigate Juvenile Delin-
      quency.   Protection of Children Against Sexual Ex-
      ploitation.   95th Congress, 1st Session.   Washington,
      D. C. :   Government Printing Office, 1978.   158 pp.

486) Verstraete, Beert C. (comp.).   Homosexuality in
      Ancient Greek and Roman Civilization: A Critical
      Bibliography with Supplement.   Toronto, Ont. :   Cana-
      dian Gay Archives, 1982.   14 pp.

487) Walter, Nicolas.   Blasphemy in Britain: The Prac-
      tice and Punishment of Blasphemy, and the Trial of
      "Gay News. "   London: Rationalist Press Association,
      1977.   16 pp.

488) Weininger, Otto.   Physical Attraction and the Theory
      of Homosexuality.   Albuquerque, N. M. :   Gloucester
      Art Press, 1979.   52 pp.

489) Wyland, Francie.   Motherhood, Lesbianism, and

Child Custody. New York: Falling Wall Press, 1977. 36 pp.

490) Ziebold, Thomas O. , and John E. Mongeon. Ways to Gay Sobriety. Washington, D. C. : Whitman-Walker Clinic, 1980. 15 pp.

DOCTORAL DISSERTATIONS

491) Adelman, Marcy R. Adjustment to Aging and Styles of Being Gay: A Study of Elderly Gay Men and Lesbians. Ph. D. , Psychology, Wright Institute, 1980. 100 pp. (Summary in Dissertation Abstracts International, 41/02-B, p. 679).

492) Aguerro, Joseph E. The Effects of Attitudinal Similarity on Heterosexual Dislike of Homosexuals. Ph. D. , Psychology, Purdue University, 1982. 95 pp. (Summary in Dissertation Abstracts International, 43/12-B, p. 4193.)

493) Alpert, Peter H. Internalized Stigma Among Homosexual Men. Ph. D. , Psychology, California School of Professional Psychology, 1978. 122 pp. (Summary in Dissertation Abstracts International, 30/07-B, p. 3580.)

494) Amodia, Anthony J. The Gay Men's Health Project: An Institutional Case Study of a Community as an Educational System. Ed. D. , Education, Columbia University Teachers College, 1982. 123 pp. (Summary in Dissertation Abstracts International, 43/05-A, p. 1400.)

495) Anderson, Carla L. The Effect of a Workshop on Attitudes of Female Nursing Students Toward Male Homosexuality. Ph. D. , Psychology, University of Missouri at Columbia, 1978. 142 pp. (Summary in Dissertation Abstracts International, 40/01-B, p. 427.)

496) Bailey, Paul J. An Analysis of the Utilization of Organization Rhetoric: The United Church of Christ's Rhetorical Construction of Postures Toward Homosexuality. Ph. D. , Speech, Pennsylvania State University,

44

1978.   279 pp.   (Summary in Dissertation Abstracts
International, 39/10-A, p. 5799.)

497)   Baker, Andrea J.   Ideology and Structure of Social
Movement Organizations: A Case Study of Lesbian-
Feminism.   Ph. D. , Sociology, Case Western Reserve
University, 1979.   274 pp.   (Summary in Dissertation
Abstracts International, 40/02-A, p. 826.)

498)   Barnard, Robert J.   Detection and Control of Sexually
Transmitted Diseases Among Male Homosexuals: A
Human Ecology Approach.   Ph. D. , Health Sciences,
George Washington University, 1980.

499)   Barton, Richard W.   Education and the Politics of
Desire: A Semiotic Analysis of the Discourse on Male
Homosexualities.   Ph. D. , Education, University of
Illinois at Urbana, 1982.   239 pp.   (Summary in Dis-
sertation Abstracts International, 43/03-A, p. 752.)

500)   Basch, Dennis B.   The Male Role, Homophobia, and
Coping Styles in Gay Males.   Ph. D. , Psychology,
California School of Professional Psychology, 1982.
120 pp.   (Summary in Dissertation Abstracts International, 43/12-B, p. 4135.)

501)   Beach, Berdena J.   Lesbian and Nonlesbian Women:
Profiles of Development and Self-Actualization.   Ph. D. ,
Psychology, University of Iowa, 1980.   253 pp.   (Summary in Dissertation Abstracts International, 42/03-B,
p. 1199.)

502)   Beebe, Leo P.   Acceptance, Sexual Orientation, and
Psychological Health: A Study of Gay Males.   Ph. D. ,
Psychology, Kent State University, 1981.   139 pp.
(Summary in Dissertation Abstracts International,
42/05-B, p. 2041.)

503)   Belkin, Beth M.   Homophobia in Women.   Ph. D. ,
Psychology, Adelphi University, 1982.   157 pp.   (Summary in Dissertation Abstracts International, 42/05-B,
p. 2041.)

504)   Benitez, John C.   The Effect of Gay Identity Acquisition on the Psychological Adjustment of Male Homosexuals.   Ph. D. , Psychology, Northwestern Univer-

sity, 1982. 177 pp. (Summary in Dissertation Abstracts International, 43/10-B, p. 3350.)

505) Bernard, Larry C. Sexual Preference and Sex Role Identification of Homosexual and Heterosexual Males. Ph. D., Psychology, University of Southern California, 1980. (Summary in Dissertation Abstracts International, 40/11-B, p. 5387.)

506) Beverley, Gay S. Some Factors in the Development of Homosexual Object Choice. Ph. D., Psychology, University of Pittsburgh, 1976. 233 pp. (Summary in Dissertation Abstracts International, 37/07-B, p. 3577.)

507) Bilotta, Vincent M., III. An Existential-Phenomenological Study of Gay Male Permanent Lover Relationships. Ph. D., Psychology, Duquesne University, 1976. 388 pp. (Summary in Dissertation Abstracts International, 38/01-B, p. 345.)

508) Blacher, Jill. An Exploration of Androgyny, Self-actualization, and Field Independence in Lesbian Feminist and Non-Feminist and Non-Lesbian Feminist and Non-Feminist Women. Ph. D., Psychology, California School of Professional Psychology, 1977. 221 pp. (Summary in Dissertation Abstracts International, 39/09-B, p. 4568.)

509) Blum, Adria C. Lesbians' Sexual Preference: The Meaning of the Origins Question in the Lives of Gay Women. Ph. D., Psychology, Wright Institute, 1982. 276 pp. (Summary in Dissertation Abstracts International, 43/04-B, p. 1299.)

510) Booth, Harold. Psychological Health and Sexual Orientation in Males. Ph. D., Psychology, California School of Professional Psychology, 1977. 133 pp. (Summary in Dissertation Abstracts International, 38/06-B, p. 2844.)

511) Bozett, Frederick W. Gay Fathers: The Convergence of a Dichotomized Identity Through Integrative Sanctioning. D. N. S., Nursing, University of California at San Francisco, 1979. 229 pp. (Summary in Dissertation Abstracts International, 40/06-B, p. 2680.)

512) Braverman, June E. T. An Examination of the

Constitutional Validity of Discriminating Practices in Cases Involving Homosexual Teachers. Ph. D. , Education, University of Iowa, 1979. 199 pp. (Summary in Dissertation Abstracts International, 40 /05-A, p. 2368.)

513)   Brooks, Virginia R. Minority Stress and Adaptation Among Lesbian Women. Ph. D. , Sociology, University of California at Berkeley, 1977.

514)   Brown, Arthur A. The Philosophical Assumption Underlying Homosexuality: A Frame of Reference for Advisors to Students. Ph. D. , Psychology, Boston College, 1977. 128 pp. (Summary in Dissertation Abstracts International, 37 /11-B, p. 5808.)

515)   Burdt, Eric T. The Self-Concept of Adult Male Homosexuals: A Comparison of a Homosexual Population with a Normative Population. Ed. D. , Education, Memphis State University, 1980. 103 pp. (Summary in Dissertation Abstracts International, 41 /07-A, p. 2938.)

516)   Cavin, Susan E. An Hystorical and Cross-Cultural Analysis of Sex Ratios, Female Sexuality, and Homosexual Segregation versus Hetero-sexual Integration Patterns in Relation to the Liberation of Women. Ph. D. , Sociology, Rutgers University, 1978. 362 pp. (Summary in Dissertation Abstracts International, 39 / 11-A, p. 7005.)

517)   Cervantes-Gutierrez, Jose J. Sexual Attitudes and Behaviors of the Latino Gay Male. Ph. D. , Psychology, Wright Institute, 1981. 105 pp. (Summary in Dissertation Abstracts International, 42 /03-B, p. 1164.)

518)   Chaffee, Paul N. Personality Factors Relating to Stability in Male Homosexual Relationships. Ph. D. , Psychology, Boston University, 1976. 176 pp. (Summary in Dissertation Abstracts International, 37 /03-B, p. 1401.)

519)   Chitwood, Karen L. The Relation of Attitudes Toward the Male Role, Attitudes Toward Homosexuality, and Sex-typed Characteristics to Traditionality of Occupation Choice Among College Men. Ph. D. , Psychology, New York University, 1980. 199 pp. (Summary in Dissertation Abstracts International, 42 /01-B, p. 353.)

520)   Clark, Mary F.   Attitudes, Information and Behavior
        of Counselors Toward Homosexual Clients.   Ed. D. ,
        Education, Wayne State University, 1979.   110 pp.
        (Summary in Dissertation Abstracts International, 40/
        11-A, p. 5729.)

521)   Clemens, Daryl J.   Homosexuality: A Desensitization
        Workshop for Homophobic Clergy-Counselors.   D. Min. ,
        Religion, Colgate Rochester Divinity School, 1979.

522)   Clevenger, Lyle J. , Jr.   Some Determinants of the
        Attitudes and Responses of Selected Protestant Chris-
        tians to Homosexuality and Their Implications for
        Christian Adult Education.   Ph. D. , Education, Boston
        University, 1982.   219 pp.   (Summary in Dissertation
        Abstracts International, 43/01-A, p. 46.)

523)   Cornelius, David L.   An Application of a Rules-based
        Theory of Interpersonal Communication: The Rules of
        Taboo Communication with a "Gay Community. "
        Ph. D. , Sociology, Florida State University, 1980.
        212 pp.   (Summary in Dissertation Abstracts Inter-
        national, 41/03-A, p. 1239.)

524)   Corzine Harold J.   The Gay Press.   Ph. D. , Soci-
        ology, Washington University, 1977.   277 p.   (Sum-
        mary in Dissertation Abstracts International, 38/12-A,
        p. 7606.)

525)   Crane, Richard W.   Problems of the Homosexual in
        Relation to the Church.   D. Min. , Religion, Fuller
        Theological Seminary, 1977.

526)   Crouch, Altha M.   A Comparison of Parental Home
        and Family Relationships and Family Constellations
        of Adult Female Homosexuals and Adult Female Het-
        erosexuals.   Ed. D. , Education, University of New
        Mexico, 1977.   119 pp.   (Summary in Dissertation
        Abstracts International, 38/09-A, p. 5264.)

527)   Delph, Edward W.   Homosexual Eroticism in Urban
        Public Places: An Ethnographic Study of Silent Langu-
        age Communication.   Ph. D. , Sociology, New School
        for Social Research, 1976.   332 pp.   (Summary in
        Dissertations Abstracts International, 37/06-A, p.
        3922.)

528) DeMonteflores, Carmen. Lesbian Sexuality: A
      Phenomenologically Based Approach. Ph. D. , Psy-
      chology, California School of Professional Psychology,
      1978. 138 pp. (Summary in Dissertation Abstracts
      International, 39 /07-B, p. 3503.)

529) Dugger, Ronald B. Fantasy Ideation in Men: Gay
      Male Fantasies During Sex with Their Partners.
      Ph. D. , Psychology, Georgia State University, 1980.
      123 pp. (Summary in Dissertation Abstracts Inter-
      national, 41 /10-B, p. 3885.)

530) Elliot, Phyllis E. Lesbian Identity and Self-Disclosure.
      Ph. D. , Psychology, University of Windsor, Canada,
      1981. (Summary in Dissertation Abstracts Interna-
      tional, 42 /08-B, p. 3494.)

531) Emond, Norma J. The Consequences of the Lesbian
      Label on Social Workers' Judgments of the Lesbian.
      D. S.W. , Social Work, University of Denver, 1978.
      297 pp. (Summary in Dissertation Abstracts Inter-
      national, 39 /11-A, p. 6970.)

532) Emplaincourt, Marilyn. La Femme Damnée: A Study
      of the Lesbian in French Literature from Diderot to
      Proust. Ph. D. , French, University of Alabama, 1977.
      445 pp. (Summary in Dissertation Abstracts Inter-
      national, 39 /04-A, p. 2316.)

533) Epstein, David J. Implications of New Sex Role For-
      mulations for Homosexual Males. Ph. D. , Psychology,
      University of California at Los Angeles, 1980. 128
      pp. (Summary in Dissertation Abstracts International,
      41 /04-B, p. 1500.)

534) Feinstein, Nancy J. Caught in the Middle: Parental
      Response to Their Adult Children's Homosexuality.
      Ph. D. , Psychology, Wright Institute, 1982. 351 pp.
      (Summary in Dissertation Abstracts International.
      43 /04-B, p. 1301.)

535) Fennessey, Alice. An Exploration of the Domain of
      Attitudes Toward Homosexuality. Ph. D. , Psychology,
      Columbia University, 1976. 127 pp. (Summary in
      Dissertation Abstracts International, 37 /07-B, p.
      3578.)

536) Fischer, Thomas R.   A Study of Educators' Attitudes
      Toward Homosexuality.   Ed. D. , Education, University
      of Virginia, 1982.   157 pp.   (Summary in Dissertation
      Abstracts International, 43/10-A, p. 3294.)

537) Fitzgerald, William A.   Pseudoheterosexuality in
      Prison and Out: A Study of the Lower Class Black
      Lesbian.   Ph. D. , Sociology, City University of New
      York, 1977.   357 pp.   (Summary in Dissertation Ab-
      stracts International, 39/04-A, p. 2582.)

538) Fogarty, Elizabeth L.   "Passing as Straight:" A
      Phenomenological Analysis of the Experience of the
      Lesbian Who is Professionally Employed.   Ph. D. ,
      Psychology, University of Pittsburgh, 1980.   182 pp.
      (Summary in Dissertation Abstracts International,
      41/06-B, p. 2384.)

539) Follett, Richard J.   On Teaching Gay Literature.
      A. D. , General Literature, University of Michigan,
      1980.   265 pp.   (Summary in Dissertation Abstracts
      International, 41/05-A, p. 2093.)

540) Fradkin, Howard R.   An Exploratory Study of the
      Effects of Specific Training in Counseling Lesbian and
      Gay Clients on the Counseling Behaviors and Attitudes
      of Counselors-in-Training.   Ph. D. , Education, Uni-
      versity of North Carolina at Chapel Hill, 1980.   266
      pp.   (Summary in Dissertation Abstracts International,
      42/02-A, p. 548.)

541) Furgeri, Lena M. B.   The Lesbian/Feminist Move-
      ment and Social Change: Female Homosexuality, A
      New Consciousness.   Ed. D. , Sociology, Columbia Uni-
      versity Teachers College, 1977.   257 pp.   (Summary
      in Dissertation Abstracts International, 37/12-A, p.
      7999.)

542) Garfinkle, Ellen M.   Psychotherapist Attitudes Toward
      Homosexual Clients.   Ph. D. , Psychology, California
      School of Professional Psychology, 1978.   187 pp.
      (Summary in Dissertation Abstracts International, 39/
      07-B, p. 3585.)

543) Germain, Edward J.   A Comparative Analysis of Psy-
      chological Adaptation to Aging Between Gay Men and
      Gay Women.   Ph. D. , Psychology, University of Oregon

1981. 134 pp. (Summary in Dissertation Abstracts International, 42/08-B, p. 3420.)

544) Goldberg, Raymond. The Effects of Three Different Types of Audiovisual Programs on Attitudes Toward Homosexuality. Ph.D., Education, University of Toledo, 1981. 123 pp. (Summary in Dissertation Abstracts International, 42/06-A, p. 2514.)

545) Goldyn, Lawrence M. Legal Ideology and the Regulation of Homosexual Behavior. Ph.D., Political Science, Stanford University, 1979. 274 pp (Summary in Dissertation Abstracts International, 40/09-A, p. 5167.)

546) Gorman, Edward M. A New Light on Zion: A Study of Three Homosexual Religious Congregations in Urban America. Ph.D., Anthropology, University of Chicago, 1980.

547) Grzelkowski, Kathryn P. Who Am I to Me? Homosexual Self-Identity in a World of Role Versatility. Ph.D., Sociology, Indiana University, 1976. 252 pp. (Summary in Dissertation Abstracts International, 37/04-A, p. 2429.)

548) Guido, Paul A. A Comparison of Heterosexual and Homosexual Single and Cohabiting Male Masturbation Fantasies. Ph.D., Psychology, California Professional School of Psychology, 1981. 272 pp. (Summary in Dissertation Abstracts International, 42/05-B, p. 2056.)

549) Hall, Marny. Gays in Corporations: The Invisible Minority. Ph.D., Psychology, Union for Experimenting Colleges and Universities, 1981. 161 pp. (Summary in Dissertation Abstracts International, 42/09-B, p. 3872.)

550) Haltiwanger, Charles D. Discriminants of Psychological Adjustment Within a Homosexual Population. Ph.D., Psychology, University of North Carolina at Chapel Hill, 1979. 158 pp. (Summary in Dissertation Abstracts International, 40/05-B, p. 2366.)

551) Hart, Maureen T. Gender Attitudes and Adjustment in Homosexual Men. Ph.D., Psychology, George

Peabody College, 1978.   180 pp.   (Summary in Dissertation Abstracts International, 39/08-B, p. 4031.)

552)   Harvey, James J.   A Study of Employment Discrimination and Reeducation of a Selected Group of Homosexuals.   Ed. D. , Education, East Texas State University, 1978.   185 pp.   (Summary in Dissertation Abstracts International, 39/11-A, p. 6612.)

553)   Hensel, William C.   Attributed Sexual Preference and Attitude Similarity of a Social Other as Factors Influencing Interpersonal Attraction: A Social Psychological Investigation of the Homosexual Label.   Ed. D. , Psychology, Ball State University, 1976.   300 pp.   (Summary in Dissertation Abstracts International, 37/10-B, p. 5436.)

554)   Hill, Lorie E.   The Baby Dilemma: How Homosexual and Heterosexual Women Are Handling This Decision.   Ph. D. , Psychology, Wright Institute, 1980.   181 pp.   (Summary in Dissertation Abstracts International, 41/05-B, p. 1974.)

555)   Hill, Marjorie J.   Effects of Conscious and Unconscious Factors on Child Rearing Attitudes of Lesbian Mothers.   Ph. D. , Psychology, Adelphi University, 1981.   111 pp.   (Summary in Dissertation Abstracts International, 42/04-B, p. 1608.)

556)   Hoeffer, Beverly.   Lesbian and Heterosexual Single Mothers' Influence on Their Children's Acquisition of Sex-Role Traits and Behavior.   D. N. S. , Nursing, University of California at San Francisco, 1979.   255 pp.   (Summary in Dissertation Abstracts International, 40/10-B, p. 4738.)

557)   Howard, Holly L.   Prejudice Against Women and Homosexuals.   Ph. D. , Psychology, University of Washington, 1981.   78 pp.   (Summary in Dissertation Abstracts International, 41/05-B, p. 1917.)

558)   Hyman, Ralph A.   A Comparison of Methods for Changing Homophobic Attitudes of Mental Health Professionals: The Effects of Cognitive vs. Affective and Homosexuality vs. Homophobia Approaches.   Ed. D. , Education, Auburn University, 1980.   148 pp.   (Summary in Dissertation Abstracts International, 40/12-A, p. 6201.)

559)   Istvan, Joseph A.   Attitudes Toward Homosexuality
       and the Male Sex Role: Effects of Normative Stan-
       dards.   Ph. D. , Psychology, Kansas State University,
       1980.   103 pp.   (Summary in Dissertation Abstracts
       International, 41/07-B, p. 2825.)

560)   James, Elizabeth C.   Treatment of Homosexuality:
       A Re-analysis and Synthesis of Outcome Studies.
       Ph. D. , Psychology, Brigham Young University, 1978.
       317 pp.   (Summary in Dissertation Abstracts Interna-
       tional, 39/08-B, p. 4035.)

561)   Jenkins, David P.   Demographic Variations in So-
       cietal Response to Homosexuality.   Ed. D. , Education,
       State University of New York at Albany, 1976.   152
       pp.   (Summary in Dissertation Abstracts International,
       37/01-A, p. 133.)

562)   Johnson, Julius M.   The Influence of Assimilation on
       the Psychological Adjustment of Black Homosexual
       Men.   Ph. D. , Psychology, California School of Pro-
       fessional Psychology, 1981.   200 pp.   (Summary in
       Dissertation Abstracts International, 42/11-B, p.
       4620.)

563)   Julian, Brigham R.   Male Homosexuality: A Theoret-
       ical and Philosphical Analysis and Integration of Eti-
       ology.   Ph. D. , Psychology, Brigham Young Univer-
       sity, 1978.   156 pp.   (Summary in Dissertation Ab-
       stracts International, 38/08-B, p. 3887.)

564)   Kanner, Ellen B.   Contemporary Standards of Gender
       Characteristics of Heterosexuals, Homosexuals, and
       Bisexuals as Evaluated by Mental Health Practitioners.
       Ph. D. , Psychology, Fordham University, 1980.   133
       pp.   (Summary in Dissertation Abstracts International,
       40/12-B, p. 5814.)

565)   Kasl, Charlotte E.   Psychotherapy Outcome of Lesbian
       Women as Related to Therapist Attitude Toward and
       Knowledge of Lesbianism.   Ph. D. , Psychology, Ohio
       State University, 1982.   235 pp.   (Summary in Dis-
       sertation Abstracts International, 43/04-B, p. 1256.)

566)   Keener, James D.   Homophobia: Irrational Beliefs
       and Death Concern: A Correlational Investigation.
       Ph. D. , Psychology, U. S. International University,

1979. 117 pp. (Summary in Dissertation Abstracts International, 41/02-B, p. 692.)

567) King, William M. The Etiology of Homosexuality as Related to Childhood Experiences and Adult Adjustment: A Study of the Perceptions of Homosexual Males, Their Parents and Siblings. Ed. D., Psychology, Indiana University, 1980. 267 pp. (Summary in Dissertation Abstracts International, 41/02-B, p. 734.)

568) Knapp, Gail I. A Reconstituted Lesbian Family: An Ethnographic Study to Formulate a Grounded Theory of Closeting Behavior. Ph. D., Psychology, Michigan State University, 1982. 113 pp. (Summary in Dissertation Abstracts International, 43/02-B, p. 557.)

569) Knutsen, Marla T. The Power of Mr. Compson in "Absalom, Absalom!": Heroism/Homoeroticism/Approach-Avoidance Toward Women. Ph. D., Modern Literature, University of Southern California, 1978. (Summary in Dissertation Abstracts International, 41/02-A, p. 668.)

570) Koller, Michael. A. A Comparison of the Satisfaction with a Residence Hall Living Situation of Gay/Lesbian Residents with Heterosexual Residents as Measured by the University Residence Environment Scale and a Gay/Lesbian Awareness Program for University Residence Hall Assistants. Ed. D., Education, University of Tennessee, 1980. 99 pp. (Summary in Dissertation Abstracts International, 41/11-A, p. 4653.)

571) Kuba, Sue A. Being-in-a-Lesbian Family: The Preadolescent Child's Experience. Ph. D., Psychology, California School of Professional Psychology, 1981. 255 pp. (Summary in Dissertation Abstracts International, 42/10-B, p. 4196.)

572) Kus, Robert J. Gay Freedom; An Ethnography of Coming Out. Ph. D., Sociology, University of Montana, 1980. 423 pp. (Summary in Dissertation Abstracts International, 42/02-A, p. 864.)

573) Larson, Paul C. Sexual Identity and Self-Concept. Ph. D., Psychology, University of Utah, 1977. 118 pp. (Summary in Dissertation Abstracts International, 38/04-B, p. 1889.)

574) Leonard, Howard E. Homophobia and Self-Disclosure: The Result of Sex-Role Socialization. Ph. D. , Psychology, California School of Professional Psychology, 1981. 189 pp. (Summary in Dissertation Abstracts International, 42/05-B, p. 2134.)

575) Levy, Terri. The Lesbian: As Perceived by Mental Health Workers. Ph. D. , Psychology, California School of Professional Psychology, 1978. 140 pp. (Summary in Dissertation Abstracts International, 39/07-B, p. 3524.)

576) Licata, Salvatore J. Gay Power: A History of the American Gay Movement, 1908-1974. Ph. D. , History, University of Southern California, 1978. (Summary in Dissertation Abstracts International, 39/01-A, p. 407.)

577) Lieberman, Joseph A. The Emergence of Lesbians and Gay Men as Characters in Plays Produced on the American Stage from 1922 to 1954. Ph. D. , Theater, City University of New York, 1981. 592 pp. (Summary in Dissertation Abstracts International, 41/12-A, p. 4889.)

578) Lindquist, Neil E. Adaptation to Marginal Status: The Case of Gay Males. Ph. D. , Sociology, University of Alberta, Canada, 1976.

579) Lisagor, Nancy L. Lesbian Identity in the Subculture of Women's Bars. Ph. D. , Sociology, University of Pennsylvania, 1980. 244 pp. (Summary in Dissertation Abstracts International, 41/03-A, p. 1237.)

580) Loftin, Elizabeth C. The Study of Disclosure and Support in a Lesbian Population. Ph. D. , Sociology, University of Texas at Austin, 1981. 257 pp. (Summary in Dissertation Abstracts International, 42/03-A, p. 1348.)

581) Ludd, Steven O. Law, Morals, and Constitutional Decision-Making: An Evaluation of the Constitutional Validity of Placing Criminal Sanctions on Adult Consensual Homosexual Behavior. Ph. D. , Political Science, Syracuse University, 1976. 228 pp. (Summary in Dissertation Abstracts International, 37/11-A, p. 7279.)

582) Marotta, Robert P. The Politics of Homosexuality:
      Homophile and Early Gay Liberation Organizations in
      New York City. Ph. D., Sociology, Harvard Univer-
      sity, 1979.

583) McBride, Max F. Effect of Visual Stimuli in Electric
      Aversion Therapy. Ph. D., Psychology, Brigham
      Young University, 1976. 111 pp. (Summary in Dis-
      sertation Abstracts International, 37/08-B, p. 4154.)

584) McCandlish, Barbara M. Object Relations and Dream
      Content of Bisexual, Homosexual, and Heterosexual
      Women. Ph. D., Psychology, Harvard University,
      1976.

585) McGirr, Marilyn V. Gender Characteristics At-
      tributed to Heterosexual, Homosexual, and Bisexual
      Persons by Therapists and Non-Therapists. Ph. D.,
      Psychology, Fordham University, 1980. 133 pp.
      (Summary in Dissertation Abstracts International, 41/
      03-B, p. 1094.)

586) McGovern, Robert H. P sychological Androgyny and
      Its Relation to Psychological Adjustment in the Homo-
      sexual Male. Ph. D., Psychology, Case Western Re-
      serve University, 1977. 105 pp. (Summary in Dis-
      sertation Abstracts International, 38/03-B, p. 1410.)

587) Mead, Stanley W. Men Loving Men: A Phenomeno-
      logical Exploration of Committed Gay Relationships.
      Ph. D., Psychology, California School of Professional
      Psychology, 1979. 416 pp. (Summary in Dissertation
      Abstracts International, 40/08-B, p. 3952.)

588) Mercer, Barbara L. Attitudes Toward Female Ho-
      mosexuality: A Phenomenological Study of Caucasian
      Heterosexual Women with Different Educational Back-
      grounds. Ph. D., Psychology, California School of
      Professional Psychology, 1980. 222 pp. (Summary
      in Dissertation Abstracts International, 41/12-B, p.
      4795.)

589) Miller, D'Lane S. Homosexualities: A Study of
      Types. Ph. D., Education, Louisiana State Univer-
      sity, 1981. 286 pp. (Summary in Dissertation Ab-
      stracts International, 42/03-A, p. 1064.)

590)   Mitchell, Judith N.   Changes in Adolescent Literature
         with Homosexual Motifs, Themes, and Characters.
         Ph. D. , Education, University of Connecticut, 1982.
         121 pp.   (Summary in Dissertation Abstracts Inter-
         national, 43/01-A, p. 133.)

591)   Montgomery, Kathryn C.   Gay Activists and the Net-
         works: A Case Study of Special Interest Pressure on
         Television.   Ph. D. , Communications, University of
         California at Los Angeles, 1979.   243 pp.   (Summary
         in Dissertation Abstracts International, 40/10-A, p.
         5236.)

592)   Moses, Alice E.   Playing It Straight: A Study of
         Identity Management in a Sample of Lesbian Women.
         D. S. W. , Social Work, University of California at
         Berkeley, 1977.   197 pp.   (Summary in Dissertation
         Abstracts International, 39/02-A, p. 1149.)

593)   Nachbar, Gemma M.   Gender Role and Sexuality in
         Transsexual Women as Compared to Homosexual and
         Heterosexual Women.   Ph. D. , Psychology, Catholic
         University of America, 1977.   114 pp.   (Summary in
         Dissertation Abstracts International, 38/03-B, p.
         1412.)

594)   Nash, Laura J.   Relation Between Sexual Object Choice
         of Women and Ego Development, Neuroticism, and
         Conscious and Unconscious Sexual Identity.   Ph. D. ,
         Psychology, Hofstra University, 1976.   140 pp.   (Sum-
         mary in Dissertation Abstracts International, 36/12-B,
         p. 6394.)

595)   Nelson, Audrey A.   A Qualitative Assessment of Per-
         ceived Communication Correlates of Female Homo-
         sexuality and Success.   Ph. D. , Sociology, University
         of Colorado, 1980.   184 pp.   (Summary in Disserta-
         tion Abstracts International, 41/04-A, p. 1795.)

596)   Newcomb, Michael D.   Development of a Measurement
         Device That Allows the Retrospective Personality As-
         sessment of Mother Relative to Father, and Validation
         of This Instrument on Heterosexuals, Homosexuals, and
         Male Transvestites.   Ph. D. , Psychology, University
         of California at Los Angeles, 1979.   196 pp.   (Sum-
         mary in Dissertation Abstracts International, 40/09-B,
         p. 4497.)

597)   Nickeson, Suzanne S.   A Comparison of Gay and
        Heterosexual Teachers on Professional and Personal
        Dimensions.   Ph. D. , Education, University of Flori-
        da, 1980.   137 pp.   (Summary in Dissertation Ab-
        stracts International, 41/09-A, p. 3956.)

598)   Nye, William R.   Attitudes Toward Homosexuality
        in a Group of Clergymen.   Ph. D. , Psychology,
        Adelphi University, 1981.   157 pp.   (Summary in
        Dissertation Abstracts International, 42/04-B, p.
        1616.)

599)   O'Carolan, Roberta J.   An Investigation of the Rela-
        tionship of Self-Disclosure of Sexual Preference to
        Self-Esteem, Feminism, and Locus of Control in
        Lesbians.   Ph. D. , Psychology, University of Missouri
        at Kansas City, 1982.   91 pp.   (Summary in Disser-
        tation Abstracts International, 43/03-B, p. 915.)

600)   Oliver, Lawrence S.   Male Homosexual Dyads: A
        Study of Thirty Couples.   Ph. D. , Psychology, George
        Washington University, 1976.   132 pp.   (Summary in
        Dissertation Abstracts International, 37/01-B, p. 471.)

601)   Omark, Richard C.   The Social Organization of a Gay
        Male Community.   Ph. D. , Sociology, Michigan State
        University, 1979.   252 pp.   (Summary in Dissertation
        Abstracts International, 40/09-A, p. 5211.)

602)   Painter, Dorothy S.   A Communicative Study of Humor
        in a Lesbian Speech Community: Becoming a Member.
        Ph. D. , Speech, Ohio State University, 1978.   237 pp.
        (Summary in Dissertation Abstracts International, 39/
        10-A, p. 5805.)

603)   Perkins, Muriel W.   Biobehavioral Aspects of Female
        Homosexuality.   Ph. D. , Anthropology, Southern Meth-
        odist University, 1976.   148 pp.   (Summary in Dis-
        sertation Abstracts International, 37/11-A, p. 7187.)

604)   Peterson, Anne V.   Emotional Intimacy Among College
        Males: A Construct Validation Study of the Personal
        Anxiety Factor of Homosexuality Attitude Scale.
        Ph. D. , Psychology, Ohio University, 1980.   203 pp.
        (Summary in Dissertation Abstracts International, 42/
        01-B, p. 432.)

605) Pinka, Allan. Gay Men and Their Parents: A Study
      of Self-Disclosure and Its Meaning. Ph. D. , Psy-
      chology, California School of Professional Psychology,
      1977. 119 pp. (Summary in Dissertation Abstracts
      International, 39 /08-B, p. 4048.)

606) Pledger, Raymond, H. , Jr. Early Parent-Child Rela-
      tionships of Male Homosexuals and Heterosexuals.
      Ph. D. , Psychology, University of Texas at Austin,
      1977. 201 pp. (Summary in Dissertation Abstracts
      International, 38 /12-B, p. 6169.)

607) Ponse, Barbara. Identities in the Lesbian World.
      Ph. D. , Sociology, University of Southern California,
      1976. (Summary in Dissertation Abstracts Interna-
      tional, 38 /01-A, p. 504.)

608) Propper, Alice M. L. Importation and Deprivation
      Perspectives on Homosexuality in Correctional In-
      stitutions: An Empirical Test of Their Relative Ef-
      ficacy. Ph. D. , Sociology, University of Michigan,
      1976. 315 pp. (Summary in Dissertation Abstracts
      International, 37 /10-A, p. 6783.)

609) Pryor, Eugene P. , Jr. Human Figure Drawing in
      Identifying Practicing Male Homosexuals. Psych. D. ,
      Psychology, Nova University, 1982. 204 pp. (Sum-
      mary in Dissertation Abstracts International, 43 /10-B,
      p. 3372.)

610) Read, Daniel V. A Touching Case of Attitude Change
      Toward the Homosexual Experimenter. Ph. D. , Psy-
      chology, University of Wyoming, 1978. 77 pp. (Sum-
      mary in Dissertation Abstracts International, 40 /10-B,
      p. 508.)

611) Rector, Phillip K. The Acceptance of a Homosexual
      Identity in Adolescence: A Phenomenological Study.
      Ph. D. , Psychology, U. S. International University,
      1982. 210 pp. (Summary in Dissertation Abstracts
      International, 43 /03-B, p. 883.)

612) Reece, Rex W. The Relationship of Selected Sex Role
      Variables to Longevity in Gay Male Couples. Ph. D. ,
      Sociology, Purdue University, 1979. 166 pp. (Sum-
      mary in Dissertation Abstracts International, 40 /09-A,
      p. 5205.)

613)   Rees, Richard L. A Comparison of Children of Les-
        bian and Single Heterosexual Mothers on Three Meas-
        ures of Socialization. Ph. D. , Psychology, California
        School of Professional Psychology, 1979. 179 pp.
        (Summary in Dissertation Abstracts International, 40 /
        07-B, p. 3418.)

614)   Rhoads, Allan H. Personality Characteristics of
        Single and Coupled Male Homosexuals. Ph. D. ,
        Psychology, California School of Professional Psy-
        chology, 1982. 225 pp. (Summary in Dissertation
        Abstracts International, 43 /06-B, p. 2000.)

615)   Richter, Robert W. Measures of Maladjustment and
        Guilt and Their Relationship to Behavior in Two Ho-
        mosexual Groups. Ph. D. , Psychology, Southern Il-
        linois University, 1976. 128 pp. (Summary in Dis-
        sertation Abstracts International, 37 /09-B, p. 4700.)

616)   Rodriguez, Gabriel J. A Comparison of Male Hetero-
        sexual and Homosexual Sexual Fantasies and Tentative
        Norms for the Meaning of Sexual Experience. Ph. D. ,
        Psychology, University of Florida, 1981. 153 pp.
        (Summary in Dissertation Abstracts International, 43 /
        01-B, p. 261.)

617)   Rossiter, William T. III. Homophobia: A Construct
        Validity Study of MacDonald's Attitude Toward Homo-
        sexuality Scale--Male. Ph. D. , Psychology, California
        School of Professional Psychology, 1979. 103 pp.
        (Summary in Dissertation Abstracts International, 41 /
        06-B, p. 2344.)

618)   Russo, Anthony J. Power and Influence in the Homo-
        sexual Community: A Study of Three California Cities.
        Ph. D. , Psychology and Sociology, Claremont Graduate
        School, 1982. 186 pp. (Summary in Dissertation Ab-
        stracts International, 43 /02-B, p. 561.)

619)   Rutter, Elliot R. An Exploration of Intimacy Between
        Gay Men. Ph. D. , Psychology, City University of
        New York, 1982. 362 pp. (Summary in Dissertation
        Abstracts International, 42 /12-B, p. 4940.)

620)   Sallee, Dock T. Relationship Between Sex-Role Iden-
        tification and Self-Concept in a Comparison of Homo-
        sexual and Heterosexual Males. Ph. D. , Psychology,

U. S. International University, 1976.   197 pp.   (Summary in Dissertation Abstracts International, 39/11-B, p. 5583.)

621)   SantaVicca, Edmund F.   The Treatment of Homosexuality in Current Encyclopedias.   Ph. D. , Library Science, University of Michigan, 1977.   323 pp.   (Summary in Dissertation Abstracts International, 38/11-A, p. 6375.)

622)   Scallen, Raymond M.   An Investigation of Paternal Attitudes and Behaviors in Homosexual and Heterosexual Fathers.   Ph. D. , Psychology, California School of Professional Psychology, 1981.   133 pp.   (Summary in Dissertation Abstracts International, 42/09-B, p. 3809.)

623)   Schwartz, Barry D.   The Jewish Tradition and Homosexuality.   D. H. L. , Religion, Jewish Theological Seminary of America, 1979.   173 pp.   (Summary in Dissertation Abstracts International, 40/08-A, p. 4637.)

624)   Shachar, Sandra A.   Lesbianism and Role Conflict: An Investigation of Coping Strategies.   Ph. D. , Psychology, University of Texas at Austin, 1979.   265 pp. (Summary in Dissertation Abstracts International, 40/ 03-B, p. 1385.)

625)   Shapiro, Stephen R.   The Theme of Homosexuality in Selected Theatrical Events Produced in the United States Between 1967 and 1974.   Ph. D. , Theater, University of California at Santa Barbara, 1976.   234 pp. (Summary in Dissertation Abstracts International, 37/ 03-A, p. 1300.)

626)   Siegel, Paul.   Privacy and the First Amendment: The Development and Application (to the Gay Rights Controversy) of an Original Model of Privacy.   Ph. D. , Speech Communications, Northwestern University, 1982. 293 pp.   (Summary in Dissertation Abstracts International, 43/06-A, p. 1748.)

627)   Smith, Katharine V.   Children Raised by Lesbian Mothers.   Ph. D. , Psychology, University of California at Los Angeles, 1981.   219 pp.   (Summary in Dissertation Abstracts International, 42/08-B, p. 3444.)

628) Sommers, Mason A. The Relationship Between Pres-
      ent Support Networks and Current Levels of Inter-
      personal Congruency of Gay Identity. Ph.D., Psy-
      chology, California School of Professional Psychology,
      1982. 146 pp. (Summary in Dissertation Abstracts
      International, 43/06-B, p. 1962.)

629) Spak, David J. An Exploratory Study of Gay Male
      Sexual Fantasies. Ph.D., Psychology, U.S. Inter-
      national University, 1982. 96 pp. (Summary in Dis-
      sertation Abstracts International, 43/02-B, p. 536.)

630) Spaulding, Elaine C. The Formation of Lesbian Iden-
      tity During the "Coming Out" Process. Ph.D., Social
      Work, Smith College, 1982. 230 pp. (Summary in
      Dissertation Abstracts International, 43/06-A, p.
      2106.)

631) Stokes, Melvin K. The Relationship of Gender Iden-
      tity, Gender Role and the I-E Locus of Control to
      Specific Sexual Behaviors of Males and Females Who
      Engage in Homosexual Behavior. Ph.D., Psychology,
      University of South Carolina, 1978. 130 pp. (Sum-
      mary in Dissertation Abstracts International, 39/12-B,
      p. 6146.)

632) Swartz, Shoshanna S. Counseling Lesbian Couples:
      Significant Factors Involved in Maintaining a Lesbian
      Dyad. Ed.D., Psychology, Boston University, 1980.
      182 pp. (Summary in Dissertation Abstracts Interna-
      tional, 41/05-B, p. 1933.)

633) Swerling, Judith B. A Study of Police Officers' Values
      and Their Attitudes Toward Homosexual Officers.
      Ph.D., Psychology, California School of Professional
      Psychology, 1977. 190 pp. (Summary in Dissertation
      Abstracts International, 38/10-B, p. 5103.)

634) Tanner, Donna M. The Formation and Maintenance of
      Lesbian Dyadic Households in an Urban Setting. Ph.D.,
      Sociology, University of Illinois at Chicago Circle,
      1976. 216 pp. (Summary in Dissertation Abstracts
      International, 37/10-A, p. 6777.)

635) Taylor, Clark L. Jr. El Ambiente: Male Homosexual
      Social Life in Mexico City. Ph.D., Anthropology, Uni-
      versity of California at Berkeley, 1978. 232 pp.

(Summary in <u>Dissertation Abstracts International</u>, 39/
10-A, p. 6208.)

636)   Teitge, Joyce E.   <u>Self-Realization and Social Estrange-</u>
       <u>ment: Employment and the Gay Dilemma.</u> Ph.D.,
       Sociology, University of Notre Dame, 1981. 180 pp.
       (Summary in <u>Dissertation Abstracts International</u>, 42/
       03-A, p. 1344.)

637)   Tinker, Dorris E.   <u>Personality Characteristics and</u>
       <u>Perception of Family Dynamics of Transsexuals, Ho-</u>
       <u>mosexuals, and Heterosexuals and Their Siblings.</u>
       Ph.D., Psychology, Case Western Reserve University,
       1979. 101 pp.   (Summary in <u>Dissertation Abstracts</u>
       <u>International</u>, 40/05-B, p. 2389.)

638)   Towne, William S.   <u>Beliefs, Attitudes, Intentions, and</u>
       <u>Behavior: The Gay Rights Issue.</u> Ph.D., Psychology,
       University of Hawaii, 1979. 216 pp. (Summary in
       <u>Dissertation Abstracts International</u>, 40/12-B, p. 5834.)

639)   Travis, Norma J.   <u>A Study of the Relationship of</u>
       <u>Certain Variables to Sex Characteristic Identification</u>
       <u>from the Speech of Heterosexual and Homosexual In-</u>
       <u>dividuals.</u> Ph.D., Sociology, Louisiana State Univer-
       sity, 1981. 163 pp. (Summary in <u>Dissertation Ab-</u>
       <u>stracts International</u>, 42/06-B, p. 2323.)

640)   Troiden, Richard R.   <u>Becoming Homosexual: Research</u>
       <u>on Acquiring a Gay Identity.</u> Ph.D., Sociology, State
       University of New York at Stony Brook, 1977. 366 pp.
       (Summary in <u>Dissertation Abstracts International</u>, 38/
       11-A, p. 6955.)

641)   Tubach, Sally P.   <u>Female Homoeroticism in German</u>
       <u>Literature and Culture.</u> Ph.D., Germanic Literature,
       University of California at Berkeley, 1980. 582 pp.
       (Summary in <u>Dissertation Abstracts International</u>, 41/
       07-A, p. 3125.)

642)   Turner, Alice P.   <u>Religiosity, Sex Role Attitudes,</u>
       <u>Previous Association with Homosexuals, Demographic</u>
       <u>Characteristics and Attitudes Toward Homosexuals in</u>
       <u>a Church Affiliated Population.</u> Ph.D., Psychology,
       University of Virginia, 1981. 111 pp. (Summary in
       <u>Dissertation Abstracts International</u>, 43/05-B,
       p. 1668.)

643) Tye, William L. The Praxis of Lonergan's Method
      for Pastoral Theology: A Study of Self-Affirmation:
      A Conversion Process in Counseling Christian Homo-
      sexuals. Ph. D. , Theology, Graduate Theological
      Union, 1982. 218 pp. (Summary in Dissertation Ab-
      stracts International, 43/03-A, p. 843.)

644) Vance, Brenda K. Female Homosexuality: A Social
      Psychological Examination of Attitudinal and Etiological
      Characteristics of Different Groups. Ph. D. , Psy-
      chology, Oklahoma State University, 1977. 145 pp.
      (Summary in Dissertation Abstracts International, 39/
      01-B, p. 451.)

645) VanCleave, Carolyn. Self-Identification, Self-Identifi-
      cation Discrepancy, and Environmental Perspectives of
      Women with a Same-Sex Sexual Preference. Ed. D. ,
      Guidance and Counseling, Ball State University, 1977.
      178 pp. (Summary in Dissertation Abstracts Inter-
      national, 38/10, p. 5932.)

646) VanWyk, Paul H. Developmental Factors Associated
      with Heterosexual, Bisexual, and Homosexual Out-
      comes. Ph. D. , Health Sciences, Illinois Institute of
      Technology, 1982. 120 pp. (Summary in Dissertation
      Abstracts International, 43/04-B, p. 1033.)

647) Wagner, Richard. Gay Catholic Priests: A Study of
      Cognitive and Affective Dissonance. Ph. D. , Human
      Sexuality, Institute for the Advanced Study of Human
      Sexuality, San Francisco, 1981.

648) Wall, Robert W. The Nature of Obedience in the
      Ethics of Paul: With Special Application to the Prob-
      lem of Homosexual Ordination for the Ministry.
      Th. D. , Theology, Dallas Theological Seminary, 1979.

649) Weinberg, Thomas S. Becoming Homosexual: Self-
      Discovery, Self-Identity, and Self-Maintenance. Ph. D. ,
      Sociology, University of Connecticut, 1977. 615 pp.
      (Summary in Dissertation Abstracts International, 38/
      01-A: p. 506.)

650) Weinrich, James D. Human Reproductive Strategy:
      I. Environmental Predictability and Reproductive
      Strategy: Effect of Social Class and Race. II. Ho-
      mosexuality and Non-Reproduction: Some Evolutionary

Models. Ph. D. , Psychology, Harvard University, 1976. 236 pp. (Summary in Dissertation Abstracts International, 37/10-B, p. 5339.)

651)   Weinrich, Robert J. The Effects of Disclosure of Gay Identity on Social Interaction and Anti-homosexual Attitudes. Ph. D. , Psychology, U. S. International University, 1981. 169 pp. (Summary in Dissertation Abstracts International, 42/05-B, p. 2140.)

652)   Weis, Charles B. , Jr. A Comparative Study of Level of Ego Development and Sex-Role Attributes in Hetero- sexual and Homosexual Men and Women. Ph. D. , Psy- chology, University of Texas Health Sciences Center, 1977. 125 pp. (Summary in Dissertation Abstracts International, 39/06-B, p. 2894.)

653)   Weston, Amy E. Sexual and Social Interaction Pat- terns in Lesbian and Heterosexual Women. Ph. D. , Psychology, University of California at Berkeley, 1978. 165 pp. (Summary in Dissertation Abstracts International, 40/01-B, p. 468.)

654)   White, Evelyn E. M. Effects of a Unit of Instruction in Human Sexuality on Freshmen Students. Ed. D. , Education, Auburn University, 1980. 149 pp. (Sum- mary in Dissertation Abstracts International, 41/12-A, p. 5047.)

655)   Wilkins, Jane L. A Comparative Study of Male Ho- mosexual Personality Factors: Brief Cruising En- counters vs. Ongoing Relationships. Ph. D. , Psy- chology, Florida Institute of Technology, 1981. 127 pp. (Summary in Dissertation Abstracts International, 42/06-B, p. 2555.)

656)   Wolf, Deborah G. Contemporary Amazons: A Study of a Lesbian Feminist Community. Ph. D. , Anthro- pology, University of California at Berkeley, 1977. 271 pp. (Summary in Dissertation Abstracts Inter- national, 38/08-A, p. 4915.)

657)   Wong, Michael J. Long-Term Homosexual and Hetero- sexual Couple Relationship Effects on Self-Concept and Relationship Adjustment. Ph. D. , Psychology, U. S. International University, 1980. 152 pp. (Sum- mary in Dissertation Abstracts International, 41/03-B, p. 1169.)

658)   Woods, Colmcille P. Alcohol Abuse Among Lesbians:
        An Investigation of Possible Contributing Factors.
        Ph. D. , Psychology, U. S. International University,
        1981.   100 pp.   (Summary in Dissertation Abstracts
        International, 42 /06-B, p. 2558.)

659)   Woolfson, Leonie R.   Psychological Androgyny and
        Gender Identity in Adult Homosexual and Heterosexual
        Females.   D. Phil. , Psychology, University of South
        Africa, 1980.   (Summary in Dissertation Abstracts
        International, 42 /01-B, p. 396.)

ARTICLES IN BOOKS

660) Abbitt, Diane, and Bobbie Bennett. "Being a Lesbian Mother," in Berzon and Leighton, no. 3, pp. 123-29.

661) Abbott, Sidney. "Lesbians and the Women's Movement," in Vida, no. 33, pp. 139-44.

662) Adam, Barry D. "A Social History of Gay Politics," in Levine, no. 22, pp. 285-300.

663) _____. "Systematic Restriction of Life Chances," in The Survival of Domination: Inferiorization and Everyday Life (New York: Elsevier North Holland, 1978), pp. 18-53.

664) Alhonte, Michael. "Confronting Ageism," in Tsang, no. 31, pp. 156-60.

665) Altman, Dennis. "Fear and Loathing and Hepatitis on the Path of Gay Liberation," in Richmond and Noguera, no. 28, pp. 199-203.

666) _____. "What Changed in the Seventies?" in Gay Left Collective, no. 13, pp. 52-63.

667) Amneus, Daniel. "The Homosexual Militants," in Back to Patriarchy (New Rochelle, N.Y.: Arlington House, 1979), pp. 177-203.

668) Anon. "From sh'ma--Must Homosexuals Be Jewish Outcasts?" in Batchelor, no. 1, pp. 33-36.

669) Apuzzo, Ginny, and Batya Bauman. "The Spectrum of Lesbian Experience: Religion," in Vida, no. 33, pp. 235-37.

670) Avedon, Burt. "Out of the Closet: Homosexuality and Bisexuality," in Ah Men! What Do Men Want?

(New York: A and W Publishers, 1980), pp. 164-74.

671) Avicolli, Tommi. "Images of Gays in Rock Music," in Jay and Young, no. 18, pp. 182-94.

672) Barnhouse, Ruth T. "Homosexuality: A Symbolic Confusion," in Batchelor, no. 1, pp. 79-85.

673) Barrett, Ellen M. "Gay People and Moral Theology," in Crew, no. 7, pp. 329-34.

674) Barth, Karl. "Church Dogmatics," in Batchelor, no. 1, pp. 48-51.

675) Baum, Gregory. "Catholic Homosexuals," in Batchelor, no. 1, pp. 22-27.

676) Bearchell, Chris. "Trading on Secrets: The Making of a TV Documentary [on Homosexuality in Canada]," in Jackson and Persky, no. 17, pp. 111-21.

677) Beck, Evelyn T. "I. B. Singer's Misogyny," in Beck, no. 2, pp. 243-49.

678) _____. "Teaching About Jewish Lesbians in Literature," in Cruikshank, no. 9, pp. 81-87.

679) Bell, Alan P. "The Homosexual as Patient," in Martin S. Weinberg (ed.), Sex Research: Studies from the Kinsey Institute (New York: Oxford University Press, 1976), pp. 202-12.

680) _____. "Homosexuality: An Overview," in Ruth T. Barnhouse and Urban T. Holmes III (eds.), Male and Female: Christian Approaches to Sexuality (New York: Seabury Press, 1976), pp- 131-42. (Reprinted in Twiss, no. 32.)

681) Bell, Arthur. "The Bath Life Gets Respectability," in Jay and Young, no. 18, pp. 77-84.

682) Bell, Robert R. "Male Homosexuality" and "Female Homosexuality," in Social Deviance: A Substantive Analysis (Rev. ed.; New York: Dorsey Press, 1976), pp. 265-307 and 308-33.

683) Bennett, Curtis. "Sappho's Hymn to Aphrodite," in

God as Form: Essays in Greek Theology (Edison,
N. J. : State Universities of New York Press, 1976),
pp. 74-97.

684)   Bennett, Paula. "Dyke in Academe (II), " in Cruikshank, no. 9, pp. 3-8.

685)   Berzon, Betty. "Developing a Positive Gay Identity"
and "Achieving Success as a Gay Couple, " in Berzon
and Leighton, no. 3, pp. 1-14 and 30-40.

686)   _____. "Sharing Your Lesbian Identity with Your
Children, " in Vida, no. 33, pp. 69-77.

687)   Birch, Keith. "The Politics of Autonomy, " in Gay
Left Collective, no. 13, pp. 85-92.

688)   Biren, Jean E. "That's Funny, You Don't Look Like
a Jewish Lesbian, " in Beck, no. 2, pp. 122-29.

689)   Birk, Lee. "The Myth of Classical Homosexuality:
Views of a Behavioral Psychotherapist, " in Marmor,
no. 24, pp. 376-90.

690)   Blachford, Gregg. "Looking at Pornography: Erotica
and the Socialist Morality, " in Mitchell, no. 25, pp.
57-71.

691)   _____. "Male Dominance and the Gay World, " in
Plummer, no. 27, pp. 184-210.

692)   Blasius, Mark. "Sexual Revolution and the Liberation
of Children ... An Interview with Kate Millett, " in
Tsang, no. 31, pp. 80-83.

693)   Body Politic Staff. "Victories and Defeats: A Gay
and Lesbian Chronology, 1964-1982, " in Jackson and
Persky, no. 17, pp. 224-43.

694)   Boucher, Sandy. "Clinging Vine, " in Heartwoman:
An Urban Feminist's Odyssey Home (San Francisco:
Harper and Row, 1982), pp. 212-30.

695)   Bowman, Frank P. "The Religious Metaphors of a
Married Homosexual: Marcel Jouhandeau's Chronique
d'une Passion" in Stambolian and Marks, no. 30, pp.
295-311.

696)   Bowman, Richard. "Public Attitudes Toward Homo-
        sexuality in New Zealand, " in Harry and Das, no. 16,
        pp. 92-101.

697)   Brian, Robert. "Female Husbands and Male Wives, "
        in Friends and Lovers (New York: Basic Books,
        1976), pp. 55-74.

698)   Brick, Barrett L. "Judaism in the Gay Community, "
        in Berzon and Leighton, no. 3, pp. 79-87.

699)   Brogan, Jim. "Teaching Gay Literature in San Fran-
        cisco, " in Crew, no. 7, pp. 152-63.

700)   Brooks, Kenneth W. , and others. "Homosexuality,
        the Law, and Public Schools, " in M. A. McGhehey
        (ed.), School Law Update--1977 (Topeka, Kans. :
        National Organization on Legal Problems of Education,
        1978), pp. 160-78.

701)   Brown, Rita M. "The Lesbian Woman: ... A Woman's
        Place Is Wherever She Wants It to Be, " in Harvey L.
        and Jean S. Gochros (eds.), The Sexually Oppressed
        (New York: Association Press, 1977), pp. 152-59.

702)   _____. "Take a Lesbian to Lunch, " in Grier and
        Reid, no. 15, pp. 119-33.

703)   Brummett, Barry. "Ideologies in Two Gay Rights
        Controversies, " in Chesebro, no. 6, pp. 291-302.

704)   Bucher, Glenn R. "The Enemy: He Is Us, " in
        Glenn R. Bucher (ed.), Straight /White /Male (Phila-
        delphia: Fortress Press, 1976), pp. 2-10.

705)   Bulkin, Elly. "A Look at Lesbian Poetry, " in
        Cruikshank, no. 9, pp. 32-54.

706)   Bullough, Vern L. "Sex in History: A Virgin
        Field, " "Attitudes Toward Deviant Sex in Ancient
        Mesopotamia, " "Heresy, Witchcraft, and Sexuality, "
        and "Homosexuality and the Medical Model, " in Sex,
        Society, and History (New York: Science History
        Publications, 1976), pp. 1-16, 17-36, 74-92, and
        161-72.

707)   _____. "Homosexuality in Nineteenth-Century

English Public Schools," in Harry and Das, no. 16, pp. 123-32.

708)   . "Transvestism in the Middle Ages," "The Sin Against Nature and Homosexuality," and "Postscript: Heresy, Witchcraft, and Sexuality," in Vern L. Bullough and James Brundage (eds.), Sexual Practices and the Medieval Church (Buffalo, N. Y.: Prometheus Books, 1982), pp. 43-54, 55-85, and 206-17.

709)   , and Bonnie Bullough. "Unnatural Sex" and "Homosexuality, Sex Labeling, and Stigmatized Behavior," in Sin, Sickness, and Sanity: A History of Sexual Attitudes (New ed.; New York: Garland Publishing Co., 1977), pp. 24-40 and 197-212.

710)   Bunch, Charlotte. "Learning from Lesbian Separatism," in Jay and Young, no. 18, pp. 433-44.

711)   Burgess-Kohn, Jane. "What About Homosexuality?" in Straight Talk About Love and Sex for Teenagers (Boston: Beacon Press, 1979), pp. 153-82.

712)   Burton, Peter. "Interview of Robin Maugham," in Robert Maugham, The Boy from Beirut and Other Stories (San Francisco: Gay Sunshine Press, 1982), pp. 109-60.

713)   Cahill, Lisa S. "Homosexuality," in Batchelor, no. 1, pp. 222-31.

714)   Califia, Pat. "Man/Boy Love and the Lesbian/Gay Movement," in Tsang, no. 31, pp. 133-46.

715)   Cant, Bob, and Nigel Young. "New Politics, Old Struggle," in Gay Left Collective, no. 13, pp. 116-27.

716)   Carlson, James W. "Images of Gay Men in Contemporary Drama," in Chesebro, no. 6, pp. 165-74.

717)   Carrier, Joseph M. "Homosexual Behavior in Cross-Cultural Perspective," in Marmor, no. 24, pp. 100-22.

718)   Cartledge, Sue. "... Lesbian-Feminist Morality," in Gay Left Collective, no. 13, pp. 93-103.

719)   Cartnal, Alan. "Boystown--The Weekend," in

California Crazy: The Ins and Outs ... of Los
Angeles (Boston: Houghton Mifflin, 1981), pp. 33-
34, 67-74, and 147-54.

720)   Chance, Paul. "Facts That Liberated the Gay Com-
munity [Interview with Dr. Evelyn Hooker]," in Focus:
Human Sexuality 1977-78 (Guilford, Conn.: Dushkin
Publishing Co., 1978), pp. 192-95.

721)   Chase, Wilda. "Men Are the Second Sex" and "Lesbianism and Feminism," in Grier and Reid, no. 15,
pp. 39-42 and 98-103.

722)   Chesebro, James W. "Views of Homosexuality Among
Social Scientists," in Chesebro, no. 6, pp. 175-88.

723)   _____, and Kenneth L. Kleuk. "Gay Masculinity
in Gay Disco," in Chesebro, no. 6, pp. 87-103.

724)   _____, and others. "Consciousness-raising Among
Gay Males," in Chesebro, no. 6, pp. 211-23.

725)   Clark, Don. "Being a Gay Father," in Berzon and
Leighton, no. 3, pp. 112-22.

726)   Clarke, Cheryl. "Lesbianism: An Act of Resistance,"
in Cherrie Moraga and Gloria Anzaldua (eds.), This
Bridge Called My Back: Writings by Radical Women
of Color (Watertown, Mass.: Persephone Press,
1981), pp. 128-37.

727)   Clayborne, Jon L. "Blacks and Gay Liberation," in
Jay and Young, no. 18, pp. 458-65.

728)   Cobhan, Linni. "Lesbians in Physical Education and
Sport," in Cruikshank, no. 9, pp. 179-86.

729)   Cockshut, A. O. J. "The Male Homosexual," "The
Male Homosexual: Forster," "The Male Homosexual:
Satire," and "The Lesbian Theme," in Man and Wom-
an: A Study of Love and the Novel, 1740-1940 (New
York: Oxford University Press, 1977), pp. 161-69,
170-81, 182-85, and 186-208.

730)   Coffin, William S. "Homosexuality," in The Courage
to Love (New York: Harper and Row, 1982), pp. 39-
48.

731)   Cohen, Derek, and Richard Dyer. "The Politics of
       Gay Culture," in Gay Left Collective, no. 13, pp.
       172-86.

732)   Cohen, Philip K. "In the End Is the Beginning: De
       Profundis," in The Moral Vision of Oscar Wilde
       (Rutherford, N.J.: Fairleigh Dickinson University
       Press, 1978), pp. 235-64.

733)   Cohl, K. A. "Homosexuality," in Sexuality and the
       Law (Toronto, Ont.: I.P.I. Publishing Division,
       1978), pp. 67-76.

734)   Coleman, Eli. "Changing Approaches to Treatment
       of Homosexuality: A Review" and "Developmental
       Stages of the Coming-Out Process," in Paul, no. 26,
       pp. 81-88 and 149-58.

735)   Cornwell, Anita. "Open Letter to a Black Sister,"
       "Letter to a Friend," and "From a Soul Sister's Note-
       book," in Grier and Reid, no. 15, pp. 225-31, 249-
       55, and 279-82.

736)   _____. "Three for the Price of One: Notes from
       a Gay Black Feminist," in Jay and Young, no. 18,
       pp. 466-76.

737)   Coulson, Margaret. "The Struggle for Femininity,"
       in Gay Left Collective, no. 13, pp. 21-37.

738)   Crew, Louie. "Before Emancipation: Gay Persons
       as Viewed by Chairpersons in English," in Crew, no.
       7, pp. 3-48.

739)   Crocker, Lawrence. "Meddling with the Sexual Orien-
       tation of Children," in Onora O'Neil (ed.), Having
       Children (New York: Oxford University Press, 1979),
       pp. 145-54.

740)   Crompton, Louis. "Gay Genocide: From Leviticus
       to Hitler," in Crew, no. 7, pp. 67-91.

741)   Cruikshank, Margaret. "Is This the Reward of a
       Catholic Girlhood?" in Wolfe and Stanley, no. 36,
       pp. 31-35.

742)   _____. "Lesbians in the Academic World," in
       Vida, no. 33, pp. 164-67.

743)   Curran, Charles E. "Homosexuality and Moral Theology: Methodological and Substantive Considerations,"
        in Batchelor, no. 1, pp. 89-95 and 171-85.

744)   Dank, Barry. "Coming Out in the Gay World," in
        Levine, no. 22, pp. 103-33.

745)   Darsey, James. "From 'Commies' to 'Queer' to 'Gay
        Is Good,'" in Chesebro, no. 6, pp. 224-47.

746)   Daum, Annette. "Blaming the Jews for the Death of
        the Goddess," in Beck, no. 2, pp. 255-61.

747)   Davenport, Doris. "Black Lesbians in Academia:
        Visible Invisibility," in Cruikshank, no. 9, pp. 9-11.

748)   Davis, Madelaine. "Learning Through Teaching: A
        Lesbian Course in 1972," in Cruikshank, no. 9, pp.
        88-92.

749)   Davison, Gerald. "Politics, Ethics, and Therapy
        for Homosexuality," in Paul, no. 26, pp. 89-98.

750)   Day, Connie, and Ben W. Morse. "Communication
        Patterns in Established Lesbian Relationships," in
        Chesebro, no. 6, pp. 80-86.

751)   DeBaugh, R. Adam. "Using Gay Voting Power," in
        Berzon and Leighton, no. 3, pp. 199-208.

752)   DeCecco, John P. "A Short History of the Task
        Force on Sexual Orientation," in Paul, no. 26, pp.
        15-17.

753)   _____, and Michael Shively. "Conflict over Rights
        and Needs in Homosexual Relationships," in Crew,
        no. 7, pp. 305-14.

754)   DeCrescenzo, Teresa, and Lillene Fifield. "The
        Changing Lesbian Scene," in Berzon and Leighton,
        no. 3, pp. 15-23.

755)   D'Emilio, John. "Dreams Deferred: The Early
        American Homophile Movement," in Jackson and Per-
        sky, no. 17, pp. 127-38.

756)   Denniston, R. H. "Ambisexuality in Animals," in
        Marmor, no. 24, pp. 25-40.

757)   Derbyshire, Philip.   "Sects and Sexuality: Trotskyism
       and the Politics of Homosexuality," in Gay Left Col-
       lective, no. 13, pp. 104-15.

758)   DeVall, William.   "Leisure and Lifestyles Among Gay
       Men: An Exploratory Essay," in Harry and Das, no.
       16, pp. 44-60.

759)   DeVito, Joseph A.   "Educational Responsibilities to
       Gay Male and Lesbian Students," in Chesebro, no. 6,
       pp. 197-208.

760)   Dobson, Rob.   "Dance Liberation," in Jay and Young,
       no. 18, pp. 171-81.

761)   Donnelly, Jerry.   "The Courts and the Out-of-School
       Activities of Teachers," in McGhehey, no. 700, pp.
       318-32.

762)   Dostourian, Ara.   "Gayness and a Radical Christian
       Approach," in Crew, no. 7, pp. 335-49.

763)   Doughty, Frances.   "Lesbian Biography, Biography of
       Lesbians," in Cruikshank, no. 9, pp. 122-27.

764)   Driver, Tom.   "The Contemporary and Christian Con-
       texts," in Batchelor, no. 1, pp. 14-21.

765)   Dyer, Richard.   "Stereotyping" and "Camp and Sensi-
       bility," in Dyer, no. 10, pp. 27-39 and 40-58.

766)   Elkind, David.   "Choosing to Be Gay: The Roots of
       Homosexuality," in The Child and Society: Essays in
       Applied Child Development (New York: Oxford Uni-
       versity Press, 1978), pp. 48-61.

767)   Elliott, S. James.   "Homosexuality in the Crucial
       Decade: Three Novelists' Views [Mailer, Merrick,
       and Vidal]," in Crew, no. 7, pp. 164-77.

768)   Endleman, Robert.   "Gay Liberation Confronts Psycho-
       analysis and the Social Sciences," in Psyche and So-
       ciety: Explorations in Psychoanalytic Sociology (New
       York: Columbia University Press, 1981), pp. 235-
       340.

769)   Erlich, Larry G.   "[Homophobia:]   The Pathogenic
       Secret," in Chesebro, no. 6, pp. 130-41.

770)   Ettorre, E. M.   "Lesbianism," in W. H. G. Armytage
       and others (eds.), Changing Patterns of Sexual Be-
       haviour (London: Academic Press, 1980), pp. 123-
       35.

771)   "Evidence of Attitudes Toward and Punishment (In-
       cluding Execution) of Homosexual Activities in America
       Between 1624 and 1890," in Katz, no. 250, pp. 16-39.

772)   "Excerpts from Church Statements on Homosexuality,"
       in Batchelor, no. 1, pp. 235-42.

773)   Faderman, Lillian.   "Who Hid Lesbian History?" in
       Cruikshank, no. 9, pp. 115-21.

774)   Fag Rag Collective.   "Second Five Year Plan," in
       Jay and Young, no. 18, pp. 484-91.

775)   Fairchild, Betty.   "For Parents of Gays: A Fresh
       Perspective," in Berzon and Leighton, no. 3, pp. 101-
       11.

776)   _____.   "When Your Child Is Gay," in Richmond
       and Noguera, no. 28, pp. 63-69.

777)   Faith, Karlene.   "Love Between Women in Prison," in
       Cruikshank, no. 9, pp. 187-93.

778)   Faraday, Annabel.   "Liberating Lesbian Research,"
       in Plummer, no. 27, pp. 112-29.

779)   Fernbach, David.   "Toward a Marxist Theory of Gay
       Liberation," in Mitchell, no. 25, pp. 148-63.

780)   Fischli, Ronald D.   "Religious Fundamentalism and
       the Democratic Process," in Chesebro, no. 6, pp.
       303-13.

781)   Fone, Byrne R. S.   "Sons and Lovers: Three English
       Portraits [Isherwood, Ackerley, and Nicolson]," in
       Crew, no. 7, pp. 200-15.

782)   Forrester, Randal G., and James Huggins.   "Homo-
       sexuality and Homosexual Behavior," in Dinah Shore
       and Harvey L. Gochros (eds.), Sexual Problems of
       Adolescents in Institutions (Springfield, Ill: C. C.
       Thomas, 1981), pp. 154-66.

783)   Frank, Bernhard.   "Homosexual Love in Four Poems
       of Rilke," in Crew, no. 7, pp. 244-54.

784)   Freedman, Alfred M., and others.   "Homosexuality
       and Sexual Orientation Disturbances," in Modern Synop-
       sis of Comprehensive Textbook of Psychiatry (2d ed.;
       Baltimore: Williams and Wilkins, 1976), pp. 757-63.

785)   Freedman, Estelle.   "Resources for Lesbian History,"
       in Cruikshank, no. 9, pp. 110-14.

786)   Freedman, Marcia.   "A Lesbian in the Promised
       Land," in Beck, no. 2, pp. 211-21.

787)   Freedman, Mark.   "Toward a Gay Psychology," in
       Crew, no. 7, pp. 315-28.

788)   Friday, Nancy.   "Straight Men, Gay Fantasies" and
       "Bisexuals, Homosexuals, and Transvestites," in Men
       in Love: Men's Sexual Fantasies (New York: Dell,
       1980), pp. 359-436.

789)   Friedenberg, Edgar Z.   "Gaiety and Laity: Avoiding
       the Excesses of Professionalism," in Crew, no. 7,
       pp. 49-56.

790)   Frye, Marilyn.   "A Lesbian Perspective on Women's
       Studies," in Cruikshank, no. 9, pp. 194-98.

791)   Furnish, Victor P.   "Homosexuality," in The Moral
       Teaching of Paul: Selected Issues (Nashville, Tenn.:
       Abingdon Press, 1979), pp. 52-83.

792)   Garnett, Blynn.   "Memoirs of a Lesbian Daughter,"
       in Jay and Young, no. 18, pp. 315-24.

793)   Gartrell, Nanette K.   "Hormones and Homosexuality,"
       in Paul, no. 26, pp. 169-82.

794)   Gaver, Charles R.   "Gay Liberation and Straight
       White Males," in Bucher, no. 704, pp. 51-70.

795)   Gay Left Collective." "Happy Families? Paedophilia
       Examined," in Mitchell, no. 25, pp. 78-89 and in
       Tsang, no. 31, pp. 53-64.

796)   _____.   "Why Marxism?" in Mitchell, no. 25, pp.
       98-106.

797)   Gearhart, Sally M.   "Gay Civil Rights and the Roots
        of Oppression," in Chesebro, no. 6, pp. 275-85.

798)   Gee, Stephen.   "Gay Activism," in Gay Left Collective,
        no. 13, pp. 189-204.

799)   Geiser, Robert L.   "Sexual Misuse of Male Children"
        and "Child Prostitution," in Hidden Victims: The
        Sexual Abuse of Children (Boston: Beacon Press,
        1979), pp. 73-106 and 132-38.

800)   Gerber, Henry.   "Thoughts and Experiences of an
        Early American Gay Activist," in Katz, no. 250,
        pp. 386-97.

801)   Gilbert, J. Allen.   "Report on His Treatment of Al-
        berta Hunt, a Lesbian," in Katz, no. 250, pp. 258-
        79.

802)   Gittings, Barbara.   "Combatting the Lies in the Li-
        brary," in Crew, no. 7, pp. 107-20.

803)   _____, and Kay Tobin.   "Lesbians and the Gay
        Movement," in Vida, no. 33, pp. 149-54.

804)   Glenn, John D.   "Gay Fantasies in Gay Publications,"
        in Chesebro, no. 6, pp. 104-14.

805)   Gonsiorek, John.   "Introduction," "Results of Psy-
        chological Testing on Homosexual Populations," and
        "Social Psychological Concepts in the Understanding
        of Homosexuality," in Paul, no. 26, pp. 57-70, 71-
        80, and 115-19.

806)   Goodman, Bernice.   "The Lesbian Woman: ... The
        Problems of Lesbians," in Gochros, no. 701, pp. 145-
        51.

807)   Gordis, Robert.   "Homosexuality and the Homosexual,"
        in Love and Sex: A Modern Jewish Perspective (New
        York: Farrar, Straus, and Giroux, 1978), pp. 149-
        61.   (Reprinted in Batchelor, no. 1, pp. 52-60.)

808)   Gough, Jamie.   "Childhood Sexuality and Paedophilia,"
        in Mitchell, no. 25, pp. 90-97 and in Tsang, no. 31,
        pp. 65-71.

809) Gould, Meredith. "Statutory Oppression: An Overview of Legalized Homophobia," in Levine, no. 22, pp. 51-67.

810) Gould, Robert E. "What We Don't Know About Homosexuality," in Levine, no. 22, pp. 36-50.

811) Green, Richard. "Patterns of Sexual Identity in Childhood: Relationship to Subsequent Sexual Partners Preference " in Marmor, no. 24, pp. 255-66.

812) Gregory-Lewis, Sasha. "Lesbians in the Military," in Vida, no. 33, pp. 211-16.

813) Guidon, Andre. "Homosexuality," in The Sexual Language: An Essay in Moral Theology (Ottawa: University of Ottawa Press, 1976), pp. 299-377.

814) Hall, Richard. "Elements of Gay Theatre," "Gay Theatre: Notes for a Diary," and "The Transparent Closet: Gay Theatre for Straight Audiences," in Three Plays (San Francisco: Grey Fox Press, 1982), pp. 147-64, 165-70, and 171-77.

815) Hanley, Susan, and others. "Lesbianism: Knowns and Unknowns," in Benjamin Schlesinger (ed.), Sexual Behaviour in Canada: Patterns and Problems (Toronto, Ont.: University of Toronto Press, 1977), pp. 126-47.

816) Hannon, Gerald. "Gay Youth and the Question of Consent," in Jay and Young, no. 18, pp. 342-64.

817) _____. "No Sorrow, No Pity: The Gay Disabled," "Men Loving Boys Loving Men," and "Raids, Rage and Bawdy Houses [Gay Baths in Toronto]," in Jackson and Persky, no. 17, pp. 64-72, 147-59, and 273-94.

818) Harnik, Noreen, and Jill Boskey. "Lesbians and the Left," in Vida, no. 33, pp. 154-56.

819) Hass, Aaron. "Homosexuality," in Teenage Sexuality (New York: Macmillan, 1979), pp. 139-44.

820) Hayes, Joseph J. "Lesbians, Gay Men, and Their Languages," in Chesebro, no. 6, pp. 28-42.

821)   _____, and James Darsey. "Gayspeak" and "Gay-speak: A Response," in Chesebro, no. 6, pp. 28-43 and 45-67.

822)   Hemmings, Susan. " ... How Lesbians Were Presented in the Newspapers of 1978," in Gay Left Collective, no. 13, pp. 157-71.

823)   Hencken, Joel D. "Homosexuality and Psychoanalysis: Toward a Mutual Understanding," in Paul, no. 26, pp. 121-47.

824)   Hennegan, Alison. " ... Some Thoughts on Lesbians in Literature," in Gay Left Collective, no. 13, pp. 187-97.

825)   "Herman Melville," in Katz, no. 250, pp. 467-80.

826)   Hickok, Kathy. "Lesbian Images in Women's Literature Anthologies," in Cruikshank, no. 9, pp. 132-47.

827)   Hiltner, Seward. "Homosexuality and the Churches," in Marmor, no. 24, pp. 219-31.

828)   Hite, Shere. "Lesbianism," in The Hite Report: A Nationwide Study of Female Sexuality (New York: Macmillan, 1976), pp. 257-80.

829)   _____. "Sex and Love Between Men," in The Hite Report on Male Sexuality (New York: Knopf, 1981), pp. 805-64.

830)   Hodges, Andrew. "Divided We Stand [The Relationship Between Lesbians and Gays]," in Jackson and Persky, no. 17, pp. 178-84.

831)   Hoffman, Martin. "Homosexuality," in Frank Beach (ed.), Human Sexuality in Four Perspectives (Baltimore: Johns Hopkins University Press, 1977), pp. 164-89.

832)   _____. "The Male Prostitute," in Levine, no. 22, pp. 275-84.

833)   Holland, Isabelle. "Tilting at Taboos," in Paul Heins (ed.), Crosscurrents of Criticism: Horn Book Essays 1968-1977 (Boston: Horn Book, 1977), pp. 137-43.

834)   Hollibaugh, Amber.   "The Right to Rebel," in Gay
        Left Collective, no. 13, pp. 205-15.

835)   "The Homosexual Underground in American Cities,
        1892-1915," in Katz, no. 250, pp. 39-68.

836)   Honoré, Tony.   "Liking Your Own Sex," in Sex Law
        in England (London: Duckworth, 1978), pp. 84-110.

837)   Hotvedt, Mary E. , and Jane B. Mandel.   "Children
        of Lesbian Mothers," in Paul, no. 26, pp. 275-85.

838)   Huggins, James and Randel G. Forrester.   "The Gay
        Male," in Gochros, no. 701, pp. 130-44.

839)   Humphreys, Laud.   "Exodus and Identity: The Emerg-
        ing Gay Culture," in Levine, no. 22, pp. 134-47.

840)   _____, and Brian Miller.   "Identities in the Emerg-
        ing Gay Culture," in Marmor, no. 24, pp. 142-56.

841)   Hunter, J. F. M.   "What Are the Ethics of Birth Con-
        trol, Abortion, and Homosexuality?" in Thinking About
        Sex and Love (New York: St. Martin's, 1980), pp. 110-
        42.

842)   Hyde, Janet S.   "Homosexuality and Bisexuality," in
        Understanding Human Sexuality (2d ed.; New York:
        McGraw-Hill, 1980), pp. 359-94.

843)   Hynes, H. Patricia.   "Toward a Laboratory of One's
        Own: Lesbians in Science," in Cruikshank, no. 9,
        pp. 174-78.

844)   Ihara, Toni, and Ralph Warner.   "Gay Couples," in
        The Living Together Kit (2d ed.; Occidental, Cal. :
        Nolo Press, 1979), pp. 184-200.

845)   Interview of Alma Routsong, Author of Lesbian Novel
        "Patience and Sarah," in Katz, no. 250, pp. 433-43.

846)   Interview of Lesbian Activist Barbara Gittings, in
        Katz, no. 250, pp. 420-33.

847)   Interview of Henry Hay, Founder of the Los Angeles
        Mattachine Society, in Katz, no. 250, pp. 406-20.

848)   Interview of a Man Involved in the Homosexual Scandal
       in Boise, Idaho, in 1955, in Katz, no. 250, pp. 109-
       19.

849)   Interview of a Young Man Given Shock Treatment for
       His Homosexuality, in Katz, no. 250, pp. 201-07.

850)   Irle, Roger D.   "Minority Ministry: A Definition of
       Territory," in Harry and Das, no. 16, pp. 61-77.

851)   Isherwood, Christopher. "Living with the Backlash,"
       in Richmond and Noguera, no. 28, pp. 195-98.

852)   Jackman, Jim. "Missing the Ports of Call [A Gay
       Bar in Worcester]," in Jay and Young, no. 18,
       pp. 150-54.

853)   Jackson, Bruce. "Deviance as Success: The Double
       Inversion of Stigmatized Roles," in Barbara A. Bab-
       cock (ed.), The Reversible World: Symbolic Inversion
       in Art and Society (Ithaca, N.Y.: Cornell University
       Press, 1978), pp. 258-75.

854)   Jackson, Dolores. "Prison Ministry," in Vida, no.
       33, pp. 171-73.

855)   Jackson, Ed. "Close but Not Enough: The 1980
       Toronto Municipal Election," in Jackson and Persky,
       no. 17, pp. 258-72.

856)   Jackson, Graham. "The Theatre of Implication: Ho-
       mosexuality in Drama," in Young, no. 377, pp. 246-
       58.

857)   _____. "Toeing the Line: In Search of the Gay
       Male Image in Contemporary Classical Ballet," in
       Jay and Young, no. 18, pp. 157-70.

858)   Jackson, Margaret, and Pat Mahony. "Lesbian,
       Socialist, Feminist," in Gay Left Collective, no. 13,
       pp. 128-39.

859)   Jacobson, Ronald J. "Gay Issues in Financial Plan-
       ning," in Berzon and Leighton, no. 3, pp. 188-98.

860)   Jandt, Fred E., and James Darsey. "Coming Out as
       a Communicative Process," in Chesebro, no. 6, pp.
       12-27.

861)   Jay, Karla. "Coming Out as Process, " in Vida, no.
        33, pp. 28-37.

862)   _____. "Male Homosexuality and Lesbianism in
        the Works of Proust and Gide, " in Crew, no. 7, pp.
        216-43.

863)   _____. "No Man's Land: A Little Herstory" and
        "X-rated Bibliography: A Spy in the House of Sex, "
        in Jay and Young, no. 18, pp. 48-65 and 257-61.

864)   Jenkyns, Richard. "Change and Decay, " in The
        Victorians and Ancient Greece (Cambridge, Mass. :
        Harvard University Press, 1980), pp. 264-97.

865)   Jennings, Theodore W. "Homosexuality and Chris-
        tian Faith: A Theological Reflection, " in Batchelor,
        no. 1, pp. 211-21.

866)   Johnson, Bill. "Protestantism and Gay Freedom, " in
        Berzon and Leighton, no. 3, pp. 65-78.

867)   Joint Council for Gay Teenagers. "I Know What I
        Am: Gay Teenagers and the Law, " in Tsang, no. 31,
        pp. 84-91.

868)   Jones, Clinton R. "Christopher Iserhwood and the
        Religious Quest, " in Crew, no. 7, pp. 350-60.

869)   Jones, H. Kimball. "Toward a Christian Understand-
        ing of the Homosexual, " in Batchelor, no. 1, pp. 105-
        13.

870)   Julty, Sam. "Men Loving Men, " in Men's Bodies,
        Men's Selves: The Complete Guide to the Health and
        Well-being of Men's Bodies, Minds, and Spirits (New
        York: Dell Publishing Co. , 1979), pp. 85-123.

871)   Kappelman, Murray M. "Homosexuality, Bisexuality,
        and the Teenager, " in Sex and the American Teenager
        (New York: Reader's Digest Press, 1977), pp. 195-
        215.

872)   Karlen, Arno. "Homosexuality in History, " in Mar-
        mor, no. 24, pp. 75-99.

873)   _____. "Homosexuality: The Scene and Its Stu-
        dent, " in James M. Henslin and Edward Sagarin (eds.),

The Sociology of Sex: An Introductory Reader (New York: Shocken Books, 1978), pp. 223-48.

874)   Karr, Rodney G. "Homosexual Labeling and the Male Role," in Chesebro, no. 6, pp. 3-11.

875)   Katchadourian, Herant A. , and Donald T. Lunde. "Homosexuality and Other Sexual Behaviors," in Understanding Human Sexuality (3d ed.; New York: Holt, Rinehart and Winston, 1980), pp. 349-86.

876)   Kauffmann, Stanley. "Homosexual Drama and Its Disguises" and "On the Acceptability of the Homosexual," in Persons of the Drama: Theater Criticism and Comment (New York: Harper and Row, 1976), pp. 291-94 and 295-98.

877)   Kaye, Melanie. "Some Notes on Jewish Lesbian Identity" and "Notes on an Immigrant Daughter: Atlanta," in Beck, no. 2, pp. 28-45 and 109-13.

878)   Keane, Philip S. "Moral Considerations in Homosexuality," in Sexual Morality: A Catholic Perspective (New York: Paulist Press, 1977), pp. 71-91.

879)   Kelly, James. "The Aging Male Homosexual," in Gochros, no. 701, pp. 160-69. (See also no. 2333.)

880)   _____. "Homosexuality and Aging," in Marmor, no. 24, pp. 176-93.

881)   Kelly, Raymond C. "Witchcraft and Sexual Relations," in Paula Brown and Georgeda Buchbinder (eds.), Man and Woman in the New Guinea Highlands (Washington, D.C.: American Anthropological Association, 1976), pp. 36-53.

882)   Kelsey, John. "The Cleveland Bar Scene in the Forties," in Jay and Young, no. 18, pp. 146-49.

883)   Kiell, Norman. "Male Homosexuality" and "Female Homosexuality," in Varieties of Sexual Experience: Psychosexuality in Literature (New York: International Universities Press, 1976), pp. 217-72 and 272-321.

884)   Kierman, Robert F. "The Early Successes: Williwaw, The City and the Pillar," in Gore Vidal (New York:

Ungar Publishing Co. , 1982), pp. 32-44.

885)   Killinger, Marc.   "Lesbian and Gay Oppression in
       the '80s: Androgyny, Men, and Power, " in Mitchell,
       no. 25, pp. 171-87.

886)   Kimmel, Douglas C.   "Adjustments to Aging Among
       Gay Men, " in Berzon and Leighton, no. 3, pp. 146-
       58.

887)   King, Dave.   "Gender Confusions: Psychological and
       Psychiatric Conceptions of Transvestism and Trans-
       sexualism, " in Plummer, no. 27, pp. 155-83.

888)   Kirkpatrick, Martha, and Carole Morgan.   "Psycho-
       dynamic Therapy of Female Homosexuality, " in Mar-
       mor, no. 24, pp. 357-75.

889)   Kirsch, John A. W. , and James E. Rodman.   "Selec-
       tion and Sexuality: The Darwinian View of Homosexu-
       ality, " in Paul, no. 26, pp. 183-95.

890)   Klepfisz, Irena.   "AntiSemitism in the Lesbian-
       Feminist Movement" and "Resisting and Surviving
       America, " in Beck, no. 2, pp. 45-51 and 100-08.

891)   Knutson, Donald C.   "Job Security for Gays: The
       Legal Aspects, " in Berzon and Leighton, no. 3, pp.
       171-87.

892)   Kolodny, Robert C. , and others.   "Homosexuality, "
       in Textbook of Sexual Medicine (Boston: Little, Brown,
       1979), pp. 447-62.

893)   Kopkind, Andrew.   "The Boys in the Barracks, " in
       Jay and Young, no. 18, pp. 367-84.

894)   Kosnik, Anthony, and others.   "Homosexuality, " in
       Human Sexuality: New Directions in American Catholic
       Thought (New York: Paulist Press, 1977), pp. 7-74
       and 186-218.

895)   Kraft, William F.   "Homogenitalism, " in Sexual Dimen-
       sions of the Celibate Life (Kansas City, Kans. : An-
       drews and McMeel, 1979), pp. 151-62.

896)   Kyper, John.   "Coming Out: Toward a Social Analy-
       sis, " in Crew, no. 7, pp. 387-414.

897)   Lachman, Linda. "Electoral Politics: Interview
        with Elaine Noble," in Vida, no. 33, pp. 128-34.

898)   Laner, Mary R. and Roy H. "Personal Style and
        Sexual Preference: Why Gay Men Are Disliked,"
        in Harry and Das, no. 16, pp. 78-91.

899)   Laporte, Rita. "Causes and Cure of Homosexuality,"
        "Can Women Unite?" and "Sex and Sexuality," in
        Grier and Reid, no. 15, pp. 43-48, 107-15, and 197-
        219.

900)   Larson, Paul. C. "Gay Male Relationships," in Paul,
        no. 26, pp. 219-32.

901)   Lauritsen, John. "Disruptions, Censorship, Bigotry,"
        in Richmond and Noguera, no. 28, pp. 155-63.

902)   Lee, John A. "Meeting Males by Mail," in Crew,
        no. 7, pp. 415-27.

903)   Lehman, J. Lee. "Gay Students," in Crew, no. 7,
        pp. 57-66.

904)   Lehne, Gregory K. "Homophobia Among Men," in
        Deborah S. David and Robert Brannon (eds.), The
        Forty-Nine Percent Majority: The Male Sex Role
        (Reading, Mass.: Addison-Wesley Publishing Co.,
        1976), pp. 66-88.

905)   Leighton, Robert. "For Men: New Social Oppor-
        tunities," in Berzon and Leighton, no. 3, pp. 24-29.

906)   "The Letters of Almeda Sperry to Emma Goldman,"
        in Katz, no. 250, pp. 523-30.

907)   Levine, Martin P. "Employment Discrimination
        Against Gay Men," in Harry and Das, no. 16, pp.
        18-30.

908)   _____. "Introduction" and "Gay Ghetto," in
        Levine, no. 22, pp. 1-16 and 182-204.

909)   Levitt, Eugene E., and Albert D. Klassen, Jr.
        "Public Attitudes Toward Homosexuality," in
        Levine, no. 22, pp. 19-35.

910)   Lewin, Ellen, and Terrie A. Lyons. "Everything in
        Its Place: Lesbianism and Motherhood," in Paul,
        no. 26, pp. 249-73.

911)   Linedecker, Clifford. "North Fox Island," "Scout
        Troop 137," "The Meat Rack," and "Chicken Hawk,"
        in Children in Chains (New York: Everest House,
        1981), pp. 37-50, 73-89, 167-81, and 227-42.

912)   Lockwood, Daniel. "Victims of Prison Rape," in
        Prison Sexual Violence (New York: Elsevier North
        Holland, 1980), pp. 87-101.

913)   Los Angeles Research Group. "Toward a Scientific
        Analysis of the Gay Question," in Mitchell, no. 25,
        pp. 117-35.

914)   Lottman, Loretta. "Gay Plus Art Equals Renaissance,"
        in Berzon and Leighton, no. 3, pp. 130-33.

915)   _____. "I Was a Dyke at My High School Reunion,"
        in Jay and Young, no. 18, pp. 332-41.

916)   Luria, Zella, and Mitchel D. Rose. "Homosexuality,"
        in The Psychology of Human Sexuality (New York:
        Wiley and Sons, 1979), pp. 349-81.

917)   Lynch, Michael. "Forgotten [Gay] Fathers," in
        Jackson and Persky, no. 17, pp. 54-63.

918)   Lyon, Phyllis, and Del Martin. "Reminiscences
        of Two Female Homophiles," in Vida, no. 33, pp.
        124-28.

919)   MacCowan, Lyndall, and Margaret Cruikshank. "Bib-
        liography: Books and Articles [on Lesbianism]," in
        Cruikshank, no. 9, pp. 237-73.

920)   Maggid, Aliza. "Lesbians in the International Move-
        ment of Gay/Lesbian Jews," in Beck, no. 2, pp.
        114-19.

921)   Manahan, Nancy. "Homophobia in the Classroom,"
        in Cruikshank, no. 9, pp. 66-69.

922)   Margolis, Joseph Z. "Homosexuality," in Tom Regan
        and Donald Van De Veer (eds.), And Justice for All:

New Introductory Essays in Ethics and Public Policy
(Totowa, N.J.: Rowman and Littlefield, 1982), pp.
42-63.

923)   Marmor, Judd. "Overview: The Multiple Roots of
        Homosexual Behavior," "Clinical Aspects of Male Ho-
        mosexuality," and "Epilogue: Homosexuality and the
        Issue of Mental Illness," in Marmor, no. 24, pp. 3-
        24, 267-79, and 391-401.

924)   Marshall, John. "Pansies, Perverts, and Macho-Men:
        Changing Conceptions of Male Homosexuality," in
        Plummer, no. 27, pp. 133-54.

925)   _____. "The Politics of Tea and Sympathy," in
        Gay Left Collective, no. 13, pp. 77-84.

926)   Martin, Del, and Phyllis Lyon. "The Older Les-
        bian," in Berzon and Leighton, no. 3, pp. 134-45.

927)   Matt, Hershel. "Sin, Crime, or Alternative Life
        Style? A Jewish Approach to Homosexuality," in
        Batchelor, no. 1, pp. 114-24.

928)   Mayer, Hans. "A Chronicle of Murders and Scandal,"
        "Christopher Marlowe and King Edward II of England,"
        "Winckelmann's Death and the Discovery of a Double
        Life," "Conflict Between Heine and Platen," "Alterna-
        tives in the Nineteenth Century," "Concerning the
        Typology of Homosexual Literature," "The Alternatives
        of Klaus Mann and Maurice Sachs," and "The Turning
        Point of Jean Genet," in Outsiders: A Study in Life
        and Letters, Translated from the German by Denis M.
        Sweet (Cambridge: Massachusetts Institute of Tech-
        nology Press, 1982), pp. 143-53, 155-66, 167-74, 175-
        89, 191-221, 223-41, 243-52, and 253-65.

929)   McCarthy, Barry. "Within the Normal Range--Under-
        standing Male Homosexuality," in What You Still Don't
        Know About Male Sexuality (New York: Crowell,
        1977), pp. 106-18.

930)   McDaniel, Judith. "Coming Out: Ten Years of
        Change," in Lyn Lifshin (ed.), Ariadne's Thread:
        A Collection of Contemporary Women's Journals
        (New York: Harper and Row, 1982), pp. 168-76.

931)   McIntosh, Mary.   "The Homosexual Role," in Plum-
        mer, no. 27, pp. 30-43.

932)   McNaron, Toni A. H.   " 'Out' at the University:
        Myth and Reality" and "A Journey into Otherness:
        Teaching 'The Well of Loneliness,' " in Cruikshank,
        no. 9, pp. 12-15 and 88-92.

933)   McNaught, Brian.   "Gay and Catholic," in Berzon
        and Leighton, no. 3, pp. 56-64.

934)   Meyer-Bahlburg, Heino.   "Homosexual Orientation
        in Women and Men: A Hormonal Basis?" in Jaquelynne
        B. Parsons (ed.), The Psychology of Sex Differences
        and Sex Roles (Washington, D.C.: Hemisphere Pub-
        lishing Corp., 1980), pp. 105-30.

935)   Milhaven, John G.   "Homosexuality and Love," in
        Batchelor, no. 1, pp. 63-70.

936)   Miller, Brian.   "Unpromised Paternity: The Life
        Styles of Gay Fathers," in Levine, no. 22, pp. 239-
        52.

937)   Miller, Rhea.   "Religion and the Lesbian," in Vida,
        no. 33, pp. 167-71.

938)   Miller, Robert K.   "Feasting with Panthers: The
        Rise and Fall of Oscar Wilde," in Oscar Wilde (Lon-
        don: Frederick Ungar, 1982), pp. 1-24.

939)   Mitchell, Pam.   "Lesbians and Gay Men: Hetero
        Sexualities, Common Cause," in Mitchell, no. 25,
        pp. 48-56.

940)   Mitzel, John.   "Recipe for a Witchhunt [Pedophilia],"
        in Tsang, no. 31, pp. 116-24.

941)   _____.   "Sports and the Macho Male," in Jay and
        Young, no. 18, pp. 385-95.

942)   Money, John.   "Genetic and Chromosomal Aspects of
        Homosexual Etiology," in Marmor, no. 24, pp. 59-74.

943)   Moody, Roger.   "Man/Boy Love and the Left," in
        Tsang, no. 31, pp. 147-55.

944)   Moraga, Cherrie, and Barbara Smith. "Lesbian
       Literature: A Third World Feminist Perspective,"
       in Cruikshank, no. 9, pp. 55-64.

945)   Morin, Stephen F., and Ellen M. Garfinkle. "Male
       Homophobia," in Chesebro, no. 6, pp. 117-29.

946)   _____, and Lonnie Nungesser. "Can Homophobia
       Be Cured?" in Robert A. Lewis (ed.), Men in Dif-
       ficult Times: Masculinity Today and Tomorrow (Engle-
       wood Cliffs, N.J.: Prentice-Hall, 1981), pp. 264-74.

947)   Mort, Frank. "Sexuality: Regulation and Contestation,"
       in Gay Left Collective, no. 13, pp. 38-51.

948)   Moss, Leland. "Sense and the Gay Sensibility," in
       Richmond and Noguera, no. 28, pp. 73-80.

949)   Muehl, William. "Some Words of Caution," in Barn-
       house and Holmes, no. 680, pp. 167-74. (Reprinted
       in Batchelor, no. 1, and in Twiss, no. 32.)

950)   Murray, Stephen O. "Institutional Elaboration of the
       Quasi-Ethnic Community in Canada," in Harry and
       Das, no. 16, pp. 31-43.

951)   "Native Americans--Gay Americans, 1528-1976," in
       Katz, no. 250, pp. 281-334.

952)   Nelson, James B. "Gayness and Homosexuality:
       Issues for the Church," in Embodiment: An Approach
       to Sexuality and Christian Theology (Minneapolis:
       Augsburg Publishing House, 1978), pp. 180-210. (Re-
       printed in Batchelor, no. 1, pp. 186-210.)

953)   Nelson, Jeffrey. "Media Reaction to the 1979 Gay
       March on Washington," in Chesebro, no. 6, pp. 189-
       96.

954)   Nichols, Jack. "Butcher Than Thou: Beyond Mach-
       ismo," in Richmond and Noguera, no. 28, pp. 167-
       78 and in Levine, no. 22, pp. 328-46.

955)   Noeller, Bruce. "Society and the Gay Movement," in
       Marmor, no. 24, pp. 232-54.

956)   Nogle, Vicki. "Lesbianfeminist Rhetoric as a Social
       Movement," in Chesebro, no. 6, pp. 260-72.

957) Noll, Dolores. "Professional and Union Caucuses," in Vida, no. 33, pp. 173-77.

958) North American Man/Boy Love Association. "The Case for Abolishing the Age of Consent Laws," in Tsang, no. 31, pp. 92-106.

959) Norton, Rictor. "Ganymede Raped: Gay Literature-- The Critic as Censor," in Young, no. 377, pp. 277- 89.

960) Novak, Michael. "A Sense of Evil," in The Joy of Sports (New York: Basic Books, 1976), pp. 311-14.

961) Oaks, Robert. "'Things Fearful to Name:' Sodomy and Buggery in Seventeenth Century England," in Elizabeth and Joseph Pleck (eds.), The American Man (Englewood Cliffs, N.J. : Prentice-Hall, 1980), pp. 53-76.

962) O'Leary, Jean. "Legal Problems and Remedies," in Vida, no. 33, pp. 196-207.

963) Operation Socrates Handbook. "Male Homosexuality," in Schlesinger, no. 815, pp. 148-61.

964) Ovesey, Lionel, and Sherwyn M. Woods. "Pseudo- homosexuality and Homosexuality in Men: Psychody- namics as a Guide to Treatment," in Marmor, no. 24, pp. 325-41.

965) Painter, Dorothy S. "Recognition Among Lesbians in Straight Settings," in Chesebro, no. 6, pp. 68-79.

966) "Parents of Gays [Interviews]," in Vida, no. 33, pp. 272-79.

967) Park, Jan C. "Referendum Campaigns Against Gay Rights," in Chesebro, no. 6, pp. 286-90.

968) Patton, Frank, Jr. "Sex and the Law," in Barnhouse and Holmes, no. 680, pp. 116-30 at 118-23.

969) Paul, William. "Social Issues and Homosexual Be- havior: A Taxonomy of Categories and Themes in Anti-Gay Argument" and "Minority Status for Gay People: Majority Reaction and Social Context," in Paul, no. 26, pp. 29-54 and 351-69.

970)   _____, and James D. Weinrich. "Whom and What We
         Study: Definition and Scope of Sexual Orientation," in
         Paul, no. 26, pp. 23-28.

971)   Peplau, Letitia A. , and Hortensia Amaro. "Under-
         standing Lesbian Relationships," in Paul, no. 26, pp.
         233-47.

972)   Petras, John W. "Unapproved Sexuality ... Homo-
         sexuality," in The Social Meaning of Human Sexuality
         (2d ed.; Boston: Allyn and Bacon, 1978), pp. 187-94.

973)   Phelps, Linda. "Female Sexual Alienation," in Grier
         and Reid, no. 15, pp. 161-70.

974)   Pieper, Richard. "Identity Management in Adolescent
         Male Prostitution in West Germany," in Harry and
         Das, no. 16, pp. 101-22.

975)   Pillard, Richard C. "Psychotherapeutic Treatment for
         the Invisible Minority," in Paul, no. 26, pp. 99-113.

976)   Pittenger, Norman. "Evils and God--From a 'Process'
         to a Perspective," in Crew, no. 7, pp. 361-68.

977)   _____. "The Morality of Homosexual Acts," in
         Batchelor, no. 1, pp. 139-45.

978)   _____. "A Theological Approach to Understanding
         Homosexuality," in Barnhouse and Holmes, no. 680,
         pp. 157-66.

979)   Plaskow, Judith. "Blaming the Jews for the Birth of
         Patriarchy," in Beck, no. 2, pp. 250-54.

980)   Plummer, Kenneth. "Building a Sociology of Homo-
         sexuality" and "Homosexual Categories: Some Research
         Problems in the Labelling Perspective of Homosexu-
         ality," in Plummer, no. 27, pp. 17-29 and 53-75.

981)   Ponse, Barbara. "Lesbians and Their World," in
         Marmor, no. 24, pp. 157-75.

982)   Poor, Matile. "Older Lesbians," in Cruikshank, no.
         9, pp. 165-73.

983)   Pope, Marvin H. "Homosexuality," in The Interpre-
         ters' Dictionary of the Bible: Supplementary Volume

(Nashville, Tenn.: Abingdon Press, 1976), pp.
415-17.

984)   Porter, John R.   "Race and Homosexuality," in
Dating Habits of Young Black Americans and Almost
Everybody Else Too (Dubuque, Ia.: Kendall-Hunt
Co., 1979), pp. 75-77.

985)   Potter, Clare. "The Lesbian Periodicals Index,"
in Cruikshank, no. 9, pp. 152-61.

986)   Powell, Betty J. "Lesbians at Work," in Vida, no.
33, pp. 37-65.

987)   Presland, Eric. "Whose Power, Whose Consent?"
in Tsang, no. 31, pp. 72-79.

988)   Rechy, John. "An Open Letter to Anita Bryant,"
in Richmond and Noguera, no. 28, pp. 213-19.

989)   Reece, Rex. "Coping with Couplehood," in Levine,
no. 22, pp. 211-21.

990)   Reeves, Tom. "Loving Boys," in Tsang, no. 31,
pp. 25-37.

991)   Rice, Lee C. "Homosexuality and the Social Order,"
in Alan Soble (ed.), The Philosophy of Sex: Contemporary Readings (Totowa, N.J.: Rowman and
Littlefield, 1980), pp. 256-80.

992)   Rich, Adrienne C. "It Is the Lesbian in Us" and
"The Meaning of Our Love for Women Is What We
Have Constantly to Expand," in On Lies, Secrets,
and Silence: Selected Prose, 1966-1978 (New York:
Norton, 1979), pp. 199-202 and 223-30.

993)   _____. "Split at the Root," in Beck, no. 2,
pp. 67-84.

994)   Riddiough, Christine. "Culture and Politics" and
"Some Thoughts on Gay/Lesbian Oppression," in
Mitchell, no. 25, pp. 14-33 and 136-47.

995)   Riddle, Dorothy I. "Finding Supporting Therapy [for
Lesbians]," in Vida, no. 33, pp. 87-93.

996)   Riess, Bernard F.   "Psychological Tests in Homo-
        sexuality," in Marmor, no. 24, pp. 296-311.

997)   Riordon, Michael.   "Capital Punishment: Notes of
        a Willing Victim," in Levine, no. 22, pp. 78-99.

998)   _____.   "The Mirror of Violence," in Jackson
        and Perksy, no. 17, pp. 33-40.

999)   Risch, Stephen.   "Towards a Gay Analysis of Sci-
        ence and Education," in Crew, no. 7, pp. 369-86.

1000)   Rivaldo, Jim, and Dick Pabish.   "Learning from
        Harvey Milk," in Richmond and Noguera, no. 28,
        pp. 205-11.

1001)   Rivera, Rhonda.   "Homosexuality and the Law,"
        in Paul, no. 26, pp. 323-36.

1002)   Rizzi, Joseph A. , and Robert W. Jacobs.   "Speech
        and Expression Outside the Classroom as Elements
        of a School Board's Determination of Teaching Fit-
        ness: A Case Study of a Gay Activist [The Gish
        Case]," in McGhehey, no. 700, pp. 179-98.

1003)   Roberts, J. R.   "Black Lesbians Before 1970: A
        Biographical Essay," in Cruikshank, no. 9, pp.
        103-10.

1004)   Robinson, David J.   "[Rev.] Troy Perry: Gay Ad-
        vocate," in Chesebro, no. 6, pp. 248-59.

1005)   Rochlin, Martin.   "Becoming a Gay Professional,"
        in Berzon and Leighton, no. 3, pp. 159-70.

1006)   Rogers, Martin.   "Critical Incidents in the Evolution
        of a Gay Liberation Group," in Levine, no. 22, pp.
        317-27.

1007)   Rorem, Ned.   "Letter to Claude," in Michael Rubin
        (ed.), Men Without Masks: Writings from the Jour-
        nals of Modern Man (Reading, Mass. : Addison-
        Wesley, 1980), pp. 107-16.

1008)   Rosan, Lawrence J.   "Philosophies of Homophobia
        and Homophilia," in Crew, no. 7, pp. 255-81.

1009)   Rose, Frank. "Norm Rathweg," in Real Men: Sex
        and Style in an Uncertain Age (New York: Double-
        day, 1980), pp. 58-75.

1010)   Rosen, Raymond and Linda R. "Homosexual Pat-
        terns and Relationships," in Human Sexuality (New
        York: Knopf, 1981), pp. 104-16.

1011)   Ross, Charles L. "Homoerotic Feeling in 'Women
        in Love': Lawrence's Struggle for Verbal Conscious-
        ness in the Manuscripts," in Robert B. Partlow, Jr.
        and Harry T. Moore (eds.), D. H. Lawrence: The
        Man Who Lived (Carbondale, Ill.: Southern Illinois
        University, 1979), pp. 168-82.

1012)   Rubin, Gayle. "Sexual Politics, the New Right, and
        the Sexual Fringe," in Tsang, no. 31, pp. 108-15.

1013)   Rueling, Anna. "What Interest Does the Women's
        Movement Have in the Homosexual Question?" in
        Faderman and Eriksson, no. 11, pp. 81-91.

1014)   Ruether, Rosemary R. "From Machismo to Mutu-
        ality," in Batchelor, no. 1, pp. 28-32.

1015)   Rush, Florence. "Greek Love" and 'The Sexual
        Abuse of Boys," in The Best Kept Secret: Sexual
        Abuse of Children (Englewood Cliffs, N.J.: Prentice-
        Hall, 1981), pp. 48-55 and 170-82.

1016)   Russo, Vito. "Camp," in Levine, no. 22, pp. 205-
        10.

1017)   Sage, Wayne. "Inside the Colossal Closet," in
        Levine, no. 22, pp. 148-63.

1018)   Saghir, Marcel T., and Eli Robins. "Clinical As-
        pects of Female Homosexuality," in Marmor, no. 24,
        pp. 280-95.

1019)   St. Joan, Jackie. "Survey of Lesbian Publications,"
        in Vida, no. 33, pp. 246-49.

1020)   Salzman, Leon. "Latent Homosexuality," in Marmor,
        no. 24, pp. 312-24.

1021)   Sanders, David S. "A Psychotherapeutic Approach to
        Homosexual Men," in Marmor, no. 24, pp. 342-56.

1022)   Sang, Barbara E.   "Lesbian Research: A Critical
        Evaluation, " in Vida, no. 33, pp. 80-87.

1023)   Saslow, James M.   "Closets in the Museums: Ho-
        mophobia and Art History, " in Jay and Young, no.
        18, pp. 215-27.

1024)   Schoenfeld, Eugene.   "Groups, Gays and Other Ways, "
        in Jealousy: Taming the Green-Eyed Monster (New
        York: Holt, Rinehart, and Winston, 1979), pp. 83-
        104.

1025)   Secor, Neale.   "A Brief for a New Homosexual
        Ethic, " in Batchelor, no. 1, pp. 154-64.

1026)   Sheed, Wilfrid.   "On Keeping Closets Closed, " in
        The Good Word and Other Words (New York: E. P.
        Dutton, 1978), pp. 73-76.

1027)   Sheldon, Caroline.   "Lesbians and Film: Some
        Thoughts, " in Dyer, no. 10, pp. 5-26.

1028)   Shelley, Martha.   "Is Heterosexuality Normal? " and
        "Confessions of a Pseudo-Male Chauvinist, " in Grier
        and Reid, no. 15, pp. 55-60 and 93-97.

1029)   Shewey, Don.   "Theatre: Gays in the Marketplace
        Versus Gays for Themselves, " in Jay and Young,
        no. 18, pp. 230-45.

1030)   Shiers, John.   "Two Steps Forward, One Step Back, "
        in Gay Left Collective, no. 13, pp. 140-56.

1031)   Shinn, Roger.   "Homosexuality: Christian Conviction
        and Inquiry, " in Batchelor, no. 1, pp. 3-13.

1032)   Shively, Charley.   "Cosmetics as an Act of Revolu-
        tion" and "Old and Gay, " in Mitchell, no. 25, pp.
        34-47 and 72-77.

1033)   _____.   "Phantasy Revolution, " in Jay and Young,
        no. 18, pp. 118-32.

1034)   Siegel, Paul.   "Androgyny, Sex-Role Rigidity, and
        Homophobia, " in Chesebro, no. 6, pp. 142-52.

1035)   Silverstein, Charles.   "Homosexuality and the Ethics
        of Behavioral Intervention" and "Sexual Problems

of Gay Men," in Richmond and Noguera, no. 28, pp. 131-38 and 179-83.

1036)   Simms, Steven A.   "Gay Images on Television," in Chesebro, no. 6, pp. 153-62.

1037)   Sklepowich, E. A.   "In Pursuit of the Lyric Quarry: The Image of the Homosexual in Tennessee Williams' Prose Fiction," in Jac Thorpe (ed.), Tennessee Williams: A Tribute (Jackson: University of Mississippi Press, 1977), pp. 525-44

1038)   Slovenko, Ralph.   "Homosexuality and the Law: From Condemnation to Celebration," in Marmor, no. 24, pp. 194-218.

1039)   Smedes, Lewis B.   "Distorted Sexuality--Homosexuality," in Sex for Christians: The Limits and Liberties of Sexual Living (Grand Rapids, Mich.: Eerdmans, 1976), pp. 62-73.

1040)   Smith, Barbara.   "Sample Syllabi from Courses on Lesbianism," in Cruikshank, no. 9, pp. 217-35.

1041)   _____.   "Toward a Black Feminist Criticism," in Gloria T. Hull and others (eds.), But Some of Us Are Brave: Black Women's Studies (Old Westbury, N.Y.: Feminist Press, 1982), pp. 157-75.

1042)   _____, and Beverly Smith.   "Lesbian Separatism" and "Homophobia in the Black Community," in Moraga and Anzaldua, no. 726, pp. 120-26.

1043)   Soares, John V.   "Black and Gay," in Levine, no. 22, pp. 263-74.

1044)   Socarides, Charles W.   "Homosexuality Is Not Just an Alternative Life Style," in Barnhouse and Holmes, no. 680, pp. 145-56.

1045)   Somerville, James W. F.   "The Aesthetic and Sexual Relativity," in Crew, no. 7, pp. 282-304.

1046)   Sonenschein, David.   "Male Homosexual Relationship," in Weinberg, no. 679, pp. 140-55.

1047)   Stanley, Julia P.   "Lesbian Separatism: The Linguistic

and Social Sources of Separatist Politics," in
Crew, no. 7, pp. 121-34.

1048)   _____, and Susan W. Robbins. "Mother Wit:
         Tongue in Cheek," in Jay and Young, no. 18, pp.
         299-307.

1049)   Stanton, Robert J., and Gore Vidal. "Sexuality,"
         in Robert J. Stanton (ed.), Views from a Window:
         Conversations with Gore Vidal (Secaucus, N.J.:
         Lyle Stuart, 1980), pp. 217-46.

1050)   Steakley, James. "Homosexuals and the Third
         Reich," in Jackson and Persky, no. 17, pp. 84-91.

1051)   Steinem, Gloria. "The Politics of Supporting Les-
         bianism," in Vida, no. 33, pp. 266-69.

1052)   Stivison, David. "Homosexuals and the Constitution,"
         in Paul, no. 26, pp. 303-21.

1053)   Stockinger, Jacob. "Homosexuality: A Proposal,"
         in Crew, no. 7, pp. 135-51.

1054)   Stoltenberg, John. "Toward Gender Justice," in
         John Snodgrass (ed.), For Men Against Sexism (Al-
         bion, Cal.: Times Change, 1977), pp. 74-83.

1055)   Symonds, John A. "Dantesque and Platonic Ideals
         of Love," in Fone, no. 12, pp. 145-60.

1056)   Szasz, Thomas S. "Sex as Treatment--In Theory,"
         in Sex by Prescription (New York: Anchor Books,
         1980), pp. 37-45

1057)   Thielicke, Helmut. "The Theologico-ethical Aspect
         of Homosexuality," in Batchelor, no. 1, pp. 96-104.

1058)   Thomas Aquinas. "Summa Theologica--Questions
         152 and 154," in Batchelor, no. 1, pp. 39-47.

1059)   Thomas, David J. "San Francisco's 1979 White
         Night Riot: Injustice, Vengeance, and Beyond," in
         Paul, no. 26, pp. 337-50.

1060)   Toder, Nancy. "Lesbian Couples: Special Issues,"
         in Berzon and Leighton, no. 3, pp. 41-55.

1061)   _____ . "Sexual Problems of Lesbians," in
             Vida, no. 33, pp. 105-13.

1062)   Toronto Gay Action.   "We Demand [A Brief Pre-
             sented to the Canadian National Government]," in
             Jackson and Persky, no. 17, pp. 217-20.

1063)   Tourney, Garfield.   "Hormones and Homosexuality,"
             in Marmor, no. 24, pp. 41-58.

1064)   Trilling, Diana.   "Our Upcomplaining Homosexuals,"
             in We Must March My Darlings: A Critical Decade
             (New York: Harcourt Brace Jovanovich, 1977), pp.
             157-71.

1065)   Tsang, Daniel.   "Men and Boys: The Boston Con-
             ference" and "Struggling Against Racism," in Tsang,
             no. 31, pp. 38-43 and 161-66.

1066)   Tucker, Scott.   "Sex, Death and Free Speech: The
             Fight to Stop [the Filming of William] Friedkin's
             'Cruising,'" in Jackson and Persky, no. 17, pp.
             197-206.

1067)   Valents, Michael F.   "A New Direction--Homosexual
             Acts Are Natural and Good," in Batchelor, no. 1,
             pp. 149-53.

1068)   Van Buren, Abigail.   "The Homosexual Hassle," in
             The Best of Dear Abby (Kansas City, Kans. : An-
             drews and McMeel, 1981), pp. 61-76.

1069)   Vida, Ginny.   "The Lesbian Image in the Media,"
             in Vida, no. 33, pp. 240-45.

1070)   Vidal, Gore.   "Pink Triangle and Yellow Star," in
             The Second American Revolution and Other Essays
             (1976-1982) (New York: Random House, 1982), pp.
             167-84.   (See no. 1582.)

1071)   "Walt Whitman, John Addington Symonds, and Ed-
             ward Carpenter," in Katz, no. 250, pp. 337-65.

1072)   Warren, Carol A. B.   "Homosexuality and Stigma,"
             in Marmor, no. 24, pp. 123-41.

1073)   _____ .   "Women Among Men: Females in the

Male Homosexual Community," in Levine, no. 22, pp. 222-38.

1074)   _____, and Barbara Ponse. "The Existential Self in the Gay World," in Jack D. Douglas and J. M. Johnson (eds.), Existential Sociology (New York: Cambridge University Press, 1977), pp. 273-89.

1075)   Watney, Simon. "The Ideology of the Gay Liberation Front," in Gay Left Collective, no. 13, pp. 64-76.

1076)   Weeks, Jeffrey. "Capitalism and the Organization of Sex," in Gay Left Collective, no. 13, pp. 11-20.

1077)   _____. "Discourse, Desire and Sexual Deviance: Some Problems in a History of Homosexuality," in Plummer, no. 27, pp. 76-111.

1078)   Weinberg, George. "The Madness and Myths of Homophobia," in Richmond and Noguera, no. 28, 185-93.

1079)   Weinberg, Martin S. , and Colin J. Williams. "Gay Baths and the Social Organization of Impersonal Sex," in Levine, no. 22, pp. 164-81.

1080)   _____, and _____. "Homosexuals and the Military" and "Male Homosexuals and Their Adaptations" in Weinberg, no. 679, pp. 233-45 and 246-57.

1081)   Weinrich, James D. "Is Homosexuality Biologically Normal?" and "Task Force Findings: Overview and Prospect," in Paul, no. 26, pp. 197-209 and 377-82.

1082)   Whitam, Frederick L. , and Mary J. Dizon. "Occupational Choice and Sexual Orientation in Cross-Cultural Perspective," in Harry and Das, no. 16, pp. 5-17.

1083)   White, Edmund. "The Political Vocabulary of Homosexuality," in Leonard Michaels and Christopher Ricks (eds.), The State of Language (Berkeley: University of California Press, 1980), pp. 235-46.

1084)   White, Robert W. , and Norman F. Watt. "Homosexuality," in The Abnormal Personality (5th ed. :

New York: Wiley and Sons, 1981), pp. 445-57.

1085) Whitehead, Harriet. "The Bow and the Burden Strap: A New Look at Institutionalized Homosexuality in Native North America," in Sherry B. Ortner and Harriet Whitehead (eds.), Sexual Meanings: The Cultural Construction of Gender and Sexuality (New York: Cambridge University Press, 1981), pp. 80-115.

1086) Whitmore, George. "Gay Theater in the 'Real World,'" in Jay and Young, no. 18, pp. 246-54.

1087) Whitworth, Sarah. "The Independent Women of Winslow Homer," "Romaine Brooks: Portrait of an Epoch," "Audrey Flack: Three Views," "Lesbian and Feminist Images in Greek Art and Mythology," "The Other Face of Love," and "The Feminist Movement and Political Art," in Grier and Reid, no. 15, pp. 300-05, 307-17, 318-25, 327-37, 338-44, and 345-57.

1088) Williams, Susan. "Lesbianism: A Socialist Feminist Perspective," in Mitchell, no. 25, pp. 107-16.

1089) "Witch-Hunt: The U. S. Government versus Homosexuals, 1950-55," in Katz, no. 250, pp. 91-108.

1090) Witters, Weldon L. and Patricia. "Homosexuality," in Human Sexuality: A Biological Perspective (New York: D. Van Nostrand, 1980), pp. 271-78.

1091) Wolfe, Susan J. "Jewish Lesbian Mother," in Beck, no. 2, pp. 164-73.

1092) Wood, Robert. "Christ and the Homosexual," in Batchelor, no. 1, pp. 165-67.

1093) Yearwood, Lennox, and Thomas S. Weinberg. "Black Organizations, Gay Organizations: Sociological Parallels," in Levine, no. 22, pp. 301-16.

1094) Young, Allen. "No Longer the Court Jesters," in Jay and Young, no. 18, pp. 23-47.

1095) Young, Ian. "The Flower Beneath the Foot: A Short History of the Gay Novel," "The Poetry of

Male Love," and "Some Notes on Gay Publishing: The 1980s and Before," in Young, no. 377, pp. 233-45, 259-76, and 290-94.

1096)   , and others. "Forum on Sadomasochism," in Jay and Young, no. 18, pp. 85-117.

1097)   Young, Perry D. "Victory in Miami; First Beachhead of the New Right" and "Homosexuals and Anti-Homosexuals," in God's Bullies: Native Reflections on Preachers and Politics (New York: Holt, Rinehart, and Winston, 1982), pp. 36-54 and 132-52.

1098)   Youth Liberation. "Children and Sex," in Tsang, no. 31, pp. 46-57.

1099)   Zimmerman, Bonnie. "One Out of Thirty: Lesbianism in Women's Studies Textbooks," in Cruikshank, no. 9, pp. 128-31.

1100)   Zoglin, Richard. "The Homosexual Executive," in Levine, no. 22, pp. 68-77.

NEWSPAPER ARTICLES

1101) Advertising Directed to Gays, San Francisco Chronicle, May 25, 1982, p. 15.

1102) AIDS [Acquired Immune Deficiency Syndrome]: A Serious Disorder Affecting Primarily Male Homosexuals, New York Times May 11, 1982, p. III-1, and August 8, 1982, p. 31.

1103) Amdur, Neil. "Homosexuality [in Sports] Sets Off Tremors," New York Times, May 12, 1981, pp. II-11+.

1104) American Bar Association Rejects Gay Rights Resolution, New York Times, Aug. 8, 1978, p. 16.

1105) American Catholic Bishops Approve Pastoral Letter Stating That Homosexual Orientation Is Not Sinful but Homosexual Acts Are, New York Times, Nov. 12, 1976, p. I-1.

1106) American Hebrew Congregations Union Adopts Resolution Opposing Discrimination Against Homosexuals in Employemnt and Housing, New York Times, Nov. 23, 1977, p. 13.

1107) Anchorage (Alaska) City Assembly Approves Ordinance Prohibiting Discrimination Against Homosexuals, New York Times, Jan. 4, 1976, p. 43.

1108) Antoine, Rick. "Gay Pride Week, Time for Self-Respect, Education," Fort Wayne News Sentinel, Jun. 16, 1982, pp. D1+.

1109) Archbishop Quinn Stops Gay Men's Choral Concert at St. Ignatius Catholic Church, San Francisco Chronicle, Apr. 7, 1981, p. 1.

1110)   Arrests for Prostitution in Male Sex Ring, Boston
        Globe, May 3, 1982, pp. 13+; May 4, 1982, p. 19;
        and May 10, 1982, pp. 13+.

1111)   Arrowsmith, Keith. "The Real History of Gay Peo-
        ple," Village Voice, Mar. 11, 1981, pp. 44+.

1112)   Austin (Texas) Voters Reject Housing Measure Au-
        thorizing Discrimination Against Gays, Austin
        American-Statesman, Jan 17, 1982, pp. 1+.

1113)   Bay Area Homosexual Physicians Form First "Gay
        Doctors" Group, San Francisco Chronicle, Jul. 25,
        1978, p. 2.

1114)   Bell, Arthur. "The Gay Double Agent [Mafia Owned
        Gay Bars]," Village Voice, May 8, 1978, pp. 1+.

1115)   _____. Murder Stalks the New York City Gay
        Community, Village Voice, Nov. 28, 1980, p. 1+.

1116)   _____, and others. "Gay Rights After Miami,"
        Village Voice, Jun. 20, 1977, pp. 11-13.

1117)   Berkeley (California) Council Votes Ban on Discrimi-
        nation Against Gays, Los Angeles Times, Sep. 21,
        1978, p. I-2.

1118)   Billie Jean King Involved in Lesbian Relationship
        with Marilyn Barnett, New York Times, May 1,
        1981, p. 12; May 2, 1981, p. 9; and Dec. 12,
        1981, p. 10.

1119)   Black Gays Begin to Make Themselves Known on
        Campus: Lambda Student Alliance at Howard Uni-
        versity Denied Recognition, Washington Post, Mar.
        22, 1980, p. A-2.

1120)   Bonwit Teller in Chicago Sponsors "Gay Fashion"
        Show, New York Times, Dec. 22, 1977, p. 14.

1121)   Brigham Young University Security Police Staked
        Out Gay Bars in Salt Lake City to Investigate Ho-
        mosexual Activity at the School, New York Times,
        Sep. 27, 1979, p. 16.

1122)   Brookband, David, and others. "Police Officer's
        Attitude Endangers Rights and Safety of Gays,"
        Minneapolis Star, Oct. 26, 1981, p. A-6.

1123)   Bush, Larry. "Homosexuality and the New Right,"
        Village Voice, Apr. 14, 1982, pp. 16+.

1124)   _____. "Naming [Gay] Names--The Ethics of
        Disclosure," Village Voice, Apr. 27, 1982, pp. 22-
        25.

1125)   _____, and Richard Goldstein. "The Anti-Gay
        Backlash--It's Not Just Coming from the Right,"
        Village Voice, Apr. 8, 1981, pp. 1+.

1126)   California Legislature Outlaws Marriages Between
        Homosexuals, Los Angeles Times, Aug. 12, 1977,
        p. I-33.

1127)   Campaign Against Homosexuality in Turkey, New
        York Times, May 7, 1981, p. 11.

1128)   Carter Administration Official Meets with Gay
        Task Force Group, New York Times, Feb. 16,
        1977, p. 14 and Mar. 27, 1977, p. 13; Washington
        Post, Dec. 21, 1979, p. A-8.

1129)   Circulation of Magazines for Gay Males Grows in
        Size and Publishers Seek National Advertisers, New
        York Times, Jul. 13, 1976, p. 55.

1130)   Cockburn, Alexander. "Homosexuals, Witch-Hunts,
        and the Cold War," Village Voice, Nov. 21, 1977,
        p. 23.

1131)   _____, and James Ridgeway. "The Social Politics
        of Homosexuality," Village Voice, Jun. 20, 1977,
        p. 15.

1132)   Congressional Committee on Immigration and Refugee
        Policy Decides Not to Recommend Any Changes in
        Law Excluding Homosexual Aliens, New York Times,
        Feb. 15, 1981, p. 28.

1133)   Congressman Jon Hinson of Mississippi Re-elected
        After Admitting Homosexual Acts, But Resigns After
        Subsequent Arrest, New York Times, Aug. 24, 1980,

p. 24; Oct. 8, 1980, p. II-8; Oct. 26, 1980, p. IV-3; Nov. 6, 1980, p. 28; Feb. 5, 1981, p. 19; and Mar. 18, 1981, p. 18.

1134) Congressman Robert E. Bauman, Conservative Republican from Maryland and Opponent of Homosexual Rights, Defeated for Re-election After Being Charged with Solicitation of Sex from a Teenage Boy, New York Times, Oct. 9, 1980, p. 27 and Nov. 5, 1980, p. 19.

1135) Connecticut House of Representatives Defeats Homosexual Rights Bill, New York Times, Mar. 4, 1976, p. 35 and Apr. 6, 1977, p. 22.

1136) Crouch, Stanley. "Gay Pride, Gay Prejudice [Black Homosexuals]," Village Voice, Apri 27, 1982, pp. 1+.

1137) Dade County (Miami) Florida Voters Decisively Repeal Gay Rights Ordinance After Heated Campaign Led by Anita Bryant, Miami Herald, Jun. 8, 1977, pp. A-1+.

1138) "Democrats Adopt Gay Rights Plank," San Francisco Chronicle, Jun. 25, 1980, p. 14.

1139) Department of Defense Threatens to Deny Contracts and Reserve Training Units to University Law Schools Refusing to Permit U.S. Army Recruiting Because Armed Services Will Not Accept Homosexuals, New York Times, Jul. 25, 1982, p. 26.

1140) Dignity, a Catholic Homosexual Group--Its Activities and Aims, New York Times, Feb. 22, 1976, p. 26.

1141) Dismissed Homosexual Pilot Files Discrimination Complaint Against Northwest Orient Airlines, New York Times, Jun. 25, 1976, p. I-24.

1142) Disneyland Bars Boy and Male Date from Night Dance, Los Angeles Times, Sep. 15, 1980, p. II-5.

1143) Dublin's High Court Upholds Ireland's Law Against Homosexual Acts, New York Times, Oct. 11, 1980, p. 2.

1144)   Dullea, Georgia. "Homosexual Couples: Therapy
        for Problems of Living Together," New York Times,
        May 8, 1979, p. C-11.

1145)   Dying Gay Rights Bill Stirs Hot Debate in Congress,
        Washington Post, Jan. 28, 1982, p. A-2.

1146)   Editor of London's Gay News Convicted for Blasphemy
        and Sentenced to Prison, New York Times, Dec. 11,
        1976, p. 7 and Jul. 13, 1977, p. 4.

1147)   Editorial Opposing Dade County Gay Rights Ordi-
        nance, Miami Herald, Jun. 5, 1977, p. E-2.

1148)   Editorial Opposing Initiative to Prohibit Homosexual
        Teachers in California Public Schools, Los Angeles
        Times, Aug. 21, 1978, p. II-6 and Oct. 30, 1978,
        pp. II-6.

1149)   Editorials in Support of Gays Rights Bill in New
        York City, New York Times, May 24, 1977, p. 34;
        Jan. 5, 1978, p. 26; and May 3, 1978, p. 24.

1150)   Emerald City--Cable TV Show for Gays, New York
        Times, Jun. 2, 1977, p. III-21.

1151)   Eugene (Oregon) Voters Repeal Gay Rights Ordinance,
        New York Times, May 25, 1978, p. 13.

1152)   Fear of AIDS [Acquired Immune Deficiency Syndrome]
        Causes Many Gays to Change Their Lifestyles, San
        Francisco Chronicle, Oct. 12, 1982, p. 17.

1153)   Federal Government routinely Spied on Gay Groups
        and Compiled Long Lists of Homosexuals in the '50s,
        '60s, and Early '70s, New York Times, Sep. 9, 1982,
        p. IV-26.

1154)   Federal Judge Rules Gay Games Cannot Use Term
        "Olympic," San Francisco Chronicle, Aug. 10, 1982,
        p. 3 and Aug. 21, 1982, p. 12.

1155)   Field, Mervin D. "California Poll: Sharp Split on
        Gay Issues," San Francisco Chronicle, Aug. 12,
        1977, p. 10.

1156)   Florida Forbids Same Sex Marriage and Adoption of
        Children by Gay Persons, Miami Herald, Jun. 9,
        1977, p. A-27.

1157)   Florida High Court Upholds Right of Homosexuals to
        Practice Law, New York Times, Mar. 21, 1978, p.
        20.

1158)   Frazier, Deborah.   "Aspen [Colorado] Bar Owners
        at War with Homosexuals," Denver Rocky Mountain
        News, Mar. 1, 1982, pp. 10+.

1159)   Fundamentalist Ministers Protest Effort to Improve
        Gay Rights, Washington Post, Mar. 22, 1980, p. A-
        2.

1160)   Gallop Poll on Attitudes About Gays, San Francisco
        Chronicle, Jul. 18, 1977, p. 1+ and Nov. 9, 1982,
        p. 7.

1161)   Garfield, Robert.   "Gays Garner Economic Support,"
        USA Today, Nov. 23, 1982, pp. B-1+.

1162)   Gay Activist Mel Boozer Withdraws Name as Vice
        Presidential Nominee at Democratic National Con-
        vention, New York Times, Aug. 16, 1980, p. 7.

1163)   Gay Activist Robert Livingstone Appointed to New
        York City Human Rights Commission, New York
        Times, Mar. 21, 1977, p. 24.

1164)   Gay Man (Richard Heakin of Lincoln, Nebraska)
        Beaten to Death Outside Tucson Gay Bar by Gang of
        Teenage Boys Out to "Hassle Queers"--Four Youths
        Found Guilty of Involuntary Manslaughter Given Pro-
        bation, Arizona Daily Star, Jun. 7, 1976, p. A-1;
        Sep. 9, 1976, p. A-1; and Oct. 21, 1976, p. A-1.

1165)   Gay March in Seattle, Seattle Post-Intelligencer,
        Jun. 28, 1981, p. F-1.

1166)   Gay Olympic Games Held in San Francisco, San
        Francisco Chronicle, Aug. 28, 1982, p. 2; Aug. 29,
        1982, p. B-1; Aug. 30, 1982, p. 2; and Sep. 6,
        1982, p. 2.

1167)   Gay Republicans Form Group to Protect Gay Rights,
        San Francisco Chronicle, Feb. 19, 1981, p. 62.

1168) Gay Rights Referendum Loses for Second Time in Miami, <u>Miami Herald</u>, Nov. 8, 1978, pp. B-1+.

1169) Gay Savings and Loan to Open in San Francisco-- First in the Nation, <u>San Francisco Chronicle</u>, Mar. 20, 1980, p. 29.

1170) Georgetown University Claims Religious Exemption from District of Columbia Human Rights Act Pro- hibiting Discrimination Against Gays, <u>Washington Post</u>, Feb. 23, 1982, p. C-20.

1171) Goldstein, Richard. "Gay New Wave [Recent Gay Movies]," <u>Village Voice</u>, Dec. 7, 1982, pp. 48-49.

1172) _____. "Whose Holocaust? [Discussion of Martin Sherman's "Bent" Which Deals with Nazi Persecution of Homosexuals]," <u>Village Voice</u>, Dec. 10, 1979, p. 46.

1173) GOP Presidential Candidate John Anderson Supports Gay Rights, <u>San Francisco Chronicle</u>, Apr. 12, 1980, p. 7.

1174) Governor Reubin Askew of Florida Opposes Gay Rights Ordinance, <u>Miami Herald</u>, Apr. 30, 1977, p. 1.

1175) Green, Blake, "Why They [Female Singers and Movie Stars] Attract Gay Audiences," <u>San Francisco Chroni- cle</u>, Mar. 13, 1978, p. 16.

1176) Greenfield, Jeff. "Why Is Gay Rights Different from All Other Rights?" <u>Village Voice</u>, Feb. 6, 1978, pp. 1+.

1177) Guerneville--Gay Resort in Northern California, <u>San Francisco Chronicle</u>, Apr. 26, 1981, p. A-1.

1178) Hager, Philip. "Emergence of the Gay Teacher Issue," <u>San Francisco Examiner and Chronicle</u>, Sep. 4, 1977, Sunday Punch Section, p. 7.

1179) Hall, Richard. "The Unnatural History of Homo- sexual Literature," <u>Village Voice</u>, Aug. 22, 1977, pp. 40-42.

1180)   Harris, Louis.   Harris Poll Shows Gays "Suffer
        Most Bias, " Chicago Tribune, Jul. 18, 1977, p.
        I-13.

1181)   Hartford (Connecticut) Mayor Vetoes Gay Rights
        Ordinance, New York Times, Jul. 26, 1978, p. 22.

1182)   Harvard University Gay Students' Association Pro-
        tests Views of Faculty Member, Boston Globe, May
        7, 1982, p. 15 and May 15, 1982, p. 24.

1183)   Harvey Milk, Open Gay Activist, Elected Supervisor
        in San Francisco, New York Times, Jan. 12, 1978,
        p. 14.

1184)   Hechinger, Grace and Fred.   "Homosexuality on Cam-
        pus [University Gay Organization], " New York Times,
        Mar. 12, 1978, pp. VI-15+.

1185)   High Incidence of Venereal Disease Among New York
        Homosexuals, New York Times, Jul. 26, 1976, p.
        19.

1186)   Holden, Stephen.   "The Village People Liberate
        Main Street, " Village Voice, Apr. 23, 1979, p. 61.

1187)   Hollywood's Failure to Present Positive Images of
        Gays, Los Angeles Times, Apr. 30, 1978, Califor-
        nia Section, p. 1.

1188)   Homosexual (Sheldon Andelson) Appointed to Cali-
        fornia Board of Regents, San Francisco Chronicle,
        Feb. 20, 1982, p. 1.

1189)   Homosexual Engineer to Keep Defense Department
        Security Clearance, San Francisco Chronicle, Jul. 2,
        1976, p. 2.

1190)   Homosexual Rights Groups Assist Cuban Refugees,
        New York Times, Jul. 8, 1980, p. 13.

1191)   Homosexuals Allowed to Adopt Children, New York
        Times, Aug. 28, 1982, p. 27 and San Francisco
        Chronicle, Dec. 22, 1982, p. 24.

1192)   "Homosexuals: A Cincinnati Report, " Cincinnati
        Enquirer, Apr. 4, 1982, Supplement, pp. 1-28.

1193) Homosexuals' Double Life in Israel, San Francisco Chronicle, Dec. 14, 1980, p. E-9.

1194) House Amendment Prohibits Legal Services Attorneys from Representing Homosexuals in Discrimination Cases, New York Times, Jul. 3, 1977, p. 32 and Jun. 21, 1981, p. 26.

1195) Houston's Homosexual Community Has Become an Important Political Force, New York Times, Nov. 2, 1981, p. 16.

1196) HUD [U.S. Department of Housing and Urban Development] to Open Public Housing to Homosexual Couples, New York Times, May 29, 1977, p. 22.

1197) Hudgins, Christine. "Gay Foster Parents: They Care About Children," Minneapolis Star, Dec. 4, 1980, pp. A-1+.

1198) Important Political Leaders Attend Dinner to Raise Funds for Human Rights Campaign Which Seeks to Advance Gay Rights, New York Times, Sep. 4, 1982, p. 25.

1199) "[International Association of] Chiefs [of Police] Oppose Hiring Gay Cops," Los Angeles Times, Oct. 7, 1977, p. 2.

1200) International Gay Games in San Francisco Open August 28th, New York Times, Aug. 22, 1982, p. 25.

1201) IRS [Internal Revenue Service] Grants Tax Exemption to Organizations with Gay Concerns, Wall Street Journal, Aug. 31, 1978, p. 1.

1202) Jewish Homosexuals Form Own Synagogue, Washington Post, Dec. 29, 1979, p. A-17.

1203) John Wayne Gacy Arrested, Tried, and Convicted in Chicago for the Killing of Some Thirty Young Men, New York Times, Jan. 1, 1979, p. 6 and Apr. 24, 1979, p. 16.

1204) Knox, Richard A. "Mysterious Disease Afflicts Gays," Boston Globe, Dec. 10, 1981, p. 3.

1205)   Kopkind, Andrew. "The Dialectic of Disco: Gay
        Music Goes Straight," Village Voice, Feb. 12, 1979,
        pp. 1+.

1206)   _____, and others. "Gay Life Ten Years After
        Stonewall," Village Voice, Jun. 25, 1979, pp. 61-82.

1207)   Legal Services Corporation Ex-Chief, Dan J. Brad-
        ley, Admits Homosexuality, Washington Post, Apr. 1,
        1982, p. A-10.

1208)   Lesbian Mary Morgan Appointed Judge, San Francisco
        Chronicle, Sep. 25, 1981, p. 15.

1209)   Lichtenstein, Grace. "Homosexuals Move Toward
        Open Life as Tolerance Rises," New York Times,
        Jul. 17, 1977, pp. 1+.

1210)   Lieutenant Governor of Nevada Castigates Gay Rodeo
        in Reno, San Francisco Chronicle, Mar. 26, 1981,
        p. 3.

1211)   Lincoln (Nebraska) Voters Reject Charter Amendment
        Prohibiting Discrimination Against Homosexuals, New
        York Times, May 12, 1982, p. 24.

1212)   Linn, Amy. "A Jubilant End to the Gay Games,"
        San Francisco Examiner, Sep. 6, 1982, p. A-4.

1213)   Longcope, Kay "Aesthetic Realism [and the Cure of
        Homosexuality]," Boston Globe, Apr. 18, 1982, pp.
        21-22.

1214)   Los Angeles Council and Mayor Approve Gay Rights
        Ordinance, Los Angeles Times, May 24, 1979, p.
        I-3 and Jun. 2, 1979, p. II-1.

1215)   Los Angeles Court Rules Boy Scouts Not Required to
        Permit a Homosexual to Become Adult Troop Leader
        New York Times, Jul. 8, 1981, p. 10.

1216)   Los Angeles Police Department Rejects Proposal to
        Recruit Homosexuals, Los Angeles Times, Nov. 7,
        1982, p. I-3.

1217)   Los Angeles Police Raid Homosexual "Slave Market,"
        San Francisco Chronicle, Apr. 12, 1976, p. 1.

1218)   Los Angeles Policemen Consider the Gay Community
        "A Real Threat," Los Angeles Times, Dec. 18, 1977,
        p. VIII-14.

1219)   Male Teenage Prostitution, Boston Herald American,
        Jul. 25, 1977, pp. 1+; San Francisco Chronicle,
        Mar. 22, 1976, p. 12; Jan. 27, 1978, p. 21; and
        Jun. 14, 1981, California Section, p. 16; Minneapolis
        Tribune, Nov. 28, 1981, pp. A-1+.

1220)   Mayo, Anna.   Harvey Fierstein and "Torch Song
        Trilogy" on Broadway, Village Voice, Oct. 12, 1982,
        pp. 43-47.

1221)   Meg.   "The West Was Wild with Gay Indians," New
        York Post, Mar. 13, 1982, p. 28.

1222)   Miami Gay Support Group Urges Nationwide Boycott
        of Florida Orange Juice in Protest to Anita Bryant's
        Anti-Gay Campaign, San Francisco Chronicle, Apr.
        21, 1977, p. 6.

1223)   Minneapolis Court Grants Child Custody to Lesbian
        Mother, New York Times, Jun. 3, 1978, p. 8.

1224)   Moral Majority Opposition and House of Representa-
        tives' Vote to Reject District of Columbia Sexual
        Reform Measure, Washington Post, Sep. 24, 1981,
        p. B-4 and Oct. 2, 1981, p. A-1.

1225)   Mormon Church Leader Calls Homosexuality "Ad-
        dictive," New York Times, Apr. 6, 1981, p. 12.

1226)   Morrow, Barbara O., and Dave Beery.   Gays in
        Fort Wayne, Fort Wayne Journal Gazette, Dec. 13,
        1981, pp. A-1+ and Dec. 14, 1981, pp. A-1+.

1227)   National Council of Churches Delays Action on Mem-
        bership Application of Metropolitan Community Church,
        Boston Globe, May 14, 1982, p. 8.

1228)   National Security Agency Allows Homosexual to Keep
        Job and Security Clearance, Washington Post, Dec.
        30, 1980, p. A-1.

1229)   New York City Council Defeats Gay Rights Bill for
        Ninth Time in Ten Years, New York Times, Nov.
        24, 1981, p. II-1 and Dec. 11, 1981, p II-3.

1230) New York City Judge Rules Sexual Preference Cannot
       Be Cause for Excluding Person from Jury, New
       York Times, Sep. 24, 1980, p. IV-23.

1231) New York City Mayor Ed Koch Issues Executive
       Order Banning Discrimination Against Homosexuals
       by City Government, New York Times, Jan. 24,
       1978, pp. 1+.

1232) New York Governor Hugh Carey Opposes Banning Dis-
       crimination Against Homosexuals in State Govern-
       ment, New York Times, Jan. 25, 1978, p. 17.

1233) New York Times/CBS Poll Indicates More Liberal
       Attitudes on Homosexuality, New York Times, Aug.
       3, 1977, p. IV-15.

1234) Oklahoma Governor David Boren Denies Charge Made
       by Political Rivals That He Is Homosexual or Bi-
       sexual, San Francisco Chronicle, Aug. 11, 1978, p.
       9.

1235) Opposition of Political and Religious Leaders to Prop-
       osition 6 Which Would Bar Homosexual Teachers
       from California's Public Schools, Los Angeles Times,
       Jun. 2, 1978, p. I-3; Jul. 13, 1978, p. II-1; Oct. 8,
       1978, p. I-3; and Nov. 6, 1978, p. I-34.

1236) Ordination of Ellen M. Barrett, Avowed Lesbian, As
       Episcopal Priest Arouses Opposition, New York Times,
       Jan. 11, 1977, p. 40; Jan. 24, 1977, p. 12; Feb. 4,
       1977, p. II-3; Oct. 2, 1977, p. 24; Oct. 4, 1977,
       p. 41; Oct. 19, 1977, p. II-3; Nov. 9, 1977, p. 24;
       and Dec. 4, 1977, p. 59.

1237) Over 250,000 People Attend Annual San Francisco
       Lesbian/Gay Freedom Day Parade, San Francisco
       Chronicle, Jun. 29, 1981, p. 1.

1238) Palo Alto (California) Voters Reject Gay Rights
       Ordinance, San Francisco Chronicle, Nov. 4, 1981,
       p. 4.

1239) Patrick Kearney, Suspect in Homosexual Trash Bag
       Murders of as Many as 21 Young Men, Pleads Guilty
       to 3 Killings and Is Sentenced to Life, New York
       Times, Dec. 22, 1977, p. 14.

1240)   Philadelphia City Council Bans Discrimination Against
        Homosexuals, Washington Post, Aug. 6, 1982, p. A-
        7.

1241)   Political Candidates Seek Gay Votes, Wall Street
        Journal, Oct. 20, 1976, p. 1.

1242)   Police Officer in Charge of Protecting Queen Eliza-
        beth of England Resigns After Admitting Homosexual
        Relationship, New York Times, Jul. 22, 1982, p. 1.

1243)   Princeton University Gay Activist Candidate Loses
        Student Election, New York Times, Mar. 3, 1977,
        p. 71.

1244)   Probe of Homosexuality at Annapolis Naval Academy,
        San Francisco Chronicle, Jul. 2, 1981, p. 49.

1245)   Prominent Europeans Publish Advertisement in Time
        Protesting Discrimination Against Homosexuals in the
        United States, New York Times, Jan. 4, 1978, p. 10.

1246)   "Rabbis Condemn Gay Rights Bill [Being Considered
        by New York City Council]," Jewish Press, Jul. 14,
        1978, p. 10.

1247)   Recent Protests and Boycotts of Homosexuality in
        World of Entertainment, Christian Science Monitor,
        Feb. 13, 1981, p. 19.

1248)   Ricklefs, Roger. "A New Constituency: Political
        Candidates Seek Out Gay Votes: In Cities Where
        Homosexuals Are Well Organized, Risks of Such
        Campaigns Fade," Wall Street Journal, Oct. 20,
        1976, p. 1+.

1249)   Reilly, Robert R. "Homosexuals and Nature's Laws,"
        Wall Street Journal, Jan. 22, 1979, p. 20.

1250)   Roiphe, Anne. "[Lesbianism:] The Trouble at Sarah
        Lawrence [College]," New York Times, Mar. 20,
        1977, pp. VI-21+.

1251)   Ronald Reagan Opposes California Proposition to
        Ban Homosexual Teachers, Los Angeles Times,
        Sep. 26, 1978, p. II-4.

1252)   Rose, Frank. "Men and Boys Together [Sex Scandal in Boston]," Village Voice, Feb. 27, 1978, pp. 1+.

1253)   Rosenbaum, Art. "Gay Sports--Divided Ranks [in San Francisco's Gay Sports World]," San Francisco Chronicle, Dec. 20, 1977, pp. 43+.

1254)   Rothenberg, David. "Bathhouse Fire [Everard Baths in New York City]," Village Voice, Jun. 6, 1977, p. 17.

1255)   Safire, William. "Now Ease Up, Anita," New York Times, Jun. 9, 1977, p. 21.

1256)   St. Paul (Minnesota) Voters Repeal Gay Rights Ordinance, New York Times, Apr. 26, 1978, p. 1.

1257)   San Francisco City Government Adopts Measure Banning Bias Based on Sexual Orientation, San Francisco Chronicle, Mar. 21, 1978, p. 1 and Apr. 12, 1978, p. 3.

1258)   San Francisco Gay Men's Chorus Makes Nationwide Tour, San Francisco Chronicle, Jun. 6, 1981, p. 4 and Jun. 22, 1981, p. 5.

1259)   San Francisco Mayor George Moscone and Gay Supervisor Harvey Milk Shot and Killed in City Hall Offices, San Francisco Chronicle, Nov. 28, 1978, pp. 1+.

1260)   San Francisco Police Commission Approves Plan for Hiring Gay Policemen, San Francisco Chronicle, Aug. 25, 1977, p. 1.

1261)   San Francisco School Board Approves Resolution Adding Study of Homosexual Lifestyle to Sex Education Curriculum, New York Times, May 26, 1977, p. 18.

1262)   Santa Clara County and San Jose (California) Voters Oppose Gay Rights Ordinance, San Francisco Chronicle, Jun. 4, 1980, p. 8.

1263)   Scheer, Robert. "[California State] Senator John Briggs on Homosexuality," Los Angeles Times, Oct. 6, 1978, pp. 1+.

1264)   Senior Citizen Center for Gays and Lesbians Opens
        in Los Angeles--First Such in the Nation, Los
        Angeles Times, Jul. 18, 1982, p. II-1.

1265)   Seventh-Day Adventists' President Condemns Homo-
        sexual Behavior, New York Times, Aug. 22, 1977,
        p. 17.

1266)   "75,000 March in Capital in Drive to Support Homo-
        sexual Rights," New York Times, Oct. 15, 1979, p.
        14.

1267)   Severson, Ed.   "Tucson Gays Walk Thin Line Between
        Tolerance, Terror," Arizona Daily Star, Jan. 13,
        1980, p. J-4.

1268)   Showing of Gay TV Health Spots Halted, San Fran-
        cisco Chronicle, Oct. 24, 1981, p. 7.

1269)   Sioux Falls (South Dakota) High School Senior Per-
        mitted to Take His Male Date to the Prom, New
        York Times, May 24, 1979, p. III-14.

1270)   Southern Baptist Convention Opposes Ordination of
        Overt Homosexuals, New York Times, Jun. 18,
        1976, p. I-11.

1271)   Spanish Police Disperse Homosexual Rights Demon-
        stration in Barcelona, New York Times, Jun. 27,
        1977, p. 20.

1272)   State Official Named to Protect Gay Rights, San
        Francisco Chronicle, May 28, 1981, p. 12.

1273)   Steele, Mike.   "Gay Theater Finds There Is an
        Audience in Twin Cities," Minneapolis Tribune,
        Jul. 29, 1979, pp. G-1+.

1274)   Study Shows 9% of San Francisco's Electorate Is
        Gay, San Francisco Chronicle, Apr. 30, 1982, p.
        20.

1275)   Swedish Parliament Ends Discrimination Against
        Homosexuals, San Francisco Chronicle, Mar. 11,
        1978, p. 10.

1276)   Teal, Donn.   "Straight Father, Gay Son: A Memoir of
        Reconciliation," Village Voice, Jun. 26, 1978, pp. 1+.

1277)   Texas Law Prohibiting Homosexual Acts Struck Down
        by Federal Judge, New York Times, Aug. 18, 1982,
        p. 8.

1278)   Times Square (New York City) Demonstration Pro-
        testing Police Brutality Against Homosexuals at
        Blues Bar, New York Times, Oct. 16, 1982, p. 31.

1279)   Trebay, Guy.   "$100, Non-negotiable [Male Hus-
        tlers]," Village Voice, Sep. 23, 1981, pp. 13-15.

1280)   Tucson (Arizona) Passes Ordinance Prohibiting Dis-
        crimination Against Homosexuals, Arizona Daily Star,
        Feb. 8, 1977, p. A-8.

1281)   United States Justice Department Tells Immigration
        Service to Bar Homosexuals, Washington Post,
        Dec. 28, 1979. p. A-6.

1282)   United States Navy Probe of Alleged Lesbianism
        Aboard the "Norton Sound," Los Angeles Times,
        Jun. 13, 1980, p. I-3; Jun. 14, 1980, p. I-23;
        and Jun. 21, 1980, p. II-7.

1283)   United States Supreme Court Lets Stand Dismissal
        of Gay Police Officer in Mesa, Arizona, Washington
        Post, Feb. 11, 1982, p. A-17.

1284)   United States Supreme Court Lets Stand Dismissal
        of Gay Teacher, New York Times, Oct. 4, 1977,
        pp. 1+.

1285)   United States Supreme Court Remaining Silent on
        Cases Involving Gay Rights, Washington Post, Dec.
        11, 1979, p. A-3.

1286)   United States Supreme Court Upholds Right of States
        to Prosecute and Imprison People for Committing
        Private Consensual Adult Homosexual Acts, New
        York Times, Mar. 30, 1976, p. 1.

1287)   University of Arkansas Asked to Stop Course on
        Homosexuality, San Francisco Chronicle, Mar. 7,
        1981, p. 2.

1288)   University of San Francisco's Anti-Gay Policy Pro-
        tested, San Francisco Chronicle, Oct. 20, 1980, p. 3.

1289)   Vatican Orders Jesuit John J. McNeil to Keep Silent
        on His Views on Homosexuality, New York Times,
        Sep. 2, 1977, p. IV-13.

1290)   Vatican Reasserts Views on Sex and Homosexuality,
        San Francisco Chronicle, Jan. 15, 1976, p. 24.

1291)   "Violent Crime and Gays--San Francisco Report,"
        San Francisco Chronicle, Nov. 12, 1982, p. 2.

1292)   Washington State Highway Patrol to No Longer Con-
        sider Homosexuality a Bar to Employment, New
        York Times, Mar. 10, 1976, p. 17.

1293)   White House Conference on Families Approves Defi-
        nition of Family Which Excludes Homosexuals, New
        York Times, Jun. 22, 1980, p. 24.

1294)   Winn, Steven.   Theater Rhinoceros, San Francisco's
        Gay Theater, San Francisco Chronicle, Nov. 22,
        1981, Datebook Section, pp. 17+.

1295)   Wisconsin Governor Signs First Statewide Gay Civil
        Rights Bill, San Francisco Chronicle, Feb. 26,
        1982, p. 2.

1296)   Wichita (Kansas) Voters Repeal Gay Rights Ordinance,
        New York Times, May 10, 1981, p. 18.

1297)   Wolcott, James.   "Sidney Shorr, [TV's] Gay Baby-
        sitter," Village Voice, Sep. 30, 1981, p. 54.

1298)   Women Dismissed from Boise (Idaho) Police Depart-
        ment Because of Allegations of Lesbianism Granted
        Unemployment Compensation, New York Times,
        Apr. 10, 1977, p. 32.

1299)   Yudelman, Micahl.   "Gays Demonstrate in Tel Aviv
        Against Denial of Rights," Jerusalem Post, Jul. 22,
        1979, p. 3.

ARTICLES IN POPULAR MAGAZINES

1300) Abse, Leo. "Ten Years After Homosexual Reform," Spectator, 239:11-12, Jul. 9, 1977.

1301) Adams, Jane. "When Your Friend Tells You She's Gay," Glamour, 80:264+, Apr. 1982.

1302) Altman, Dennis. "The Gay Movement Ten Years Later," Nation, 235:494-96, Nov. 13, 1982.

1303) "And Now, Gay Family Rights? [Proposed San Francisco Ordinance]," Time, 120:74, Dec. 13, 1982.

1304) Anita Bryant and the Successful Campaign to Repeal Miami's Gay Rights Ordinance, Time, 109:76, May 2, 1977; 109:20, Jun. 13, 1977; 109:59-60, Jun. 20, 1977.

1305) "Anita Bryant's Hollow Victory," Progressive, 41:8, Sep. 1977.

1306) Anita Bryant's Successful Campaign Encourages Other Cities to Oppose Gay Rights, Newsweek, 91:14, 14-16, Mar. 13, 1978.

1307) Anon. "My Husband Was Different [Marriage to a Homosexual]," Good Housekeeping, 182:214+, May 1976.

1308) "[Anthony Blunt] The Spy with a Clear Conscience," Time, 114:61, Dec. 3, 1979.

1309) "Are Homosexuals Illegal Aliens?" Newsweek, 94:25, Aug. 27, 1979.

1310) Assassination of San Francisco Mayor George Moscone and Supervisor Harvey Milk; Trial of Dan White

and the Rage Following Jury's Verdict of Voluntary
Manslaughter, Time, 112:24-26, Dec. 11, 1978;
113:57, May 28, 1979; 113:15, Jun. 4, 1979.

1311)   "At Bay in San Francisco: A Task Force Criticizes
Catholic Teachings on Homosexuality," Time, 120:
67, Oct. 11, 1982.

1312)   Axthelm, Pete. "The Case of Billie Jean King,"
Newsweek, 97:133, May 18, 1981.

1313)   "The Band Gets Bigger [Increasing Openness of
American Homosexuals]," Time, 110:30, Jul. 11,
1977.

1314)   "Battle over Gay Rights [Anita Bryant's Campaign in
Miami]," Newsweek, 89:39-40, Apr. 11, 1977; 89:
16-22, Jun. 6, 1977; 89:27-30, Jun. 20, 1977.

1315)   Battle over Gay Rights in Eugene, Oregon. People
Weekly, 9:43, May 22, 1978.

1316)   Beks, Herman. "Learning to Say 'I Am a Homosexual," New Society, Jan. 13, 1977, pp. 58-60.

1317)   Bell, Arthur. "Sex Goes Public--the Gays Pioneer,"
Playboy, 24:98-100, Jul. 1977.

1318)   Billie Jean King Faces "Galimony" Suit Filed by Her
Ex-Secretary, Time, 117:77, May 11, 1981.

1319)   "Billie Jean's Odd Match [Palimony Suit Brought by
Ms. Barnett]," Newsweek, 97:36, May 11, 1981.

1320)   "The Bisexual [Ensign Vernon Berg] and the Navy,"
Time, 107:49, Feb. 2, 1976.

1321)   Blanford, Linda. "A Song in Their Hearts, and
Homophobia in the Wings," Guardian, Jul. 10, 1981,
p. 10.

1322)   Blazer, Fred. "Clayton Ruby's People Power [Law-
yer for The Body Politic, a Gay Canadian Journal],"
Maclean's, 92:14+, Oct. 22, 1979.

1323)   Branch, Taylor. "Closets of Power: The Double
Lives of Homosexuals in Politics," Harper's, 265:34-
50, Oct. 1982.

1324)   Braudy, Susan.   'The 'Cruising' Controversey--Gay
        Activists Protest Media Violence, " Ms. , 8:34, Dec.
        1979.

1325)   Brett, Philip.   "[Benjamin] Britten and [Peter]
        Grimes, " Musical Times, 118:995-1000, 1977.

1326)   British Government Committee Recommends Lowering
        Age of Consent for Homosexuals from 21 to 18.
        Economist, 271:26, Jun. 30, 1979.

1327)   Buckley, William F. , Jr.   "Who Speaks for the
        Gays? " National Review, 31:578-79, 1979.

1328)   Bunch, Charlotte.   Dismissal of Lesbian Joan L.
        Clark by the United Methodist Church, Ms. , 8:29,
        Oct. 1979.

1329)   _____ .   "Learning from Lesbian Separatism, "
        Ms. , 5:60-61, Nov. 1976.

1330)   Burgess-Kohn, Jane.   'Why Parents Worry About
        Homosexuality, " Parents Magazine, 52:40-41+,
        Jan. 1977.

1331)   Butts, June D.   'Is Homosexuality a Threat to the
        Black Family? " Ebony, 36:138-44, Apr. 1981.

1332)   "California Travesty: Proposition 6 [Against Gay
        Teachers], " New Republic, 179:8, Oct. 28, 1978.

1333)   Calvert, Catherine.   "Homosexuality on Campus:
        Out of the Closet, Into the Dorm, " Mademoiselle,
        84:152+, Feb. 1978.

1334)   "Can a Homosexual Work for the CIA? " Newsweek,
        100:29, Sep. 20, 1982.

1335)   "Capitol Scandal [Charges that Congressmen Solicited
        Pages for Sex], " Time, 120:17, Jul. 12, 1982 and
        120:12, Jul. 26, 1982.

1336)   Cassill, Kay.   "Rhode Island Town Survives Its
        Night to Remember as Aaron [Fricke] Takes Paul
        [Guilbert] to the Prom, " People Weekly, 13:98+,
        Jun. 16, 1980.

1337)   Castleman, Michael. "Scapegoating the Gays: Propo-
        sition 6 [Against Gay Teachers] and the Rights of Us
        All, " Nation, 227:403-05, 1978.

1338)   "Catch as Catch Can [Arrest on Homosexual Charges
        of Judge Harold Carswell and General Edwin Walker], "
        Time, 107:59, Jun. 26, 1976.

1339)   Chappell, Helen. "No Job for a Gay, " New Society,
        Jul. 29, 1982, pp. 169-70.

1340)   "Charting the Gay Life [Kinsey Institute Study], "
        Newsweek, 91:98-100, Mar. 27, 1978.

1341)   Child Pornography, Time, 109:55, Apr. 4, 1977.

1342)   Chippendale, Peter, and David Leigh.   "Anatomy of
        a Political Animal [Jeremy Thorpe], " New Statesman,
        98:44-46, 1979.

1343)   Clarke, Gerald. Drama Review: Harvey Fierstein's
        "Torch Song Trilogy, " Time, 119:70, Feb. 22, 1982.

1344)   Coburn, Judith. "California's Proposition 6 [Against
        Gay Teachers], " Mademoiselle, 85:94+, Feb. 1979.

1345)   Cockburn, Alexander. "Not So Gay America [Miami
        and Gay Rights], " New Statesman, 93:802+, 1977.

1346)   _____ . "Sex, Politics, and the Family [Homo-
        sexuality and American Politics], " New Statesman,
        94:644-45, 1977.

1347)   Coleman, Ray. "Power in the Darkness: Tom
        Robinson's Greatest Hit, " Melody Maker, 52:30-32+,
        Oct. 22, 1977.

1348)   Congress: The Page Scandal and an Accuser Who
        Lied, Newsweek, 100:30, Jul. 12, 1982 and 100:19,
        Sep. 6, 1982.

1349)   Conservative Congressman Robert Bauman and His
        Homosexuality, National Review, 32:1308-09 and
        1349, 1980.

1350)   Conviction of Editor of London's Gay News for Blas-
        phemy, Economist, 264:20, Jul. 16, 1977; 266:22,
        Mar. 25, 1978; 270:26, Feb. 24, 1979.

1351)   "A Cooler Crusader [Anita Bryant]," Newsweek,
        90:11, Oct. 3, 1977.

1352)   Corning, Peg.   "Hardest Hurt to Heal, Losing Your
        Husband to a Man," Glamour, 76:140+, Apr. 1978.

1353)   Cotton, Janet.   "Sad Day at Bishop's [Controversy
        over Inclusion of Homosexual Material in the Uni-
        versity's Student Handbook]," Maclean's, 93:40-41,
        Oct. 6, 1980.

1354)   Coulter, Carol.   "No Earthquake in Dublin [Trial of
        Homosexual Activists Challenging Ireland's Gross
        Indecency Between Males Statute]," New Statesman,
        100:34-35, 1980.

1355)   "The Deadly Spread of AIDS [Acquired Immune De-
        ficiency Syndrome]," Time, 120:55, Sep. 6, 1982.

1356)   Decter, Midge.   "Boys on the Beach--Fire Island,"
        Commentary, 70:35-48, Sep. 1980.   (Responses: 70:
        6+, Dec. 1980.)

1357)   Deer, Brian.   "Trust Is a Two-Way Street [Homo-
        sexuals and Police Harassment]," New Statesman,
        99:954, 1980.

1358)   Demaret, Kent.   Tennessee Williams at Center in
        Furor over Gays in Key West.   People Weekly,
        11:32-35, May 7, 1979.

1359)   Denby, David.   "Movie Bashing [Gay Protests
        Against the Filming of 'Cruising']," New York, 12:
        64-65, Aug. 6, 1979.

1360)   "Deviant Customs; Immigration and Naturalization
        Act Ban of Homosexual from Entering the U. S. "
        New Republic, 181:8-9, Jul. 21, 1979.

1361)   Dey, Wendy.   "The Boys in the Band Play On [Trial
        of Publishers of Body Politic, a Gay Journal]," Mac-
        lean's, 92:26, Feb. 26, 1979.

1362)   "Director of Gay Film Touring U. S. Colleges with
        Complications," Variety, 283:7, Jun. 2, 1976.

1363)   "Diseases that Plague Gays," Newsweek, 98:51-52,
        Dec. 21, 1981 and 100:10, Aug. 23, 1982.

1364)   Durbin, Karen. "The Homosexual Experience,"
        Mademoiselle, 82:46, Jun. 1976.

1365)   Dyer, Richard. "Gays in Film," Jump Cut, 18:
        15-16, Aug. 1978.

1366)   Election of Dianne Feinstein as Mayor of San Fran-
        cisco with Strong Support from the Gay Community,
        Time, 114:20, Dec. 24, 1979.

1367)   Emerson, Ken. "The Village People: America's
        Male Ideal?" Rolling Stone, 275:26-27+, Oct. 5,
        1978.

1368)   Eskow, John. "Mirage on the Mountain [Motel for
        Homosexuals]," New Times, 10:44-46, Mar. 6,
        1978.

1369)   Faber, Nancy. "Couples: Lesbian Mothers Made-
        leine Isaacson and Sandy Schuster Find Marriage
        Happy but Hardly Untroubled," People Weekly, 12:
        53-54+, Jul. 9, 1979.

1370)   _____. "Never in the Closet or on the Charts;
        Holly Near Sings Uncompromisingly of Gay Love,"
        People Weekly, 16:103-04, Jul. 13, 1981.

1371)   _____. "Psychiatrist David Kessler Organizes
        a Gay Doctors' Movement," People Weekly, 11:101-
        02, May 21, 1979.

1372)   Fain, Nathan. "Gay Lit Today: For Better and
        Worse," After Dark, 11:52-56, Apr. 1979.

1373)   Farber, Stephen. "Hollywood Comes out of the
        Closet [Gay Movies]," Saturday Review, 8:48-51,
        Oct. 1981.

1374)   Flower, Joe. "Gays in Business," San Francisco,
        22:41-45, Sep. 1980.

1375)   "Football as Erotic Ritual--Are the Guys on the
        Gridiron Really Gay?" Time, 112:112, Nov. 13,
        1978.

1376)   Frank, Arthur and Stuart. "Homosexuality,"
        Mademoiselle, 83:108, Oct. 1977.

1377)   "French Ultra-Rightists Break Up Gay Film Fest,"
        Variety, 290:1, Feb. 8, 1978.

1378)   Gallagher, Nora. "The San Francisco Experience ...
        The Straight Community Finally Lets Its Fear and
        Loathing Out of the Closet," Playboy, 27:116-17+;
        Jan. 1980, Responses: 27:15+, Apr. 1980; 27:72,
        May 1980; and 27:75, Jun. 1980.

1379)   "Gay Parents and Teachers: A Questionnaire,"
        Glamour, 77:34, Sept. 1979.

1380)   "Gay Power in Macho Houston," Newsweek, 98:29,
        Aug. 10, 1981.

1381)   "Gay Power in San Francisco," Newsweek, 89:25-26,
        Jun. 6, 1977.

1382)   "Gay Teachers--Prop. 6 in California," Newsweek,
        92:56, Oct. 2, 1978.

1383)   "Gay U.S.A.: Gay Pride Marches, 1977 [A Film on
        the Gay Movement]," Variety, 288:2+, Aug. 24, 1977.

1384)   "The Gay World's Leather Fringe," Time, 115:74-75,
        Mar. 24, 1980.

1385)   "The Gaycott Turns Ugly: Homosexual Militants Are
        Tormenting Foe Anita Bryant," Time, 110:33, Nov.
        21, 1977.

1386)   "Gays and Lesbians on Campus," Newsweek, 99:75-
        77, Apr. 5, 1982.

1387)   "Gays and the Law," Newsweek, 88:101, Oct. 25,
        1976.

1388)   "Gays Are Born, Not Made [Report from the Kinsey
        Institute]," Newsweek, 98:42, Sep. 7, 1981.

1389)   "Gays, Gals, Boys and All Other Minorities in
        Media," Variety, 281:22, Jan. 7, 1976.

1390)   "Gays in the Military," Playboy, 27:55, Oct. 1980.

1391)   Gerard, Warren. "Straight Talk in Gay Town [Police
        Raids on Homosexual Bath Houses in Toronto]," Mac-
        lean's, 94:27-28, Feb. 23, 1981.

1392)   "Going Wrong [Repeal of Gay Rights Ordinances in a
        Number of American Cities]," Economist, 267:28+,
        Jun. 3, 1978.

1393)   Gold, Herbert. "A Walk on San Francisco's Gay
        Side," New York Times Magazine, Nov. 7, 1977,
        pp. 67-69+.

1394)   Goodman, Walter. "Homosexuals," New Leader,
        61:12, Nov. 6, 1978

1395)   "Gore Vidal: Laughing Cassandra," Time, 107:59-
        64, Mar. 1, 1976.

1396)   Gould, Robert. "A Psychiatrist Answers Teen Ques-
        tions About Homosexuality," Seventeen, 36:152-53+,
        Sep. 1977.

1397)   Grabowicz, Paul. "Bay Area Physicians for Human
        Rights--1st in the Annals of Medicine," New Times
        11:20, Nov. 13, 1978

1398)   _____. "California's Latest Right Wing Spasm:
        The Anti-Gay Briggs Amendments," New Times,
        11:19, Jul. 24, 1978.

1399)   _____. "Gay Frights in 'Frisco--'White' Back-
        lash," Politics Today, 6:6, Jul.-Aug. 1979.

1400)   Grey, Antony. "Anglicans and Homosexuals," New
        Humanist, 95:145-47, Mar. 1980.

1401)   _____. "Homosexual Rights and Wrongs," New
        Humanist, 94:91-92, Nov. 1978.

1402)   Gross, Amy. "If Lesbians Make You Nervous...."
        Mademoiselle, 84:126-27, Feb. 1978.

1403)   "The Growing Terror of Gay Bashing," Newsweek,
        97:30, Mar. 23, 1981.

1404)   Gusfield, Joseph R. "Proposition 6 [Against Gay
        Teachers]; Political Ceremony in California,"
        Nation, 227:633-35, 1978.

1405)   Harris, Max. "[Bali:] A Hell for Homosexuals,"
        Spectator, 239:16-17, Nov. 12, 1977.

1406) _____. "Should Homosexuals Be Allowed to
       Teach?" McCalls, 105:100+, Mar. 1978.

1407) Hendrickson, Paul. "Fear of Faggotry: Growing
       Up in the Seminary," Playboy, 29:103-04+, Oct.
       1982.

1408) Herrick, Jim. "Homosexuality and Humanism,"
       New Humanism, 94:158, Mar. 1979.

1409) Heymont, George. "Parents of Gays [An Organiza-
       tion] Come Out," Progressive, 46:66, Mar. 1982.

1410) Hofsess, John. "The Sexual Niggers [Homosexuals],"
       Content: Canada's National News Magazine, Aug.
       1977, pp. 15+.

1411) Holland, Mary. "Gay Time in Belfast [Raids and
       Arrests of Homosexuals in Northern Ireland]," New
       Statesman, 91:763-64, 1976.

1412) "Homophobia in Oklahoma [Proposed Law Against
       Homosexual Teachers]," Playboy, 25:74, Jun. 1978.

1413) "Homosexual Adoption," Playboy, 26:87, Dec. 1979
       and 27:72, Jun. 1980.

1414) "The Homosexual Economy [Affluence of Homosex-
       uals]," Economist, 282:71-72, Jan. 23, 1982.

1415) "The Homosexual Teacher," Newsweek, 92:91, Dec.
       18, 1978.

1416) "Homosexuality and the Clergy: A Presbyterian
       Task Force Proposes a Policy of Toleration,"
       Time, 111:85, Jan. 30, 1978.

1417) "Homosexuality as Sin [Position of American
       Protestant Churches]," Time, 111:53, Jun. 5, 1978.

1418) "Homosexuals in the Churches," Newsweek, 100:113-
       14, Oct. 11, 1982.

1419) Hoover, Eleanor. "Author John Rechy Describes--
       and Defends--His Shocking Life as a 'Sexual Outlaw,'"
       People Weekly, 9:61-62, May 22, 1978.

1420)   "Hormones and Homosexuality," Playboy, 25:248,
          Mar. 1978.

1421)   "How Gay Is Gay? Homosexual Men and Women
          Are Making Progress Toward Equality," Time,
          113:72-76, Apr. 23, 1979.

1422)   "Inside J. Edgar Hoover's X-Rated Files," Time,
          108:24, Dec. 6, 1976.

1423)   Ireland, Doug. "New Homophobia: Open Season on
          Gays," Nation, 229:207-10, Sep. 15, 1979.

1424)   _____. "Rendezvous in the Ramble [Crimes
          Against Homosexuals in Central Park]," New York,
          11:39-42, Jul. 24, 1978.

1425)   Irish Laws Against Homosexuality Bring About
          Inquiry from European Commission on Human Rights,
          Economist, 277:60-61+, Nov. 8, 1980.

1426)   "Italian Gay Group Files Slander Suit Against Pope
          Paul VI," Playboy, 23:48, Sep. 1976.

1427)   Jahr, Cliff. "Anita Bryant's Startling Reversal,"
          Ladies' Home Journal, 97:60-68, Dec. 1980.

1428)   _____. "Dog Day Aftermath [John Wojtowicz
          Imprisoned for Bank Robbery]," Playboy, 23:128-
          31+, Aug. 1976. (Responses: 23:11-12, Nov.
          1978.)

1429)   Jay, Karla. "Lesbianism from the Bible On," Ms. ,
          5:21, Jul. 1976.

1430)   Jeremy Thorpe--Arrest, Trial, and Acquittal of
          Prominent English Political Leader on Charges
          Associated with Homosexuality, Time, 107:30-31,
          May 24, 1976; 112:35, Aug. 14, 1978; 112:63, Dec.
          4, 1978; 112:62, Dec. 11, 1978; 113:53, May 21,
          1979; 114:47, Jul. 2, 1979.

1431)   "[Jeremy]Thorpe's Sad Fall," Newsweek, 87:44,
          May 24, 1976.

1432)   Kalem, T. E. Drama Review: David Rabe's
          "Streamers, " Time, 107:75, May 3, 1976.

1433) _____. Drama Review: Lanford Wilson's "The Fifth of July," Time, 116:109, Nov. 17, 1980.

1434) _____. Drama Review: Martin Sherman's "Bent," Time, 114:84, Dec. 17, 1979.

1435) Kazin, Alfred. "Gay Genius and the Gay Mob," Esquire, 88:33-34+, Dec. 1977.

1436) Kelley, Ken. "Cruising with Anita [Bryant]," Playboy, 25:97+, Mar. 1978.

1437) Kimmelman, Marsha. "I Had a Lesbian Lover," Cosmopolitan, 19:84-86, Jul. 1981.

1438) Kirby, Fred. "Gay Market No Longer Peripheral: Content Comes Out of the Closet," Variety, 286:111, Apr. 20, 1977.

1439) Kirshenbaum, Jerry. "Facing Up to Billie Jean's Revelations [Relationships Between Women Athletes]," Sports Illustrated, 54:13, May 11, 1981.

1440) Kondracke, Morton. "Anita Bryant Is Mad About Gays," New Republic, 176:13-15, May 7, 1977.

1441) Lafferty, Elaine. "Lavender Pages: A Guide to Lesbian Resources," Ms., 4:99-102, Mar. 1976.

1442) Lahr, John. "Political Fag and Drag," New Society, May 24, 1979, p. 462-63.

1443) Larkin, Joan. "Coming Out [Lesbianism]," Ms., 4:72-74+, Mar. 1976.

1444) Larry and Billie Jean King--An Interview, People Weekly, 15:73-79, May 25, 1981 and 16:111, Dec. 28, 1981.

1445) LaValley, Al, and others. "Out of the Closet and On to the Screen [Gay Movies]," American Film, 7:57-64+, Sep. 1982.

1446) "Lea Hopkins: Just Different [Black Lesbian Unwed Mother]," Essence, 10:88-89+, Apr. 1980.

1447) "Leapin' Lizards [Lesbianism in Reptiles]," Time, 115:50, Feb. 18, 1980.

1448)   Leo, John. "Homosexuality: Tolerance vs. Approval," Time, 113:48-51, Jan. 8, 1979.

1449)   "[Leonard Matlovich] A Career Man in Gay Politics," Newsweek, 93:18-19, Apr. 9, 1979.

1450)   "Leonard Matlovich--The Sergeant Who Came Out of the Closet Embarks on a Crusade," People Weekly, 4:51, Jan. 5, 1976

1451)   Levine, Richard. "How the Gay Lobby Has Changed Television," TV Guide, 29:2-6, May 30, 1981 and 29:49-54, Jun. 6, 1981.

1452)   Lieber, Jill, and Jerry Kirshenbaum. "Stormy Weather at South Carolina [Pam Parsons, Former Women's Basketball Coach, Faces Charges of Lesbianism and Other Misdeeds]," Sports Illustrated, 56:30-37, Feb. 8, 1982.

1453)   "Love Among the Ruins [Review of Martin Sherman's 'Bent']," Newsweek, 94:115, Dec. 17, 1979.

1454)   "Love with an Improper Stranger [Deprogramming a Lesbian]," Time, 119:22, May 3, 1982.

1455)   MacCracken, Samuel. "Are Homosexuals Gay?" Commentary, 67:19-29, Jan. 1979. (Responses: 67:8, 12, 16-30, Apr. 1979.)

1456)   Malcolm, Sarah. "I Am a Second-Generation Lesbian," Ms., 6:13-16, Oct. 1977.

1457)   Malinovich, Myriam M. "On Lesbianism and Peer Group Pressure," Mademoiselle, 82:84, Apr. 1976.

1458)   Mano, D. Keith. "Gay Beauty Contests [Blueboy's Man of the Year]," National Review, 31:1509-10, 1979.

1459)   _____. "United Fruit [American Loathing of Homosexuals]," National Review, 29:898-99, 1977.

1460)   Marcus, Greil. "San Francisco's Day of Rage [Anger at Acquittal of Dan White of Murder]," Rolling Stone, 295:50, Jul. 12, 1979.

1461) Masters and Johnson, Sexual Therapists and Re-
       searchers, on Homosexuality, Time, 113:77-78,
       Apr. 23, 1979.

1462) Maynor, Joe S. "Acid Test for the Fairness Doc-
       trine [Clash Between Gay Rights Group and Funda-
       mentalist Ministers]," TV Guide, 28:16-20, Nov. 15-
       21, 1980.

1463) McCall, Cheryl. "The Billie Jean King Case: A
       Friend's Outrage," Ms., 10:100, Jul. 1981.

1464) McCray, Chirlane. "I Am a Lesbian," Essence,
       10:90-91+, Sep. 1979.

1465) Merrow, John. "Gay Sex in the Schools," Parents
       Magazine, 52:66+, Sep. 1977.

1466) "Miami Vote; Tide Turning Against Homosexuals?"
       U.S. News and World Report, 82:46, Jun. 20, 1977.

1467) Middleton, Thomas H. "[Homosexuality:] Choice of
       Lifestyle," Saturday Review, 5:99, Apr. 15, 1978;
       5:61, Aug. 1978; 5:49, Sep. 2, 1978.

1468) Milson, Fred. "Face to Faith [The Church and Ho-
       mosexuals]," Guardian, Jul. 31, 1976, p. 8.

1469) Mitchener, Larry. "The St. Louis Gay Community:
       Hidden and Still Hiding," St. Louis, Feb. 1980, pp.
       66-67 and 89-92.

1470) Mithers, Carol L. "Why Gay Men Make Me Mad,"
       Mademoiselle, 88:20, Jul. 1982.

1471) Moore, Winston E. "How to End Sex Problems in
       Our Prisons," Ebony, 32:83-84+, Nov. 1976.

1472) Murphy, Mary. "I Felt a Lot of Rage [Billy Crys-
       tal Plays Gay Character in TV's 'Soap']," TV Guide,
       28:30, 32, 34, Nov. 15-21, 1980.

1473) Naylor, Gloria. "A Message to Winston--To Black
       Men Who Are Gay," Essence, 13:78-85, Nov. 1982.

1474) Neier, Aryeh. "Statues Have Free Speech Too [Op-
       position to Placing Statues of Gay Couples in Park in
       New York City]," Nation, 231:375-76, 1980.

1475)   "A New Big Push for Homosexuals' Rights," U.S.
        News and World Report, 88:93-95, Apr. 14, 1980.

1476)   "A New Kinsey Report: Researchers Look at Gays,"
        Time, 112:53, Jul. 17, 1978.

1477)   "New Power Bloc: Urban Homosexuals," U.S.
        News and World Report, 86:13, Jun. 4, 1979.

1478)   Newman, Patricia. Teacher Larry Bernes and Op-
        position to California's Anti-Gay Teachers' Initiative,
        People Weekly, 10:110-12, Nov. 6, 1978.

1479)   "Night of Rage [Protest Following Verdict in Dan
        White Murder Trial in San Francisco]," Newsweek,
        93:30-31, Jun. 4, 1979.

1480)   "No Handicapped and Gays in FCC Ascertainment,"
        Variety, 298:108, Mar. 19, 1980.

1481)   "No Risk: A Gay Analyst Keeps His Job [At the
        National Security Administration]," Time, 117:22,
        Jan. 12, 1981.

1482)   "A No to Sodomy [U.S. Supreme Court Upholds Vir-
        ginia's Sodomy Law]," Time, 107:50, Apr. 12, 1976.

1483)   Nobile, Philip. "The Meaning of Gay--An Interview
        with C. A. Tripp," New York, 12:36-41, Jun. 25,
        1979.

1484)   Northcott, Cecil. "The Homosexual Debate," Con-
        temporary Review, 236:40-42, Jan. 1980.

1485)   "Not So Gay Times with Nabe Vandals at 55th Street
        Playhouse," Variety, 291:7+, Jun. 21, 1978.

1486)   "Not So Gay; Vote to Repeal [Florida's] Homosexual
        Rights Bill," National Review, 29:763-64, 1977.

1487)   "The NOW Debates [On Lesbian and Gay Rights],"
        Ms., 10:88, Mar. 1982.

1488)   "Of Human Bondage [Homosexual Slave Auction in
        Los Angeles]," Newsweek, 87:35, Apr. 26, 1976.

1489)   "Oh, Billy Jean [Palimony Suit Against Billy Jean
        King]," National Review, 33:598-600, 1981.

1490)   "On Trial for Blasphemy [Editor of London's Gay
        News]," Time, 110:54, Jul. 15, 1977.

1491)   "Opportunistic Diseases: A Puzzling New Syndrome
        Afflicts Homosexual Men," Time, 118:68, Dec. 21,
        1981.

1492)   Opposition to Gay Rodeo in Reno, Nevada. Playboy,
        28:58, Aug. 1981.

1493)   Ordination of Lesbian Priest in Episcopal Church in
        New York City, Time, 109:58, Jan. 24, 1977.

1494)   Orlando (pseud.). "Bisexuality: A Choice and Not
        an Echo? A Very Personal Confession," Ms.,
        7:60-62+, Oct. 1978.

1495)   "Out of the Closet," Nation, 225:34-35, 1977.

1496)   "Out of the Closet, In from the Cold [Re-instatement
        of Security Clearance of Avowed Homosexual in the
        National Security Administration]," Newsweek, 97:30,
        Jan. 12, 1981.

1497)   Packman, David. "Jack Smith's 'Flaming Creatures,'"
        Film Culture, 63:51-56, 1977.

1498)   Pennsylvania House of Representatives Votes to
        Censure the Governor for Proclaiming Gay Pride
        Week, Playboy, 26:61, Oct. 1979.

1499)   "Perplexing Question [What Churches Should Do About
        Homosexuals]," Time, 107:88, Jun. 7, 1976.

1500)   Persky, Stan. "From Dade County to Davie Street:
        The Rightwing Crusade Against Gay Rights," Ca-
        nadian Dimension, 12:17-19, 1977.

1501)   Playboy Interview: Anita Bryant, Playboy, 25:73-96,
        232-50, Mar. 1978. (Responses: 25:17-20, Aug.
        1978; 25:20-22, Sep. 1978; 25:72-73, Nov. 1978.)

1502)   Playboy Interview: David Bowie, Playboy, 23:57-
        72, Sept. 1976.

1503)   Playboy Interview: "Masters and Johnson: A Candid
        Conversation About the Newest Findings in Sex Re-

search--And What Heterosexuals Can Learn from
Homosexuals About Lovemaking," Playboy, 26:87-
88, 92-122, Nov. 1979.

1504)   Playboy Letters: Views on Anita Bryant's Campaign
Against Gay Rights, Playboy, 25:57, Jan. 1978; 25:55,
Feb. 1978; Mar. 1978; 25:63, Apr. 1978.

1505)   Podell, Judith. "About Gay Men ... and Me,"
Mademoiselle, 86:88+, Feb. 1980.

1506)   Podhoretz, Norman. "The Culture of Appeasement
[Homosexuality as a Cause for Much of the Pacifism
Between World Wars I and II]," Harper's, 255:25-
32, Oct. 1977.

1507)   Pogrebin, Letty C. "Growing Up Free [Fear of Homosexuality and Raising Children in the 1980s],"
Ms., 9:49-54, Oct. 1980.

1508)   Pollack, Andrew. Homosexual Scandal at Kincora
Boys Home in East Belfast, New Statesman, 103:
6-7, Feb. 12, 1982.

1509)   Powell, Leslie. "The Gay Writer," Progressive,
45:46-47, Nov. 1981.

1510)   "Protestants Echo Catholic Distaste for 'Norman [Is
That You?],'" Variety, 284:24, Nov. 3, 1976.

1511)   Rainer, Pete. "Why Heterosexual Males Feel
Threatened by Gays," Mademoiselle, 86:16+, Jan.
1980.

1512)   Raskin, Richard. "Protecting the Aural Majority
[Suit Charging Homosexual with Disseminating Ma-
terial Harmful to Minors on his Cincinnati Radio
Show]," Progressive, 45:17, Dec. 1981.

1513)   Real, Jere, and M. J. Sobran. "Gay Rights and
Conservative Politics," National Review, 30:392-47+,
1978.

1514)   Rensin, David. "Can't Stop the Muse [The Village
People]," Playboy, 27:106-08+, Jul. 1980.

1515)   Repeal of Gay Rights Ordinance in Miami, Economist,
263:52, Jun. 11, 1977.

1516)   Richards, Mary.   "The Gay Deception [Gayness in
         Recent Films]," Film Comment, 18:15-16, May-
         Jun. 1982.

1517)   "Rights for Homosexuals?   Controversy Surrounding
         the Acceptance of Homosexuals in the Catholic
         Church," Newsweek, 87:71, Mar. 8, 1976.

1518)   Roberts, Shelley.   "Bad Form, Billie Jean [King],"
         Newsweek, 97:19, May 25, 1981.

1519)   Roberts, Yvonne.   "Gay Night Out [In London's
         Largest Gay Discothèque]," New Statesman, 92:204,
         1976.

1520)   Robinson, Paul.   "Gays in the Streets [Protest After
         Verdict in the Dan White Murder Trial in San Fran-
         cisco]," New Republic, 180:9-10, Jun. 9, 1979.

1521)   _____.   "Invisible Men: [The Gay Rights] Issue
         Is Visibility, Not Discrimination," New Republic,
         178:9-11, Jun. 3, 1978.

1522)   Roddick, Nick.   "Gay Cinema: A New Cinema Club
         Against the Grain in London's Soho," Sight and
         Sound, 51:80, Apr. 1982.

1523)   Roiphe, Anne.   "Who's Afraid of Lesbian Sex?"
         Vogue, 167:150-51, Aug. 1977.

1524)   Ross, Ken.   "Gay Rights: The Coming Struggle,"
         Nation, 225:526-30, 1977.

1525)   Rowes, Barbara.   "Ned Rorem [Composer, Author,
         and Critic]," People Weekly, 10:38-43, Aug. 21,
         1978.

1526)   "Rumbles of New Sex Scandals in Congress [Homo-
         sexual Acts Between Congressmen and Pages Al-
         leged]," U. S. News and World Report, 93:11, Jul.
         12, 1982.

1527)   Russo, Vito.   "'Cruising' [A Movie]: The Contro-
         versy Continues," New York, 12:46-47+, Aug. 13,
         1979.

1528)   _____.   "On the Set [Of 'Making Love']," Es-
         quire, 96:102-03, Oct. 1981.

1529)   Ryle, John.   "Out of the Closet, Into the Streets
         [Gay Pride March in Great Britain]," New States-
         man, 98:3, 1979.

1530)   Salter, Michael.   "Moving to Resolve an Unthinkable
         Paradox [Ordination of Non-Practicing Homosexuals
         as Priests]," Maclean's, 92:49-49, Mar. 26, 1979.

1531)   San Francisco Mourns Its Murdered Mayor and
         Supervisor, People Weekly, 10:161, Dec. 11, 1978.

1532)   Satchell, Michael.   "How to Cope If Your Child Is
         Gay," Parade, Jun. 4, 1978, pp. 6-7.

1533)   "Scapegoating Homosexuals [California's Proposition
         6 Against Gay Teachers]," Progressive, 42:7, Aug.
         1978.

1534)   Scheer, Robert.   "The [Ronald] Reagan Question,"
         Playboy, 27:121-22+ at 230, Aug. 1980.

1535)   Schickel, Richard.   "Gays to the Fore, Cautiously
         [Review of 8 Movies]," Time, 119:78-79, Mar. 22,
         1982.

1536)   _____. Movie Review: "Personal Best." Time,
         119:72, Feb. 8, 1982.

1537)   Schofield, Michael.   "Why Is Homosexuality Still
         Something to Hide?" New Society, Feb. 15, 1979,
         pp. 348-50.

1538)   Schrag, Peter.   "Education Now [Influence of Gay
         Teachers]," Saturday Review, 5:53-54, Nov. 12,
         1977.

1539)   Schwartz, Pepper, and Philip Blumstein.   "Bi-
         sexuals: Where Love Speaks Louder Than Labels,"
         Ms., 5:80-81, Nov. 1976.

1540)   Scobie, William.   "Unholy Crusade on a Sexual Bat-
         tlefront [Moral Majority Protests Against Homo-
         sexuals in San Francisco]," Maclean's, 94:13+,
         May 4, 1981.

1541)   Scotland Legalizes Adult Consensual Homosexual
         Acts, Economist, 276:59-60, Jul. 26, 1980.

1542)   "Sculpture [Controversy over Placing Gay Liberation
        Sculptures in Greenwich Village]," New Yorker, 56:
        42-45, Oct. 27, 1980.

1543)   "[Sergei Diaghilev] The Genghis Khan of Ballet,"
        Time, 114:80, Sep. 10, 1979.

1544)   "Sex and the Homosexual [Study by Masters and
        Johnson]," Newsweek, 93:81-82, Apr. 30, 1979.

1545)   Sex Researcher C. A. Tripp Comments on New
        Book by Masters and Johnson, New York, 12:89,
        Apr. 30, 1979.

1546)   "Sexual Dissent [Views of Jesuit John McNeill],"
        Time, 108:93, Sep. 20, 1976.

1547)   "Sexual Tolerance in Mississippi? [Homosexual
        Charges Against Congressman Hinson]," Newsweek,
        96:38, Oct. 20, 1980.

1548)   "[Shirley] MacLaine Calls for Shobiz to Come Out
        in Support of Gays [And Against Anita Bryant],"
        Variety, 287:2+, Jun. 22, 1977.

1549)   Shrum, Robert. "Gay-baiting in the Classroom:
        Sexual Politics in California," New Times, 11:20-
        27, Sep. 4, 1978.

1550)   "Sins of Billy James [Hargis, Moral Crusader],"
        Time, 107:52, Feb. 16, 1976.

1551)   "Smearing the Pope [Paul VI]," Time, 107:53,
        Apr. 19, 1976.

1552)   Smith, Michael J.   "The Double Life of a Gay
        Dodger [Glenn Burke]," Inside Sports, 4:57-63,
        Oct. 1982.

1553)   Smith, Richard.   "The Gay Geordies," New Society,
        Feb. 12, 1976, pp. 317-18.

1554)   Smith, Richard W.   "Research and Homosexuality,"
        Humanist, 38:20-22, Mar. 1978.

1555)   "Sodom and Kincora [Pederasty in Northern Ireland],"
        Economist, 282:33, Feb. 6, 1982.

1556)   "Sodomy Law Repeal [in Washington]," Playboy,
         23:44, Jan. 1976.

1557)   "Sodomy Squad [Moral Majority Opposition Kills
         Law Reform in District of Columbia]," Playboy,
         29:53-54, Feb. 1982.

1558)   Somerset Maugham's Homosexuality, Time, 112:
         78-79, Jul. 24, 1978.

1559)   Spector, Malcolm. "Legitimizing Homosexuality,"
         Society, 14:52-56, Jul.-Aug. 1977.

1560)   Stabiner, Karen. "Tapping the Homosexual Market,"
         New York Times Magazine, May 2, 1982, pp. 34+.

1561)   Steinem, Gloria. "Anita Bryant's Crusade," Pro-
         gressive, 41:37, Jun. 1977.

1562)   _____. Interview with Feminist Charlotte Bunch,
         Ms., 6:54+, Jul. 1977.

1563)   Stone, Laurie. "Women Who Live with Gay Men,"
         Ms., 10:103-08, Oct. 1981.

1564)   Strouse, Joan. "Homosexuality since Rome [Review
         of John Boswell's Christianity, Social Tolerance, and
         Homosexuality]," Newsweek, 96:79-81, Sep. 29,
         1980.

1565)   Taylor, Alice. "Women in Love: Straight Talk
         from a Gay Woman," Mademoiselle, 84:124-26, Feb.
         1978.

1566)   Texas' Law Prohibiting Homosexual Acts Struck Down
         by Federal Judge, Playboy, 29:67, Dec. 1982.

1567)   Thorson, Scott. "Liberace Bombshell--Boyfriend
         Tells All About Their Six Year Romance," National
         Enquirer, Nov. 2, 1982, pp. 48-51.

1568)   "Time for Judgment [Trial Involving Samuel Bronf-
         man II and Melvin Lynch]," Time, 108:21, Dec. 13,
         1976.

1569)   "Toujours Gai [Comments on Norman Podhoretz's Arti-
         cle in Harper's]," National Review, 29:1160-61, 1977.

1570) Toynbee, Polly. "What Makes Lesbians so Particu-
       larly Dangerous as Parents?" Guardian, Jan. 16,
       1978, p. 9.

1571) "The Trash-bag Murders [Case of D. D. Hill and
       P. W. Kearney in Los Angeles]," Newsweek, 90:
       22, Jul. 18, 1977.

1572) Trash-bag Murders of Gay Males in Los Angeles,
       Time, 110:49, Jul. 18, 1977.

1573) Trial and Conviction of Mass Murderer John Gacy
       of Chicago, Time, 113:23, Jan. 8, 1979 and 115:28,
       Mar. 24, 1980.

1574) Trillin, Calvin. Reassignment of Homosexual
       Methodist Minister Julian Rush of Boulder, Colorado,
       New Yorker, 57:80-88, Jan. 25, 1982.

1575) Tucker, Carll. "Returning Sex to the Bedroom [Neg-
       ative Influence of Anita Bryant]," Saturday Review,
       4:60, Jul. 23, 1977.

1576) "Two Small Scores for Gay Rights [Immigration
       Policy and Back Pay for Leonard Matlovich]," News-
       week, 96:31-32, Sep. 22, 1980.

1577) U. S. Immigration Officials and the Exclusion of
       Homosexuals, Playboy, 23:47 May 1976; 25:63, Jul.
       1978; 29:55, Sep. 1982.

1578) VanGelder, Lindsy. "Anita Bryant on the March:
       The Lessons of Dade County," Ms. , 6:75-78+,
       Sep. 1977.

1579) _____ . "Lesbian Custody: A Tragic Day in
       Court [Case of Mary Jo Risher]," Ms. , 5:72-73,
       Sept. 1976.

1580) Vatican Condemnation of Homosexuality, Premarital
       Sex, and Masturbation, Time, 107:41, Jan. 26, 1976.

1581) VerMeulen, Michael. "The Gay Plague: A Mys-
       terious Immune Disorder Is Spreading Like Wildfire,"
       New York, 15:52-62, May 31, 1982.

1582)   Vidal, Gore.   "Neo-Con Homophobia: Some Jews
        and the Gays," Nation, 233:489, 509-17, 1981.
        (Responses: 234:2+, 1982.)

1583)   Vinocur, Barry.   "Being Gay Is a Health Hazard:
        The 'Gay Plague' Is a Frightening Epidemic," Satur-
        day Evening Post, 254:26+, Oct. 1982.

1584)   "Voting Against Gay Rights [Wichita, Kansas]," Time,
        111:21-22, May 22, 1978.

1585)   Walter Mondale Speaks at Manhattan Dinner to Gay
        Rights Political Action Committee, Time, 120:14,
        Oct. 11, 1982.

1586)   Ward, Michael, and Mark Freeman.   "Defending
        Gay Rights: The Campaign Against the Briggs
        Amendment in California," Radical American, 13:
        11-26, 1979.

1587)   Waters, Craig.   "24 Men Indicted for Abuse of 70
        Boys in Boston Hired-Sex Ring," New Times, 10:
        21, Jan. 23, 1978.

1588)   Waugh, T.   "The Gay Cultural Front," Jump Cut,
        18:36-37, Aug. 1978.

1589)   Waxman, Ken.   "The Rise of Gay Capitalism,"
        Toronto Life, Sept. 1976, pp. 34+.

1590)   "The Weekend Poll: Most Canadians Think Homo-
        sexuals are 'Sick People,'" Weekend Magazine,
        Dec. 17, 1977, p. 2.

1591)   Weiss, Michael.   "Trial and Error [The Dan White
        Trial in San Francisco]," Rolling Stone, 295:47-49,
        Jul. 12, 1979.

1592)   Wheen, Francis.   "Homosexuals Unite Against Anglo-
        Saxon Attitudes [Politics and Homosexuality in Great
        Britain]," New Statesman, 96:266, 1978.

1593)   _____.   "A Menace to Pupils? [Attitude of Edu-
        cator Toward Homosexuals]," New Statesman, 99:
        45, 1980.

1594)   _____ . "Michael Foot and Queers [Britain's Labor
            Party and Its Anti-homosexual Attitude]," New States-
            man, 98:259, 1979.

1595)   "Where the Boys Are [Gay Resorts]," Newsweek,
            94:62-64, Jul. 30, 1979.

1596)   White, Edmund. "Sado-Machismo: The Politics of
            Gay S and M," New Times, 12:54-55, Jan. 8, 1979.

1597)   Whittingham, Anthony. "The Gay Boys of Summer
            [Gay Softball Teams in Canada]," Maclean's, 94:38-
            39, Sep. 14, 1981.

1598)   "Why Tide Is Turning Against Homosexuals," U.S.
            News and World Report, 84:29, Jun. 5, 1978.

1599)   Wilhelm, Maria. "John Schmidt, Founder of First
            Gay Savings and Loan Gives Credit Where Credit Is
            Due," People Weekly, 17:117-18, Feb. 22, 1982.

1600)   Wilkins, Roger. "Institutional Bigotry [Leonard
            Matlovich]," Progressive, 44:12, Nov. 1980.

1601)   Will, George F. "How Far Out of the Closet?"
            Newsweek, 89:92, May 30, 1977.

1602)   Willenbecher, Thom. "No More Fun and Games
            [Hostility Between Gays and Police in San Francisco],"
            Progressive, 46:18-19, Sep. 1982.

1603)   Williams, Elaine. European Commission's Court
            of Human Rights Hears Its First Gay Rights Case,
            New Statesman, 101:3, May 1, 1981.

1604)   Williams, Roger M. "Turning the Tide on Gay
            Rights [A Victory in Seattle]," Saturday Review,
            6:21-24, Feb. 17, 1979.

1605)   "Witch-hunting [Proposition Against Gay Teachers
            in California]," Economist, 269:50, Oct. 28, 1978.

1606)   Witt, Linda. Interview of Sex Researcher Alan P.
            Bell, People Weekly, 10:109+, Oct. 30, 1978.

1607)   Woffinden, Bob. "Gay Rights Test Case [Dismissal
            of Homosexual Worker] Goes to Appeal," New States-
            man, 99:660, 1980.

1608)   Wood, Robin.   "Responsibilities of a Gay Film
         Critic, " Film Comment, 14:12-17, Jan. 1978.

1609)   Young, Gavin.   "Frisco Brings Gaiety to the
         Nation, " Observer, May 3, 1981, p. 10.

1610)   Young, Ian.   "Gay in the Seventies, " Weekend
         Magazine, Dec, 17, 1977, pp. 10-14.

1611)   Young, Perry D.   "She Said: 'He's a Fag. You
         Know. ' I Smiled and Said: 'So Am I,' " Ms. ,
         4:37-38, Jun. 1976.

ARTICLES IN RELIGIOUS JOURNALS

1612) Adell, Arvid. "Process Thought and the Liberation of Homosexuals," Christian Century, 96:46-48, 1979.

1613) Aden, Leroy. "Homosexuality: What Can the Church Say?" The Lutheran, 17:14-16, May 2, 1979.

1614) The American Friends Service Committee (Quaker Agency) Includes Gays, Christian Century, 95:528, 1978.

1615) The American Lutheran Church Holds Homosexual Behavior Is Wrong. Christian Century, 96:843, 1979.

1616) Andersen, W. E., and B. B. Hill. "Homosexuality and the Education of Persons," Journal of Christian Education, 59:3-82, Sep. 1977.

1617) Ard, Roger H. "Why the Conservatives Won in Miami," Christian Century, 94:677-79, 1977.

1618) Baltimore Archdiocese Task Force. "Baltimore's Ministry to Lesbian and Gay Catholics," Origins, 11:549-53, 1982.

1619) Barnhouse, Ruth T. "Homosexuality," Anglican Theological Review, Supplemental Series, 6:107-34, Jun. 1976.

1620) Barrett, Ellen, and others. "Gays in the Church Speak for Themselves," The Witness, 60: 4-9 and 14-18, Oct. 1977.

1621) Bartlett, David L. "A Biblical Perspective on Homosexuality," Foundations, 20:133-47, Apr.-Jun. 1977. (Reprinted in Twiss, no. 32.)

1622) Batteau, John M. "Sexual Differences; A Cultural Convention?" Christianity Today, 21:1064-66, 1976-77. (Reprinted in Twiss, no. 32.)

1623) Bauer, Paul F. "Homosexual Subculture at Worship: A Participant Observation Study," Pastoral Psychology, 25:115-27, Winter 1976.

1624) Beeson, Trevor. "Sexuality Issues--No Edifying Debate [Reports of Methodist Church and Church of England]," Christian Century, 96:1164-65, 1979.

1625) Beifuss, Joan T. "Gays 1980: Out of Both Closet and Confessional," National Catholic Reporter, 17:7-9+, Nov. 21, 1980.

1626) Bennett, John C., and others. "Gay Questions, Straight Answers," Christianity and Crisis, 38:98-100, 1978.

1627) Bergman, Jerry. "The Genetic Basis of Homosexuality," Journal of the American Scientific Affiliation, 33:153-57, 1981.

1628) Berrigan, Daniel. "The Leveling of John McNeill," Commonweal, 104:778-83, 1977.

1629) Birchard, Roy. "Metropolitan Community Church: Its Development and Significance," Foundations, 20:127-32, Apr.-Jun. 1977.

1630) Borhek, Mary V. "Can the National Council of Churches Accept a Gay Denomination?" Christian Century, 99:461-62, 1982.

1631) Boyd, Malcolm, and Edward J. Curtin. "Mask-wearing: Spiritually Stifling," Christian Century, 96:79-81, 1979.

1632) _____, and Virginia Mollenkott. "Homosexual Love: An Explanation/An Exploration," Insight: A Quarterly of Lesbian/Gay Christian Opinion, 3:5-8, Fall 1979.

1633) British Methodist Report Favors Acceptance of Homosexuality, Christian Century, 96:583, 1979.

1634)   Brown, Robert M.   "The Religious Right and
         Political/Economic Conservatism," Radical Religion,
         5:37-43, 1981.

1635)   Browning, Don S.   "Homosexuality, Theology, the
         Social Sciences, and the Church," Encounter, 40:
         223-43, Summer 1979.

1636)   Cahill, Lisa S.   "Sexual Issues in Christian The-
         ological Ethics: A Review of Recent Studies,"
         Religious Studies Review, 4:1-14, Jan. 1978.

1637)   "A Call to Responsible Ecumenical Debate on Abor-
         tion and Homosexuality," Engage/Social Action, 7:41-
         44, Oct. 1979.

1638)   Callahan, Daniel, and others.   "Homosexual Husband
         and Physician Confidentiality," Hastings Center Re-
         port, 7:15-17, Apr. 1977.

1639)   Cameron, Paul, and Kenneth P. Ross.   "Social and
         Psychological Aspects of the Judeo-Christian Stance
         Toward Homosexuality," Journal of Psychology and
         Theology, 9:40-57, 1981.

1640)   Campion, Michael A., and Alfred A. Barrow.   "When
         Was the Last Time You Hugged a Homosexual?"
         Journal of the American Scientific Affiliation, 29:10-
         11, 1977.

1641)   Campolo, Anthony.   "A Christian Sociologist Looks
         at Homosexuality," Wittenberg Door, 39:16-17, Nov.
         1977.

1642)   "The Church and Homosexuals," Christian Century,
         94:528, 1977.

1643)   Clark, Joan L.   "Coming Out: The Process and the
         Price," Christianity and Crisis, 39:149-53, 1979.

1644)   "Climate of Readiness for Gay Ordination?" Chris-
         tian Century, 95:475-76, 1978.

1645)   Coffin, William S.   "Homosexuality Revisited: Whose
         Problem?" Christianity and Crisis, 41:290, 300-02,
         1981.

1646) "A Colloquy on Homosexuality and the Church,"
Circuit Rider, 4:3-13, Mar. 1980.

1647) "Confronting the Homosexual Issue," Christianity
Today, 21:1092, 1976-77.

1648) Cook, E. David. "Homosexuality: A Review of the
Debate," The Churchman, 94:297-313, 1980.

1649) Court, John H., and O. Raymond Johnston. "Psychosexuality: A Three-Dimensional Model," Journal of Psychology and Theology, 6:90-97, 1978.

1650) Craddock, Fred. "How Does the New Testament
Deal with Homosexuality," Encounter, 49:197-208,
Summer 1979.

1651) Crew, Louie. The Church and Gays, Christianity and
Crisis, 37:140-44, 1977; 40:2+, 1980; and 41:290+,
1981.

1652) _____. "Homosexuality: An Integrity Leader's
View," The Living Church, 173:8+, Aug. 1, 1976.

1653) Cromey, Robert W. "A Clerical Fantasy [Gay
Episcopal Priests and Bishops Coming Out of the
Closet]," The Witness, 64:13, Mar. 1981.

1654) BeBlassie, R. "Pastoral Concern for the Adolescent
Homosexual," Priest, 36:32-34, Apr. 1980.

1655) Dismissal of Lesbian Joan Clark from United
Methodist Board, Christian Century 96:520, 1979.

1656) Doughty, Darrell J. "Homosexuality and Obedience
to the Gospel," Church and Society, 67:12-23, May-
June 1977.

1657) Duncan, Celena M. "Metropolitan Community
Churches vs. National Council of Churches," Christian Century, 99:1319-20, 1982.

1658) Early, Tracy. 'The Struggle in the Denominations:
Shall Gays Be Ordained?" Christianity and Crisis,
37:118-22, 1977. (Reprinted in Twiss, no. 32.)

1659)   Editor of the Virginia Churchman Takes a Strong
        Stand Against Homosexuality, Christianity Today,
        23:876, 1978-79.

1660)   Editorial: California's Proposition 6 [Against Ho-
        mosexual Teachers] Is Not Necessary, America,
        139:325-26, 1978.

1661)   Editorial: "Debate on Homosexuality: We Vote
        for Change," Christianity and Crisis, 37:114-15,
        1977.

1662)   Editorial: "Homosexuality and Civil Rights--[No
        Need for Gay Rights Ordinances]," America, 137:
        558, 1977.

1663)   Editorial: "Supporting Human Rights for Gays,"
        National Catholic Reporter, 17:11, Nov. 21, 1980.

1664)   Edmonds, Patty. "New York Parish May Be Sold
        to Obstruct Gay Ministry," National Catholic Re-
        porter, 15:5+, Aug. 24, 1979.

1665)   Episcopal Church Commission Recommends Per-
        mitting Homosexuals to Become Priests, Christian
        Century, 96:665, 1979.

1666)   Espy, John W. , and James B. Nelson. "Homo-
        sexuality and the Church," Christianity and Crisis,
        37:116-18, 1977.

1667)   Eyrich, Howard A. "Hope for the Homosexual: The
        Case for Nouthetic Help," Journal of Pastoral Prac-
        tice, 1:19-33, Summer 1977.

1668)   Fisher, David H. "The Homosexual Debate: A
        Critique of Some Critics," St. Luke's Journal of
        Theology, 22:176-84, Jun. 1979.

1669)   Floerke, Jill D. "Ministering to Gay Christians,"
        Christian Century, 93:854-56, 1976.

1670)   Fortunato, John E. "Gay Ministry Vital as Violence
        Escalates," The Witness, 65:10-11, May 1982.

1671)   Garrett Evangelical Theological Seminary Expells
        Homosexuals from Master of Divinity Program,
        Christian Century, 95:584 and 1128, 1978.

1672)   Gay, Calvin [pseud.].   'To the Presbyterians on
        Homosexuality: You Spoke from Ignorance," Chris-
        tianity and Crisis, 38:254-59, 1978.

1673)   Gay Priest Suspended in Virginia, Christian Century,
        96:336, 1979.

1674)   "Gay Scouts Ousted [in Mankato, Minn.]," Christian
        Century, 95:231, 1978.

1675)   Gay Students Sue Georgetown University for Refusing
        to Recognize Their Organization, Christian Century,
        97:936, 1980.

1676)   "Gay Week in San Jose [Cal.]," Christianity Today,
        22:875, 1977-78.

1677)   Gibson, E. Lawrence.   "Homosexuals in the Mili-
        tary," Engage /Social Action, 7:19-22, Apr. 1979.

1678)   Glaser, Chris.   "A Newly Revealed Christian Ex-
        perience," Church and Society, 67:5-11, Jun. 1977.

1679)   Gordon, Sol.   'It's Not OK to Be Anti-gay," The
        Witness, 60:10-13+, Oct. 1977.

1680)   Greenburg, Alcuin E.   "How Can Pastors Minister
        to Homosexuals?" Homiletic and Pastoral Review,
        77:52-58, Jan. 1977.

1681)   Griffin, David R.   "Ordination for Homosexuals?
        Yes. " Encounter, 40:265-72, Summer 1979.

1682)   Haas, Harold I.   "Homosexuality," Currents in
        Theology and Mission, 5:82-104, Apr. 1978.

1683)   Harrison, James.   'Building Bonds: The Church
        and the Gays," Christian Century, 96:500-04, 1979.

1684)   _____.   "[Homosexuality and] the Dynamics of
        Sexual Anxiety," Christianity and Crisis, 37:136-40,
        1977.   (Reprinted in Twiss, no. 32.)

1685)   Harvey, John.   "Chastity and the Homosexual: Psy-
        chological and Moral Considerations Are Keys to
        Counseling," Priest, 33:10+, Jul.-Aug. 1977.

1686)   _____. "The Impact of Gay Propaganda upon
        Adolescent Boys and Girls," Priest, 36:15+, Mar.
        1980.

1687)   _____. "Reflections on a Retreat for Clerics
        with Homosexual Tendencies," Linacre Quarterly,
        46:6-40, May 1979.

1688)   Healy, P. W. J.   "Uranisme et Unisexualité: A
        Late Victorian View of Homosexuality," New Black-
        friars, 59:56-65, 1978.

1689)   Hencken, Joel D.   "Homosexuals and Heterosexuals:
        We Are All Apologists," Anglican Theological Re-
        view, 59:191-93, Apr. 1977.

1690)   Henry, Patrick.   "Homosexuals: Identity and Dig-
        nity," Theology Today, 33:33-39, 1976-77.

1691)   Herring, Reuben,   "Southern Baptist Convention
        Resolutions on the Family," Baptist History and
        Heritage, 17;36-45+, Jan. 1982.

1692)   Heyward, Carter.   "Coming Out: Journey Without
        Maps," Christianity and Crisis, 39:153-56, 1979.

1693)   _____. "Theological Explorations of Homosex-
        uality," The Witness, 62:12-15, Jun. 1979.

1694)   Higgs, Roger and others.   "Lesbian Couples: Should
        Help Extend to AID [Artificial Insemination]?" Jour-
        nal of Medical Ethics, 4:91-95, Jun. 1978.

1695)   Hildebrand, Alice J. von.   "Plato and the Homo-
        sexuals," Homiletic and Pastoral Review, 82:19-23,
        Dec. 1981.

1696)   "Homosexual Ordination," Christianity Today, 21:525,
        958-59, and 1138, 1976-77.

1697)   "Homosexual Rights and Ordination," America, 137:
        346, 1977.

1698)   "Homosexuality: Biblical Guidance Through a Moral
        Morass," Christianity Today, 24:489, 1980.

1699)   "Homosexuality: A Re-examination," Engage/Social
        Action, 8:9-56, Mar. 1980.

1700)   Horner, Tom.   "The Centurion's Servant," Insight:
         A Quarterly of Gay Catholic Opinion, 2:9, Summer
         1978.

1701)   Humm, Andy, and others.   "Silencing of Gay Issues
         in the Christian Churches," Insight: A Quarterly
         of Gay Catholic Opinion, 3:5-13, Summer 1979.

1702)   Hyde, Clark and Janet.   "Homosexuality and the
         Theological Uses of Social Science," Anglican Theo-
         logical Review, 59:187-90, Apr. 1977.

1703)   Iliff School of Theology in Denver Bars Gay Ap-
         plicant, Christian Century, 95:1033, 1978.

1704)   "Invitation to Character Assassination [California
         Voters and Proposition 6]," Christian Century, 95:
         1028-29, 1978.

1705)   Jennings, Theodore W.   "Homosexuality and the
         Christian Faith: A Theological Reflection," Chris-
         tian Century, 94:137-42, 1977.   (Reprinted in Twiss,
         no. 32.)

1706)   Jesuits Reject Homosexual Candidate for the Priest-
         hood," Christian Century, 94:1087, 1977.

1707)   Johnson, Dick.   "Homosexuals and the Seminaries,"
         Engage/Social Action, 6:44-45, 1978.

1708)   Jones, Alan W.   "When Is a Homosexual Not a Ho-
         mosexual?" Anglican Theological Review, 59:183-86,
         Apr. 1977.

1709)   Jones, Arthur, and Jim McManus.   "Bishops Speak
         on Homosexuality and Gay Symposium," National
         Catholic Reporter, 18:3, Nov. 13, 1981.

1710)   Jones, Joe R.   "Christian Sensibility with Respect
         to Homosexuality," Encounter, 40:209-21, Summer
         1979.

1711)   Kavanagh, Julia [pseud.].   "My Son Is Gay," U.S.
         Catholic, 45:14-15, Jun. 1980.

1712)   Kenkelen, Bill.   "Gay Rights Ally Heads San Fran-
         cisco Parish," National Catholic Reporter, 15:5,
         Aug. 24, 1979.

1713)   _____. "Report on Gays Casts Church as Unjust,
Unresponsive," National Catholic Reporter, 18:1+,
Sep. 24, 1982.

1714)   _____. "San Francisco Gays [and Catholic
Church]: An Uneasy Truce," National Catholic Reporter, 17:13, Nov. 21, 1980.

1715)   _____. "Priest Faces Ouster; Views on Gays
Cited," National Catholic Reporter, 17:3-4, Jul. 31,
1981.

1716)   Kleinig, John. "Reflections on Homosexuality,"
Journal of Christian Education, 58:32-57, 1977.

1717)   Koskella, Roger. "Open Door to Gays [San Jose
Metropolitan Community Church Admitted to Mem-
bership in Santa Clara County Council of Churches],"
Christianity Today, 20:1622, 1975-76.

1718)   Kraft, William F. "Homosexuality and Religious
Life," Review for Religious, 40:370-81, 1981.

1719)   Kratt, Mary. "Church 'Always Resistant to Change'
[Lesbian Priest Visits Her Home Town Church in
North Carolina]," Christian Century, 97:237-38, 1980.

1720)   Krody, Nancy E. "An Open Lesbian Looks at the
Church," Foundations, 20:148-62, Apr.-Jun. 1977.

1721)   _____. "Woman, Lesbian, Feminist, Christian,"
Christianity and Crisis, 37:131-36, 1977.

1722)   Kuehnelt-Leddhin, Erik von. "The Problem of Homosexuality: A Christian View," Human Life Review, 4:61-75, Spring 1978.

1723)   Larsen, Paul E., and others. "Christian Answers
on Homosexuality," Journal of the American Scientific Affiliation, 31:48-53, 1979.

1724)   Larue, Gerald. "The Bible and Homosexuality,"
Religious Humanism, 14:78-86, 1980.

1725)   "Lesbians and Politics: A Group Discussion," Radical Religion, 3:44-51, 1977.

1726)   Lewis, Dean H.   "Homosexuality: Resources for
        Reflection," Church and Society, 67:3-40 and 59-79,
        May-Jun. 1977.

1727)   Lewis, Jeffrey.   "One California Bishop Pans
        Proposition 6; Others Demur," National Catholic Re-
        porter, 15:15, Oct. 13, 1978.

1728)   Lexington Theological Seminary Refuses to Grant
        Degree to Homosexual; Court Challenges Ahead.
        Christian Century, 96:633-34 and 783, 1979.

1729)   Lovelace, Richard F.   "The Active Homosexual Life-
        style and the Church," Church and Society, 67:12-23,
        May-Jun. 1977.

1730)   Martin, Enos D. , and Ruth K. Martin.   "Develop-
        mental and Ethical Issues in Homosexuality: Pastoral
        Implications," Journal of Psychology and Theology,
        9:58-68, 1981.

1731)   Marty, Don.   "The Church and the Homosexuals,"
        Christian Herald, 101:41-45+, Jan. 1978.

1732)   Marty, Martin E.   Criticisms of Anita Bryant's
        Campaign Against Homosexuals, Christian Century,
        94:584, 639, and 1047, 1977.

1733)   Mathers, James.   "Homosexuality," Theology, 83:
        131-33, Mar. 1980.

1734)   Matt, Hershel J.   "Sin, Crime, Sickness, or Alterna-
        tive Life Style: A Jewish Approach to Homosexual-
        ity," Judaism, 27:13-24, Winter 1978.

1735)   Matthews, Arthur H.   "United Presbyterian Church:
        Deciding the Homosexual Issue," Christianity Today,
        22:1162-65, 1977-78.

1736)   Matzkin, William L.   "Homosexuality," Linacre
        Quarterly, 43:259-63, 1976.

1737)   Maust, John.   "Episcopalians' Great Debate on the
        Ordination of Homosexuals," Christianity Today,
        23:1411-13, 1978-79.

1738)   McClory, Robert J.   "Episcopal Bishop Cody Pro-

hibits Gay Workshop," National Catholic Reporter, 17:2, May 15, 1981.

1739)   McGraw, James R.   "Anita and the Gays," Christianity and Crisis, 37:147-49, 1977.

1740)   McKenzie, Thomas.   "Why Gay Catholics Won't Be Locked Out of the Church," U. S. Catholic, 47:6-12, Aug. 1982.

1741)   McNaught, Brian.   "Is Our Church Big Enough for Gay Catholics?" U. S. Catholic, 45:6-13, Jun. 1980.

1742)   _____.   "Why Bother with Gay Rights," Humanist, 37:34-36, Sep.-Oct. 1977.

1743)   Mehler, Barry.   "Gay Jews," Moment, 2:22+, Feb.-Mar. 1977.

1744)   Messer, Alfred A.   "The Family and Homosexual Behavior," Marriage and Family Living, 60:11-14, Jul. 1978.

1745)   Methodist Church Committee of Investigation Drops Charges Against Bishop Who Refused to Dismiss Homosexual Minister, Christianity Today, 26:44, Jul. 16, 1982.

1746)   Methodists Reappoint Gay Minister, Christian Century, 95:672, 724, 1201, 1978.

1747)   Michaels, James W., Jr.   "Baltimore Bishop's Role in Ordinance Defeat Angers Homosexuals," National Catholic Reporter, 16:7, Aug. 15, 1980.

1748)   Minnery, Tom.   "Homosexuals Can Change," Christianity Today, 25:172-77, 1981.

1749)   Minnesota Council of Churches Voice Strong Support for Gays," Christian Century, 99:1225, 1982.

1750)   Mitchell, Basil.   "The Homosexuality Report [of the Working Party of the Anglican Church]," Theology, 83:184-90, May 1980.

1751)   Moberly, Elizabeth.   "Homosexuality: Structure and Evaluation," Theology, 83:177-84, May 1980.

1752)   Mollenkott, Virginia. "Joyful Worship in the Midst
        of Danger [Los Angeles' Metropolitan Community
        Church]," Christian Century, 96:910, 1979.

1753)   _____, and Letha Scanzoni. "Homosexuality: It's
        Not as Simple as We Think," Faith at Work, 91:8+,
        Apr. 1978.

1754)   Moorehead, Lee C. Right-wing Minister Threatens
        Repeal of Gay Rights Ordinance in Madison, Wis.,
        Christian Century, 95:846, 1978.

1755)   Mount, Eric, and Johanna Bos. "Scripture on Sexu-
        ality: Shifting Authority," Journal of Presbyterian
        History, 59:219-42, Summer 1981.

1756)   Mugavero, Francis J. "Sexuality--God's Gift: Pas-
        toral Letter of the Most Reverend Francis J. Muga-
        vero, Bishop of Brooklyn," Insight: A Quarterly of
        Gay Catholic Opinion, 1:5-7, Spring 1977.

1757)   Muehl, William. "The Myth of Self-Evident Truths
        [Justifying Repeal of the Dade County Gay Rights
        Ordinance]," Christian Century, 94:1000-02, 1977.

1758)   Murphy, John F. "The Teacher and the Homosexual,"
        Linacre Quarterly, 43:249-58, 1976.

1759)   National Council of Churches of Christ in the U.S.A.
        Calls for Responsible Ecumenical Debate on Abortion
        and Homosexuality, Ecumenical Trends, 8:45-48,
        Mar. 1979.

1760)   Nelson, James B. "Homosexuality and the Church,"
        St. Luke's Journal of Theology, 22:197-211, Jun.
        1979.

1761)   _____. "Toward a Sexual Ethics of Love: Ho-
        mosexuality and the Church," Christianity and Crisis,
        37:63-69, 1977.

1762)   "New York Diocese Opposes Gay Job Equality,"
        National Catholic Reporter, 14:3, Jan. 27, 1978.

1763)   Nugent, Robert. "Homosexuality and the Hurting
        Family," America, 144:154-57, 1981.

1764)   _____ . "Sex Education Guidelines: New Gay In-
           sights, " National Catholic Reporter, 17:11, Aug. 14,
           1981.

1765)   O'Brien, Charles R. , and Josephine Johnson.   "A
           Counseling Approach to the Homosexual Client, "
           Pastoral Psychology, 29:262-69, Summer 1981.

1766)   Ohio Episcopal Diocesan Report on Homosexuality,
           Christian Century, 94:1024, 1977.

1767)   Oliver, Kay, and Wayne Christianson.   "Unhappily
           'Gay': From Closet to Front Page, " Moody Monthly,
           78:62-68, Jan. 1978.

1768)   Olsen, Glenn W.   "The Gay Middle Ages: A Response
           to Professor [John] Boswell, " Communio: Interna-
           tional Catholic Review, 8:119-38, Summer 1981.

1769)   Orr, Kenneth, and Michael W. Ross.   "Homosexual-
           ity in Clinical and Biblical Context, " Journal of Chris-
           tian Education Papers, 69:37-48, Dec. 1980.

1770)   Osborn, Ronald E.   "Ordination for Homosexuals? A
           Negative Answer Qualified by Some Reflections, " En-
           counter, 40:245-63, Summer 1979.

1771)   Papa, Mary.   "Catholic Clergy Take Opposite Sides
           as St. Paul [Minn.] Voters Repeal Gay Rights, " Na-
           tional Catholic Reporter, 14:24, May 5, 1978.

1772)   Patterson, Ben.   "A Belated Answer, " Wittenberg
           Door, 39:18-19+, Oct. -Nov. 1977.

1773)   Pattison, E. Mansell, and others.   "Understanding
           Homosexuality: A Symposium, " Pastoral Psychology,
           24:231-44, Spring 1976.

1774)   Phillips, Anthony.   "Uncovering the Father's Skirt
           [Prohibition of Homosexual Acts Between Father and
           Son], " Vetus Testamentum, 30:38-43, Jan. 1980.

1775)   Pinney, Gregory W.   The Metropolitan Community
           Church Is Not Welcome, The Witness, 61:10-13,
           Oct. 1978.

1776)   Presbyterians and the United Church of Christ Oppose

Proposition 6 in California, Christian Century,
95:977, 1978.

1777)   Preston, John.   "White Candles at the Ramrod
[Shooting of Homosexuals in New York City]," The
Witness, 64:18-19, Nov. 1981.

1778)   Rayner, DeCourcey H.   Anglicans Ordain Celibate
Homosexual as Minister, Christianity Today, 23:
760-61, 1978-79.

1779)   "Resettling Gay Cubans," Christian Century, 98:
504-05, 1981.

1780)   "Rome Silences McNeill [Jesuit Priest for His Views
on Homosexuality]," National Catholic Reporter, 13:
1+, Sep. 9, 1977.

1781)   Ross, John C., and John M. Gessell.   "Report on
the Documentation Program on Diocesan and Other
Materials in the Area of Human Sexuality," St.
Luke's Journal of Theology, 22:212-16, Jun. 1979.

1782)   St. Paul [Minn.] Voters Reject Gay Rights Ordinance,
Christianity Today, 22:1063, 1977-78.

1783)   Samuel, K. Mathew.   "A Judeo-Christian Attitude to
Homosexuality: An Historical View," AME [African
Methodist Episcopal] Zion Quarterly Review, 93:24-
31, Apr. 1981.

1784)   Scanzoni, Letha.   "Conservative Christians and Gay
Civil Rights," Christian Century, 93:857-62, 1976.
(Reprinted in Twiss, no. 32.)

1785)   _____.   "Gay Confrontation [Bloomington, Indiana
Prohibits Discrimination Based on Sexual Preference],"
Christianity Today, 20:633-35, 1975-76.

1786)   Schaibley, Robert W.   "Evaluation of the Australian
Lutheran 'Statement on Homosexuality,'" Concordia
Theological Quarterly, 42:1-7, Jan. 1978.

1787)   Schindler, Ruben.   "Homosexuality, the Halacha, and
the Helping Professions," Journal of Religion and
Health, 18:132-38, Apr. 1979.

1788)   Scott, David A.   "Ordaining a Homosexual Person:
         A Policy Proposal," St. Luke's Journal of Theology,
         22:185-96, Jun. 1979.

1789)   "Seminaries: Glum over 'Gays,'" Christianity Today,
         23:375-76, 1978-79.

1790)   Shelp, Earl E.   "Pastor, I Think I'm Gay," Chris-
         tian Ministry, 10:18-19, Mar. 1979.

1791)   Siegel, Paul.   "Homophobia: Types, Origins, and
         Remedies," Christianity and Crisis, 39:280-84, 1979.

1792)   Sims, Bennett J.   "Sex and Homosexuality: A Pas-
         toral Statement [of the Episcopal Bishop of Atlanta],"
         Christianity Today, 22:651-58, 1977-78.

1793)   Smedes, Lewis, B.   "Homosexuality: Sorting Out
         the Issues," Reformed Journal 28:9-12, Jan. 1978.

1794)   _____.   "The San Diego Decision: Presbyterians
         and Homosexuality," Reformed Journal, 28:12-16,
         Aug. 1978.

1795)   Smith, Dwight C.   Presbyterians on Homosexuality,
         Christianity and Crisis, 38:22-27, 1978.

1796)   Smith, Richard W.   "Research and Homosexuality,"
         Humanist, 38:20-22, Mar.-Apr. 1978.

1797)   Snow, John H.   "Gay People and Parish Life," The
         Witness, 61:4-9, Oct. 1978.

1798)   Solheim, James E.   "She's Still Our Daughter,"
         A.D., 8:31-32, May 1979.

1799)   Souster, Howard.   "Data Sheet on Homosexuality,"
         Epworth Review, 7:22-25, May 1979.

1800)   Southern Baptists Retain Homosexuality as Sin, Chris-
         tian Century, 93:621, 1976.

1801)   Spero, Moshe H.   "Homosexuality: Clinical and
         Ethical Challenges," Tradition, 17:53-73, 1979.

1802)   Springer, R.   "Holy God, Gays Want In," Today's
         Parish, 12:10-13, Jan. 1980.

1803)   Steinbeck, A. W.   "Of Homosexuality: The Current
          State of Knowledge, " Journal of Christian Education,
          58:58-82, 1977.

1804)   Stowe, W. McFerin, and others.   "The Church and
          Homosexuals, " Christianity and Crisis, 39:206-08,
          1979.

1805)   Strong, Stanley R.   "Christian Counseling with Ho-
          mosexuals, " Journal of Psychology and Theology, 8:
          279-87, 1980.

1806)   Thomas, Susan.   "Palo Alto [Cal.] Voters Reject
          Gay Rights Ordinance, " Christianity Today, 26:39,
          Jan. 1, 1982.

1807)   Tjetje, Louis, and Gary Schuler.   "Setting 'Cruising'
          Straight, " Union Seminary Quarterly Review, 35:211-
          16, Spring-Summer 1980.

1808)   Tracy, James D.   "Behind St. Paul's Affectional
          Preference Vote, " Commonweal, 105:434-36, 1978.

1809)   "Understanding Homosexuality, " Canadian Churchman,
          102:8-14, Oct. 1976.

1810)   "United Church of Christ Anti-Gay Caucus, " Chris-
          tian Century, 95:440, 1978.

1811)   United Presbyterian Church and the Issue of Ordina-
          tion of Homosexual Ministers, Christian Century 95:
          379-80, 603-04, and 636-38, 1978.

1812)   United Presbyterian Church, USA General Assembly.
          Policy Statements and Recommendations.   Church
          and Society, 68:3-78, May-Jun. 1978.

1813)   United Universalist Association Convention Call for
          Hiring of Openly Gay and Bisexual Persons for Lead-
          ership Positions, Christian Century, 97:727, 1980.

1814)   Unsworth, Richard. P.   "Theological Table-Talk:
          Human Sexuality, " Theology Today, 36:58-65, Apr.
          1979.

1815)   "U.S. Group [New Ways Ministry] Issues Dutch
          Statement on Homosexuality, " National Catholic Re-
          porter, 16:3, Mar. 7, 1980.

1816)   Vacek, Edward.   "Christian Homosexuality?" Common-
        weal, 107:681-84, 1980.

1817)   Wagenaar, Theodore C. , and Patricia E. Bartos.
        "Orthodoxy and Attitudes of Clergymen Towards Ho-
        mosexuality and Abortion," Review of Religious
        Research, 18:114-25, Winter 1977.

1818)   Wagner, Richard.   "Being Gay and Celibate--Another
        View," National Catholic Reporter, 17:16, Nov. 21,
        1980.

1819)   Wagner, Roman.   "Moving into Unchartered Territory
        [Gay Ministers]," Counseling and Values, 22:184-96,
        Apr. 1978.

1820)   Wall, James M.   "On Being Consistent in Polity--
        A Question of Ordination of Homosexual Ministers,"
        Christian Century, 95:379-80, 1978.

1821)   Way, Peggy.   "Homosexual Counseling as a Learning
        Ministry," Christianity and Crisis, 37:123-31, 1977.

1822)   White, Richard and Rosalie.   "When Homosexuality
        Hits a Marriage: His Story and Her Story," Chris-
        tian Life, 40:24-25+, Jun. 1978.

1823)   Wilkening, Norma, and others.   "Tracing a Biblical
        Sex Ethic," Christian Century, 97:20-27, 1980.

1824)   Wilkinson, L. P.   "Classical Approaches: Homo-
        sexuality," Encounter, 51:20-31, Sep. 1978.

1825)   Williams, Peter.   The Church of England's Glou-
        cester Report on Homosexuality, The Churchman,
        94:4-6, 1980.

1826)   Williamson, Clark M.   "Disciple Theology: Or-
        dination and Homosexuality," Encounter, 40:197-
        272, Summer 1979.

1827)   Willimon, William H.   "Coming Out of the Closet,"
        Christian Century, 95:1076, 1978.

1828)   Wink, Walter.   "Biblical Perspectives on Homo-
        sexuality," Christian Century, 96:1082-86, 1979.

1829)   Woggon, Harry A.   "A Biblical and Historical Study
        of Homosexuality," Journal of Religion and Health,
        20:156-73, Summer 1981.

1830)   Woods, Richard, and others.   "Toward a Gay Chris-
        tian Ethic," Insight: A Quarterly of Lesbian/Gay
        Catholic Opinion, 3:5-12, Spring-Summer 1979.

1831)   York, Richard H.   "How Gay Issues Fared at
        General Convention," St. Luke's Journal of Theology,
        20:34-38, Dec. 1976.

1832)   Zaas, Peter.   "I Corinthians 6:9ff.: Was Homo-
        sexuality Condoned in the Corinthian Church?" So-
        ciety of Biblical Literature: Papers, 17:205-12,
        1979.

ARTICLES IN LEGAL JOURNALS

1833) Bader, Louise. "Commonwealth v. Bonadio--Unconstitutionality of Pennsylvania's Deviate Sexual Intercourse Statute," Duquesne Law Review, 19:793-800, 1980-81.

1834) Barnhart, Debra M. "Commonwealth v. Bonadio: Voluntary Deviate Sexual Intercourse--A Comparative Analysis," University of Pittsburgh Law Review, 43: 253-84, 1981-82.

1835) Barrett, Ellen M. "Legal Homophobia and the Christian Church," Hastings Law Journal, 30:1019-27, 1978-79.

1836) Black, W. W. "Gay Alliance Toward Equality v. Vancouver Sun (1979) (2 N R 117)," Osgoode Hall Law Journal, 17:649-75, 1979.

1837) Blackburn, Catherine E. "Human Rights in an International Context: Recognizing the Right of Intimate Association," Ohio State Law Journal, 43:143-63, 1982.

1838) Blackford, Barbara. "Good Moral Character and Homosexuality," Journal of the Legal Profession, 5:139-49, 1980.

1839) Blair, Jerry D. "Sex Offender Registration for [Section] 647 Disorderly Conduct Convictions Is Cruel and Unusual Punishment," San Diego Law Review, 13:391-409, 1975-76.

1840) Bogatin, Marc. "Immigration and Nationality Act and the Exclusion of Homosexuals: Boutilier v. I. N. S. Revisited," Cardoza Law Review, 2:359-96, 1981.

162

1841)   Boggan, E. Carrington. "Securing Gay Rights
        Through Constitutional Litigation," New York Uni-
        versity Review of Law and Social Change, 8:309-10,
        1978-79.

1842)   Brant, Jonathan. "Bezio v. Patenaude: The 'Coming
        Out' Custody Controversy of Lesbian Mothers," New
        England Law Review, 16:331-65, 1980-81.

1843)   Browell, Douglas K. "M.T. v. J.T.: An Enlightened
        Perspective on Transsexualism," Capital University
        Law Review, 6:403-27, 1977.

1844)   Brownstone, Harvey. "The Homosexual Parent in
        Custody Disputes," Queen's Law Journal, 5:199-240,
        1979-80.

1845)   "Burton v. Cascade School District Union High School:
        Re-instatement as a Remedy in Section 1983 Actions,"
        Brigham Young University Law Review, 1976:531-48.

1846)   Camazine, Alisse C. "Gay Lib v. University of
        Missouri," St. Louis University Law Journal. 22:711-
        20, 1978-79.

1847)   Campbell, Rose W. "Child Custody When One
        Parent Is a Homosexual," Judges' Journal, 17:38-
        41 and 51-52, Spring 1978.

1848)   Canepa, Theresa J. "Aftermath of Saal v. Midden-
        dorf: Does Homosexuality Preclude Military Fit-
        ness?" Santa Clara Law Review, 22:491-511, 1982.

1849)   Cardwell, Gary L. "Doe v. Doe: Destroying the
        Presumption that Homosexual Parents Are Unfit--
        The New Burden of Proof," University of Richmond
        Law Review. 16:851-66, 1981-82.

1850)   Clark, Penny M. "Homosexual Public Employee:
        Utilizing Section 1983 to Remedy Discrimination,"
        Hastings Constitutional Law Quarterly, 8:255-311,
        1980-81.

1851)   Cohn, Steven F., and James E. Gallagher. "Crime
        and the Creation of Criminal Law [The Decriminaliza-
        tion of Homosexuality in Maine]," British Journal of
        Law and Society, 4:220-36, 1977.

1852)   Cole, Wayne S.   "Transsexuals in Search of Legal
         Acceptance: The Constitutionality of the Chromosome
         Test," San Diego Law Review, 15:331-55, 1978.

1853)   Coleman, Thomas F.   "Procedure and Strategy in
         Gay Rights Litigation," New York University Review
         of Law and Social Change, 8:317-23, 1978-79.

1854)   Connelly, A. M.   "A Note on 7215/75 X v. United
         Kingdom: Report of the European Commission of
         Human Rights, 12 October 1978," Human Rights
         Review, 5:202-04, 1980.

1855)   "Constitutional Protection of Private Sexual Conduct
         Among Consenting Adults: Another Look at the
         Sodomy Statutes," Iowa Law Review, 62:568-90,
         1976-77.

1856)   Cooney, Leslie L.   "Doe v. Commonwealth's At-
         torney [Supreme Court's Summary Affirmance of
         Virginia's Sodomy Statute]," Duquesne Law Review,
         15:123-32, 1976-77.

1857)   Craft, Laura R., and Matthew A. Hodel.   "City
         of Chicago v. Wilson and Constitutional Protection
         for Personal Appearance: Cross-Dressing as an
         Element of Sexual Identity," Hastings Law Journal,
         30:1151-81, 1978-79.

1858)   Cullem, Catherine M.   "Fundamental Interests and
         the Question of Same-sex Marriage," Tulsa Law
         Journal, 15:141-63, 1979-80.

1859)   Deiter, Lawrence R.   "Employment Discrimination
         in the Armed Services--An Analysis of Recent
         Decisions Affecting Sexual Preference Discrimination
         in the Military," Villanova Law Review, 27:351-73,
         1981-82.

1860)   Dressler, Joshua.   "Gay Teachers: A Disesteemed
         Minority in an Overly Esteemed Profession," Rut-
         gers Camden Law Journal, 9:399-445, 1977-78.

1861)   _____.   "Judicial Homophobia: Gay Rights' Biggest
         Roadblock," Civil Liberties Review, 5:19-27, Jan. -
         Feb. 1979.

1862)   Duban, Patricia D.   "Matlovich v. Secretary of the
        Air Force [Military Discharge]," Duquesne Law Re-
        view, 18:150-60, 1979-80.

1863)   "Dudgeon v. United Kingdom 7525/76, Report, Mar.
        13, 1980, European Commission of Human Rights,"
        Human Rights Review, 6:69-70, 1981.

1864)   Dunlap, Mary C.   "The Constitutional Rights of
        Sexual Minorities: A Crisis of the Male/Female
        Dichotomy," Hastings Law Journal, 30:1131-49,
        1978-79.

1865)   Elliott, Chris. "Gay Lib. v. University of Missouri:
        1st Amendment Rights in the School Environment,"
        University of Missouri at Kansas City Law Review,
        46:489-506, 1978.

1866)   Evans, Marie W. "M.J.P. v. J.G.P.: An Analysis
        of the Relevance of Parental Homosexuality in Child
        Custody Determination," Oklahoma Law Review, 35:
        633-58, 1982.

1867)   Friedman, Joel W.   "Constitutional and Statutory
        Challenges to Discrimination in Employment Based on
        Sexual Orientation," Iowa Law Review, 64:527-72,
        1978-79.

1868)   "The Gaylord Case--Dismissal of a Homosexual
        Teacher," Journal of Family Law, 16:129-34, 1977.

1869)   Goodman, Ellen. "Homosexuality of a Parent: A
        New Issue in Custody Disputes," Monash Law Re-
        view, 5:305-15, 1978-79.

1870)   Goreham, Richard A. "Human Rights Code of
        British Columbia ... Discrimination Against Homo-
        sexuals," Canadian Bar Review, 59:165-79, 1981.

1871)   Hansen, Kent A. "Gaylord v. Tacoma School District
        No. 10: Homosexuality Held Immoral for Purposes
        of Teacher Discharge," Willamette Law Journal, 14:
        101-14, 1977-78.

1872)   Harkavy, Jeffrey M. "Defending of Accused Homo-
        sexuals: Will Society Accept Their Use of the Bat-
        tered Wife Defense?" Glendale Law Review, 4:208-
        32, 1979-80.

1873)   Harry, Joseph.   "Derivative Deviance: The Cases
         of Extortion, Fag-bashing, and Shakedown of Gay
         Men, " Criminology, 19:546-64, 1981-82.

1874)   Heilman, John.   "Constitutionality of Discharging Ho-
         mosexual Military Personnel, " Columbia Human Rights
         Law Review, 12:191-204, 1980-81.

1875)   Hindes, Thomas L.   "Morality Enforcement Through
         the Criminal Law and the Modern Doctrine of Sub-
         stantive Due Process, " University of Pennsylvania
         Law Review, 126:344-84, 1977.

1876)   Hitchens, Donna, and Barbara Price.   "Trial Strate-
         gy in Lesbian Mother Custody Cases: The Use of
         Expert Testimony, " Golden Gate University Law Re-
         view, 9:451-79, 1978-79.

1877)   Hoffman, Stephen C.   "Analysis of Rationales in Ho-
         mosexual Public Employment Cases, " South Dakota
         Law Review, 23:338-57, 1978.

1878)   "Homosexuals' Right to Marry: A Constitutional Test
         and a Legislative Solution, " University of Pennsylvania
         Law Review, 128:198-216, 1979-80.

1879)   Howarth, Joan W.   "Rights of Gay Prisoners: A
         Challenge to Protective Custody, " Southern California
         Law Review, 53:1225-76, 1980.

1880)   Hunter, Nan D. , and Nancy D. Polikoff.   "Custody
         Rights of Lesbian Mothers: Legal Theory and Liti-
         gation Strategy, " Buffalo Law Review, 25:691-733,
         1976.

1881)   "Immigration and Naturalization: 'Good Moral
         Character' Requirement Is a Question of Federal
         Law [Nemetz v. INS 647 F. 2d 432], " Suffolk Trans-
         national Law Journal, 1982:383-94.

1882)   Johnson, Lee A.   "Gay Law Students Association
         v. Pacific Telephone and Telegraph Co. ... Dis-
         crimination Against Homosexuals by Public Utilities, "
         California Law Review, 68:680-715, 1980.

1883)   Katz , Katheryn D.   "Sexual Morality and the Con-
         stitution: People v. Onofre, " Albany Law Review,
         46: 311-62, 1982.

1884)   Katzer, Peggy R.   "Civil Rights--Title VII and
        Section 1985(3)--Discrimination Against Homosexuals,"
        Wayne Law Review, 26:1611-23, 1980.

1885)   Knutson, Donald, and others.   "Representing the Un-
        popular Client ... Gays," Law Library Journal, 72:
        674-89 at 677-79, 1979.

1886)   Knutson, Kirbie.   "Dismissal of a Transsexual from
        a Tenured Teaching Position in a Public School,"
        Wisconsin Law Review, 1976:670-89.

1887)   Kopyto, Harry.   "Gay Alliance [Gay Alliance Toward
        Equality v. Vancouver Sun] Case Reconsidered," Os-
        goode Hall Law Journal, 18:639-52, 1980-81.

1888)   Lasson, Kenneth.   "Homosexual Rights: The Law in
        Flux and Conflict," University of Baltimore Law Re-
        view, 9:47-74, 1979-80.

1889)   Lavine, Karen S.   "Free Speech Rights of Homosexual
        Teachers," Columbia Law Review, 80:1513-34, 1980.

1890)   Leggett, Walter E., Jr.   "In Re Brodie--Court
        Rules Alien Cannot Be Denied Citizenship Solely on
        Basis of His Homosexuality," Georgia Journal of
        International and Comparative Law, 6:333-38, 1976.

1891)   Leitch, Patricia.   "Custody: Lesbian Mothers in the
        Courts," Gonzaga Law Review, 16:147-70, 1980-81.

1892)   Levine, Ellen.   "Legal Rights of Homosexuals in
        Public Employment," Annual Survey of American
        Law, 1978:455-91.

1893)   Levine, Lawrence C.   "Pryor v. Municipal Court:
        California's Narrowing Definition of Solicitation for
        Public Lewd Conduct," Hastings Law Journal, 32:
        461-98, 1980-81.

1894)   Levy, Martin R., and C. Thomas Hectus.   "Privacy
        Revisited: The Downfall of Griswold," University
        of Richmond Law Review, 12:627-46, 1977-78.

1895)   Lodge, Thomas E.   "... Homosexual Solicitation and
        the Fighting Words Doctrine," Case Western Reserve
        Law Review, 30:461-93, 1980.

1896)   Lowe, John H.   "Homosexual Teacher Dismissal
         [The Gaylord Case]: A Deviant Decision," Washing-
         ton Law Review, 53:499-510, 1977-78.

1897)   Lynch, A. C. E.   "Counselling and Assisting Ho-
         mosexuals," Criminal Law Review, 1979:630-44.

1898)   McLeod, Richard E.   "Denial of Recognition to Ho-
         mosexual Group [Gay Lib v. University of Missouri]
         Abridges Freedom of Association," Missouri Law
         Review, 43:109-15, 1978.

1899)   Morris, Katrina K.   "Gay Students Association v.
         Pacific Telephone and Telegraph Company," Santa
         Clara Law Review, 20:263-67, 1980.

1900)   Mullins, Charles E.   "Fricke v. Lynch [Preventing
         Male Student from Bringing Male Date to High
         School Prom]," Journal of Family Law, 19:541-44,
         1980-81.

1901)   Myers, John E. B.   "Singer v. U. S. Civil Service
         Commission: Dismissal of Government Employee
         for Advocacy of Homosexuality," Utah Law Review,
         1976:172-85.

1902)   O'Leary, Jean, and Bruce Voeller.   "Gay Rights
         Law: Confusion En Route to Equality," Juris Doc-
         tor, 8:36-42, Jun.-Jul. 1978.

1903)   Olt, Schyler J.   "M. P. v. S. P.: Mother's Homo-
         sexuality ... Held Not Proper Grounds for Removal
         of Custody," Journal of Family Law, 18:629-32,
         1979-80.

1904)   O'Neill, Tim.   "Doe v. Commonwealth's Attorney:
         A Set-back for the Right of Privacy," Kentucky Law
         Journal, 65:748-63, 1976-77.

1905)   Orbach, William.   "Homosexuality and Jewish Law,"
         Journal of Family Law, 14:353-81, 1976.

1906)   Palais, Douglas M.   "Recent Trends in Criminal
         Law ... Sexual Privacy," Journal of Criminal Law
         and Criminology, 68:70-82, 1977.

1907)   Payne, Anne T.   "Law and the Problem Parent:
         Custody and Parental Rights of Homosexual,

Mentally Ill, Mentally Retarded, and Incarcerated
Parents," Journal of Family Law, 16:797-818, 1978.

1908)   Pearldaughter, Andra.   "Employment Discrimination
        Against Lesbians: Municipal Ordinance and Other
        Remedies," Golden Gate University Law Review, 8:
        537-58, 1977-79.

1909)   Perry, Michael J.   "Substantive Due Process Re-
        visited: Reflections on (and Beyond) Recent Cases,"
        Northwestern University Law Review, 71:417-69,
        1976.

1910)   "Remedial Balancing Decisions and the Rights of Ho-
        mosexual Teachers: A Pyrrhic Victory," Iowa Law
        Review, 60:1080-98, 1975-76.

1911)   Richards, David A. J.   "Homosexuality and the Con-
        stitutional Right to Privacy," New York University
        Review of Law and Social Change, 8:311-16, 1978-
        79.

1912)   _____.   "Sexual Autonomy and the Constitutional
        Right to Privacy: A Case Study in Human Rights
        and the Unwritten Constitution," Hastings Law Jour-
        nal, 30:957-1018, 1978-79.

1913)   _____.   "Unnatural Acts and the Constitutional
        Right to Privacy: A Moral Theory," Fordham Law
        Review, 45:1281-1348, 1976-77.

1914)   Richstone, Jeff, and J. Stuart Russell.   "Shutting
        the Gate: Gay Civil Rights in the Supreme Court
        of Canada," McGill Law Journal, 27:92-117, 1981-82.

1915)   Ritter, George P.   "Property Rights of a Same-sex
        Couple: The Outlook after Marvin," Loyola Univer-
        sity (Los Angeles) Law Review, 12:409-23, 1978-79.

1916)   Rivera, Rhonda R.   "Our Straight-Laced Judges:
        The Legal Position of Homosexual Persons in the
        United States," Hastings Law Journal, 30:799-955,
        1978-79.

1917)   _____.   "Recent Developments in Sexual Preference
        Law," Drake Law Review, 30:311-46, 1980-81.

1918)   Rizzo, James J.   "The Constitutionality of Sodomy
         Statutes," Fordham Law Review, 45:553-95, 1976-77.

1919)   Roberts, Leslie J.   "Private Homosexual Activity
         and Fitness to Practice Law: Florida Board of Bar
         Examiners in re N. R. S. " Nova Law Journal, 6:519-
         34, 1981-82.

1920)   Roberts, Maurice A.   "Sex and the Immigration
         Laws," San Diego Law Review, 14:9-41, 1976-77.

1921)   Rosen, Steven A.   "Police Harassment of Homo-
         sexual Women and Men in New York City 1960-80,"
         Columbia Human Rights Law Review, 12:159-90,
         1980-81.

1922)   Rubenstein, R. A., and P. B. Fry.   "Of a Homo-
         sexual Teacher: Beneath the Mainstream of Con-
         stitutional Equalities," Texas Southern University
         Law Review, 1981:183-275.

1923)   Scholz, Jeanne L.   "Out of the Closet, Out of a
         Job: Due Process in Teacher Disqualification,"
         Hastings Constitutional Law Quarterly, 6:663-717,
         1978-79.

1924)   Seidenberg, Faith.   "Military Justice Is to Jus-
         tice ... ," Criminal Law Bulletin, 17:45-59, 1981.

1925)   Shaffer, John S., Jr.   "The Boundaries of a
         Church's First Amendment Rights as an Employer,"
         Case Western Reserve Law Review, 31:363-85,
         1981.

1926)   Sherman, Jeffrey G.   "Undue Influence and the Ho-
         mosexual Testator," University of Pittsburgh Law
         Review, 42:225-67, 1981.

1927)   Siniscalco, Gary R.   "Homosexual Discrimination
         in Employment," Santa Clara Law Review, 16:495-
         512, 1976.

1928)   "State Statute Prohibiting Private Consensual Sodomy
         Is Constitutional," Brigham Young University Law
         Review, 1977:170-88.

1929)   Taber, Carleton H. A.   "Consent, Not Morality,
         as the Proper Limitation on Sexual Privacy,"

Hastings Constitutional Law Quarterly, 4:631-64, 1977.

1930) Tayrien, Mary L. "California's 'Consenting Adults' Law: The Sex Act in Perspective," San Diego Law Review, 13:439-53, 1976

1931) Tewksbury, Michael D. "Gaylord and Singer: Washington's Place in the Stream of Emerging Law Concerning Homosexuals," Gonzaga Law Review, 14:167-96, 1978-79.

1932) Veitch, Edward. "Essence of Marriage--A Comment on the Homosexual Challenge," Anglo-American Law Review, 5:41-49, 1976.

1933) Von Beitel, Randy. "Criminalization of Private Homosexual Acts: A Jurisprudential Case Study of a Decision by the Texas Bar Penal Code Revision Committee," Human Rights, 6:23-73, 1976-77.

1934) Walmsley, Roy. "Indecency Between Males and the Sexual Offences Act of 1967," Criminal Law Review, 1978:400-07.

1935) Wein, Stuart A. , and Cynthia L. Remmers. "Employment Protection and Gender Dysphoria: Legal Definitions of Unequal Treatment on the Basis of Sex and Disability," Hastings Law Journal, 30:1075-1129, 1978-79.

1936) Wilkinson, J. Harvie, III and G. Edward White. "Constitutional Protection for Personal Lifestyles," Cornell Law Review, 62:563-625 at 587-600, 1976-77.

1937) Williams, Mark A. "Homosexuality and the Good Moral Character Requirement," University of Detroit Journal of Urban Law, 56:123-39, 1978-79.

1938) Wilson, Lawrence A. and Raphael Shannon. "Homosexual Organizations and the Right of Association," Hastings Law Journal, 30:1029-74, 1978-79.

1939) Wise, Donna L. "Challenging Sexual Preference Discrimination in Private Employment," Ohio State Law Journal, 41:501-31, 1980.

1940)   Wolff, Bennett.   "Expanding the Right of Sexual
         Privacy [People v. Onofre]," Loyola Law Review,
         27:1279-1300, 1981.

COURT CASES INVOLVING CONSENTING ADULTS

1941)   Adams v. Howerton.   486 F. Supp. 1119 (Cal.,
1980).   Affirmed 673 F. 2d 1036 (9th Cir., 1982).
Certiorari denied 102 S. Ct. 3494 (1982).   Refusal
to recognize marriage of two males and deportation
of gay male alien "married" to American male citizen upheld.

1942)   Adult Anonymous, In the Matter of.   435 N.Y.S. 2d
527 (N.Y., 1981).   Adoption of adult homosexual by
his adult homosexual partner granted.

1943)   Adult Anonymous II, In re.   452 N.Y.S. 2d 198
(N.Y., 1982).   Adoption of adult homosexual by his
adult homosexual partner granted.

1944)   Alaska Gay Coalition v. Sullivan.   578 P. 2d 951
(Alas., 1978).   Access of gay group to public
forum granted.

1945)   Ashton v. Civiletti.   613 F. 2d 923 (D.C. Cir.,
1979).   Summary dismissal of homosexual federal
employee overruled.

1946)   Aumiller v. University of Delaware.   434 F. Supp.
1273 (Del., 1977).   Dismissed homosexual professor
ordered reinstated with back pay and damages.

1947)   Baker v. Wade.   553 F. Supp. 1121 (Tex., 1982).
State's statute prohibiting homosexual conduct held
unconstitutional.   (On appeal)

1948)   Bateman, State v. 547 P. 2d 6 (Ariz., 1976).
Certiorari denied 429 U.S. 864 (1976).   State's
statute prohibiting private, consensual, adult, homosexual acts held constitutional.

1949)   benShalom v. Secretary of the Army.   489 F.
        Supp. 964 (Wis. , 1980).   Lesbian ordered reinstated
        in United States Army Reserves.

1950)   Berg v. Claytor.   436 F. Supp. 76 (D. C. , 1977).
        Vacated and remanded 591 F. 2d 849 (D. C. Cir. ,
        1981).   Discharge of homosexual Navy officer over-
        ruled.

1951)   Bezio v. Patenaude.   410 N. E.   2d 1207 (Mass. ,
        1980).   Remand to determine whether lesbian mother
        or child's guardian should have custody.

1952)   Big Brothers, Inc. v. Minneapolis Commission on
        Civil Rights.   284 N. W. 3d 823 (Minn. , 1979).   In-
        quiring into the sexual orientation of a candidate
        for Big Brothers and passing that information on to
        others held not a prohibited discrimination.

1953)   Board of Bar Examiners v. Eimers.   358 So. 2d 7
        (Fla. , 1978).   Admission of homosexual lawyer to
        State Bar ordered.

1954)   Board of Education of Long Beach Unified School
        District v. Millette.   133 Cal. Rptr. 275 (1976).
        Vacated 566 P. 2d 602 (Cal. , 1977) sub nom.
        Board of Education v. Jack M.   A sex offense held
        not per se to be evidence of unfitness to teach.
        Homosexual teacher ordered reinstated with back
        pay.

1955)   Bonadio, Commonwealth v.   415 A 2d 47 (Pa. , 1980).
        State's statute prohibiting voluntary deviate sexual
        intercourse held unconstitutional.

1956)   Bramlett v. Selman.   597 S. W. 2d 80 (Ark. , 1980).
        Constructive trust between homosexual male and his
        deceased lover held valid.

1957)   Chicago v. Wilson.   389 N. E. 3s 522 (Ill. , 1978).
        State's statute forbidding appearing in public dressed
        as a member of the opposite sex held unconstitutional
        when applied to transsexuals.

1958)   Childers v. Dallas Police Department.   513 F. Supp.
        134 (Tex. , 1981).   Refusal to hire open homosexual
        upheld.

1959) Ciufinni, State v. 164 N. J. 145, Superior Court
(N. J. , Dec. 6, 1978). State's sodomy statute held
unconstitutional when applied to consensual, adult
acts performed in private.

1960) Clark, People v. 241 N. W. 2d 756 (Mich. , 1976).
State's gross indecency statute held constitutional.

1961) Cooper v. Commonwealth. 550 S. W. 2d 478 (Ky. ,
1977). Conviction for adult sodomy upheld.

1962) Cyr v. Walls. 439 F. Supp. 697 (Tex. , 1977).
Right of gay persons and groups to file suit against
police for alleged violation of their constitutional
rights upheld and police ordered to cease surveillance
and harassment of gays.

1963) Department of Education v. Lewis. 416 So. 2d 455
(Fla. , 1982). State's statute denying funds to any
college recognizing or assisting any group recom-
mending or advocating sexual relations between persons not married to one another held unconstitutional.

1964) DeSantis v. Pacific Telephone and Telegraph Co. 608
F. 2d 327 (9th Cir. , 1979). Dismissal of homosexual
employee found not a violation of the Civil Rights Act
of 1964.

1965) DeStefano v. DeStefano. 401 N. Y. S. 2d 636 (N. Y. ,
1978). Denial of child custody to lesbian mother
upheld.

1966) Doe v. Commonwealth's Attorney. 403 F. Supp.
1199 (Va. , 1975). Affirmed 425 U. S. 901 (1976).
Rehearing denied 425 U. S. 985 (1976). State's
sodomy statute held constitutional.

1967) Doe v. Doe. 284 S. E. 2d 799 (Va. , 1981). Lesbian mother's refusal to permit adoption of her child
upheld.

1968) Doe v. McConn. 489 F. Supp. 76 (Tex. , 1980).
State's statute forbidding cross-dressing held unconstitutional when applied to a transsexual.

1969) Elliott, State v. 551 P. 2d 1352 (N. Mex. , 1976).
State's sodomy statute held constitutional.

1970)   Ferguson, Commonwealth v.   422 N. E. 2d 1365
          (Mass. , 1981).   State's unnatural acts statute held
          not applicable to consensual, private, adult sexual
          conduct.

1971)   Florida Board of Bar Examiners, In re.   358 So.
          2d 7 (Fla. , 1978).   Admission of homosexual lawyer
          to the State Bar upheld.

1972)   Florida Board of Bar Examiners re N.R.S.   403 So.
          2d 1315 (Fla. , 1981).   Admission of homosexual
          lawyer to State Bar granted.

1973)   Fricke v. Lynch.   491 F. Supp.   381 (R. I. , 1980),
          Vacated and remanded 627 F. 2d 1088 (1st Cir. ,
          1981).   Male student permitted to take his male date
          to high school prom.

1974)   Garcia-Jaramillo v. Immigration and Naturalization
          Service.   604 F. 2d 1236 (9th Cir. , 1979).   Cer-
          tiorari denied 449 U. S. 828 (1980).   Deportation of
          homosexual male alien married to a woman upheld.

1975)   Gay Activists Alliance v. Board of Regents of Uni-
          versity of Oklahoma.   638 P. 2d 1116 (Okla. , 1981).
          Right of gay student group to be recognized as an
          official campus organization.

1976)   Gay Activists Alliance v. Washington Metropolitan
          Area Transit Authority.   48 U. S. Law Week 2053
          (D. C. , 1979).   Access to a public forum for gay
          rights advertisement upheld.

1977)   Gay Alliance of Students v. Matthews.   544 F. 2d
          162 (4th Cir. , 1976).   Right of gay student group
          to be recognized as an official campus organization.

1978)   Gay Law Students' Association v. Pacific Telephone
          and Telegraph Co.   595 P. 2d 592 (Cal. , 1979).   A
          Public utility cannot discriminate against homosexuals
          in employment.

1979)   Gay Lib v. University of Missouri.   558 F. 2d 848
          (8th Cir. , 1977).   Certiorari denied sub nom.   Ratch-
          ford v. Gay Liberation 434 U. S. 1080 (1978).   Re-
          hearing denied 435 U. S. 981 (1978).   Right of gay
          student group to be recognized as an official campus
          organization.

1980)   Gay Student Services v. Texas A. and M. University.
        612 F. 2d 160 (5th Cir., 1980). Rehearing denied
        620 F. 2d 300 (5th Cir., 1980). Certiorari denied
        449 U.S. 1034 (1980). Right of gay student group
        to be recognized as an official campus organization.

1981)   Gaylord v. Tacoma School District No. 10. 559 P.
        2d 1340 (Wash., 1977). Certiorari denied 434 U.S.
        879 (1977). Dismissal of homosexual teacher up-
        held.

1982)   Gish v. Board of Education of the Borough of
        Paramus. 366 A. 2d 1337 (N.J., 1976). Certiorari
        denied 434 U.S. 879 (1977). Requirement that ho-
        mosexual teacher undergo psychiatric examination
        upheld.

1983)   Hatheway v. Secretary of the Army. 641 F. 2d
        1376 (9th Cir., 1981). Conviction for sodomy and
        discharge from the Armed Forces for homosexuality
        upheld.

1984)   Hill v. Immigration and Naturalization Service. 541
        F. Supp. 569 (Cal., 1982). Affirmed 714 F. 2d 1470
        (9th Cir., 1983). Immigration and Naturalization
        Service must obtain a Public Health Medical Cer-
        tificate (which the Public Health Service refuses to
        issue) before a self-declared homosexual can be
        excluded from the United States.

1985)   Hubert v. Williams. 184 Cal. Rptr. 161 (Cal.,
        1982). Eviction of lesbian from apartment held
        a violation of state's Unruh Act.

1986)   Jane B., In re. 380 N.Y.S. 2d 848 (N.Y., 1976).
        Child custody transferred from lesbian mother to
        divorced father.

1987)   Johnsen v. State. 332 So. 2d 69 (Fla., 1976).
        State's unnatural acts statute held constitutional.

1988)   Jones v. Daly. 176 Cal. Rptr. 130 (Cal., 1978).
        Oral cohabitation agreement between two men held
        unenforceable where it rests on the rendering of
        sexual services.

1989)   Kallas v. Kallas. 614 P. 2d 641 (Utah, 1980). Lesbian
        mother's visitation rights with her children restricted.

1990)   Kimball v. Florida Bar.   537 F. 2d 1305 (5th Cir.,
        1976).   Disbarment of homosexual lawyer for acting
        contrary to good morals upheld.

1991)   Ledenbach, People v.   132 Cal. Rptr. 643 (Cal.,
        1976).   State's statute forbidding loitering near a
        public toilet for the purpose of soliciting a lewd
        act held constitutional.

1992)   Lemons, U. S. v.   697 F. 2d 832 (8th Cir., 1983).
        Conviction of Arkansas man for consensual sodomy
        upheld.

1993)   Lesbian/Gay Freedom Day Committee v. Immigration
        and Naturalization Service.   541 F. Supp. 569 (Cal.,
        1982).   Vacated 714 F. 2d 1470 (9th Cir., 1983).   Ho-
        mosexuality held not sufficient reason to exclude gay
        alien.

1994)   Levitt, State v.   371 A. 2d 596 (R. I., 1977).   State's
        crime against nature statute held constitutional at
        least in cases of forcible acts.

1995)   Lexington Theological Seminary v. Vance.   596 S. W.
        2d 11 (Ky., 1979).   Denial of degree to homosexual
        student upheld.

1996)   Loveland v. Leslie.   583 P. 2d 664 (Wash., 1978).
        Refusal to rent apartment to two males held violation
        of state's antidiscrimination law.

1997)   Lundin v. Pacific Telephone and Telegraph Co.   608
        F. 2d 327 (9th Cir., 1979).   Dismissal of homo-
        sexual employee upheld.

1998)   M. J. P. v. J. G. P.   640 P. 2d 966 (Okla., 1982).
        Transfer of child custody from lesbian mother to
        child's father upheld.

1999)   M. P. v. S. P.   404 A. 2d 1256 (N. J., 1979).   Grant
        of child custody to lesbian mother upheld.

2000)   Macauley v. Massachusetts Commission Against Dis-
        crimination.   397 N. E. 2d 670 (Mass., 1979).   State
        Commission held to lack authority to consider claims
        of employment discrimination based on sexual pre-
        ference.

2001)   Marriage of Ashling, In the Matter of.   599 P. 2d
        475 (Ore. , 1979).   Change of joint child custody to
        custody of divorced father with restricted visitation
        rights for lesbian mother.

2002)   Martinez v. Brown.   449 F. Supp. 207 (Cal. , 1978).
        Navy ordered not to discharge sailor for homosex-
        uality.

2003)   Matlovich v. Secretary of the Air Force.   414 F.
        Supp. 690 (D. C. , 1976).   Vacated and remanded 591
        F. 2d 852 (D. C. Cir. , 1978).   Discharge of homo-
        sexual sergeant by Air Force vacated.

2004)   Mays, State v.   329 So. 2d 65 (Miss. , 1976).   Cer-
        tiorari denied 429 U. S. 864 (1976).   State's sodomy
        statute held constitutional.

2005)   McCoy, State v.   337 So. 2d 192 (La. , 1976).
        State's crime against nature statute held constitu-
        tional.

2006)   Mississippi Gay Alliance v. Goudelock.   536 F. 2d
        1073 (5th Cir. , 1976).   Certiorari denied 430 U. S.
        982 (1977).   Refusal of student newspaper to print
        Gay Alliance advertisement upheld.

2007)   National Gay Task Force v. Board of Education.
        Civil No. 80-1174-E (Okla. , Jun. 29, 1982).   State's
        statute authorizing dismissal of any teacher promoting
        homosexuality held constitutional.

2008)   Neal v. Secretary of the Navy.   472 F. Supp. 763
        (Pa. , 1979).   Reversed 639 F. 2d 1029 (3d Cir. ,
        1981).   Discharge of Marine for homosexuality up-
        held.

2009)   Newsome v. Newsome.   256 S. E. 2d 849 (N. Car. ,
        1979).   Transfer of child custody from lesbian
        mother to divorced father upheld.

2010)   Onofre, People v.   415 N. E. 2d 936 (N. Y. , 1980).
        Certiorari denied 451 U. S. 987 (1981).   State's
        statute prohibiting consensual sodomy /deviate sexual
        intercourse held unconstitutional.

2011)   Pederson v. City of Richmond.   254 S. E. 2d 95
         (Va. , 1979).   State's statute forbidding solicitation
         of sodomy held constitutional.

2012)   Penn, People v.   247 N. W. 2d 575 (Mich. , 1976).
         State's gross indecency statute held constitutional in-
         sofar as it pertains to acts in public, with minors,
         or without consent.

2013)   Petition of Horst Nemetz.   485 F. Supp. 470 (Va. ,
         1980).   Reversed sub nom. Nemitz v. Immigration
         and Naturalization Service 647 F. 2d 432 (4th Cir. ,
         1981).   Homosexuality held not grounds for denying
         an alien U. S. citizenship.

2014)   Phipps, State v.   389 N. E. 2d 1128 (Ohio, 1979).
         State's statute forbidding solicitation of a deviate
         sexual act held to apply only when injury or a breach
         of the peace is likely to result.

2015)   Preston v. Brown.   No. C-80-0994 (Cal. , 1980).
         Dispute over revocation of security clearance settled
         in favor of homosexual employee.

2016)   Pryor v. Municipal Court.   599 P. 2d 636 (Cal. ,
         1979).   Solicitation of a sex act to be performed in
         private held not illegal.

2017)   Rowland v. Mad River Local School District.   No.
         C-3-75-125 (Ohio, 1981).   Bisexual female guidance
         counselor's retention of her job upheld.

2018)   Saal v. Middendorf; Beller v. Middendorf; Miller v.
         Rumsfeld.   632 F. 2d 788 (9th Cir. , 1980).   Cer-
         tiorari denied 102 S. Ct. 304 (1981).   Rehearing
         denied 102 S. Ct. 621 (1981).   Discharge of homo-
         sexuals from the Armed Forces upheld.

2019)   Sandstrom, State v.   344 S o. 2d 554 (Fla. , 1976).
         State's statute prohibiting unnatural and lascivious
         acts held constitutional.

2020)   Scargliatti, Commonwealth v.   371 N. E. 2d 726
         (Mass. , 1977).   State's unnatural acts statute held
         not to apply to consensual, private, adult, sexual
         conduct.

2021) Schuster v. Schuster; Isaacson v. Isaacson. 585 P.
       2d 130 (Wash., 1978). Child custody retained by
       lesbian mother.

2022) Sefranka, Commonwealth v. 414 N.E. 2d 602
       (Mass., 1980). Statute prohibiting lewd persons
       in speech or behavior held to apply only to public
       solicitation or commission of conduct performed in
       public in the presence of persons offended by the
       act.

2023) Singer v. U.S. Civil Service Commission. 530 F.
       2d 247 (9th Cir., 1976). Vacated and remanded
       429 U.S. 1034 (1977). Civil Service Commission
       ordered to reconsider its dismissal of a homosexual
       federal employee. (Subsequently employee was re-
       instated.)

2024) Stewart v. U.S. 364 A. 2d 1205 (D.C., 1976).
       District's sodomy statute held constitutional.

2025) Strailey v. Happy Times Nursery School. 608 F.
       2d 327 (9th Cir., 1979). Dismissal of homosexual
       employee upheld.

2026) Student Coalition for Gay Rights v. Austin Peay
       State University. 477 F. Supp. 1267 (Tenn., 1979)
       Right of gay student group to be recognized as of-
       ficial campus organization.

2027) Toward a Gayer Bicentennial Committee v. Rhode
       Island Bicentennial Foundation. 417 F. Supp. 632
       and 642 (R.I., 1976). Denial of access to a public
       forum to a gay group upheld.

2028) Tusek, State v. 630 P. 2d 892 (Ore., 1981).
       State's statute prohibiting accosting for deviate
       purposes held unconstitutional.

2029) Uplinger, People v. 449 N.Y.S. 2d 916 (N.Y.,
       1982). State's statute proscribing loitering for
       solicitation of deviate sexual intercourse held con-
       stitutional.

2030) Van Ooteghem v. Gray. 628 F. 2d 488 (5th Cir.,
       1980). Rehearing en banc 640 F. 2d 12 (5th Cir.,
       1981). Affirmed 654 F. 2d 304 (5th Cir., 1981).

Certiorari denied 451 U. S. 935 (1981). Reinstatement of homosexual public employee dismissed for exercising his right of free speech upheld.

2031)   Walker v. First Orthodox Presbyterian Church.   No. 760-028 San Francisco Superior Court (Apr. 3, 1980). Dismissal of homosexual employee upheld.

2032)   Weekes v. Gay.   256 S. E. 2d 901 (Ga. , 1979). Fiduciary relationship between (homosexual?) couple recognized.

2033)   Williams, People v.   130 Cal. Rptr. 460 (Cal. , 1976).   Conviction for public lewd act upheld.

2034)   Woodruff v. Woodruff.   260 S. E. 2d 775 (N. Car. , 1979).   Gay father granted visitation rights.

ARTICLES IN MEDICAL AND SCIENTIFIC JOURNALS

2035)   Abel, Gene G. , and others.   "Measurement of
        Sexual Arousal in Several Paraphilias: The Effects
        of Stimulus Modality, Instructional Set, and Stimulus
        Control on the Objective," Behaviour Research and
        Therapy, 19:25-33, 1981.

2036)   Abele, Lawrence G. , and Sandra Gilchrest.   "Homo-
        sexual Rape and Sexual Selection--Acanthocephalan
        Worms," Science, 197:81, Jul. 1, 1977.

2037)   Abramson, Harold A.   "The Historical and Cultural
        Spectra of Homosexuality and Their Relationship to
        the Fear of Being a Lesbian," Journal of Asthma Re-
        search, 17:177-88, 1980.

2038)   _____ .   "Reassociation of Dreams III and IV:
        LSD Analysis ... Fear of Lesbianism," Journal of
        Asthma Research, 14:131-58 and 15:23-62, 1977.

2039)   Adams, Henry E. , and Ellie T. Sturgis.   "Status
        of Behavioral Reorientation Techniques in the Modi-
        fication of Homosexuality: A Review," Psychological
        Bulletin, 84:1171-88, 1977.

2040)   Adelman, H.   "Publicizing Pedophilia: Legal and
        Psychiatric Discourse," International Journal of Law
        and Psychiatry, 4:311-25, 1981.

2041)   Adelman, Marcy R.   "A Comparison of Profession-
        ally Employed Lesbians and Heterosexual Women on
        the MMPI," Archives of Sexual Behavior, 6:193-201,
        1977.

2042)   Allen, Donald M.   "Young Male Prostitutes: A Psy-
        chosocial Study," Archives of Sexual Behavior, 9:
        399-426, 1980.

2043)   Altshuler, Kenneth Z.   "Some Notes on an Exercise
        with Regard to Male Homosexuality," Journal of the
        American Academy of Psychoanalysis, 4:237-48,
        1976.

2044)   Atkins, Merrilee, and others.   "Brief Treatment of
        Homosexual Patients," Comprehensive Psychiatry,
        17:115-24, 1976.

2045)   Atkinson, Donald R., and others.   "Sexual Prefer-
        ence Similarity, Attitude Similarity, and Perceived
        Counselor Credibility and Attractiveness," Journal
        of Counseling Psychology, 28:504-09, 1981.

2046)   Auerbach, Stephen M., and Jack D. Edinger.   "Fac-
        tor Structure of Rorschach Prognostic Rating Scale
        and Its Relation to Therapeutic Outcome," Journal
        of Consulting and Clinical Psychology, 44:682, 1976.

2047)   Austin, T. W., and others.   "Gonorrhea in Homo-
        sexual Men," Canadian Medical Association Journal,
        119:731-32, 1978.

2048)   Awad, George A.   "Father-Son Incest: A Case Re-
        port," Journal of Nervous and Mental Disease, 162:
        135-39, 1976.

2049)   Babb, Richard R.   "Sexually Transmitted Infections
        in Homosexual Men," Post-Graduate Medicine, 65:
        215-18, Mar. 1979.

2050)   Bachman, Robert.   "Homosexuality: The Cost of
        Being Different," Canadian Nurse, 77:20-23, Feb.
        1981.

2051)   Baker, Andrea J.   "The Problem of Authority in
        Radical Movement Groups: A Case Study of Lesbian-
        Feminist Organization," Journal of Applied Behavioral
        Science, 18:323-41, 1982.

2052)   Baker, Robert W., and Mark A. Peppercorn.   "Gas-
        trointestinal Ailments of Homosexual Men," Medi-
        cine, 61:390-405, 1982.

2053)   Barr, Ron, and others.   "Autonomic Responses of
        Transsexual and Homosexual Males to Erotic Film
        Sequences," Archives of Sexual Behavior, 5:211-22,
        1976.

2054) Barrios, Billy A., and others. "Effect of Social Stigma on Interpersonal Distance [Bisexuality]," Psychological Record, 26:343-48, 1976.

2055) Bartholomew, Allen A., and others. "Homosexual Necrophilia," Medicine, Science, and Law, 18:29-35, 1978.

2056) Bass, Christopher M. "Homosexual Behavior After Vasectomy," British Medical Journal, 281:1460, 1980.

2057) Bath, Richard, and John Sketchley. "Homosexuality: Misconceptions and Problems," British Medical Journal, 283:768-69, 1981.

2058) _____, and _____. "Homosexuality: Treating Patients in General Practice," British Medical Journal, 283:827-30, 1981.

2059) Bellezza, Francis S., and Gordon H. Bower. "Person Stereotypes and Memory for People," Journal of Personality and Social Psychology, 41:856-65, 1981.

2060) Belote, Deborah, and Joan Joestling. "Demographic and Self-Report Characteristics of Lesbians," Psychological Reports, 39:621-22, 1976.

2061) Bennett, Keith C., and Norman L. Thompson. "Social and Psychological Functioning in the Aging Male Homosexual," British Journal of Psychiatry, 137: 361-70, 1980.

2062) Bernard, Larry C., and David J. Epstein. "Sex Role Conformity in Homosexual and Heterosexual Males," Journal of Personality Assessment, 42: 505-11, 1978.

2063) Bieber, Irving. "A Discussion of Homosexuality: The Ethical Challenge," Journal of Consulting and Clinical Psychology, 44:163-66, 1976.

2064) _____. "Psychodynamics and Sexual Object Choice: I. A Reply to Dr. Richard C. Friedman's Paper," Contemporary Psychoanalysis, 12:366-69, 1976.

2065) _____. "Sexuality: 1956-1976," Journal of the American Academy of Psychoanalysis, 5:195-205, 1977.

2066)   _____, and Toby Bieber. "Male Homosexuality,"
             Canadian Journal of Psychiatry, 24:409-21, 1979.

2067)   Bierer, Joshua. " 'A Generation of Homosexuals'--
             An Unusual Case of Anorexia Nervosa," International
             Journal of Social Psychiatry, 26:153-57, 1980.

2068)   Bleeker, A. N. S., and others. "Prevalence of
             Syphilis and Hepatitis B Among Homosexual Men in
             Two Saunas in Amsterdam," British Journal of
             Venereal Diseases, 57:196-99, 1981.

2069)   Bloch, Dorothy. "The Threat of Infanticide and Ho-
             mosexual Identity," Psychoanalytic Review, 62:579-
             600, 1976.

2070)   Blumstein, Philip W., and Pepper Schwartz. "Bi-
             sexuality in Women," Archives of Sexual Behavior,
             5:171-81, 1976.

2071)   Bobys, Richard S., and Mary R. Laner. "On the
             Stability of Stigmatization: The Case of Ex-
             homosexual Males," Archives of Sexual Behavior, 8:
             247-61, 1979.

2072)   Bolan, Robert K., and others. "Hepatitis B and
             Sexual Practices," Annals of Internal Medicine,
             96:678, 1982.

2073)   _____. "Sexual Transmission of Hepatitis A in
             Homosexual Men," New England Journal of Medicine,
             303:282-83, 1980.

2074)   Borkovic, Steven P., and Robert A. Schwartz. "Ka-
             posi's Sarcoma Presenting in the Homosexual Man--
             A New and Striking Phenomenon," Arizona Medicine,
             38:902-04, 1981.

2075)   Bowie, William R., and others. "Etiologies of Post-
             gonococcal Urethritis in Homosexual and Heterosexual
             Men: Roles of Chlamydia Trachomatis and Urea-
             plasma Urealyticum," Sexually Transmitted Diseases,
             5:151-54, 1978.

2076)   Bozett, Frederick W. "Gay Fathers: Evolution of
             the Gay-Father Identity," American Journal of Ortho-
             psychiatry, 51:536-44, 1981.

2077)   Brass, Alister.   "His Terrible Bright Sword,"
         British Journal of Hospital Medicine, 27:662, 1982.

2078)   _____.   "Hunting Season in America [Against
         Homosexuals]," British Journal of Hospital Medicine,
         20:86, 1978.

2079)   Brennan, Robert O., and David T. Durack.   "Gay
         Compromise Syndrome," Lancet, 2:1338-39, 1981.

2080)   British Cooperative Clinical Group.   "Homosexuality
         and Venereal Disease in the United Kingdom: A
         Second Study," British Journal of Venereal Diseases,
         56:6-11, 1980.

2081)   Brossart, Jeanne.   "The Gay Patient: What You
         Should Be Doing," RN, 42:50-52, Apr. 1979.

2082)   Brown, Lawrence. J.   "Paranoid Schizophrenia and
         Homosexuality: A Case Study," Bulletin of the
         Menninger Clinic, 46:414-28, 1982.

2083)   Brown, Richard K., and others.   "Pulmonary Fea-
         tures of Kaposi Sarcoma," American Journal of
         Roentgenology, 139:659-60, 1982.

2084)   Buhrich, N., and N. McConaghy.   "Bisexual Feelings
         and Opposite-sex Behavior in Male Malaysian Medical
         Students," Archives of Sexual Behavior, 11:387-93,
         1982.

2085)   _____, and _____.   "Parental Relationships
         During Childhood in Homosexuality, Transvestism,
         and Transsexualism," Australian and New Zealand
         Journal of Psychiatry, 12:103-08, 1978.

2086)   _____, and _____.   "Tests of Gender Feelings
         and Behavior in Homosexuality, Transvestism, and
         Transsexualism," Journal of Clinical Psychology, 35:
         187-91, 1979.

2087)   _____, and _____.   "Two Clinically Discrete
         Syndromes of Transsexualism," British Journal of
         Psychiatry, 132:73-76, 1978.

2088)   Burnham, W. R., and others.   "Entamoeba His-
         tolytica Infection in Male Homosexuals," Gut: The

British Journal of Gastroenterology, 21:1097-99, 1980.

2089)   Bygdeman, Solgun.   "Gonorrhea in Men with Ho-
        mosexual Contacts.   Serogroups of Isolated Gono-
        coccal Strains Related to Antibiotic Susceptibility,
        Site of Infection, and Symptoms," British Journal
        of Venereal Diseases, 57:320-24, 1981.

2090)   Calicchia, Christy A. , and Joseph F. Governali.
        "Attitudes Toward Homosexuality: Does Role-Playing
        Have an Impact?" Health Values, 4:176-82, Jul. -
        Aug. 1980.

2091)   Cantom-Dutari, Alejandro.   "Combined Intervention
        for Controlling Unwanted Homosexual Behavior,"
        Archives of Sexual Behavior, 5:323-25, 1976.

2092)   Cardell, Mona, and others.   "Sex-Role Identity,
        Sex-Role Behavior, and Satisfaction in Heterosexual,
        Lesbian, and Gay Male Couples," Psychology of Wom-
        en Quarterly, 5:488-94, 1981.

2093)   Carey, P. B. , and E. P. Wright.   "Campylobacter
        Jejuni in a Male Homosexual," British Journal of
        Venereal Diseases, 55:380, 1979.

2094)   Carrier, Joseph M.   "Cultural Factors Affecting
        Urban Mexican Male Homosexual Behavior," Archives
        of Sexual Behavior, 5:103-24, 1976.

2095)   _____.   "Sex-Role Preference as an Explanatory
        Variable in Homosexual Behavior," Archives of
        Sexual Behavior, 6:53-65, 1977.

2096)   Carroll, Michael P.   "Freud on Homosexuality and
        the Super-ego: Some Cross-Cultural Tests," Be-
        havior Science Research, 13:255-71, 1978.

2097)   Catterall, R. D.   "Homosexuality and Freedom of
        Speech," Journal of Medical Ethics, 6:128-29, 1980.

2098)   Caukins, Sivan E. , and Neil R. Coombs.   "The Psy-
        chodynamics of Male Prostitution," American Jour-
        nal of Psychotherapy, 30:441-51, 1976.

2099)   "CDC [Center for Disease Control] Sets Probe of
         Kaposi's in Homosexuals," Hospital Practice, 17:
         106+, May 1982.

2100)   Centers for Disease Control. "Acquired Immune
         Deficiency Syndrome (AIDS): Precautions for
         Clinical and Laboratory Staffs," Morbidity and
         Mortality Weekly Report, 31:577-80, Nov. 5, 1982.

2101)   _____. "A Cluster of Kaposi's Sarcoma and
         Pneumocystis Carinii Pneumonia Among Homosexual
         Male Residents of Los Angeles and Orange Counties,
         California," Morbidity and Mortality Weekly Report,
         31:305-07, Jun. 18, 1982.

2102)   _____. "Diffuse Undifferentiated Non-Hodgkin
         Lymphoma Among Homosexual Males--United States,"
         Morbidity and Mortality Weekly Report, 31:277-79,
         Jun. 4, 1982.

2103)   _____. "Kaposi's Sarcoma and Pneumocystis
         Pneumonia Among Homosexual Men--New York City
         and California," Morbidity and Mortality Weekly Re-
         port, 30:305-08, Jul. 3, 1981.

2104)   _____. "Persistent, Generalized Lymphadenopathy
         Among Homosexual Males," Morbidity and Mortality
         Weekly Report, 31:249-51, May 21, 1982.

2105)   Chambers, Jay L., and Mary B. Surmo. "Motiva-
         tion Concepts and Sexual Identity," Journal of Re-
         search in Personality. 10:228-36, 1976.

2106)   Chapel, Thomas A., and others. "Neisseria Men-
         ingitidis in the Anal Canal of Homosexual Men,"
         Journal of Infectious Diseases, 136:810-12, 1977.

2107)   Chevalier-Skolnikoff, Suzanne. "Homosexual Be-
         havior in a Laboratory Group of Stumptail Monkeys
         (Macaca Arctoides): Forms, Contexts, and Possible
         Social Functions," Archives of Sexual Behavior, 5:
         511-27, 1976.

2108)   "Children of Gays; Sexually Normal," Science Notes,
         113:389, Jun. 17, 1978.

2109)   Clark, Leslie F. , and Stanley B. Woll. "Stereotype
        Biases: A Reconstructive Analysis of Their Role in
        Reconstructive Memory," Journal of Personality and
        Social Psychology, 41:1064-72, 1981.

2110)   Clemmesen, Johannes. "Kaposi Sarcoma in Homo-
        sexual Men: Is It a New Disease?" Lancet, 2:51-
        52, 1982.

2111)   Climent, Carlos E. , and others. "Epidemiological
        Studies of Female Prisoners. IV: Homosexual Be-
        havior," Journal of Nervous and Mental Disease,
        164:25-29, 1977.

2112)   Clingman, Joy, and Marguerite G. Fowler. "Gender
        Roles and Human Sexuality," Journal of Personality
        Assessment, 40:276-84, 1976.

2113)   Cohen, Debra R. "Children of Homosexuals Seem
        Headed Straight," Psychology Today, 12:44+, Nov. 1978.

2114)   Coleman, Eli. "Changing Approaches to the Treat-
        ment of Homosexuality" and "Developmental Stages of
        the Coming Out Process," American Behavioral Sci-
        entist, 25:397-406 and 469-82, 1981-82.

2115)   Coleman, J. C. , and others. "Hepatitis B. Antigen
        and Antibody in a Male Homosexual Population,"
        British Journal of Venereal Diseases, 53:132-34, 1977.

2116)   Comfort, Alex. "Homosexual Practices and Immune
        Deficits," Lancet, 1:1422, 1982.

2117)   Conant, Marcus A. , and others. "Squamous Cell
        Carcinoma in Sexual Partner of Kaposi Sarcoma
        Patient," Lancet, 1:286, 1982.

2118)   Conrad, Stanley R. , and John P. Wincze. "Orgasmic
        Reconditioning: A Controlled Study of Its Effects upon
        the Sexual Arousal and Behavior of Adult Male Homo-
        sexuals," Behavior Therapy, 7:155-66, 1976.

2119)   Cooper, Harry S. , and others. "Cloacogenic Carci-
        noma of the Anorectum in Homosexual Men: An Ob-
        servation of Four Cases," Diseases of the Colon and
        Rectum, 22:557-58, 1979.

2120)   Corey, Lawrence, and King K. Holmes. "Sexual

Transmission of Hepatitis A in Homosexual Men: Incidence and Mechanism," New England Journal of Medicine, 302:435-38, 1980.

2121)   Cosgrove, I. M.   "AID for Lesbians," British Medical Journal, 2:495, 1979.

2122)   Council on Scientific Affairs.   "The Health Care Needs of a Homosexual Population," Journal of the American Medical Association, 248:736-39, 1982.

2123)   Coutinho, Elsimar M.   "Kaposi's Sarcoma and the Use of Oestrogen by Male Homosexuals," Lancet, 1:1362, 1982.

2124)   Crown, S.   "Male Homosexuality: Perversion, Deviation, or Variant?" Ciba Foundation Symposium, 62:145-64, Mar. 1978.

2125)   Crown, Sidney.   "Psychosocial Aspects of Homosexuality," Journal of Medical Ethics, 6:130-32, 1980.

2126)   Cuenot, R. G., and S. S. Fugita.   "Perceived Homosexuality: Measuring Heterosexual Attitudinal and Non-verbal Reactions," Personality and Social Psychology Bulletin, 8:100-06, 1982.

2127)   Dailey, Dennis M.   "Adjustment of Heterosexual and Homosexual Couples in Pairing Relationships: An Exploratory Study," Journal of Sex Research, 15: 143-57, 1979.

2128)   Daling, Janet R., and others.   "Correlates of Homosexual Behavior and the Incidence of Anal Cancer," Journal of the American Medical Association, 247: 1988-90, 1982.

2129)   Darkick, Larry, and Kathleen E. Grady.   "Openness Between Gay Persons and Health Professionals," Annals of Internal Medicine, 93:115-19, 1980.

2130)   Darrow, William W., and others.   "Gay Report on Sexually Transmitted Diseases," American Journal of Public Health, 71:1004-11, 1981.

2131)   Davison, Gerald C.   "Homosexuality: The Ethical Challenge," Journal of Consulting and Clinical Psychology, 44:157-62, 1976.

2132)   _____. "Not 'Can' but 'Ought': The Treatment
of Homosexuality, " Journal of Consulting and Clinical
Psychology, 46:170-72, 1978.

2133)   _____. "Politics, Ethics, and Therapy for Homosexuality, " American Behavioral Scientist, 25:423-34,
1981-82.

2134)   Deb, Subimal. "On Bisexuality: An Overview, "
Samiksa, 33:53-57, 1979.

2135)   _____. "Repressed Homosexuality and Symptom
Formation Like Paranoid Jealousy and Erotomania, "
Samiksa, 30:41-46, 1976.

2136)   DeFries, Zira. "A Comparison of Political and
Apolitical Lesbianism, " Journal of the American
Academy of Psychoanalysis, 7:57-66, 1979.

2137)   _____. "Political Lesbianism and Sexual Politics, "
Journal of the American Academy of Psychoanalysis,
6:71-78, 1978.

2138)   _____. "Pseudohomosexuality in Feminist Students, " American Journal of Psychiatry, 133:400-04,
1976.

2139)   DeMott, Benjamin. "Outsidedness Is In, " Psychology
Today, 15:80+, May 1981.

2140)   DeStefano, E. , and others. "Acid-labile Human
Leukocyte Interferon in Homosexual Men with Kaposi's
Sarcoma and Lymphadenopathy, " Journal of Infectious
Diseases, 146:451-59, 1982.

2141)   DeWys, William D. , and others. "Workshop on
Kaposi's Sarcoma: Meeting Report, " Cancer Treatment Reports, 66:1387-90, 1982.

2142)   DiBella, Geoffrey H. "Family Psychotherapy with
the Homosexual Family: A Community Psychiatry
Approach to Homosexuality, " Community Mental
Health Journal, 15:41-46, 1979.

2143)   Dietz, P. E. "Medical Criminology Note No. 5:
Male Homosexual Prostitution, " Bulletin of the
American Academy of Psychoanalysis, 6:468-71,
1978.

2144)   Dietzman, Dale E., and others. "Hepatitis B Surface
        Antigen (HBsAg) and Antibody to HBsAg. Prevalence
        in Homosexual and Heterosexual Men," Journal of the
        American Medical Association, 238:2625-26, 1977.

2145)   Dixler, Elsa. "Positive Thinking on Lesbians [Re-
        view of Four Books]," Psychology Today, 13:106-07,
        Aug. 1979.

2146)   Dixon, Katharine N., and others. "Father-Son In-
        cest: Underreported Psychiatric Problem?" Ameri-
        can Journal of Psychiatry, 135:835-38, 1978.

2147)   Doerner, Guenter, and others. "Prenatal Stress as
        Possible Aetiogenetic Factor of Homosexuality in Hu-
        man Males," Endokrinologie, 75:365-68, 1980.

2148)   Doerr, Peter, and others. "Further Studies on Sex
        Hormones in Male Homosexuals," Archives of General
        Psychiatry, 33:611-14, 1976.

2149)   Doll, Donald C., and Alan F. List. "Burkitt's
        Lymphoma in a Homosexual," Lancet, 1:1026-27,
        1982.

2150)   Donnelly, F. C. "The Doctor and the Homosexual,"
        New Zealand Medical Journal, 83:322-24, 1976.

2151)   Drew, W. Lawrence, and others. "Cytomegalovirus
        and Kaposi's Sarcoma in Young Homosexual Men,"
        Lancet, 2:125-27, 1982.

2152)   _____. "Prevalence of Cytomegalovirus Infection
        in Homosexual Men," Journal of Infectious Diseases,
        143:188-92, 1981.

2153)   Dritz, Selma K. "Medical Aspects of Homosexuality,"
        New England Journal of Medicine, 302:463-64, 1980.
        (Responses: 303:50-51, 1980.)

2154)   _____, and Erwin H. Braff. "Sexually Transmitted
        Typhoid Fever," New England Journal of Medicine,
        296:1359-60, 1977.

2155)   _____, and others. "Patterns of Sexually Trans-
        mitted Enteric Diseases in a City," Lancet, 2:3-4,
        1977.

2156)   DuBois, R. M., and others. "Primary Pneumocystis
        Carinii and Cytomegalovirus Infections," Lancet, 2:
        1339, 1981.

2157)   Dunk, A., and others. "Guillain-Barré Syndrome
        Associated with Hepatitis A in a Male Homosexual,"
        British Journal of Venereal Diseases, 58:269-70,
        1982.

2158)   Duracks, David T. "Opportunistic Infections and
        Kaposi's Sarcoma in Homosexual Men," New England
        Journal of Medicine, 305:1465-57, 1981.

2159)   Ehrhardt, Anke A., and others. "Female to Male
        Transsexuals Compared to Lesbians' Behavioral Pat-
        terns of Childhood and Adolescent Development,"
        Archives of Sexual Behavior, 8:48-90, 1979.

2160)   Eisenbud, Ruth J. "Early and Later Determinants
        of Lesbian Choice," Psychoanalytic Review, 69:85-
        109, 1982.

2161)   Ellis, W. R., and others. "Liver Disease Among
        Homosexual Males," Lancet, 1:903-05, 1979.

2162)   Enright, Michael F., and Bruce V. Parsons.
        "Training Crisis Intervention Specialists and Peer
        Group Counselors as Therapeutic Agents in a Gay
        Community," Community Mental Health Journal, 12:
        383-91, 1976.

2163)   "Epidemiologic Aspects of the Current Outbreak of
        Kaposi's Sarcoma and Opportunistic Infections," New
        England Journal of Medicine, 306:248-52, 1982.

2164)   Epstein, David M., and others. "Lung Disease in
        Homosexual Men," Radiology, 143:7-10, 1982.

2165)   Escoffier, Jeffrey, and others. "Homophobia: Ef-
        fects on Scientists," Science, 209:340, Jul. 18, 1980.

2166)   Etchegoyen, Ricardo H. "Some Thoughts on Trans-
        ference Perversion," International Journal of Psycho-
        analysis, 59:45-63, 1978.

2167)   Everaerd, Walter, and others. "Treatment of Homo-
        sexual and Heterosexual Sexual Dysfunction in Male-

only Groups of Mixed Sexual Orientation," Archives of Sexual Behavior, 11:1-10, 1982.

2168) "'Ex-Gays': Religious Abuse of Psychiatry?" American Journal of Psychiatry, 138:852-53, 1981.

2169) Fainstein, V., and others. "Disseminated Infection Due to Mycobacterium Avium-Intracellulare in a Homosexual Man with Kaposi's Sarcoma," Journal of Infectious Diseases, 145:586, 1982.

2170) Falbo, Toni, and Letitia A. Peplau. "Power Strategies in Intimate Relationships," Journal of Personality and Social Psychology, 38:618-28, 1980.

2171) Fauci, Anthony S. "The Syndrome of Kaposi's Sarcoma and Opportunistic Infections: An Epidemiologically Restricted Disorder of Immunoregulation," Annals of Internal Medicine, 96:777-79, 1982.

2172) Faur, Yvonne C., and others. "Isolation of N Meningitidis from Patients in a Gonorrhea Screening Program: A Four Year Study in New York City," American Journal of Public Health, 71:53-58, 1981.

2173) Fawaz, Karim A., and Daniel S. Matloff. "Viral Hepatitis in Homosexual Men," Gastroenterology, 81; 537-38, 1981.

2174) Felman, Yehudi M. "Approaches to Sexually Transmitted Amebiasis," Bulletin of the New York Academy of Medicine, 57:201-06, 1981.

2175) _____. "Homosexual Hazards," Practitioner, 224: 1151-56, 1980.

2176) _____, and John M. Morrison. "Examining the Homosexual Male for Sexually Transmitted Diseases," Journal of the American Medical Association, 238: 2046-47, 1977.

2177) _____, and others. "Sexually Transmitted Diseases in the Male Homosexual Community," Cutis, 30:706-20, 1982.

2178) _____, and others. "Spectinomycin in the Treatment of Anal Gonorrhea," Sexually Transmitted Diseases, 5:158-59, 1978.

2179) Ferguson, K. D. , and Deanna Finkler. "An Involvement and Overtness Measure for Lesbians: Its Development and Relation to Anxiety and Social Zeit-
geist, " Archives of Sexual Behavior, 7:211-27, 1978.

2180) Finch, Roger, and others. "Amoebic Liver Abscess, "
British Medical Journal, 283:1545-46, 1981.

2181) Finkbeiner, Walter E. , and others. "Kaposi's Sarcoma in Young Homosexual Men: A Histopathologic
Study with Particular Reference to Lymph Node Involvement, " Archives of Pathology and Laboratory
Medicine, 106:261-64, 1982.

2182) Fischer, Robert B. , and Ronald D. Nadler. "Af-
filiative, Playful, and Homosexual Interactions of
Adult Female Lowland Gorillas, " Primates, 19:657-
64, 1978.

2183) Fishbain, David A. , and Adolfo Vilasuso. "Exclusive Adult Lesbianism Associated with Turner's Syndrome Mosaicism, " Archives of Sexual Behavior, 9:
349-53, 1980.

2184) Fiumara, Nicholas J. "The Treatment of Gonococcal
Proctitis, " Journal of the American Medical Association, 239;735-39, 1978.

2185) Fluker, J. L. "Homosexuality and Sexually Transmitted Diseases, " British Journal of Hospital Medicine, 26:265-66, 269, 1981.

2186) _____. "A Ten Year Study of Homosexually Transmitted Infection, " British Journal of Venereal Diseases, 52:155-60, 1976.

2187) _____, and others. "Rectal Gonorrhea in Male
Homosexuals: Presentation and Therapy, " British
Journal of Venereal Diseases, 56:397-99, 1980.

2188) Follansbee, Stephen E. , and others. "An Outbreak
of Pneumocystis Carinii Pneumonia in Homosexual
Men, " Annals of Internal Medicine, 96:705-13, 1982.

2189) Forester, Donald. "Disease Entities in the Homosexual Population, " Annals of Emergency Medicine,
11:456, 1982.

2190)   . "Hepatitis A in Homosexual Men," Annals
        of Emergency Medicine, 10:499-500, 1981.

2191)   Foster, G. D. "Sexual Deviations," British Journal
        of Hospital Medicine, 26:434, 1981.

2192)   Fowler, Marguerite G. , and Franz R. Epting.   "The
        Person in Personality Research: An Alternate Life
        Style Case Study," Journal of Clinical Psychology,
        32:159-67, 1976.

2193)   Francioli, Patrick, and François Clement. "Beta 2-
        Microglobulin and Immunodeficiency in a Homosexual
        Man," New England Journal of Medicine, 307:1402-
        03, 1982.

2194)   Francis, Donald P. , and others.   "The Prevention
        of Hepatitis B with Vaccine: Report of the Centers
        for Disease Control Multi-center Efficacy Trial
        Among Homosexual Men," Annals of Internal Medi-
        cine, 97:362-66, 1982.

2195)   Freund, Kurt, and Ron Langevin. "Bisexuality in
        Homosexual Pedophilia," Archives of Sexual Behavior,
        5:415-23, 1976.

2196)   , and others.   "Heterosexual Interest in
        Homosexual Males," Archives of Sexual Behavior,
        4:309-18, 1976.

2197)   Friedman, Alan H. , and others.   "Cytomegalovirus
        Retinitis and Immunodeficiency in Homosexual Males,"
        Lancet, 1:958, 1982.

2198)   Friedman, Richard C.   "Psychodynamics and Sexual
        Object Choice: III.   A Re-Reply to Drs. I. Bieber
        and C. W. Socarides," Contemporary Psychoanalysis,
        12:379-85, 1976.

2199)   , and Andrew G. Frantz.   "Plasma Pro-
        lactin Levels in Male Homosexuals," Hormonal Be-
        havior, 9:19-22, Aug. 1977.

2200)   , and others.   "Fathers, Sons, and Sexual
        Orientation: Replication of a Bieber Hypothesis,"
        Psychiatric Quarterly, 52:175-89, 1980.

2201) _____, and others. "Hormones and Sexual Orientation in Men," American Journal of Psychiatry,
134:571-72, 1977.

2202) _____, and others. "Psychological Development
and Blood Levels of Sex Steroids in Male Twins of
Divergent Sexual Orientation," Journal of Nervous
and Mental Disease, 163:282-88, 1976.

2203) _____, and others. "Reassessment of Homosexuality and Transsexualism," Annual Review of Medicine,
27:57-62, 1976.

2204) _____, and Lenore O. Stern. "Juvenile Aggres-
sivity and Sissiness in Homosexual and Heterosexual
Males," Journal of the American Academy of Psychoanalysis, 8:427-40, 1980.

2205) Friedman-Kien, Alvin E. "Disseminated Kaposi's
Sarcoma Syndrome in Young Homosexual Men," Journal of the American Academy of Dermatology, 5:468-
71, 1981.

2206) _____, and others. "Disseminated Kaposi's Sarcoma in Homosexual Men," Annals of Internal Medicine, 96:693-700, 1982.

2207) Frommer, D. "Hepatitis A in Homosexual Men,"
Gastroenterology, 83:1333, 1982.

2208) Frosch, John. "The Role of Unconscious Homosexuality in the Paranoid Constellation," Psychoanalytic Quarterly, 50:587-613, 1981.

2209) Futuyma, Doug. "Is There a Gay Gene? Does It
Matter?" Science for the People, 12:10-15, Jan.-
Feb. 1980.

2210) Gadpaille, Warren J. "Cross-Species and Cross-
Cultural Contributions to Understanding Homosexual
Activity," Archives of General Psychiatry, 37:349-
56, 1980.

2211) Gamsu, Gordon, and others. "Pneumocystis Carinii
Pneumonia in Homosexual Men," American Journal
of Roentgenology, 139:647-51, 1982.

2212)   Gardiner, Richard. "Incidence of Nodular Lymphoid
        Hyperplasia in Homosexual Men," American Journal
        of Roentgenology, 138:593, 1982.

2213)   _____. "Nodular Lymphoid Hyperplasia in Ho-
        mosexual Males," Gastrointestinal Radiology, 7:291,
        1982.

2214)   Garner, Brian, and Richard W. Smith. "Are There
        Really Any Gay Athletes? An Empirical Survey,"
        Journal of Sex Research, 13:22-34, 1977.

2215)   Gartrell, Nanette. "The Lesbian as a 'Single' Wom-
        an," American Journal of Psychotherapy, 35:502-16,
        1981.

2216)   _____. "Testosterone Levels and Women's Sexual
        Preference," American Journal of Psychiatry, 135:
        1067-69, 1978.

2217)   _____, and others. "Plasma Testosterone in Ho-
        mosexual and Heterosexual Women," American Jour-
        nal of Psychiatry, 134:1117-18, 1977.

2218)   Gay, George R., and others. "Love and Haight: The
        Sensuous Hippie Revisited: Drug/Sex Practices in
        San Francisco, 1980-81," Journal of Psychoactive
        Drugs, 14:111-23, 1982.

2219)   Gelfand, M. "The Infrequency of Homosexuality in
        Traditional Shora Society," Central African Journal
        of Medicine, 25:201-02, 1979.

2220)   Geller, Joseph J., and others. "A Psychoanalytic
        View of Homosexuality," Perspectives in Psychiatric
        Care, 16:76-79, 1978.

2221)   Gershman, Harry. "Homosexual Marriages," Ameri-
        can Journal of Psychoanalysis, 41:149-59, 1981.

2222)   Gerstoft, J., and others. "Severe Acquired Immuno-
        deficiency in European Homosexual Men," British
        Medical Journal, 285:17-19, 1982.

2223)   Gilberg, Arnold L. "Psychosocial Considerations in
        Treating Homosexual Adolescents," American Jour-
        nal of Psychoanalysis, 38:355-58, 1978.

2224)   _____ . "Treatment of Young Adults with Sexual
           Maladaptation," American Journal of Psychoanalysis,
           41:45-50, 1981.

2225)   Giordano, Frank L, and Renée E. Lemieux, "Hetero-
           sexual Panic: Case Report," Military Medicine,
           146:650-51, 1981.

2226)   Glasser, Mervin. "Homosexuality and Adolescence,"
           British Journal of Medical Psychology, 50:217-25,
           1977.

2227)   Glenn, Norval D. , and Charles N. Weaver. "At-
           titudes Toward Premarital, Extramartial, and Homo-
           sexual Relations in the United States in the 1970s,"
           Journal of Sex Research, 15:108-18, 1979.

2228)   Godwin, J. David, and others. "Fatal Pneumocystis
           Pneumonia, Cryptococcosis, and Kaposi Sarcoma in
           a Homosexual Man," American Journal of Roentgenol-
           ogy, 138:580-81, 1982.

2229)   Goedert, James J. , and others. "Amyl Nitrate May
           Alter T Lymphocytes in Homosexual Men," Lancet,
           1:412-16, 1982.

2230)   Goldbaum, John. "Gay Bowel Syndrome," Medical
           Journal of Australia, 2:699, 1979.

2231)   Golden, Jeffrey. "Pneumocystis Lung Disease in
           Homosexual Men," Western Journal of Medicine,
           137:400-07, 1982.

2232)   Goldmeier, David. "Herpetic Proctitis and Sacral
           Radiculomyelopathy in Homosexual Men," British
           Medical Journal, 2:549, 1979.

2233)   _____ . "Proctitis and Herpes Simplex Virus in
           Homosexual Men," British Journal of Venereal Dis-
           eases, 56:111-14, 1980.

2234)   _____ , and S. Darougar. "Isolation of Chlamydia
           Trachomatis from Throat and Rectum of Homosexual
           Men," British Journal of Venereal Diseases, 53:184-
           85, 1977.

2235)   Gomez, Joan. "Homosexuality and Sexually Trans-
        mitted Diseases," British Journal of Hospital Medi-
        cine, 26:654, 1981.

2236)   Gonsiorek, John C. "An Introduction to Mental
        Health Issues and Homosexuality" and "Social Psy-
        chological Concepts in Understanding Homosexuality,"
        in American Behavioral Scientist, 25:367-96 and
        483-96, 1981-82.

2237)   Good, Raphael S. "The Gynecologist and the Les-
        bian," Clinical Obstetrics and Gynecology, 19:473-
        82, 1976.

2238)   Goode, Erich. "Comments on the Homosexual Role"
        and "The Homosexual Role: Rejoinder to Omark and
        Whitam," Journal of Sex Research, 17:54-65 and 76-
        83, 1981.

2239)   _____, and Lynn Haber. "Sexual Correlates of
        Homosexual Experience: An Exploratory Study of
        College Women," Journal of Sex Research, 13:12-21,
        1977.

2240)   _____, and Richard R. Troiden. "Amyl Nitrate
        Use Among Homosexual Men," American Journal of
        Psychiatry, 136:1067-69, 1979.

2241)   _____, and _____. "Correlates and Accom-
        paniments of Promiscuous Sex Among Male Homo-
        sexuals," Psychiatry, 43:51-59, 1980.

2242)   Goodyear, Rodney K., and others. "Ascription of
        Negative Traits Based on Sex Role and Sexual Ori-
        entation," Psychological Reports, 49:194, 1981.

2243)   Gorin, Isabelle, and others. "Kaposi's Sarcoma
        Without the United States, or the 'Popper' Connec-
        tion," Lancet, 1:908, 1982.

2244)   Gottlieb, Geoffrey J., and others. "A Preliminary
        Communication on Extensively Disseminated Kaposi's
        Sarcoma in Young Homosexual Men," American Jour-
        nal of Dermatopathology, 3:111-14, 1981.

2245)   Gottlieb, Michael S., and others. "Pneumocystis
        Carinii Pneumonia and Mucosal Candidiasis in Previ-

ously Healthy Homosexual Men; Evidence of a New Acquired Cellular Immunodeficiency," New England Journal of Medicine, 305:1425-31, 1981.

2246) Götz, F., and others. "Homosexual Behavior in Prenatally Stressed Male Rats After Castration and Oestrogen Treatment in Adulthood," Endokrinologie, 76:115-17, 1980.

2247) Green, Richard. "Childhood Cross-Gender Behavior and Subsequent Sexual Preference," American Journal of Psychiatry, 136:106-08, 1979.

2248) _____. "Sexual Identity of 37 Children Raised by Homosexual or Transsexual Parents," American Journal of Psychiatry, 135:692-97, 1978.

2249) Greene, Jeffrey B., and others. "Mycobacterium Avium-Intracellulare: A Cause of Disseminated Life-Threatening Infection in Homosexuals and Drug Abusers," Annals of Internal Medicine, 97:539-46, 1982.

2250) _____, and others. "Salmonella Enteritidis Genitourinary Tract Infection in a Homosexual Man," Journal of Urology, 128:1046-48, 1982.

2251) Grellert, Edward A. "Childhood Play Behavior of Homosexual and Heterosexual Men," Psychological Reports, 51:607-10, 1982.

2252) _____, and others. "Childhood Play Activities of Male and Female Homosexuals and Heterosexuals," Archives of Sexual Behavior, 11:451-78, 1982.

2253) Gross, Alan E., and others. "Disclosure of Sexual Orientation and Impressions of Male and Female Homosexuals," Personality and Social Psychology Bulletin, 6:307-14, 1980.

2254) Gross, Mary J. "Changing Attitudes Toward Homosexuality--Or Are They?" Perspectives in Psychiatric Care, 16:71-75, 1978.

2255) Groth, A. Nicholas, and H. Jean Birnbaum. "Adult Sexual Orientation and Attraction to Underage Persons," Archives of Sexual Behavior, 7:175-81, 1978.

2256)   _____, and Ann W. Burgess. "Male Rape: Offenders and Victims," American Journal of Psychiatry, 137:806-10, 1980.

2257)   Gunby, Phil. "Clinical Trial of Vaccine for Type B Hepatitis to Begin Next Month [Among Homosexual Men]," Journal of the American Medical Association, 241:979-80, 1979.

2258)   _____. "Cytomegalovirus Vaccine Work Progressing," Journal of the American Medical Association, 248:1424-25, 1982.

2259)   Gundlach, Ralph H. "Birth Order Among Lesbians: New Light on an Only Child," Psychological Reports, 40:250, 1977.

2260)   _____. "Sibship Size, Sibsex, and Homosexuality Among Females," Transnational Mental Health Research Newsletter, 19:3-7, 1977.

2261)   Gurwitz, Sharon B., and Melinda Marcus. "Effects of Anticipated Interaction, Sex, and Homosexual Stereotypes on First Impressions," Journal of Applied Social Psychology, 8:47-56, 1978.

2262)   Hadden, Samuel B. "Homosexuality: Its Questioned Classification," Psychiatric Annals, 6:165-69, 1976.

2263)   Haeberle, Erwin J. "Swastika, Pink Triangle, and Yellow Star--The Destruction of Sexology and Persecution of Homosexuals in Nazi Germany," Journal of Sex Research, 17:270-87, 1981.

2264)   Halbreich, Uriel, and others. "Day-to-day Variations in Serum Levels of Follicle-stimulating Hormone and Luteinizing Hormone in Homosexual Males," Biological Psychiatry, 13:541-49, 1978.

2265)   Halleck, Seymour L. "Another Response to 'Homosexuality: The Ethical Challenge,'" Journal of Consulting and Clinical Psychology, 44:167-70, 1976.

2266)   Hamilton-Farrell, Martin R. "Advice for the Homosexual Patient," Journal of Medical Ethics, 8:162-63, 1982.

2267)   Handsfield, H. Hunter.   "Acquired Immunodeficiency
        in Homosexual Men," American Journal of Roentgen-
        ology, 139:832-33, 1982.

2268)   _____.   "Sexually Transmitted Diseases in Homo-
        sexual Men," American Journal of Public Health, 71:
        989-90 and 72:496-97, 1981.

2269)   Hansen, Gary L.   "Androgyny, Sex-Role Orientation
        and Homosexism [Homophobia]," Journal of Psy-
        chology, 112:39-45, 1982.

2270)   _____.   "Measuring Prejudice Against Homo-
        sexuality (Homosexism) Among College Students,"
        Journal of Social Psychology, 117:233-36, 1982.

2271)   Hare, E. H. and P. A. Moran.   "Parental Age and
        Birth Order in Homosexual Patients: A Replication
        of Slater's Study," British Journal of Psychiatry,
        134:178-82, 1979.

2272)   Harris, B. S. "Lesbian Mother Child Custody: Legal
        and Psychiatric Aspects," Bulletin of the American
        Academy of Psychiatry and Law, 5:75-89, 1977.

2273)   Harry, Joseph, and William DeVall.   "Age and Sexual
        Culture Among Homosexually Oriented Males," Ar-
        chives of Sexual Behavior, 7:199-209, 1978.

2274)   Hart, Maureen, and others.   "Psychological Adjust-
        ment of Nonpatient Homosexuals: Critical Review of
        the Research Literature," Journal of Clinical Psy-
        chiatry, 39:604-08, 1978.

2275)   Haselton, P. S. and A. Curry.   "Pneumocystis
        Carinii: The Continuing Enigma," Thorax, 37:481-85,
        1982.

2276)   Hauser, William E., and others.   "Central-nervous-
        system Toxoplasmosis in Homosexual and Heterosexu-
        al Adults," New England Journal of Medicine, 307:
        498-99, 1982.

2277)   Haverkos, Harry W., and James W. Curran.   "The
        Current Outbreak of Kaposi's Sarcoma and Opportun-
        istic Infections," CA: A Cancer Journal for Clini-
        cians, 32:330-39, 1982.

2278) Haynes, Stephen N., and L. Jerome Oziel, "Homosexuality: Behaviors and Attitudes," Archives of
Sexual Behavior, 5:283-89, 1976.

2279) Headings, Verle E. "Etiology of Homosexuality,"
Southern Medical Journal, 73:1024-27+, 1980.

2280) Hedblom, Jack H., and John J. Hartman. "Research
on Lesbianism: Selected Effects of Time, Geographic
Location, and Data Collection Techniques," Archives
of Sexual Behavior, 9:217-34, 1980.

2281) Heller, Michael. "The Gay Bowel Syndrome: A
Common Problem of Homosexual Patients in the
Emergency Department," Annals of Emergency Medi-
cine, 9:487-93, 1980.

2282) Hellman, Ronald E., and others. "Childhood Sexual
Identity, Childhood Religiosity, and 'Homophobia' as
Influences in the Development of Transsexualism, Homosexuality, and Heterosexuality," Archives of General Psychiatry, 38:910-15, 1981.

2283) Hemming, Jan. "A Clue to Homosexuality? Stress
During Pregnancy," Science Digest, 88:69-70, Aug.
1980.

2284) Hencken, Joel D. "Homosexuality and Psychoanalysis," American Behavioral Scientist, 25:435-68, 1981-
82.

2285) Hendin, Herbert. "Homosexuality: The Psychosocial
Dimension," Journal of the American Academy of
Psychoanalysis, 6:479-96, 1978.

2286) Henley, Nancy M., and Fred Pincus. "Interrela-
tionship of Sexist, Racist, and Anti-Homosexual Attitudes," Psychological Reports, 42:83-90, 1978.

2287) Hentzer, Bent, and others. "Viral Hepatitis in a
Venereal Clinic Population. Relation to Certain Risk
Factors," Scandinavian Journal of Infectious Dis-
eases, 12:245-49, 1980.

2288) Herbert, W. "Homosexuality Roots: Precocious
Puberty?" Science News, 122;151, Sep. 4, 1982.

2289) Hess, Eckhard H. , and Slobodan B. Petrovich. "A
       Response to Nicholas F. Skinner's 'The Hess et al.
       Study of Pupillary Activity in Heterosexual and Homo-
       sexual Males: A Reevaluation,'" Perceptual and
       Motor Skills, 51:845-46, 1980.

2290) Hetrick, Emery S. , and A. Damien Martin. "More
       on 'Ex-Gays,'" American Journal of Psychiatry,
       138:1510-11, 1981.

2291) Higdon, John F. "Paranoia: Power Conflict or Ho-
       mosexual Projection?" Journal of Operational Psy-
       chiatry, 7:32-45, 1976.

2292) Hines, Maryjo T. "Classification of Homosexuality,"
       Journal of Family Practice, 10:742, 1980.

2293) Hinton, J. W. , and others. "Psychophysiological
       Assessment of Sex Offenders in a Security Hospital,"
       Archives of Sexual Behavior, 9:205-16, 1980.

2294) Hoeffer, Beverly. "Children's Acquisition of Sex
       Role Behavior in Lesbian-Mother Families," Ameri-
       can Journal of Orthopsychiatry, 51:536-44, 1981.

2295) _____. "Gay Motherhood--Reports by Ellen Lewin
       and Terrie A. Lyons," Science News, 116:198, Sep.
       22, 1979.

2296) _____. "Resolution on Gay Rights," Perspectives
       in Psychiatric Care, 16:113, 1978.

2297) Hoenig, J. "Sigmund Freud's Views on Sexual Dis-
       orders in Historical Perspective," British Journal
       of Psychiatry, 129:193-200, 1976.

2298) Hogan, Robert A. , and others. "The Only Child
       Factor in Homosexual Development," Psychology: A
       Quarterly Journal of Human Behavior, 17:19-33,
       1980.

2299) Holbreich, Uriel, and others. "Day-to-day Variations
       in Serum Levels of Follicle-Stimulating Hormone and
       Luteinizing Hormone in Homosexual Males," Biologi-
       cal Psychiatry, 13:541-49, 1978.

2300) Holland, Gary N., and others. "Ocular Disorders
       Associated with a New Severe Acquired Cellular
       Immunodeficiency Syndrome," American Journal of
       Ophtalmology, 93:393-402, 1982.

2301) "Homosexual Transmission of Amoebiasis," Journal
       of the Royal Society of Medicine, 75:564-65, 1982.

2302) "Homosexuality: Help for Those Who Want It--Study
       by Masters and Johnson," Science News, 115:275-76,
       Apr. 28, 1979.

2303) Hooberman, Robert E. "Psychological Androgyny,
       Feminine Gender Identity, and Self-Esteem in Homo-
       sexual and Heterosexual Males," Journal of Sex Re-
       search, 15:306-15, 1979.

2304) Horn, Jack C. "Does a Boy Have the Right to Be
       Effeminate?" Psychology Today, 12:34+, Apr. 1979.

2305) Høybye, Gerda, and others. "An Epidemic of Acute
       Viral Hepatitis in Male Homosexuals. Etiology and
       Clinical Characteristics," Scandinavian Journal of In-
       fectious Diseases, 12:241-44, 1980.

2306) Hunt, Samuel P. "Homosexuality from a Contem-
       porary Perspective," Connecticut Medicine, 42:105-
       08, 1978.

2307) Hurwitz, Alfred L, and Robert L. Owen. "Venereal
       Transmission of Intestinal Parasites," Western Jour-
       nal of Medicine, 128:89-91, 1978.

2308) Hymes, Kenneth B., and others. "Kaposi's Sarcoma
       in Homosexual Men--A Report of Eight Cases," Lan-
       cet, 2:598-600, 1981.

2309) Ibrahim, Azmy. "The Home Situation and the Homo-
       sexual," Journal of Sex Research, 12:263-82, 1976.

2310) "Immunocompromised Homosexuals," Lancet, 2:1325-
       26, 1981.

2311) Israelstam, Stephen, and others. "Use of Isobutyl
       Nitrite as a Recreational Drug," British Journal of
       Addiction, 73:319-20, 1978.

2312)   Jaffe, Leslie R. , and Joan E. Morgenthau. "Syphi-
        lis and Homosexuality in Adolescents, " Journal of
        Pediatrics, 95:1062-64, 1979.

2313)   James, Sheelah.   "Treatment of Homosexuality: II.
        Superiority of Desensitization /Arousal as Compared
        with Anticipatory Avoidance Conditioning.   Results
        of a Controlled Trial, " Behavior Therapy, 9:28-36,
        1978.

2314)   _____, and others. "Significance of Androgen
        Levels in the Aetiology and Treatment of Homosexu-
        ality, " Psychological Medicine, 7:427-29, 1977.

2315)   Janda, William M. , and others.   "Prevalence and
        Site-Pathogen Studies of Neisseria Meningitidis and
        N Gonorrhoeas in Homosexual Men, " Journal of the
        American Medical Association, 244:2060-64, 1980.

2316)   Jefferiss, F. J. G.   "Venereal Disease and the Ho-
        mosexual, " Practitioner, 217:741-45, 1976.

2317)   Jensen, Ole M. and others.   "Kaposi's Sarcoma in
        Homosexual Men: Is It a New Disease?" Lancet,
        1:1027, 1982.

2318)   Johnson, Richard, and others.   "Disseminated Kapo-
        si's Sarcoma in a Homosexual Man, " Journal of the
        American Medical Association, 247:1739-41, 1982.

2319)   Johnson, Susan R. , and others.   "Factors Influencing
        Lesbian Gynecologic Care: A Preliminary Study, "
        American Journal of Obstetrics and Gynecology, 140:
        20-28, 1981.

2320)   Jorgensen, Karl A. , and Sven O. Lawesson.   "Amyl
        Nitrate and Kaposi's Sarcoma in Homosexual Men, "
        New England Journal of Medicine, 307:893-94, 1982.

2321)   Judson, Franklyn N. , and others.   "Anogenital In-
        fection with Neisseria Meningitidis in Homosexual
        Men, " Journal of Infectious Diseases, 137:455-63,
        1978.

2322)   _____, and others. "Comparative Prevalence
        Rates of Sexually Transmitted Diseases in Hetero-
        sexual and Homosexual Men, " American Journal of
        Epidemiology, 112:836-43, 1980.

2323)   _____, and others. "Screening for Gonorrhea and Syphilis in the Gay Baths--Denver, Colorado," American Journal of Public Health, 67:740-42, 1977.

2324)   Kalcheim, Chaya, and others. "Bisexual Behavior in Male Rats Treated Neonatally with Antibodies to Luteinizing Hormone-Releasing Hormone," Journal of Comparative and Physiological Psychology, 95:36-44, 1981.

2325)   Kang, J. Y., and others. "Proctocolitis Caused by Concurrent Amoebiasis and Gonococcal Infection. The 'Gay Bowel Syndrome,'" Medical Journal of Australia, 2:496-97, 1979.

2326)   Kappelman, Murray M. "When Your Teenager Needs You Most: Learning to Talk Openly About Homosexuality," Family Health, 9:44-46, Aug. 1977.

2327)   Kaslow, Florence, and others. "Homosexual Incest," Psychiatric Quarterly, 53:184-93, 1981.

2328)   Kaufman, Arthur, and others. "Male Rape: Non-institutionalized Assault," American Journal of Psychiatry, 137:221-23, 1980.

2329)   Kaufman, J. C., and others. "Shigellosis and the Gay Bowel Syndrome: An Endoscopic Point of View and a Review of the Literature," Gastrointestinal Endoscopy, 28:250-51, 1982.

2330)   Kayal, Philip M. "Researching Behavior: Sociological Objectivity and Homosexual Analysis," Corrective and Social Psychiatry and Journal of Behavioral Technology, Methods, and Therapy, 22:25-31, 1976.

2331)   Kazal, Henry L., and others. "The Gay Bowel Syndrome: Clinico-Pathologic Correlation in 260 Cases," Annals of Clinical and Laboratory Science, 6:184-92, 1976.

2332)   Keller, David, and Edna B. Foa. "Phenothiazines Combined with Systematic Desensitization in a Psychotic Patient with Obsessions About Homosexuality," Journal of Behavior Therapy and Experimental Psychiatry, 9:265-68, 1978.

2333) Kelly, James. "The Aging Male Homosexual. Myth and Reality," Gerontologist, 17:328-32, 1977.

2334) Kenyon, Frank E. "Homosexuality in Gynaecological Practice," Clinical Obstetrics and Gynaecology, 7: 363-86, 1980.

2335) Keystone, Jay S. , and others. "Intestinal Parasitic Infections in Homosexual Men: Prevalence, Symptoms and Factors in Transmission," Canadian Medical Association Journal, 123:512-14, 1980.

2336) Kimmel, Douglas C. "Life-History Interviews of Aging Gay Men," International Journal of Aging and Human Development, 10:239-48, 1979-80.

2337) _____. "Psychotherapy and the Older Gay Man," Psychotherapy: Theory, Research, and Practice, 15:386-402, 1978.

2338) Kirkpatrick, Martha, and others. "Lesbian Mothers and Their Children: A Comparative Survey," American Journal of Orthopsychiatry, 51:545-51, 1981.

2339) Koenig, Frederick. "Dominant Parent as Projected by Homosexual and Heterosexual Males," Journal of Sex Research, 15:316-20, 1979.

2340) Kondlapoodi, P. "Anorectal Cancer and Homosexuality," Journal of the American Medical Association, 248:2114-15, 1982.

2341) Kornfield, Hardy, and others. "T-Lymphocyte Subpopulations in Homosexual Men," New England Journal of Medicine, 307:729-31, 1982.

2342) Kraemer, W. P. "Homosexuality--Is It an Illness?" Midwife, Health Visitor, and Community Nurse, 12: 147-53, May 1976.

2343) Krajeski, James. "About Homosexualism," Connecticut Medicine, 42:749, 1979.

2344) Kreutzer, Erik, and John Hansbrough. "Superimposed Traumatic and Gonococcal Proctitis," Sexually Transmitted Diseases, 6:75-76, 1979.

2345)   Krulewitz, Judith E. , and Janet E. Nash. "Effects
        of Sex Role Attitudes and Similarity on Men's Rejec-
        tion of Male Homosexuals," Journal of Personality
        and Social Psychology, 38:67-74, 1980.

2346)   Kurtz, Richard M. , and Sol L. Garfield. "Illusory
        Correlation: A Further Exploration of Chapman's
        Paradigm," Journal of Consulting and Clinical Psy-
        chology, 46:1009-15, 1978.

2347)   Kuschner, Harvey, and others. "The Homosexual
        Husband and Physician Confidentiality," Hastings
        Center Report, 7:15-17, Apr. 1977.

2348)   Kwawer, Jay S. "Male Homosexual Psychodynamics
        and the Rorschach Test," Journal of Personality As-
        sessment, 41:10-18, 1977.

2349)   _____. "Transference and Countertransference in
        Homosexuality--Changing Psychoanalytic Views,"
        American Journal of Psychotherapy, 34:72-80, 1980.

2350)   Lanahan, Colleen C. "Homosexuality: A Different
        Sexual Orientation," Nursing Forum, 15:314-19, 1976.

2351)   Langevin, Ron, and others. "The Clinical Profile
        of Male Transsexuals Living as Females vs. Those
        Living as Males," Archives of Sexual Behavior, 6:
        143-54, 1977.

2352)   _____, and others. "Personality Characteristics
        of Sexual Anomalies in Males," Canadian Journal of
        Behavioural Science, 10:222-38, 1978.

2353)   Larsen, Knud S. , and others. "Attitudes of Hetero-
        sexuals Toward Homosexuality: A Likert-Type Scale
        and Construct Validity," Journal of Sex Research,
        16:245-57, 1980.

2354)   Latimer, Paul. "A Case of Homosexuality Treated
        In Vivo Desensitization and Assertive Training,"
        Canadian Psychiatric Association Journal, 22:185-
        89, 1977.

2355)   Laurens, Richard G. , Jr. and others. "Pneumocystis
        Carinii Pneumonia in a Male Homosexual," Southern
        Medical Journal, 75:638-39, 1982.

2356)   Lawrence, John C.   "Gay Peer Counseling," Journal
        of Psychiatric Nursing, 15:33-37, Jun. 1977.

2357)   Lawrence, Susan.   "AIDS [Acquired Immune Deficien-
        cy Syndrome]--No Relief in Sight," Science News,
        122:202-03, Sept. 25, 1982.

2358)   Laws, D. R.   "Treatment of Bisexual Pedophilia by
        a Biofeedback-assisted Self-Control Procedure," Be-
        haviour Research and Therapy, 18:207-11, 1980.

2359)   Leach, R. D., and H. Ellis.   "Carcinoma of the
        Rectum in Male Homosexuals," Journal of the Royal
        Society of Medicine, 74:490-91, 1981.

2360)   Learner, J. M., and others.   "Pneumocystis Carinii
        Pneumonitis and Esophageal Moniliasis in a Previ-
        ously Unknown Homosexual Host," Journal of the
        American Osteophathic Association, 82:109-14, 1982.

2361)   Lego, Suzanne M.   "Beginning Resolution of the Oedi-
        pal Conflict in a Lesbian About to Become a 'Parent'
        to a Son," Perspectives of Psychiatric Care, 19:107-
        11, 1981.

2362)   Leitner, L. M., and Suzana Cado.   "Personal Con-
        structs and Homosexual Stress," Journal of Person-
        ality and Social Psychology, 43:869-72, 1982.

2363)   "Lesbian Couples: Should Help Extend to AID?"
        Journal of Medical Ethics, 4:91-95, 1978.

2364)   Lester, David, and others.   "Sex-Deviant Hand-
        writing, Femininity, and Homosexuality," Per-
        ceptual and Motor Skills, 45:1156, 1977.

2365)   Levine, Arthur S.   "The Epidemic of Acquired
        Immune Dysfunction in Homosexual Men and Its
        Sequelae--Opportunistic Infections, Kaposi's Sar-
        coma, and Other Malignancies: An Update and
        Interpretation," Cancer Treatment Reports, 66:
        1391-95, 1982.

2366)   Levine, Edward M.   "Male Transsexuals in the
        Homosexual Subculture," American Journal of Psy-
        chiatry, 133:1318-21, 1976.

2367)   _____, and others. "Behavioral Differences and
             Emotional Conflict Among Male-to-Female Trans-
             sexuals," Archives of Sexual Behavior, 5:81-86,
             1976.

2368)   _____, and Nathaniel Ross. "Sexual Dysfunction
             and Psychoanalysis," American Journal of Psychiatry,
             134:646-51, 1977.

2369)   Levine, Joel S., and others. "Chronic Proctitis in
             Male Homosexuals Due to Lymphogranuloma Venere-
             um," Gastroenterology, 79:563-65, 1980.

2370)   Levy, Norman J. "The Middle-aged Male Homo-
             sexual," Journal of the American Academy of Psy-
             choanalysis, 7:405-18, 1979.

2371)   Lewis, Collins E., and others. "Drinking Patterns
             in Homosexual and Heterosexual Women," Journal of
             Clinical Psychiatry, 43:277-79, 1982.

2372)   Li, Frederick P., and others. "Anorectal Squamous
             Carcinoma in Two Homosexual Men," Lancet, 2:391,
             1982.

2373)   Lim, K. S., and others. "Role of Sexual and Non-
             sexual Practices in the Transmission of Hepatitis B,"
             British Journal of Venereal Diseases, 53:190-92,
             1977.

2374)   Limentani, A. "Object Choice and Actual Bisexual-
             ity," International Journal of Psychoanalysis and Psy-
             chotherapy, 5:205-17, 1976.

2375)   _____. "The Differential Diagnosis of Homosexu-
             ality," British Journal of Medical Psychology, 50:209-
             16, 1977.

2376)   Lipsedge, Maurice S., and J. Christie Brown. "Psy-
             chopathology of Sexual Behavior," Journal of the Royal
             Society of Medicine, 71:73, 1978.

2377)   Livingstone, I. R., and others. "The Effect of
             Luteinizing Hormone Releasing Hormone (LRH) on
             Pituitary Gonadotropins in Male Homosexuals," Hor-
             mone and Metabolic Research, 10:248-49, 1978.

2378)   Lohrenz, Leander J., and others. "Alcohol Problems
        in Several Midwestern Homosexual Communities,"
        Journal of Studies on Alcohol, 39:1959-63, 1978.

2379)   Lumey, L. H., and others. "Screening for Syphilis
        Among Homosexual Men in Bars and Saunas in Am-
        sterdam," British Journal of Venereal Diseases, 58:
        402-04, 1982.

2380)   MacCulloch, Malcolm. "Biological Aspects of Homo-
        sexuality," Journal of Medical Ethics, 6:133-38,
        1980.

2381)   _____, and others. "Avoidance Latencies Reliably
        Reflect Sexual Attitude Change During Aversion Thera-
        py for Homosexuality," Behavior Therapy, 9:562-77,
        1978.

2382)   _____, and John L. Waddington. "Neuroendocrine
        Mechanisms and the Aetiology of Male and Female
        Homosexuality," British Journal of Psychiatry, 139:
        341-45, 1981.

2383)   Macek, Catherine. "Acquired Immunodeficiency Syn-
        drome Cause(s) Still Elusive," Journal of the Ameri-
        can Medical Association, 248:1423-31, 1982.

2384)   Macherski, Hazel. "Nursing Care Study: A Teenage
        Homosexual," Nursing Mirror, 147:29-32, Oct. 5,
        1978.

2385)   MacKenzie, K. Roy. "Gender Dysphoria Syndrome:
        Towards Standardized Diagnostic Criteria," Archives
        of Sexual Behavior, 7:251-62, 1978.

2386)   Maddox, Brenda. "Homosexual Parents," Psychology
        Today, 16:62-69, Feb. 1982.

2387)   Malcolm, Shirley M. "Who Are the Gay Scientists?"
        Science, 213:1100-01, Sep. 4, 1981.

2388)   Maletzky, Barry M. "Booster Sessions in Aversion
        Therapy: The Permanency of Treatment," Behavior
        Therapy, 8:460-63, 1977.

2389)   Marano, Hara. "New Light on Homosexuality," Medi-
        cal World News, 20:8+, Apr. 30, 1979.

2390)   Marmor, Michael, and others.   "Risk Factors for
         Kaposi's Sarcoma in Homosexual Men," Lancet, 1:
         1083-87, 1982.

2391)   Marr, John S.   "Amebiasis in New York City: A
         Changing Pattern of Transmission," Bulletin of the
         New York Academy of Medicine, 57:188-20, 1981.

2392)   Marx, Jean L.   "New Disease [Acquired Immune
         Deficiency Syndrome] Baffles Medical Community,"
         Science, 217:618-21, Aug. 13, 1982.

2393)   Masur, Henry, and others.   "An Outbreak of
         Community-acquired Pneumocystis Carinii Pneumonia;
         Initial Manifestation of Cellular Immune Dysfunction,"
         New England Journal of Medicine, 305:1431-38, 1981.

2394)   _____, and others.   "Opportunistic Infection in
         Previously Healthy Women, Initial Manifestations of
         a Community-acquired Cellular Immunodeficiency,"
         Annals of Internal Medicine, 97:533-39, 1982.

2395)   Maurer, Tom.   "Health Care and the Gay Commu-
         nity," Nursing Dimensions, 7:83-85, Apr. 1979.

2396)   Maurice, P. D. L., and others.   "Kaposi's Sarcoma
         with Benign Course in a Homosexual," Lancet, 1:
         571, 1982.

2397)   May, Eugene.   "Discussion of Recent Trends and New
         Developments in the Treatment of Homosexuality,"
         Psychotherapy: Theory, Research, and Practice,
         14:18-20, 1977.

2398)   Maze, J. R.   "Dostoyevsky: Epilepsy, Mysticism,
         and Homosexuality," American Imago, 38:155-83,
         1981.

2399)   McCauley, Dorothy I., and others.   "Radiographic
         Patterns of Opportunistic Lung Infections and Kaposi
         Sarcoma in Homosexual Men," American Journal of
         Roentgenology, 139:653-58, 1982.

2400)   McCauley, Elizabeth, and Anke A. Ehrhardt.   "Sexu-
         al Behavior in Female Transsexuals and Lesbians,"
         Journal of Sex Research, 16:202-11, 1980.

2401)   McConaghy, N.   "Heterosexual Experience, Marital
         Status, and Orientation of Homosexual Males," Ar-
         chives of Sexual Behavior, 7:575-81, 1978.

2402)   _____. "Is a Homosexual Orientation Irrever-
         sible?" British Journal of Psychiatry, 129:556-63,
         1976.

2403)   _____, and A. Blaszczynski. "A Pair of Mono-
         zygotic Twins Discordant for Homosexuality: Sex-
         dimorphic Behavior and Penile Volume Responses,"
         Archives of Sexual Behavior, 9:123-31, 1980.

2404)   _____, and others. "Controlled Comparison of
         Aversive Therapy and Covert Sensitization in Com-
         pulsive Homosexuality," Behavioral Research and
         Therapy, 19:425-34, 1981.

2405)   McManus, T. J., and others. "Amyl Nitrate Use
         by Homosexuals," Lancet, 1:503, 1982.

2406)   McMillan, Alexander. "Gonorrhea in the Homosexual
         Man.   Frequency of Infection by Culture Site," Sexu-
         ally Transmitted Diseases, 5:146-50, 1978.

2407)   _____. "Threadworms in Homosexual Males,"
         British Medical Journal, 1:367, 1978.

2408)   _____, and F. D. Lee. "Sigmoidoscopic and
         Microscopic Appearance of the Rectal Mucosa in
         Homosexual Men," Gut: The British Journal of
         Gastroenterology, 22:1035-41, 1981.

2409)   _____, and others. "Chlamydial Infection in Ho-
         mosexual Men," British Journal of Venereal Dis-
         eases, 57:47-49, 1981.

2410)   _____, and others. "Sexually Transmitted Dis-
         eases in Homosexual Males in Edinburgh," Health
         Bulletin, 35:266-71, 1977.

2411)   McWhirter, David P., and Andrew M. Mattison.
         "The Treatment of Sexual Dysfunction in Gay Male
         Couples," Journal of Sex and Marital Therapy, 4:
         213-18, 1978.

2412)   Meredith, R. L., and Robert W. Riester. "Psy-
         chotherapy, Responsibility, and Homosexuality:

Clinical Examination of Socially Deviant Behavior,"
Professional Psychology, 11:174-93, 1980.

2413)   Merino, Hernando I. , and others.   "Screening for
Gonorrhea and Syphilis in Gay Bath Houses in Denver and Los Angeles," Public Health Reports, 94:
376-79, 1979.

2414)   Meyer-Bahlberg, Heino F.   "Hormones and Psycho-
sexual Differentiation: Implications for the Management of Intersexuality, Homosexuality, and Trans-
sexuality," Clinics in Endocrinology and Metabolism,
11:681-701, 1982.

2415)   _____.   "Sex Hormones and Female Homosexuality: A Critical Examination," Archives of Sexual
Behavior, 8:101-19, 1979.

2416)   _____.   "Sex Hormones and Male Homosexuality
in Comparative Perspective," Archives of Sexual
Behavior, 6:297-325, 1977.

2417)   Meyers Joel D. , and others.   "Giardia Lamblia
Infection in Homosexual Men," British Journal of
Venereal Diseases, 54:53-55, 1977.

2418)   Mildvan, Donna, and others.   "Opportunistic Infections and Immune Deficiency in Homosexual Men,"
Annals of Internal Medicine, 96:700-04, 1982.

2419)   _____, and others.   "Venereal Transmission of
Enteric Pathogens in Male Homosexuals: Two Case
Reports," Journal of the American Medical Associa-
tion, 238:1387-89, 1977.

2420)   Miller, Frank.   "Etiologic Factors in a Case of
Female Homosexuality," American Journal of Psychoanalysis, 39:273-78, 1979.

2421)   Miller, James R. , and others.   "Progressive Multi-
focal Leukoencephalopathy in a Male Homosexual with
T-cell Immune Deficiency," New England Journal of
Medicine, 307:1436-38, 1982.

2422)   Miller, Judith, and others.   "Comparison of Family
Relationships: Homosexual versus Heterosexual Wom-
en," Psychological Reports, 46:1127-32, 1980.

2423)   Miller, Robert D.   "Pseudohomosexuality in Male
         Patients with Hysterical Psychosis: A Preliminary
         Report," American Journal of Psychiatry, 135:112-
         13, 1978.

2424)   Mills, A. F.   "Kaposi Sarcoma and Oestrogens,"
         Lancet, 1:1465, 1982.

2425)   Mindel, Adrian.   "Changing Patterns of Communi-
         cable Disease in England and Wales," British Medi-
         cal Journal, 281:616, 1980.

2426)   _____, and Richard Tedder.   "Hepatitis A in
         Homosexuals," British Medical Journal, 282:1666,
         1981.

2427)   Mitchell, Stephen A.   "Psychodynamics, Homosexu-
         ality, and the Question of Pathology," Psychiatry,
         41:254-63, 1978.

2428)   Mohl, Paul C., and others.   "Prepuce Restoration
         Seekers: Psychiatric Aspects," Archives of Sexual
         Behavoir, 10:383-93, 1981.

2429)   Money, John, and Carol Bohmer.   "Prison Sexology:
         Two Personal Accounts of Masturbation, Homosexu-
         ality, and Rape," Journal of Sex Research, 16:258-
         66, 1980.

2430)   _____, and Jean Dalery.   "Iatrogenic Homosexu-
         ality," Annual Progress in Child Psychiatry and
         Child Development 1977:215-29.

2431)   _____, and Anthony J. Russo.   "Homosexual Out-
         come of Discordant Gender Identity/Role in Child-
         hood: Longitudinal Follow Up," Journal of Pediatric
         Psychology, 4:29-41, 1979.

2432)   Montagu, Ashley.   "A 'Kinsey Report' on Homosexu-
         alities [A Study by Alan Bell and Martin Weinberg],"
         Psychology Today, 12:62-66+, Aug. 1978.

2433)   Morin, Stephen F.   "Heterosexual Bias in Psychologi-
         cal Research on Lesbianism and Male Homosexuality,"
         American Psychologist, 32:629-37, 1977.

2434)   Morris, Lynn, and others. "Autoimmune Thrombo-
        cytopenic Purpura in Homosexual Men," Annals of
        Internal Medicine, 96:714-17, 1982.

2435)   Morse, Stephen A., and others. "Gonococcal Strains
        from Homosexual Men Have Outer Membranes with
        Reduced Permeability to Hydrophobic Molecules,"
        Infection and Immunity, 37:432-38, 1982.

2436)   Mosher, Donald L., and Kevin E. O'Grady. "Ho-
        mosexual Threat, Negative Attitudes Toward Mastur-
        bation, Sex Guilt, and Males' Sexual and Affective
        Reactions to Explicit Sexual Films," Journal of Con-
        sulting and Clinical Psychology, 47:860-73, 1979.

2437)   Moss, C. Scott, and others. "Sexual Assault in
        Prison," Psychological Reports, 44:823-28, 1979.

2438)   Mucklow, Bonnie M., and Gladys K. Phelan. "Les-
        bian and Traditional Mothers' Responses to Adult
        Response to Child Behavior and Self-Concept," Psy-
        chological Reports, 44:880-82, 1979.

2439)   Mukherjee, J. B. "Castration--A Means of Induction
        into the Hijirah Group of the Eunuch Community in
        India. A Critical Study of 20 Cases," American
        Journal of Forensic Medicine and Pathology, 1:61-
        65, 1980.

2440)   Mundy, P. E. and others. "Microbiological Study
        of Non-gonococcal Proctitis in Passive Male Homo-
        sexuals," Postgraduate Medical Journal, 57:705-11,
        1981.

2441)   Munroe, Robert L. and Ruth H. "Male Transvestism
        and Subsistence Economy," Journal of Social Psy-
        chology, 103:307-08, 1977.

2442)   Murphy, Bert. L., and others. "Serological Testing
        for Hepatitis B in Male Homosexuals: Special Em-
        phasis on Hepatitis B e Antigen and Antibody by
        Radioimmunoassay," Journal of Clinical Microbiology,
        11:301-03, 1980.

2443)   "My Child Is a Homosexual [Excerpt from Book for
        Parents by Fairchild and Hayward]," Family Health,
        12:38+, Jun. 1980.

2444)   Myers, Michael F.   "Common Psychiatric Problems
        in Homosexual Men and Women Consulting Family
        Physicians," Canadian Medical Association Journal,
        123:359-63, 1980.

2445)   _____.   "Homosexuality, Sexual Dysfunction and
        Incest in Male Identical Twins," Canadian Journal
        of Psychiatry, 27:144-47, 1982.

2446)   Myskowski, Patricia L., and others.   "Kaposi's
        Sarcoma in Young Homosexual Men," Cutis, 29:31-
        34, 1982.

2447)   Nardi, Peter M.   "Alcohol Treatment and the Non-
        traditional Family Structures of Gays and Lesbians,"
        Journal of Alcohol and Drug Education, 27:83-89,
        1982.

2448)   Natterson, Joseph M.   "The Self as a Transitional
        Object: Its Relationship to Narcissism and Homo-
        sexuality," International Journal of Psychoanalysis
        and Psychotherapy, 5:131-43, 1976.

2449)   Neumann, Hans H.   "Use of Steroid Creams as a
        Possible Cause of Immunosuppression in Homo-
        sexuals," New England Journal of Medicine, 306:935,
        1982.

2450)   Neuwirth, Jerry, and others.   "Cytomegalovirus
        Retinitis in a Young Homosexual Male with Acquired
        Immunodeficiency," Ophthalmology, 89:805-08, 1982.

2451)   "New Outbreak of Serious Diseases Focuses on Ho-
        mosexual Men [Study by Jeffrey Greene and Others],"
        Science News, 120:309, Nov. 14, 1981.

2452)   Newmark, Steven R., and others.   "Gonadotropin
        Estradial and Testosterone Profiles in Homosexual
        Men," American Journal of Psychiatry, 136:767-71,
        1979.

2453)   Newmeyer, John A.   "The Sensuous Hippy: II. Gay/
        Straight Differences in Regard to Drugs and Sexuality,"
        Drug Forum, 6:49-55, 1977-78.

2454)   Novak, Michael J.   "Genetic Predisposition to Ka-
        posi's Sarcoma," American Academy of Dermatology,
        7:806-07, 1982.

2455)   O'Leary, Virginia. "Lesbianism," Nursing Dimen-
        sions, 7:78-82, Spring 1979.

2456)   Olson, Kate. "The Masculinity and Femininity of
        Homosexuals [Study by Michael Storms]," Psychology
        Today, 15:98-101, Oct. 1981.

2457)   Omark, Richard C. "A Comment on the Homosexual
        Role" and "A Further Comment ... A Reply to
        Goode," Journal of Sex Research, 14:273-74, 1978
        and 17:73-75, 1981.

2458)   O'Neill, Michael T., and John W. Hinton. "Pupil-
        lographic Assessment of Sexual Interest and Sexual
        Arousal," Perceptual and Motor Skills, 44:1278,
        1977.

2459)   "Opportunistic Infections and Kaposi's Sarcoma in
        Homosexual Men," New England Journal of Medicine,
        306:932-35, 1982.

2460)   Ostrow, David G., and Walter J. Lear. "Sexually
        Transmitted Diseases," American Journal of Public
        Health, 72:495-96, 1982.

2461)   Oswald, George A., and others. "Attempted Immune
        Stimulation in the 'Gay' Compromise Syndrome,"
        British Medical Journal, 285:1082, 1982.

2462)   Owen, William F., Jr. "The Clinical Approach to
        the Homosexual Patient," Annals of Internal Medi-
        cine, 93:90-92, 1980.

2463)   _____. "Sexually Transmitted Diseases and
        Traumatic Problems in Homosexual Men," Annals
        of Internal Medicine, 92:805-08, 1980.

2464)   Paitich, Daniel, and Ron Langevin. "The Clarke
        Parent-Child Relations Questionnaire: A Clinically
        Useful Test for Adults," Journal of Consulting and
        Clinical Psychology, 44:428-36, 1976.

2465)   Paradinas, F. J., and others. "Histopathology and
        Localization of Viral Antigens in the Liver of HBsAg
        Positive Homosexuals," Histopathology, 5:623-37,
        1981.

2466) Parolski, Paul A. , Jr. "The Unique Considerations and Concerns of the Homosexual Patient Receiving Care for Sexually Transmitted Diseases," Sexually Transmitted Diseases, 9:214-15, 1982.

2467) Pattison, E. Mansell and Myrna L. "'ExGays': Religiously Mediated Change in Homosexuals," American Journal of Psychiatry, 137:1553-62, 1980.

2468) Peplau, Letitia A. "What Homosexuals Want in Relationships," Psychology Today, 15:28-34+, Mar. 1981.

2469) Peretti, Peter O. "Dysfunctions and Eufunctions of Prison Homosexuality. A Structural-Functional Approach," Panminerva Medicine, 21:135-40, 1979.

2470) _____, and others. "Self-Image and Emotional Stability of Oedipal and Non-Oedipal Male Homosexuals," Acta Psychiatrica Belgica, 76:46-55, 1976.

2471) _____, and others. "Self-Perceptions of Oedipal and Non-Oedipal Homosexuals," Indian Journal of Psychology, 51:98-105, 1976.

2472) Perkins, Muriel W. "Female Homosexuality and Body Build," Archives of Sexual Behavior, 10:337-45, 1981.

2473) _____. "On Birth Order Among Lesbians," Psychological Reports, 43:814, 1978.

2474) Pettyjohn, R. D. "Health Care of the Gay Individual," Nursing Forum, 18:366-93, 1979.

2475) Phillips, Debora, and others. "Alternative Behavioral Approaches to the Treatment of Homosexualty," Archives of Sexual Behavior, 5:223-28, 1976.

2476) Pillard, Richard C. "Psychotherapeutic Treatment for the Invisible Minority," American Behavioral Scientist, 25:407-22, 1981-82.

2477) _____, and others. "Is Homosexuality Familial? A Review, Some Data, and a Suggestion," Archives of Sexual Behavior, 10:465-75, 1981.

2478)   Pinta, Emil R.   "Treatment of Obsessive Homo-
        sexual Pedophilic Fantasies with Medroxyprogesterone
        Acetate," Biological Psychiatry, 13:369-73, 1978.

2479)   Pogorcheff, Elaine.   "The Gay Patient: What Not to
        Do," RN, 42:46-50, Apr. 1979.

2480)   Poleski, Martin H.   "Kaposi's Sarcoma and Hepatitis
        B Vaccine," Annals of Internal Medicine, 97:786,
        1982.

2481)   Pollack, Stephen, and others.   "The Dimensions of
        Stigma: The Social Situation of the Mentally Ill Per-
        son and the Male Homosexual," Journal of Abnormal
        Psychology, 85:105-12, 1976.

2482)   Pomerantz, Barry M., and others.   "Amebiasis in
        New York City 1958-1978:   Identification of the Male
        Homosexual High Risk Population," Bulletin of the
        New York Academy of Medicine, 56:232-44, 1980.

2483)   Porter, Jeannie F.   "Homosexuality Treated Adven-
        titiously in a Stuttering Therapy Program: A Case
        Report Presenting a Heterophobic Orientation,"
        Australian and New Zealand Journal of Psychiatry,
        10:185-89, 1976.

2484)   Power, D. J.   "Paedophilia," Practitioner, 218:805-
        11, 1977.

2485)   Prytula, Robert E., and others.   "Body Self-Image
        and Homosexuality," Journal of Clinical Psychology,
        35:567-72, 1979.

2486)   "The Psychoanalytic Treatment of Male Homosexu-
        ality," Journal of the American Psychoanalytic As-
        sociation, 25:183-99, 1977.

2487)   Quinn, Thomas C., and others.   "Campylobacter
        Proctitis in a Homosexual Man," Annals of Internal
        Medicine, 93:458-59, 1980.

2488)   _____, and others.   "The Etiology of Anorectal
        Infections in Homosexual Men," American Journal of
        Medicine, 71:395-406, 1981.

2489) Rasmussen, E. O. , and others. "Immunosuppression
       in a Homosexual Man with Kaposi's Sarcoma," Jour-
       nal of the American Academy of Dermatology, 6:870-
       79, 1982.

2490) Reiche, Reimut, and Martin Dannecker. "Male Ho-
       mosexuality in West Germany--A Sociological Inves-
       tigation," Journal of Sex Research, 1:35-53, 1977.

2491) Reiner, Neil E. , and others. "Asymptomatic Rectal
       Mucosal Lesions and Hepatitis B Surface Antigen at
       Sites of Sexual Contact in Homosexual Men with Per-
       sistent Hepatitis B Virus Infection," Annals of Inter-
       nal Medicine, 96:170-73, 1982.

2492) Rekers, George A. , and others. "Genetic and Phys-
       ical Studies of Male Children with Psychological Gen-
       der Disturbances," Psychological Medicine, 9:373-75,
       1979.

2493) _____, and others. "Sex-Role Stereotypes and
       Professional Intervention for Childhood Gender Dis-
       turbance," Professional Psychology, 9:127-36, 1978.

2494) Renton, P. H. "Hepatitis B Antigen and Antibody in
       a Male Homosexual Population," British Journal of
       Venereal Diseases, 54:206, 1978.

2495) Rickards, Frank S. "Homosexuality: Victims of
       Society," Nursing Mirror, 149:28-30, Nov. 1, 1979.

2496) Rigg, C. A. "Homosexuality in Adolescence," Pedi-
       atric Annals, 11:826-28+, 1982.

2497) Rister, Esther S. "The Male Homosexual Style of
       Life: A Contemporary Adlerian Interpretation,"
       Journal of Individual Psychology, 37:86-94, 1981.

2498) Ritchey, Michael G. "Venereal Disease Among Ho-
       mosexuals," Journal of the American Medical Asso-
       ciation, 237:767, 1977.

2499) Rizzo, Albert A. , and others. "Mosher Guilt Scores
       and Sexual Preference," Journal of Clinical Psychol-
       ogy, 37:827-30, 1981.

2500) Robertiello, Richard C. "The 'Fag Hag,'" Journal
       of Contemporary Psychotherapy, 10:10-11, 1978.

2501)   Roberts, Lorraine A.   "Female Homosexuality,"
        Nursing Times, 73:1426-29, 1977.

2502)   Robertson, D. H. H., and others.   "Sexual Trans-
        mission of Enteric Pathogens," Lancet, 1:393, 1982.

2503)   Robinson, Bryan E., and others.   "Sex Role Endorse-
        ment Among Homosexual Men Across the Life Span,"
        Archives of Sexual Behavior, 11:355-60, 1982.

2504)   Robinson, Lillian H.   "Adolescent Homosexual Pat-
        terns: Psychodynamics and Therapy," Adolescent
        Psychiatry, 8:422-36, 1980.

2505)   Rodrigue, Roger B.   "Amebic Balantis," Journal of
        the American Medical Association, 239:109, 1978.

2506)   Roedell, R. F., Jr.   "Affirmative Gay Material in
        the Hospital Library," Bulletin of the Medical Li-
        brary Association, 64:423, 1976.

2507)   Rogers, Carl, and others.   "Group Psychotherapy
        with Homosexuals: A Review," International Journal
        of Group Psychotherapy, 26:3-27, 1976.

2508)   Rohde, W., and others.   "Plasma Levels of FSH,
        LH, and Testosterone in Homosexual Men," Endo-
        krinologie, 70:241-48, 1977.

2509)   Rose, Henry S., and others.   "Alimentary Tract In-
        volvement in Kaposi's Sarcoma: Radiographic and
        Endoscopic Findings in 25 Homosexual Men," Ameri-
        can Journal of Roentgenology, 139:661-66, 1982.

2510)   Rosen, Raymond C., and Steven A. Kopel.   "Penile
        Plethysmography and Biofeedback in the Treatment of
        a Transvestite Exhibitionist," Journal of Consulting
        and Clinical Psychology, 45:908-16, 1977.   (Replies:
        46:1515-16 and 1519-21, 1978.)

2511)   Rosenthal, Franz.   "Ar-Râzi on the Hidden Illness
        [Homosexuality]," Bulletin of the History of Medicine,
        52:45-60, 1978.

2512)   Ross, Michael W.   "Attitudes of Male Homosexuals
        to Venereal Disease Clinics," Medical Journal of
        Australia, 2:670-71, 1981.

2513) _____. "Retrospective Distortion in Homosexual
Research," Archives of Sexual Behavior, 9:523-31,
1980.

2514) _____. "Social Factors in Homosexually Acquired
Venereal Disease. Comparison Between Sweden and
Australia," British Journal of Venereal Diseases,
58:263-68, 1982.

2515) _____, and Olli W. Stalstrom. "Exorcism as
Psychiatric Treatment: A Homosexual Case Study,"
Archives of Sexual Behavior, 8:379-83, 1979.

2516) Roth, Nathan. "The Roots of Mary Wollstonecraft's
Feminism," Journal of the American Academy of
Psychoanalysis, 7:67-77, 1979.

2517) Rozenbaum, Willy, and others. "Multiple Opportunistic Infection in a Male Homosexual in France,"
Lancet, 1:572-73, 1982.

2518) Rubin, B., and others. "Gonococcal Endocarditis in
a Male Homosexual: Report of Case," Journal of
the American Osteopathic Association, 80:534-37,
1981.

2519) Russell, A., and R. Winkler. "Evaluation of Assertive Training and Homosexual Service Groups
Designed to Improve Homosexual Functioning," Journal of Consulting and Clinical Psychology, 45:1-13,
1977.

2520) Sagarin, Edward. "Prison Homosexuality and Its
Effect on Post-Prison Sexual Behavior," Psychiatry,
39:245-57, 1976.

2521) Salit, Irving S., and Carl E. Frasch. "Seroepi-
demiologic Aspects of Neisseria Meningitidis in
Homosexual Men," Canadian Medical Association
Journal, 126:38-41, 1982.

2522) Salvage, Jane. "Suitable to Nurse?" Nursing
Mirror, 152:6-7, Apr. 23, 1981.

2523) Samarasinghe, P. L., and others. "Herpetic
Proctitis and Sacral Radiomyelopathy--A Hazard
for Homosexual Men," British Medical Journal,
278:365-66, 1979.

2524)   Sambrooks, Jean E. , and others. "Incubation of
        Sexual Attitude Change Between Sessions of Instru-
        mental Aversion Therapy: Two Case Studies," Be-
        havior Therapy, 9:477-85, 1978.

2525)   "San Francisco Gays Well Adjusted," Science News,
        114:37, Jul. 15, 1978.

2526)   Sarwer-Foner, G. J. "Some Psychodynamic Aspects
        of Transsexual, Homosexual, and Transvestite Pa-
        tients Presenting Themselves to a Psychiatric Gender
        Clinic," Bulletin of the American Academy of Psy-
        chiatry and Law, 7:249-58, 1979.

2527)   Schaefer, Siegrid. "Sexual and Social Problems of
        Lesbians," Journal of Sex Research, 12:50-69, 1976.

2528)   _____. "Sociosexual Behavior in Male and Female
        Homosexuals: A Study in Sex Differences," Archives
        of Sexual Behavior, 6:355-64, 1977.

2529)   Schiavi, Raul C. , and Daniel White. "Androgens
        and Male Sexual Function: A Review of Human Stud-
        ies," Journal of Sex and Marital Therapy, 2:214-28,
        1976.

2530)   Schmerin, Michael J. , and others. "Amebiasis, an
        Increasing Problem Among Homosexuals in New York
        City," Journal of the American Medical Association,
        238:1386-87, 1977.

2531)   _____, and others. "Giardiasis' Association with
        Homosexuality," Annals of Internal Medicine, 88:801-
        03, 1978.

2532)   Schmidt, Gunter. "Childhood Indicators of Male Ho-
        mosexuality," Archives of Sexual Behavior, 7:73-75,
        1978.

2533)   Schneider, Laurie. "Donatello and Caravaggio: The
        Iconography of Decapitation," American Imago, 33:
        76-91, 1976.

2534)   Schreeder, M. T. , and others. "Hepatitis B in Ho-
        mosexual Men: Prevalence of Infection and Factors
        Related to Transmission," Journal of Infectious Dis-
        eases, 146:7-15, 1982.

2535)   Scott, James M., and Kenneth N. Anchor. "Male
        Homosexual Behavior and Ego Function Strategies in
        the Group Encounter," Journal of Clinical Psychology,
        33:1079-84, 1977.

2536)   Seigal, Frederick P., and others. "Severe Acquired
        Immunodeficiency in Male Homosexuals, Manifested
        by Chronic Perianal Ulcerative Herpes Simplex Le-
        sions," New England Journal of Medicine, 305:1439-
        44, 1981.

2537)   Sesso, D. J., and others. "Pneumocystis Carinii
        Pneumonia in a Male Homosexual: Report of a
        Case," Journal of the American Osteopathic Asso-
        ciation, 82:256-60, 1982.

2538)   "Sexual Transmission of Enteric Pathogens," Lancet,
        2:1328-29, 1981.

2539)   Shaffer, David R., and Thomas Case. "On the
        Decision to Testify in One's Own Behalf: Effects
        of Withheld Evidence, Defendant's Sexual Preferences,
        and Juror Dogmatism on Juridic Decisions," Journal
        of Personality and Social Psychology, 42:335-46,
        1982.

2540)   Sharma, R. P. "Light-dependent Homosexual Ac-
        tivity in Males of a Mutant of Drosophilia Melano-
        gaster," Experientia, 33:171-73, 1977.

2541)   Shaw, Phyllis. "Medical Sequelae of a Lifestyle--
        An Interview with Dr. Joyce I. Wallace," Journal of
        the American Medical Women's Association, 37:199-
        202, 1982.

2542)   Shoham, S. Giora, and others. "Personality Core
        Dynamics and Predisposition Toward Homosexuality,"
        British Journal of Medical Psychology, 51:161-75,
        1978.

2543)   Sider, Lee, and others. "Radiographic Findings of
        Infectious Proctitis in Homosexual Men," American
        Journal of Roentgenology, 139:667-71, 1982.

2544)   Siegal, Reva L., and David D. Hoefer. "Bereave-
        ment Counseling for Gay Individuals," American Jour-
        nal of Psychotherapy, 35:517-25, 1981.

2545)   Siegelman, Marvin.   "Adjustment of Homosexual and
        Heterosexual Women: A Cross-National Replication,"
        Archives of Sexual Behavior, 8:121-25, 1979.

2546)   _____. "Parental Backgrounds of Homosexual
        and Heterosexual Women: A Cross-National Repli-
        cation," Archives of Sexual Behavior, 10:371-78 and
        505-12, 1981.

2547)   _____. "Psychological Adjustment of Homosexual
        and Heterosexual Men: A Cross-Cultural Replication,"
        Archives of Sexual Behavior, 7:1-11, 1978.

2548)   Sigusch, Volkmar, and others.   "Official Statement
        by the German Society for Sex Research on the Re-
        search of Prof. Dr. Günter Dörner on the Subject
        of Homosexuality," Archives of Sexual Behavior,
        11:445-49, 1982.

2549)   Silverman, Lloyd H., and others.   "The Further
        Use of the Subliminal Psychodynamic Activation Meth-
        od for the Experimental Study of the Clinical Theory
        of Psychoanalysis: On the Specificity of the Rela-
        tionship Between Symptoms and Unconscious Con-
        flicts," Psychotherapy: Theory, Research, and Prac-
        tice, 13:2-16, 1976.

2550)   Simari, C. Georgia, and David Baskin.   "Incestuous
        Experiences Within Homosexual Populations: A Pre-
        liminary Study," Archives of Sexual Behavior, 11:
        329-44, 1982.

2551)   Simmons, P. D.   "Campylobacter Species in Male
        Homosexuals," British Journal of Venereal Diseases,
        55:66, 1979.

2552)   _____. "Homosexuals and Enteric Infections in
        a London Health District," Public Health, 96:164-67,
        1982.

2553)   _____, and others.   "E Antigen Among Male Ho-
        mosexual Patients," British Medical Journal, 2:1458,
        1977.

2554)   Skinhøj, P., and others.   "Chronic Hepatitis B In-
        fection in Male Homosexuals," Journal of Clinical
        Pathology, 32:783-85, 1979.

2555) Skinner, Nicholas F. "The Hess et al. Study of
      Pupillary Activity in Heterosexual and Homosexual
      Males: A Re-evaluation" and "Pupillary Activity and
      Male Sexuality: Reply to Hess and Petrovich, " Per-
      ceptual and Motor Skills, 51:844 and 897-98, 1980.

2556) Skrapec, Candice, and K. R. McKenzie. "Psycho-
      logical Self-Perception in Male Transsexuals, Homo-
      sexuals, and Heterosexuals, " Archives of Sexual Be-
      havior, 10:357-70, 1981.

2557) Small, Edward J. , Jr. and Barry Leach. "Coun-
      seling Homosexual Alcoholics: Ten Case Histories, "
      Journal of Studies on Alcohol, 38:2077-86, 1977.

2558) Smith, David E. , and others. "PCP and Sexual Dys-
      function, " Journal of Psychedelic Drugs, 12:269-73,
      1980.

2559) Smith, Jaime. "Ego-Dystonic Homosexuality, " Com-
      prehensive Psychiatry, 21:119-27, 1980.

2560) Socarides, Charles W. "Psychoanalytic Perspectives
      on Female Homosexuality, " American Journal of Psy-
      chotherapy, 35:510-15, 1981.

2561) _____. "Psychodynamics and Sexual Object Choice.
      II. A Reply to Dr. Richard C. Friedman's Paper, "
      Contemporary Psychoanalysis, 12:370-78, 1976.

2562) _____. "The Sexual Deviations and the Diagnostic
      Manual, " American Journal of Psychotherapy, 32:414-
      26, 1978.

2563) _____. "Some Problems Encountered in the Psy-
      choanalytic Treatment of Overt Male Homosexuality, "
      American Journal of Psychotherapy, 33:506-20, 1979.

2564) _____, and others. "Challenging the Diagnostic
      Status of Homosexuality, " American Journal of Psy-
      chiatry, 138:1256-58, 1981.

2565) Sohn, Norman, and James G. Robilotti, Jr. "The
      Gay Bowel Syndrome. A Review of Colonic and
      Rectal Conditions in 200 Male Homosexuals, " Ameri-
      can Journal of Gastroenterology, 67:478-84, 1977.

2566)   Soloff, Paul H.   "Pseudohomosexual Psychosis in
        Basic Military Training," Archives of Sexual Be-
        havior, 7:501-10, 1978.

2567)   Spiers, Alexander S., and Chester L. Robbins.
        "Cytomegalovirus Infection Simulating Lymphoma in
        a Homosexual Man," Lancet, 1:1248-49, 1982.

2568)   Spitzer, Robert L.   "The Diagnostic Status of Ho-
        mosexuality in DSM-III: A Reformulation of the
        Issue," American Journal of Psychiatry, 138:210-
        15, 1981.

2569)   Stahl, F., and others.   "Significantly Decreased
        Apparently Free Testosterone Levels in the Plasma
        of Male Homosexuals," Endokrinologie, 68:115-17,
        1976.

2570)   Stahl, Rosalyn E., and others.   "Immunologic Ab-
        normalities in Homosexual Men.   Relationship to
        Kaposi's Sarcoma," American Journal of Medicine,
        73:171-78, 1982.

2571)   Stoller, Robert J.   "Boyhood Gender Aberrations:
        Treatment Issues," Journal of American Psycho-
        analytic Association, 26:541-58, 1978.

2572)   _____.   "Problems with the Term 'Homosexu-
        ality,'" Hillside Journal of Clinical Psychiatry,
        2:3-25, 1980.

2573)   Stone, Alan A.   "Conceptual Ambiguity and Mor-
        ality in Modern Psychiatry," American Journal of
        Psychology, 137:887-99, 1980.

2574)   Stone, Norman M.   "On the Assessment of Sexual
        Orientation: A Reply," Journal of Personality As-
        sessment, 40:54-56, 1976.

2575)   Storms, Michael D.   "Theories of Sexual Orienta-
        tion," Journal of Personality and Social Psychology,
        38:783-92, 1980.

2576)   _____.   "Theory of Erotic Orientation Develop-
        ment," Psychological Review, 88:340-53, 1981.

2577)   Strassberg, Donald S. , and others.   "Psychopatholo-
        gy in Self-Identified Female-to-Male Transsexuals,
        Homosexuals, and Heterosexuals," Archives of Sexual
        Behavior, 8:491-96, 1979.

2578)   Stringer, Peter, and Tadeusz Grygier.   "Male Homo-
        sexuality, Psychiatric Patient Status, and Psycholog-
        ical Masculinity and Femininity," Archives of Sexual
        Behavior, 5:15-27, 1976.

2579)   Sturgis, Ellie T. , and Henry E. Adams.   "The Right
        to Treatment: Issues in the Treatment of Homosexu-
        ality," Journal of Consulting and Clinical Psychology,
        46:165-69, 1978.

2580)   Suarez, B. K. , and T. R. Przybeck.   "Sibling Sex
        Ratio and Male Homosexuality," Archives of Sexual
        Behavior, 9:1-12, 1980.

2581)   Suhonen, R. , and others.   "Syphilis, Homosexuality,
        and Legislation," Dermatologica, 152:363-66, 1976.

2582)   Swigert, V. L. , and others.   "[Homo]Sexual Suicide:
        Social, Psychological, and Legal Aspects," Archives
        of Sexual Behavior, 5:391-401, 1976.

2583)   Taff, M. L. , and others.   "Outbreak of an Acquired
        Immunodeficiency Syndrome Associated with Oppor-
        tunistic Infections and Kaposi's Sarcoma in Male Ho-
        mosexuals: An Epidemic with Forensic Implications,"
        American Journal of Forensic Medicine and Pathology,
        3:259-64, 1982.

2584)   Tavris, Carol.   "Gay Is Beautiful--At a Distance:
        Study of Stephen F. Morin," Psychology Today, 9:
        101-02, Jan. 1976.

2585)   Tedder, R. S. , and others.   "Contrasting Patterns
        and Frequency of Antibodies to the Surface, Core,
        and e Antigens of Hepatitis B Virus in Blood Donors
        and in Homosexual Patients," Journal of Medical
        Virology, 6:323-32, 1980.

2586)   Thomas, Sandra P.   "Bisexuality: A Sexual Orien-
        tation of Great Diversity," Journal of Psychiatric
        Nursing and Mental Health Services, 18:19-27, Apr.
        1980.

2587) Thomsen, Henrik K. , and others. "Kaposi Sarcoma Among Homosexual Men in Europe," Lancet, 2:688, 1981.

2588) Thor, D. H. "Reciprocal Homosexual Mounting Behavior in Paired Anosmic Rats," Psychological Reports, 47:349-50, 1980.

2589) Tompkins, D. S. , and others. "Isolation of Intestinal Spirochaetes from Homosexuals," Journal of Clinical Pathology, 34:1385-87, 1981.

2590) Trappler, Brian. "Therapist Conflict and Management Bias," Canadian Journal of Psychiatry, 26:140-41, 1981.

2591) Trent, Michael. "On Being a Gay Teacher: My Problems--and Yours," Psychology Today, 11:136, Apr. 1978.

2592) Troiden, Richard R. "Becoming Homosexual: A Model of Gay Identity Acquisition," Psychiatry, 42: 362-73, 1979.

2593) Turnbull, Debi, and Marvin Brown. "Attitudes Toward Homosexuality and Male and Female Reactions to Homosexual and Heterosexual Slides," Canadian Journal of Behavioural Science, 9:68-80, 1977.

2594) Turner, William J. "Alcoholism, Homosexuality, and Bipolar Affective Disorder," American Journal of Psychiatry, 138:262-63, 1981.

2595) Urmacher, C. , and others. "Outbreak of Kaposi's Sarcoma with Cytomegalovirus Infection in Young Homosexual Men," American Journal of Medicine, 72: 569-75, 1982.

2596) Vaisrub, Samuel. "Homosexuality--A Risk Factor in Infectious Disease," Journal of the American Medical Association, 238:1402, 1977.

2597) VanBaal, J. G. , and P. Leguit, Jr. "Peri-anal Abscess--The Relationship Between Peri-anal Abscess, Hepatitis B. , and Sexual Behavior," Netherlands Journal of Surgery, 33:32-33, 1981.

2598) Vanley, Gregory T., and others. "Atypical Pneu-
       mocystis Carinii Pneumonia in Homosexual Men with
       Unusual Immunodeficiency," American Journal of
       Roentgenology, 138:1037-41, 1982.

2599) Vilaseca, J., and others. "Kaposi's Sarcoma and
       Toxoplasma Gondii Brain Abscess in a Spanish Ho-
       mosexual," Lancet, 1:572, 1982.

2600) Waldhorn, Richard E., and others. "Pneumocystis
       Carinii Pneumonia in a Previously Healthy Adult,"
       Journal of the American Medical Association, 247:
       1860-61, 1982.

2601) Wallace, Joyce I., and others. "T-Cell Ratios in
       Homosexuals," Lancet, 1:908, 1982.

2602) Warren, Carol A. B. "Women Among Men: Females
       in the Male Homosexual Community," Archives of
       Sexual Behavior, 5:157-69, 1976. (Reprinted in Le-
       vine, no. 22, pp. 222-38.)

2603) Waugh, M. A. "Hepatitis B Surface Antigen in Ho-
       mosexuals," British Journal of Venereal Diseases,
       54:352, 1978.

2604) Weis, Charles B., Jr. and Robert N. Dain. "Ego
       Development and Sex Attitudes in Heterosexual and
       Homosexual Men and Women," Archives of Sexual
       Behavior, 8:341-56, 1979.

2605) Weissman, Gerald. "A Gut Reaction: The Cells of
       Pleasure [Opportunistic Diseases in Gay Men]," Hos-
       pital Practice, 17:24-28+, Jul. 1982.

2606) Whitam, Frederick L. "Childhood Indicators of Male
       Homosexuality," Archives of Sexual Behavior, 6:89-
       96, 1977.

2607) _____. "The Homosexual Role: A Reconsidera-
       tion," Journal of Sex Research, 13:1-11, 1977.

2608) _____. "The Prehomosexual Male Child in Three
       Societies: The United States, Guatemala, Brazil,"
       Archives of Sexual Behavior, 9:87-99, 1980.

2609)   . "Rejoinder to Omark's Comment on the Homosexual Role" and "A Reply to Goode," Journal of Sex Research, 14:274-75, 1978 and 17:66-72, 1981.

2610)   White, Terri A. "Attitudes of Psychiatric Nurses Toward Same Sex Orientations," Nursing Research, 28:276-80, 1979.

2611)   Whitehead, George I., and Susan C. Metzger. "Helping Behavior in Urban and Non-Urban Settings," Journal of Social Psychology, 114:295-96, 1981.

2612)   Whitman, Roy M., and Harry E. Morgan. "Group Process During a Consultation: An Institution Copes with Perceived Homosexual Onslaught," Social Psychiatry, 16:105-09, 1981.

2613)   Whyte, John, and Lisa Capaldini. "Treating the Lesbian or Gay Patient," Delaware Medical Journal, 52:271-77, 1980.

2614)   Willcox, R. R. "Epidemiology of Anorectal Disease: A Review," Journal of the Royal Society of Medicine, 73:508-09, 1980.

2615)   . "The Rectum as Viewed by the Venereal-ogist," British Journal of Venereal Diseases, 57:1-6, 1981.

2616)   , and others. "Sexual Behavior and Sexually Transmitted Disease Patterns in Male Homosexuals," British Journal of Venereal Diseases, 57:167-69, 1981.

2617)   William, Daniel C. "Sexually Transmitted Diseases in Gay Men: An Insider's View," Sexually Transmitted Diseases, 6:278-80, 1979.

2618)   , and others. "High Rates of Enteric Protozoal Infections in Selected Homosexual Men Attending a Venereal Disease Clinic," Sexually Transmitted Diseases, 5:155, 1978.

2619)   , and others. "Sexually Transmitted Enteric Pathogens in Male Homosexual Population," New York State Journal of Medicine, 77:2050-52, 1977.

2620)   Williams, Stephen G.   "Male Homosexual Responses
        to MMPI Combined with Subscales Mf and Mf2,"
        Psychological Reports, 49:606, 1981.

2621)   Williams, Thomas.   "When Your Patient Is a Homo-
        sexual," Journal of Practical Nursing, 26:34, Aug.
        1976.

2622)   Wilson, D. H.   "AID for Lesbians," British Medical
        Journal, 2:669, 1979.

2623)   Wilson, M. Lee.   "Neuroticism and Extraversion of
        Female Homosexuals," Psychological Reports, 51:
        559-62, 1982.

2624)   Wise, Thomas N. , and others.   "Partners of Dis-
        tressed Transvestites," American Journal of Psy-
        chology, 138:1221-24, 1981.

2625)   Wright, Rex A. , and Michael D. Storms.   "Male
        Sexual Schemata and Responses to Male Homosexu-
        ality," Personality and Social Psychology Bulletin,
        7:444-50, 1981.

2626)   Young, Michael, and Jean Whertvine.   "Attitudes of
        Heterosexual Students Toward Homosexual Behavior,"
        Psychological Reports, 51:673-74, 1982.

2627)   Zalewska, Marina.   "Can Primal Therapy Cure Ho-
        mosexuality?" Journal of Primal Therapy, 3:226-29,
        1976.

2628)   Ziebold, Thomas O.   "Ethical Issues in Substance-
        Abuse Treatment Relevant to Sexual Minorities,"
        Contemporary Drug Problems, 8:413-18, 1980.

2629)   Ziegler, John L. , and others.   "Outbreak of Burkitt-
        like Lymphoma in Homosexual Men," Lancet, 2:631-
        33, 1982.

2630)   Zuger, Bernard.   "Effeminate Behavior Present in
        Boys from Childhood: Ten Additional Years of Follow-
        up," Comprehensive Psychiatry, 19:363-69, 1978.

2631)   _____.   "Homosexuality and Parental Guilt," Brit-
        ish Journal of Psychiatry, 137:55-57, 1980.

2632)   _____ . "Homosexuals Who Give No History of
            Effeminacy," Journal of the American Academy of
            Psychoanalysis, 9:483-87, 1981.

2633)   _____ . "Monozygotic Twins Discordant for Homo-
            sexuality: A Report of a Pair and Significance of the
            Phenomenon," Comprehensive Psychiatry, 17:661-69,
            1976.

2634)   _____ . "A Neglected Source-Book on Homosexu-
            ality," British Journal of Psychiatry, 133:87-88,
            1978.

ARTICLES IN OTHER SPECIALIZED JOURNALS

2635) Adam, Barry D. "Some Continuities in Out-Group Stereotypes," Gai Saber, 1:72-76, 1977-78.

2636) _____. "Stigma and Employability: The Discrimination by Sex and Sexual Orientation in the Ontario Legal Profession," Canadian Review of Sociology and Anthropology, 18:216-21, 1981.

2637) Addelson, Kathryn P. "Words and Lives," Signs, 7:187-99, 1981.

2638) Adelman, Marcy R. "Sexual Orientation and Violations of Civil Liberties," Journal of Homosexuality, 2:327-30, 1976-77.

2639) Africa, Thomas. "Homosexuals in Greek History," Journal of Psychohistory, 9:401-20, 1982.

2640) Albro, Joyce C., and Carol Tully. "A Study of Lesbian Lifestyles in the Homosexual Micro-culture and the Heterosexual Macro-culture," Journal of Homosexuality, 4:331-44, 1978-79.

2641) Allen, Paula G. "Lesbians in American Indian Cultures," Conditions, 7:67-87, 1981.

2642) Alter, Robert. "Proust and the Ideological Reader," Salmagundi, 58-59:347-57, 1982.

2643) Anderson, Carla L. "The Effect of a Workshop on Attitudes of Female Nursing Students Toward Male Homosexuality," Journal of Homosexuality, 7:57-69, 1981-82. (Reprinted in Gonsiorek, no. 14, pp. 57-62.)

2644) Anderson, Craig L. "Males as Sexual Assault Victims: Multiple Levels of Trauma," Journal of Ho-

mosexuality, 7:145-62, 1981-82. (Reprinted in
Gonsiorek, no. 14, pp. 145-62.)

2645) Anthony, Bronwyn D. "Lesbian Client-Lesbian
Therapist Opportunities and Challenges in Working
Together," Journal of Homosexuality, 7:45-57,
1981-82. (Reprinted in Gonsiorek, no. 14, pp.
45-57.)

2646) Arkin, Stephen. "The Man in the Deerstalker
Cap: The Mysteries of Biographical Discovery,"
Modern Fiction Studies, 26:628-30, 1980-81.

2647) Armstrong, E. N. "American Scene as Satire:
The Art of Paul Cadmus in the 1930s," Arts Magazine, 56:122-25, Mar. 1982.

2648) Atwell, Lee. "'Word Is Out' and 'Gay USA,'"
Film Quarterly, 32:50-57, Winter 1978-79.

2649) Baker, A. L. "Chronic Type B Hepatitis in Gay
Men: Experience with Patients Referred from the
Howard Brown Memorial Clinic to the University
of Chicago," Journal of Homosexuality, 5:311-15,
1979-80.

2650) Baker, Donald F., and others. "Are High School
Teachers Ready for Homosexual Students?" Phi
Delta Kappan, 63:67, Sep. 1981.

2651) Banes, Sally. "Men Together," Dance Magazine,
55:31-32+, Mar. 1981.

2652) Bartley, W. W., III. "Wittgenstein and Homosexuality," Salmagundi, 58-59:166-96, 1982.

2653) Barton, Bruce C. "Peer Counseling for Gay and
Other Alternative Life-styles," Journal of College
Student Personnel, 21:370, 1980.

2654) Bayer, Ronald, and Robert L. Spitzer. "Edited
Correspondence on the Status of Homosexuality in
DSM-III [Diagnostic and Statistical Manual, 3d
edition]," Journal of the History of the Behavioral
Sciences, 18:32-52, 1982.

2655) Beane, Jeffrey. "'I'd Rather Be Dead Than Gay':
Counseling of Gay Men Who Are Coming Out."

Personnel and Guidance Journal, 60:222-26,
1981.

2656)   Beaton, Stephen, and Naome Guild.   "Treat-
         ment for Gay Problem Drinkers," Social Case-
         work, 57:302-08, 1976.

2657)   Beaver, Harold.   "Homosexual Signs," Critical
         Inquiry, 8:99-119, 1981-82.

2658)   Bedient, Calvin.   "Walt Whitman Overruled,"
         Salmagundi, 58-59:326-46, 1982.

2659)   Begelman, D. A.   "Homosexuality and the Eth-
         ics of Behavioral Intervention," Journal of Homo-
         sexuality, 2:213-19, 1976-77.

2660)   Bell, Joseph J.   "Public Manifestations of Per-
         sonal Morality: Limitations on the Use of Solic-
         itation Statutes to the Control of Homosexual
         Cruising," Journal of Homosexuality, 5:97-114,
         1979-80.   (Reprinted in Knutson, no. 20, pp.
         97-114.)

2661)   Bender, V. Lee, and others.   "Patterns of Self-
         Disclosure in Homosexual and Heterosexual Col-
         lege Students," Sex Roles, 2:149-60, 1976.

2662)   Bennett, Paula.   "The Language of Love: Emily
         Dickinson's Homoerotic Poetry," Gai Saber, 1:13-
         17, 1977-78.

2663)   Bentley, Eric.   "The Homosexual Question," Ca-
         nadian Theatre Review, Fall 1976, pp. 15-23.
         (Reprinted in American Review, 26:288-303, 1977.)

2664)   Berger, Raymond M.   "An Advocate Model for
         Intervention with Homosexuals," Social Work, 22:
         280-83, 1977.

2665)   _____.   "Psychological Adaptation of the Older
         Homosexual Male," Journal of Homosexuality, 5:
         161-75, 1979-80.

2666)   _____.   "The Unseen Minority: Older Gays
         and Lesbians," Social Work, 27:236-41, 1982.

2667)   _____, and James J. Kelly. "Do Social Work
Agencies Discriminate Against Homosexual Job
Applicants?" Social Work, 26:193-98, 1981.

2668)   Bernard, Jessie. "Homosexuality and Female Depression," Journal of Social Issues, 32: no. 4:213-38,
1976.

2669)   Bernard, Larry C., and David J. Epstein. "Androgyny Scores of Matched Homosexual and Heterosexual
Males," Journal of Homosexuality, 4:169-78, 1978-79.

2670)   Bernstein, Barton E. "Legal and Social Interface in
Counseling Homosexual Clients," Social Casework,
58:36-40, 1977.

2671)   Biemiller, Lawrence. "Homosexual Academics Say
Coming Out Could Jeopardize Careers," Chronicle of
Higher Education, 25:9-10, Oct. 20, 1982.

2672)   Binder, C. V. "Affection Training: An Alternative
to Sexual Reorientation," Journal of Homosexuality,
2:251-59, 1976-77.

2673)   Birke, Linda I. A. "Is Homosexuality Hormonally
Determined?" Journal of Homosexuality, 6:35-49,
Summer 1981. (Reprinted in Koertge, no. 21, pp.
35-49.)

2674)   Bittle, William E. "Alcoholics Anonymous and the
Gay Alcoholic," Journal of Homosexuality, 7:81-88,
1981-82. (Reprinted in Ziebold and Mongeon, no.
37, pp. 81-88.)

2675)   Blau, Herbert. "Politics and the Presentation of
Self: Disseminating Sodom," Salmagundi, 58-59:221-
51, 1982.

2676)   Blumstein, Philip, and Pepper Schwartz. "Bisexuality in Men," Urban Life, 5:339-58, 1976-77.

2677)   _____, and _____. "Bisexuality: Some Social
Psychological Issues," Journal of Social Issues, 33:
no. 2: 30-45, 1977.

2678)   Boswell, John. "Towards the Long View: Revolu-
tions, Universals, and Sexual Categories," Salmagundi, 58-59:89-113, 1982.

2679)   Bowles, James K.   "Dealing with Homosexuality: A
        Survey of Staff Training Needs," Journal of College
        Student Personnel, 22:276-77, 1981.

2680)   Boyette, Purvis E.   "Wanton Humor and Wanton
        Poets: Homosexuality in Marlowe's Edward II,"
        Tulane Studies in English, 22:33-50, 1977.

2681)   Boyum, Richard.   "Gay Counseling Group: The Uni-
        versity of Wisconsin-Eau Claire Counseling Center in
        Cooperation with the University Ecumenical Religious
        Center," Journal of College Student Personnel, 19:75,
        1978.

2682)   Bozett, Frederick W.   "Gay Fathers: How and Why
        They Disclose Their Homosexuality to Their Chil-
        dren," Family Relations, 29:173-79, 1980.

2683)   _____. "Gay Fathers: Identity Conflict Resolution
        Through Integration Sanctioning," Alternative Life-
        styles, 4:90-107, 1981.

2684)   Briggs, H. Carson.   "Coalition Building for Gay
        Rights," Social Policy, 9:57, May 1978.

2685)   Brown, Douglas F.   "The Health Service and Gay
        Students," Journal of the American College Health
        Association, 24:272-73, 1975-76.

2686)   Brudnoy, David.   "Homosexuality in America: At
        200 Years," Homosexual Counseling Journal, 3:10-
        22, 1976.

2687)   Brummett, Barry.   "A Pentadic Analysis of Ideologies
        in Two Gay Rights Controversies," Central States
        Speech Journal, 30:250-61, 1979.

2688)   Bulkin, Elly.   "Whole New Poetry Beginning Here:
        Teaching Lesbian Poetry," College English, 40:874-
        88, 1979.

2689)   Bullough, Vern L.   "Challenges to Societal Attitudes
        Toward Homosexuality in the Late Nineteenth and
        Early Twentieth Centuries," Social Science Quarterly,
        58:29-44, Jun. 1977.

2690)   _____, and Bonnie Bullough. "Lesbianism in the
            1920s and 1930s: A Newfound Study," Signs, 2:895-
            904, 1977.

2691)   Burg, B. Richard. "Ho Hum, Another Work of the
            Devil: Buggery and Sodomy in Early Stuart England,"
            Journal of Homosexuality, 6:69-78, 1980-81. (Re-
            printed in Licata and Peterson, no. 23, pp. 69-78.)

2692)   Burnett, Anne. "Desire and Memory [Sappho Frag-
            ment 94]," Classical Philology, 74:16-27, 1979.

2693)   Cady, Joseph. "Homosexuality and the Calamus
            Poems," American Studies, 19:5-22, 1978.

2694)   Califia, Pat. "Feminism and Sadomasochism," Co-
            Evolution Quarterly, 33:33-40, Spring 1982.

2695)   _____. "Lesbian Sexuality," Journal of Homosexu-
            ality, 4:255-66, 1978-79.

2696)   Carrier, Joseph M. "Family Attitudes and Mexican
            Male Homosexuality," Urban Life, 5:359-75, 1976-77.

2697)   Carroll, Leo. "Humanitarian Reform and Biracial
            Sexual Assault in a Maximum Security Prison," Ur-
            ban Life, 5:417-37, 1976-77.

2698)   Cass, Vivienne C. "Homosexual Identity Formation:
            A Theoretical Model," Journal of Homosexuality, 4:
            219-35, 1978-79.

2699)   Chalus, Gary A. "An Evaluation of the Validity of
            the Freudian Theory of Paranoia," Journal of Homo-
            sexuality, 3:171-88, 1977-78.

2700)   Chauncey, George, Jr. "From Sexual Inversion to
            Homosexuality: Medicine and the Changing Conceptu-
            alization of Female Deviance," Salmagundi, 58-59:
            114-46, 1982.

2701)   Chesebro, James W. "Paradoxical Views of 'Homo-
            sexuality' in the Rhetoric of Social Scientists: A
            Fantasy Theme Analysis," Quarterly Journal of
            Speech, 66:127-39, 1980.

2702)   Childs, Maggie. "Japan's Homosexual Heritage,"
         Gai Saber, 1:41-45, 1977-78.

2703)   Chng, Chwee Lye. "Adolescent Homosexual Be-
         havior and the Health Educator," Journal of School
         Health, 50:517-21, 1980.

2704)   "The Church and Homosexuality," Journal of Cur-
         rent Social Issues, 15:79-81, Spring 1978.

2705)   Clay, James W. "Self and Roles in Relation to the
         Process Writing in Jean Genet's Journal du Voleur
         and John Rechy's City of Night," Gai Saber, 1:112-
         31, 1977-78.

2706)   Clayborne, Jon. "Blacks and Gay Liberation," Gai
         Saber, 1:55-57, 1977-78.

2707)   Cohan, A. S. "Obstacles to Equality: Government
         Responses to the Gay Rights Movement in the United
         States," Political Studies, 30:59-76, 1982.

2708)   Cohn, Jack R., and Thomas J. O'Donnell. "Inter-
         view with Robert Duncan," Contemporary Literature,
         21:513-48, 1980.

2709)   Colcher, Ronnie W. "Counseling the Homosexual
         Alcoholic," Journal of Homosexuality, 7:43-52, 1981-
         82. (Reprinted in Ziebold and Mongeon, no. 37,
         pp. 43-52.)

2710)   Coleman, Eli. "Bisexual and Gay Men in Hetero-
         sexual Marriage: Conflicts and Resolutions in Thera-
         py," Journal of Homosexuality, 7:93-103, 1981-82.
         (Reprinted in Gonsiorek, no. 14, pp. 93-103.)

2711)   _____. "Developmental Stages of the Coming Out
         Process," Journal of Homosexuality, 7:31-43, 1981-
         82. (Reprinted in Gonsiorek, no. 14, pp. 31-43.)

2712)   _____. "Toward a New Model of Treatment of
         Homosexuality: A Review," Journal of Homosexuality,
         3:345-59, 1977-78.

2713)   Conlin, David, and Jaime Smith. "Group Psycho-
         therapy for Gay Men," Journal of Homosexuality, 7:
         105-12, 1981-82. (Reprinted in Gonsiorek, no. 14,
         pp. 105-12.)

2714)   Connor, Edward. "Film in Drag: Transvestism on
        the Screen," Films in Review, 32:398-405, 1981.

2715)   Cook, Blanche W.   "The Historical Denial of Les-
        bianism," Radical History Review, 20:60-65, 1979.

2716)   _____.   "Women Alone ... Lesbianism and the
        Cultural Tradition," Signs, 4:718-39, 1979.

2717)   Cooper, Janet. "Female Crushes, Affections, and
        Friendships in Children's Literature," Gai Saber,
        1:83-88, 1977-78.

2718)   Corbett, Sherry L. , and others. "Tolerance as a
        Correlate of Experience with Stigma: The Case of
        the Homosexual," Journal of Homosexuality, 3:3-13,
        1977-78.

2719)   Corzine, Jay, and Richard Kirby.   "Cruising the
        Truckers: Sexual Encounters in a Highway Rest
        Area," Urban Life, 6:171-92, 1977-78.

2720)   Coser, Lewis. "Midge Dector and the Boys on the
        Beach," Dissent, 28:217-18, 1981.

2721)   Coughlin, Ellen K.   "Homosexual Professors Find
        Bias Plagues Their Life on Campuses," Chronicle
        of Higher Education, 19:1, 8-9, Sep. 24, 1979.

2722)   Coward, D. A.   "Attitudes to Homosexuality in
        Eighteenth Century France," Journal of European
        Studies, 10:231-55, 1980.

2723)   Crew, Louie. "Honey, Let's Talk About the Queen's
        English," Gai Saber, 1:240-43, 1977-78.

2724)   _____, and K. Keener.   "Homophobia in the
        Academy--A Report of the Committee on Gay/Lesbian
        Concerns," College English, 43:682-89, 1981.   Re-
        sponses: 44:433-34, 1982.

2725)   Crompton, Louis. "Homosexuals and the Death
        Penalty in Colonial America," Journal of Homosexu-
        ality, 1:277-93, 1975-76.

2726)   _____.   "Jeremy Bentham's Essay on 'Paederasty,'"
        Journal of Homosexuality, 3:383-405, 1977-78 and 4:
        91-107, 1978-79.

2727) _____ . "The Myth of Lesbian Impunity: Capital
Laws from 1270 to 1791," Journal of Homosexuality,
6:11-25, 1980-81. (Reprinted in Licata and Peterson, no. 23, pp. 11-25.)

2728) _____ . "Offenses Against One's Self: Paederasty.
Part I. Jeremy Bentham," Journal of Homosexuality,
3:389-405, 1977-78.

2729) Cronin, Denise M. "Female Homosexuality: Behavior Following the Social Script Model of Sexuality,"
National Association of Student Personnel Administra-
tors' Journal, 13:57-61, 1976.

2730) Cruikshank, Margaret. "Notes on Recent Lesbian
Autobiographical Writing," Journal of Homosexuality,
8:19-26, 1982-83.

2731) Cunningham, P. G., and A. J. Parker. "Two
Selves, Two Sexes: Deference and the Interpretation
of a Homosexual Presence," Sociology and Social Research, 63:90-111, 1978-79.

2732) Cushman, Keith. "A Note on Lawrence's Fly in the
Ointment," English Language Notes, 15:47-51, 1977-
78.

2733) Dailey, Dennis M. "Legitimacy and Performance in
the Gay Relationship: Some Intervention Alternatives,"
Journal of Social Welfare, 4:81-88, 1977.

2734) Dank, Barry M. "The Social Construction and Destruction of the Homosexual," Humanity and Society,
4:133-47, June 1980.

2735) David, Pam, and Lois Helmbold. "San Francisco:
Courts and Cops vs. Gays," Radical America, 12:
27-32, 1979.

2736) Davies, Christie. "Sexual Taboos and Social Boundaries," American Journal of Sociology, 87:1032-63,
1982.

2737) Davison, Gerald C. "Homosexuality and the Ethics
of Behavioral Intervention: Homosexuality, the Ethical Challenge," Journal of Homosexuality, 2:195-204,
1976-77.

2738)   _____, and Friedman, Steven. "Sexual Orientation
          Stereotypy in the Distortion of Clinical Judgment,"
          Journal of Homosexuality, 6:37-44, Summer 1981.
          (Reprinted in Koertge, No. 21, pp. 37-44.)

2739)   Deats, Sara M. "Myth and Metamorphosis in Mar-
          lowe's Edward II," Texas Studies in Literature and
          Language, 22:304-21, 1980.

2740)   DeBoer, Connie. "The Polls: Attitudes Toward Ho-
          mosexuality [in Various Countries]," Public Opinion
          Quarterly, 42:265-76, 1978.

2741)   DeCecco, John P. "Definition and Meaning of Sexual
          Orientation," Journal of Homosexuality, 6:51-67,
          Summer 1981. (Reprinted in Koertge, no. 21, pp.
          51-67.)

2742)   _____. "Studying Violations of Civil Liberties of
          Homosexual Men and Women," Journal of Homosexu-
          ality, 2:315-22, 1976-77.

2743)   _____, and Mary C. Figliulo. "Methodology for
          Studying Discrimination Based on Sexual Orientation
          and Social Sex-Role Stereotypes," Journal of Homo-
          sexuality, 3:235-41, 1977-78.

2744)   _____, and Michael G. Shively. "A Study of Per-
          ceptions of Rights and Needs in Interpersonal Con-
          flicts in Homosexual Relationships," Journal of Ho-
          mosexuality, 3:205-16, 1977-78.

2745)   Decker, Phillip J. "Homosexuality and Employment:
          A Case Law Review," Personnel Journal, 59:756-60,
          1980.

2746)   Dector, Midge. "Boys on the Beach [Fire Island],"
          Commentary, 70:35-48, Sep. 1980.

2747)   DeMonteflores, Carmen, and Stephen J. Shultz.
          "Coming Out: Similarities and Differences for Les-
          bians and Gay Men," Journal of Social Issues, 34:
          no. 3:59-72, 1978.

2748)   Diamond, Deborah L., and Sharon C. Wilsnack. "Al-
          cohol Abuse Among Lesbians: A Descriptive Study,"
          Journal of Homosexuality, 4:123-42, 1978-79.

2749)   "Do Homosexuals Have the Right to Teach in Our
        Schools?" Instructor, 87:29, Apr. 1978.

2750)   Domino, George. "Homosexuality and Creativity,"
        Journal of Homosexuality, 2:261-67, 1976-77.

2751)   Donovan, Josephine. "The Unpublished Love Prob-
        lems of Sarah Orne Jewett," Frontiers, 4:26-31,
        1979.

2752)   Doughty, Frances. "Lesbian Biography, Biography
        of Lesbians," Frontiers, 4:76-79, 1979.

2753)   Dressler, Joshua. "Study of Law Student Attitudes
        Regarding the Rights of Gay People to Be Teachers,"
        Journal of Homosexuality, 4:315-29, 1978-79.

2754)   Driscoll, Rosanne. "A Gay-Identified Alcohol Treat-
        ment Program: A Follow-up Study," Journal of Ho-
        mosexuality, 7:71-80, 1981-82. (Reprinted in Zie-
        bold and Mongeon, no. 37, pp. 71-80.)

2755)   Duberman, Martin B. "Gay in the Fifties," Sal-
        magundi, 58-59:42-75, 1982.

2756)   _____. "'I Am Not Contented': Female Masochism
        and Lesbianism in Early Twentieth Century New Eng-
        land," Signs, 5:825-41, 1980.

2757)   _____. "'Writhing Bedfellows': 1826 Two Young
        Men from Antebellum South Carolina's Ruling Elite
        Share 'Extravagant Delight,'" Journal of Homosexu-
        ality, 6:85-101, 1980-81. (Reprinted in Licata and
        Peterson, no. 23, pp. 85-101.)

2758)   Dubro, James R. "The Third Sex: Lord Hervey and
        His Coterie," Eighteenth Century Life, 2:89-95, 1976.

2759)   Duehm, Wayne D., and Nazneen Mayadas. "The Use
        of Stimulus/Modeling Videotapes in Assertive Train-
        ing for Homosexuals," Journal of Homosexuality, 1:
        373-81, 1975-76.

2760)   Duggan, Lisa. "Lesbianism and American History:
        A Brief Source Review," Frontiers, 4:80-85, 1979.

2761)   Dulaney, Diana D., and James Kelly. "Improving
        Services to Gay and Lesbian Clients," Social Work,
        27:178-83, 1982.

2762)   Dundes, Alan. "Into the Endzone for a Touchdown:
        A Psychoanalytic Consideration of American Football,"
        Western Folklore, 37:75-88, 1978.

2763)   Dynes, Wayne. "Orpheus Without Eurydice," Gai
        Saber, 1:268-78, 1977-78.

2764)   Ellem, Elizabeth W. "E. M. Forster's Greenwood,"
        Journal of Modern Literature, 5:89-98, 1976.

2765)   Elshtain, Jean B. "Homosexual Politics: The Para-
        dox of Gay Liberation," Salmagundi, 58-59:252-80,
        1982.

2766)   Epstein, Joseph. "What Makes [Gore] Vidal Run?"
        Commentary, 63:72-75, Jun. 1977.

2767)   Eriksson, Birgitte (trans.). "A Lesbian Execution
        in Germany, 1721: The Trial Records," Journal of
        Homosexuality, 6:27-40, 1980-81. (Reprinted in
        Licata and Peterson, no. 23, pp. 27-40.)

2768)   Ettore, E. M. "Sappho Revisited: A New Look at
        Lesbianism," Women's Studies International Quarter-
        ly, 3:415-28, 1980.

2769)   Evans, Medford. "There's No Such Thing as a Good
        Fairy," American Opinion, 20:23-28+, May 1977.

2770)   "Eye-opening Survey: A Kinsey Institute Study by
        Bell and Weinberg," Human Behavior, 7:58-59, Dec.
        1978.

2771)   Faderman, Lillian. "Emily Dickinson's Letters to
        Sue Gilbert," Massachusetts Review, 18:197-225,
        1977.

2772)   _____. "Female Same-Sex Relationships in Novels
        by Longfellow, Holmes, and James," New England
        Quarterly, 51:309-22, 1978.

2773)   _____. "Lesbian Magazine Fiction in the Early
        Twentieth Century," Journal of Popular Culture, 11:
        800-17, 1978.

2774) _____. "The Morbidification of Love Between Women by Nineteenth Century Sexologists," Journal of Homosexuality, 4:73-90, 1978-79.

2775) _____. "Who Hid Lesbian History?" Frontiers, 4:74-76, 1979.

2776) Farber, Stephen. "From Sissies to Studs," American Film, 6:72+, Sep. 1981.

2777) Farrell, Ronald A., and James F. Nelson. "A Causal Model of Secondary Deviance: The Case of Homosexuality," Sociological Quarterly, 17:109-20, 1976.

2778) Fassler, Barbara. "Theories of Homosexuality as Sources of Bloomsbury's Androgyny," Signs, 5:237-51, 1979.

2779) Fein, Sara B., and Elane M. Nuehring. "Intrapsychic Effect of Stigma: A Process of Breakdown and Reconstruction of Social Reality," Journal of Homosexuality, 7:3-13, 1981-82. (Reprinted in Gonsiorek, no. 14, pp. 3-13.)

2780) Feinbloom, Deborah H., and others. "Lesbian/ Feminist Orientation Among Male-to-Female Transsexuals," Journal of Homosexuality, 2:59-71, 1976-77.

2781) Feldman, Philip. "Helping Homosexuals with Problems: A Commentary and a Personal View," Journal of Homosexuality, 2:241-49, 1976-77.

2782) Felman, Shoshana. "Rereading Femininity [Lesbianism]," Yale French Studies, 62:19-44, 1981.

2783) Ferguson, Ann. "Patriarchy, Sexual Identity, and the Sexual Revolution," Signs, 7:158-72, 1981.

2784) Fernbach, David. "Toward a Marxist Theory of Gay Liberation," Socialist Revolution, 6:28, Apr.-Jun. 1976.

2785) Figliulo, Mary C., and others. "The Relationship of Departures in Social Sex-Role to the Abridgment of Civil Liberties," Journal of Homosexuality, 3: 249-55, 1977-78.

2786)   Firmat, Gustavo P.   "Descent into Paradiso: A
        Study of Heaven and Homosexuality," Hispania,
        59:247-57, 1976.

2787)   Fischli, Ronald.   "Anita Bryant's Stand Against
        'Militant Homosexuality': Religious Fundamentalism
        and the Democratic Process," Central States Speech
        Journal, 30:262-71, 1979.

2788)   Fitzgerald, Thomas K.   "A Critique of Anthropologi-
        cal Research on Homosexuality," Journal of Homo-
        sexuality, 2:385-97, 1976-77.

2789)   "Florida Law Denying Funds to Campus Homosexuals
        Overturned," Chronicle of Higher Education, 23: 9,
        Feb. 17, 1982.

2790)   Flygare, Thomas J.   "Supreme Court Refuses to
        Hear Case of Discharged Homosexual Teacher,"
        Phi Delta Kappan, 59:482-83, 1978.

2791)   Flynn, Charles P.   "Sexuality and Insult Behavior,"
        Journal of Sex Behavior, 12:1-13, Feb. 1976.

2792)   Follett, Richard J.   "Censors in our Midst [Teaching
        Gay Literature]," College English, 43:690-93, 1981.

2793)   _____, and Rayna Larson.   "It Is Dishonest of
        English Teachers to Ignore the Homosexuality of
        Literary Figures Whose Works They Teach [Pro
        and Con]," English Journal, 71:18-21, Apr. 1982.

2794)   Francher, Jay S. , and Serena Nanda.   "Cultural
        Patterning and Sex Roles: Evolution in Long-term
        Relationships Among Male Homosexuals," Gai Saber,
        1:207-10, 1977-78.

2795)   Freudenberger, Herbert J.   "The Gay Addict in a
        Drug and Alcohol Abuse Therapeutic Community,"
        Homosexual Counseling Journal, 3:34-45, 1976.

2796)   Freund, Kurt.   "Should Homosexuality Arouse
        Therapeutic Concern?" Journal of Homosexuality,
        2:235-40, 1976-77.

2797)   Friend, Richard A.   "GAYging: Adjustment and
        the Older Gay Male," Alternative Lifestyles, 3:
        231-48, 1980.

2798)   Fryer, Jonathan H.   "Sexuality in Isherwood, " Twen-
         tieth Century Literature, 22:343-53, 1976.

2799)   Fussell, Mark E. B.   "Billy Budd: Melville's Happy
         Ending," Studies in Romanticism, 15:43-57, 1976.

2800)   Gardner, Philip.   "E. M. Forster and the Possession
         of England," Modern Language Quarterly, 42:166-83,
         1981.

2801)   Garfinkle, Ellen M. , and Stephen F. Morin.   "Psy-
         chotherapists' Attitudes Toward Homosexual Psycho-
         therapy Clients, " Journal of Social Issues, 34: no.
         3:101-12, 1978.

2802)   "Gay Ghettos--A Study by Martin P. Levine," Hu-
         man Behavior, 7:41, Sep. 1978.

2803)   "Gays, a Major Force in the Market Place," Busi-
         ness Week, Sep. 3, 1979, pp. 118-20.

2804)   Geis, Gilbert, and others.   "Reported Consequences
         of Decriminalization of Consensual Adult Homosexu-
         ality in Seven American States," Journal of Homo-
         sexuality, 1:419-26, 1975-76.

2805)   George, Bill.   "Young Homosexuals and the Corrup-
         tion Theory," Social Work Today, 8:11-13, Nov. 16,
         1976.

2806)   Gibbs, Annette.   "Gay Student Organization on Cam-
         pus: The Controversy Continues," Journal of Col-
         lege Student Personnel, 20:485-89, 1979.

2807)   Gibson, E. Lawrence.   "Homosexuality in the Navy:
         The Suppressed Findings of the Crittenden Board,"
         Gai Saber, 1:132-35, 1977-78.

2808)   Gilbert, Arthur N.   "Buggery and the British Navy,
         1700-1861," Journal of Social History, 10:72-98,
         1976-77.

2809)   _____.   "Conceptions of Homosexuality and Sodomy
         in Western History," Journal of Homosexuality, 6:
         57-68, 1980-81.   (Reprinted in Licata and Peterson,
         no. 23, pp. 57-68.)

2810)   Glassner, Barry, and Carol Owen. "Variations in
         Attitudes Toward Homosexuality," Cornell Journal
         of Social Relations, 11:161-76, 1976.

2811)   Glazier, Lyle. "Who Are the Homosexuals?" Hu-
         manist, 36:20-24, Nov. -Dec. 1976.

2812)   Goldberg, Raymond. "Attitude Change Among Col-
         lege Students Toward Homosexuality," Journal of
         the American College Health Association, 30:260-
         68, 1982.

2813)   Goldberg, Steven. "Is Homosexuality Normal?"
         Policy Review, 21:119-38, 1982.

2814)   Goldhaber, Gerald M. "Gay Talk: Communication
         Behavior of Male Homosexuals," Gai Saber, 1:136-
         49, 1977-78.

2815)   Goldstein, Melvin. "Some Tolerant Attitudes Toward
         Female Homosexuality Throughout History," Journal
         of Psychohistory, 9:437-60, 1982.

2816)   Goldstein, William. "Interview with Novelist Edmund
         White," Publishers Weekly, 222:6-8, Sep. 24, 1982.

2817)   Gonos, George, and others. "Anonymous Expres-
         sion: A Structural View of [Anti-Homosexual] Graf-
         fiti," Journal of American Folklore, 89:40-48, 1976.

2818)   Gonsiorek, John C. "Organizational and Staff Prob-
         lems in Gay/Lesbian Mental Health Agencies," Jour-
         nal of Homosexuality, 7:193-208, 1981-82. (Re-
         printed in Gonsiorek, no. 14, pp. 193-208.)

2819)   _____. "Present and Future Directions in Gay/
         Lesbian Mental Health," Journal of Homosexuality,
         7:5-7, 1981-82. (Reprinted in Gonsiorek, no. 14,
         pp. 5-7.)

2820)   _____. "Use of Diagnostic Concepts in Working
         with Gay and Lesbian Populations," Journal of Ho-
         mosexuality, 7:9-20, 1981-82. (Reprinted in Gon-
         siorek, no. 14, pp. 9-20.)

2821)   Gonzales, R. M. "Hallucinogenic Dependency During
         Adolescence as a Defense Against Homosexual Fanta-
         sies," Journal of Youth and Adolescence, 8:63-71, 1979.

2822)   Goodich, Michael.   "Sodomy in Ecclesiastical Law
         and Theory," Journal of Homosexuality, 1:427-34,
         1975-76.

2823)   _____.   "Sodomy in Medieval Secular Law," Jour-
         nal of Homosexuality, 1:295-302, 1975-76.

2824)   Gould, Karen.   "Censored Word and 'The Body Poli-
         tic': \ Reconsidering the Fiction of Marie-Claire
         Blais," Journal of Popular Culture, 15:14-27, Win-
         ter 1981.

2825)   Graves, John C.   "Philosophy and Sexuality," Gai
         Saber, 1:23-26, 1977-78.

2826)   Green, Martin.   "Homosexuality in Literature," Sal-
         magundi, 58-59:393-405, 1982.

2827)   Green, Richard.   "The Best Interests of a Child
         with a Lesbian Mother," Bulletin of the American
         Academy of Psychiatry and Law, 10:7-15, 1982.

2828)   Greenberg, Jerrold S.   "The Effects of a Homophile
         Organization on the Self-Esteem and Alienation of Its
         Members," Journal of Homosexuality, 1:313-17, 1975-
         76.

2829)   Gubar, Susan.   "Blessings in Disguise: Cross-
         Dressing as Redressing for Female Modernists,"
         Massachusetts Review, 22:477-508, 1981.

2830)   Gundlach, Ralph H.   "Sexual Molestation and Rape
         Reported by Homosexual and Heterosexual Women,"
         Journal of Homosexuality, 2:367-84, 1976-77.

2831)   Gutstadt, Joseph P.   "Male Pseudoheterosexuality
         and Minimal Sexual Dysfunction," Journal of Sex and
         Marital Therapy, 2:297-302, 1976.

2832)   Haeberle, Erwin J.   "'Stigmata of Degeneration:'
         Prisoner Markings in Nazi Concentration Camps,"
         Journal of Homosexuality, 6:135-39, 1980-81.   (Re-
         printed in Licata and Peterson, no. 23, pp. 135-39.)

2833)   Hall, Marny.   "Lesbian Families: Cultural and Clin-
         ical Issues," Social Work, 23:380-85, 1978.

2834)   Hanckel, Frances, and John Cunningham.   "Can
        Young Gays Find Happiness in Young Adult Books?"
        Wilson's Library Bulletin, 50:528-34, 1975-76.   Re-
        sponses: 50:777 and 51:300-04, 1976-77.

2835)   Hansen, Bert.   "The Historical Construction of Ho-
        mosexuality," Radical History Review, 20:66-73,
        1979.

2836)   Harry, Joseph.   "Decision Making and Age Differ-
        ences Among Gay Male Couples," Journal of Homo-
        sexuality, 8:9-21, 1982-83.

2837)   _____. "The 'Marital' Liaisons of Gay Men,"
        Family Coordinator, 28:622-29, 1979.

2838)   _____. "On the Validity of Typologies of Gay
        Males," Journal of Homosexuality, 2:143-52, 1976-
        77.

2839)   _____, and Robert Lovely.   "Gay Marriages and
        Communities of Sexual Orientation," Alternative
        Lifestyles, 2:177-200, 1979.

2840)   Hayes, Joseph J.   "Gayspeak," Quarterly Journal
        of Speech, 62:256-66, 1976.

2841)   _____.   "Language and Language Behavior of Les-
        bian Women and Gay Men: A Selected Bibliography,"
        Journal of Homosexuality, 4:201-12 and 299-309,
        1978-79.

2842)   Haynes, Alphonso W.   "Challenge of Counseling the
        Homosexual Client," Personnel and Guidance Journal,
        56:243-46, 1977.

2843)   Heasman, D. J.   "Sexuality and Civil Liberties,"
        Political Quarterly, 48:313-27, 1977.   Response:
        49:99-102 and Rejoinder: 49:227-31, 1978.

2844)   Hedgpeth, Judith M.   "Employment Discrimination
        Law and the Rights of Gay Persons," Journal of Ho-
        mosexuality, 5:67-79, 1979-80.   (Reprinted in Knut-
        son, no. 20, pp. 67-79.)

2845)   Heilbrun, Alfred B., and Norman L. Thompson, Jr.
        "Sex-Role Identity and Male and Female Homosexu-
        ality," Sex Roles, 3:65-79, 1977.

2846)   Helbing, Terry.   "Gay Plays, Gay Theatre, Gay Per-
        formance, " Drama Review, 25:35-46, Mar. 1981.

2847)   Hencken, Joel D. , and William T. O. O'Dowd.
        "Coming Out as an Aspect of Identity Formation, "
        Gai Saber, 1:18-22, 1977-78.

2848)   Henderson, Ann F.   "College Age Lesbianism as a
        Developmental Phenomenon, " Journal of the American
        College Health Association, 28:176-78, 1979-80.

2849)   Henderson, Susan W.   "Frederick the Great of Prus-
        sia: A Homophile Perspective, " Gai Saber, 1:46-54,
        1977-78.

2850)   Hendlin, Steven J.   "Homosexuality in the Rorschach:
        A New Look at the Old Signs, " Journal of Homosexu-
        ality, 1:303-12, 1975-76.

2851)   Hendryx, Steven W.   "In Defense of the Homosexual
        Teacher, " Viewpoints in Teaching and Learning, 56:
        74-84, Fall 1980.

2852)   Heron, Liz.   "[Homosexual Teachers:] Glad to Be
        Gay--But Still Nervous About Admitting It, " Times
        Educational Supplement, no. 3464, p. 11, Nov. 19,
        1982.

2853)   Herron, William G. , and others.   "New Psycho-
        analytic Perspectives on the Treatment of a Homo-
        sexual Male, " Journal of Homosexuality, 5:393-403,
        1979-80.   (Reprinted in Gonsiorek, no. 14, pp. 393-
        403.)

2854)   _____, and others.   "Psychoanalytic Psycho-
        therapy for Homosexual Clients: New Concepts, "
        Journal of Homosexuality, 7:177-92, 1981-82.

2855)   Herz, Judith S.   "The Double Nature of Forster's
        Fiction: A Room with a View and The Longest
        Journey, " English Literature in Transition, 21:254-
        65, 1978.

2856)   Hidalgo, Hilda A. , and Elia H. Christensen.   "The
        Puerto Rican Lesbian and the Puerto Rican Commu-
        nity, " Journal of Homosexuality, 2:109-21, 1976-77.

2857)   Hilliard, David. "Unenglish and Unmanly, Anglo-
         Catholicism and Homosexuality," Victorian Studies,
         25:181-210, Winter 1982.

2858)   Hippler, Mike. "In the Closet Doorway," Learning:
         The Magazine for Creative Teaching, 8:10+, May-
         Jun. 1980.

2859)   Hitchens, Donna. "Social Attitudes, Legal Standards,
         and Personal Trauma in Child Custody Cases," Jour-
         nal of Homosexuality, 5:89-95, 1979-80. (Reprinted
         in Knutson, no. 20, pp. 89-95.)

2860)   Hodges, Robert R. "Deep Fellowship: Homosexu-
         ality and Male Bonding in the Life and Fiction of Jo-
         seph Conrad," Journal of Homosexuality, 4:379-93,
         1978-79.

2861)   Hoffman, Richard J.   "Some Cultural Aspects of
         Greek Male Homosexuality," Journal of Homosexu-
         ality, 5:217-26, 1979-80.

2862)   Hogan, Robert A. , and others.   "Attitudes, Opinions,
         and Sexual Development of 205 Homosexual Women, "
         Journal of Homosexuality, 3:123-26, 1977-78.

2863)   Holmes, K. K.   "Future Directions in Research on
         Sexually Transmitted Diseases in Homosexual Men, "
         Journal of Homosexuality, 5:317-24, 1979-80.

2864)   _____ .   "Nongonococcal Urethritis: General Con-
         siderations and Specific Considerations for Homosexu-
         al Men, " Journal of Homosexuality, 5:295-98, 1979-
         80.

2865)   "Homosexual Is Named as California Regent [Sheldon
         Andelson]," Chronicle of Higher Education, 23:2,
         Mar. 3, 1982.

2866)   "A Homosexual Teacher's Argument and Plea, " Phi
         Delta Kappan, 59:93-94, 1977-78.

2867)   "Homosexuality in America--Poll Findings, " Gallop
         Opinion Index, Oct. 1977, pp. 1-24.

2868)   Hongisto, Richard D.   "Why Are There No Gay
         Choir Boys? Ask Your Friendly Chief of Police, "

Perspectives: The Civil Rights Quarterly, 12:39-
42, Summer 1980.

2869)   Hoover, Eleanor L. "An Open Letter to Anita Bryant," Human Behavior, 7:11-12, Jul. 1978.

2870)   Hudson, Walter W., and Wendell A. Ricketts. "A
Strategy for the Measurement of Homophobia," Journal of Homosexuality, 5:357-72, 1979-80.

2871)   Humm, Andrew. "Personal Politics of Lesbian and
Gay Liberation," Social Policy, 11:40-45, Sep. 1980.

2872)   "Interview of Jonathan Katz: First Step Toward a
Documented Gay History," Publishers' Weekly, 209:
73, Jun. 21, 1976.

2873)   Irwin, Patrick, and Norman L. Thompson. "Acceptance of the Rights of Homosexuals: A Social Profile," Journal of Homosexuality, 3:107-21, 1977-78.

2874)   Itkin, Mikhail. "Edward Carpenter: Prophet of Gay
Freedom," Gai Saber, 1:99-103, 1977-78.

2875)   _____, and Margaret Anderson. "Gay Seeker for
an Unimaginable Freedom," Gai Saber, 1:261-62,
1977-78.

2876)   Jacobs, John A., and William H. Tedford, Jr.
"Factors Affecting the Self-Esteem of the Homosexual
Individual," Journal of Homosexuality, 5:373-82,
1979-80.

2877)   Janda, W. M., and others. "Epidemiology of Pathogenic Neisseria in Homosexual Men," Journal of Homosexuality, 5:289-90, 1979-80.

2878)   Jay, Karla. "The X-Rated Bibliographer: The Story
of Dr. Jeanette H. Foster," Gai Saber, 1:93-94,
1977-78.

2879)   Johnson, Miriam M. "Heterosexuality, Male Dominance, and the Father Image," Sociological Inquiry,
51:129-39, 1981.

2880)   Johnston, Craig, and Pauline Garde. "The Political
Sociology of Gay Activists," Australian and New Zea-
land Journal of Sociology, 17:76-77, Jul. 1981.

2881)   Johnston, Jill. "Lesbian Feminism Reconsidered,"
        Salmagundi, 58-59:76-88, 1982.

2882)   Jones, Gerald P. "Counseling Gay Adolescents,"
        Counselor Education and Supervision, 18:144-52, 1978.

2883)   _____. "The Social Study of Pederasty: In Search
        of a Literature Base: An Annotated Bibliography of
        Sources in English," Journal of Homosexuality, 8:61-
        95, 1982-83.

2884)   Jones, Randall W., and John E. Bates. "Satisfaction
        in Male Homosexual Couples," Journal of Homosexu-
        ality, 3:217-24, 1977-78.

2885)   _____, and John P. DeCecco. "The Femininity
        and Masculinity of Partners in Heterosexual and Ho-
        mosexual Relationships," Journal of Homosexuality,
        8:37-44, 1982-83.

2886)   Karlen, Arno. "The New Lesbian Politics and the
        Decline of Social Science," Salmagundi, 58-59:300-07,
        1982.

2887)   Karr, Rodney, G. "Homosexual Labeling and the Male
        Role," Journal of Social Issues, 34: no. 3: 73-83,
        1978.

2888)   Katz, Jonathan. "The Founding of the Mattachine So-
        ciety: An Interview with Henry Hay," Radical Amer-
        ica, 11:27-40, 1977.

2889)   Kayal, Philip M. "Homophobia and Society," Gai
        Saber, 1:95-98, 1977-78.

2890)   Keller, Karl. "The Whitman Issue in American Lit-
        erature: A Review Essay," Texas Studies in Litera-
        ture and Language, 22:576-86, 1980.

2891)   Kelly, James. "The Aging Male Homosexual: Myth
        and Reality," Gerontologist, 8:328-32, 1977. (Re-
        printed in Levine, no. 22, pp. 253-62.)

2892)   Kennedy, Hubert C. "The Case for James Mills
        Pierce," Journal of Homosexuality, 4:179-84, 1978-
        79.

2893)   _____ . "The 'Third Sex' Theories of Karl Hein-
             rich Ulrichs," Journal of Homosexuality, 6:103-11,
             1980-81. (Reprinted in Licata and Peterson, no. 23,
             pp. 103-11.)

2894)   Kim, Young Ja. "Korean Narmsadang [A Gay Acting
             Community]," Drama Review, 25:9-16, Mar. 1981.

2895)   Kimmel, Douglas C. "Adult Development and Aging:
             A Gay Perspective," Journal of Social Issues, 34:
             no. 3:113-30, 1978.

2896)   King, Dixie. "The Influence of Forster's Maurice
             on Lady Chatterley's Lover," Contemporary Litera-
             ture, 23:65-82, 1982.

2897)   Kirkendall, Lester, and Len Tritsch. "Educational
             Implications of the Dade County [Florida] Imbroglio,"
             Phi Delta Kappan, 59:94-97, Oct. 1977.

2898)   Kitsuse, John I. "Coming Out All Over: Deviants
             and the Politics of Social Problems," Social Prob-
             lems, 28:1-13, 1980.

2899)   Knutson, Donald C. "The Civil Liberties of Gay
             Persons' Present Status," Journal of Homosexuality,
             2:337-42, 1976-77.

2900)   _____ . "Introduction to Homosexuality and the
             Law," Journal of Homosexuality, 5:5-23, 1979-80.
             (Reprinted in Knutson, no. 20, pp. 5-23.)

2901)   Krestan, JoAnn, and Claudia S. Bepko. "The Prob-
             lem of Fusion in the Lesbian Relationship," Family
             Process, 19:277-89, 1980.

2902)   Lambert, Deborah G. "Defeat of a Hero: Autonomy
             and Sexuality in My Antonia," American Literature,
             53:676-90, 1982.

2903)   Laner, Mary R. "The Growing Older Female: Het-
             erosexual and Homosexual," Journal of Homosexual-
             ity, 4:267-75, 1978-79.

2904)   _____ . "The Growing Older Male: Heterosexual
             and Homosexual," Gerontologist, 18:496-501, 1978.

2905)   . "Permanent Partner Priorities: Gay and
        Straight," Journal of Homosexuality, 3:32-39, 1977-
        78.

2906)   . "'Personals' Advertisements of Lesbian
        Women," Journal of Homosexuality, 4:41-61, 1978-
        79.

2907)   , and G. W. Levi Kamel. "Media Mating
        I: Newspaper 'Personals' Ads of Homosexual Men,"
        Journal of Homosexuality, 3:149-62, 1977-78.

2908)   , and Roy H. Laner. "Sexual Preference or
        Personal Style: Why Lesbians Are Disliked," Jour-
        nal of Homosexuality, 5:339-56, 1979-80.

2909)   Larson, Paul. "Sexual Identity and Self-Concept,"
        Journal of Homosexuality, 7:15-32, 1981-82. (Re-
        printed in Gonsiorek, no. 14, pp. 15-32.)

2910)   Latham, J. David, and Geoffrey D. White.   "Coping
        with Homosexual Expression Within Heterosexual Mar-
        riages: Five Case Studies," Journal of Sex and Mar-
        ital Therapy, 4:198-212, 1978.

2911)   Lautmann, Rüdiger. "The Pink Triangle: The Per-
        secution of Homosexual Males in Concentration Camps
        in Nazi Germany," Journal of Homosexuality, 6:141-
        60, 1980-81. (Reprinted in Licata and Peterson, no.
        23, pp. 141-60.)

2912)   Lee, John A. "Forbidden Colors of Love: Patterns
        of Gay Love and Gay Liberation," Journal of Homo-
        sexuality, 1:401-18, 1975-76.

2913)   . "The Gay Connection," Urban Life, 8:175-
        98, 1979.

2914)   . "Going Public: A Study in the Sociology
        of Homosexual Liberation," Journal of Homosexuality,
        3:49-78, 1977-78.

2915)   Lee, Mary. "Homosexuality and the Police in Hong-
        kong," Far Eastern Economic Review, 109:18-20,
        Jul. 18, 1980; 109:17-18, Aug. 29, 1980; 112:18-19,
        Jun. 26, 1981; and 114:46-47, Oct. 9, 1981.

2916)   Lehne, Gregory K.   "Gay Male Fantasies and Real-
         ities," Journal of Social Issues, 34:no. 3:28-37,
         1978.

2917)   Levin, James.   "Butterflies, Pansies, Twilight Men,
         and Strange Brothers: The American Male Homo-
         sexual Novel Between the Wars," Gai Saber, 1:244-
         60, 1977-78.

2918)   Levine, Martin P.   "The Gay Ghetto," Journal of
         Homosexuality, 4:363-77, 1978-79.   (See Levine,
         no. 22, pp. 182-204 for another version of this
         article.)

2919)   _____.   "The Sociology of Male Homosexuality
         and Lesbianism: An Introductory Bibliography,"
         Journal of Homosexuality, 5:249-75, 1979-80.

2920)   Lewin, Ellen.   "Lesbianism and Motherhood: Impli-
         cations for Child Custody," Human Organization, 40:
         6-14, 1981.

2921)   Lewis, Karen G.   "Children of Lesbians: Their
         Point of View," Social Work, 25:198-203, 1980.

2922)   Lewis, Robert A., and others.   "Commitment in
         Same-Sex Love Relationships," Alternative Lifestyles,
         4:22-42, 1981.

2923)   Lewis, Thomas S. W.   "The Brothers of Ganymede
         [Homosexuality in the Classical World]," Salmagundi,
         58-59:147-65, 1982.

2924)   Licata, Salvatore J.   "The Homosexual Rights Move-
         ment in the United States: A Traditionally Overlooked
         Area of American History," Journal of Homosexual-
         ity, 6:161-89, 1980-81.   (Reprinted in Licata and
         Peterson, no. 23, pp. 161-89.)

2925)   Liljestrand, Petra and others.   "The Effects of So-
         cial Sex-Role Stereotypes and Sexual Orientation in
         Psychotherapeutic Outcomes," Journal of Homosexu-
         ality, 3:361-72, 1977-78.

2926)   _____, and others.   "The Relationship of Assump-
         tion and Knowledge of the Homosexual Orientation to
         the Abridgment of Civil Liberties," Journal of Ho-
         mosexuality, 3:243-48, 1977-78.

2927)   Lindquist, Neil, and Gordon Hirabayashi.   "Coping
        with Marginal Situations: The Case of Gay Males,"
        Canadian Journal of Sociology, 4:87-104, 1979.

2928)   Lineham, Peter.   "Growing Hostile to Gays [Review
        of John Boswell's Christianity, Social Tolerance, and
        Homosexuality]," Times Literary Supplement, no.
        4060, p. 73, Jan. 23, 1981.

2929)   Lipman-Blumen, Jean.   "Toward a Homosexual Theo-
        ry of Sex Roles," Signs, 1:15-31, 1976.

2930)   Lloyd, Chris E.   "In Defense of Billie Jean [King],"
        World Tennis, 29:8, Jul. 1981.

2931)   Loewenstein, Sophie F.   "Understanding Lesbian Wom-
        en," Social Casework, 61:29-38, 1980.

2932)   Lorde, Audre.   "Scratching the Surface: Some Notes
        on Barriers to Women and Loving," Black Scholar,
        9:31-35, Apr. 1978.

2933)   Lucie-Smith, Edward.   "Gay Seventies?" Art and
        Artists, 14:4-11, Dec. 1979.

2934)   Lumby, Malcolm E.   "Code Switching and Sexual
        Orientation: A Test of Bernstein's Sociolinguistic
        Theory," Journal of Homosexuality, 1:383-99, 1975-
        76.

2935)   _____.   "Homophobia: The Quest for a Valid
        Scale," Journal of Homosexuality, 2:39-47, 1976-77.

2936)   _____.   "Men Who Advertise for Sex," Journal
        of Homosexuality, 4:63-72, 1978-79.

2937)   MacDonald, A. P.   "Bisexuality: Some Comments
        on Research and Theory," Journal of Homosexuality,
        6:21-35, 1980-81.

2938)   _____.   "Homophobia: Its Roots and Meaning,"
        Homosexual Counseling Journal, 3:23-33, 1976.

2939)   Macklin, Eleanor D.   "Non-Traditional Family
        Forms: A Decade of Research," Journal of Mar-
        riage and the Family, 42:905-22, 1980.

2940)   Malek, James S.   "Salvation in Forster's Dr. Woola-
        cott," Studies in Short Fiction, 18:319-20, 1981.

2941)   Maloney, Stephen R.   'The Lavender Menace: Though
        Many Homosexuals Are Harmless and Even Goodly,
        the Gay Liberation Movement Is Tawdry, Libertine,
        and Barbaric," Alternative, 10:12-15, Dec. 1976.

2942)   Malyon, Alan K.   'The Homosexual Adolescent: De-
        velopmental Issues and Social Bias," Child Welfare,
        60:321-30, 1981.

2943)   _____.   "Psychotherapeutic Implications of Inter-
        nalized Homophobia in Gay Men," Journal of Homo-
        sexuality, 7:59-69, 1981-82. (Reprinted in Gonsiorek,
        no. 14, pp. 59-69.)

2944)   Manford, Morty.   "Gay Columbia [University], Yes-
        terday and Today," Gai Saber, 1:263-67, 1977-78.

2945)   Marecek, Jeanne, and others.   "Gender Roles in
        Relationships of Lesbians and Gay Men," Journal of
        Homosexuality, 8:45-49, 1982-83.

2946)   Martin, A. Damien.   'The Minority Question,"
        Etc.: A Review of General Semantics, 39:22-42,
        Spring 1982.

2947)   Martin, David L.   "Abortion and Homosexuality:
        Issues of Controversy," Learning: A Magazine for
        Creative Teaching, 6:34, May-Jun. 1978.

2948)   Martin, Robert K.   "Criticizing the Critics: A Ho-
        mosexual Perspective," Gai Saber, 1:203-06, 1977-
        78.

2949)   _____.   'Oscar Wilde and the Fairy Tale: The
        Happy Prince as Self Dramatization," Studies in
        Short Fiction, 16:74-77, 1979.

2950)   Maryles, Daisy, and Robert Dahlin.   'Books on Ho-
        mosexuality: A Current Checklist," Publishers' Week-
        ly, 212:50-54, Aug. 8, 1977.

2951)   Massing, Michael.   'Invisible Cubans [Gay Refugees],"
        Columbia Journalism Review, 19:49-51, Sep. -Oct.
        1980.

2952)   Mayadas, Nazneen S., and Wayne D. Duehn. "Chil-
        dren in Gay Families: An Investigation of Services,"
        Homosexual Counseling Journal, 3:70-83, 1976.

2953)   McAlpine, Monica E. "The Pardoner's Homosexual-
        ity and How It Matters," Modern Language Associa-
        tion Publications, 95:8-22, 1980.

2954)   McCandish, Barbara M. "Therapeutic Issues with
        Lesbian Couples," Journal of Homosexuality, 7:71-
        78, 1981-82. (Reprinted in Gonsiorek, no. 14, pp.
        71-78.)

2955)   McCauley, Elizabeth A., and Anke A. Ehrhardt.
        "Role Expectations and Definitions: A Comparison
        of Female Transsexuals and Lesbians," Journal of
        Homosexuality, 3:137-47, 1977-78.

2956)   McConaghy, N. "Behavioral Intervention in Homo-
        sexuality," Journal of Homosexuality, 2:221-27, 1976-
        77.

2957)   McCoy, Sherry, and Maureen Hicks. "A Psycho-
        logical Retrospective on Power in the Contemporary
        Lesbian-Feminist Community," Frontiers, 4:65-69,
        1979.

2958)   McCracken, Samuel. "Are Homosexuals Gay?"
        Commentary, 67:19-29, Jan. 1979. Responses: 67:
        12-31, Apr. 1979.

2959)   McCrary, Jerel, and Lewis Gutierrez. "The Homo-
        sexual Person in the Military and in National Securi-
        ty Employment," Journal of Homosexuality, 5:115-
        46, 1979-80. (Reprinted in Knutson, no. 20, pp.
        115-46.)

2960)   McCurdy, Jack. "University [of San Francisco],
        Opposed to Lesbians, Bars Women's Studies," Chron-
        icle of Higher Education, 22:2, Mar. 2, 1981.

2961)   McDonald, Gary J. "Individual Differences in the
        Coming Out Process for Gay Men: Implications for
        Theoretical Models," Journal of Homosexuality, 8:
        47-60, 1982-83.

2962)   _____. "Misrepresentation, Liberalism, and
         Heterosexual Bias in Introductory Psychology Text-
         books," Journal of Homosexuality, 6:45-60, 1980-81.

2963)   _____, and Robert J. Moore. "Sex-Role Self-
         Concepts of Homosexual Men and Their Attitudes
         Toward Both Women and Male Homosexuality," Jour-
         nal of Homosexuality, 4:3-14, 1978-79.

2964)   McGreivy, Susan. "How the Military Hunts for Ho-
         mosexuals," Civil Liberties, Jun. 1981, p. 6.

2965)   McKinlay, Thomas, and others. "Teaching Assertive
         Skills to a Passive Homosexual Adolescent: An Il-
         lustrative Case," Journal of Homosexuality, 3:163-
         70, 1977-78.

2966)   McNally, Emily B., and Dana G. Finnegan. "Work-
         ing Together: The National Association of Gay Alco-
         holism Professionals," Journal of Homosexuality, 7:
         101-03, 1981-82. (Reprinted in Ziebold and Mongeon,
         no. 37, pp. 101-03.)

2967)   McNaught, Brian. "Why Bother with Gay Rights?"
         Humanist, 37:34-36, Sep.-Oct. 1977.

2968)   McWhirter, David P., and Andrew M. Mattison.
         "Psychotherapy for Gay Male Couples," Journal of
         Homosexuality, 7:79-91, 1981-82. (Reprinted in
         Gonsiorek, no. 14, pp. 79-91.)

2969)   Meyer, Robert G. "Legal and Social Ambivalence
         Regarding Homosexuality," Journal of Homosexuality,
         2:281-87, 1976-77.

2970)   _____, and William M. Freeman. "A Social Epi-
         sode Model of Human Sexual Behavior," Journal of
         Homosexuality, 2:123-31, 1976-77.

2971)   "Michigan State Fraternity's Ouster of Homosexual
         Upheld," Chronicle of Higher Education, 24:3, Aug.
         11, 1982.

2972)   Middleton, Lorenzo, and Anne C. Roark. "Campus
         Homosexuals [at Texas A and M University] Out of
         the Closet but Not Out of Trouble," Chronicle of
         Higher Education, 22:3-4, Jul. 13, 1981.

2973)   Milham, Jim, and others. "A Factor-Analytic Con-
        ceptualization of Attitudes Toward Male and Female
        Homosexuals," Journal of Homosexuality, 2:3-10,
        1976-77.

2974)   _____, and Linda E. Weinberger. "Sexual Pref-
        erence, Sex Role Appropriateness, and Resolution of
        Social Access," Journal of Homosexuality, 2:343-57,
        1976-77.

2975)   Miller, Brian. "Adult Sexual Resocialization: Ad-
        justment Toward a Stigmatized Identity," Alternative
        Lifestyles, 1:207-34, 1978.

2976)   _____. "Gay Fathers and Their Children," Fam-
        ily Coordinator, 28:544-52, 1979.

2977)   _____, and Laud Humphreys. "Lifestyles and
        Violence: Homosexual Victims of Assault and Mur-
        der," Quantitative Sociology, 3:169-85, 1980.

2978)   Miller, Judith A., and others. "The Child's Home
        Environment for Lesbian vs. Heterosexual Mothers:
        A Neglected Area of Research," Journal of Homosex-
        uality, 7:49-56, 1981-82. (Reprinted in Gonsiorek,
        no. 14, pp. 49-56.)

2979)   Miller, Patricia M. "The Individual Life [Lesbian
        Biography]," Frontiers, 4:70-74, 1979.

2980)   Miller, Rhoda. "Counseling the Young Adult Les-
        bian," Journal of the National Association for Women
        Deans, Administrators, and Counselors, 43:44-48,
        Spring 1980.

2981)   Minnigerode, Fred A. "Age-Status Labeling in Ho-
        mosexual Men," Journal of Homosexuality, 1:273-76,
        1975-76.

2982)   _____. "Attitudes Toward Homosexuality: Femi-
        nist Attitudes and Sexual Conservatism," Sex Roles,
        2:347-52, 1976.

2983)   _____. "Rights or Repentance?" Journal of Ho-
        mosexuality, 2:323-26, 1976-77.

2984)   _____, and Marcy R. Adelman. "Elderly Homosexual Women and Men: Report on a Pilot Study,"
Family Coordinator, 27:451-56, 1978.

2985)   Moberly, Elizabeth. "Homosexuality: Restating the
Conservative Case," Salmagundi, 58-59:281-99, 1982.

2986)   Mohr, R. D. "Gay Rights," Social Theory and Practice, 8:31-41, Spring 1982.

2987)   Money, John. "Bisexual, Homosexual, and Heterosexual: Society, Law, and Medicine," Journal of
Homosexuality, 2:229-33, 1976-77.

2988)   _____. "Statement on Antidiscrimination Regarding Sexual Orientation," Journal of Homosexuality,
2:159-61, 1976-77.

2989)   _____, and Jean Dalery. "Iatrogenic Homosexuality: Gender Identity in Seven 46, XX Chromosomal Females ... ," Journal of Homosexuality, 1:357-
71, 1975-76.

2990)   Mongeon, John E. , and Thomas O. Ziebold. "Pre-
venting Alcohol Abuse in the Gay Community: Toward
a Theory and Model," Journal of Homosexuality, 7:
89-99, 1981-82. (Reprinted in Ziebold and Mongeon,
no. 37, pp. 89-99.)

2991)   Monter, E. William. "Sodomy and Heresy in Early
Modern Switzerland," Journal of Homosexuality, 6:
41-55, 1980-81. (Reprinted in Licata and Peterson,
no. 23, pp. 41-55.)

2992)   Montgomery, Kathryn. "Gay Activists and the Networks," Journal of Communication, 31:49-57, Summer
1981.

2993)   Morgan, M Gwym. "Catullus 112: A Pathicus in
Politics," American Journal of Philology, 100:477-
80, 1979.

2994)   Morin, Stephen. "Psychology and the Gay Community: An Overview," Journal of Social Issues, 34:
no. 3:1-6, 1978.

2995)   _____, and Ellen M. Garfinkle. "Male Homophobia,"
Journal of Social Issues, 34:no. 1:29-47, 1978.

2996)   _____, and S. J. Schultz.   "Gay Movement and
             the Rights of Children, " Journal of Social Issues,
             34:no. 2:137-48, 1978.

2997)   Morrison, James K.   "Homosexual Fantasies and the
             Reconstructive Use of Imagery, " Journal of Mental
             Imagery, 4:165-68, 1980.

2998)   Morrison, Kristin.   "Lawrence, Beardsley, Wilde:
             The White Peacock and Sexual Ambiguity, " Western
             Humanities Review, 30:241-48, 1976.

2999)   Moses, Alice E. , and J. A. Buckner.   "Special
             Problems of Rural Gay Clients, " Human Services in
             the Rural Environment, 5:22-27, 1980.

3000)   Mosse, George L.   "Nationalism and Responsibility:
             Normal and Abnormal Sexuality in the Nineteenth Cen-
             tury, " Contemporary History, 17:221-46, 1982.   Re-
             sponse by Isabel V. Hull: 17:247-68, 1982.

3001)   Moufarrege, N. A.   "Lavender: On Homosexuality
             and Art, " Arts Magazine, 57:78-87, Oct. 1982.

3002)   Muecke, Frances.   "Portrait of the Artist as a
             Young Woman, " Classical Quarterly, 32:41-55, 1982.

3003)   Myers, Michael F.   "Counseling the Parents of
             Young Homosexual Male Patients, " Journal of Homo-
             sexuality, 7:131-43, 1981-82.   (Reprinted in Gon-
             siorek, no. 14, pp. 131-43.)

3004)   Nacci, Peter L.   "Sexual Assault in Prisons, " Amer-
             ican Journal of Corrections, 40:30-31, Jan. 1978.

3005)   Nachman, Larry D.   "Genet: Dandy of the Lower
             Depths, " Salmagundi, 58-59:358-72, 1982.

3006)   Nanda, Serena, and J. Scott Francher.   "Culture
             and Homosexuality: A Comparison of Long Term
             Gay Male and Lesbian Relationships, " Eastern An-
             thropologist, 33:139-52, 1980.

3007)   Nardi, Peter M.   "Alcoholism and Homosexuality:
             A Theoretical Perspective, " Journal of Homosexuality,
             7:9-25, 1981-82.   (Reprinted in Ziebold and Mongeon,
             no. 37, pp. 9-25.)

3008)   "National Gay Rights Project Begins Work," Civil
        Liberties, Apr. 1980, p. 6.

3009)   Navin, Helen.   "Medical and Surgical Risks in
        Handballing: Implications of an Inadequate Sociali-
        zation Process," Journal of Homosexuality, 6:67-
        76, 1980-81.

3010)   Needham, Russell.   "Casework Intervention with a
        Homosexual Adolescent," Social Casework, 58:387-
        94, 1977.

3011)   Nelson, James B.   "Religious and Moral Issues in
        Working with Homosexual Clients," Journal of Ho-
        mosexuality, 7:163-75, 1981-82.   (Reprinted in Gon-
        siorek, no. 14, pp. 163-75.)

3012)   Newton, David E.   "Homosexual Behavior and Child
        Molestation: A Review of the Evidence," Adolescence,
        8:29-43, 1978.

3013)   _____ .   "A Note on the Treatment of Homosexual-
        ity in Sex Education Classes in the Secondary
        Schools," Journal of Homosexuality, 8:97-99, 1982-
        83.

3014)   _____ .   "Representations of Homosexuality in
        Health Science Textbooks," Journal of Homosexuality,
        4:247-54, 1978-79.

3015)   _____ , and Stephen J. Risch.   "Homosexuality and
        Education: A Review of the Issue," High School Jour-
        nal, 64:191-202, 1980-81.

3016)   Nicolson, Joe.   "Coming Out at the New York Post,"
        Columbia Journalism Review, 20:26-27, Mar. -Apr.
        1982.

3017)   Noel, Thomas J.   "Gay Bars and the Emergence of
        the Denver Homosexual Community," Social Science
        Journal, 15:59-74, Apr. 1978.

3018)   Northcott, Cecil.   "The Homosexual Debate," Con-
        temporary Review, 236:40-42, 1980.

3019)   Norton, Joseph L.   "The Homosexual and Counseling,"
        Personnel and Guidance Journal, 54:374-77, 1976.

3020) _____. "Integrating Gay Issues into Counselor
       Education," Counselor Education and Supervision,
       21:208-12, 1982.

3021) Nungesser, Lonnie G. "Theoretical Bases for Re-
       search on the Acquisition of Social Sex-Role by
       Children of Lesbian Mothers," Journal of Homosexu-
       ality, 5:177-87, 1979-80.

3022) Nyberg, Kenneth L. "Sexual Aspirations and Sexual
       Behaviors Among Homosexually Behaving Males and
       Females: The Impact of the Gay Community," Jour-
       nal of Homosexuality, 2:29-38, 1976-77.

3023) _____, and Jon P. Alston. "Analysis of Public
       Attitudes Toward Homosexual Behavior," Journal of
       Homosexuality, 2:99-107, 1976-77.

3024) _____, and _____. "Homosexual Labeling by
       University Youths," Adolescence, 12:541-46, 1977.

3025) Oaks, Robert F. "Defining Sodomy in Seventeenth
       Century Massachusetts," Journal of Homosexuality,
       6:79-83, 1980-81. (Reprinted in Licata and Peter-
       son, no. 23, pp. 79-83.)

3026) _____. "Perceptions of Homosexuality by Justices
       of the Peace in Colonial Virginia," Journal of Homo-
       sexuality, 5:35-41, 1979-80. (Reprinted in Knutson,
       no. 20, pp. 35-41.)

3027) O'Higgins, James. "Sexual Choice, Sexual Act: An
       Interview with Michael Foucault," Salmagundi, 58-59:
       10-24, 1982.

3028) Oldham, Sue, and others. "Sex-Role Identity of
       Female Homosexuals," Journal of Homosexuality, 8:
       41-46, 1982-83.

3029) Olson, Ray. "Gay Film Work: Affecting But Too
       Evasive," Jump Cut, 20:9-12, May 1979.

3030) Ostrow, David G. (comp. and ed.). "Synopses of
       Papers Delivered at the Conference on Current As-
       pects of Sexually Transmitted Diseases, June 1979,"
       Journal of Homosexuality, 5:281-332, 1979-80.

3031)   Padgag, Robert A.   "Sexual Matters: On Concep-
        tualizing Sexuality in History," Radical History Re-
        view, 20:3-33, 1979.

3032)   Pagelow, Mildred D.   "Heterosexual and Lesbian
        Single Mothers: A Comparison of Problems, Coping,
        and Solutions," Journal of Homosexuality, 5:189-204,
        1979-80.

3033)   Panton, James H.   "Characteristics Associated with
        Male Homosexuality Within a State Correctional Popu-
        lation," Corrections, 2:26-31, 1978.

3034)   Parker, Jack B., and Robert A. Perkins.   "The In-
        fluence of Type of Institution on Attitudes Toward the
        Handling of the Homosexual Among Inmates," Offender
        Rehabilitation, 2:245-54, 1978.

3035)   Parker, William.   "Homosexuality in History: An
        Annotated Bibliography," Journal of Homosexuality,
        6:191-210, 1980-81.   (Reprinted in Licata and Peter-
        son, no. 23, pp. 191-210.)

3036)   Patrick, Robert.   "Gay Analysis," Drama Review,
        22:67-72, Sep. 1978.

3037)   Peplau, Letitia.   "Research on Homosexual Couples:
        An Overview," Journal of Homosexuality, 8:1-8,
        1982-83.

3038)   _____, and Susan D. Cochran.   "Value Orienta-
        tions in the Intimate Relationships of Gay Men,"
        Journal of Homosexuality, 6:1-19, 1980-81.

3039)   _____, and others.   "Loving Women: Attachment
        and Autonomy in Lesbian Relationships," Journal of
        Social Issues, 34:no. 3:7-27, 1978.

3040)   _____, and others.   "Satisfaction in Lesbian Re-
        lationships," Journal of Homosexuality, 8:23-35,
        1982-83.

3041)   Peretti, O., and others.   "Dysfunctions and Eufunc-
        tions of Prison Homosexuality: A Structural-
        Functional Approach," Acta Criminologiae et Medi-
        cine Legalis Japonica, 45:22-29, 1979.

3042)   Peterson, Robert P., and Salvatore Licata. "The
        Collection and Analysis of Documents for the Civil
        Liberties and Sexual Orientation Project," Journal
        of Homosexuality, 4:277-82, 1978-79.

3043)   Pierson, Ransdell. "Uptight on Gay News--Can the
        Straight Press Get the Gay Story Straight? Is Any-
        one Even Trying?" Columbia Journalism Review,
        20:25-33, Mar.-Apr. 1982.

3044)   "Police Come to Terms with Gays," Police Magazine,
        Jan. 1980, pp. 28-31+.

3045)   Ponse, Barbara. "Secrecy in the Lesbian World,"
        Urban Life, 5:313-38, 1976.

3046)   Ponting, K. G. "Rediscovering Forrest Reid," Con-
        temporary Review, 237:34-37, 1980.

3047)   Potter, Sandra J., and Trudy E. Darty. "Social
        Work and the Invisible Minority: An Exploration of
        Lesbianism," Social Work, 26:187-92, 1981.

3048)   Price, James H. "High School Students' Attitudes
        Toward Homosexuality," Journal of School Health,
        52:469-74, 1982.

3049)   Propper, Alice M. "Lesbianism in Female and Coed
        Correctional Institutions," Journal of Homosexuality,
        3:265-74, 1977-78.

3050)   _____. "Make-Believe Families and Homosexuality
        Among Imprisoned Girls," Criminology, 20:127-38,
        1982.

3051)   Rader, Dotson. "Art of Theater: Tennessee Wil-
        liams" and "Tennessee Williams: A Friendship,"
        Paris Review, 81:145-85 and 186-96, Fall 1981.

3052)   Rafferty, Max. "Should Gays Be Permitted to Teach
        School?" Phi Delta Kappan, 59:91-92, 1977-78.

3053)   Rand, Catherine, and others. "Psychological Health
        and Factors Court Seeks to Control in Lesbian Mother
        Custody Trials," Journal of Homosexuality, 8:27-39,
        1982-83.

3054)   Raphael, Sharon M. , and Mina K. Robinson. "The
        Older Lesbian: Love Relationships and Friendship
        Patterns, " Alternative Lifestyles, 3:207-29, 1980.

3055)   Rechy, John.   "The New Censorship and Repression, "
        Books West, 1:no. 7:24-25+, Fall 1977.

3056)   Reece, Rex.   "Group Treatment of Sexual Dysfunction
        in Gay Men, " Journal of Homosexuality, 7:113-29,
        1981-82.   (Reprinted in Gonsiorek, no. 14, pp. 113-
        29.)

3057)   _____, and Allen E. Segrist.   "The Association of
        Selected 'Masculine' Sex-Role Variables in Gay Male
        Couples, " Journal of Homosexuality, 7:33-47, 1981-
        82.   (Reprinted in Gonsiorek, no. 14, pp. 33-47.)

3058)   Reich, Wendy, and others.   "Notes on Women's
        Graffiti, " Journal of American Folklore, 90:188-91,
        Apr. 1977.

3059)   Reinhardt, Karl J.   "The Image of Gays in Chicano
        Prose Fiction, " Explorations in Ethnic Studies, 4:
        41-55, 1981.

3060)   Reynolds, William T.   "The Immigration and Nation-
        ality Act and the Rights of Homosexual Aliens, " Jour-
        nal of Homosexuality 5:79-87, 1979-80.   (Reprinted
        in Knutson, no. 20, pp. 79-87.)

3061)   Rich, Adrienne.   "On 'Compulsory Heterosexuality'
        and Lesbian Existence, " Signs, 5:631-60, 1980.

3062)   Richards, David A. J.   "The Concept of the Unnatural
        and the Constitutional Right of Privacy, " Gai Saber,
        1:211-14, 1977-78.

3063)   _____.   "The Constitutionality of Laws Prohibiting
        Unnatural Acts, " Gai Saber, 1:225-39, 1977-78.

3064)   _____.   "Homosexual Acts and the Constitutional
        Right to Privacy, " Journal of Homosexuality, 5:43-
        65, 1979-80.   (Reprinted in Knutson, no. 20, pp. 43-
        65.)

3065)   Richmond, Katy.   "Fear of Homosexuality and Modes
        of Rationalisation in Male Prisons, " Australian and
        New Zealand Journal of Sociology, 14:51-57, 1978.

3066)   Riddle, Dorothy I.   "Relating to Children: Gays as
        Role Models," Journal of Social Issues, 34:no. 3:38-
        58, 1978.

3067)   _____, and Barbara Sang.   "Psychotherapy with
        Lesbians," Journal of Social Issues, 34:no. 3:84-100,
        1978.

3068)   Rieff, Philip.   "The Impossible Culture: Wilde as
        a Modern Prophet," Salmagundi, 58-59:406-26, 1982.

3069)   Rivlin, Mark.   "The Disabled Gay: An Appraisal,"
        Sexuality and Disability, 3:221-22, 1980.

3070)   Roback, Howard B. , and others.   "Self-Concept and
        Psychological Adjustment Differences Between Self-
        Identified Male Transsexuals and Male Homosexuals,"
        Journal of Homosexuality, 3:15-20, 1977-78.

3071)   Robinson, Bryan E. , and others.   "Gay Men's and
        Women's Perceptions of Early Family Life and Their
        Relationships with Parents," Family Relations, 31:
        79-83, Jan. 1982.

3072)   Robinson, Paul.   "In the First Person--Dear Paul:
        An Exchange Between Teacher and Student," Sal-
        magundi, 58-59:25-41, 1982.

3073)   Roby, Douglas.   "Early Medieval Attitudes Toward
        Homosexuality," Gai Saber, 1:67-71, 1977-78.

3074)   Rochlin, Martin.   "Sexual Orientation of the Therapist
        and Therapeutic Effectiveness with Gay Clients,"
        Journal of Homosexuality, 7:21-29, 1981-82.   (Re-
        printed in Gonsiorek, no. 14, pp. 21-29.)

3075)   Rollison, David.   "Property, Ideology and Popular
        Culture in a Gloucestershire Village, 1660-1740,"
        Past and Present, 93:70-97, 1981.

3076)   Rosecrance, Barbara.   "Forster's Comrades,"
        Partisan Review 47:591-603, 1980.

3077)   Rosenbaum, S. P.   "Keynes, Lawrence, and Cam-
        bridge Revisited," Cambridge Quarterly, 11:252-64,
        1982.

3078)   Ross, Michael W.   "Heterosexual Marriage of Homo-
         sexual Males: Some Associated Factors," Journal of
         Sex and Marital Therapy, 5:142-51, 1979.

3079)   _____. "The Relationship of Perceived Societal
         Hostility, Conformity, and Psychological Adjustment
         in Homosexual Males," Journal of Homosexuality, 4:
         157-68, 1978-79.

3080)   _____, and others.   "Stigma, Sex and Society: A
         New Look at Gender Differentiation and Sexual Varia-
         tion," Journal of Homosexuality, 3:315-30, 1977-78.

3081)   Roth, Norman.   "Deal Gently with the Young Man:
         Love of Boys in Medieval Hebrew Poetry in Spain,"
         Speculum: A Journal of Medieval Studies, 57:20-51,
         1982.

3082)   Rubin, Marc.   "Gay Teachers in New York City,"
         Gai Saber, 1:89-92, 1977-78.

3083)   Ruse, Michael.   "Are There Gay Genes? Sociobiolo-
         gy and Homosexuality," Journal of Homosexuality, 6:
         5-34, Summer 1981.   (Reprinted in Koertge, no. 21,
         pp. 5-34.)

3084)   _____. "Medicine as Social Science: The Case
         of Freud on Homosexuality," Journal of Medicine and
         Philosophy, 6:361-86, 1981.

3085)   Saladin, Kenneth S.   "Toward a Biology of Homosexu-
         ality," Humanist, 42:57-58, Jan.-Feb. 1982.

3086)   Sanders, Geert.   "Homosexualities in the Nether-
         lands," Alternative Lifestyles, 3:278-312, 1980.

3087)   Sandholzer, T. A.   "Physician Attitudes and Other
         Factors Affecting the Incidence of Sexually Trans-
         mitted Diseases in Homosexual Males," Journal of
         Homosexuality, 5:325-27, 1979-80.

3088)   San Miguel, Christopher L. , and Jim Millham.   "The
         Role of Cognitive and Situational Variables in Aggres-
         sion Toward Homosexuals," Journal of Homosexuality,
         2:11-27, 1976-77.

3089)   Saperstein, Sue. "Lesbian and Gay Adolescents: The
        Need for Family Support," Catalyst: A Socialist
        Journal of the Social Sciences, Jan. 1982, pp. 3-5.

3090)   Saslow, James M. "The Tenderest Love: St. Sebas-
        tian in Renaissance Painting," Gai Saber, 1:58-66,
        1977-78.

3091)   Satterfield, Ben. "John Rechy's Tormented World,"
        Southwest Review, 67:78-85, 1982.

3092)   Savage, D. S. "Christopher Isherwood: The Novel-
        ist as Homosexual," Literature and Psychology, 29:
        71-88, 1979.

3093)   Schindler, Ruben. "Homosexuality, Halacha, and So-
        cial Work (Hebrew)," Society and Welfare, 4:50-55,
        1981.

3094)   Schofield, Michael. "Why Is Homosexuality Still
        Something to Hide?" New Society, 47:no. 854:348-
        50, Feb. 1979.

3095)   Schreeder, M. T., and others. "Epidemiology of
        Hepatitis B Infection in Gay Men," Journal of Homo-
        sexuality, 5:307-10, 1979-80.

3096)   Schuster, Marilyn R. "Strategies for Survival: The
        Subtle Subversion of Jane Rule," Feminist Studies,
        7:431-50, 1981.

3097)   Schwarz, Judith. "Questionnaire on Issues in Les-
        bian History," Frontiers, 4:1-12, 1979.

3098)   _____. "Yellow Clover: Katharine Lee Bates and
        Katharine Coman," Frontiers, 4:59-67, 1979.

3099)   Sedgwick, Peter. "Out of Hiding: The Comradeships
        of Daniel Guérin," Salmagundi, 58-59:197-220, 1982.

3100)   Segrest, M. "Lines I Dare to Write: Lesbian Writ-
        ing in the South," Southern Exposure, 9:53-55 and 57-
        62, 1981.

3101)   Shapiro, H. A. "Courtship Scenes in Attic Vase
        Painting," American Journal of Archaeology, 85:133-
        43, 1981.

3102)   Shavelson, Eileen, and others. "Lesbian Women's
        Perceptions of Their Parent-Child Relationships,"
        Journal of Homosexuality, 5:205-15, 1979-80.

3103)   Sherrill, Kenneth. "Homophobia: Illness or Dis-
        ease?" Gai Saber, 1:27-40, 1977-78.

3104)   Shively, Michael, and John P. DeCecco. "Compo-
        nents of Sexual Identity," Journal of Homosexuality,
        3:41-48, 1977-78.

3105)   _____, and _____. "Sexual Orientation Survey
        of Students on the San Francisco State University
        Campus," Journal of Homosexuality, 4:29-39, 1978-
        79.

3106)   _____, and others. "The Identification of Social
        Sex-Role Stereotypes," Journal of Homosexuality, 3:
        225-34, 1977-78.

3107)   Silverstein, Charles. "Even Psychiatry Can Profit
        from Its Past Mistakes," Journal of Homosexuality,
        2:153-61, 1976-77.

3108)   _____. "Homosexuality and the Ethics of Be-
        havioral Intervention," Journal of Homosexuality, 2:
        205-11, 1976-77.

3109)   Simmons, Christina. "Companionate Marriage and
        the Lesbian Threat," Frontiers, 4:54-59, 1979.

3110)   Sisley, Emily L. "Notes on Lesbian Theatre,"
        Drama Review, 25:47-56, Mar. 1981.

3111)   Small, Ian, and Lawrence F. Schuetz. "Pater and
        the Suppressed 'Conclusion' to The Renaissance,"
        English Literature in Transition, 19:313-21, 1976.

3112)   Smith, F. B "LaBouchière's Amendment to the
        Criminal Law Amendment Bill," Historical Studies,
        17:165-75, 1976.

3113)   Smith, Richard W. "Research and Homosexuality,"
        Humanist, 38:20-22, Mar. 1978.

3114)   Smith, Tom. M. "Specific Approaches and Techniques
        in the Treatment of Gay Male Alcohol Abusers,"

Journal of Homosexuality, 7:53-69, 1981-82. (Reprinted in Ziebold and Mongeon, no. 37, pp. 53-69.)

3115)   Smith Wendy. "Un-authorized Life of Novelist Felice
        Picano," Publishers' Weekly, 219:48-49+, Jan. 30,
        1981.

3116)   Snyder William P., and Kenneth L. Nyberg. "Gays
        and the Military: An Emerging Policy Issue," Jour-
        nal of Political and Military Sociology, 8:71-84, 1980.

3117)   Sobel, Harry J. "Adolescent Attitudes Toward Homo-
        sexuality in Relation to Self-Concept and Body Satis-
        faction," Adolescence, 11:443-53, 1976.

3118)   Solomon, Donald M. "The Emergence of Associa-
        tional Rights for Homosexual Persons," Journal of
        Homosexuality, 5:147-55, 1979-80. (Reprinted in
        Knutson, no. 20, pp. 147-55.)

3119)   Sophie, Joan. "Counseling Lesbians," Personnel
        and Guidance Journal, 60:341-45, 1982.

3120)   Spector, Malcolm. "Legitimizing Homosexuality,"
        Society, 14:52-56, Jul.-Aug. 1977.

3121)   Spiegelman, Willard. "Progress of a Genre: Gay
        Journalism and Its Audience," Salmagundi, 58-59:
        308-25, 1982.

3122)   Staats, Gregory R. "Stereotype Context and Social
        Distance: Changing Views of Homosexuality," Jour-
        nal of Homosexuality, 4:15-27, 1978-79.

3123)   Stein, Theodore J. "Gay Service Organizations: A
        Survey," Homosexual Counseling Journal, 3:84-97,
        1976.

3124)   Steinhorn, Audrey I. "Lesbian Adolescents in
        Residential Treatment," Social Casework, 60:494-
        98, 1979.

3125)   Stenson, Leah D. "Playing Favorites: The Trouble
        with Sex Education Guides," School Library Journal,
        23:34-35, Nov. 1976.

3126)   Stephan, G. Edward, and Douglas R. McMullin.
        "Tolerance of Sexual Nonconformity: City Size as
        a Situational and Early Learning Determinant," Amer-
        ican Sociological Review, 47:411-15, 1982.

3127)   Steuernagel, Trudy.   "Another Nail in the Closet
        Door: Introductory American Government Textbooks
        and the Gay Rights Movement," Teaching Political
        Science, 8:493-97, 1981.

3128)   Stimpson, Catharine R.   "The Beat Generation and
        the Trials of Homosexual Liberation," Salmagundi,
        58-59:373-92, 1982.

3129)   Stone, Wilfred.   "Overleaping Class: Forster's Prob-
        lem in Connection," Modern Language Quarterly, 39:
        386-404, 1978.

3130)   Storms, Michael D.   "Attitudes Toward Homosexu-
        ality and Femininity in Men," Journal of Homosexu-
        ality, 3:257-63, 1977-78.

3131)   _____, and others.   "Sexual Scripts for Women,"
        Sex Roles, 7:699-707, 1981.

3132)   Styles, Joseph.   "Outsider/Insider: Researching
        Gay Baths," Urban Life, 8:135-52, 1979-80.

3133)   Suarez-Orozco, Marcelo M.   "A Study of Argentine
        Soccer: The Dynamics of Its Fans and Their Folk-
        lore," Journal of Psychoanalytic Anthropology, 5:7-
        28, 1982.

3134)   Summers, Darryl.   "Juvenile Male Prostitutes: Run-
        aways Become 'Situational Hustlers,'" Sexuality To-
        day, 5:20+, Mar. 8, 1982.

3135)   Suppe, Frederick.   "The Bell and Weinberg Study:
        Future Priorities for Research," Journal of Homo-
        sexuality, 6:69-97, Summer 1981.   (Reprinted in
        Koertge, no. 21, pp. 69-97.)

3136)   Sutherland, Allen T.   "Setting Up of [the Movie]
        'Nighthawks,'" Sight and Sound, 48:50-52, Winter
        1978-79.

3137)   Tapia, Ralph J.   "Human Sexuality: The Magister-
        ium and Moral Theologians," Thought: A Review of
        Culture and Ideas, 54:405-18, 1979.

3138)   Tartagni, Donna.   "Counseling Gays in a School
        Setting," School Counselor, 26:26-32, 1978-79.

3139)   Taub, Diane, and Robert G. Leger.   "Social Identities
        in a Young Gay Community," Sociological Forum, 3:
        47-61, Fall, 1980.

3140)   Taylor, Brian.   "Motives for Guilt-Free Pederasty:
        Some Literary Considerations," Sociological Review,
        24:97-114, 1976.

3141)   Taylor, John R.   "Terence Rattigan and the Sorrows
        of Success," Drama: the Quarterly Theatre Review,
        no. 135:19-22, Jan. 1980.

3142)   Taylor, Lindsay I.   "Aspects of the Ideology of the
        Gay Liberation Movement in New Zealand," Australian
        and New Zealand Journal of Sociology, 13:126-32,
        1977.

3143)   Thayer, James S.   "The Berdache of the Northern
        Plains: A Socioreligous Perspective," Journal of
        Anthropological Research, 36:287-93, 1980.

3144)   Thomas, Keith.   "Rescuing Homosexual History,"
        New York Review of Books, 27:26-29, Dec. 4, 1980.

3145)   Thompson, George H., and William R. Fishburn.
        "Attitudes Toward Homosexuality Among Graduate
        Counseling Students," Counselor Education and
        Supervision, 17:121-30, 1977.

3146)   Tindall, Ralph H.   "The Male Adolescent Involved
        with a Pederast Becomes an Adult," Journal of Ho-
        mosexuality, 3:373-82, 1977-78.

3147)   Townes, Brenda D., and others.   "Differences in
        Psychological Sex, Adjustment, and Familial Influences
        Among Homosexual and Nonhomosexual Populations,"
        Journal of Homosexuality, 1:261-72, 1975-76.

3148)   Troiden, Richard R.   "Androgyny: A Neglected Di-
        mension of Homosexuality," Humanity and Society,
        3:122-35, May 1979.

3149)   _____, and Erich Goode. "Variables Related to Acquisition of Gay Identity," Journal of Homosexuality, 5:383-92, 1979-80.

3150)   Trumbach, Randolph. "London's Sodomites: Homosexual Behavior and Western Culture in the Eighteenth Century," Journal of Social History, 11:1-33, 1977-78.

3151)   Tuller, Neil R. "Couples: The Hidden Segment of the Gay World," Journal of Homosexuality, 3:331-43, 1977-78.

3152)   Tully, C., and J. C. Albro. "Homosexuality: A Social Worker's Imbroglio," Journal of Sociology and Social Welfare, 6:154-67, 1979.

3153)   Turnbull, Debi, and Marvin Brown. "Attitudes Toward Homosexuality and Male and Female Reactions to Homosexual and Heterosexual Slides," Canadian Journal of Behavioral Science, 9:68-80, 1977.

3154)   Ungaretti, John R. "Demoralizing Morality: Where Dover's Greek Homosexuality Leaves Us," Journal of Homosexuality, 8:1-17, 1982-83.

3155)   _____. "Pederasty, Heroism, and the Family in Classical Greece," Journal of Homosexuality, 3:291-300, 1977-78.

3156)   VanWormer, Katherine S., and Frederick L. Bates. "Study of Leadership Roles in an Alabama Prison for Women," Human Relations, 32:793-801, 1979.

3157)   Verstraete, Beert C. "Homosexuality in Ancient Greek and Roman Civilization: A Critical Bibliography," Journal of Homosexuality, 3:79-89, 1977-78.

3158)   _____. "Slavery and the Social Dynamics of Male Homosexual Relations in Ancient Rome," Journal of Homosexuality, 5:227-36, 1979-80.

3159)   Vetere, Victoria A. "The Role of Friendship in the Development and Maintenance of Lesbian Love Relationships," Journal of Homosexuality, 8:51-65, 1982-83.

3160)   Vetri, Dominick. "The Legal Arena: Progress for
         Gay Civil Rights," Journal of Homosexuality, 5:25-
         33, 1979-80. (Reprinted in Knutson, no. 20, pp.
         25-33.)

3161)   Voeller, Bruce, and James Walters. "Gay Fathers,"
         Family Coordinator, 27:149-57, 1978.

3162)   Wagner, Ramon. "Moving into Uncharted Territory
         [the Gay Ministry]," Counseling and Values, 22:184-
         96, 1977-78.

3163)   Ward, Michael, and Mark Freeman. "Defending Gay
         Rights: The Campaign Against the Briggs Amendment
         [Against Gay Teachers] in California," Radical Amer-
         ica, 13:11-26, 1979.

3164)   Ward, Russell A. "Typifications of Homosexuals,"
         Sociological Quarterly, 20:411-23, 1979.

3165)   Warren, Carol A. B. "Fieldwork in the Gay World:
         Issues in Phenomenological Research," Journal of
         Social Issues, 33:no. 4:93-107, 1977.

3166)   _____, and Joann S. DeLora. "Student Protest
         in the 1970s: The Gay Student Union and the Mili-
         tary," Urban Life, 7:67-90, 1978-79.

3167)   _____, and Barbara Laslett. "Privacy and
         Secrecy: A Conceptual Comparison," Journal of
         Social Issues, 33:no. 3:43-51, 1977.

3168)   Watkins, Beverly T. "Widespread Bias Against
         Homosexuals Called Bar to Academic Work in
         Sociology," Chronicle of Higher Education, 23:10,
         Sep. 2, 1981.

3169)   Weeks, Jeffrey. "In Days of Yore When Knights
         Were Gay," History Today, 30:49+, Jul. 1980.

3170)   _____. "Inverts, Perverts, and Mary-Annes:
         Male Prostitution and the Regulation of Homosexu-
         ality in England in the Nineteenth and Early Twen-
         tieth Centuries," Journal of Homosexuality, 6:113-
         34, 1980-81. (Reprinted in Licata and Peterson,
         no. 23, pp. 113-34.)

3171)   . "'Sins and Diseases:' Some Notes on
Homosexuality in the Nineteenth Century," History
Workshop Journal, 1:211-19, 1976.

3172)   Weightman, Barbara A. "Gay Bars as Private
Places," Landscape, 24:no. 1:9-16, 1980.

3173)   Weinberg, Thomas S. "On 'Doing' and 'Being'
Gay: Sexual Behavior and Homosexual Male Self-
Identity," Journal of Homosexuality, 4:143-56, 1978-
79.

3174)   Weinberger, Linda E., and Jim Millham. "Attitudinal Homophobia and Support of Traditional Sex
Roles," Journal of Homosexuality, 4:237-46, 1978-
79.

3175)   Weinrich, James D. "Nonreproduction, Homosexuality, Transsexualism, and Intelligence: I. A
Systematic Literature Search," Journal of Homosexuality, 3:275-89, 1977-78.

3176)   Wellisch, David K., and others. "A Study of Therapy of Homosexual Adolescent Drug Users in a Res-
idential Treatment Setting," Adolescence, 16:689-
700, 1981.

3177)   Werner, Dennis. "A Cross-Cultural Perspective
on Theory and Research on Male Homosexuality,"
Journal of Homosexuality, 4:345-62, 1978-79.

3178)   West, Donald J. "The Gay Dimension," Times
Literary Supplement, no. 4000, p. 1391, Dec. 1,
1978.

3179)   West, Richard. "Homosexuality and the Police in
Hongkong," Far Eastern Economic Review, 108:
140, Apr. 4, 1980.

3180)   West, Walter G. "Public Tolerance of Homosexual
Behavior," Cornell Journal of Social Relations, 12:
25-36, 1977.

3181)   "What Happens to Those Initiated into Homosexuality
in Jail?" Behavior Today, 7:3-4, Aug. 30, 1976.

3182) Whitemore, George. "Friendship in New England: Henry Thoreau," Gai Saber, 1:104-11 and 187-202, 1977-78.

3183) Whitney, Scott. "The Ties that Bind: Strategies for Counseling the Gay Male Co-Alcoholic," Journal of Homosexuality, 7:37-41, 1981-82. (Reprinted in Ziebold and Mongeon, no. 37, pp. 37-41.)

3184) Wikan, Unni. "Man Becomes Woman: Transsexualism in Oman as a Key to Gender Roles," Man: Journal of the Royal Anthropological Society, 12:304-19, 1977.

3185) William D. C. "Sexual Transmission of Parasitic Infections in Gay Men," Journal of Homosexuality, 5:291-94, 1979-80.

3186) Wilson, Colin. "Integrity Born of Hope: Notes on Christopher Isherwood," Twentieth Century Literature, 22:312-31, 1976.

3187) Wilson, Des. "A Case for Shame and Sympathy," Observer Magazine, Jan. 18, 1976, pp. 5-6.

3188) Winkelpleck, Judy M., and John S. Westfield. "Counseling Considerations with Gay Couples," Personnel and Guidance Journal, 60:294-96, 1982.

3189) Wise, Thomas N., and Jane Lucas. "Pseudotranssexualism: Iatrogenic Gender Dysphoria," Journal of Homosexuality, 6:61-66, 1980-81.

3190) Wood, Robin. "'Cruising' [the Movie] and Gay Life," Canadian Forum, 60:41+, May 1980.

3191) _____. "Dyer's Hand: Stars and Gays," Film Comment, 16:70-72, Jan.-Feb. 1980.

3192) _____. "Responsibilities of a Gay Film Critic," Film Comment, 14:12-17, Jan.-Feb. 1978.

3193) Zakarewsky, George T. "Patterns of Support Among Gay and Lesbian Deaf Persons," Sexuality and Disability, 2:178-91, 1979.

3194)   Ziebold, Thomas O. , and John E. Mongeon.   "Intro-
         duction: Alcoholism and the Homosexual Community"
         and "Preventing Alcohol Abuse in the Gay Commu-
         nity: Toward a Theory and Model," Journal of Ho-
         mosexuality, 7:3-7, and 89-99, 1981-82.   (Reprinted
         in Ziebold and Mongeon, no. 37, pp. 3-7 and 89-99.)

3195)   Zigrang, Tricia A.   "Who Should Be Doing What
         About the Gay Alcoholic?" Journal of Homosexuality,
         7:27-35, 1981-82.   (Reprinted in Ziebold and Mon-
         geon, no. 37, pp. 27-35.)

3196)   Zimmerman, Bonnie.   "What Never Has Been: An
         Overview of Lesbian Feminist Literary Criticism,"
         Feminist Studies, 7:451-75, 1981.

3197)   Zita, Jacquelyn N.   "Historical Amnesia and the
         Lesbian Continuum," Signs, 7:172-87, 1981.

ARTICLES IN GAY PUBLICATIONS

3198) Agger, Ellen. "Lesbian Mother and Custody Rights," Body Politic, Oct. 1979, pp. 26-27.

3199) Alaska Revises Penal Code Effective Jan. 1, 1980, Advocate, No. 246, Jul. 26, 1978, p. 11.

3200) Allen, Dan. "Blowing Catullus' Cover Two Thousand Years Later," Vector, Apr. 1976, pp. 29-30 and 35-36.

3201) Altman, Dennis. "The Gay Lifestyle: Myth or Reality?" Christopher Street, Apr. 1979, pp. 55-57.

3202) _____. "How Much Do Gay Men and Lesbians Really Have in Common?" Advocate, No. 315, Apr. 16, 1981, pp. 21-22.

3203) _____. Interview: Gore Vidal, Christopher Street, Jan. 1978, pp. 4-12.

3204) American Association of University Professors Adopts Non-discrimination Policy Against Gay People, Advocate, No. 195, Jul. 28, 1976, p. 21.

3205) Anderson, Scott. "The Gay Press Proliferates--And So Do Its Problems," Advocate, No. 282, Dec. 13, 1979, pp. 19-20+.

3206) _____. "The Hows of Worship [--The Gay Religious Movement]," Advocate, No. 343, May 27, 1982, pp. 19+.

3207) _____. "San Francisco Grieves the Slaying of Mayor George Moscone and Supervisor Harvey Milk," Advocate, No. 258, Jan. 11, 1979, pp. 7+.

3208)   _____. "Wayland Flowers Pulls No Strings (or
        Punches) on 'Madame's Place,'" _Advocate_, No. 357,
        Dec. 9, 1982, p. 45.

3209)   _____, and others. "Doing the Continent: Fronts
        and Frontiers of Europe's Gay Movement," _Advocate_,
        No. 308, Dec. 25, 1980, pp. 16-19.

3210)   _____, and _____. "Gay Sports," _Advocate_,
        No. 273, Aug. 9, 1979, pp. 49-54.

3211)   _____, and _____. "Riot in San Francisco
        After Verdict in Dan White Trial," _Advocate_, No.
        270, Jun. 28, 1979, pp. 7-9+.

3212)   Anti-gay Discrimination Provision Incorporated into
        Quebec's Charter, _Advocate_, No. 234, Feb. 8,
        1978, pp. 10-11.

3213)   April, Wayne. "Business Boom for Gay Savings
        and Loan," _New York Native_, Dec. 6, 1982. pp.
        24-25.

3214)   Archbishop of Canterbury Refuses Ordination of Open
        Gays, _Body Politic_, May 1980, p. 19.

3215)   Arkansas Reinstates Sodomy Statutes, _Advocate_, No.
        214, Apr. 20, 1977, p. 36.

3216)   Armstrong, James. Interview: Charles Pierce,
        Female Impersonator, _Advocate_, No. 190, May 19,
        1976, pp. 19-21.

3217)   Arsenault, Joseph. "Uncloseted Theater" and "Gay
        Theater," _Mandate_, Oct. 1980, pp. 46-49+ and Aug.
        1981, pp. 23-25+.

3218)   Austrian Nazi Concentration Camp Victims Denied
        Compensation, _Body Politic_, Dec. 1982, p. 17.

3219)   Averill, Brett, and Lenny Giteck. "On the Beat
        with Gay Cops [in New York City and San Francis-
        co]," _Advocate_, No. 317, May 14, 1981, pp. 15-17.

3220)   Avicolli, Tommy. "Barbara Gittings [Lesbian Ac-
        tivist]," _Advocate_, No. 321, Jul. 9, 1981, pp. 24+.

3221)   Bailey, Jeffrey. Interview: Gore Vidal, Advocate, No. 291, May 1, 1980, pp. 19-23.

3222)   Baker, Joe. "Refugees from Communism: Miami's Gay Cubans," Advocate, No. 203, Nov. 17, 1976, pp. 7-8.

3223)   _____, and Robert McQueen. "Miami [Defeat of Gay Rights Ordinance]: What Did We Learn?" Advocate, No. 219, Jul. 13, 1977, pp. 6-7.

3224)   "Baron von Gloeden [Photographer]," Mandate, Oct. 1977, pp. 20-23.

3225)   Barrett, Connie. "Wearing of the Gay [Gay Life in Ireland]," Christopher Street, No. 70, Nov. 1982, pp. 32-38.

3226)   Beame, Thom. "From a Black Perspective: Racism," Advocate, No. 339, Apr. 1, 1982, pp. 23-25.

3227)   Beery, Steve. Interview: Rita Mae Brown, Lesbian Author, Advocate, No. 347, Jul. 22, 1982, pp. 35-37.

3228)   Bernstein, Mal. "When a Cop Comes Out [--Steve Horn of Mesa, Az.]," Mandate, Jul. 1981, pp. 48-52.

3229)   Berube, Allan. "Marching to a Different Drummer: Lesbian and Gay GIs in World War II," Advocate, No. 328, Oct. 15, 1981, pp. 20-24.

3230)   Blasius, Mark. Interview: Guy Hocquenghem, Christopher Street, Apr. 1980, pp. 36-45.

3231)   Block, Adam. "Rebel, Rebel: Confessions of a Gay Rocker" and "Cracks in the Closet," Advocate, No. 340, Apr. 15, 1982, pp. 43-47 and No. 358, Dec. 23, 1982, pp. 43-47+.

3232)   Body Politic Acquitted for the Third Time, Body Politic, Dec. 1982, p. 11.

3233)   Boston Mayor Issues Order Banning Discrimination Against Gay People, Advocate, No. 190, May 19, 1976, p. 7.

3234)   Boultonhouse, Charles, and others.   "Time Capsules:
        The Fifties, the Darker Side of the Fifties, the Six-
        ties, and Fantasia on the Seventies," Christopher
        Street, Sep. 1977, pp. 13-21.

3235)   Boyd, Malcolm.   "An Ambiguous Synthesis: Gay
        Religious Consciousness," Advocate, No. 208, Jan.
        26, 1977, pp. 13-14.

3236)   Boylan, Robert G.   "[Paul Cadmus,] America's
        Greatest Gay Artist," Vector, Jan.-Feb. 1976, pp.
        18-20.

3237)   Breslo, Robert.   "[Joe] Orton Revived," Mandate,
        Dec. 1981, pp. 29-33+.

3238)   Britton, Jeff, and Scott Anderson.   "A Tale of
        Two [Gay] Community Centers [Philadelphia and Los
        Angeles]," Advocate, No. 309, Jan. 8, 1981, pp. 24-
        27.

3239)   Burns, Robert J.   "'Queer Doings:' Attitudes Toward
        Homosexuality in Nineteenth Century Canada," Body
        Politic, Jan. 1977, pp. 4-7 of Our Image Section.

3240)   Bush, Larry.   "The Anatomy of a Scandal: [The
        Congressional Page] Who Created It? For What Pur-
        pose?" Advocate, No. 353, Oct. 14, 1982, pp. 21-25.

3241)   _____ .   "Gay Research Gets the Ax: Back to the
        '50s with Reaganomics," Advocate, No. 329, Oct.
        29, 1981, pp. 14-17+.

3242)   _____ .   "Has the FBI Been in Your Closet? In-
        vestigations of Gay People Confirmed," Advocate,
        No. 346, Jul. 8, 1982, pp. 16-20.

3243)   _____ .   "King Koch [Mayor of New York] Talks
        to the Native," New York Native, Oct. 5, 1981, pp.
        12-13.

3244)   _____ .   "New Right Leader Terry Dolan," Ad-
        vocate, No. 340, Apr. 15, 1982, pp. 15-17+.

3245)   _____ .   "The New Separatism in Gay America,"
        Christopher Street, Aug. 1981, pp. 10-15.

3246)   _____, and Richard Goldstein. "A Chill Wind
             for Gay Rights. Where Have All the Liberals Gone?"
             Advocate, No. 321, Jul. 9, 1981, pp. 17-19.

3247)   _____, and others. "Gayscam: The Biggest
             Scandal of All, " New York Native, Aug. 16, 1982,
             pp. 12-17.

3248)   Cabral, John. "Gay Life in Mainland China, "
             Christopher Street, No. 62, Mar. 1982, pp. 27-34.

3249)   Cagle, Charles H. "Dancing Dragonfly: The Life
             of Jean Cocteau, " Mandate, Dec. 1982, pp. 34-36+.

3250)   Califia, Pat, and others. "Queer Bashing, " Ad-
             vocate, No. 314, Apr. 2, 1981, pp. 20-26.

3251)   Canada's Liberal Party Reaffirms Gay Rights Pro-
             tection, Body Politic, Aug. 1980, p. 17.

3252)   Censorship Kills Gay Magazine in Brazil, Gay Commu-
             nity News, May 22, 1982, p. 1.

3253)   Chesley, Robert. "A Perfect Relationship with Gay
             Theatre: Playwright Doric Wilson, " Advocate, No.
             264, Apr. 5, 1979, pp. 33-34.

3254)   _____, and David Glassberg. "See Me! Hear
             Me! [Gay Blind and Deaf Ask to Be Heard], " Ad-
             vocate, No. 274, Aug. 23, 1979, pp. 17-20.

3255)   "Christian Leaders Launch 'Moral War' on Homo-
             sexuals, " Advocate, No. 313, Mar. 19, 1981, p. 9.

3256)   "CIA [Central Intelligence Agency] Keeps Gay Lists, "
             Advocate, No. 207, Jan. 12, 1977, p. 7.

3257)   Collins, Gary. "Yukio Mishima and the War of
             Emotion, " Vector, Aug. 1976, pp. 19-21.

3258)   "Communist Workers Do About-Face on Gay Rights, "
             New York Native, Dec. 20, 1982, p. 11.

3259)   Cops in New Hampshire Seize Gay Mailing List, Gay
             Community News, Apr. 3, 1982, p. 1.

3260) Costner, Tom. "Homo-Economics: Cowboy Money
       Talks at the Reno Gay Rodeo," New York Native,
       Aug. 30, 1982, p. 25.

3261) Courouve, Claude. "Aspects of Male Love in the
       French Language" and "The Word 'Berdache,'"
       Gay Books Bulletin, No. 7, 1982, pp. 13-14 and
       No. 8, 1982, pp. 18-19.

3262) _____. "Sodomy Trials in France," Gay Books
       Bulletin, No. 1, 1978, pp. 22-26.

3263) Crompton, Louis. "What Do You Say to Someone
       Who Claims That Homosexuality Caused the Fall of
       Greece and Rome?" Christopher Street, Mar. 1978,
       pp. 49-52.

3264) Daniels, Matthew. "Breaking the Color Barriers--
       Black and White Men Together," Advocate, No. 331,
       Nov. 26, 1981, pp. 17-18.

3265) _____. "The Moral Majority, Inc., and the Tar-
       geting of Gays," New York Native, Apr. 20, 1981,
       p. 10.

3266) Deiter, Newt. Interview: Poet Rod McKuen. Ad-
       vocate, No. 198, Sep. 8, 1976, pp. 19-20.

3267) D'Emilio, John. "Countless Gay Men and Lesbians
       Were Victims of McCarthyism--Could It Happen
       Again?" Advocate, Dec. 23, 1982, pp. 25-27.

3268) _____. "Dreams Deferred [Early Phases of the
       American Gay Rights Movement]," Body Politic,
       Nov. 1978, pp. 19-24; Dec. 1978-Jan. 1979, pp.
       24-29; and Feb. 1979, pp. 22-27.

3269) DeMoss, Virginia. "Disco: From High Camp to
       High Tech--Gay Got It All Together," Advocate,
       No. 259, Jan. 25, 1979, pp. 17-19.

3270) DeVere, John. "Gay Images: Television and Film,"
       Mandate, Dec. 1976, pp. 10-11+.

3271) _____. "Why Billy Joe Jumped Off the Talla-
       hatchee Bridge," Mandate, Aug. 1976, pp. 6-7+.

3272)   District of Columbia Decriminalization of Consensual
        Sodomy Defeated with Opposition of Moral Majority,
        Advocate, No. 330, Nov. 12, 1981, p. 8.

3273)   Dlugos, Tim. "A Cruel God: The Gay Challenge
        to the Catholic Church," Christopher Street, Sep.
        1979, pp. 20-39.

3274)   _____. "Hunting Gays in Government: An Inter-
        view with Christopher Wallace," Christopher Street,
        Oct. 1978, pp. 29-34.

3275)   Dodge, T. P. N. "The Origins of 'Faggot' etc.,"
        Christopher Street, May 1977, pp. 61-62.

3276)   Donald, Christine. "Going Back to Growing Up Gay,"
        Body Politic, Jun. 1982, pp. 29-33.

3277)   Duberman, Martin B. "About Time: 1960--The In-
        ternational Homosexual Conspiracy," New York Na-
        tive, Sep. 21, 1981, p. 13.

3278)   _____. "Hunting Sex Perverts," Christopher
        Street, No. 60, Jan. 1982, pp. 43-48.

3279)   _____. "1933: The New Deal--Sex in the CCC
        [Civilian Conservation Corps] Camps," New York Na-
        tive, Nov. 16, 1981, pp. 13-14.

3280)   _____. "The Therapy of C. M. Otis, 1911,"
        Christopher Street, Nov. 1977, pp. 33-37.

3281)   Ebert, Alan. "Sex in the Soviet [Union]: Sublimate
        or Siberia," Advocate, No. 215, May 4, 1977, pp.
        11-12.

3282)   Edwards, Douglas. "R. W. Fassbinder [Filmmaker],
        Artist as Activist," Advocate, No. 347, Jul. 22,
        1982, p. 53.

3283)   _____, and others. "Gay and the Art of Motion
        Picture Making," Advocate, No. 285, Feb. 7, 1980,
        pp. 28-32+.

3284)   Epstein, Renée. "Children of Gays," Christopher
        Street, Jun. 1979, pp. 43-50.

3285)   Evans, Arthur. "Gay Business vs. Gay Liberation:
        All We Get from Business Is a Raw Deal," New
        York Native, Mar. 1, 1982, pp. 10, 31.

3286)   Evans, Len. "'For Centuries We Hid Alone':   A
        Chronicle of Our Invisible Years," Advocate. No.
        182, Jan. 28, 1976, pp. 36-40.

3287)   Faber, Charles. "Los Angeles-Based 'One, Inc.,'
        Thirty [Years Old] and Going Strong," Advocate, No.
        349, Aug. 19, 1982, pp. 32-35.

3288)   Fain, Nathan. "Is Our 'Lifestyle' Hazardous to Our
        Health?" Advocate, No. 338, Mar. 18, 1982, pp.
        17-21 and No. 339, Apr. 1, 1982, pp. 17-21.

3289)   _____, and Brandon Judell. "The Gay Market:
        A Sign of Progress?" Advocate, Oct. 14, 1982, pp.
        37-42.

3290)   Feineman, Neil. Joseph Hansen, Author of Gay
        Detective Novels, Advocate, No. 328, Oct. 15,
        1982, pp. 39-40.

3291)   _____. "Talking with Tennessee [Williams]," Ad-
        vocate, No. 270, Jun. 28, 1979, p. 31.

3292)   Fields, Steve. "Gay Business Groups Are Growing,"
        Advocate, No. 236, Mar. 8, 1978, pp. 17-18.

3293)   "Finnish Gay Freedom of Speech Curtailed," New
        York Native, Feb. 1, 1982, p. 8.

3294)   Fone, Byrne R. S. "Some Notes Toward a History
        of Gay People," Advocate, No. 259, Jan. 25, 1979,
        pp. 17-19 and No. 260, Feb. 8, 1979, pp. 11-13.

3295)   Foster, Stephen W. "Beauty's Purple Flame: Some
        Minor American Gay Poets, 1786-1936," Gay Books
        Bulletin, No. 7, 1978, pp. 14-18.

3296)   France Lowers Age of Homosexual Consent to 15,
        Body Politic, Mar. 1982, p. 19.

3297)   Frank, Leah D. "'Torch Song [Trilogy]' Lights Up
        Broadway; First Gay Play to Go Legit," Advocate,
        No. 347, Jul. 22, 1982, pp. 41-43.

3298)   Franklin, Patrick.   "Religion: Bond or Bondage for
        Gays?"   Advocate, No. 306, Nov. 27, 1980, pp. 21-
        23.

3299)   _____.   Artist David Hockney, Advocate, No. 269,
        Jun. 14, 1979, pp. 35-36.

3300)   "G. " "The Secret Life of Moscow," Christopher
        Street, Jun. 1980, pp. 15-22.

3301)   Galligan, David.   "Barry Sandler [Hollywood Screen-
        writer]," and "Brideshead Revisited," Advocate, No.
        337, Mar. 4, 1982, pp. 31-32 and 35-36.

3302)   Garber, Eric.   "Tain't Nobody's Business: Homo-
        sexuality in Harlem in the 1920s," Advocate, No.
        342, May 13, 1982, pp. 39-43+.

3303)   Garrett, Thomas "Pain and Pride of Gay Fathers,"
        New York Native, Nov. 16, 1981, pp. 1, 12.

3304)   Gay Liberation in Japan, Gay Community News, Jul.
        4, 1981, p. 5 and Jan. 30, 1982, p. 10.

3305)   Gay Mennonites, Gay Community News, Aug. 8, 1981,
        p. 13.

3306)   Gay Olympic Games in San Francisco, Body Politic,
        Nov. 1982, pp. 11-13.

3307)   Gay Press Association Formed, Advocate, No. 311,
        Feb. 19, 1981, p. 9.

3308)   "Gay Vote Emerges as Important Force in Australian
        Politics," Body Politic, Dec. 1981, p. 16.

3309)   Gengle, Dean.   Beth Chayim Chadashim, Gay Jewish
        Temple in Los Angeles, Advocate, No. 197, Aug.
        25, 1976, pp. 16-17.

3310)   _____.   "Ending the Doctors' Dilemma: Bay Area
        Physicians Come Out," Advocate, No. 249, Sep. 6,
        1978, p. 12.

3311)   _____.   Interviews: Psychiatrist Thomas Szasz
        and Rev. Malcolm Boyd, Advocate, No. 231, Dec.
        28, 1977, pp. 37-40 and No. 244, Jun. 28, 1978,
        pp. 23-26.

3312)   _____ . "Troy Perry and the Universal Fellowship of Metropolitan Community Churches: The Trip
of a Lifetime," Advocate, No. 218, Jun. 29, 1977,
pp. 33-34 and No. 219, Jul. 13, 1977, pp. 33-35.

3313)   _____ . W. Dorr Legg of One, Inc., Advocate,
No. 203, Nov. 17, 1976, p. 17.

3314)   _____ , and Norman C. Murphy. "Why Are We
Gay: Revolutionary Extinction? An Emerging Model
of the Origin of Sexualities," Advocate, No. 253,
Nov. 1, 1978, pp. 15-21.

3315)   Gerson, Philip. "Homosexuality on Television,"
Christopher Street, Aug. 1977, pp. 47-49.

3316)   Gibson, E. Lawrence, and Vernon E. Berg III. "A
Personal View of the Pentagon's Homophobia," Advocate, No. 217, Jun. 15, 1977, pp. 6-7+.

3317)   Giteck, Lenny. "Academics: Chalking Up Lessons,"
Advocate, No. 325, Sep. 3, 1981, pp. 17-19+.

3318)   _____ . "Do Your Parents Know: Some Expert
Advice on Coming Out," Advocate, No. 300, Sep. 4,
1980, pp. 14-19.

3319)   _____ . "Gay Humor: Comedy Comes Out of the
Closet," Advocate, No. 289, Apr. 3, 1980, pp. 23-
26.

3320)   _____ . "Gay Parents in Profile," Advocate, No.
269, Jun. 14, 1979, pp. 16-18.

3321)   _____ . "Gay Siblings--All in the Family," Advocate, No. 293, May 29, 1980, pp. 15-16.

3322)   _____ . "How Gay Are the Ghettos?" Advocate,
No. 275, Sep. 6, 1979, pp. 15-18.

3323)   _____ . "[Judge] Mary Morgan: A Lesbian for
Justice," Advocate, No. 331, Nov. 26, 1981, pp.
22-23.

3324)   _____ . "Recruiting Gay Rookies [for the Police
Force]," Advocate, No. 276, Sep. 20, 1979, pp.
20-23.

3325)   _____. "Strike Up the Gay Band! [San Francisco's
              Gay Freedom Day Marching Band and Twirling Corps],"
              Advocate, No. 255, Nov. 29, 1978, pp. 13-14.

3326)   Gold, Sandy. "Lesbians and the Gay Community,"
              Christopher Street, Jan. 1978, pp. 39-40.

3327)   Goodstein, David B. "Fighting the Briggs Brigade:
              The California Teachers Initiative Battle--An Apprais-
              al," Advocate, No. 243, Jun. 14, 1978, pp. 6-8.

3328)   Gravett, John. "[Tommy Tune] Tuned in," Mandate,
              May 1977, pp. 26-29+.

3329)   Greco, Stephen. Interviews: Musician Ned Rorem
              and French Author and Philosopher Guy Hocquenghem,
              Advocate, No. 277, Oct. 4, 1979, pp. 35-37 and No.
              286, Feb. 21, 1980, pp. 17-19.

3330)   _____, and Charles Faber. "In Search of Our
              History: Archives, Libraries and Projects History
              [in New York City, San Francisco, and Los Angeles],"
              Advocate, No. 330, Nov. 12, 1981, pp. 22-27.

3331)   _____, and others. "Merry Musicmakers [Gay
              Men's Choruses in New York City, Los Angeles,
              Chicago, and San Francisco]," Advocate, No. 312,
              Mar. 5, 1981, pp. T-7-10.

3332)   "Greek Police Given Broad Anti-gay Power," Body
              Politic, Jun. 1981, p. 19.

3333)   Gregory-Lewis, Sasha. "Gay Liberation Movement
              FBI Files Released to Advocate," Advocate, No. 222,
              Aug. 24, 1977, pp. 36-38.

3334)   _____. "The Republicans: Embracing Homophobes
              and Gay Rights Backers: A Fresh Look at the Grand
              Old Party," Advocate, No. 200, Oct. 6, 1976, pp. 7-
              8+.

3335)   _____. "Revelations of a Gay Informant: 'I Spied
              for the FBI,'" Advocate, No. 210, Feb. 23, 1977,
              pp. 12-15; No. 211, Mar. 9, 1977, pp. 13-16+; and
              No. 215, May 4, 1977, pp. 7-9+.

3336)   _____. "Secret Investigations of Gay People: A
Gay Bugaboo or a Reality?" Advocate, No. 199,
Sep. 22, 1976, pp. 6-9.

3337)   _____. "Unraveling the Anti-Gay Network,"
Advocate, No. 223, Sep. 7, 1977, pp. 8-9.

3338)   Grillo, Rudy. "Gay Moments in Straight Music,"
Gay Books Bulletin, No. 8, 1982, pp. 22-26.

3339)   Grossman, Paul. "Gay in the Kaiser's Germany,"
New York Native, Jun. 29, 1981, p. 18.

3340)   Gunter, Freeman. "Gay History on Stamps," Mandate, Aug. 1982, pp. 51-55.

3341)   Guthmann, Edward. "Gay Film Festivals," Advocate,
No. 345, Jun. 24, 1982, pp. 59-63.

3342)   Haddad-Garcia, George. "Box-Office Gays," In
Touch for Men, No. 50, Dec. 1980, pp. 68-72+.

3343)   _____. "Lily Tomlin: The Woman with One
Thousand Faces," Mandate, Mar. 1981, pp. 12-16.

3344)   Hall, Richard. "Gay Books: From the Furtive
World of the '50s to the Fad-style of the '70s," Advocate, No. 243, Jun. 14, 1978, pp. 17-19.

3345)   _____. Interview: Historian John Boswell, Advocate, No. 318, May 28, 1981, pp. 20-23 and 26-
27.

3346)   _____. "The Perils of Publishing Gay Books"
and "Will Gay Books Muscle into the Mainstream?"
Advocate, No. 209, Feb. 9, 1977, pp. 24-27 and
No. 268, May 31, 1979, pp. 17+.

3347)   _____. "Reclaiming Our Gay American Past
[Work of Jonathan Katz]," Advocate, No. 207, Jan.
12, 1977, pp. 19-21.

3348)   _____. "The Translucent Closet: Gay Theater
for Straight Audiences--Sort of," New York Native,
Jun. 21, 1982, pp. 18, 39.

3349)   _____. "The Work and Words of Marguerite Your-
cenar," Advocate, No. 344, Jun. 10, 1982, pp. 36-41.

3350)   _____, and others. "An Assessment of the Past,
Present and Future of Gay Liberation," Advocate,
No. 320, Jun. 25, 1981, pp. 29-31+.

3351)   Hamilton, Wallace. "The Boston Sex Scandal," New
York Native, Feb. 9, 1981, p. 13.

3352)   _____. "Gay Colonists at Jamestown. Were We
There?" Advocate, No. 332, Dec. 10, 1981, pp.
51-53.

3353)   Hannon, Gerald. "Calgary: Growing Pains in Boom-
town: Can Gay Business, Gay Activism ... Find
Happiness in Canada's Fastest Growing City?" Body
Politic, Sep. 1980, pp. 19-25.

3354)   _____. "No Sorrow, No Pity--A Report on the
Gay Disabled," Body Politic, Mar. 1980, pp. 19-22.

3355)   Hartmann, Paul F. "Arabian Knight: T. E. Lawrence," Mandate, Aug. 1977, pp. 45-48.

3356)   Hasbany, Dick, and Barry Laine. "Men Dancing
[in San Francisco and New York City]," Advocate,
No. 352, Sep. 30, 1982, pp. 35-40.

3357)   Helbing, Terry. "A Boom Time for [Gay] Theater,"
Advocate, No. 335, Jan. 21, 1982, pp. 43, 51-55.

3358)   _____. "Playwright Martin Sherman--Behind the
Scenes at Broadway's Big Schocker 'Bent,'" Advocate,
No. 284, Jan. 10, 1980, pp. 29+.

3359)   Hepworth, John. "[Alfred] Hitchcock's Homophobia,"
Christopher Street, No. 64, May 1982, pp. 42-49.

3360)   Heymont, George. "There's Nothing Queer About a
$3 Bill: The Gay Business Community Flexes Its
Muscle," New York Native, Mar. 1, 1982, pp. 11-
13.

3361)   Hicks, Betty. "Lesbian Athletes" and "The Billie
Jean King Affair," Christopher Street, Oct. 1979,
pp. 42-50 and Jul. 1981, pp. 13-17.

3362)   Hippler, Mike. "Herb Donaldson [California Judge],"
Christopher Street, No. 70, Nov. 1982, pp. 10-11.

3363) Holley, Steve. Interview: Jean O'Leary, Lesbian Activist, _Advocate,_ No. 321, Jul. 9, 1981, pp. 20-22.

3364) Hornak, Richard W. Interview: Quentin Crisp, _Christopher Street,_ Jan. 1979, pp. 33-35.

3365) Howe, Frederick, "The American Musical: Grand, Gaudy, and Guardedly Gay," _Advocate,_ No. 213, Apr. 6, 1977, pp. 17-19.

3366) _____. "An Exploration of the History of Female Impersonators," _Advocate,_ No. 224, Sep. 21, 1977, pp. 26-29 and No. 225, Oct. 5, 1977, pp. 28-29.

3367) _____. "Gay Theater USA," _Advocate,_ No. 234, Feb. 8, 1978, pp. 29-30.

3368) _____. "Homosexuality in English Drama" and "Homosexuality in American Drama," _Advocate,_ No. 210, Feb. 23, 1977, pp. 43-45 and No. 211, Mar. 9, 1977, pp. 41-43.

3369) Hughes, Jeremy. "Cole Porter--Larry Hart: Making Beautiful Music," _In Touch for Men,_ No. 42, Aug. 1979, pp. 38-40+.

3370) _____. "David Kopay," _In Touch for Men,_ No. 29, Jun. 1977, pp. 28-29+.

3371) _____. "Gay Mythology," _In Touch for Men,_ No. 36, Aug. 1978, pp. 25-26, 94-97 and No. 40, Apr. 1979, pp. 30-32, 68-74.

3372) _____. "[Rudolf] Nureyev," _In Touch for Men,_ No. 33, Feb. 1978, pp. 36-38.

3373) _____. "Sal Mineo: The Eternal Original," _In Touch for Men,_ No. 23, Jun. 1976, pp. 22-25.

3374) Humm, Andy. "Midtown Cops Go Berserk in Gay Bar," _New York Native,_ Oct. 11, 1982, pp. 1+.

3375) Hunter, Bill. "The Greenwich Village Story [A History]," _Mandate,_ Mar. 1980, pp. 16-21+.

3376) Indiana Penal Code Reform, _Advocate,_ No. 188, Apr. 21, 1976, p. 10.

3377)   Iowa Repeals Sodomy Statute, Advocate, No. 195,
        Jul. 28, 1976, p. 21.

3378)   Iran Executes Two Men for Homosexual Acts, Body
        Politic, May 1981, p. 16.

3379)   Israeli Government Reduces Penalty for Homosexual
        Act from Ten Years to One Year, Body Politic, Oct.
        1980, p. 18.

3380)   Jackson, Ed. "Gay Issue Heats Up Toronto Campaign
        for Mayor," Body Politic, Nov. 1980, pp. 14-15.

3381)   Johnson, R. Charles. "A Gay Vet? Here's How to
        Upgrade Your Discharge," Advocate, No. 274, Aug.
        23, 1979, p. 10.

3382)   Johnston, Gordon. "Keys to the [Gay] Ghetto," Chris-
        topher Street, Jan. 1980, pp. 21-32.

3383)   Judell, Brandon. Interview: James Baldwin, New
        York Native, Jan. 25, 1981, pp. 9-11.

3384)   Kantrowitz, Arnie. "The Good Gay Poet: Walt
        Whitman," Advocate, No. 350, Sep. 2, 1982, pp.
        38-42+.

3385)   _____. "The Price of Gay Visibility," Advocate,
        No. 318, May 28, 1981, pp. 17-19+.

3386)   _____. "Teachers: The Human Cost of Coming
        Out," Advocate, No. 277, Oct. 4, 1979, pp. 22-23.

3387)   Karlinsky, Simon. "Gay Life Before the Soviets:
        Revisionism Revised," Advocate, No. 339, Apr. 1,
        1982, pp. 31-34.

3388)   _____. "Sergei Diaghilev: Public and Private,"
        Christopher Street, Mar. 1980, pp. 48-54.

3389)   Karr, M. A. Feature Articles on Pat Bond (Lesbian
        Comedian), Robin Tyler (Lesbian Comedian), and
        Holly Near (Lesbian Singer and Songwriter), Advocate,
        No. 256, Dec. 13, 1978, pp. 27-28; No. 268, May
        31, 1979, pp. 26+; and No. 283, Dec. 27, 1979, p.
        41.

3390) Katz, Jonathan. "Why Gay History?" Body Politic,
       Aug. 1979, pp. 19-20.

3391) Kepner, Jim. "[Harry Otis Remembers:] 'Those
       Were the Days,'" In Touch for Men, No. 22, Apr.
       1976, pp. 60-61+.

3392) _____. "Our Heritage of Pride--Gay Women and
       Men Who Made History," In Touch for Men, No. 56,
       Jun. 1981, pp. 70-73.

3393) Kikel, Rudy, and Steve Abbott. "In Search of a
       Muse: The Politics of Gay Poetry," Advocate,
       No. 342, May 13, 1982, pp. 23-27.

3394) Kimmel, Douglas C. "Patterns of Aging Among
       Gay Men," Christopher Street, Nov. 1977, pp. 28-
       31.

3395) Klein, Howard. "They're Playing Our Song: Rock
       Grooves on Gay," Advocate, No. 239, Apr. 19, 1978,
       pp. 25-26.

3396) Kleinberg, Seymour. "Gay Prisoners," Christopher
       Street, Jan. 1979, pp. 23-32.

3397) _____. "It Is 1690 and You Have Been Accused
       of Sodomy," Christopher Street, No. 63, Apr. 1982,
       pp. 46-53.

3398) _____. "Passing: Gay Men Posing as Straight,"
       Christopher Street, Aug. 1979, pp. 28-40.

3399) _____. "Where Have All the Sissies Gone?"
       Christopher Street, Mar. 1978, pp. 4-12.

3400) Knutson, Donald C. "Homophobia in the American
       Judicial System," Advocate, No. 272, Jul. 26, 1979,
       pp. 15-17.

3401) Kulieke, Stephen, and Pat Califia. "In the True
       'Olympic' Tradition: The Gay Games," Advocate,
       No. 353, Oct. 14, 1982, pp. 29-34.

3402) Laine, Barry. "Diaghilev: The Imprint of a Gay
       Impresario on Twentieth Century Art," Advocate,
       No. 297, Jul. 24, 1980, pp. 27-28+.

3403)   _____ . "Gay Poetry Reaches Adolescence," Christopher Street, Dec. 1976, pp. 34-42.

3404)   Lehman, J. Lee.   "The Lesbian Herstory Archives,"
Advocate, No. 264, Apr. 5, 1979, pp. 15-17.

3405)   Lemon, Brendan.   "A Conversation with [Sociologist]
Richard Sennett," Christopher Street, No. 63, Apr.
1982, pp. 22-29.

3406)   Lennox, David R.   "Gay Life in Macho Mexico,"
Christopher Street, Jul. 1977, pp. 6-18 and Aug.
1977, pp. 34-42.

3407)   Levin, Jim.   "The Homosexual Rights Movement in
the United States to 1959: Some Basic Questions,"
Gay Books Bulletin, No. 7, 1978, pp. 19-22+.

3408)   _____ . "Pervo Killers and Gay Dicks: Gays in
American Mystery Novels," New York Native, May
10, 1982, pp. 26-27+.

3409)   Licata, Sal J.   "The Emerging Gay Presence," Advocate, No. 245, Jul. 12, 1978, pp. 7-8+. No. 246,
Jul. 26, 1978, pp. 7-8; and No. 247, Aug. 9, 1978,
pp. 17-18.

3410)   Llewellyn, Michael.   "Homosex in the Cinema,"
Mandate, Sep. 1976, pp. 22-23, 49-53; Oct. 1976,
pp. 28-29; Dec. 1976, pp. 23-25+; and Jan. 1977,
pp. 19-21, 55-70.

3411)   _____ . "Lou Reed: Wanted Dead or Alive for
Transforming a Whole Generation of Young Americans
into Faggot Junkies," Mandate, Jun. 1977, pp. 9-11.

3412)   _____ . "Next Stop, Greenwich Village," Mandate,
May 1977, pp. 36-43.

3413)   Lynch, Michael.   "Bent Under Hitler; Bent Under
Ackroyd [of the Toronto Police]," Body Politic,
Apr. 1981, pp. 28-29.

3414)   _____ . "Walt Whitman in Ontario [1800]," Body
Politic, Oct. 1980, pp. 29-31.

3415) MacLean, Judy. "National Conference on Lesbian and Gay Aging," Advocate, No. 334, Jan. 7, 1982, pp. 15-17.

3416) Marks, Neil A. "New York Gaycult: The Jewish Question and Me," Christopher Street, No. 58, Nov. 1981, pp. 8-21.

3417) Martin, Robert K. "Christopher Marlowe, Elizabethan Gay," In Touch for Men, No. 31, Oct. 1977, pp. 66-68.

3418) _____. "[Herman] Melville" and "Oscar Wilde," In Touch for Men, No. 27, Feb. 1977, pp. 22-23 and No. 32, Dec. 1977, pp. 28-29+.

3419) _____. "Walt Whitman" and "[Poet] A. E. Housman," In Touch for Men, No. 26, Dec. 1976, pp. 54-55+ and No. 30, Aug. 1977, pp. 20-21+.

3420) Mass, Lawrence. "The [Acquired Immune Deficiency Syndrome] Epidemic Continues," New York Native, Mar. 29, 1982, pp. 12-15.

3421) _____. "Congress Looks at the [Acquired Immune Deficiency Syndrome] Epidemic," New York Native, May 10, 1982, pp. 16-17+.

3422) _____. "Homophobia on the Couch," Advocate, No. 277, Oct. 4, 1977, pp. 18-19+.

3423) _____. "The New Narcissism and Homosexuality: The Psychiatric Connection," Christopher Street, Jan. 1980, pp. 14-19.

3424) _____. "Sanity in Chicago--The Trial of John Wayne Gacy and American Psychiatry," Christopher Street, Jun. 1980, pp. 24-30.

3425) _____. "Shrinking Homophobia: American Medical Association Report Echoes the Same Old Prejudice," New York Native, Apr. 12, 1982, pp. 10-11+.

3426) _____. "A Talk with [Psychiatrist] Thomas Szasz," Christopher Street, Mar.-Apr. 1981, pp. 32-39.

3427)   McCaskell, Tim. "Gay in Colombia: Hiding,
        Hustling, and Coming Together," Body Politic,
        Dec. 1980-Jan. 1981, pp. 25-27.

3428)   . "Gay Life in the New Nicaragua,"
        Body Politic, May 1981, pp. 19-21.

3429)   . "International Gay Association Meets
        in Barcelona, Spain" and "Out in Basque Country,"
        Body Politic, Jul. 1980, pp. 25-28 and Aug. 1980,
        pp. 25-28.

3430)   . "West German Police Said to Maintain
        Lists of German Homosexuals," Body Politic, Nov.
        1980, p. 20.

3431)   McCollough, Roy L. "Out of the Locker: For a
        Lot of Pro Athletes, It's Safer Inside," In Touch
        for Men, No. 25, Oct. 1976, pp. 54-55+.

3432)   McDowell, Michael S. "The New Gay Conservatism
        on Campus," Christopher Street, Dec. 1980, pp. 26-
        33.

3433)   McKuen, Rod. "The Squeeze Goes on: A Report
        from the [Florida] Battlefield," Christopher Street,
        Jun. 1977, pp. 3-14.

3434)   McQueen, Robert and others. "Gay Sports Illus-
        trated," Advocate, No. 250, Sep. 20, 1978, pp.
        23-27.

3435)   , and   . "Gays in the Country,"
        Advocate, No. 183, Feb. 11, 1976, pp. 18-29.

3436)   , and   . "Perspectives on Growing
        Older," Advocate, No. 257, Dec. 27, 1978, pp. 24-
        27.

3437)   Mehl, Robert. "International Gay Group [Campaign
        for Homosexual Equality] Formed," Advocate, No.
        255, Nov. 29, 1978, p. 7.

3438)   Mehler, Barry. "In Neo-Nazi Germany," Christopher
        Street, Jun. 1979, pp. 60-67. Response by Simon
        Karlinsky, Sep. 1979, pp. 17-18.

3439)   Meic, Robert K.   "Sexuality and the Human Commu-
         nity," Christopher Street, Jul.-Aug. 1980, pp. 8-10.

3440)   Mexico's First Gay Group Dies After Four Years,
         Body Politic, Dec. 1981, p. 16.

3441)   Miller, Jesse S.   Interview: Armistead Maupin,
         Advocate, No. 200, Oct. 6, 1976, pp. 24-26.

3442)   Missouri Reduces Homosexual Acts from Felonies
         to Misdemeanors, Advocate, No. 222, Aug. 24,
         1977, p. 36.

3443)   Moore, Gerald.   "Television Turns Vicarious--Gay
         Going Down the Tube?" Queens' Quarterly, May-
         Jun. 1977, pp. 23-25+.

3444)   "Mormons Excommunicate Editor of Advocate," Ad-
         vocate, No. 273, Aug. 9, 1979, pp. 10-11.

3445)   Morrison, Cheryl.   "Lesbian Marketplace: Changing
         a Career," Christopher Street, Feb. 1979, pp. 17-
         18.

3446)   "National Gay Archives Open in Los Angeles," Ad-
         vocate, No. 289, Apr. 3, 1980, p. 8.

3447)   Nebraska Repeals Sodomy Law, Advocate, No. 219,
         Jul. 13, 1977, p. 40.

3448)   New Hampshire Repeals Sodomy Law, Advocate, No.
         199, Sep. 22, 1976, p. 10.

3449)   "New York Bathhouse Blaze Kills Nine," Advocate,
         Jun. 29, 1977, p. 15.

3450)   "New York High Court Rules Sodomy Statute Uncon-
         stitutional," Advocate, No. 310, Jan. 22, 1981, p.
         6.

3451)   Nicholas, Ted.   "Pootahs in English Prisons," Chris-
         topher Street, Jun. 1977, pp. 31-34.

3452)   Nichols, Jack.   "The Days and Dreams of Edward
         Carpenter, England's Gay Visionary," Advocate, No.
         352, Sep. 30, 1982, pp. 25-27.

3453)   Nicholson, Joe. "Confessions of a Closeted News-
        paperman," New York Native, Jan. 8, 1981, pp.
        14-17.

3454)   "Norway Leads Way with Anti-bias Law," Body
        Politic, Jun. 1981, p. 20.

3455)   O'Loughlin, Ray. "On the Radio: The Airways
        Are Crackling with Messages of Gay Liberation,"
        Advocate, No. 340, Apr. 15, 1982, pp. 50-52.

3456)   Ontario Rejects Gay Rights; Vancouver Passes Strong
        Gay Rights Law, Body Politic, Feb. 1982, pp. 8-9
        and Dec. 1982, p. 17.

3457)   Ortlieb, Charles. "God and Gays: A New Team?
        Interview with Rev. John J. McNeill [Jesuit Priest],"
        Christopher Street, Oct. 1976, pp. 25-34.

3458)   _____. Interview: John Rechy, Christopher
        Street, Dec. 1979, pp. 59-62.

3459)   _____. Interview: "Masters and Johnson in Per-
        spective," Christopher Street, Jul. 1979, pp. 55-61.

3460)   _____. "Sharing the Holocaust," Christopher
        Street, Jan. 1980, pp. 10-13.

3461)   _____. "The West Street Massacre [and the
        Moral Majority]," New York Native, Dec. 5, 1980,
        pp. 4-8.

3462)   Pally, Marcia. "Protecting the Children: Is There
        Room for Gays in Young Adult Books?" New York
        Native, Jul. 19, 1982, pp. 27-28.

3463)   Paraguayan Police Round Up City's Gays, Body Poli-
        tic, Nov. 1982, p. 23.

3464)   Patton, Joseph. "D. H. Lawrence and His Men,"
        In Touch for Men, No. 63, Jan. 1982, pp. 74-77.

3465)   Peters, J. "Gay and Young [Youth Support Group],"
        Christopher Street, May 1979, pp. 47-49.

3466)   Pevnik, Stefan. "Gay Filmmakers Confront Media
        Homophobia in the United States," Advocate, No.
        331, Nov. 26, 1981, pp. 37-38.

3467)   Phillips, Gene.   "The Last Taboo: We Gays Have
        Reason to Fear," Queens' Quarterly, Jan. -Feb.
        1977, pp. 14-21+.

3468)   Picano, Felice.   "Hot-l Wilson: A Conversation with
        Lanford Wilson," Christopher Street, May 1981, pp.
        20-26.

3469)   Pierson, Ransdell.   "Gay News: How Good Are the
        Mainstream Media?" Advocate, No. 347, Jul. 22,
        1982, pp. 25-27+.

3470)   Plant, Richard.   "The Men with the Pink Triangles,"
        Christopher Street, Feb. 1977, p. 4-10.

3471)   _____, and others.   "Gay Germany's Resurrection,"
        Advocate, No. 358, Dec. 23, 1982, pp. 28-31+.

3472)   Pliner, Roberta.   "Fag-hags, Friends or Fellow-
        travelers?" Christopher Street, Oct. 1979, pp. 17-
        25.

3473)   Pogrebin, Letty C.   "Homosexuality, Hysteria, and
        Children: How Not to Be a Homophobic Parent,"
        New York Native, Feb. 9, 1981, Supplement, pp.
        15-21.

3474)   "Police Purge in Utah," Advocate, No. 188, Apr.
        21, 1976, pp. 11-12.

3475)   Potter, Mark.   Interview: John Gonsiorek, Mental
        Health Therapist, Advocate, No. 357, Dec. 9, 1982,
        pp. 30-31.

3476)   Preston, John.   "Goodbye, Sally Gearhart: Gay Men
        and Feminists Have Reached a Fork in the Road,"
        Christopher Street, No. 58, Nov. 1981, pp. 17-26.

3477)   _____.   "Trouble in Paradise: Does Ogunquit
        [Maine] Want Gay Tourists?" New York Native, Jun.
        7, 1982, p. 16.

3478)   "Public Housing for Gay Couples," Advocate, No.
        220, Jul. 27, 1977, p. 14.

3479)   Quinn, Brian.   "Christian Science: Homophobia
        Strikes the Hierarchy," Advocate, No. 205, Dec.
        15, 1976, pp. 15-17.

3480) Racelis, Felix. "Gay Asians: Visible, Vocal at Last," Advocate, No. 326, Sep. 17, 1981, pp. 42-43.

3481) Rector, Frank. "The [Ottoman] Empire That Was Ruled by Homosexuals," Queens' Quarterly, Sep. - Oct. 1977, pp. 5-8+.

3482) _____. "The Pink Triangle: Homosexuality in Nazi Germany," Queen's Quarterly, Aug. 1976, pp. 18, 47-50.

3483) Redfern, Jon. "[Canadian] Gay Television Drama: 'Friday Night Adventures,'" Mandate, Sep. 1976, pp. 24-26+.

3484) Reed, David. "The Persian Boy Today: Sexual Politics in Teheran," Christopher Street, Aug. 1978, pp. 15-17.

3485) "Remos, Vincenzio." "Guatemala Gay," New York Native, Aug. 30, 1982, pp. 16-17.

3486) "Report of Presidential Commission on the Holocaust Ignores Gays," Body Politic, Apr. 1980, p. 19.

3487) Rhynsburger, Mark. "On the Road with the San Francisco Gay Men's Chorus," Advocate, No. 324, Aug. 20, 1981, pp. 27-31.

3488) Rice, Jerry. "Village People [Music Group]," In Touch for Men, No. 36, Aug. 1978, pp. 69-71.

3489) Riordon, Michael. "The Mirror of Violence [Self-Defense and Toronto Gay Men]," Body Politic, May 1980, pp. 25-28.

3490) Roca, Ana. "Interview: Eduardo--After the [Cuban] Revolution," Christopher Street, Feb. 1980, pp. 44-46.

3491) Rofes, Eric. "A Gay Issue That Cannot Be Ignored ... Suicide," Advocate, No. 273, Aug. 9, 1979, pp. 15-19.

3492) Rothenberg, David. "Can Gays Save New York City?" Christopher Street, Sep. 1977, pp. 7-12.

3493)   _____. "Gay Prisoners Rebel," Advocate, No.
240, May 3, 1978, pp. 13-15.

3494)   _____. "Group Rip-off: The Prison Rape," Advocate, No. 189, May 5, 1976, pp. 9-11.

3495)   _____. "Homophobia and the New York [Theater]
Critics" and "Homophobia at the New York Times,"
New York Native, Jan. 10, 1981, pp. 24-25 and Jun.
1, 1981, pp. 1, 14-15.

3496)   Russo, Tony. Interview: Christopher Isherwood,
Christopher Street, Mar. 1977, pp. 7-10.

3497)   Russo, Vito. "Gay Filmography [A List of Movies],"
In Touch for Men, No. 58, Aug. 1981, pp. 76-83.

3498)   Russo, William. "Horatio, Mr. Alger and His Boys"
and "James M. Barrie; The Secret Life of Peter
Pan," In Touch for Men, No. 38, Dec. 1978, pp.
30-31 and No. 49, Oct. 1980, pp. 61-64.

3499)   _____. "Lawrence of Arabia" and "[General
Charles] Gordon of Khartoum: A Military Mind,"
In Touch for Men, No. 44, Dec. 1979, pp. 61-64
and No. 48, Aug. 1980, pp. 21-23.

3500)   _____. "Leonardo [da Vinci], A Brush with
Gayness" and "Caravaggio," In Touch for Men, No.
37, Oct. 1978, pp. 39, 92-95 and No. 39, Feb.
1979, pp. 74-75+.

3501)   _____. "Son of Pan: Arthur Rimbaud," Mandate, Jan. 1979, pp. 50-52+.

3502)   _____. "[Theodore] Gericault ... A Man's Painter" and "Hart Crane [Poet]," In Touch for Men, No.
40, Apr. 1979, pp. 18-19+ and No. 41, Jun. 1979,
pp. 69-72+.

3503)   _____. "The Tragic History of Edward II, England's Gay King," In Touch for Men, No. 43, Oct.
1979, pp. 61-63.

3504)   Rutledge, Leigh W. "Oscar Wilde in Paris," Mandate, Nov. 1982, pp. 14-17+.

3505)   . "Uncut Scenes from Gay History," Mandate, Aug. 1982, pp. 10-13.

3506)   Sarver, Tony. "The Decline and Fall of Britain's Jeremy Thorpe, M.P.," Advocate, No. 263, Mar. 22, 1979, pp. 12-14+.

3507)   Saslow, James M. "Ars Gratia Erotica: The Laid-back Leslie-Lohman Gallery Is Home for Homoerotic Art," Advocate, No. 252, Oct. 18, 1978, pp. 38-39.

3508)   . "'Bent:' Gay Holocaust," Advocate, No. 277, Oct. 4, 1979, p. 46.

3509)   . "Charles Henri Ford: A Traveler Without Touchstone," Advocate, No. 317, May 14, 1981, pp. 30-32.

3510)   . "[Gay Presses:] Getting the Word Out and About," Advocate, No. 332, Dec. 10, 1981, pp. 30-31.

3511)   . "The New York School: The Avant-Garde Painters of the '40s and '50s," Advocate, No. 191, Jun. 2, 1976, pp. 23-24+.

3512)   . "Romaine Brooks: In Retrospect," Advocate, No. 223, Sep. 7, 1977, pp. 34-35.

3513)   . "Rosa Bonheur: Allowed to Be Unusual Because She Was Successful," Advocate, No. 199, Sep. 22, 1976, pp. 14-16.

3514)   . "Slave to Beauty and Master of Photography: F. Holland Day," Advocate, No. 330, Nov. 12, 1981, pp. 28-30.

3515)   , and Neil Feineman. "Tom Robinson: Gay, Punk, and Glad to Be Out-of-Bounds," Advocate, No. 315, Apr. 16, 1981, pp. T-1-3+.

3516)   , and others. "Gay Art and the Galleries," Advocate, No. 263, Mar. 22, 1979, pp. 20-23.

3517)   Sawatsky, John. "Security Paranoia and the Fruit Machine [Activities of the Royal Canadian Mounted Police]," Body Politic, May 1980, p. 21.

3518)   Schauer, John. "[Gerald] Arpino: Dance and the
        Male Mystique," Advocate, No. 237, Mar. 22, 1978,
        pp. 32-33.

3519)   _____. "Sylvester: A Sterling [Singing] Talent
        Turns Gold into Platinum," Advocate, No. 259, Jan.
        25, 1979, pp. 32-33.

3520)   _____. "The Tiptoeing Trockadero [Ballet]," Ad-
        vocate, No. 203, Nov. 17, 1976, pp. 24-26+.

3521)   Schultz, Mark. "Survivors Pay Tribute to Holocaust
        Victims," New York Native, Nov. 22, 1981, p. 8.

3522)   Schuvaloff, George. "Gay Life in Russia," Chris-
        topher Street, Sept. 1976, pp. 14-23.

3523)   Schwartz, William C. "Allen Ginsberg and the
        Homoerotic Sensibility," Mandate, Jan. 1978, pp.
        54-70.

3524)   _____. "André Gide: Homosexuality and Litera-
        ture," Mandate, Nov. 1976, pp. 8-10, 56-68 and
        Dec. 1976, pp. 57-72.

3525)   _____. "André Gide's 'Corydon,'" Mandate,
        Sep. 1977, pp. 38-39+.

3526)   _____. "Phallic Consciousness and D. H. Law-
        rence: Men in Love," Mandate, Jun. 1976, pp. 28-
        30, 48-51.

3527)   Scobie, W. I. Interview: Martin Duberman, Ad-
        vocate, No. 229, Nov. 30, 1977, pp. 41-42.

3528)   _____. "Pier Paolo Pasolini," Advocate, No.
        189, May 5, 1976, pp. 45-47.

3529)   _____. "W. H. Auden," Advocate, No. 243, Jun.
        14, 1978, pp. 23-27.

3530)   Shapiro, Ellen. "Three Women on Lesbians and
        Fathers," Christopher Street, Apr. 1977, pp. 24-40.

3531)   Shewey, Don. Feature Articles on Broadway Stars
        Tommy Tune and Harvey Fierstein, Advocate, No.
        213, Apr. 6, 1977, pp. 24-25 and No. 243, Jun. 14,
        1978, pp. 35-36.

3532)   Shilts, Randy. "Alcoholism: A Look in Depth at
        How a National Menace is Affecting the Gay Commu-
        nity," Advocate, No. 184, Feb. 25, 1976, pp. 16-25.

3533)   _____. "Big Bill Tilden [Tennis Player], Triumph
        Then Tragedy," Advocate, No. 195, Jul. 28, 1976,
        pp. 11-12.

3534)   _____. "Big Business: Gay Bars and Baths Come
        Out of the Bush Leagues," Advocate, No. 191, Jun.
        2, 1976, pp. 37-38+.

3535)   _____. "Gay Campus Movement," Advocate, No.
        198, Sep. 8, 1976, pp. 6-7.

3536)   _____. "Gay Youth: The Lonely Young," Advo-
        cate, No. 216, Jun. 1, 1977, pp. 31-34+.

3537)   _____. "Hepatitis," Advocate, No. 207, Jan. 12,
        1977, pp. 23-26.

3538)   _____. "The Life and Death of Harvey Milk,"
        Christopher Street, Mar. 1979, pp. 25-43.

3539)   _____. "Mecca or Ghetto: Castro Street [San
        Francisco] thru Residents' Eyes," Advocate, No.
        209, Feb. 9, 1977, pp. 20-23.

3540)   _____. "A New Plague on Our House: Gastro-
        intestinal Diseases," Advocate, No. 214, Apr. 20,
        1977. pp. 12-13.

3541)   _____. "Paul Ferguson Remembers the Ramon
        Novarro Murder," Advocate, No. 225, Oct. 5, 1977,
        pp. 14-15.

3542)   _____. "Plain Brown Wrappers: Peddling Gay
        Porn by Mail Is A Million Dollar Business," Ad-
        vocate, No. 193, Jun. 30, 1976, pp. 16-19.

3543)   _____. "Pop Music: Strictly Between the Lines,"
        Advocate, No. 187, Apr. 7, 1976, pp. 25-27.

3544)   _____. "Unethical Lawyers--Some of Them Are
        Gay," Advocate, No. 218, Jun. 29, 1977, pp. 10-11.

3545)   _____. "V. D. and Other Sexually Transmitted
        Diseases in the Gay Community," Advocate, No.
        188, Apr. 21, 1976, pp. 14-18.

3546) Sloan, David. "Did the Homophobic Media Force
      Paul Lynde to Assume the Role of a Faggoty Man?"
      Mandate, Aug. 1982, pp. 62-64+.

3547) Soares, John V. "Black and Gay: Problems and
      Possibilities," Advocate, No. 203, Nov. 17, 1976,
      pp. 13-16.

3548) South African Gays Form National Group, Body Poli-
      tic, May 1980, p. 20.

3549) Sowers, Prudence. "The Habits of Love: Lesbians
      Who Were Nuns," Advocate, No. 343, May 27, 1982,
      pp. 29-30+.

3550) Spain Still Outlaws Gay Organizations, Body Politic,
      Apr. 1980, p. 19.

3551) Stambolian, George. "We Are in History: An Inter-
      view with Eric Bentley," Christopher Street, Dec.
      1977, pp. 29-36.

3552) Staton, Robert W. "Tennessee Williams: The Play-
      wright as Painter," Advocate, No. 253, Nov. 1,
      1978, pp. 40-41.

3553) Steakley, James. "Gays Under Socialism: Male Ho-
      mosexuality in the German Democratic Republic,"
      Body Politic, Dec. 1976-Jan. 1977, pp. 15-18.

3554) Stein, David. "Why Are Gays Smarter Than
      Straights? Homosexuality and Sociobiology," Chris-
      topher Street, Jul. 1978, pp. 9-14.

3555) Stephen Lachs of Los Angeles Becomes First Openly
      Gay Judge in the United States, Advocate, No. 280,
      Nov. 15, 1979, p. 7.

3556) Steward, Samuel M. "Cardinal Newman and
      Friends," Advocate, No. 331, Nov. 26, 1981, pp.
      25-27.

3557) Stone, Charles. "The Semantics of 'Gay,'" Ad-
      vocate, No. 325, Sep. 3, 1981, pp. 20-22.

3558) Stone, Christopher. Interview: Johnny Mathis,
      Advocate, No. 184, Feb. 25, 1976, pp. 35-36.

3559)   Stoneman, Donnell. Interview: Paul Cadmus, Amer-
        ican Painter, Advocate, No. 191, Jun. 2, 1976, pp.
        25-29.

3560)   "Sudanese Gays Sent to Labor Camps," New York
        Native, Feb. 1, 1982, p. 8.

3561)   Taylor, Clark L., Jr. "Mexican Gaylife in His-
        torical Perspective," Gay Sunshine, Nos. 26-27,
        1975-76, pp. 1-3.

3562)   Taylor, Clarke. "Contemporary Elegance at 74:
        Sir John Gielgud," Advocate, No. 216, Jun. 1, 1977,
        pp. 19-20.

3563)   Thompson, Mark. Drama Review: "Crimes Against
        Nature," Advocate, No. 221, Aug. 10, 1977, pp. 22-
        23.

3564)   _____. "RFD: A [Gay] Magazine for the Heart-
        land," Advocate, No. 334, Jan. 1, 1982, pp. 21+.

3565)   _____, and others. "The Western Range [Gay
        Cowboys and Rodeos]," Advocate, No. 315, Apr. 16,
        1981, pp. T-11-14.

3566)   Trefzger, Paul. "The Gay Olympic Games," Ad-
        vocate, No. 348, Aug. 5, 1982, pp. 18-19.

3567)   Treimel, Scott. "Win or Lose ... The Gay Olympics
        Redefine Victory," New York Native, Aug. 16, 1982,
        p. 36.

3568)   Tress, Arthur. "Victims of Male Rape," Mandate,
        May 1981, pp. 30-33.

3569)   Tucker, Scott. "Sex, Death and Free Speech: The
        Fight to Stop Friedkin's [Filming of] 'Cruising,'"
        Body Politic, Nov. 1979, pp. 23-27.

3570)   Turtell, Stephen. "Emerald City, New York City's
        Cable TV Show for Gays," Advocate, No. 260,
        Feb. 8, 1979, pp. 40-41.

3571)   Tuveson, Roger. "First Gay Tour of China," Man-
        date, Dec. 1982, pp. 10-13+.

3572)   Twyford, Neal.   "The Double Closet: Disabled Gays
        Who Cope with Coming Out--Twice," Advocate, No.
        336, Feb. 18, 1982, pp. 18-21.

3573)   United States State Department Ends Ban on Employ-
        ment of Gay People, Advocate, No. 211, Mar. 9,
        1977, p. 17.

3574)   University of Southern California Law School Adopts
        Policy of Non-discrimination Against Gay People,
        Advocate, No. 188, Apr. 21, 1976, p. 10.

3575)   Varady, Mike.   "If You're Young, Gay and Draft
        Bait--How Not to Get Hooked," Advocate, No. 318,
        May 28, 1981, pp. 15-16.

3576)   Vennard, Jane.   "My Husband Is a Homosexual,"
        Christopher Street, No. 65, Jun. 1982, pp. 18-25.

3577)   Vidal, Gore.   "Some Jews and the Gays," Chris-
        topher Street, No. 59, Dec. 1981, pp. 29-37.

3578)   Vining, Donald.   "The Advantage of Age," Advocate,
        No. 313, Mar. 19, 1981, pp. 22-23

3579)   Walter, Kate.   "Glad to Be Gray: Old and Gay Is
        Not Alone," New York Native, Sep. 27, 1982, pp.
        14-15.

3580)   Weinstein, Jeff.   "Uneasy Days on Old Cape Cod
        [Provincetown]," Body Politic, Aug. 1979, pp. 23-
        25.

3581)   Weissman, Eric.   "Kids Who Attack Gays," Chris-
        topher Street, Aug. 1978, pp. 9-13.

3582)   West Virginia Repeals Sodomy Law, Advocate, No.
        196, Apr. 11, 1976, p. 11.

3583)   Willenbecher, Thom.   "Gay Atheists Come Out,"
        Advocate, No. 284, Jan. 10, 1980, pp. 19-21.

3584)   _____.   "Gentrification: Has the Gay Role in
        Urban Restoration Led to Hostile Reactions?" Ad-
        vocate, No. 298, Aug. 7, 1980, pp. 17-19.

3585)   _____, and Scott Anderson.   "Police-Gay Rela-
        tions," Advocate, No. 291, May 1, 1980, pp. 13-15.

3586)   Wilson, Barbara. "Lesbian Writer Jane Rule," Advocate, No. 279, Nov. 1, 1979, pp. 30-31.

3587)   Wilson, Edward O. "Gay as Normal: Homosexuality and Human Nature. A Sociobiological View," Advocate, No. 266, May 3, 1979, pp. 15+.

3588)   Wisconsin First State to Pass Gay Rights Law, Advocate, No. 339, Apr. 1, 1982, p. 9.

3589)   Wood, B. Ayer. "The Gay Olympics," In Touch for Men, No. 74, Dec. 1982, pp. 26-43.

3590)   Wyoming Repeals Sodomy Statute, Advocate, No. 213, Apr. 6, 1977, p. 11.

3591)   Young Ian. "The Gay Monarchs of England: The Kings Who Would Be Queens," Advocate, No. 299, Aug. 21, 1980, pp. 25-27.

3592)   _____. "Gay Presses [c. 1890 to the Present]," Advocate, No. 242, May 31, 1978, pp. 28-29.

3593)   _____. "Gays Against Hitler," Advocate, No. 303, Oct. 16, 1980, pp. 28-31+.

3594)   Young, Scott. "Forty Years of 'Gay' in the USA," Queens' Quarterly, Nov.-Dec. 1979, pp. 10-13+.

3595)   Youngman, Barry. "Gay Life in Israel," Advocate, No. 272, Jul. 26, 1979, pp. 20-22.

3596)   Yousling, Jim, and Rob Rae. Out-of-the-Closet Gay Athletes: Interviews with Glenn Burke, George Frenn, and Richard Hunter, In Touch for Men, No. 74, Dec. 1982, pp. 44, 78-83.

3597)   Zemel, Sue. "Fun Folk of Gay Comix," Advocate, No. 343, May 27, 1982, pp. 45-46.

3598)   _____. "Learning to Deal with Death and Dying," Advocate, No. 343, May 27, 1982, pp. 31-33.

3599)   Ziebold, Thomas O. "Alcoholism and Recovery: Gays Helping Gays," Christopher Street, Jan. 1979, p. 36+.

3600)   Zweigler, Mark. "Gay Theater: 'Crimes Against Nature,'" Mandate Sep. 1978, pp. 18-20.

MOVIES

With a Major Homosexual Theme

"Army of Lovers or Revolt of the Perverts" (German, 1979)

"The Best Way" (French, 1977)

"La Cage aux Folles" (French, 1978)

"La Cage aux Folles II" (French, 1980)

"The Consequence" (German, 1977)

"Cruising" (Lorimar, 1980)

"Deathtrap" (Columbia, 1982)

"The Deputy" (Spanish, 1977)

"A Different Story" (Enterprise, 1978)

"Ernesto" (Italian, 1979)

"Happy Birthday, Gemini" (United Artists, 1980)

"Making Love" (20th Century-Fox, 1981)

"Nighthawks" (Cinegate, 1978)

"Norman, Is That You?" (Metro-Goldwyn-Mayer, 1976)

"Outrageous" (Film Consortion of Canada, 1977)

"Partners" (United International, 1982)

"Personal Best" (Columbia, 1982)

"Querelle" (German, 1982)

"The Ritz" (Warner, 1976)

"Sebastiani" (Latin-Italian, 1976)

"Taxi zum Klo" (German, 1981)

"To an Unknown God" (Spanish, 1981)

"Victor/Victoria" (United International, 1982)

With a Minor Homosexual Theme

"American Gigolo" (Paramount, 1980)

"The Betsy" (Allied Artists, 1978)

"The Big Sleep" (Warner, 1978)

"Bloodbrothers" (Warner, 1978)

"California Suite" (Columbia, 1978)

"Caligula" (Penthouse Films, 1979)

"Can't Stop the Music" (Columbia, 1980)

"Car Wash" (Universal, 1976)

"Choirboys" (Lorimar, 1977)

"Drum" (London Films, 1976)

"Evil Under the Sun" (Titan, 1981)

"Fame" (Metro-Goldwyn-Mayer, 1980)

"Fellini's Casanova" (20th Century-Fox, 1976)

"Gator" (United Artists, 1976)

"Hair" (United Artists, 1979)

"The Last Married Couple in America" (Universal, 1979)

"Logan's Run" (Metro-Goldwyn-Mayer, 1976)

"Looking for Mr. Goodbar" (Paramount, 1977)

"Madam Kitty" (German, 1976)

"The Man Who Fell to Earth" (British Lion, 1976)

"Manhattan" (United Artists, 1979)

"Midnight Express" (Columbia, 1978)

"Murder by Death" (Columbia, 1976)

"Next Stop, Greenwich Village" (TCF, 1976)

"Nijinsky" (Paramount, 1980)

"Ode to Billy Joe" (Columbia, 1976)

"The Onion Field" (Black Marble, 1979)

"A Perfect Couple" (20th Century-Fox, 1979)

"Pixotte" (Spanish, 1981)

"The Rose" (20th Century-Fox, 1978)

"St. Jack" (New World, 1979)

"Saturday Night Fever" (Paramount, 1977)

"Short Eyes" (Harris-Fox, 1977)

"Slap Shot" (Universal, 1977)

"A Special Day" (Italian, 1977)

"Spetters" (Dutch, 1981)

"Swashbuckler" (Universal, 1976

"Valentino" (United Artists, 1977)

"The World According to Garp" (Columbia, 1982)

TELEVISION PROGRAMS

Series

ABC   "Soap. " Fall 1977-Spring 1980.

ABC   "Dynasty. " Jan. 1981 to present

ABC   "Nancy Walker Show. " Fall 1976-Spring 1977.

ABC   "Three's Company. " Fall 1977 to present.

NBC   "Fame. " Fall 1981-Spring 1982.

NBC   "Love, Sidney. " Fall 1981-Spring 1982 and Fall 1982.

Individual Programs

ABC   "Baretta: The Reunion. " Feb. 2, 1977.

ABC   "Barney Miller. " Apr. 22, 1976; Sep. 30, 1976, Oct. 7, 1976, Dec. 16, 1976; Feb. 24, 1977, Sep. 13, 1979; Jan. 24, 1980.

ABC   "Carter Country. " Sep. 29, 1977.

ABC   "Close Up: ERA-- The War Between Women. " Jan. 22, 1977.

ABC   "Donahue. " Jan. 30, 1980 (Bisexuality); Feb. 22, 1980 (Gays and Job Discrimination); Jul. 14, 1980 (Gay High School Student and Senior Prom); Mar. 3, 1981 (Gay Couples); Sep. 2, 1981 (Gay Senior Citizens); Apr. 8, 1982 (Married Homosexuals and Bisexual Couples); Oct. 13, 1982 (Homosexual

Rights--Pro and Con); Nov. 21, 1982 (Homosexuals and Acquired Immune Deficiency Syndrome); Nov. 24, 1982 (Lesbians and Sperm Banks); Nov. 25, 1982 (Spousal Rights for Homosexuals and Unmarried Couples); Dec. 1, 1982 (Homosexuals and Acquired Immune Deficiency Syndrome).

ABC   "Family: Rites of Friendship. "   Sep. 28, 1976.

ABC   "Family. "   Nov. 1, 1977

ABC   "Fish. "   Oct. 1, 1977.

ABC   "Geraldo Rivera: Good Night America. "   Apr. 28, 1977 (Guests: David Kopay and Christine Jorgensen).

ABC   "Good Morning America. "   Dec. 16, 1981 (Interview with Billie Jean King); Jan. 1, 1982 (Interview with Al Corley of "Dynasty").

ABC   "The Jim Ferguson Show. "   Feb. 28, 1982 (Interview with Harry Hamlin of "Making Love").

ABC   "News Close-up: Homosexuals. "   Dec. 18, 1979.

ABC   "Nightline. "   Sep. 9, 1980 (The Armed Forces and Discharge of Homosexuals); Sep. 29, 1982 (Homosexuality and Politics); Nov. 10, 1982 (Homosexual Rape in Prison); Dec. 17, 1982 (Acquired Immune Deficiency Syndrome).

ABC   "Prime Time Saturday. "   May 16, 1980 (Gentrification of parts of San Francisco by Gays).

ABC   "Starsky and Hutch: Death in a Different Place. "   Oct. 15, 1977.

ABC   "The Streets of San Francisco: Thrill Killers. "   Sep. 30, 1976.

ABC   "The Streets of San Francisco: A Good Cop--But. "   Feb. 10, 1977.

ABC   "The Streets of San Francisco: A Trout in the Milk. "   May 2, 1977.

ABC   "Sunday Night Movie: A Question of Love. "   Nov. 26, 1978.

ABC   "Taxi." Nov. 21, 1978; Dec. 10, 1980.

ABC   "20/20." Oct. 18, 1978 (The Village People);
             May 7, 1981 (Billie Jean King); May 6, 1982
             (Recent Movies Dealing with Homosexuality).

CBS   "Alice." Sep. 29, 1976.

CBS   "All in the Family." Dec. 18 and 25, 1977.

CBS   "Archie Bunker's Place." Aug. 17, 1980.

CBS   "The Bob Newhart Show." Oct. 16, 1976.

CBS   "CBS Reports: Gay Power, Gay Politics."
             Apr. 26, 1980.

CBS   "Hour Magazine." Dec. 22, 1980 (Gay Children).

CBS   "Kojak: A Need to Know." Oct. 24, 1976.

CBS   "The Last Resort." Dec. 17, 1979.

CBS   "Lou Grant." May 1, 1978, and Sep. 17, 1979.

CBS   "Maude." Dec. 3, 1977.

CBS   "Sixty Minutes." May 15, 1977 (Kiddie Porn and
             Boy Prostitution); Jun. 5, 1977 (Gay Rights--Pro
             and Con); Sep. 24, 1977 (Jeremy Thorpe and Ho-
             mosexual Scandal in England); Oct. 16, 1977 (Wives
             of Homosexuals); Oct. 28, 1978 (Coptic Church and
             Opposition to Homosexuality); May 5, 1979 (Up-
             coming Trial of Jeremy Thorpe); Dec. 11, 1981
             (Prison Goon Squads and Homosexuality in Prison).

CBS   "Stockard Channing and Just Friends." Mar. 25,
             1979.

CBS   "Thirty Minutes." Feb. 16, 1980 (Teen-age Homo-
             sexuals).

CBS   "Trapper John, M.D.: Straight and Narrow." Dec.
             11, 1981.

CBS   "The White Shadow." Jan. 27, 1979.

CBS   "Who's Who." Apr. 12, 1977 (Anita Bryant and Her Anti-gay Campaign in Miami).

CBS   "WKRP in Cincinnati." Oct. 2, 1978.

CBS   "Your Turn--Letters to CBS." Jun. 11. 1980 (Criticisms of CBS Reports Special on "Gay Power, Gay Politics").

KBHK   San Francisco. "Mary Hartman, Mary Hartman." Sep. 28, 1976; Oct. 11, 1976.

KGO   San Francisco. "Lesbians: The Invisible Minority." Jan. 12, 1981.

KGO   San Francisco. "Say What You Think." Nov. 6, 1982 (San Francisco--The Gay Capital?).

KNBC   Los Angeles. "Gay: A Documentary." Mar. 28, 1977.

KNBC   Los Angeles. "Proposition 6: The Briggs Initiative." Aug. 26, 1978.

KQED   San Francisco. "Pride, Prejudice, and Gay Politics." Oct. 27, 1982.

KUID   Moscow, Idaho. "Sweet Land of Liberty." Jul. 31, 1977.

NBC   "The American Family: An Endangered Species?" Jan. 2, 1978.

NBC   "The Big Event: In the Glitter Palace." Feb. 27, 1977.

NBC   "CPO Sharkey." Mar. 16, 1977.

NBC   "Entertainment Tonight." Jan. 15, 1982 (Hostility to Song, "Johnny Are You Queer?"); Mar. 10, 1982 (Interview with Al Corley of "Dynasty").

NBC   "James Dean--Portrait of a Friend." Feb. 19, 1976.

NBC   "Meet the Press." Nov. 20, 1977 (Homosexuality and Opposition to Equal Rights Amendment).

NBC   "Monday Night at the Movies: Dawn--Portrait of
           a Teenage Runaway. " Sep. 27, 1976.

NBC   "Monday Night at the Movies: Alexander--The
           Other Side of Dawn, " May 16, 1977.

NBC   "Monday Night at the Movies: Sergeant Matlovich
           Versus the U. S. Air Force, " Aug. 21, 1978.

NBC   "Nightly News. " Sep. 12-16, 1977 (Daily Segment
           on Homosexuality).

NBC   "Police Woman: Trial by Prejudice. " Oct. 12,
           1976.

NBC   "Real People. " Apr. 14, 1982 (Gay Rodeo in
           Reno); Apr. 28, 1982 (Mr. and Ms. Gay America).

NBC   "The Runaways. " Aug. 21, 1979.

NBC   "Saturday Night Live. " Sep. 24, 1977 (Segment on
           Anita Bryant and Her Opposition to Gays).

NBC   "Sidney Shorr. " Oct. 5, 1981.

NBC   "Today. " Jun. 3, 1977 (Anita Bryant and Her
           Campaign Against Gay Rights); Nov. 3, 1977
           (Anita Bryant); Apr. 20, 1979 (Masters and John-
           son and Their Study on Homosexuality); Aug. 18,
           1980 (The Navy and Lesbianism); May 26, 1981
           (The Gay Lobby and Television); Oct. 14-15, 1981
           (Phil Donahue on Homosexuality); Oct. 27-28, 1981
           (Phil Donahue on Gay Rights); Feb. 25, 1982 (Re-
           cent Movies on Homosexuality); Sep. 13, 1982 (In-
           terview of Glenn Burke, Gay Athlete and Former
           Major League Baseball Player).

NBC   "Tomorrow Show. " Apr. 30, 1976 (Interview with
           David Kopay); Jun. 25, 1976 (The Gay Business
           World); Jun. 2, 1980 (Interview with Quentin Crisp).

PBS   "Brideshead Revisited. " Jan. -Apr. 1982.

PBS   "Christopher Marlowe's 'Edward II. ' " Feb. 24,
           1977.

PBS   "The Dick Cavett Show. " Dec. 25, 1979 (Inter-
           view with Bishop Paul Moore, Jr.).

PBS   "Firing Line: The Question of Gay Rights. "
           Apr. 26, 1981.

PBS   "Great Performances: Harold Pinter's 'The Col-
           lection.'"   Oct. 25, 1978.

PBS   "Greetings from Washington, D. C. :   The National
           Gay March, 1981. "   Jun. 22, 1982.

PBS   "The Life of Cecil J. Rhodes: A Touch of Church-
           ill, a Touch of Hitler. "   Jul. 15, 1981.

PBS   "The MacNeil-Lehrer Report: A. I. D. S. :   The
           Mysterious Disease. "   Aug. 26, 1982.

PBS   "Nova: The Elusive Disease--Hepatitis. "   Jan.
           15, 1980.

PBS   "Sneak Previews with Gene Siskel and Robert
           Ebert. "   May 13, 1982 (Review of recent movies
           dealing with Homosexuality).

PBS   "Third Avenue: Only the Strong Survive. "   Apr.
           11, 1980 (Case studies including a New York City
           Male Hustler).

PBS   "The Tom Cottle Show: Gay Adolescents. "   Jul.
           15, 1981.

PBS   "Word Is Out: Stories of Some of Our Lives. "
           Oct. 10, 1978.   (26 Homosexual Men and Women).

WCBS   New York City.   "Eye On: Lesbians--Women
           Without Rights?"   Feb. 7, 1978.

WCBS   New York City.   "The Lives We Live. "   Oct. 29
           and 30, 1982.   (Gay Life).

WNET   New York City.   "Gerty Stein Is Back, Back,
           Back. "   Jun. 22, 1981.

WNET   New York City.   "Lesbian and Gay Update 1981. "
           Jun. 22, 1981.

WPIX   New York City.   "Open Mind.   Homosexuality. "
           Nov. 13, 1981.

AUDIOVISUAL AIDS

Angels of Mercy. Charles M. Crann. New York, N.Y. 16-minute film. 1976.

Boys Beware. Charles Cahill and Associates. AIMS In-structional Media, Glendale, Calif. 14-minute film. 1980.

Counseling the Homosexual Person. Lester A. Kirkendall. National Catholic Reporter Publishing Co., P.O. Box 281, Kansas City, Mo. 2 cassette tapes

Early Homosexual Fears. Dimension Films. Little Red Film-house, Los Angeles, Calif. 11-minute film. 1977.

Gay, Proud, and Sober. Image Associates. Santa Barbara, Calif. 21-minute film. 1978.

Greetings from Washington, D.C. Iris Films. Berkeley, Calif. 28-minute film. 1981. (See also Appendix II, PBS.)

The Hidden Minority: Homosexuality in Our Society. Guid-ance Associates. White Plains, N.Y. Filmstrip of 208 frames or 2 cassettes. 1979.

Homosexuality. Lee Thorn. Lansford Publishing Co., San Jose, Calif. 12 transparencies. 1976.

Homosexuality and Lesbianism: Gay or Straight, Is There a Choice? Hobel-Leiterman Productions. Document Asso-ciates, New York, N.Y. 26-minute film. 1976.

Issues in Sexual Behavior: Homosexuality. Peter Schnitzler Productions. Harper and Row, New York, N.Y. Film-strip of 85 frames. 1976.

<u>Michael, A Gay Son.</u> Film-makers Library, New York, N.Y.
   27-minute film. 1981.

<u>Mixed Marriages: Homosexual Husbands.</u> CBS News. Car-
   ousel Films, New York, N.Y. 13-minute film. 1978.

<u>Our Lesbian Roots.</u> Valerie Taylor. Mosaic Press, Box
   41502, Tucson, Ariz. 85717. 8 one-hour cassettes on
   Lesbian literature. 1980.

<u>Pink Triangles: A Study of Prejudice Against Lesbians and
   Gay Men.</u> Cambridge Documentary Films, Inc. , Cambridge, Mass. 34-minute film. 1982.

<u>Sergeant Matlovich Versus the U.S. Air Force.</u> Tomorrow
   Entertainment, Inc. Learning Corporation of America,
   New York, N.Y. 98-minute film. 1979. (<u>See also</u> Ap-
   pendix II, NBC, "Monday Night at the Movies. ")

<u>Sharing the Secret.</u> Canadian Broadcasting Corporation. In-
   ternational Film Exchange, New York, N.Y. 84-minute
   film. 1981.

<u>Teenage Homosexuality.</u> CBS News. Carousel Films, New
   York, N.Y. 11-minute film. 1979. (<u>See also</u> Appendix
   II, CBS, "Thirty Minutes. ")

<u>Who Happen to Be Gay.</u> Direct Cinema Ltd. , Franklin Lakes,
   N.J. 23-minute film. 1979.

<u>You [Gay Parents] Just Love Your Children.</u> Temple Univer-
   sity, Department of Radio-Television-Film, Philadelphia,
   Pa. 12-minute film. 1979.

Appendix IV:

AMERICAN LAWS APPLICABLE TO CONSENSU AL
ADULT HOMOSEXUAL ACTS (1982)

Offenses and Criminal Codes	Penalties

ALABAMA (Revision effective Jan. 1, 1980.)

Sexual misconduct--deviate sexual intercourse 13A-6-65(a)(3). 13A-5-2, 13A-5-7(a)(1), 13A-5-12(a)(1).	up to 1 yr, up to $2000, or both
Indecent exposure 13A-6-68. 13A-5-2, 13A-5-7(a)(1), 13A-5-12(a)(1).	up to 1 yr, up to $2000, or both
Disorderly conduct--obscene language or gesture 13A-11-7. 13A-5-2, 13A-5-7(a)(3), 13A-5-12(a)(3).	up to 3 mos, up to $500, or both
Loitering for solicting or engaging in deviate sex act 13A-11-9(3). 13A-5-7(b), 13A-5-12(b).	up to 30 days, up to $200
Failure to register as sex offender 13A-11-200 and 203.	1-5 yrs & (optional) up to $1000
Public lewdness 13A-12-135. 13A-5-2, 13A-5-7(a)(3), 13A-5-12(a)(3).	up to 3 mos, up to $500, or both

ALASKA (Revision effective Jan. 1, 1980. Age of consent: 18.)

Disorderly conduct--indecent exposure 11.61.110(a)(7). 11.05.010.	up to 1 yr or up to $500

ARIZONA (Revision effective Oct. 1, 1978.)

Indecent exposure 13-1402. 13-603D, 13-707(3), 13-802C.	up to 30 days, up to $500, or both

Offenses and Criminal Codes	Penalties
Public sexual indecency 13-1403. 13-603D, 13-707 (2), 13-802B.	up to 4 mos, up to $750, or both
Crime against nature (anal) with person 15 or over 13-1411. 13-603D, 13-707 (3), 13-802C.	up to 30 days, up to $500, or both
Lewd and lascivious acts 13-1412. 13-603D, 13-707 (3), 13-802C.	up to 30 days, up to $500, or both
Loitering for sexual solicitation 13-2905A(1). 13-603D, 13- 707(3), 13-802C.	up to 30 days, up to $500, or both

ARKANSAS (Revision effective Jan. 1, 1976.)

Public sexual indecency--deviate sex act 41-1811b. 41-803(3), 41-901 (2)(a), 41-1101(2)(a).	up to 1 yr. up to $1000
Indecent exposure 41-1812. 41-803(3), 41-901 (2)(a), 41-1101(2)(a).	up to 1 yr, up to $1000
Sodomy (anal or oral) with per- son of same sex 41-1813. 41-803(3), 41- 901(2)(a), 41-1101(2)(a).	up to 1 yr, up to $1000
Disorderly conduct--obscene language or gesture, sexual exposure 41-2908(c)&(i). 41-803(3), 41-901(2)(c), 41-1101(2)(c).	up to 30 days, up to $100
Loitering for soliciting or en- gaging in deviate sexual ac- tivity 41-2914(e). 41-803(3), 41- 901(2)(c), 41-1101(2)(c).	up to 30 days, up to $100

CALIFORNIA (Revision effective Jan. 1, 1976. Age of consent: 18.)

Sodomy (anal) & oral copulation in prison 286(e) & 288a(3).	up to 1 yr
Failure to register as sex of- fender 290	90 days to 1 yr
Arrest of teachers & school employees for sex offenses 291 & 291.1.	notification of school officials

Offenses and Criminal Codes	Penalties

Indecent exposure--1st offense
   314. 18, 19, 672.

up to 6 mos, up to $500, or
   both, or up to 1 yr

Indecent exposure--subsequent
   offense 314. 18, 672.

16 mos, or 2-3 yrs, up to
   to $5000, or both

Public solicitation or commission of a lewd act in public
   647(a). 18, 19, 672

up to 6 mos, up to 12 mos, up
   to $500, or both

Loitering for soliciting or committing a lewd act 647(d).
   18, 19, 672.

up to 6 mos, up to 12 mos, up
   to $500, or both

Outraging public decency
   650 1/2. 18, 19, 672.

up to 6 mos, up to 12 mos, up
   $500, or both

COLORADO (Revision effective Jan. 1, 1972. Age of consent: 15.)

Public indecency
   18-7-301. 18-1-107.

up to $500, up to 6 mos, or
   both

Indecent exposure
   18-7-302. 18-1-106.

3-24 mos, $250-$5000, or both

Disorderly conduct--offensive
   gesture or comment
   18-9-106(a). 18-1-107.

up to $500, up to 6 mos, or
   both

Loitering for deviate sexual
   intercourse
   18-9-112(c). 18-1-107.

up to $500, up to 6 mos, or
   both

CONNECTICUT (Revision effective Aug. 1, 1972. Age of consent: 18.)

Public indecency
   53a-186. 53a-28, 53a-36
   (2), 53a-42(1).

up to 6 mos, up to $1000, or
   both

DELAWARE (Revision effective Jul. 1, 1973. Age of consent: 16.)

Indecent exposure
   11-768. 11-4206(b).

up to 6 mos & up to $500

Disorderly conduct--offensive
   comment or gesture
   11-1301. 11-4206(b).

up to 6 mos & up to $500

Loitering for engaging in or
   soliciting deviate sexual intercourse
   11-1321(5). 11-2407(d).

up to $250

Public lewdness
   11-1341. 11-4206(b).

up to 6 mos & up to $500

Offenses and Criminal Codes   Penalties

DISTRICT OF COLUMBIA

Disorderly conduct--obscene gestures or comments 22-1107.	up to $250, up to 90 days, or both
Indecent exposure, lewd acts 22-1112.	up to $300, up to 90 days, or both
if in presence of person under 16 22-1112.	up to 1 yr, up to $1000, or both
Disorderly conduct--offensive acts 22-1121.	up to $250, up to 90 days, or both
Disorderly conduct--unlawful acts in public 22-3111.	up to $500, up to 6 mos, or both
Sodomy (anal and oral) 22-3502.	up to $1000 or up to 10 yrs
if with person under 16 22-3502.	up to $1000 or up to 20 yrs
Sexual psychopath 22-3503-11.	commitment to St. Elizabeth's Hospital

FLORIDA (Revision effective Oct. 1, 1974.)

Unnatural and lascivious acts (anal & oral) 800.02 775.082 and 083.	up to 60 days, up to $500, or both
Indecent exposure 800.03. 775.082 and 083.	up to 1 yr, up to $1000, or both

GEORGIA (Revision effective Jul. 1, 1979.)

Sodomy (anal and oral) 16-6-2.	1-20 yrs
Public indecency 16-6-8. 17-10-3.	up to $1000, up to 1 yr, or both
Solicitation of sodomy 16-6-15. 17-10-3.	up to $1000, up to 1 yr, or both

HAWAII (Revision effective Jan. 1, 1973. Age of consent: 14.)

Indecent exposure 37-707-738. 37-706-640 & 663.	up to $500 or up to 30 days

Offenses and Criminal Codes	Penalties

Disorderly conduct--offensive
language & display
37-711-1101.   37-706-640 &
663.

up to $500, or up to 30 days

IDAHO (Revision effective Apr. 1, 1972.)

Crime against nature (oral and
anal)
18-6605.

not less than 5 yrs

Disturbing the peace--offensive
conduct
18-6409.   18-113.

up to 6 mos, up to $300, or
both

ILLINOIS (Revision effective Jan. 1, 1962.   Age of consent: 18.)

Public indecency
38.11-9.   38.1005-8-3, 38.
1005-9-1.

up to 1 yr, up to $1000, or
both

Obscene act or exhibition
38.11-20.   38.1005-8-3, 38.
1005-9-1.

up to 1 yr, up to $1000, or
both

INDIANA (Revision effective Jan. 21, 1976.   Age of consent: 18.)

Public indecency
35-45-4-1.   35-50-3-2.

up to 1 yr, up to $5000, or
both

IOWA (Revision effective Jan. 1, 1978.   Age of consent: 18.)

Indecent exposure
709.9.   903.1.

up to 1 yr, up to $1000, or
both

KANSAS (Revision effective Jul. 1, 1970.)

Consensual sodomy (anal and
oral)
21-3105.   21-4502 & 4503.

up to 6 mos, up to $1000, or
both

Open lewd & lascivious behavior
indecent exposure
21-3508.   21-4502 & 4503.

up to 6 mos, up to $1000, or
both

Disorderly conduct--offensive
language
21-4101.   21-4502 & 4503.

up to 1 mo, up to $500, or
both

Offenses and Criminal Codes	Penalties

KENTUCKY (Revision effective Jan. 1, 1975.)

Fourth degree consensual sodomy (anal and oral) 510.100. 532.090.	up to 1 yr, up to $500, or both
Indecent exposure 510.150. 534.040.	up to 90 days, up to $250, or both

LOUISIANA

Crime against nature (anal and oral) 14.89.	up to $2000, up to 5 yrs, or both
Disturbing the peace--offensive words 14.103A(2).	up to $100, up to 90 days, or both
Indecent exposure 14.106A(1).	$1000-$2500, 6 mos to 3 yrs, or both
Vagrancy--loitering 14.107(7).	up to $200, up to 6 mos, or both

MAINE (Revision effective May 1, 1976.   Age of consent: 16.)

Disorderly conduct--offensive words and gestures 17A.501. 17A.1152, 17A. 1252, 17A.1301.	up to 6 mos or up to $500
Public indecency--indecent exposure 17A.854. 17A.1152, 17A. 1252, 17A.1301.	up to 6 mos or up to $500

MARYLAND

Indecent exposure 27.335A.	up to 3 yrs, up to $1000, or both
Sodomy (anal) 27.553.	up to 10 yrs
Unnatural or perverted sexual practices 27.554.	up to $1000, up to 10 yrs, or both
Lewdness and solicitation 27.15e & 15g, 16, 17.	up to $500, up to 1 yr, or both
Disturbance--disorderly manner 27.122.	up to $100, up to 30 days, or both

Offenses and Criminal Codes   Penalties

MASSACHUSETTS

Resorting for immoral purposes $25-$500, up to 1 yr, or both
  and acts
  272. 26.
Sodomy and buggery (anal)   up to 20 yrs
  272. 34.
Unnatural and lascivious acts $100-$1000, up to 2 1/2
  272. 35.   or 5 yrs
  [In Commonwealth v. Balthazar (318 NE 2d 478, 1974) the Supreme
  Judicial Court of Massachusetts has ruled that this statute does
  not prohibit consensual private conduct between adults. See also
  Commonwealth v. Scargliotti, 371 NE 2d, 726, 1977 and Commonwealth v. Ferguson, 422 NE 2d 1365, 1981. Age of consent: 18.]
Lewdness and indecent expo-   up to 1 mo or up to $50
  sure
  272. 53.   272. 40

MICHIGAN

Sodomy, crime against nature   up to 15 yrs
  (anal)
  28. 355.
  if sexually delinquent person   1 day to life
Disorderly persons--indecent   up to 90 days, up to $100, or
  conduct in public   both
  28. 364-65.   28. 772.
Open or indecent exposure   up to 1 yr or up to $500
  28. 567(1).   28. 200 (1)
  if sexually delinquent person   1 day to life
Gross indecencies between   up to 5 yrs or up to $2500
  males, & attempts
  28. 570.   28. 200(1).
  if sexually delinquent person   1 day to life
Gross indecencies between fe-   up to 5 yrs or up to $2500
  males, & attempts
  28. 570(1).   28. 200(1)
  if sexually delinquent person   1 day to life
Public solicitation & accosting   up to 90 days, up to $100, or
  for lewd acts   both
  28. 703.   28. 772.

MINNESOTA (Revision effective May 18, 1967.)

Disorderly conduct--offensive   up to 90 days, up to $500, or
  language   both
  609. 72   609. 02.

Offenses and Criminal Codes   Penalties

Consensual sodomy (anal and   up to 1 yr, up to $1000, or
    oral)   both
    609.293(1 & 5).
Indecent exposure, lewdness   at least $5 or at least 10 days
    617.23.

MISSISSIPPI

Indecent exposure in public   up to $500, up to 6 mos, or
    97-29-31   both
Unnatural intercourse, crime   up to 10 yrs
    against nature (anal & oral)
    97-29-59.
Disorderly conduct--indecent   up to $200, up to 4 mos, or
    remarks and gestures   both
    97-35-3(1)(b).
Disturbing the peace--offensive   up to $500, up to 6 mos, or
    language or conduct   both
    97-35-13 & 15.
Failure to register as a felon   up to 3 mos, up to $100, or
    97-35-27.   both
Vagrancy--immoral life--1st of-   10-30 days or bond of at least
    fense $201
    97-35-37 & 39.

MISSOURI (Revision effective Jan. 1, 1979.)

Sexual misconduct (anal and   up to 1 yr, up to $1000, or
    oral)   both
    566.090.   557.011, 558.011,
    560.016.
Indecent exposure   up to 1 yr, up to $1000, or
    566.130.   557.011, 558.011,   both
    560.016.

MONTANA (Revision effective Jan. 1, 1974.)

Indecent exposure   up to $500, up to 6 mos, or
    45-5-504   both
Deviate sexual conduct   up to 10 yrs, up to $50,000,
    45-5-505   or both

NEBRASKA (Revision effective Jan. 1, 1979. Age of consent: 18.)

Public indecency   up to 6 mos, up to $1000, or
    28-806.   28-106.   both

Offenses and Criminal Codes   Penalties

Disturbing the peace   up to 3 mos, up to $500, or
28-1322.   28.106.   both

NEVADA (Revision effective Jul. 1, 1967.)

Crime against nature (anal and   1-6 yrs
oral)
201.190.
Open lewdness--first offense   up to 1 yr, up to $2000, or
201.210.   193.140   both
Indecent exposure--first offense   up to 1 yr, up to $2000, or
201.220.   193.140.   both
Vagrancy--soliciting or engaging   up to 6 mos, up to $1000, or
in lewd conduct--first offense   both
207.030.   193.150.
Loitering about schools   up to 6 mos, up to $1000, or
207.070.   193.150.   both
Failure to register as sex of-   up to 6 mos, up to $1000, or
fender   both
207.151.   193.150.

NEW HAMPSHIRE (Revision effective Aug. 6, 1975.   Age of consent:
                        18.)

Indecent exposure, lewdness   up to 1 yr, up to $1000, or
645.1.   651.2.   both
Solicitation   up to 1 yr, up to $1000, or
645.2.   651.2.   both

NEW JERSEY (Revision effective Sep. 1, 1979.   Age of consent: 16.)

Indecent exposure   up to $1000, up to 6 mos, or
2C:14-4.   2C:43-2, 2C:43-   both
3, 2C:43-8.

NEW MEXICO (Revision effective Jul. 1, 1975.   Age of consent: 16.)

Indecent exposure before per-   up to 6 mos, up to $500 or
son under 18   both
30-9-14.   31-19-1.
Disorderly conduct--indecent   up to 6 mos, up to $500, or
conduct   both
30-20-1.   31-19-1.

Offenses and Criminal Codes   Penalties

NEW YORK (Revision effective Sep. 1, 1967.)

Consensual sodomy--deviate   up to 3 mos, up to $500, or
  sexual intercourse   both
  39.130.38.   39.60.10, 39.
  70.15, 39.80.105.
  [The N.Y. Court of Appeals in People v. Onofre, 415 NE 2d 963
  (1980) declared this statute unconstitutional. Age of consent: 17.]
Disorderly conduct--obscene   up to 15 days, up to $250, or
  words or gestures   both
  39.240.20.   39.60.01, 39.
  70.15, 39.80.05.
Loitering for soliciting or en-   up to 15 days, up to $250, or
  gaging in deviate sexual   both
  intercourse
  39.240.35.3.   39.60.01, 39.
  70.15, 39.80.05.
Public lewdness or exposure   up to 3 mos, up to $500, or
  39.245.00.   39.60.01, 39.   both
  70.15, 39.80.05

NORTH CAROLINA (Revision effective Jul. 1, 1981.)

Crime against nature (anal and   up to 10 yrs, fine, or both
  oral)
  14-177.
Indecent exposure   up to $500, up to 6 mos, or
  14-190.9   both
Disorderly conduct, loitering,   up to $50 or up to 30 days
  obscene language
  14-275.1.
Vagrancy--idle and immoral   up to $50 or up to 30 days
  life--first offense
  14-336.

NORTH DAKOTA (Revision effective Jul. 1, 1975. Age of consent:
                  15.)

Disorderly conduct--obscene   up to 30 days, up to $500, or
  language or gesture, loiter-   both
  ing to solicit sexual contact
  12.1-31-01.   21.1-32-01.
Indecent exposure   up to 30 days, up to $500, or
  12.1-20-12.1.   12.1-32-01.   both

Offenses and Criminal Codes   Penalties

OHIO (Revision effective Jan. 1, 1974. Age of consent: 16.)

Offensive solicitation of person   up to 6 mos, up to $1000, or
  of same sex   both
  2907.07B.   2929.21-22.
Public sexual indecency   up to 30 days, up to $250, or
  2907.09.   2929.21-22.   both
Disorderly conduct--offensive   up to 30 days, up to $250, or
  language or gesture   both
  2917.11.
Failure to register as habitual   up to 6 mos, up to $1000, or
  sex offender -- first offense   both
  subsequent offense   6 mos to 5 yrs, up to $2500,
  2950.01, 2950.99.   2929.   or both
  21-22, 2929.11.

OKLAHOMA

Outraging public decency   up to 1 yr, up to $500, or
  21.22,   21.10.   both
Crime against nature (anal and   up to 10 yrs
  oral)
  21.886.
Indecent exposure $100-$10,000, 30 days to 10
  21.1021.   yrs, or both
Lewdness, solicitation   30 days to 1 yr
  21.1029-31.

OREGON (Revision effective Jan. 1, 1972. Age of consent: 18.)

Public accosting for deviate   up to 30 days or up to $500
  sexual intercourse
  163.455.   161.615 & 635.
Public indecency, public sex   up to 1 yr or up to $2500
  acts, indecent exposure
  163.465.   161.615 & 635.
Obscene language or gesture   up to 6 mos or up to $1000
  166.025(1)(c).   161.615 &
  635.
Loitering near a school   up to 30 days or up to $500
  166.045. 161.615 & 635.

PENNSYLVANIA (Revision effective Jun. 6, 1973.)

Voluntary aeviate sexual inter-   up to 2 yrs or up to $5000
  course
  18.3124.   18.1101 & 1104.

Offenses and Criminal Codes	Penalties

[The Pennsylvania Supreme Court in Commonwealth v. Bonadio, 415 A. 2d 47, 1980, declared this statute unconstitutional. Age of consent: 16. See also Commonwealth v. Walters, 422 A. 2d 598, 1980.]

Indecent exposure 18. 3127. 18. 1101 & 1104.	up to 2 yrs or up to $5000

Disorderly conduct--obscene
  language or gesture
  18. 5503.   18. 1101 & 1104.
	up to 1 yr or up to $2500

Open lewdness 18. 5901. 18. 1101 & 1104.	up to 1 yr or up to $2500

RHODE ISLAND

Crime against nature (anal and
  oral)
  11. 10. 1.
	7-20 yrs

Disorderly conduct--offensive
  language, indecent exposure
  11. 45. 1.
	up to 6 mos, up to $500, or
	  both

SOUTH CAROLINA (Revision effective Jan. 1, 1967.)

Buggery 16-15-120.	5 yrs, at least $500, or both

Indecent exposure
  16-15-130.
	fine, imprisonment, or both at
	  discretion of the court

Public disorderly conduct--
  obscene language
  16-17-530.
	up to $100 or up to 30 days

SOUTH DAKOTA (Revision effective Apr. 1, 1977. Age of consent: 15.)

Indecent exposure
  22-24-1.   22-6-2.
	up to 30 days, up to $100, or
	  both

TENNESSEE

Crime against nature (anal and
  oral)
  39-2-612.
	5-15 yrs

Disturbing the peace--offensive
  language & conduct
  39-6-301.
	$20-$200 & (optional) up to
	  30 days

Offenses and Criminal Codes   Penalties

TEXAS (Revision effective Jan. 1, 1975.)

Homosexual conduct--deviate   up to $200
   sexual intercourse
   21.06.   12.23.
   [A federal district court, in Baker v. Wade (553 F. Supp. 1121,
   1982), has declared this statute unconstitutional.   Age of consent:
   17.   This case is on appeal before the 5th U.S. Circuit Court.]
Public lewdness   up to $2000, up to 1 yr, or
   21.07.   12.21.   both
Indecent exposure   up to $200
   21.08.   12.23.
Disorderly conduct--indecent   up to $200
   language, offensive gesture
   or display
   42.01.   12.23.

UTAH (Revision effective Jul. 1, 1973.)

Consensual sodomy (anal and   up to 6 mos, up to $299, or
   oral)   both
   76-5-403.   76-3-201, 204,
   & 301.
Disorderly conduct--obscene   up to 90 days, up to $299, or
   language or gesture   both
   76-9-102.   76-3-201, 204,
   & 301.
Public lewdness, public sex act,   up to 6 mos, up to $299, or
   indecent exposure   both
   76-9-702.   76-3-201, 204, &
   301.

VERMONT (Revision effective Jul. 1, 1977.   Age of consent: 16.)

Disorderly conduct--obscene   up to 60 days, up to $500, or
   language   both
   13.1026.
Open lewd and lascivious conduct   up to 5 yrs or up to $300
   13.2601.

VIRGINIA (Revision effective Aug. 1, 1975.)

Crime against nature (anal and   1-5 yrs
   oral)
   18.2-361.   18.2-10.
   [This statute has been upheld as constitutional by the U.S. Supreme
   Court in Doe v. Commonwealth's Attorney, 425 U.S. 901, 1976.]

Offenses and Criminal Codes	Penalties
Indecent exposure 18. 2-387. 19. 2-11.	up to 1 yr, up to $1000, or both

WASHINGTON (Revision effective Jul. 1, 1976.   Age of consent: 18.)

Public indecency, obscene expo- sure 9A. 88. 011. 9A. 20. 020.	up to 90 days, up to $1000, or both

WEST VIRGINIA (Revision effective Jun. 2, 1976.   Age of consent:
16.)

Loitering on or near school property--1st offense 61-6-14a.	up to $100, up to 30 days, or both
Indecent exposure 61-8B-10.	up to 90 days, up to $250, or both
Public indecency 61-8B-11.	up to $250

WISCONSIN (Revision effective May 12, 1983.   Age of consent: 18.)

Sexual gratification in public 944. 17. 939. 51.	up to $10,000, up to 9 mos, or both
Public lewd behavior, indecent exposure 944. 20. 939. 51.	up to $10,000, up to 9 mos, or both

WYOMING (Revision effective May 27, 1977.   Age of consent: 16.)

Public indecency, indecent ex- posure, obscene language 6-5-301.	up to $100 & (optional) up to 3 mos
Breach of the peace--obscene language 6-6-201.	up to $50, up to 30 days, or both
Vagrancy--immoral life 9-9-402 & 403.	up to $100, up to 3 mos, or both

Historical 170, 220, 706-09, 740, 771, 2689, 2815, 3073, 3171,
    3239
Professional 162, 381, 520, 531, 536, 540, 542, 558, 565, 575,
    585, 621, 633, 706, 722, 768, 2150, 2610, 2738, 2801, 2994,
    3087, 3145, 3168, 3422, 3425
Public 330, 404, 414, 457-58, 463-64, 476, 492, 535, 544, 557,
    559, 561, 588, 610, 617, 644, 651, 696, 704, 745, 794, 898,
    909, 924, 967, 969, 972, 1155, 1160, 1178, 1180, 1209, 1233,
    1267, 1313, 1358, 1378, 1399, 1410, 1448, 1474, 1484, 1498,
    1542, 1547, 1590, 1598, 2090, 2126, 2227, 2254, 2286, 2353,
    2593, 2740, 2769, 2810, 2867, 2973, 3023, 3126, 3130, 3153,
    3180, 3267
Student 495, 519, 2270, 2626, 2753, 2812, 3048, 3145
See also Anita Bryant; California Campaign; Christian Church;
    Federal policy; Gay demonstrations; Gay public officials; Gay
    rights bills; Gay vote; Homophobia; The Law; Law reform; Po-
    lice attitudes; Stigmatization; and Violence
Auden, W. H. 54, 112, 119, 3529
Audiovisual aids 544; See also Appendix III
Austin, Texas 1112
Australia 1786, 3308
Austria 3218
Autobiographies 38-39, 45, 51-52, 56, 59-60, 62, 64-68, 71, 75,
    77, 86-87, 91, 95, 100, 105-06, 108, 113, 115, 118, 123-24,
    128-29, 137-38, 140-41, 143-45, 147, 149-51

Baldwin, James 3383
Bali 1405
Barcelona, Spain 1271
Barney, Natalie C. 57, 146
Barrett, Ellen M. 1236
Barrie, James M. 47, 3498
Bauman, Robert E. 1134, 1349
Beardsley, Aubrey V. 2998
Behan, Brendan 41
Belfast, Northern Ireland 1411
Bell, Alan P. 1606
Bentham, Jeremy 2726, 2728
Bentley, Eric 3551
Berg, Vernon E. , III 76, 1320, 1677
The Bible 160, 216, 237, 386, 405, 408, 419, 740, 1429, 1621,
    1650, 1656, 1698, 1724, 1755, 1769, 1823, 1828-29, 1832; See
    also Christian Church, Judaism, Religion
Bibliographies 181, 236, 301, 321, 350, 377, 380, 402, 436, 440,
    443, 450-52, 455, 486, 863, 919, 2841, 2883, 2919, 2950,
    3035, 3157
Big Brothers, Inc. 1952
Biographies 40-44, 46-50, 53-55, 57-58, 61, 63, 69-70, 72-74, 76,
    78-85, 88-90, 91-94, 96-99, 101-04, 107, 109-12, 114, 116-17,
    119-22, 125-27, 130-36, 139, 142, 146, 148, 241, 2646
Biology and Sociobiology 26, 603, 1090, 2387, 3083, 3085, 3554,
    3587

Caravaggio 2533, 3500
Carey, Hugh 1232
Carpenter, Edward 327, 1071, 2874, 3452
Carswell, Harold 1338
Castration 2439
Castro Street (San Francisco) 132, 356, 3539
Catullus 2993, 3200
Causation, genesis, or etiology 21, 187, 509, 563, 567, 766, 899,
    923, 942, 1388, 1627, 2147, 2160, 2209, 2279, 2283, 2288,
    2298, 2314, 2382, 2420, 2606, 2777; See also Theories of ho-
    mosexuality
Cavafy, C. P. 107, 120, 251
Censorship 901, 2792, 2824, 3055, 3252
Central Intelligence Agency (CIA) 1153, 1334, 3256
Chaucer 2953
Cheney, Russell 86
Chicago 3331, 3424
Child custody 75, 489, 1223, 1579, 1844, 1847, 1866, 1869, 1876,
    1880, 1891, 1903, 1907, 1951, 1965, 1986, 1998-99, 2001,
    2009, 2021, 2272, 2827, 2859, 2920, 3053, 3198; See also
    Gay fathers, Gay parents, Lesbian mothers
Childhood play 2251-52
Children, sexual exploitation of 483-85, 799, 911, 1341, 3012; See
    also Pedophilia
Children and adolescents 71, 228, 265, 435, 555-56, 571, 590, 611,
    613, 627, 686, 692, 711, 739, 811, 819, 837, 871, 974, 1191,
    1197, 1396, 1507, 1532, 1654, 1686, 2108, 2159, 2223, 2226,
    2247-48, 2282, 2298, 2312, 2326, 2338, 2384, 2492-93, 2496,
    2504, 2532, 2606, 2608, 2703, 2821, 2952, 2996, 3066, 3117,
    3146, 3176, 3462, 3473, 3581; See also Children of homosex-
    uals, Gay children, Gay youth, Gay adoption, Male Prostitution,
    Pedophilia
Children of homosexuals 2113, 2294, 2338, 2921, 2976, 2978, 3021,
    3284; See also Child custody
China 3248, 3571
The Christian Church
    Church statements on homosexuality 382, 396-97, 400, 462, 469,
        471-72, 772, 1105, 1290, 1417, 1580, 1615, 1633, 1709, 1749-
        50, 1756, 1766, 1786, 1792, 1812, 1815, 1825
    Counseling, pastoral care, and ministry to homosexuals 397, 410,
        417, 438, 462, 466, 643, 850, 1105, 1618, 1623, 1654, 1664,
        1669-70, 1680, 1685, 1730, 1756, 1790, 1792, 1797
    Denominations
        African Methodist Episcopal 1783
        Christian Scientist 3479
        Church of England 400, 1400, 1624, 1778, 1825
        Episcopalian 115, 472, 673, 1493, 1665, 1737, 1766, 1792
        Fundamentalist Protestant 780, 1159, 1224, 1540, 1557, 1634,
            2787
        Lutheran 1615, 1786
        Methodist 1328, 1574, 1624, 1633, 1655, 1745
        Presbyterian 253, 469, 1416, 1672, 1735, 1776, 1794-95,
            1811-12

Gay drama reviews 1343 (Torch Song Trilogy), 1432 (Streamers),
   1433 (Fifth of July), 1434 and 1453 (Bent), 3563 (Crimes
   Against Nature)
Gay etiquette 193, 447
Gay fashion show 1120
Gay fathers 422, 511, 622, 725, 917, 936, 2034, 2076, 2682-83,
   2976, 3161, 3303
Gay foster homes 1197
Gay ghettos 908, 2802, 2918, 3322, 3382
Gay guides and handbooks 33, 185-86, 192-93, 212, 219, 225, 260,
   286, 290, 326, 332, 341-42, 345, 357, 394, 407, 423-25, 437,
   439, 447, 449, 459, 473, 475, 1441
Gay history 693, 1223, 3330, 3340, 3347, 3390-92, 3505
Gay humor 602, 1048, 3319, 3597
Gay Jews and synagogues 2, 668, 698, 1202, 1743, 3309; See also
   Lesbian Jews, Judaism
Gay judges 1208 and 3323 (Mary Morgan), 3362 (Herbert Donaldson),
   3555 (Stephen Lachs)
Gay language, vocabulary, and rhetoric 6, 322, 478, 527, 750, 820-
   21, 956, 1083, 2723, 2814, 2840-41
Gay Latinos 517
Gay lawyers 1157, 1919, 1953, 1971-72, 1990, 3544
Gay liberation and Gay Liberation Movement 4, 13, 18, 25, 28, 34,
   153-54, 217, 274, 283, 310, 434, 444, 479, 576, 582, 665,
   667, 693, 714-15, 727, 755, 768, 779, 794, 798, 803, 955,
   1006, 1075, 1302, 2706, 2765, 2784, 2871, 2912, 2914, 2924,
   2941, 2996, 3127-28, 3142, 3268, 3285, 3304, 3333, 3350,
   3407, 3409; See also Gay activists, Gay organizations, Gay
   rights
Gay life as seen by homosexuals 3, 8, 18, 28, 36, 38, 141, 143,
   145, 151, 158, 171, 185-86, 193, 207, 217, 243, 247, 255,
   280, 286, 290, 294, 310, 342, 345, 349, 356-57, 415, 447, 665-
   66, 691, 697, 774, 1206, 1419, 1610, 3022, 3201, 3288
Gay life as seen by others 206, 225, 330, 670, 704, 758, 1340,
   1356, 1393, 1405
Gay literature 539, 959, 1095, 1179, 1372, 2705, 3290, 3295, 3393,
   3403; See also Gay drama and theater
Gay lobby 1451
Gay love signs 244
Gay marriage 1126, 1156, 1858, 1878, 1932, 1491, 2221, 2839;
   See also Gay couples
Gay Mennonites 3305
Gay ministers and priests 647, 850, 1546, 1574, 1631, 1673, 1745-
   46, 1780, 1818-19, 3162; See also Ordination
Gay movies and films 1171, 1362, 1377, 1383, 1497, 1522, 1608,
   2648, 3029; See also Movies
Gay music and musicians 1205, 1325, 1347, 1370, 3231; See also
   Gay bands, Gay choruses
Gay mythology 358, 3371
Gay (Olympic) Games 418, 1154, 1166, 1200, 1212, 3306, 3401,
   3566-67, 3589
Gay organizations 477, 1075, 1093, 1944, 2027, 2818, 2828, 3287,
   3429, 3437, 3440, 3548, 3550; See also Gay Liberation Move-
   ment

Homosexual incest 1774, 2048, 2146, 2327, 2445, 2550
Homosexual labeling 531, 553, 709, 874, 980, 2887, 2981, 3024
Homosexual offenses 367, 406, 1134, 1839, 1856, 1893, 1895, 1904,
     1918, 1928, 1933-34, 1947-48, 1959-61, 1966, 1969, 1983,
     1987, 1991-92, 1994, 2004-05, 2011-12, 2014, 2019, 2022,
     2024, 2029, 2033, 2660, 3062-63; See also Appendix IV
Homosexual patients 679, 2081, 2266, 2444, 2462, 2466, 2479, 2613,
     2621; See also Health care
Homosexual relationships 518, 587, 655, 750, 753, 829, 870, 900,
     971, 1010, 1046, 2468, 2733, 2744, 2794, 2885, 2922, 2945
Homosexual scandals 240, 285, 343, 848, 928, 1110, 1252, 1335,
     1348, 1508, 1526, 1555, 1567, 1587, 3240, 3247, 3351
Homosexual tendencies 1687
Homosexual types 589, 924, 954, 1384
Hong Kong 2915, 3179
Hooker, Evelyn 720
Hoover, J. Edgar 1422
Hormones see Endocrine factors
Horn, Steve 3228
Housman, A. E. 78, 3419
Houston, Texas 1195, 1380
Humanism 1408
Hunt, Alberta 801
Hunter, Richard 3596

Immigration and naturalization--alien residence and citizenship 1132,
     1281, 1309, 1360, 1576-77, 1840, 1881, 1890, 1920, 1941,
     1974, 1984, 1993, 2013, 3060; See also Federal policy
Internal Revenue Service 1201
Iran 3378, 3484
Ireland 1143, 1354, 1425, 1508, 3225; See also Northern Ireland
Isherwood, Christopher 70, 72, 88-89, 105, 139, 781, 868, 2798,
     3092, 3186, 3496
Israel 1193, 1299, 3379, 3595
Italy 1426

Japan 2702, 3304
Jewett, Sarah Orne 2751
Johnson, Virginia see Masters, William
Judaism and homosexuality 623, 698, 746, 807, 927, 977, 1070,
     1246, 1582, 1639, 1734, 1787, 1905, 3081, 3093, 3416, 3577;
     See also Gay Jews and synagogues
Jury service and homosexuals 1250, 2539

Katz, Jonathan 2872
Kessler, David 1371
Keynes, John Maynard 3077
King, Billie Jean 93, 1118, 1312, 1318-19, 1439, 1444, 1463, 1489,
     1518, 2930, 3361; See also Sports
Knight, John 46

Koch, Edward   1231, 3243
Kopay, David   96, 2370; See also Sports
Korea   2894

Labor unions   957
LaBouchière Amendment   3112
Latent or repressed homosexuality   1020, 2135, 2208
Laughton, Charles   82
The Law and homosexuality   20, 44, 319, 329, 344, 409, 425, 439,
    473, 487, 512, 545, 581, 626, 700, 733, 761, 809, 836, 867,
    891, 962, 968, 997, 1001, 1038, 1052, 1132, 1157, 1194, 1215,
    1277, 1283-86, 1354, 1361, 1387, 1412, 1425, 1482, 1490, 1512,
    1579, 1591, 1839, 1856, 1872, 1875, 1909, 1917, 1937, 2539,
    2581-82, 2660, 2745, 2789, 2900, 2969, 2987, 3026, 3053,
    3062-64, 3112, 3160, 3400; See also Appendix IV, Court cases,
    Federal policy, Gay rights, Homosexual offenses, Immigration
    and naturalization, Law reform.
Law reform   1224 (failure in Washington, D. C.), 1277 (Texas), 1300
    (England), 1326 (Britain), 1541 (Scotland), 1556-57 (failure in
    Washington, D. C.), 1566 (Texas), 1833 (Pennsylvania), 1851
    (Maine), 1883 (New York), 1930 (California), 1955 (Pennsyl-
    vania), 1970 (Massachusetts), 2010 (New York), 2016 (Califor-
    nia), 2020 (Massachusetts), 2028 (Oregon), 2804, 3199 (Alaska),
    3272 (failure in Washington, D. C.), 3376 (Indiana), 3377 (Iowa),
    3379 (Israel), 3442 (Missouri), 3447 (Nebraska), 3448 (New
    Hampshire), 3450 (New York), 3582 (West Virginia), 3590 (Wy-
    oming)
Lawrence, D. H.   1011, 2998, 3077, 3464, 3526
Lawrence, T. E.   3355, 3499
Legal guides   192, 425, 439, 473
Legg, W. Dorr   3313
Leonardo da Vinci   3500
Lesbians and lesbianism
    Anthologies   2, 5, 8, 15
    Bibliographies   321, 443, 919, 985, 2919
    Black lesbians   321, 537, 726, 735-36, 747, 1003, 1041, 1446
    Book reviews   195, 2145
    "Coming out"   1443, 1643, 1842, 2747
    Comparison with heterosexual women   501, 508, 526, 554, 556,
        2217, 2978
    General works   208, 304, 309, 344, 366, 378, 389, 432, 460,
        682, 701-02, 754, 770, 806, 815, 828, 883, 965, 971, 981,
        992, 1301, 1402, 1457, 1523, 1565, 2215, 2455, 2501, 2640,
        2695, 2716, 2908, 2931-32, 3045, 3047, 3049, 3054, 3061, 3159
    Guides and resources   5, 33, 182, 219, 263, 268, 345, 365, 373,
        407, 1441.
    Jewish lesbians   2, 678, 688, 786, 877, 920, 1091
    Lesbian academics   742, 747, 790, 932, 1250, 2980
    Lesbian activists   846, 918
    Lesbian couples   280, 353, 632, 634, 750, 1060, 1369, 1694,
        2092, 2363, 2954, 3006
    Lesbian families   568, 2833

Lesbian-feminists and the Women's Movement   11, 497, 508, 516,
    541, 656, 661, 694, 718, 721, 736, 858, 890, 956, 1013, 1041,
    1087-88, 1099, 2051, 2138, 2768, 2782, 2881, 2957, 3196
Lesbian identity   288, 530, 579, 592, 607, 630, 645, 659; See also
    Homosexual identity
Lesbian mothers   75, 227, 489, 555, 571, 613, 627, 660, 837,
    910, 1091, 1223, 1369, 1446, 1570, 1579, 1842, 1876, 1880,
    1891, 1903, 1951, 1965, 1967, 1986, 1989, 1998-99, 2001,
    2009, 2021, 2121, 2272, 2294-95, 2338, 2361, 2438, 2827,
    2920, 2978, 3021, 3032, 3053, 3102, 3198; See also Child Cus-
    tody
Lesbian oppression   726
Lesbian publications   1019
Lesbian relationships   2901, 3039-40
Lesbian research   441, 1022, 2280
Lesbian separatism   710, 1042, 1047, 1329
Lesbian studies   9, 748, 778, 1040, 2960
Lesbian theater   3110
Lesbian and artificial insemination   1694, 2121, 2363, 2622
Lesbians and counseling and therapy   888, 995, 1454, 2645, 2954,
    3067, 3119, 3124
Lesbians and employment   684, 1298, 1328, 1908, 3445
Lesbians and films   1027
Lesbians and Gay Liberation   803; See also Gay liberation
Lesbians and gay men   830, 939, 3202, 3326, 3476
Lesbians and health care   229, 2237, 2319, 2334; See also Health
    care
Lesbians and history   773, 785, 2641, 2715, 2760, 2775, 2815,
    3197, 3229, 3267, 3404; See also History
Lesbians and the Law   192, 344, 1985, 2727, 2767, 3323; See also
    Child custody
Lesbians and the Media   1069
Lesbians and the Military   812, 1282, 1949; See also The Military
Lesbians and Politics   818, 897, 1051, 2136-37, 2886
Lesbians and Religion   669, 741, 937, 1236, 1429, 1493, 1719-21,
    1725, 1798, 3549; See also The Christian Church
Lesbians and Science   843
Lesbians and Sports   728, 1439, 1452, 3361; See also Billie Jean
    King, Sports
Lesbians and stress   174, 513, 2179
Lesbians in art and literature   223, 226, 532, 678, 705, 729, 824,
    826, 845, 932, 944, 2662, 2688, 2692, 2717, 2772-73, 3100,
    3196
Lesbians in prison   777, 2111, 3049-50, 3156
Married lesbians   277
Personal experiences of lesbians   8, 36, 43, 56-57, 74, 80, 305,
    351, 369, 763, 792, 801, 915, 1003, 1437, 1456, 1464, 2690,
    2730, 2752, 2862, 2979, 3530
Other specialized works   430, 509, 531, 580, 595, 603, 644, 1018,
    1061, 2037-38, 2060, 2160, 2183, 2239, 2334, 2472, 2527,
    2623, 2700, 2729, 2774, 2848, 2856
Lhasa   122
Liberace   1567

Mesa, Arizona   1283, 3228
Metropolitan Community Churches   448-49, 1004, 1227, 1629-30,
    1657, 1717, 1752, 1775, 3312
Mexico   635, 2094, 2696, 3406, 3440, 3561
Miami   405, 1097, 1116, 1222, 1345, 1466, 1578, 1617; See also
    Anita Bryant, Gay rights bills
The Middle Ages   170, 220, 706, 708, 1768, 2822-23, 3073, 3081
The Military--attitudes, policies, and practices   76, 452, 812, 893,
    1080, 1139, 1244, 1282, 1320, 1390, 1450, 1677, 1848, 1859,
    1862, 1874, 1924, 1949-50, 1983, 2002-03, 2008, 2018, 2807,
    2959, 2964, 3116, 3166, 3229, 3316, 3381. See also Federal
    policy, Security clearance and security risks
Milk, Harvey   132, 1000, 1183, 1259, 1310, 3207, 3538
Mineo, Sal   3373
Minneapolis and St. Paul, Minnesota   1223, 1273
Mishima, Yukio   3257
Misogyny   677
Mondale, Walter   1585
Monroe, Hector H.   101
The Moral Majority and the New and Far Right   246, 1012, 1097,
    1123, 1125, 1224, 1377, 1500, 1513, 1540, 1556-57, 1754,
    1784, 3265, 3272, 3461
The Mormons   470, 1121, 1225, 3444
Moscone, George   1259, 1310, 3207
Moscow   3300
Movie review   1536 (Personal Best)
Movies and homosexuality   10, 331, 765, 1066, 1187, 1324, 1359,
    1365, 1373, 1445, 1510, 1516, 1527-28, 1535, 1588, 1807,
    2714, 2776, 3190-91, 3270, 3283, 3342, 3410, 3497, 3569; See
    also Appendix I, Gay movies, Movie review
Murders   264, 928, 1115, 1164, 1239, 1259, 1310, 1571-73, 1777,
    2977, 3541; See also Violence
Music   671, 3231, 3338, 3365, 3395, 3543

Narcissism   2448, 3423
National Council of Churches   1227, 1630, 1657, 1759
National Gay Archives   3446
National Organization for Women   1487
The Navy   see   The Military
The Nazis   231, 315, 740, 1050, 1070, 1172, 2263, 2832, 2911,
    3218, 3413, 3470, 3482, 3508, 3593; See also Germany; Holo-
    caust
Near, Holly   1370, 3389
Necrophilia   2055
The Networks   2992
Neuroticism   594, 2623
New Guinea   881
New Hampshire   3259, 3448
New York City   582, 1150, 1163, 1185, 1230-32, 1278, 1423, 1493,
    1777, 1921, 2172, 2391, 2530, 3082, 3219, 3330, 3356, 3449,
    3492, 3570; See also Gay rights bills

Baars, Conrad W. 384
Babb, Richard R. 2049
Babcock, Barbara A. 853
Babuscio, Jack 158
Bach, Gerard 159
Bachman, Robert 2050
Bader, Louise 1833
Baetz, Ruth 43
Bahnsen, Greg L. 160
Bailey, Jeffrey 3221
Bailey, Paul J. 496
Baker, A. L. 2649
Baker, Andrea J. 497, 2051
Baker, Donald F. 2650
Baker, Joe 3222-23
Baker, Robert W. 2052
Balliet, Bev 385
Banes, Sally 2651
Barnard, Robert J. 498
Barnett, Walter 386
Barnhart, Debra M. 1834
Barnhouse, Ruth T. 161, 672,
    680, 949, 968, 978, 1044,
    1619
Barr, Ron 2053
Barrett, Connie 3225
Barrett, Ellen M. 673, 1620,
    1835
Barrett, W. Elcano 181
Barrios, Billy A. 2054
Barrow, Alfred A. 1640
Barth, Karl 674
Bartholomew, Allen A. 2055
Bartlett, David L. 1621
Bartley, W. W., III 2652
Barton, Bruce C. 2653
Barton, Richard W. 499
Bartos, Patricia E. 1817
Basch, Dennis B. 500
Baskett, Edward E. 44
Baskin, David 2550
Bass, Christopher M. 2056
Basse, Laura 45
Batchelor, Edward, Jr. 1
Bates, Frederick L. 3156
Bates, John E. 2884
Bath, Richard 2057-58
Batteau, John M. 1622
Bauer, Paul F. 1623
Baum, Gregory 675
Bauman, Batya 669
Bayer, Ronald 162, 2654
Beach, Berdena J. 501

Beach, Frank 831
Beame, Thom 3226
Beane, Jeffrey 2655
Bearchell, Chris 676
Beaton, Stephen 2656
Beaver, Harold 2657
Beck, Evelyn T. 2, 677-78
Bedient, Calvin 2658
Beebe, Leo P. 502
Beer, Chris 387
Beery, Dave 1226
Beery, Steve 3227
Beeson, Trevor 1624
Begelman, D. A. 2659
Beifuss, Joan T. 1625
Beks, Herman 1316
Belkin, Beth M. 503
Bell, Alan P. 163-65, 679-80
Bell, Arthur 46, 681, 1114-
    16, 1317
Bell, Joseph J. 2660
Bell, Robert R. 682
Bellezza, Francis S. 2059
Belote, Deborah 2060
Bender, V. Lee 2661
Benitez, John C. 504
Bennett, Bobbie 660
Bennett, Curtis 683
Bennett, John C. 1626
Bennett, Keith C. 2061
Bennett, Paula 684, 2662
Bentley, Eric 2663
Bepko, Claudia S. 2901
Berg, Vernon E., III 3316
Berger, Raymond M. 166,
    2664-67
Bergman, Jerry 1627
Berkson, Bill 167
Bernard, Jessie 2668
Bernard, Larry C. 505, 2062,
    2669
Bernstein, Barton E. 2670
Bernstein, Edward 388
Bernstein, Mal 3228
Berrigan, Daniel 1628
Berube, Allan 3229
Berzon, Betty 3, 685-86
Bessell, Peter 168
Beverley, Gay S. 506
Bieber, Irving 2063-66
Bieber, Toby 2066
Biemiller, Lawrence 2671
Bierer, Joshua 2067

To my brother Alfonso for his courage, and to my wife Lola for her patience

Contents

List of Figures

List of Tables

Preface

This book analyses whether debates about civil society participation in the years preceding the European Convention (1997–2003) contributed to shape the emerging participatory mechanisms of the EU (Article 11 Treaty on European Union). It examines the frames that civil society organisations used to articulate their demands during the agenda-setting process in order to understand how the institutional configuration of the EU influences its relationship with general publics. The central questions concern what organisations were trying to achieve in the agenda-setting process and how the resulting mechanisms contribute to democracy in the EU, and what the democratic potential of these mechanisms is.

This is done via an in-depth analysis of the organisations' discourses, as expressed in their position papers, understood here as ways of making sense of the social reality operating as frames which actors use to promote their interests and projects. A distinction is thus maintained between core aspects of the discourse or *masterframes* (Ruzza 2004, 150), and more variable frames and justifications. The book analyses three categories of frames that are present, albeit with different intensities, across the consultation period: the conception of civil society, the meaning of participatory democracy at the EU level, and the role of civil society organisations in the EU institutional architecture. The book also analyses the advocacy and intention of the organisations in the process. The data come from in-depth interviews carried out with representatives of the organisations as well as from documentary and questionnaire evidence about the participation of organisations in different debates and their contact with other organisations. Qualitative interviews aimed at understanding the rationale of the organisations' strategy asked the interviewees to articulate frankly what they tried to achieve and how they did it. All interview data have been triangulated with documentary evidence or other interviews to increase reliability. Coalitions have been studied via network analysis. The method entailed the formalisation of relations between organisations into a binary matrix comprising all the contacts between all of these groups. The focus has been placed on studying the centrality of each organisation in the network, composed of 22 organisations, to analyse whether recognisable patterns of interaction revealing common action between the groups were at play.

Analysis of the way in which the demands were framed shows that the arguments of these organisations evolved over time, from dialogue with organised civil society as a way to improve European governance to a more politicised discourse focusing on participatory democracy and citizens' direct involvement. This was due to the increasing concern that EU institutions had about the democratic deficit. The European Convention provided the opportunity to formulate existing practices of civil society consultation (Pérez Solórzano-Borragán, 2007) as a response to the problem of the democratic deficit. The agenda-setting process for civil society participation preceding the Convention saw the emergence of a coalition of NGOs which sought to institutionalise their role in the EU's policymaking. This demand built on the Commission's interest in using existing structured relations with organised civil society (Smismans, 2003) to obtain legitimacy (Kohler-Koch and Finke, 2007; Saurugger, 2010). It also unleashed opposition among already institutionalised organisations, in particular social partners.

In terms of collective action, organisations advocating the institutionalisation of civil society consultation as a form of participatory democracy created a coalition sharing a common frame argument and a common demand throughout the process. Civil society position papers and the Convention documents provide evidence that the discussions on participatory democracy in the Convention were strongly influenced by the previous exchanges between institutions and civil society. However, the debate on this topic contributed to stretching the discussion on participatory mechanisms; references to participatory democracy eased the success of advocates of alternative mechanisms, such as the European Citizens' Initiative (ECI). Organisations managed to include the issues in the Convention's agenda, despite the surprising lack of support from the Commission, thanks to the Convention's mechanisms for dialogue with civil society such as hearings and working groups. These formal fora were a way for civil society organisations to frame their unity and to show their involvement and expertise in a specialised European field. Participation in these fora was important for building coalitions and framing demands for access to the EU institutions as collective demands of European civil society. Network analysis confirms strong collective action among the organisations, using a common frame around civil dialogue and participatory democracy.

The book analyses the changes in the agenda in the aftermath of the Convention. Whereas organisations expected that recognition of the principle of consultation in the Treaty would grant them secure access to the EU institutions, unify consultation practices across different departments and institutions and avoid competition with outsiders, the aftermath of the Convention (marked by the failed referenda in France and the Netherlands) moved the agenda away from the focus on consultation of a narrow group of European stakeholders and favoured the increased use of open consultation. The characteristic of the aftermath of the Convention is that the politicisation of the agenda (including the need to face the rejection of the constitution and transparency "scandals") has favoured a neo-pluralist approach, which has to some extent marginalised the original movers.

The other relevant evolution in this period is the regulation of the ECI (2009–2011) and its entry into effective force in June 2012. Although initial initiatives have not, at the time of writing, yet been presented, available evidence shows that the organisations that advocated civil dialogue in order to obtain better access to EU institutions did not show great engagement with the ECI, neither during the Convention nor during the negotiation of the regulation. Nevertheless, the first ECI to collect in excess of a million signatures was the "Water and sanitation are a human right!" initiative, organised by some of the largest civil society networks in Brussels, including the EEB, ETUC and the Social Platform.[1] In any event, it can also be expected that the ECI will bring more diversity and possibly more contestation to the field of EU–civil society relations.

This book also evaluates the contribution of civil society to democracy in the EU via the notions of participation, representation and communication. Assessment clearly shows that these mechanisms are ambiguous from the participation perspective, as it is clear that they do not offer opportunities for direct participation. However, it can be assumed that organisations do represent their members and concerns without necessarily biasing the field in favour of membership organisations, if mechanisms to evaluate the social representativeness of organisations have been developed.

In sum, this book finds that participatory democracy is characterised by having a changing agenda which is nevertheless marked by strong regularities. The aims associated with this mechanism by institutions have moved strongly from fostering input legitimacy via a strong association in a neo-corporatist setting towards a system of open consultation focusing on transparency. Nevertheless, the organisations most actively involved in the discussion of these mechanisms have stayed relatively stable, as have their goals. In this sense, despite the relative neglect of the ECI by established organisations during 2009, they were the first to be able to gather one million signatures via the ECI. As the ECI is due to be reviewed by 2015 and action on Articles 11.2 and 11.3 has not yet been taken, further developments cannot be excluded. It can thus be anticipated that most of the collective action logics that were relevant in this field in 2003 will remain so in the coming years.

Note

1. http://www.right2water.eu/ (consulted on 24 March 2013).

Acknowledgements

This research project has meant that I have lived in Brussels, Madrid and Aberdeen, where I met dozens of people and have, almost invariably, found only friendly faces in the process.

I am indebted, first and foremost, to the interviewees, who patiently gave up their precious time to discuss a subject which had long been one of their main concerns. I hope that reviving the many good memories of the Convention paid off for them. Particular thanks go to the interviewees from the European Foundation Centre, Social Platform, ATTAC Spain and RCE, who gave me access to their archives. I have maintained their anonymity here.

Thanks are due to the Robert Gordon University, which provided a research scholarship.

I thank colleagues who encouraged me to start this project, particularly Carlos Closa and the late Robert Picht, with whom I shared my ideas about the role of civil society in the European public sphere. I'm very grateful to Geir Kvaerk for facilitating access to some of the documents missing from the Convention archive. Thanks to Susana del Río Villar for sending me relevant chapters of her thesis and introducing me to some of my interviewees. I'm indebted to many colleagues that I have had the chance of meeting at different conferences and events and with whom I have discussed ideas. I would like to thank Peter McLaverty, Carlo Ruzza, Pauline Cullen, Emmanuella Lombardo, Rosa Sánchez-Salgado, Nieves Pérez-Solórzano Borragán and Rafael Vázquez García for their comments and advice on different aspects of this book. I would also like to thank the anonymous reviewers whose critical comments contributed to improve the final version of this book. My most sincere gratitude goes to Justin Greenwood, without whose expertise and encouragement I don't think I would have embarked on this journey. It goes without saying that all opinions and any mistakes are exclusively my own.

Finally, I am indebted to my family and friends. Civil society has become a "trending topic" at some friendly gatherings with Pedro, Julio, Trini, Senel and Nacho. Special thanks go to my parents, Luis and Mercedes, and my brother, Alfonso, for understanding my spending so much valuable time far away from home at difficult times. And, of course, to Lola, who's been with me throughout this entire process and I hope will be so for a long time to come.

xv

List of Abbreviations

ACN	Active Citizenship Network
ATTAC	Association for the Taxation of Financial Transactions and Aid to Citizens
CEDAG	Comité européen des associations d'intérêt général (European Council for Non-profit Organisations)
CEV	Centre Européen du Volontariat (The European Volunteer Centre)
CEMR	Council of European Municipalities and Regions
COFACE	Confederation of Family Organisations in the European Union
CONCORD	Confederation for Cooperation, Relief and Development
CPMR	Conference of Peripheral and Maritime Regions
CSCG	Civil Society Contact Group
ECAS	European Citizens Action Service
ECI	European Citizens' Initiative
EEB	European Environment Bureau
EESC	European Economic and Social Committee
EFC	European Foundation Centre
ELO	European Landowners' Organisation
ETUC	European Trade Union Confederation
EU	European Union
IGC	Intergovernmental Conference
IRI	Initiative and Referendum Institute (Europe)
PFCS	Permanent Forum of Civil Society
TCE	Treaty Establishing a European Constitution*
UEAPME	European Association of Craft, Small and Medium-Sized Enterprises
UNICE	Union of Industrial and Employers' Confederations of Europe

Note

* In this book Treaty and Constitution are used interchangeably to refer to the TCE, except where it is explicitly mentioned.

1

The Contribution of Civil Society to Bridging the Gap with EU Citizens: Reviewing a Decade of Debate

Civil society and the legitimacy of the EU

The Europa web portal – the European Union's official gateway on the Internet – contains a series of arguments aimed at convincing Europeans of the merits of the Lisbon Treaty. An entire section is entitled "A more democratic and transparent Europe", and one of the central arguments is that the Treaty brings more participatory democracy via new mechanisms of interaction.[1] However, when one searches for the words "participatory democracy" in the Lisbon Treaty they are nowhere to be found. This anecdote tells us much about the EU's agenda in this field. It conveys the way in which the EU has tried to regain legitimacy by complementing representative democracy with participatory tools. It also demonstrates the importance that political actors attach to the way in which they frame their discourses. Finally, the anecdote indicates changes in the agenda during the last years, when notions have appeared and disappeared at different times.

Questions about the democratic legitimacy of the EU have arisen since the troublesome ratification of the Maastricht Treaty in 1992. EU institutions have reacted to this by formulating the idea that the shortcomings of representative democracy at the supranational level could be tackled by creating stronger opportunities for citizens' participation. Participation can take place in different venues and forms: from involvement in an emerging "European public sphere", and the Europeanisation of civil society organisations involving citizens, to a stronger association of citizens and their organisations in the policymaking of the EU.

All these discourses have a distinct potential for legitimacy and their appropriateness has been thoroughly discussed. The evolution of this debate is related to that of the political scenario at EU level. Until the debate on the future of the EU (2000–2003) that – resulted in the Convention it was considered by some that the EU could not be legitimated by political will formation and political participation because several of the prerequisites for democracy are still lacking at EU level. As a consequence the EU should focus on producing successful policies that make it legitimate, thanks to the public goods which it produces (Scharpf 1999; Majone 2002; Moravcsik 2006). However, in the wake of the debate on the constitutionalisation of the EU (Habermas 2001; Weiler 2003) other authors argued the contrary: that the EU should be understood as a regular political system suffering from a democratic deficit problem which is related to its institutional design (Follesdal and Hix 2006). This approach assumes that input legitimacy problems are not irredeemable but are linked to the institutional set-up of the EU.

However, the rejection of the constitutional Treaty seems to have moved the debate beyond the issue of the EU's democratic deficit to point out its legitimacy crisis, which encompasses the existence of an institutional democratic deficit and a structural lack of communication, trust and accountability (Kohler-Koch and Rittberger 2007; Bertoncini and Chopin 2010; Chopin 2010;). Recently, it has been pointed out that the EU is becoming increasingly politicised and contested (Hooghe and Marks 2009; Papadopoulos and Magnette 2010; De Wilde 2011), breaking the permissive consensus of public opinions on which European integration has rested since its inception (Lindberg and Scheingold 1970). In this sense it is less a matter of objective institutional design but of a subjective perception akin to Max Weber's conception of legitimacy (de Castro Asarta 2011).

Additionally the consensus-prone nature of the EU integration process (Lijphart 1999, 7) has blurred traditional political frames (Eriksen 2000, 58–61). At EU level it is difficult to perceive and communicate a clear political framework beyond the traditional tension between member states' preferences for more or less European integration. In this sense it is not surprising that contestation and EU politicisation have been mainly left to European federalists or emerged from generally Eurosceptic national political parties and grassroots movements (Hooghe and Marks 2009).

The paradox of the debate on the democratic deficit is well summarised by the fact that every increase in the powers of the European Parliament has been matched by a decrease in participation in European Parliament elections (Costa 2009). The paradox of the EU's institutional discourse is that it has assumed the existence of a democratic legitimacy problem

(European Commission 2001) but has tried to solve it through reforms focusing on the institutional system. For instance, the Laeken declaration's mandate, which launched the European Convention, focused exclusively on the reform of EU institutions. The Constitution made the EU more democratic in several senses as it extended the powers of the European Parliament, reinforced national parliaments and recognised participatory democracy in the EU. However, this Treaty was rejected in referenda in two founding member states, the Netherlands and France. Voters may not have analysed the proposed text, but there is clear evidence that voters made up their minds according to their appraisal of European integration (Glencross and Tresschel 2011). This apparent contradiction illustrates well the insufficiency of institutional reforms to take account of a disconnected and increasingly politicised debate about the EU (Hooghe and Marks 2009; Papadopoulos and Magnette 2010; De Wilde 2011).

The EU has turned in the last decade towards civil society, with the expectation that civil society organisations can serve as the interface for and promoter of a larger public debate on EU issues. The notions of public sphere, deliberation and civil society are attractive to EU scholars and institutions because they are not necessarily but are historically linked to the nation state (Cohen and Arato 1992, 201), and can be the founding steps of a political community that is not bound to the state but is constructed by mutual recognition in a transnational public sphere (Kaldor 1995; Habermas 2000).The idea that consulting civil society contributes to the legitimacy of the EU has been built incrementally (Armstrong 2002; Sloat 2003; del Río Villar 2004; Greenwood 2007a; Kohler-Koch and Finke 2007; Pérez Solórzano-Borragán 2007; Saurugger 2010). This idea resonates with the requirement of Habermasian discourse ethics that "all the affected have an effective equality of chances to assume dialogue roles" (Cohen and Arato 1992, 348). This respects the EU's diversity of cultural and political traditions without trying to build a unified demos (Nicolaïdis 2003; Weiler 2003); rather, it promotes equal access to actors who have interests at stake. The EU has developed relations with organised civil society as a proxy, fulfilling some of the functions of the public in a democracy (Greenwood 2011b, 201–202). The EU has opted for a neo-pluralist system, if necessary by engineering the organisation of some interests (Sánchez-Salgado 2007), where groups check and balance each other thus avoiding routine domination by any of them (Greenwood 2011b).

Civil society is a multifaceted concept, as different ways of thinking emphasise different dimensions. Kohler-Koch and Quittkat (2011) analyse four distinct conceptions of civil society: the representation of different voices and interests in society; the autonomous participation of organisations in the public sphere; the emergence of organisations that mediate between other spheres of society (market and state); and organisations orientated towards the public good. This book follows a decision by these authors in a recent book (Kohler-Koch and Quittkat 2013) to use the notion of organised civil society. Organised civil society is conceived here as voluntary organisations, distinct from those active in the state and the market which aim at influencing these spheres via their activism in the European segmented public sphere. The normative assumption here is that the political process in a democracy is fundamentally open, and that all interests affected by the policy process thus have to be accounted for and have an equal chance of having their concerns considered. It is also argued that this approach is better suited to analyse the reality of the EU political system and the way in which interests are organised. First of all it accounts for the above-mentioned multiplicity of access points and fundamental plurality of interests in the EU. It also acknowledges the difficulty of drawing a clear line between organisations advocating sectoral and general interests, and better suits the way in which the EU has defined civil society. It thus has a better analytical correspondence with the object that will be analysed (Kohler-Koch and Quittkat 2013, 8–9).

Advocates of participatory democracy highlight that stronger participation has effects not only at the level of the political system but can also have positive consequences for society in the broader sense (Monaghan 2012). Authors writing from a republican perspective consider participation as a way to re-establish a dialogue between the citizen and the community (Barber 2003). Others highlight the positive effects of participation in civil society for a democratic political culture, because of its education and socialisation functions (Pateman 1970; Van Ingen and Van der Meer 2009). Stronger participation is also deemed to facilitate the inclusion of socially excluded communities and to foster the accountability of elected officials (Parés and Resende 2009; Smith 2009). In a similar vein, the EU has raised expectations that European civil society can contribute to deliberation and empowerment of citizens (Armstrong 2002; Ruzza 2004, 177; Giorgi et al. 2006; Magnette 2006). Academic literature has generally seen the institutionalisation of civil society relations as a contribution to the legitimacy of the EU (De Schutter 2002; Joerges 2002; Fazi and Smith 2006; Eder and Trenz 2007; Greenwood 2011a). The expectation that civil society organisations can be the link between international and European governance arenas and ordinary citizens (Steffek and Nanz 2008; Steffek and Hahn 2010) relies on the expectation that the participation of civil society in policymaking arenas contributes to the emergence of an "artificial public sphere" (McLaverty 2002) that will be enlarged by the very presence of public discussion and deliberation (Eder and Trenz 2007).

However, it has to be asked through which mechanisms civil society makes citizens interested in the EU. Expectations that the participation of civil society can make the EU more legitimate have been matched by negative empirical evaluations. Mechanisms that create civil society involvement in EU policymaking have been associated with incentives to civil society organisations to concentrate on lobbying EU institutions rather than in building a grassroots European civil society or public opinion (Warleigh 2001). In a nutshell, it has been suggested that the political opportunity structure at EU level provides organisations with an incentive to lobby institutions rather than to mobilise their members in order to influence EU decisionmaking (Warleigh 2001; Sudbery 2003; Mahoney 2007; Kohler-Koch 2010b). Secondly, the EU's civil society consultation model presents some weaknesses, as it overemphasises the production of outputs (Armstrong 2002; Curtin 2003) and the representativeness of organisations rather than activism in the public sphere (Greenwood and Halpin 2007; Kohler-Koch 2010). Finally, the professionalisation of these organisations (Halpin and McLaverty 2010, 59; Buth 2011) does not make them real promoters of a wider public sphere (Sudbery 2003; Maloney and Van Deth 2008). Furthermore, civil society has been mainly involved in institutional attempts to build a European sphere of communication via bureaucratic procedures (Bee 2010). Although these procedures may create opportunities for civil society to contribute to deliberation (Joerges 2002; Boucher 2007; Lindgren and Persson 2011), such deliberation may be too technical to facilitate citizens' participation.

Civil society and the European public sphere

A rich literature has already analysed the role of civil society in the development of the European public sphere and its limits (François and Neveu 1999; Kaelble 2002; Chalmers 2003; Trenz and Eder 2004; Giorgi, Von Homeyer and Parsons 2006; Fossum and Schlesinger 2007; Bee and Bozzini 2010). Some historians and sociologists have considered that the notion of the public sphere could be applied at EU level without substantially modifying the focus on the long-term emergence of a common European public, as historically publics have emerged in new spheres of economic exchange and political power (Kaelble 2002;

Delanty and Rumford 2005). However, Schlesinger and Deirdre (2000, 220–221) have suggested that a quest for a common European public is conducive to determinism about the inexistence of a European public sphere, as long as the media and the general public do not pay attention to the EU (see Ward 2002; Delanty and Rumford 2005; de Swaan 2007 for examples of such determinism). Furthermore, such a quest may neglect the study of emergent processes and marginalise the role of actors other than the media and the general public (Trenz 2010, 29; van de Steeg 2010, 35–36).

It is authors working on deliberation and deliberative democracy who have paid more attention to the role of civil society organisations in specialised consultative fora, by pointing out that by engaging in very intense information exchanges on specialised issues civil society organisations reach common answers with other groups (Joerges 2002; Chalmers 2003). Through these processes organisations start to perceive each other as co-participants in a common project. In this sense civil society organisations' participation in policymaking contributes to the emergence of a European public, by reducing the distance between and enhancing cooperation and mutual learning among civil society organisations.

Other authors, in particular in the light of the Convention, have pointed out the importance of participation in policy exchanges as a form of self-determination, in the sense that they contribute to the shaping of the EU by participating in deliberative venues (Eriksen and Fossum 2000; Chalmers 2003; Magnette 2004; Fossum and Schlesinger 2007). Some authors have argued that such participation may contribute to the emergence of a European civic identity by focusing on issues of democracy in the EU (Warleigh 2003). Counter-intuitively, by pointing out the insufficient democratic credentials of the EU, civil society organisations contribute to the democratisation of EU integration by putting the issue on the public agenda (Trenz and Eder 2004; Eder and Trenz 2007, 178–179). Eder and Trenz consider that debates about the legitimacy of the EU in specialised fora, such as the consultations about the White Paper on Governance and the Convention, may become self-sustaining and contribute to the democratisation of the EU by spilling over into general debates. Here the term participation is stretched and applied more generally to consider how the presence of civil society in debates may extend to a wider public.

However, different criticisms can be made of this literature. The first is that it seems to identify interest in the EU with consensus about it, which cannot accommodate the turn towards politicisation of the EU

(Hooghe and Marks 2009; Papadopoulos and Magnette 2010; De Wilde 2011). Secondly, it can be argued that more often than not debates in these spaces are about highly technical regulatory legislation, which is unlikely to spark the interest of the "ordinary citizen". Finally, the most significant criticism is that this literature focuses on deliberation by elite actors without sufficiently focusing on how this deliberation spills over to the general public (Trenz and Eder 2004; Giorgi et al. 2006).

Other authors have thus focused on the ways in which organisations communicate about the EU. One way in which organisations foster public debates is via "outside lobbying", The argument is that organisations which use the mobilisation of their members and supporters as a way of pursuing influence may contribute to the circulation of information about the EU. However empirical analysis finds that this is relatively rare among EU organisations (Monaghan 2007; Mahoney 2008a). However, the European Citizens' Initiative (ECI), included within the participatory democracy article by the Convention, may revitalise this approach. That said, this mechanism will require an ability to mobilise members that more established organisations seem unlikely to possess. It may thus be more attractive for outsider and more Eurosceptic organisations, making them more prone to participate in EU politics (Bouza Garcia and Greenwood 2014). There are thus considerable differences between the emergent European public sphere and the notion of a unified public sphere (Schlesinger and Deirdre 2000). Most authors foresee the constitution of different publics alongside the institutions and policies of the EU rather than the emergence of a general European public (Schlesinger and Deirdre 2000; Giorgi, Von Homeyer and Parsons 2006; Eriksen 2007; Bozzini 2010). Cohen and Arato's proposal of a theory of democratic legitimacy rooted in Habermas' discourse ethics, requiring that "all the affected have an effective equality of chances to assume dialogue roles" (Cohen and Arato 1992, 348), seems thus particularly well suited to the EU's diversity of cultural and political traditions (Nicolaïdis 2003) and its long-lasting tradition of stakeholder consultation (Kohler-Koch and Finke 2007).

Eriksen has suggested conceiving of the emergent European public sphere as a set of divided sociopolitical spaces in which the predominant actors differ (Eriksen 2007). He sees civil society organisations and expert fora (Zito 2001) as a segmented public intermediating between general publics, composed by individuals and media at the national level, and the official debates within the institutions, which are conceived as a strong public (Eriksen 2007). Ruzza (2004, 26–28) also points out the importance of designing a research strategy that takes into account the interrelated levels of governance. It is thus necessary to analyse the logic of each of these spaces, and it is particularly important to consider their interrelation and communication flows. Recently some authors have applied similar approaches in trying to analyse and map the entrepreneurship of different actors in the Europeanisation of public spheres (Trenz 2010). Generally speaking, contributions in Giorgi et al. (2006), Fossum and Schlesinger (2007), Kohler-Koch and Rittberger (2007) and Bee and Bozzini (2010) tend to see a much stronger activism among civil society organisations than in the media when it comes to linking different public spaces in the EU.

The question is whether the institutionalisation of dialogue with civil society and a relatively modest tool such as the ECI may contribute to reversing the critical remarks about the role of civil society in the public sphere. The expectation is that the institutionalisation of these new mechanisms may have a relevant effect on the actors' strategies because of a convergence of expectations and norms and competition between different actors and forms of collective action. To start with the expectations and the norms, the enforcement of the Lisbon Treaty is a further step in the decade-long process that aims to turn ad hoc mechanisms for interaction with interest groups into democratic innovations that aim to legitimise the EU. Participation is increasingly becoming a norm that EU institutions and civil society have to comply with. In this sense the mutual pressure from each actor increases, with the Commission being asked to pay more attention to the track record of participatory mechanisms and civil society organisations being watched more closely in terms of their participation. An additional mechanism at play might be the diversification of European actors and increasing competition among different types of actors and collective action strategies. The new mechanisms, and in particular the ECI, may make other actors' collective action strategies more appreciated at EU level, and thus attract them to participate in EU politics. These actors may additionally be more able to engage citizens directly at national level.

Participation and representation

The participation of organisations in policy consultations can be expected to contribute to involvement of their members and the public associated with these organisations in the process of consultation, either directly or indirectly, via internal discussions, although contributions in Steffek and Hahn (2010) suggest that there is no consensus about the effects of these internal democracy mechanisms. Furthermore other authors argue that this view is linked to outdated conceptions about internal participation in organisations, and argue that the democratic effects of civil society participation relate to their function in the public sphere (Buth 2011).

The EU's discursive turn towards civil society and participation has limited the recognition of these tools as a complement to representative democracy (Smismans 2003, 487). Dialogue with organised civil society can be linked to the development of a model of participatory democracy because it provides citizens with opportunities to contribute, thus strengthening input legitimacy in the EU (Zimmer and Freise 2008, 32–33). However, identifying the institutionalisation of civil society consultation with participatory democracy has a risk that could be called participatory autopoiesis. This happens when the mere inclusion of an existing practice in the Treaty is expected to transform a governance tool whose original aim was to improve the quality of legislation (Perez-Solorzano 2007; Friedrich 2011) into a participatory mechanism that brings the EU closer to the citizens. Civil dialogue following the 2002 standards for consultation is a relevant instrument for building relations and trust between EU officials and civil society organisations, conveying expertise and providing transparent access to the institutions at a relevant point in the policymaking process. However, it does not seem to entail wider participation by grassroots citizens. Empirical assessment of internal participation in civil society in relation to the EU does not provide evidence of positive effects. Some authors suggest that organisations do not need to or cannot involve their members and the public when taking opportunities for participation:

> organised civil society, contributes little to the formation of a grass roots based European civil society; it is instrumental to "better legislation" and in order to be efficient and effective it is becoming part of the EU elite system. (Kohler-Koch 2010b, 13)

It could be expected that the increasing usage of digital fora as a complement to stakeholders' consultation (Michailidou 2010; Bozzini 2011; Quittkat 2011) could compensate for organisations' tendency to neglect their own members. That said, it seems that these instruments suffer from the same problems as "conventional" civil dialogue. Kohler-Koch reports that practices are very variable from one Directorate-General (DG) to another, in particular with regard to inclusion of the general public:

> The market-related DGs have been hesitant to use the instrument of online-consultations and when they use it the consultation is mostly

addressed to "stakeholders" and not to the "general public". General Directorates with a broader reach such as employment and social affairs or in charge of a newly established EU policy field such as culture or public health are eager to engage the wider public in their consultations and, accordingly, use online-consultations and open hearings and conferences extensively. (Kohler-Koch 2010b, 9)

Michailidou (2010) finds that online consultation has been designed as an information and communication tool rather than a participatory one, since it remains weakly interactive and provides unclear evidence of empowerment.

It can be discussed to what extent organisations' representativeness criteria can be applied to participatory mechanisms. It has been suggested that when they contribute to consultation processes organisations are claiming a voice but not a vote (Fazi and Smith 2006, 20), and that they are thus simply expressing their freedom of expression. It therefore seems that when consultation processes are open there is no need to establish representativeness thresholds for organisations to participate. Although the Commission has never created formal accreditation systems as they exist in the UN or the Council of Europe (Fazi and Smith 2006, 25–26), it created a de facto system between 2002 and 2006 that relied on "a formalised set of procedures for exchanges with outside interests designed to address asymmetries of power" (Greenwood and Halpin 2007, 206). However, the European Transparency Initiative of 2006 saw a move away from this strategy in favour of a more open approach (de Castro Asarta 2011; Greenwood 2011a), in which the Transparency Register replaced the CONECCS database and moved away from representativeness criteria. Nevertheless this move fails to address some pending questions regarding representativeness. The first is whether EU institutions should pay more attention to opinions from representative organisations. The second is whether these criteria should be used when carrying out focused consultation if a selection of organisations has to take place beforehand. Available assessment of online consultations shows that even those open mechanisms created de facto access barriers (Quitkatt and Kotzian 2011). As will be discussed in the following chapters, representativeness has been an important issue of contention between social partners and citizen interest groups.[2] Business groups and trade unions, which have traditional internal consultation structures, have raised the stakes very high, in particular via the European Economic and Social Committee (Smismans 2003), up to the point of suggesting representativeness criteria based on their own internal structures (Michel 2007).

See for instance the stringent criteria suggested by UNICE, the main business organisation at EU level (UNICE 2002, 2).[3]

It thus seems that asking whom organisations represent has a valuable potential from a democratic perspective, even though representativeness criteria have traditionally been biased in favour of membership against cause groups (Greenwood and Halpin 2007; Halpin and McLaverty 2010). The question is thus whether organisations involved in consultation procedures are fostering participation of their members (via internal discussion) or whether they are rather representing their members, causes and even citizens in the broadest sense (Kohler-Koch 2010a; Ruzza 2011, 462–465; Pérez-Solórzano Borragán and Smismans 2012). The above-mentioned structure of political opportunities also affects the ability of civil society organisations to represent their members and constituencies. The EU has strongly encouraged the creation of large European umbrella organisations leading citizens' interests in their sectors, which can easily claim geographical representativeness (Greenwood and Halpin 2007, 201). Nevertheless most European organisations find it difficult to obtain a formal authorisation from their members (Fazi and Smith 2006; Monaghan 2007, 190–192; Ruzza 2011, 464), which makes it difficult to assume the role of trustees or delegates for a given constituency (Pitkin 1972, 38–59).

As a consequence it has been suggested that civil society organisations can play a different representative function, not acting as formally elected representatives nor as delegates, but rather standing for a cause or interest via activism in the public sphere (Greenwood and Halpin 2007; Kohler-Koch 2010a; Halpin and McLaverty 2010; Buth 2011). They provide symbolic representation and promote a cause without necessarily holding a mandate from members (Pitkin 1972, 92–143). Castiglione and Warren (2006) have argued that in transnational contexts civil society actors frequently promote causes without a formal authorisation from members. Several European organisations have adopted the attitude that their representativeness is related more closely to their expertise in a certain domain than to their relationship with a constituency. In some cases European organisations have formulated conceptions of their activity as representatives acting for a cause or an interest but without the need to consult it:

> The high level of expertise and experience of EU policy processes held by key officers in Brussels means that they are accorded a large degree of independence and are "more or less left to get on with the job". "EU work", stated one interviewee "is largely seen as work for

specialists". Actively seeking to involve supporters in the formulation of policy was generally viewed by interviewees as time-consuming and rather unrealistic, given the degree of knowledge necessary to make an effective contribution. (Sudbery 2003, 90)

In this light, Buth (2011) sees organisations' professionalisation as a factor enhancing their ability to represent causes which, like the environment, cannot cast a mandate but have to be championed. Ruzza points out that deliberation has been suggested as an alternative to consultation with members (Ruzza 2011, 464).

This formulation of the debate suggests that tension in the field is caused by a clash between formal authorisation and social representativeness in the public sphere paradigms. However, both dimensions have to be judged against empirical assessments of the role of civil society organisations in the European institutional system and in the public sphere. In reality representation practices vary between different sectors, as Ruzza notes that environmentalists are more prone to claim an authorisation from members, whereas pro-minority groups tend to put forward descriptive representativeness (Ruzza 2011, 462–463).

The main criticism of the notion that organisations' activism in the representation of causes should be considered instead of formal representativeness is that there is little evidence of their involvement in the promotion of a European public sphere. It can be suggested that the difficulties of European civil society in formally representing its members only reflects a broader difficulty in communicating. In this sense the notion that organisations represent causes in the public sphere has been criticised as failing to satisfactorily associate citizens with policymaking (Monaghan 2007, 181). It can be asked to what extent conceiving organisations as advocates independently promoting a cause or interest (Buth 2011) contributes to making the public aware of their activity. Although civil society organisations raise issues around specialised and strong publics, this does not mean that their activism is reflected among the general public, because the link between these public spaces is missing at EU level (Eriksen 2007). Furthermore, in terms of policy practice, the EU has not developed any mechanism to assess this criterion.

In this sense traditional representativeness criteria have been abandoned without being replaced by an alternative assessment of the democratic credentials of consulted organisations (Friedrich 2011). This can create a bias in the interests which are effectively represented in the policymaking process. Although it can be expected that in a neo-pluralist setting such as the EU all the constituencies having a stake in process will be mobilised, resulting in a fair representation (Greenwood 2007b), it can as well be highlighted that different constituencies have been mobilised very differently at EU level as a result of different collective action problems and access barriers (Balme and Chabanet 2008). Furthermore, recent assessment of the organisations represented in new online open consultations reveal that they are biased in favour of business interests and interests from Northern Europe (Bozzini 2011; Quittkat 2011).

The turn towards institutionalised participation

Whereas the idea that the Commission turned towards civil society as a way of improving its democratic credentials is now quite consensual in the literature, it does not explain why it has implied the institutionalisation of these mechanisms or why the stakeholders were interested in this agenda or how it has evolved. This book begins by pointing out that the origins of these ideas and the agency behind them has been somehow neglected or not entirely represented. Civil society has been widely credited with influencing the article on participatory democracy during the Convention (del Rio Villar 2004; Lamassoure 2004; Will 2005; Perez-Solorzano 2007), although to date there is no comprehensive account of the way in which this demand was introduced first on the agenda and second in the Treaty. On the other hand, one of the most detailed analyses of the discussions about the institutionalisation of participation in the last decade (Saurugger 2010) neglects the role of civil society organisations in the agenda-setting process. This book examines the evolution of the mechanisms of civil society participation in the EU in the last decade. It asks in particular which stakes influenced the institutionalisation of the role of civil society by analysing the evolution of the agenda on this topic and the aims that the actors involved in the process were trying to achieve.

The history of the institutionalisation of civil dialogue can be summarised as an evolution from ad hoc relationships between the EU institutions and interest groups towards relations structured by norms (Smismans 2003).The Lisbon Treaty has introduced in the EU's primary legislation an article that was drafted by the European Convention under the heading of participatory democracy. However, this article was drafted earlier by the European Convention (2002–2003). This "deliberative assembly" (Magnette 2004) was convened in 2001 by the European Council in the Laeken declaration, in order to change the institutional setting for the reform of the Treaties. The enlargements and deepenings from Maastricht in 1992 resulted in a piecemeal reform of the Treaties, threatening deadlock and a lack of strategic reflection. The Convention's mandate was to reflect over 18 months on all substantial matters, with the idea that a transparent venue could facilitate consensus and compromises that are rendered impossible behind the closed doors of intergovernmental conferences. The Convention also implied a significant change of personnel, since it was not only composed of representatives of national governments and the Commission but also by members of national parliaments and the European Parliament, meaning an increased diversity in issues and positions. This change in venue was made even more significant because of the openness of the Convention to outside contributions by citizens, experts and organised civil society via different forms of dialogue and websites. It is relevant to analyse whether these changes had an effect on the opportunity for civil society organisations to include a treaty article on civil dialogue and participatory democracy.

Today's Article 11 TEU reads as follows:

1. The institutions shall, by appropriate means, give citizens and representative associations the opportunity to make known and publicly exchange their views in all areas of Union action.
2. The institutions shall maintain an open, transparent and regular dialogue with representative associations and civil society.
3. The European Commission shall carry out broad consultations with parties concerned in order to ensure that the Union's actions are coherent and transparent.
4. Not less than one million citizens who are nationals of a significant number of Member States may take the initiative of inviting the European Commission, within the framework of its powers, to submit any appropriate proposal on matters where citizens consider that a legal act of the Union is required for the purpose of implementing the Treaties.

By commanding institutions to maintain an open dialogue with civil society and the Commission to consult stakeholders, this article acknowledges EU institutions' active establishment of structured relations with interest groups and in defining these groups as organised civil society (Smismans 2003). However, it is also an acknowledgement of these organisations' attempts to secure a role in the EU's policymaking process.

The most characteristic aspect of the EU's system of interest intermediation is its strong institutionalisation, including Commission funding for EU level umbrella organisations (Sánchez Salgado 2007), the creation of a system of consultation and registration of interest groups (Friedrich 2011; Greenwood 2011a). The evolution towards institutionalisation has been clear since the early 1990s. In 1992 the Commission launched a communication on the relation with special interest groups, followed by a protocol in the Amsterdam Treaty (Protocol 11) and a Commission communication on how to promote the role of associations and foundations in the EU (European Commission 1997). The 1997 communication was also preceded and followed by intense consultation with experts, national and regional institutions and civil society organisations. The institutionalisation of a system of structured relations has consisted in a mutually advantageous exchange of funding and access opportunities for interest groups (Sánchez-Salgado 2007a; Mahoney and Beckstrand 2011) against a supply of expertise and support for further integration in their policy field (Greenwood 2011b, 327).

However, the Commission has not only developed this system as a result of internal demands and strategies, but also in response to a number of external pressures. The first of these pressures explored in this book has been the demand coming from organisations in the field acting as cause entrepreneurs. The 1998 "red card" campaign – when social and citizens' interests organisations showed red cards to the president of the Commission at a public hearing to demonstrate against legal and financial challenges against mechanisms of financial support for EU civil society platforms (Alhadeff and Wilson 2002; Ruzza 2004, 47) – is telling about the early focus of the agenda, which was on definitional issues about what is European civil society and what its legal status and funding should be (Will and Kendall 2009, 309–311). The visible conflict between civil society organisations and the Commission services during the "red card" mobilisation makes it tempting to present the history of civil dialogue as civil society's conquest of the Commission (Alhadeff and Wilson 2002). However, the process is characterised by a convergence of agendas, where organisations' advocacy for securing a role in the policymaking process meets the Commission's strategy. For instance, organisations criticise the "low profile" of the Commission's discussion paper in 2000 (Alhadeff and Wilson 2002), but they then use this document recognition of one of their main demands – the adoption of a legal basis for dialogue between civil society and the Commission – as a precedent granting them access. It also reflects some of the main positions of civil society organisations, such as their role in representing categories of people and causes, and as promoters of participatory democracy in Europe; as well as the need to create clear and transparent rules on consultation.

The second external pressure that this book considers is related to concerns about the EU's democratic credentials. The structuring of EU relations with interest groups in the 1990s is related to the concerns about lack of transparency following the Danish referendum rejection of the Maastricht Treaty and the corruption accusations and subsequent resignation of the Santer Commission. These rules were aimed at improving the EU's input legitimacy by giving stakeholders and concerned organisations a bigger role in the policymaking process and structuring relations with civil society with norms about fairness and transparency as part of the consultation. The aim was to improve the opportunity for all relevant actors to have their say in order to achieve a balanced and broad policy debate: "In this context, civil society organisations play an important role as facilitators of a broad policy dialogue" (European Commission 2001, 5). EU institutions also expect participatory mechanisms to contribute to output legitimacy (Scharpf 1999), and thus these rules are elaborated at the same time as the "better regulation package" (European Commission 2002b), which considers that stakeholders' contribution to the policymaking process is their input in terms of expertise, which contributes to improving the quality of the policies rather than their ability to mobilise a constituency. Finally, EU institutions have also considered dialogue with civil society as a way of enlarging the European public sphere and engaging in an interactive dialogue on EU policies with citizens (European Parliament 2008). The literature has emphasised the discursive and strategic nature of this turn (Smismans 2003; Greenwood 2007a; Michel 2007; Kohler-Koch and Quittkat 2011) and its thin normative dimension, up to the point that the Commission has never defined its understanding of civil society. Nevertheless the 2000 and 2001 papers consolidated a clear agenda for civil society consultation from the EU institutions, contributing to the "participatory turn" that has characterised the last decade.

The agenda for consultation of organised civil society was broadened in the late 1990s from definitional issues to include notions aiming at improving legitimacy. The concept of civil dialogue appears for the first time in the institutional agenda in the follow-up documents to the 1997 communication (European Parliament 1998, 9).The increased political salience of this agenda within the Commission after the Cresson scandal is marked by the move of the responsibility for the agenda on civil society from the Social Economy Unit in DG Enterprise to the Secretariat General of the Commission in 1999 (Armstrong 2002),[4] which resulted in a new emphasis on dialogue with civil society as a way of building the legitimacy of the EU, further resulting in the communication on

"Building a stronger partnership", in which the notion of participatory democracy was used for the first time (European Commission 2000, 4).

The decisive moment in the attribution of input legitimacy purposes to this process was the fall of the Santer Commission at the turn of the century (Michel 2007). The 2000 position paper by the Commission is a key moment for its leadership regarding civil society participation, as this document formulates the notion of participatory democracy for the first time and urges the institutionalisation of consultation via a Treaty article. This event was followed by a process of administrative reform within the Commission, culminating in the White Paper on Governance (European Commission 2001) where interest groups are defined as organised civil society. A noticeable aspect is a convergence of the notions in organisations and in the Commission position papers. Organisations maintain their core demands, albeit framing them in the terms of the debate set by the EU Commission. As discussed in Chapter 3, this is precisely how civil society organisations reacted to the Commission's turn towards participatory governance in around 2000: their core demand remained a legal recognition for civil dialogue but they started framing it in terms of part of the EU's participatory model. This is clearly seen in the reactions to the White Paper on Governance (European Commission 2001): although the notion of participatory democracy was used for first time in the 2000 consultation, organisations did not react to it immediately but in the 2001 document.

The White Paper on Governance was followed by the adoption of a series of rules (European Commission 2002) ensuring the dialogue's transparency and to some extent a balanced representation of interests (Fazi and Smith 2006; Cuesta 2010). However, these rules have been also considered minimal from a political participation perspective, as they are limited to consultation rather than decisionmaking (Quittkat and Kohler-Koch 2013).

The focus of the Commission on civil society consultation together with demands from the organisations paved the way to the introduction of the abovementioned article on participatory democracy in the Treaty, establishing a European Constitution in 2003 (Article 47 TCE) and thus upgrading the Amsterdam Treaty protocol.[5] This article was maintained in the Lisbon Treaty (Article 11 TUE), albeit with the reference to participatory democracy removed from the title following the symbolic de-constitutionalisation that was undertaken in this Treaty, which entered into force in November 2009. However, in relation to this treaty article, the EU only passed legislation in 2012, on the European Citizens Initiative (Regulation 211/2011), and the rules about civil society consultation are still largely rooted on the principles established by the Commission in 2002 (European Commission 2002c), notwithstanding incremental changes related to the transparency agenda. The transparency initiative created a voluntary register of interest representatives that (despite not being mandatory) tries to provide incentives for organisations to sign up by suggesting that contributions from unregistered organisations are considered equal to contributions by individual citizens, and more recently by suggesting the provision of permanent access to the European Parliament's premises. This suggests that the agenda's emphasis has moved towards a more open approach than is implied by relations with Brussels-based organisations, with the purpose of increasing the legitimacy of the EU.

Structure of the book

Chapter 2 outlines the theoretical and analytical framework used to analyse the contribution of organisations to the making of the participatory agenda. The book is grounded in studies of agenda setting in the EU (Princen 2009) as well as in the newly emerging field approaches (Fligstein and McAdam 2012). The analytical framework is a combination of organisational agency analysis, via the study of interpretive frames, and collective action analysis, understood as the ways in which organisations approach EU institutions and the competition and cooperation between groups.

Chapter 3 analyses these interpretive frames. Chapter 4 focuses on the analysis of the competition and cooperation between organisations. Chapter 5 presents findings on access to and influence on the European Convention. Chapter 6 discusses the agenda-setting process for participation and the emergence of organisations that are actively participating. Chapter 7 provides an overview of the evolution of the field of participation between 2003 and 2012, to show that the field is still structured by similar competition and cooperation patterns to those of its establishment.Chapter 8 evaluates the contribution of participatory mechanisms to participation, representation and the public sphere. Chapter 9 concludes the book with a discussion of its two main contributions: a critical understanding of the contribution of organised civil society to democracy in the EU and a theoretical understanding of the influence of organised civil society on agenda-setting in the EU.

2

From the Regulation of Lobbies to Participatory Democracy: Agenda Setting and Civil Society in the EU

Civil society in the EU: sources of influence and models of interest intermediation

The EU's relations with interest groups have evolved with the course of EU integration, in particular as the EU has won competencies in new areas. Until the 1970s most organisations in Brussels were general business or agricultural groups. The 1980s saw an expansion and diversification of business interest groups in Brussels as the EU left the eurosclerosis years behind and started to deliver credible targets regarding the completion of the single market. However, during these years the EU also developed policies in new areas such as social affairs and the environment, attracting activists in these fields to Brussels. The EU system of interest intermediation has a number of salient features.

Interest groups are a relevant actor in the EU political system firstly because of the regulatory nature of EU politics. Whereas it is extremely difficult and rare for interest groups to have an effect in directly distributive policy decisions, regulatory politics has the characteristic of creating norms whose costs are relatively diffuse and benefits are concentrated, thus attracting groups that are able to use this opportunity to gain benefits and spread their costs.

The second reason is related to the nature of EU polity and its policy process. The EU offers multiple access opportunities to interest groups because of its divided executive and 28 national governments, its increasingly influential parliament and activist-consultative fora such as the Committee of the Regions and the Economic and Social Committee. Nevertheless the Commission remains at the centre of the policy process because of its key institutional position, its monopoly of policy initiation and the continuity of its staff in comparison with those of other institutions. However, it is a small mission administration that lacks technical expertise. It is thus required to exchange resources with interest groups, information and technical expertise being traded for access to policymaking.

Resource exchange is one of the most convincing explanations for interest group involvement in European politics. Whereas the influence of an interest group in politics is usually explained in terms of the importance of that interest in society (Lindblom 1977), this does not explain by itself involvement as an organised group in the political process. If a societal interest is important for structural reasons, decision-makers can be expected to take it into account when making policies irrespective of the involvement of interest groups. Yet, as stated above, interest groups have mobilised at the EU level as competencies have been transferred to Brussels, making it necessary to analyse which factor motivates each actor to establish relationships. The notion behind resource exchange is that institutions and groups will only engage if each of them has something that is necessary for the other. It is important to understand which resources organisations possess and are able to mobilise.

Despite the caricatures that are depicted in the media, money is not the single explanation for influence in public affairs (Kingdon 2003, 51–53; Baumgartner et al. 2009), in particular not in the EU (Mahoney 2008b). Other factors influencing political influence are the size and representativeness of an organisation, its ability to provide decision-makers with precise and accurate information, its *embeddedness* in a certain policy area and its reputation among institutions and stakeholders. Most research on civil society organisations in the EU suggests that their role is explained by their functional contribution to European integration in terms of input of expertise and legitimacy. It is important to point out the publicity around exchanges that take place in formalised consultation venues and the frequent coincidence of the same actors in these venues, which provides incentives for organisations to abide by the "rules of the game".

Even though civil society organisations are able to combine institutional and protest regimes (Ruzza 2004, 2011), the long relationship between civil society and institutions has influenced the preference of most European organisations for an insider collective action register, based on cooperation with officials rather than on contestation (Ruzza 2004; Kriesi 2007; Mahoney 2007; Balme and Chabanet 2008; Mahoney 2008a). In this sense, trust between and reputation of policymakers and other organisations is a very relevant resource for civil society influence, which is achieved by long-lasting involvement in a policy arena (Greenwood 2011b; Quittkat and Kotzian 2011). However, in concrete terms, what do citizens' interest groups provide EU institutions with?

Firstly they contribute to pluralising EU policymaking, in that they help to check business organisations' influence on the agenda (Greenwood 2011b). This means that in most policy fields the Commission can claim that legislation proposals are balanced between the interests of different stakeholders and that interest groups do not dominate EU policymaking. Secondly, they provide EU institutions with information and expertise (Klüver 2013). In the case of the Commission, this information is vital for highly technical regulatory decisions with clear economic costs, because unlike most national executives it lacks a large staff with a range of qualifications. Obviously the information provided by organisations cannot be deemed to be bias-free, but the diversity of interests in Brussels contributes to giving EU institutions contrasting pictures of policy solutions. Thirdly, civil society organisations have contributed to Europeanise policy issues. Organisations such as the European Women's Lobby or the Social Platform have successfully advocated for more EU attention on the concerns of their constituencies and have thus contributed to an assumed goal of the Commission, the extension of the realm of EU policy decisions. Finally, organised civil society provides inputs and political support to EU institutions, contributing to its legitimacy in the eyes of the European public.

It appears that through their eventual influence these organisations provide their partners in EU institutions with goods and resources that those institutions expect. From this can be derived the theoretical expectation that organisations adapt their strategies and demands to what they perceive to be the expectations of EU institutions.

What EU institutions provide in return is quite clear: organisational and financial support and regular access to the policymaking process. However, in doing so EU institutions have to make choices about which organisations can be supported and which cannot, whether access is to be granted to selected groups or whether it is to be open to all. These decisions have fluctuated according to the application of pluralist or corporatist systems of interest intermediation, and the institutions have not been the only actor in this process. Competition among institutions and their partners in civil society in defining this model can be analysed as a field of contention, cooperation and imitation among the actors who are active in the definition of participatory democracy in the EU.

Pluralist and corporatist understandings of structured relations

The effect of the Europeanisation of different types of interests and the multiplicity of access venues is that the literature tends to see the EU as a pluralistic polity where a large diversity of interests is represented in Brussels. Wonka et al. (2010) come to the figure of 3,700 groups. Greenwood (2011b, 10), using a different categorisation, finds a more modest figure of 2,200, but emphasises the diversity of these organisations – from companies to trade unions and including NGOs and think tanks. Nevertheless, both pluralism as an issue and its character are disputed. Some authors emphasise the predominance of business organisations over other actors (Bouwen 2002; Mazey and Richardson 2006; Quittkat 2011), whereas others point out that no one type of interest can routinely dominate (Greenwood 2011b). The concept of *elite pluralism* (Eising 2007; Coen 1997, 98–99) as "an interest arrangement where access is generally restricted to a few policy players" is useful because it emphasises the opposition between insiders and outsiders (Bidenkrantz 2005; Balme and Chabanet 2008), being more reminiscent of debates about corporatism and recognition and shifting attention to the way in which institutional preferences shape the field of civil society.

This elite pluralism has various implications for the actors in policy-making. On the one hand it can be understood as a neo-pluralist strategy by EU institutions, whereby interested citizens' organisations are encouraged to organise in fields where industry interests are active in order to achieve a balanced representation of interests in the policy process. However, it also has features of a corporatist system, where institutions regulate interest groups' access and recognise some but not all interest groups, thereby creating a two tier system.

The stakes are very clear in the debates about the emerging rules of civil society consultation. In the White Paper on Governance (European Commission 2001) the Commission seemed to endorse the explicit definition of civil society provided by the European Economic and Social Committee (European Commission 2002c, 6), including a representative understanding of civil society (Smismans 2003, 481–482). This focus on quasi-corporatist understandings of civil society was probably never fully shared by the Commission, but it still influenced the subsequent moves of the Commission when considering rules for consultation and transparency (Smismans 2003).

In line with the White Paper on Governance, the Commission drafted minimum standards and principles for consultation, and launched the CONECCS (Consultation, the Commission and Civil Society) website to make consultation processes transparent (European Commission 2002c) and to give stakeholders and concerned organisations a bigger role in the policymaking process, through the implementation of norms of fairness and transparency when undertaking consultation (Smismans 2003). The minimum standards (European Commission 2002c, 19–22) emphasise an open exchange between different interest groups. In a nutshell, the Commission assumes a commitment to formulate policies after the consultation of interested parties. Stakeholders must receive appropriate information on the policy options and be given the opportunity to express their opinions in a timely manner. The Commission also commits to publishing the result of the consultation and providing feedback to the stakeholders about how their contribution was used. This, together with the absence of representativeness criteria for open consultation and the "reject[ion] of an accreditation system and a wide definition of civil society" (Fazi and Smith 2006, 25–26), suggests that the Commission designed a pluralistic system of consultation.

However, the system created by the implementation of minimum standards is better understood as "a niche between accreditation and laissez-faire" (Greenwood and Halpin 2007), because until the adoption of the transparency initiative it contained a corporatist dimension based on the principle by which organisations were selected to be involved in focused consultations. In certain services of the Commission, such as Agriculture or Internal Market, there was a corporatist understanding of relations with civil society (Smismans 2003). This led to the proposal that enhanced partnerships should be created in fields where consultation was already a well-established practice (European Commission 2001), although it was not really developed (Sloat 2003). The main corporatist dimension of the focused consultation system in the aftermath of the Convention was the creation of a de facto accreditation system to give access to membership in consultative committees. CONECCS was not intended to be an accreditation system:

> The Commission believes that consultation should be undertaken as widely as possible and does not wish, as a general principle at this time, to accord certain organisations special status.[1]

Nevertheless CONECCS has been considered by some to be a de facto accreditation system (Greenwood and Halpin 2007, 206), because it was used between 2002 and 2007 to select organisations that were invited to take part in focused consultation in committees on the grounds, among others, of the representativeness criteria established in the EESC definition (Armstrong 2002; Smismans 2003) and referred to in the minimum standards (European Commission 2002c, 17, footnote 21). Registration in the database was not required for participation in focused consultations, but the Commission used it to select focused consultation partners, favouring groups that represented constituencies over cause organisations (Greenwood and Halpin 2007). Although cases of rejected registration were rare (Friedrich 2011, 106–107), non-registered organisations had to apply for involvement in consultation on a case by case principle, which created a clear distinction between insiders and outsiders. This distinction was particularly visible in that European organisations were favoured over national organisations. Furthermore, organisations selected to participate in consultative committees were in practice the most representative ones (Fazi and Smith 2006, 28).

This is not neutral from the point of the view of the strategies of access and influence by the actors of civil society. The issues of accreditation, representativeness and transparency articulate the whole agenda-setting process before 2002 and remain salient until the adoption of the transparency initiative in 2007. They are particularly salient in 2000 and 2002, and become less relevant during the Convention, although they are clearly a matter of concern for all the participants in their strategies. The Commission's early proposal is that organisations participating in consultations should be representative, without this however becoming the only selection criterion:

> For the consultation process to take place via such associations and networks, these organisations need to ensure that their structures are representative, in particular regarding their roots in the different Member States of the European Union. However, representativeness, though an important criterion, should not be the only determining factor for membership of an advisory committee, or to take part in dialogue with the Commission. Other factors, such as their track record and ability to contribute substantial policy inputs to the discussion are equally important. (European Commission 2000, 9)

The fact that the Commission has taken no action on civil dialogue since the entry into force of Article 11 in 2009, despite demands from key actors in the civil society field such as the Social Platform, is telling of the change of focus from consultation with specialised groups towards a more open approach. After the rejection of the European constitution, EU institutions sought ways to carry out the idea introduced in 2002 that civil society dialogue could facilitate "a broad policy dialogue" (European Commission 2002c, 5). In the aftermath of the Convention, the Commission and the Parliament proposed to decentralise civil dialogue and to enlarge it to ordinary citizens, in order to turn it into a mechanism of communication (European Commission 2005; European Parliament 2008). However, these proposals have not had significant outcomes, except maybe a greater focus on online consultations (Bozzini 2011; Quittkat 2011). The civil society dialogue agenda has been incrementally reformed by the transparency agenda (European Commission 2006b; European Parliament and Commission 2011), which has replaced some of the corporatist tendencies of the 2002 consultation standards towards de facto accreditation of organisations via a database into a neopluralist regime that emphasises openness to all organisations on the condition that they identify themselves (Greenwood 2011b).

A relational analysis of agenda setting: the stakes of institutionalisation of civil society consultation

Institutions and civil society organisations sought institutionalisation for different reasons, legitimacy for the institutions and access for the organisations. Because civil dialogue reinforces the position of civil society in the EU by granting organisations regular and predictable access (Fazi and Smith 2006), and given the strong profile of the Commission in its promotion by using participatory democracy framing (Sánchez-Salgado 2007; Saurugger 2010), this book researches the hypothesis that both civil society and the Commission used these discussions to improve their position in the increasingly formalised relations between the EU and civil society. From this follows a second hypothesis that the process of institutionalisation gave rise to a degree of competition among the participants in the process of defining access rules. In particular, organisations tried to use the debates to maximise their influence and to check competitors via the definition of rules about the degree of openness of the dialogue, about stakeholders' representativeness, and about the impact and the transparency required for policy discussions. These questions have structured the debate throughout this decade, and are still open today.

The need to understand how organisations relate to each other in a public context, where they have to build reputation and trust, suggests the appropriateness of using approaches informed by new institutionalism. The fact that debates are public, structured by a well-defined issue and legitimate forms of action, resonates with Pierre Bourdieu's idea of a social field (Bourdieu 1981, 1984) and more particularly with new institutional understandings of organisational and strategic fields (DiMaggio and Powell 1991, 65–66; Scott 2008, 185–190; Fligstein and McAdam 2012).

A field consists of a set of players who are endowed with differing types and levels of resources, or capitals in Bourdieu's terminology, and have stakes in a number of common issues that form a recognisable domain of institutional life (DiMaggio and Powell 1991, 65; Fligstein and McAdam 2012, 5–10), which is socially constructed by mutual recognition among the participants in the field, known as mutual awareness, or visible access barriers, such as institutional requirements to enter the field. The emergence of a field is characterised by four elements: "an extension of interaction of organizations in the field; the emergence of sharply defined interorganizational structures of domination and patterns of coalition; an increase in the information load with which organizations in the field must contend; and the development of a mutual awareness among participants" (DiMaggio and Powell 1991, 65). The actors attempt to "improve their position and to impose the principle of hierarchization most favorable to their own products" (Bourdieu and Wacquant 1992, 101). Actors' strategies depend upon the type and amount of resources they have and on their relative position within the field. However, the main object of analysis is not the individual rivalries but the ordering of the field; understanding which actors can decide what is valuable in a field, and why.

In classical neo-institutional organisation studies field analysis has been used to explain account for similarities – isomorphism – in organisations active in the policy field (DiMaggio and Powell 1991, Scott 2008). However, this approach has focused on imitation and adaptation patterns among organisations rather than on actors' strategic behaviour to impose or react to definitions of appropriate structure. Fortunately there have been major recent contributions that aim to theorise "strategic action fields" (Fligstein and McAdam 2012) in a way more akin to Bourdieu's relational understanding of social relations. This posits a greater interest on agency, as well as the importance of the stakes ("enjeux" in Bourdieu's terminology) rather than common form, and on conflict and competition rather than on isomorphism. Fligstein and McAdam (2012, 5) emphasise the way in which this elaboration of field theory contributes to bring together theorising on institutional emergence and transformation and social movement and advocacy literature. This approach thus has a strong potential for analysing relations of cooperation and competition for recognition in the field of organised civil society in the EU (Stone Sweet, Fligstein and Sandholtz 2001; Ruzza 2007; Dufour 2010; Johansson and Lee 2014).

The debates on participatory democracy constitute a very clear stake for organised civil society; that is, they establish or change regulations that decide who may access the EU institutions and how. The actions of organisations cannot only be explained in relation to the institutional agenda-setting process but also in relation to other organisations. Thus, the expectation is to observe the formation of visible alliances and oppositions along a number of clearly identified divisions. These patterns of cooperation and competition can be observed in relations between organisations, in their approach to the institutions and in the interpretive frames that these actors use.

Civil society and agenda setting in the EU

Available literature about the role and objectives of civil society in the European Convention points out that these organisations were influential in discussions on participatory democracy (del Río Villar 2004; Kværk 2007; Lombardo 2007; Pérez Solórzano-Borragán 2007; Clerck-Sachsse 2011). However, most of these analyses frequently pay more attention to the general role of these organisations in the Convention, their inability to influence it and the insufficiency of the access mechanisms, rather than to the agenda-setting process or to the analysis of influence on concrete decisions. In this sense the article on participatory democracy is frequently attributed to civil society activism (del Río Villar 2004, 282–283, 311; Will et al. 2005; Lombardo 2007; Monaghan 2007; Pérez Solórzano-Borragán 2007; del Río Villar 2008; Clerck-Sachsse 2011), but most of the empirical analysis focuses on the ECI and does not address the paragraphs on civil dialogue, let alone provide a comprehensive account of the agenda-setting process and the mechanisms of influence on the Convention.

The first exchange regarding the role of organised civil society in fostering the EU's social dimension was the social forum organised in 1996 (Friedrich 2011, 91), followed by a communication in 1997 which was open for stakeholders' comments (European Commission 1997). The question of the role of civil society in the EU and its position in the institutional system is addressed by Commission communications in 2000, 2001 and 2002. Interestingly the Laeken declaration (European Council 2001) follows up this approach by referring to the need to make the EU more democratic and granting it access to the Convention, which would include in its final version in July 2003 an article on participatory democracy with an explicit reference to civil society consultation. The time frame, extending from 1996 to 2003, is thus sufficient to observe the emergence, evolution and inclusion of the issue on the agenda, and represents a sufficiently large number of actors and institutions to give a comprehensive picture of the process.

The European Convention (2002–2003) was the culminating point of two evolutions in the relations between the European institutions and citizens' interest groups: the institutionalisation of civil society consultation via a reference in a Treaty article and the conceptualisation of this mechanism as a form of participatory democracy. Although the idea that the institutionalisation of civil society relations can legitimise the EU had been explicitly formulated by the Commission before (European Commission 2001, 2002c, 2005), and despite previous references to the inclusion of a legal basis for civil dialogue in the Treaties (European Commission 2000, 12), it is not until the Convention that an article on the consultation of civil society was included in the Treaty under the heading of "participatory democracy". This tells us two things about the agenda-setting process: it speaks about the extensive changes in frames of reference that are used in relation to civil society participation and it is also informative about the way in which the discussion venue – the consultation with different services of the Commission or in the Commission – creates different opportunities for influence and transformation of the agenda. When analysing the agenda-setting process it is thus necessary to consider two main elements: the evolution of the collective frame of reference and the agency of the actors in the venues where they can be influential.

The importance of frames and venues have begun to be taken seriously in studies of agenda setting in the EU (Princen 2009).The major characteristic of interest groups in EU agenda setting is their multi-level nature and enhanced plurality of interests. This means that there are several levels and venues that organisations can use in order to access the agenda, but it is rare that they can dominate it. Thus a typical strategy for organisations seeking to influence the agenda (Princen 2009, 155–159) is to introduce their point of view at the venue where it is most likely to be listened to. However, the EU is characterised by the Commission's monopoly of legislative initiative, so even if it is well known that the Commission is rarely the genuine initiator of the agenda (Diedrichs and Wessels 2006, 223) it is still the institution through which all proposals have to come. This is why the European Convention can be considered an exceptional opportunity for agenda setting, as the Commission is no longer the principal agenda setter in relation to civil society. It can thus be expected that this change of venue had a significant effect.

Another important characteristic of interest groups in EU agenda setting is that their contribution rarely consists of "twisting the arm" of the institutions (Kingdon 2003, 17). Greenwood (2011d) shows that interest groups' influence on policy initiation is extremely rare, with just three examples from the European Women's Lobby, the European Round Table of industrialists or ALTER-EU in recent years; more often the influence is limited to a contribution to the framing and details of generally complex and consensus-prone negotiations. EU interest groups can influence agendas in the longer term by introducing and promoting ideas in epistemic communities, policy networks or advocacy coalitions (Engel 2007; Ruzza 2007; Dreger 2008; Princen 2009). These communities are constituted by agents who are active in the same domain, "read the same publications, go to the same conferences and meetings and in these ways develop shared understandings of policy problems and the available policy options to deal with them" (Princen 2009, 151–152). From this it follows that a single group can rarely be identified as the mover behind a proposal, and that changes must often be explained as the result of the coordinated activism of a coalition.

There is growing agreement on the need for the theoretical integration of political opportunities, mobilisation structures and processes of interpretation of reality, and for assigning meanings to understand the involvement of organised civil society in agenda-setting processes (Zald 1996; Scott 2008; Schmidt 2010). The work of Irving Goffman (2006) on framing is particularly useful in trying to bridge these theories, as it aims to analyse how the reinterpretation of reality contributes to collective action. In a nutshell, this approach posits that organised groups tend to strategically and consciously define situations through "framing processes" that favour their interpretation of reality, to legitimise themselves and therefore to organise collective action to meet their interests and substantive goals.

Analysing frames of reference has started to be considered important for the analysis of EU civil society organisations advocacy (Ruzza 2004, 2007; Bozzini 2010). Both advocacy coalition (Sabatier and Jenkins 1993; Sabatier 1998; Hula 1999) and frame analysis (Snow et al. 1986; Zald 1996) coincide in pointing out that organisations have a set of core values and demands which tend to be stable and vary only in the long term – in this case the promotion of their own role and characteristics as the barrier of entry to the field – which are accompanied and framed by more incidental and flexible demands. Thus, the question is whether arguments about democracy and citizenship evolved according to advocacy and coalition-making strategies at different times. It also must be asked whether a clear and stable demand by organisations emerges, or whether their contributions are reactive to the Commission's focus. This is particularly important as changing rationales have been used in order to justify the institutionalisation of consultation procedures. Some of these legitimatising frames are the European public sphere, civil dialogue and participatory democracy. It is expected to find a significant variance in the actors involved and the framing of the different consultations that were taken into account before the Convention (1997, 2000, 2001 and 2002). It must be borne in mind that consultations are reactive processes where organisations reply to the focus of the Commission on different policy issues. This focus is volatile: although all the consultations include the question of which rules should be applied to organised civil society consultation, this is the central question only in the 2002 and to a lesser extent the 2000 consultation, whereas the 2001 White Paper has a higher political profile and the 1997 consultation's primary aim was to promote civil society in Europe in the context of enlargement.

Data and methodology

Because of its focus on how the particular topic of participatory democracy was introduced and framed in the agenda, this part of the research follows a qualitative approach. It conceives these exchanges as a process of discourse creation regarding civil society and participatory democracy in the EU. Discourse is not understood in a constructivist sense as meaning the entire social field, but rather in Fairclough's critical understanding. Although the proposal that participatory democracy is a way to answer criticisms of the lack of democratic legitimacy is a social construction, as is the idea of civil society consultation as a model of participatory democracy, this construction takes place in a social environment which is not totally flexible but constrained by resource availability (Fairclough 2005, 931). In this case the constraints are the possibilities of securing channels of access to the institutions. Organisations' ability to construct social reality is thus fundamentally mediated by their embeddedness in an institutional system. In this sense discourses, in the plural as Fairclough emphasises, are understood here as particular ways of representing, talking about and understanding the world or aspects of the world (see Jorgensen and Phillips (2002, 1) and Fairclough (2003, 24) for very similar definitions). They will be understood in a strategic way, that is as "frames acting as a way for social groups to advance their interests and projects" (Howarth 2000, 3). In this sense different discourses about participatory democracy will be identified and compared, with a particular focus on the emergence of shared discourses, similarities and differences, and convergences and divergences between organisations' discourses.

Given the relatively long time frame and the high number of organisations taking part in this process – 800 for the Convention alone (Kværk 2007) – it is impossible to carry out a qualitative analysis of contributions from the entire population. Hence it is necessary to choose a limited number of civil society actors and analyse their contribution. However, doing this by studying a representative random sample of the entire population of organisations active in the Convention would be highly inconclusive, because for a large number of organisations in such a sample their contributions to these consultations would not necessarily be regarding participatory democracy, the aspect of the agenda that is being considered. Instead, the choice has been made to focus on the most active organisations in the process. This has been done by only considering contributions by organisations active during the Convention and two of the previous consultation processes. This arbitrary boundary avoids the bias that would be introduced if a selection were made by the author according to reputation or snowballing. Setting the boundary of a field is a key aspect of field and network analysis. The aim in defining the boundary according to the number of contributions is to make the most salient actors visible. This focus on publicly available contributions follows on from the understanding that the field is structured by visible membership and the awareness of the members of each others' actions. The CONECCS database or the transparency register have not been used in setting this boundary because they were not in force when the field emerged.

The result is a picture composed of some of the core Brussels citizens' interests organisations but with a fair representation of other groups, such as business or regional interest organisations. The only exceptions that have been applied to the selection of European groups regard three organisations which failed to meet this threshold but are pointed out as particularly important in the process. Those are ETUC as a social partner, CSCG as the broadest umbrella organisation of citizens' interests and IRI, insistently pointed out as the main driver of the debate on the ECI (Lamassoure 2004; del Río Villar 2004; Clerck-Sachsse 2011). The result is a constituency of 22 organisations, the list of which can be consulted in Annex 2. The bias of this sample must be considered in order to understand the conclusions that can and cannot be derived from its analysis. This group does not represent the activism, access mechanisms, issue focus and framing of civil society in general during the agenda-setting process but rather a group of organisations particularly active and with privileged links to institutions and officials. However, it provides a very detailed picture of what civil society organisations expected to achieve by repeated involvement in these consultations. It is thus the best way to analyse the influence of organisations in the agenda-setting process, since all the actors that had a stake in the issue are likely to have been included in the study.

Analysing the frames of reference

Frames are understood both as a means of advocacy and their manifestation. Their analysis has consisted of considering in detail and coding the written contributions submitted by every organisation to the consultations in order to map the frames that structured the discussion during this process. The methodological choice is an inductive approach to the discourses of the organisations as expressed mainly in their position papers, whereas interviews focused on understanding the rationale behind organisations' activism.

The data available are 123 position papers of which 14 correspond to the 2000 consultation, 17 to the 2001, 13 to the 2002 and 79 to the Convention. Additionally 112 official documents have been analysed in order to analyse their relation to civil society framing. These were four communications by the Commission, 18 Commission staff reports on the works of the Convention, nine documents from the Secretariat of the Convention, 18 reports on the hearings regarding organised civil society held at the EESC during the Convention, 61 amendments by members of the Convention to the article on participatory democracy and two reports from national Conventions.

Although these documents are usually publicly available, two problems were encountered when gathering them. The documents for the 1997 consultation were not publicly available, but access was given to first-hand reports on condition that they were not reproduced. More seriously, the documents submitted by civil society to the Convention were not publicly available and the Commission, which was responsible for the administration of the Convention's civil society forum website, was unable to produce them. This important shortcoming was partially overcome thanks to access to data provided by other researchers and by the archives of some civil society organisations. The result is that papers from 16 out of 22 organisations were finally available, thus significantly reducing this difficulty. Interviews have also provided very complete data for 20 of the 22 organisations.

The discourses produced in the public documents have been analysed according to established practice in the field (Ruzza 2007; Princen 2009;

Bozzini 2010), by coding the data into common categories that can then be compared. In order to analyse the individual discourses and the collective frames, as well as to avoid imposing the author's interpretive schemes after the first approach to the data, these have been coded in two different ways. Firstly, a descriptive coding approach where the data were coded inductively was followed, and the codes were organised chronologically. In a second phase a more analytical coding was produced. This reduced the number of codes by organising them in more general categories. Along with the expectations that relate to the adaptation of demands from the Commission, an important distinction is made between core aspects of the discourse, or masterframes, and more variable frames and justifications (see also Sabatier and Jenkins-Smith 1993). The most straightforward way in which to recognise core aspects in the discourse is to focus on the number of references and on the persistence of a code across time. The analysis thus focuses on these collective masterframes; that is, on identifying which demands and issues organisations discuss consistently across the process and how those are formulated and evolve. Rather than analysing individual framing processes, in other words the discursive mechanisms that organisations use to present their demands in the most favourable way, the objective is to understand which topics organisations focus on as a result of collective action. In order to analyse the emergence of these collective frames, it was noted how many and which organisations were taking positions in each case, and the aggregate evolution of attention to an issue and positions was analysed. Associations of terms and values are examined as well, using Snow et al.'s (1986) notions of frame bridging, when an element is presented and justified as congruent with another, and frame amplification, when new interpretations and meanings are associated with existing frames.

The analytical method is thus fairly simple. The key aspect when deciding whether to code sections of the discourse is the preciseness of the reference; that is, how close the discourse is to the content already established in the coding. If the discourse differs from existing codes a new code is created. Notions were analysed literally without interpretation; for instance, in no case was "civil dialogue" analysed as "participatory democracy" if this aspect was not explicitly elaborated in the data. The emphasis on explicit formulations and common aspects obviously implies a trade-off between making sense of a large number of data and the consideration of detailed nuances. In this sense the strategy is not to interpret what organisations were trying to achieve, but what they were saying in each context. In order to compensate for this, aspects of interpretive discourse analysis have been applied to selected complex issues such as conceptions of representativeness and decisive frame transformations. The general focus of contributions and the general objectives and characteristics of organisations were considered while making these interpretations.

The result consists of 19 frames that are present with different intensities across the four consultations, which have been classified according to three dimensions: conceptions of civil society, conceptions of participatory democracy in the EU and the role of civil society organisations in the EU's institutional architecture. These codes are not classifications established from a theoretical point of departure, where the organisations' discourses are classified with varying scores, but are inductively created from the data. As the results are similar but not identical framings, the codes were refined and made more general, tending to be constructed as opposed positions, for instance for or against civil dialogue. Frame analysis therefore basically consisted of coding the relevant parts of European organisations into 76 frames (19 frames for each of the four consultations), creating as a result 1,596 possible positions. The NVIVO 9 software package has been used to create and analyse the codes, which have then been used to generate the collective frames. This allowed codes to be crossed with variables, such as the type of document (interviews versus public document), the type of interest represented, membership in coalitions, organisations' primary level of action (national or European) and the degree of involvement of each actor in the process (in terms of date of involvement and number of contributions). Analysis of these positions, in terms of which organisations issue the demands, when and how often, provides an accurate description of the aims that the organisations were seeking to promote and how they were justifying them.

The stakes of institutionalisation of participatory mechanisms

The second part of the work seeks to explain organisations' collective action. It will analyse whether collective action registers and framing varied according to variables such as salience, type of venue, number and kinds of actors: see Mahoney (2007) and Princen (2009, 155–156) for a discussion of the importance of these variables in EU agenda setting. Direct mobilisation of the public and supporters in media campaigns or mass demonstrations is an exception in the collective action registers of organisations active in the EU (Imig and Tarrow 2001; Della Porta 2007; Balme and Chabanet 2008). On the contrary, the organisation of coalitions and involvement in networks that promote the inclusion of ideas and causes in the EU's agenda is a frequent activity (Ruzza 2004; Mahoney 2007; Greenwood 2011b; Ruzza 2011). The literature emphasises the importance of formal venues as political opportunity structures for interest groups in the EU (Princen and Kerremans 2010). Particular importance will thus be paid to the way in which organisations' demands are justified and argued in this segmented public space. Although key aspects of the agenda-setting process are undoubtedly informal, in the context of public consultations organisations need to argue for their demands in terms that are acceptable for the rest of the actors (Naurin 2007, 20–24). It is thus important to analyse whether arguments about democracy and citizenship were used to frame the demands, and whether they evolved according to advocacy and coalition-making strategies at different times. It can be argued that the framing process helped to frame existing civil society consultation mechanisms as elements of a model of participatory democracy in the EU (Kohler-Koch and Finke 2007).

The analysis concentrates on understanding the ways in which organisations became involved in the consultations – including the framing of demands (with particular attention to their resonance in official documents), the resources exchanged with the institutions, and the relationships between organisations active in the same field – that shaped the EU agenda on civil society institutionalisation. Advocacy on civil dialogue is understood as a form of policy entrepreneurship (Kingdon 2003), whereby organisations that are involved invest significant resources to take part in consultations about participatory democracy, with the expectation of a return in terms of position in the field. It has already been pointed out that participation in consultations is important, as it is a form of "jockeying for position" in the emerging field (Fligstein and McAdam 2012, 12). Participation in consultation is also one of the resources that organisations offer to the Commission in the exchange mentioned above (Michel 2007).

In order to understand the evolution of the frames in the context of the organisations' collective action, the frames' evolution will be linked and explained according to the different ways in which organisations are active in the socially constructed field of participatory democracy. The activities that will be considered are thus participation in the formal consultation events, the submission of written documents to these exercises, the establishment of informal contacts with officials, relations with other groups and with their members, and participation in formal and informal coalitions. The data for relations between the organisations will be formalised quantitatively to provide a precise account of the evolution of the networking relations between the organisations and its relationship with the emerging frame.

Collective action has been analysed with a special focus on access to institutions and to coalition behaviour and networking, to observe how organisations promoted their views, and the formal and informal means of access. Interviews with officials are valuable sources in this respect. Finally, analysis of relationships between organisations has been made via network analysis, in particular by focusing on individual actor centralities, that is the position of actors in the network as well as structural similarities, in order to analyse the types of behaviour that similar actors adopted. Particular attention was paid to contacts between national and European organisations, to networks of communication and to the specific common action networking in contrast with simple exchanges of opinions. Furthermore, when analysing the choice of partners and of strategies of collective action, the type of actors who contributed to the eventual diffusion of discourses about participatory democracy was considered; whether the organisations lobbying more actively were also those contributing to the diffusion.

Access to data about how the organisations promoted their points of view and the patterns of relationship between them has been gained via primary and secondary sources. Firstly, all available observations about participation in fora, coalitions or consultative groups in consultation documents and on websites have been used. Additionally, it was decided to carry out in-depth semi-structured interviews with representatives of all the organisations and with officials active in the process, in order to understand how each organisation participated in the process and what its relations with the national public were. These were conducted with a broad list of topics rather than a detailed and strict questionnaire, in order to avoid missing information by imposing a closed list of questions. The list of themes always addressed the way in which organisations participated in the process, what they sought to achieve, in particular by asking explicitly what the rationale was for promoting (or eventually opposing) the inclusion of the participatory democracy principle in the Treaty, and what their relations were with members in Spain and France. Thirty interviews were carried out, of which 11 corresponded to officials and members of the Convention and 19 to European organisations. The response rate was very high, with about 90% of the target organisations responding positively. These interviews were carried out in English or French, according to the choice of the interviewee, so that they were more comfortable and the information obtained was maximised. All recorded interviews were fully transcribed and analysed in the language of origin.

Finally, a questionnaire asking interviewees about their contacts regarding participatory democracy (from exchange of opinions to common action) with the other organisations in the sample was circulated in order to complete information about collective action that was gathered from documents and interviews. The response rate for this source was lower than for interview demands but still acceptable (42%).

Evaluating participatory democracy in the EU

The last part of this work addresses the contribution of civil society participation to the legitimacy of the EU. It will analyse to what extent the debate on participatory democracy in the EU, which is still largely ongoing, has enhanced participation, representation and communication by civil society organisations. It will do so by considering the dimensions already highlighted, including issues of inclusion and exclusion, competition, diversity and communication.

In particular, the section analyses to what extent organisations involved in the agenda-setting process contributed to "download" the participatory democracy debate from the Convention to the general public and whether the evolution of the agenda at different times has contributed to change this. The expectation is that the politicisation of the venue that was induced by the Convention must have helped civil society organisations to mobilise their supporters and members at national level. The analysis of this dimension is carried out by analysing references to the debate around this issue with member organisations.

The other expectation is that the field of participatory democracy became increasingly complex as it became institutionalised. This is because of its higher profile – necessarily raising the stakes and the number of interested parties – and because of the increasing diversity of mechanisms – focused and open consultation, including online fora, transparency rules and the entirely new ECI. Increased competition is expected to have made organisations active in communicating with their members and the field more diverse.

Epistemological issues

This combination of research methods raises the issue of possible contradictions between different sources as well as the eventual bias introduced in interviews as a result of the time lapse between the time frame (1996–2005) and the fieldwork (2009–2011).

This research builds on a strongly emerging approach which seeks to use analysis of discourses and frames in order to understand organisational and institutional processes and characteristics (Grant, Hardy and Putnam 2004; Fairclough 2005; Scott 2008; Schmidt 2010).

The aim of the research is to understand whether and how arguing publicly as a strategy of civil society links the different segments of the public sphere. In this sense, although the strategies and goals of organisations are considered, emphasis is put on the effects of organisations' activism. The primary aim is not to interpret whether groups were advancing their interests or their ideologies with their activism concerning participatory democracy (Ruzza 2011, 461), but rather to understand the effects of that activism. In particular, as will be seen in Chapter 3, ideological elements about participation in the discourse of civil society organisations strongly coincide with their own interests, since the notion of participation is strongly related to the involvement of organised groups.

It could be said that this project relies on a positivist rationale that considers it possible to discern, characterise and analyse an objective action by organisations. Public discourse is understood as a form of action of organisations, but not the only one. In this sense it is argued that not all the activities of organisations are shaped by discourses, as some of their interests are formed independently of the way in which discourse is formulated. On the contrary, discourse expresses ways in which to justify those interests. Chapter 3 offers strong evidence for this, since it shows clearly that organisations have a set of core objectives which remain stable, while the manner in which the legitimacy of such objectives is presented evolves quite clearly. Frame analysis appears thus to be the most useful analytical framework. This approach relies on "empirically derived data to identify patterns and regularities within the discursive interactions of various organizational actors" (Grant, Hardy and Putnam 2004, 15) and thus finds itself on the positivist side of discursive approaches. These conceptions have been criticised as unable to uncover the power struggles related to these processes of convergence.

However, this last criticism does not seem to make much sense in the context of this research, as the aim is precisely to understand the power struggles and interests that are conveyed by organisations' discourse. Additionally it takes discourse seriously and not merely descriptively or rhetorically, as emphasis is put on the role of public discourse and publicity in the transformation of relations between organisations. In this sense, the bounded rationality context imposed on actors' strategies in terms of seeking selfish objectives is an important factor that affects individual organisations' preferred outcomes and strategies. In this sense, therefore, the positivist approach to discourse does not necessarily imply a realist or rationalist analytical approach that relies on mere interest calculation by the actors. Thus emphasis is put on achieving a reliable and replicable research framework by using, as much as possible, a clear perspective on organisations' activism. It is argued that this does not hinder but rather enhances a better understanding of such power struggles. Furthermore, this approach does not diminish the importance of discourse, as obviously organisations formulate and justify their strategies discursively. The book provides evidence that the way in which organisations frame their demands has unexpected effects on the results of their advocacy.

In relation to interviews, according to this positivist approach it is assumed "that the accounts provided by respondents are an accurate and honest reflection of their beliefs, activities and opinions" (Monaghan 2007, 46) rather than a contextual interaction between the interviewer and interviewee. When doing this, the obvious implication is that the information provided by the interviewee may not always be accurate. In addition to the possibility that the interviewee would not like to disclose his or her opinion and activities, this research faces the fact that a non-negligible time elapsed between the moments addressed in the interviews (1996–2005) and the fieldwork (2009–2011). The first risk was that interviewees could have difficulties in retrieving the processes, in particular those for which the question of participatory democracy was not primary. The second and more subtle risk was that interviewees would retrospectively justify or reconstruct their positions, in order to adjust it to match their current organisation's position on the issue.

In order to address these problems, a control mechanism has been established that consists of a triangulation of the data. In fact, two sorts of triangulations have been established: triangulation between primary and secondary sources and triangulation between the information provided by different interviewees. That is, when interview data or accounts from the actors are used in the context of subjective behaviour, the data were always analysed in the context of the general action, rather than merely in terms of the behaviour of a single actor. This allows for comparisons, making it possible to interpret what organisations were trying to achieve. Whenever possible this is compared to position papers as well. Whenever the aim is to analyse organisations' discourse, the data are not triangulated. In that case the aim is to analyse the evolution, and thus changes of opinions are analysed in relation to the time frame rather than as contradictions. Only in a few cases are the discourse in interviews and in position papers compared and contradictions highlighted (such as in the case of the complex notion of representativeness). It appears that the data were generally very reliable as there were very few contradictions between the different sources and the interviewees. Whenever contradictions appear they are highlighted and interpreted.

Interviews were recorded with the explicit agreement of interviewees, who agreed to be quoted without being identified. When the interviewee did not consent, notes were taken and only comments on general processes were used. All interview data have been anonymised to protect the interviewees' identity. Additionally, biographical data and similar have been omitted from the transcriptions for the same reasons. It turns out that none of these data are necessary for the presentation of the results. The rest of the data were either available in the public domain or obtained from legitimate sources, such as archives and repositories of EU institutions, civil society organisations or other researchers.

3
Interpretive Frames in the Agenda-Setting Process, 1997–2003

Introduction

One of the core expectations referred to in Chapter 2 is that organisations adapt the way in which they frame their demands according to the expectations of the institutions, which are themselves dynamic. Figure 3.1 confirms a strong variation in emphasis on these different frames, supporting the idea that civil society organisations were trying to achieve different things at different times (Snow et al. 1986). However, in-depth analysis of their positions suggests that the core of their demands remains quite stable. This may be because civil society organisations attempt to reframe their demands in order to better correspond with what they perceive to be the expectations of EU institutions. In order to evaluate this hypothesis, this chapter analyses the core of the discourse and demands of the organisations in each of the three dimensions, and indicates how these were adapted to each stage of the debate (see Annex 3 for the complete codebook and the detailed coding).

Position of civil society organisations in the EU institutional architecture

The topics regrouped in the "relation between the EU and civil society organisations (CSO)" variable express civil society organisations' claims for a larger role in the EU's institutional architecture. This demand has been expressed by organisations involved in consultations since the mid-1990s and has been persistent in all subsequent consultations (Fazi and Smith 2006). This section presents these demands and the ways in which they have been formulated, and secondly looks at how these groups envisage the way in which their participation in the EU should be organised.

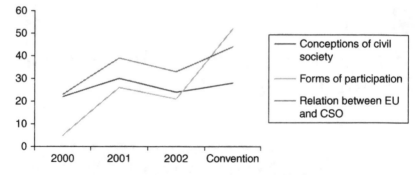

Figure 3.1   Evolution of civil society organisations' references

Note: Unlike the rest of the figures in this chapter, Figure 3.1 does not represent the number of organisations referring to one code but to a cumulative number of references to all the codes. It is based on the detailed coding of each consultation process rather than on the coding of common aspects.

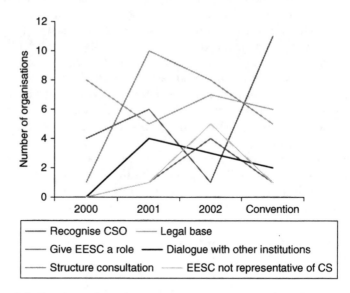

Figure 3.2   Position of civil society organisations in the EU institutional architecture

Main demands: recognition and legal rank for consultation

The call to be recognised at EU level is the oldest demand. In its original form it is strongly linked to the projects of the last Delors Commission for strengthening the third or voluntary sector at European level (Will and Kendall 2009). It is formulated in responses to the 1997 communication by the Commission in which each kind of organisation hopes to obtain recognition for its specificity. Although the focus becomes slightly more general in responses to the 2001 White Paper on Governance, the particularistic claims remain strong in the Convention. For instance, European Council for Non-Profit Organisations (CEDAG) demanded recognition of the economic importance of the third sector, whereas the EFC would have liked to see a specific recognition of the peculiarities of foundations. Two facts however suggest that the first approach by the Commission was a failure: the moving of the political initiative on the subject of Commission – civil society relations from DG Enterprise to the General Secretariat after 1997 as well as the abandonment of a proposal for a European association statute (Will and Kendall 2009).

Despite this, claims for civil society recognition became more frequent in 2001, and they acquired a new significance as they were no longer limited to the status of European association but sought to secure a consultation role. The strong decline of this topic in the 2002 consultation can be linked to the technical nature of this consultation, which was not about the principle of consultation in itself but about who specifically should be consulted. However the topic re-emerges very strongly during the Convention, and in the discourse of citizens' organisations it is clearly linked to the legal status of consultation; that is, claims for recognition are demands to be recognised as consultation partners. The high number of demands during the Convention (made by virtually all organisations) means that all the organisations used the new venue as an opportunity to raise their profile and to obtain a recognised status (Will et al. 2005; Lombardo 2007).

Citizens' groups linked their demand for a role in the policymaking process to a second core demand: legal status for consultation. This latter demand has been supported by the Commission since 2000 (European Commission 2000), although the Commission did not succeed in including it in the Nice ICG in 2001. This suggests that the claims by civil society for a strengthened and legally binding consultation met the Commission's intention to derive input legitimacy from its relations with civil society organisations (Kohler-Koch and Finke 2007; Monaghan 2007, 27–28). This was important for the organisations at least for two reasons. Firstly, it made civil dialogue mandatory, and thus ensured civil society organisations access to EU affairs without depending on the Commission's goodwill (Fazi and Smith 2006). Secondly, it recognised the legitimacy of one of the main elements of the collective action repertoire of these organisations, that is, direct access to decision-makers

(Kohler-Koch 2007; Mahoney 2007; Balme and Chabanet 2008), at the same time distinguishing it from conventional lobbying as a sort of "structured relation" (Smismans 2003) entrusted with a higher degree of legitimacy. The following quote summarises the range of expectations for the legal basis for dialogue (Caritas – Eurodiaconia 2000, 4):

19. A legal basis makes consultation mechanisms more predictable. Predictability and accountability of policy procedures are important principles.

20. A legal status safeguards the process against organisational changes of personnel in the Commission.

21. The Commission's proposal can then be extended to cover the Council and Parliament in the further development of consultation mechanisms in European policy-making.

22. This can then also put pressure on national and regional authorities to develop their own consultation mechanisms with civil society.

This recurrent demand by citizens' organisations was very strongly promoted by the Social Platform and later on by the CSCG, an alliance set up by the largest citizens' interest umbrella organisations in the wake of the Convention, which expressed some of the core demands of the organisations. In the context of the Convention this demand was clearly formulated as the need of a legal base for civil society consultation in the Treaty. On the other hand business organisations and ETUC have been sceptical about the creation of an article about consultation in the Treaty. This quote from Eurocommerce's contribution to the consultation on the 2000 paper is the most straightforward formulation:

EUROCOMMERCE sees no need to adopt the American system of accreditation and wonders how a legal basis in the Treaty could concretely contribute to improve the way these consultation forums operate. (Eurocommerce 2000, 3)

However, the endorsement of this demand by the Commission and its expression in the irresistible frame of participatory democracy contributed to a decrease in expressions of outright rejection and encouraged the social partners to attempt to influence the details as this principle developed (see Chapter 6). The role of the EESC is for instance one of the stakes of the discussions among these two emerging coalitions.

The controversial role of the EESC

The role of the EESC in the EU's dialogue with civil society is among the most controversial issues in the process. The Committee has sought to raise its profile in the wake of the debate on governance and has tried to make it the key venue for participation in the EU. According to Smismans, "the EESC had a particular interest in developing a discourse on civil society: created by the Rome Treaty [...] it had de facto been rather marginalised in the institutional setup" (Smismans 2006, 4). During this period it offered its "good offices" to the Commission and civil society organisations in order to provide expertise, and even to be the institution that hosted civil dialogue (Smismans 2003). The Committee's success in organising regular contact between the Convention and civil society (Monaghan 2007, 100) exemplifies this strategy.

However, the citizens' interests organisations which promoted civil dialogue in the first years of the process rejected proposals to institutionalise dialogue in the EESC. This confirms that for these organisations civil dialogue is essentially a way of access to decision-makers that would be weakened if it were to be limited to participation in a mere "talking shop", as the EESC is often perceived by these organisations (Green 8 2002, 4). Another argument is that the Committee is not representative of civil society since it is nominated by Member States and is composed essentially of representatives of trade unions and employers. The following quote summarises how citizens' interests organisations perceived the EESC and the strategy to make it the seat of civil dialogue:

> The Economic and Social Committee does not represent civil society and we oppose attributing such a role to it. Whether ECOSOC continues to have value for the social partners (employers and trade unions) is a matter for them to address. For our part, we prefer to devote our energies to attempting to inform and influence the decision making institutions rather than to engage with a government-appointed, consensus-based advisory body. (Green 8 2002, 4)

On the other hand, representatives of local and regional governments and business organisations, which expressed the need to subordinate participatory democracy to representative democracy, proposed to use the EESC as the forum for civil dialogue:

> The Economic and Social Committee is the place for civil dialogue. When discussing its role and status, it is essential to avoid any confusion between civil dialogue and social dialogue, which is an

autonomous process between the social partners and takes place outside the Economic and Social Committee. (Unice 2002, 7)

There is thus a clear cleavage between citizens' interest groups and the other organisations. In this sense the caricature of the EESC as a useless forum is a typical belief amplification process, which consists of constructing a stereotypical opponent in order to strengthen the coherence of the alternative frame (Snow et al. 1986, 470).

Inasmuch as they reject the idea of instituting the EESC as the "house of civil society", the organisations that promoted civil dialogue insisted in creating additional consultation mechanisms with other EU institutions, in particular the Council and the Parliament, which are pointed out as the most inaccessible institutions (see Figure 3.2):

> CEDAG particularly wishes to see a strengthening of the dialogue between civil society and the European Parliament, this being the body that represents the citizens of Europe, through more systematic consultations, particularly by means of intergroups. (CEDAG 2003, 2)

This appears as further evidence supporting the theory that by promoting participatory ideas, civil society organisations are seeking to multiply and institutionalise their access points to the EU's decision-making bodies. Thus organisations' alternative strategies for recognition were also evident in their proposals for how civil society consultation should take place.

Conception of civil society

Monaghan has summarised the main functions of European civil society organisations as their ability to communicate, represent and promote participation (Monaghan 2007). Frame analysis, below, highlights that organisations are well aware of these capacities and that they use them to convey their demand for a recognised role.

The role of civil society organisations in EU integration

References to the contribution of civil society organisations to making citizens aware of EU integration can be summarised in two major aspects, which evolve through time. Figure 3.3 indicates that at the beginning of the process the organisations' main claim was that they could be a link between the EU institutions and citizens, whereas from 2001 the focus has been more frequently on their ability to give a voice

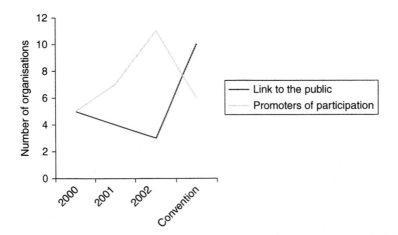

Figure 3.3 Organisations referring to the role of civil society organisations in EU integration

to citizens' concerns, values and rights claims. This resonates strongly with the focus of the Commission's agenda on participation in the 2001 and 2002 documents. However, the idea that civil society links the EU and the public returns strongly during the Convention, albeit with the caveat that it is civil society consultation which informs the public.

As the differences between these frames may appear subtle, it is worth highlighting some of them. Compare the frames as formulated in the 2000 position paper of the Commission. This paper raises expectations that CSO involvement can have two effects. One regards public opinion at large:

> By encouraging national NGOs to work together to achieve common goals, the European NGO networks are making an important contribution to the formation of a "European public opinion" usually seen as a pre-requisite to the establishment of a true European political entity. At the same time this also contributes to promoting European integration in a practical way and often at grassroots level. (European Commission 2000)

The second effect has to do with the idea that participating in an association can itself be a way to contribute to the shaping of EU integration:

> The decision making process in the EU is first and foremost legitimised by the elected representatives of the European people. However,

NGOs can make a contribution to in [*sic*] fostering a more participatory democracy both within the European Union and beyond.

[...]

Belonging to an association provides an opportunity for citizens to participate actively in new ways other than or in addition to involvement in political parties or trade unions. (European Commission 2000)

As to the manifestation of this difference in organisations' discourses, compare them in the two following statements by the Social Platform in its contribution to the 2002 consultation:

We regret that the role of European NGOs in stimulating debates among national NGOs and contributing to the emergence of a European thinking has not been highlighted. If consultation is to be effective and useful, then the need to fund spaces for discussions both at a national and European level should be acknowledged.

[...]

We believe that in recognition of the reality of millions of people within the European Union experiencing poverty, exclusion and inequalities, particular recognition should be given to the expertise that emerges from that part of civil society which organises to represent the interest of those people and in which they participate. (Social Platform 2002a: 3, 1)

Despite the strong bias towards EU umbrella groups in the agenda-setting phase it is possible to see a relevant difference between those organisations and the rest in the way in which these claims are voiced. Figure 3.4 shows clearly that EU umbrella groups voiced the participatory dimension more strongly, whereas all the other organisations continued to justify the importance of civil society organisations in terms of their ability to engage the public.

Obviously these dimensions are not opposed, but they certainly convey different expectations regarding the contribution of civil society organisations to the legitimacy of the EU. If CSOs are considered as promoters of participation because of their representativeness in society and their ability to channel grassroots demands (Friedrich 2011), the requirements on civil society are very different from those related to the ability of organisations to speak up for causes in the public sphere (Buth 2011). This is why it is significant to discover an evolution of the emphasis of

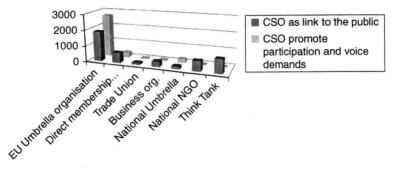

Figure 3.4   Position on role of CSO by type of organisation (number of words coded)

Note: In order to visualise the differences better, this graph represents the number of words coded instead of the number of organisations referring to one of the aspects.

organisations in each of these dimensions. These distinctions deserve some qualitative exploration, in that they suggest an evolution in the justificatory rationale provided by organisations for their role.

The argument that organisations can play an important role in raising awareness about EU policies among the public is often used to justify a closer relation between them and institutions. However, this argument is built in a very abstract way, which tends to draw a direct equivalence between the presence of civil society organisations in policy dialogue and debate between organisations from different countries and increased interest of public opinion for EU affairs:

> As the Commission has itself acknowledged, "European citizens have little sense of ownership over the structures that govern their lives". ("Shaping the new Europe", COM 2000, 154). NGOs help to **reduce the gap between the governing and the governed** by awareness raising with the public concerning the purpose, policies, and actions of the European Union (Social Platform 2001:3)[1]

These arguments resonate so strongly with some of the arguments in the literature that were reviewed in the previous chapter (Armstrong 2002; Eder and Trenz 2004; Steffek and Nanz 2008) about civil society's ability to bring the EU closer to its citizens that it has been suggested that academic thinking had an influence in this agenda-setting process (Saurugger 2010). Few organisations mention specific mechanisms, such as the ability of organisations to provide information to their members (EFC) or their contribution to communication on EU affairs (Polish Office):

> The role of civil society organisations as *facilitators* of information flow on EU policy should be encouraged. Foundations themselves have acted as information and dialogue facilitators to help address and devise effective responses to social, environmental, educational, scientific and economic challenges facing European citizens. (European Foundation Centre 2002: 2)

> The Office made a translation of the White Paper into Polish available to Polish non-governmental organisations (NGOs) last summer. It also elaborated a summary and brief comments, especially regarding those sections that concern civil society or are relevant to the concerns of NGOs in Poland. Our interest in this topic is an extension of the work of Poland's NGOs to improve the manner in which its citizens live and are governed. (Polish NGO Office in Brussels (Undated document: 1))

In this sense, it is noticeable that organisations tend to introduce the claim that they can contribute to raising awareness among the public without further elaboration of the ways in which this can happen. Furthermore, the fact that none of the organisations argued about their contribution to the public sphere in the consultations suggests that this idea is not at the core of their self-conceptions. Interviews seem to suggest that what organisations mean is that they are bringing in a new perspective based on their expertise and on members' concern rather than contributing to a generalising of the debate among their members or the media. It is even suggested that this is not the role of civil society. This approach seems to be linked to the issue of whether and how organisations represent their members when engaging in policy discussions.

The evolution of these two dimensions shows that the frames evolve according to the forum addressed and the Commission's civil society agenda. The idea that civil society organisations are able to communicate with the European public, which was not present in 1997, was strongly formulated in the wake of the emphasis given to communication weaknesses that followed the resignation of the Santer Commission (Bastin 2002; Georgakakis 2004), whereas the subsequent change of focus indicates that civil society organisations endorse the White Paper on Governance and the Laeken declaration participatory overtones. In this sense organisations seem to accept a stronger role in claiming to be vehicles for citizens' participation and contributing to the formation of the EU's general interest, rather than merely being voices in a pluralistic setting. These roles have some distinctive features in terms of internal democracy requirements which actors must fulfil (Halpin and McLaverty 2010, 58–61), and these are examined in the following section.

Characteristics of legitimate actors

The frame on the role of civil society in the EU also serves to introduce proposals about the characteristics that make the consultation of actors by EU institutions legitimate. This debate is also characterised by an evolution along the time frame and a significant shift during the Convention. In the previous fora the debate focused on the definition of civil society and which groups should be consulted. This is quite a heated and detailed debate, where all the organisations put forward their own characteristics as those of a legitimate actor (Michel 2007).

Figure 3.5 shows that issues related to the definition of civil society disappear in the wake of the Convention, whereas the main legitimacy factor of civil society organisations becomes their ability to represent their members or causes, although significant differences remain between different types of organisations. The following paragraphs analyse the evolution of each of these variables.

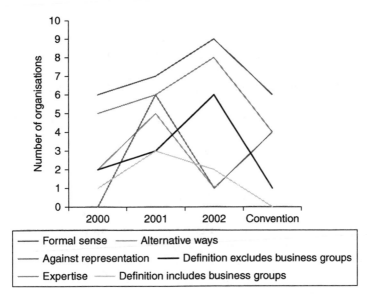

Figure 3.5 Number of organisations referring to characteristics of legitimate actors

Expertise

This is one of the rare places where the conceptions of different organisations coincide. Both citizens' organisations and business groups say that civil society organisations can contribute to the policymaking process by providing specialised knowledge in a particular field. Furthermore, this is explicitly formulated by many organisations as a necessary criterion for participating in consultations and policy dialogues, being implicit for almost all the organisations. Interestingly, this is one of the topics referred to more than once by the same organisation, as up to five organisations repeatedly formulated the point. Although there is a slight decline during the Convention, the turn towards participatory democracy does not challenge the consensus that civil society organisations contribute to the quality of European policymaking thanks to their independent expertise. Interviews reveal that the notion of expertise is not limited to technical knowledge but also encompasses grassroots experiences.

> We know that we have a very precious expertise which is unique, and we, you know that there is all these associations in Brussels working with marginal, undocumented people. (Interview 3, with a representative of the Social Platform)

The centrality of expertise suggests that there is not a complete turn towards an input-legitimacy oriented system but rather an adaptation of existing mechanisms to different purposes. Civil society organisations do not challenge the "dominant ethos of the institutionalised European project as it has developed historically: an ethos that rewards cost-benefit analysis, the professionalism of lobbyists, the quality of the information that these provide to policy-makers and an ability to address policy issues systematically and technically" (Ruzza 2004, 7).

Representation

The idea that organisations represent their members remains stable during the process, with a very strong peak in 2002 (see Figure 3.4). However, the ability of civil society organisations to represent their members is a contentious issue. Questions of representation and representativeness convey alternative conceptions of the role of civil society organisations in a democracy and have important practical implications.

As the idea of the creation of civil dialogue is advanced, the Commission points out that, since the participants will have to be selected beforehand, a criterion for deciding who should be consulted would have to be elaborated. In this respect, it suggests that organisations participating in consultations should be representative.

The best evidence for the difficulty that many NGOs find in taking sides is provided by the changes of position of the Social Platform, from its initial argument in favour of alternative criteria in 2000 to its openness to discuss this criterion in 2001, as appears in the quotes below:

> However, the Commission uses the term "representativeness" with relation to NGOs on several occasions throughout the document, particularly in section 2.2. Whilst the Platform agrees that *geographical* representativeness is an important feature for European NGOs, it is not the role of NGOs to act as elected representatives, but to advance the interests of their constituencies. The term "representativeness", when applied to NGOs, thus seems ambiguous because their "representativeness" is primarily qualitative: it is deep-rooted in the nature of the relationships established by NGOs on the ground. NGOs promote minority needs and opinion, giving the means of expression to some of the "voiceless" within society, and even advancing the interests of those whom by reason of various handicaps (intellectual, cultural, or other forms of marginalisation and exclusion) need advocates to defend their interests and needs. The Platform therefore prefers to emphasise the need for transparency in the functioning of NGOs. A real transparency permits a knowledge of who is representing people, groups, actors and ideas. It should be the right of minority groups to be represented by the NGO of their choice. (Social Platform 2000: 5)

> We therefore propose that the Secretariat General of the Commission should, together with European NGOs, examine the criteria applied in relation to NGOs in the framework of the structured civil dialogue, with regard to representativeness, transparency, accountability, and track-record. (Social Platform 2001: 5)

There is a clear move towards accepting the notion of representativeness by citizens' interest groups. This is related among other things to the high political salience of the Convention, which was underpinned by a referendum as final outcome. Since the aim of the Convention was to bring citizens closer to the EU, the "force of numbers" becomes one of the most determinant strengths of organisations during the Convention, as expressed in these two quotes:

> MILLIONS of Europeans represented by our organisations would appreciate it if the European Convention finds the missing articles and integrates them into Article 8 of the new European Constitution.

This contribution represents the views and aspirations of millions of people in Europe and we call on each individual member of the Convention to listen to these voices as they begin to discuss their **priorities for the future of Europe**. (Social Platform 2002b: 2)

That said, in these quotes organisations are not claiming to have received a mandate from their members authorising them to represent their constituency at EU level, as the social partners would demand, but simply to stand for the interests of citizens and convey causes at EU level. The idea that civil society brings the EU closer to its citizens by bringing causes and interests to the attention of EU institutions (Steffek and Nanz 2008) gains weight throughout the process. It thus appears that civil society organisations do not formally represent citizens or categories of the population, but that they are representative of their expectations (Kohler-Koch 2010a).

These quotes are therefore interesting examples of how organisations claim to be representative without necessarily arguing to represent their members, but rather some sort of social representativeness beyond their own organisations. This is interesting since it is related to the difficulty of linking participation and representation at EU level, because most European organisations have difficulties in providing evidence of regular involvement of their members in decision making (Friedrich 2011). The tensions between participation and representation mandate versus independence, and different conceptions of the role of a representative and formalistic versus descriptive or symbolic notions, can be addressed with reference to the discussion about these dimensions by Hannah Pitkin (1972).

The notion that organisations have to be representative of and able to consult a European constituency conveys the idea that representation is the result of a formalised authorisation from members, and is strongly linked with ideas that organisations have to be in touch with their members and actively consult them before responding to consultations, thus approximating the position of organisations to that of a delegate. On the other hand it is equally suggested that such an approach marginalises organisations that stand for causes or constituencies which cannot cast a mandate (Greenwood and Halpin 2007; Halpin and McLaverty 2010) because they are weak or are an idea or a cause. In this sense ideas of representation tend to imply that organisations standing for nature or the rights of marginal people have to act as trustees, thus defining by themselves the interests of such a constituency. The preference of most European organisations for this conception of representation before the

Convention is related to their insistence on the importance of expertise that was discussed above. Pitkin points out that "the more a theorist sees political issues as questions of knowledge, to which it is possible to find correct, objectively valid answers, the more inclined he will be to regard the representative as an expert and to find the opinion of the constituency irrelevant. If political issues are like scientific or even mathematical problems, it is foolish to try to solve them by counting noses in the constituency" (Pitkin 1972, 211).

Arguments that organisations contributing to participatory mechanisms have to be representative are founded on the fact that otherwise participation is limited to the persons who actually take part in the process on behalf of an organisation that does not have an actual linkage to members. In this sense, accepting representativeness criteria can be a way of stressing ownership over the consultation process of EU groups, the only representative organisations in the geographical sense at EU level (Greenwood and Halpin 2007).

It seems that the evolution of the frame from the representation of particular constituencies to the representation of general causes and interests in a more politically salient environment contributed to the evolution of the organisations' framing of the issue, making them more likely to accept the idea that they represent their members in a formal sense.

Economic versus general interest groups and European versus national organisations

Before the Convention the most contentious topic within this variable, regarding both the number of references and in relation to the differences in opinions, concerned the question of whether organisations representing economic interests should be included in the definition of civil society, and thus be involved in the civil society consultation mechanisms and given the same institutional recognition sought by citizens' organisations. It must also be noted that the Commission's approach seems to leave several organisations unsatisfied, in that it appears to give precedence to NGOs and non-economic interests without really excluding business groups or trade unions. Even today the Commission does not adhere to any definition when carrying out consultations[2]. Whereas it is true that some academics include economic life in the civil society sphere (Pérez Díaz 1994b), this can be related as well to a strategy of reframing interest representation as civil society for legitimisation purposes (Saurugger 2007).

Business organisations, UEAPME, Eurocommerce and Unice, repeatedly rejected their eventual exclusion from consultations, which should gather all relevant stakeholders. In this sense, as we will see later, they insist on the relevance of expertise as the main characteristic of a legitimate partner of EU institutions. On the other hand, almost all citizens' interests organisations insist that the working definition of civil society to be used when deciding who should be consulted should be limited to groups promoting a cause or general interest, or being part of the third sector[3]. Interestingly, although the number of references is very high, here again there are few organisations referring systematically to this topic. These contending definitions were almost always followed by proposals of alternative criteria and characteristics that should be met by organisations.

However, at the time of the Convention the attention shifts and there are virtually no references to the topic. When one considers the change of venue that the Convention signified this is less surprising than initially implied. This topic is at the core of the debates between the organisations and the Commission, since the focus of these consultations consisted of how to organise the existing practice (Greenwood 2007a, 44; Pérez Solórzano-Borragán 2007). However, the Convention was a more political forum and thus not suited for a detailed debate about the notion of European civil society but rather for a discussion about the broad contribution of civil society to European integration. In this sense, the organisations left the debate about the definition and the characteristics of legitimate partners on "stand by", in order to concentrate on the principles and recognition.

The question about the role that national organisations are to play is a detailed one but it provides interesting data for analysing the organisations' discourse and objectives. At the beginning of the period under consideration, the group of organisations involved for a longer time in the promotion of civil dialogue were either not concerned about this (CEDAG, CONCORD) or opposed to it (Social Platform and COFACE), with the only exception being the EFC. This may appear to be an attempt by Brussels-based groups to centralise the dialogue. However, their position changed, and after 2002 all these organisations supported the principle that local and national organisations should have their say in EU level consultations, whereas there were only two sceptical references coming from business organisations.

This suggests, as was the case regarding citizens' direct participation, that framing has an effect on the strategy of organisations because of the bridging and amplification effect. In this sense using the frame on participatory democracy to promote the institutionalisation of civil society consultation has the consequence that it becomes difficult for organisations to reject issues which are strongly linked with this frame, such as the idea of inclusiveness (Parés 2009; Smith 2009). That said, the evolution registered is even more relevant, since organisations argue in favour of inclusiveness rather than abstaining from opposing it. This is probably a manifestation of a certain degree of control by national organisations, or at least of the awareness by European organisations that strategically they still need to be able to act as access doors to EU institutions for their members.

Conception and role of participatory democracy in the EU

This section analyses how civil society organisations have justified the need to be involved in the policymaking process and how the notion of participatory democracy came to the fore. It must be noted that in most contributions this term is not explicit until a late stage of the agenda-setting process, in particular until the White Paper on Governance (European Commission 2001), despite the use of "participatory democracy" by the Commission in the 2000 discussion paper. Thus, this section approaches the conception of participatory democracy firstly by analysing the justifications that organisations provide for consultation of civil society organisations and secondly by exploring the emergence of a more general frame for participation and participatory democracy.

Political justification of civil society consultation

Figure 3.6 shows that organisations have provided alternative justifications for their participation in EU policymaking via consultation.

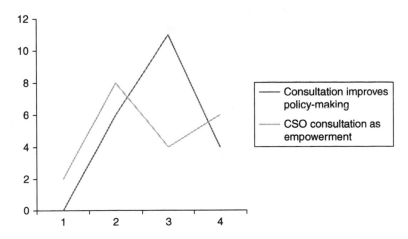

Figure 3.6 Number of organisations referring to rationale for consultation

In conceptual terms these are clearly distinct proposals. The idea that participation improves policymaking corresponds to an output legitimacy approach, whereas the consideration that participation directly makes the EU more legitimate corresponds to an input legitimacy rationale, to use Scharpf's (1999) typology. It also suggests that justifications in terms of input legitimacy were also made independently of the participatory democracy frame. Finally, the graph clearly shows the ductility of the frame: organisations adapt their arguments to the venue and the institution (Princen 2009), in that the White Paper on governance and the Convention are more oriented towards input legitimacy (Monaghan 2007, 27–28) whereas the 2002 consultation is essentially about how to use external contributions to improve policymaking.

Civil society arguments that they help European institutions to improve policymaking suggest that they provide the Commission with grassroots experience of the policy field and a measure of expertise which is not always available for EU civil servants (Greenwood 2011b). This topic is strongly correlated to arguments that a degree of expertise is one of the legitimacy thresholds to be met by any organisation, an argument that is shared by all the business organisations and also made by citizens' groups which are active in policy implementation or technical fields. In this sense, it is not participation per se which makes the EU more legitimate, but the quality of the input to the policymaking process that is made by civil society organisations. The evolution of this topic, peaking in the 2002 consultation on minimal rules of consultation and then decreasing in the wake of the Convention, suggests that there is a general politicisation of the frame evolving towards a justification of civil society involvement in a participatory perspective.

On the other hand, the majority of organisations consider that the consultation of civil society organisations makes the EU more legitimate, as it helps it to be in touch with citizens' concerns. This topic has much support, as it is uttered by up to eight organisations in the 2001 consultation on governance with no group against it (see CSO consultation as empowerment in Annexes 7 and 8). That said, this strong emergence in 2001 and in the Convention is certainly linked to the political nature of these debates, whereas the frequency of this topic is lower in the previous and following consultations. As additional evidence for the importance of the Commission's influence on the discourse of these organisations, it appears that as late as 2000 a group such as the Social Platform did not refer to the contribution that civil society consultation made to the legitimacy of the EU. A majority of organisations, including business groups such as Eurocommerce or UNICE, consider that their participation in consultation has a political nature as well and may contribute to making the EU more legitimate, although this position is clearly influenced by the venue in which it is formulated.

However, the most relevant feature regarding the content of this variable is that even during the Convention organisations tended to formulate the expectation that their involvement would directly make the EU more legitimate, without necessarily framing this as participatory democracy. This has two significant implications. The first is that the participatory democracy frame was not unanimous among civil society, although as will be seen it became the most frequent justification during the Convention. Secondly, it implies that elaborating the notion of participatory democracy is a clear form of frame bridging (Snow et al. 1986). By arguing that their involvement could contribute to bringing the EU closer to its citizens, organisations created the context where their participation could be characterised as a democratic mechanism.

Conceptions of participation

The previous section showed that during the entire process organisations have sought to provide political justification for their participation in the policymaking process via consultation. The evolution of the demands on civil dialogue, one of the most recurrent notions in the agenda of citizens' organisations, is quite telling about the way in which organisations reframed their demands as participatory democracy devices. Although the demands to create a specific procedure for dialogue with civil society remain stable (see the next section), Figure 3.6 shows a clear evolution in the justification rationale. References to the original notion of "civil dialogue" decline and civil society consultation emerges as a form of participation at the same time as there is a consolidation of the participatory democracy frame and a strong emergence of proposals focusing on direct participation by citizens rather than organisations. In this sense, the collective construction of the notion of participatory democracy, which started before the Convention (Saurugger 2010), is clearly influential in the reframing of the organisations' demands. This section examines in detail how the process of bridging civil society participation and democracy occurred.

Civil dialogue

The notion of civil dialogue has been on the agenda since the first discussions in 1996 and 1997 about how to build a stronger relation between civil society organisations and EU institutions, yet it is enormously ambiguous (Fazi and Smith 2006). On the one hand, in the most limited interpretation it may just mean any dialogue between civil society and EU institutions. On the other hand, the most ambitious version considers it as a form of formalised dialogue (similar to social dialogue) on political and horizontal issues, and not just on the thematic questions addressed in dialogue with particular Directorates-General. This distinction is clear for the officials as well, as this quote from an official of the EESC makes clear:

> You have the so-called horizontal civil dialogue and the sector-specific civil dialogue sector, that's two different issues. (Interview 20, with a representative of the EESC)

Although the organisations do not always make their claims explicit, the content of their demands implies that they propose the creation of a stable framework for direct dialogue between organisations and the Commission, thus going beyond ad hoc consultation:

> European NGOs welcome Romano Prodi's recognition of the value of civil society to Europe. However although it is unquestioned that we are an important part of the economy and have found ways of making our voices heard, we would argue that it would be more correct to say that we participate in the organisation of society, rather than being involved in the running of society. We believe that the development of good government necessitates the full participation of its citizens at all stages, and the establishment of a structured dialogue between organised civil society and the different levels of government. Such a structured civil dialogue should not detract from the importance of the political dialogue, nor from the necessity of taking action to strengthen political structures and institutions. (Social Platform 2001: 5)

Despite its ambiguous content, civil dialogue seems to encompass all the demands by citizens' interest groups for a secure access to institutions, and it is thus at the core of their demands:

> The importance of **formalising the dialogue between civil society and the EU** institutions by including an article guaranteeing the legal basis for such a *"Civil dialogue"* in the next Treaty of the European Union, through a Council Regulation or some other appropriate legal instrument. It is likely and appropriate that the dialogue will take different forms from sector to sector, but the general principle should

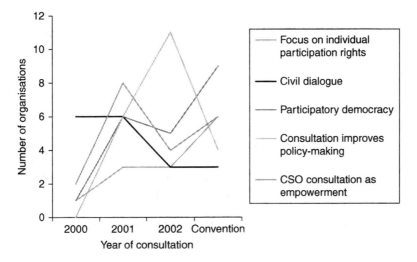

Figure 3.7 Rationales of civil society participation

be established as a formal requirement in policy areas. (Liaison Committee of Development NGOs to the European Union, 2000: 2)

The documental analysis provides good evidence that organisations aim to promote this topic. After 2002 a number of organisations insisted that consultation was not just a formal exercise to be carried out to improve the legitimacy of the EU (Fazi and Smith 2006, 48–49) but must provide them with opportunities to significantly influence the policymaking process. This implies that organisations perceived consultation as a politically important stage for the Commission, in that the Commission would tend to consult civil society in order to obtain legitimacy but also try to deny political influence to organisations. They thus requested the Commission to consult before taking any definitive decision, which appears to be an explicit recognition that organisations are above all seeking political influence.

Civil dialogue is thus a recurrent demand by the organisations that have been involved for a longer time in the debate and one that, unlike other demands, creates a degree of disagreement among organisations. It is present in all the papers of the Social Platform, the European Foundation Centre and CEDAG from 1997 until the Convention. Additionally, it is supported by nine organisations at different moments, and rejected by four business organisations, in particular on the grounds that the uncertain representativeness of NGOs makes them unable to claim a status as social partners. This position is close to that of EU institutions, which have insisted on the importance of representativeness criteria, as expressed in this quote:

> If you want to influence the course of European development or of European integration generally, that's what horizontal civil dialogue is about [...] and if you want to do so as an organisation this organisation must have some legitimacy for being able to influence the course they want to give to European integration. And that's very different from the Social Platform approach which is "let every organisation do as they want". (Interview 20, with a representative of the EESC)

This suggests that institutions see the need to agree with institutionalising civil dialogue, but that this must be done according to traditional procedures. This means that civil society organisations accept representativeness as part of the process of building consensus on civil dialogue.

Whereas the core of the demand remains stable and is shared by a number of organisations, it is worth noting that the way in which it is formulated has evolved. In the first stage (1996–2000) the Social Platform, the main actor here, formulates it as a way in which to improve social policies, without linking it to the EU's legitimacy. It is only in 2001, when the Commission expresses a need to reinforce its legitimacy, that civil society consultation appears in the civil society organisations' discourse as a way in which to give citizens a greater say in EU policies, as appears in Figure 3.6, with the strong increase in the number of references to civil dialogue in order to bring citizens closer to the EU. The Convention appears to be a further step in this reframing process, since references to the need for a structured dialogue remain at the core; but this is no longer called "civil dialogue", rather being formulated as a mechanism of participatory democracy.

Civil society consultation as participatory democracy

Figure 3.6 clearly shows that, despite the reference to participatory democracy in the Commission's 2000 paper (European Commission 2000, 4), organisations do not really start using this notion until late in the process. General references during the Convention to the need of a bigger role for citizens are very interesting in that they suggest that whereas the need for more participation by citizens was clearly on the agenda in the wake of the Laeken declaration, the notion of participatory democracy is clearly a specific frame used more frequently by specialised organisations.

Beyond the use of the notion of participatory democracy, it is relevant that organisations reframe their demand to be consulted as a form of citizens' empowerment. This quote from CEDAG's paper to the Convention is a good example of this evolution:

> One element of this participation is civil dialogue between European institutions and the organisations of civil society since citizens express themselves through the organisations in which they are active. (CEDAG 2003, 1)

This evolution is consistent with that reported in the previous section regarding evolution towards an increased insistence on the importance of civil society organisations as promoters of participation rather than as promoters of debates. It thus appears that civil society organisations adapted different aspects of their discourse to the emergent frame on participatory democracy as a response to the EU legitimacy deficit that EU institutions articulated at the turn of the century (Saurugger 2010).

Although several civil society organisations mention that civil society consultation is a way in which citizens may be brought close to the EU (Figure 3.6), most only elaborate on the idea that this mechanism is a form of participatory democracy after 2001. There may be two reasons for this. Firstly, since participatory democracy is an emergent topic, civil society organisations need some time to include it in their discourse. In this sense the evolution towards participatory democracy is more profound than it seems, in that civil dialogue focuses on the *participation* of civil society's Brussels offices, whereas considering this as a mechanism of participation by citizens would imply that civil society organisation themselves have a participatory structure and represent their members, which is difficult if we take into account organisations' initial reluctance to consider themselves as representatives of their members and critical empirical assessments of their relations with their members (Sudbery 2003). The difficulty that the Social Platform had in assuming participatory democracy, which does not appear in its papers until April 2002, is very telling of the difficulty of bridging the frames of civil society participation and the need for stronger participation by citizens:

> Now we are reviewing that, because we wonder how that comes with participatory democracy, but I think that's a different idea, participatory democracy with civil dialogue, I don't know, we have to define it. So we still have to adopt our position in our general assembly this year, and I think we still continue to use civil dialogue, because we see civil dialogue, we love participatory democracy a lot, and if

you see in the Convention it's participatory democracy, in the sense of opening up a kind of participatory processes where you bring all stakeholders together, it's not civil dialogue, it's more participatory democracy, I don't know, maybe we are...Do you know the distinction between participatory democracy and civil dialogue? (Interview 3, with a representative of the Social Platform)

This quote, as well as Interview 27 (CEDAG), confirms that the difficulty in assuming the enlargement of the frame is related to the fact that civil society organisations consider they have a bigger say in civil dialogue than participatory democracy, which is open to more actors and includes different procedures, such as the European Citizens Initiative (ECI).

The second reason why the frame of participatory democracy was particularly used during the White Paper on Governance and the Convention is certainly the higher political salience of these venues (Monaghan 2007; Princen 2009, on the importance of this variable in the EU). In this sense, there is a clear evolution from a series of discussions dominated by an administrative reform frame (Michel 2007) to more politicised venues. It is clear that participatory democracy as a policy proposal is congruent with the problem identification of the previous consultations and the Laeken declaration, and it was also pushed by institutional actors. In this sense the opportunities for frame bridging in terms of ideological closeness were clearly present, and the Convention was a window of opportunity for raising civil dialogue's profile as it would be enshrined in a Treaty article.

Citizens' participation rights

Finally, it is very interesting to point out that there is a small but significant increase in the number of references to forms of direct participation by citizens rather than participation through civil society organisations. Whereas before the Convention only three groups (ECAS, the European Foundation Centre and the European Environment Bureau) argued in favour of the recognition of participatory mechanisms, such as initiative rights or a right to receive information being a right of European citizens and not a prerogative of organisations, this kind of demand became more frequent among organisations that were actively promoting "civil dialogue" during the Convention:

> In its paper, ECAS advocated a "right to be heard based on citizenship, of which all NGO's, as organizations of citizens would take advantage". (ECAS undated: 1)

This is a clear amplification of the frame (Snow et al. 1986, 469), in that use of the frame of participatory democracy offered opportunities to introduce a series of ideas traditionally associated with it. However, it is noticeable that the only individual direct participation right recognised by the Convention, the ECI, was the result of a campaign by two organisations, the Initiative and Referendum Institute – Europe and Mehr Demokratie (Lamassoure 2004; del Río Villar 2004; Clerck-Sachsse 2011), two organisations which had not previously taken part in the agenda-setting process.

Overall, the emergence of the participatory democracy frame is very significant, in that despite the stability of the demands (see following section) the justificatory frame evolves from a focus on the legitimacy of civil society and its ability to contribute to better policymaking, via the notion of civil dialogue, to a focus on participatory democracy which concentrates on the importance of bringing the EU closer to citizens, where organisations are an interface with those citizens. In this sense it is clearly a process of frame bridging (Snow et al. 1986, 469), where the previously bureaucratic oriented tools (Kohler-Koch and Finke 2007) are identified with mechanisms of democracy and participation. This evolution is the result of the politicisation of the venues and serves to bypass rejection by some business organisations. In addition, it facilitates the expression of demands focusing on direct participation by citizens. Ruzza argues that frame bridging can arise as a result of "low intensity modifications and re-definitions of policy discourses in which cross-fertilisation occurs between political institutions (and this is typically the case of consensus formation)" or as responses to crises (Ruzza 2004, 151). In this case it is clearly the result of a consensus construction process, where the demands from organisations are adopted by the political system as a response to a different objective from its original one.

Evolution of the frame in relation to the institutional agenda

There is a clear evolution regarding the conception of civil society and its contribution to European integration. In the initial discourse organisations put forward a particularistic claim in which civil society stands for marginal interests or causes in which organisations' main contribution to the policymaking process is their expertise. This then moves to a much broader understanding of civil society organisations as promoters of the general concerns and values of citizens and their representation of millions of people across Europe (del Río Villar 2004, 281, 283). That said, this chapter has shown that the discourse and practices of organisations continue to be highly influenced by the importance of expertise, which is the dominant ethos in the close contacts between EU institutions and external interests (Ruzza 2004; Balme and Chabanet 2008). This is clearly one of the legacies of the origins of the existing mechanisms, and is seen to be a way of improving policymaking rather than promoting participation.

The importance of the frame setting process could be challenged with insights into the organisational questions of European civil society organisations, in particular by pointing to the importance of turnover in organisations' staff. It is quite well known that one of the effects of the expertise required by European civil society organisations is that their qualified personnel usually take on better remunerated opportunities after a few years, or consider work in civil society organisations to continue their career in Brussels (Baisnée 2007; Greenwood 2011c). In this sense it could be argued that it is difficult to see a clear continuity in organisations' frames, and the evolution of discourses could be related to internal organisational change. However, although this may be true, this chapter has shown that evolution in organisations' demands and framing tend to happen collectively; that is, framing processes tend to be aligned. Furthermore, interviews have shown that turnover in the Convention does not substantially affect mid to senior positions, and that these moves tend to happen among organisations in the same coalition, which may contribute to the circulation of the frame rather than to its instability.

Regarding the second variable, notions of participation, it appears that the use of the notion of participatory democracy to qualify organisations' own proposals, in particular civil dialogue, is strongly influenced by the Commission's position in this respect. Hence organisations include a contribution to the EU's legitimacy as an additional virtue of their core position on civil society consultation, whose previous justification was its contribution to a more social union and better policymaking, thus contributing to the EU's output legitimacy (Scharpf 1999).

It appears that when organisations refer to participatory democracy they mean civil dialogue to a very large extent. It has been highlighted that this was a way of bridging the institutions' problem identification (democracy) with a policy proposal by civil society and their allies in institutions (civil society consultation). In this sense the most notable discursive evolution is the formulation of civil dialogue, to a large extent using an existing mechanism (Pérez Solórzano-Borragán 2007) as a new model of participatory democracy. The imprecise focus of such dialogue (Fazi and Smith 2006) contributes to its generalisation (Ruzza 2004, 57–58 on the contribution of ambiguity to the generalisation of frames; Milton and Keller-Noëllet 2005, 48–49 as an example of how this happened with regard to the usage of the word Constitution by the Convention). However, presenting civil society consultation as a way of citizens' participation can be problematic from a normative perspective. It can be considered as a form of indirect participation, inasmuch as organisations represent their members. However, if these organisations consider that they are just contributing their expertise, it appears that civil dialogue is an extremely elitist conception of participatory democracy, where only the Brussels-based specialists actually participate (Kohler-Koch 2010b). Interestingly this is precisely the way in which the frame evolved, as organisations integrated claims that they represented their members, and citizens in general, into their discourse despite their original rejection of this.

Thus by promoting participatory democracy organisations put forward the demand that civil society organisations should be given a more important role in the EU, distinct from that of social partners and other lobby groups and with a horizontal and political nature. On the other hand, even if proposals for citizens' direct participation rights were not totally absent from these organisations' proposals, IRI, the organisation that managed to convince convention members that they should include the citizens' initiative in the Treaty (IRI 2004; Lamassoure 2004; del Río Villar 2004), had not been involved at all in the agenda-setting process.

As for the third variable, the organisations associated with the Social Platform and the CSCG to a large extent shared a discourse about the way in which the institutional profile of civil society organisations had to be promoted. The most distinctive feature of this discourse was the inclusion of a legal base, making it mandatory for EU institutions to consult civil society organisations. Such dialogue was to take place early in the policymaking cycle and consist of meetings with decision-making officials. As a consequence, these organisations strongly rejected the possibility of holding this dialogue at the EESC. Additionally, and after some hesitation, they considered that such dialogue should be open to national organisations.

It is noticeable that almost all the organisations agreed on the need to structure relations between institutions and civil society organisations and used this as a chance to promote their own profile. Although the central demand of institutionalising civil society consultation is not unanimously shared, and has even met some opposition, it was easily taken on board by the Commission and the Convention itself. However, it is necessary to analyse how this frame was put on the Convention's agenda, as it cannot be simply assumed that the "time of the idea had come" (Kingdon 2003), in particular because of the change of venue. It can be deduced that it was the result of the advocacy of civil society organisations coinciding with the new discourse of the Commission, where transparency and governance are the new keywords.

However, the opposition to civil dialogue can build on one of the critical aspects of the civil society organisations' discourse on which the organisations appear unable to reach a compromise: the representativeness of organisations involved in civil dialogue. Although it has not been thoroughly discussed here, this may be one of the reasons why the article on consultation (11 TUE) does not grant these organisations the privileged role that they were seeking, as it engages EU institutions to consult "representative associations and civil society", thus possibly allowing for the existence of diverse forms of consultation (see Chapters 4 and 5).

This chapter has shown that citizens' interests organisations were active in promoting and institutionalising their own influence, and protecting it from the "attacks" of social partners and (especially) business organisations. This is clearly evidenced by the structure of the organisations' discourse: whereas there is a clear evolution towards the participatory democracy frame in relation to the conception of civil society and the political justification of consultation, it is strongly coherent and subject to few changes in relation to the third variable; that is, the ways in which the role of civil society organisations should be institutionalised.

Qualitative analysis confirms the expectations relating to the ductility of organisations' discursive strategies: organisations are successful in adapting the frame of their discourses without substantially modifying their demands in relation to their role in the EU. However, organisations' influence strategies are remarkably stable in the time frame considered. In this sense, with very few exceptions, it appears that organisations preferred insider strategies, basically consisting of participation in structured consultation processes and lobbying of officials, with the exception of the red card campaign in 1998 (Alhadeff and Wilson 2002). Chapter 4 examines whether the Convention provided an opportunity to use a different repertoire of action.

The finding that organisations adapt their frames to the Commission's, albeit emphasising demands for access, is very similar to that of Ruzza (2007, 56) for three different advocacy coalitions. This does not mean that these results are generalisable per se but it also suggests that they are not merely a sample effect. It thus appears that these debates reproduce a common practice in the field of the Commission – civil society relations; that is, organisations perceive that possibilities for access and influence come with meeting institutions' expectations rather than confronting them.

4
Networking and Alliances

Analysing the field of organisations active in the debate about civil society institutionalisation

Figure 4.1 represents the relationships between the organisations that are considered in this book. The graph provides a number of relevant observations. Firstly, the almost complete connection of the network may be noted; that is, there is only one sub-component consisting of regional organisations, suggesting that despite the great diversity of organisations in terms of policy area (business, trade unions, social, environmental, regional, etc.) the organisations involved in the discussion on participatory democracy were regularly in touch because of their interest in the same topic. The existence of this shared interest and a system allowing regular relations suggest that exchanges between these organisations on the subject of civil society participation can be characterised as an organisational field. Figure 4.1 confirms the existence of regular exchanges and mutual awareness, and significantly that these links were established despite the strong diversity of interests and goals. The following section analyses the objectives and motivations of organisations in order to understand what was at stake in these exchanges.

Figure 4.1 reveals very significant differences in patterns of cooperation and competition, which suggests "sharply defined inter-organizational structures of domination and patterns of coalition" (DiMaggio and Powell 1991, 61). The graph portrays a clear core of organisations in the centre of the graph intensely communicating with each other and a periphery comprising those that were sceptical or opposed to the frame of participatory democracy, mainly business and regional organisations. It is noticeable that the latter are weakly connected to the rest of the

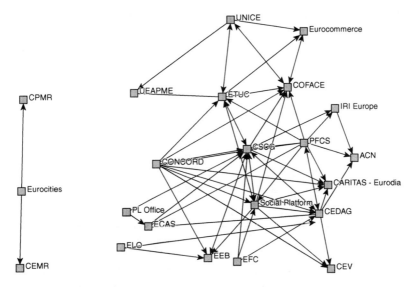

Figure 4.1 Network relations

network. This suggests that they were outside the main coalition and that they occupied a different position in the organisational field. This means that the process which has been analysed configured a space of regular exchange between organisations linked by a common interest, the definition of norms of access to the EU institutions, despite different strategies and stakes in the process.

Alliances and frame convergence

Figure 4.1 demonstrates that the field is characterised by a strong exchange of information among its participants. Given the under-standing of framing as a strategic use of discourse for collective action, it is necessary to ask whether participation in alliances played a role in the circulation of frames on participatory democracy. As has already been suggested in Chapter 3, demands for the institutionalisation of consultation are strongly articulated by members of the CSCG and the Social Platform. Table 4.1 shows that 74% of references to the need for a legal base for civil society dialogue come from members of these organi-sations, with a very significant salience of the Social Platform. At the level of individual organisations, the Social Platform, CEDAG, COFACE,

Table 4.1 Alliance membership of organisations demanding a legal base for consultation

	No coalition	CSCG	Social Platform	ERC	Regional organisations
Number of references per organisation	EFC (8), PFCS (4), ECAS (2), LDH (3), UEAPME (1),	SOCIAL PLATFORM (23), CONCORD (6), CSCG (4), ETUC (2), EEB (3)	CEDAG (9), COFACE (7), CARITAS – EURODIACONIA (5), CEV (1)	ACN (1)	CPRM (2)
Number of references	18	38	22	1	2
Percentage of total (81 references)	22.2%	46.9%	27.1%	1.3%	2.5%

CONCORD and Caritas – Eurodiaconia stand out. The EFC stands out as the only organisation intensely making this point without being a member of the coalition.

The strong correspondence between demands and membership in a coalition confirms the importance of alliances in the agenda-setting process for collective action. The quote below from CEV's position paper for the 2000 consultation process confirms the importance of the agenda-setting process for exchanges of opinion that contribute to the circulation of collective demands:

> Like CEDAG and the European Foundation Centre we believe that the NGO sector should be recognised as a social partner alongside employers and trade unions. [...] We recommend that the Commission take an approach that builds upon the Amsterdam Treaty, and that it comes out in support of a Treaty Amendment. (CEV Response to the discussion paper 'European Commission and Non-Governmental Organisations: Building A Stronger Partnership', April 2000, 3)

Analysing the broader context is also useful in understanding the importance of coalitions. From 1997 to 2002 the context of the discussions is similar; that is, a consultation based on a communication or discussion paper from the Commission. That said, the tendency is towards a significant increase in the number of contributions to each consultation. Whereas only five European organisations were involved in the 1997 discussion (Social Platform, EFC, CEDAG, CEV and CMAF), the

Table 4.2 Number of civil society organisations contributing to each consultation process[1]

	1997	2000	2001	2002	Convention
Total	5	37	225	65	528

Note: [1]The Commission documents for its consultations (Kværk 2007, 161) for the Convention. Obviously the Convention position papers do not only refer to participatory democracy.

Commission received several dozen contributions for the consultation on the White Paper on Governance. Table 4.2 shows the general increase in the number of contributions.

The organisations promoting civil dialogue, whose contributions are the oldest ones, reacted to this tendency by trying to foster their cooperation. The clearest evidence is the creation of the Civil Society Contact Group (CSCG) ahead of the European Convention. The CSCG was an important actor in framing the unity of civil society behind demands about consultation. On the other hand, and contrary to the wishes of some Convention members who wanted to "simplify" the civil society spectrum, it was never recognised as the formal voice of civil society in the Convention (del Río Villar 2004, 287–288). The CSCG could not have been a strong voice in concrete proposals on civil dialogue because of the different views on this topic among some of its members, such as the Social Platform, ETUC and the EEB. Although ETUC played a minor role in this organisation, its own perception of this role is extremely telling:

> We are not totally against this idea of having less distance between the citizen and Europe and his job [the colleague participating in the CSCG meetings] was to make sure that there were no proposals coming out that were totally counterproductive. (Interview 31, with a representative of ETUC)

The difficulty that the CSCG had in acting as a strong coalition is clearly acknowledged by a representative of the organisation:

> It was difficult enough if you think at the time, it was four sectors. Now our members are European NGOs, who then have members and that, and that. Now, to reach common positions and to have a common mission statement, you need to get there. You are very likely to be entering into a Christmas tree, where a million things

were put in and there is no line to perceive any more. It took a lot of effort to put together an arrangement that people could accept, you know, we are not going to have 10 development statements, we are going to have one. (Interview 18, with a representative of the CSCG)

Internal divisions may also explain the fact that, according to the CSCG interviewee, the main role of the organisation was not to advocate particular horizontal causes such as participatory democracy, although that was an important issue, but to provide support for the key issues for each of its sectors. In this sense the interviewee was much keener to acknowledge CSCG support for the Social Platform's call for a horizontal anti-discrimination clause than its support for participatory democracy.

Interviews suggest that the Social Platform played a more direct role in brokering the coalition and in promoting its members' activism on this topic. They also suggest that the PFCS, which describes itself as "a think tank" on European citizenship and brought together different European and national actors during the Convention, may have been important in creating the general participatory democracy frame, as it brought together advocates of civil dialogue and of more direct democratic tools.

A question related to the role of alliances is that of staff turnover. It is not infrequent that European civil society organisations see their personnel move to other positions related to the EU, although this did not visibly affect organisational framing. Six of the interviewees moved from their organisation during the research time frame. An interesting finding, although it is difficult to present precise data without endangering respondents' anonymity, is that turnover did not necessarily affect organisations' coalition roles, as several of the changes occurred among civil society organisations and more importantly, between organisations in the same alliance. In particular some interviewees held multiple positions across the organisations, which, far from hindering their coalition activity, may have promoted it.

Collective action: coalitions and interorganisational structures

These qualitative findings about the role of alliances as facilitators of collective action and frame convergence can be explored further by a quantitative analysis of two dimensions of the network. The first dimension is individual actor centralities; that is, the place of each actor in the network in terms of the number of its ties to the rest. The second dimension is a study of individual actors' structural similarities; that is, the roles played by different actors and the hierarchical composition of the network. These analyses have been carried out with the Visone and Ucinet software packages respectively.

Closeness and betweenness have been used as the main measures of individual actor centrality. Both measures point out how central an actor is in terms of contacts with the rest of the network. Closeness measures how close an actor is to the rest and betweenness calculates how many paths between pairs of actors intersect with one actor. That is, closeness measures the direct contact between one actor and the rest whereas betweenness measures the ability to broker contact between actors. Table 4.3 summarises the findings for the ten most central actors in each measure. This is illustrated in Figure 4.2, which represents actors who are close in the same areas of the graph, and scales nodes according to their distance from the centre to the periphery of the graph.

The analysis shows some relevant differences between the centrality measures. Some of these divergences are telling with regard to the structure of the network and alliances. Analysis of closeness centrality shows

Table 4.3 Centrality measures

id	closeness (std)	id	betweenness (std)
CSCG	0.63	PFCS	0.193
PFCS	0.62	CSCG	0.188
Social Platform	0.62	ETUC	0.161
CONCORD	0.60	Eurocities	0.151
ETUC	0.57	CEDAG	0.121
CEDAG	0.55	Social Platform	0.111
COFACE	0.54	CONCORD	0.082
CARITAS UE	0.5	EEB	0.076
ECAS	0.45	COFACE	0.064
EFC	0.44	EFC	0.012
EEB	0.43	ECAS	0.008
IRI Europe	0.43	IRI Europe	0.007
ACN	0.42	UNICE	0.003
CEV	0.42	ACN	0.002
Eurocities	0.41	CARITAS UE	0.0
PL Office	0.4	CEMR	0.0
Eurocommerce	0.38	CEV	0.0
UNICE	0.38	CPMR	0.0
UEAPME	0.37	ELO	0.0
ELO	0.31	Eurocommerce	0.0
CEMR	0.29	PL Office	0.0
CPMR	0.29	UEAPME	0.0

that despite finding that the PFCS and the CSCG had a minor role in the frame-setting process, they had an important role in linking other organisations, since they were the organisations that had more ties to other actors. Surprisingly ETUC appears as a central actor in the network despite its rather distant attitude towards participatory democracy and civil society involvement. Given that the betweenness centrality measure increases for nodes connecting actors that would otherwise be isolated, the most plausible explanation is that the PFCS, IRI and ETUC had more ties to the more isolated organisations than the other actors.

Figure 4.1 suggested that the network was clearly divided between the core and the periphery, with a core of organisations intensely communicating between each other and a periphery comprising less directly involved organisations. Table 4.4 confirms this intuition:

Table 4.4 Core–periphery density matrix

	Core	Periphery
Core	0.667	0.238
Periphery	0.095	0.038

The result is a clear bipartite division, placing the CSCG as the most central actor and COFACE, CEDAG, the Social Platform, PFCS, ETUC and CONCORD in very central positions as well. This is a very strong suggestion that the organisations at the core form a coalition exchanging information and acting together. All these organisations except the PFCS are members of the CSCG or the Social Platform, and they are those that advocate more strongly a legal rank for civil society consultation in the process. On the other hand regional organisations (Eurocities, CPMR and CEMR) and business organisations (ELO, UEAPME, UNICE and Eurocommerce) have stronger relations between them than with the rest of the network. Organisations advocating for a more direct role for individual citizens (ECAS, ACN or IRI Europe) are in touch with a few organisations in the core but interestingly have weak contacts between them, suggesting that their campaigns were not coordinated.

The core of the network is thus constituted by advocates of civil society consultation (see Table 4.1). This provides very strong confirmation that these organisations constitute a coalition that exchange information and act together on this topic. The most noticeable aspect is the strong role of the PFCS and ETUC in the coalition despite their distant attitude to civil dialogue and more indirectly the presence of the CSCG, since the qualitative data suggest that the organisation's role was undermined

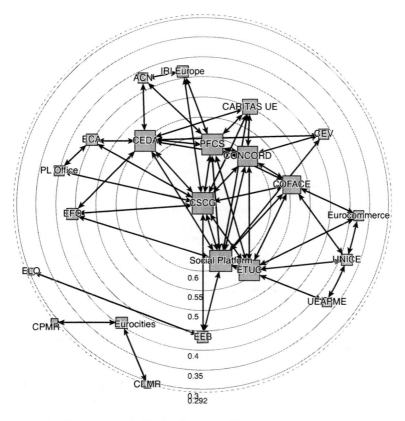

Figure 4.2 Closeness centrality in the network[1]

Note: [1]An organisation's position indicates closeness centrality in the network; the node size indicates its number of contacts.

by internal differences. The role played by ETUC means that despite the activism of some organisations most of the members of the network tended to target well-known actors. Even if it was not really supportive of civil dialogue, its importance in EU civil society and its presence in the CSCG make it a focal actor for any organisation that is active in the field of civil society dialogue. Evidence of ETUC's ability to be active in different publics and bridge institutional and contestatory discourses is well exemplified by the following quote from the General Secretary's intervention in the European Social Forum:

> I would like first to thank the Mayor of Paris for his support in arranging this tremendous Trade Union Forum, as the opening

event for the European Social Forum in Paris this week. As a left-over of the '68 generation, I remember the old slogan: "sous le pavé, la plage". [...] We need more of this kind of thinking, which brings public administration, at whatever level, closer to our citizens. [...] The principles agreed by the Convention go very much in the direction pointed-to by the European trade union Movement. It did not go all the way to meet our objectives. We have particular concerns about the need for new tools for economic governance and we would have liked more majority voting on social policy. But as trade union negotiators, we know a workable deal when we see one. We judge that it would be a disaster if the principles that have been agreed were now brought back into question. They do not consecrate competition, but rather introduce the social market economy. They provide a legal base for positive action on our public services. Those are features that distinguish Europe from the model that some, like the International Monetary Fund, would wish to impose on us. (John Monks' address to the European Trade Union Forum, Paris, 11 November 2003)

As this division was expected, a structural equivalence analysis has been carried out to understand more precisely the similarities and differences in the roles of the actors. Figure 4.3 clusters together actors with similar patterns of relations to other actors, rather than those networking intensely among themselves as in the previous analysis. This means that the ties towards other actors of organisations grouped together tend to be very similar. This figure suggests that organisations of the same size and type and those sharing similar visions of participatory democracy have a similar pattern of relations. In this sense organisations advocating a stronger dimension for individual citizens' participation and direct democracy are grouped together (except the PFCS), whereas social partners and regional organisations have similar patterns of relations. The rest of the organisations are regrouped according to their relevance in the coalition, as it seems that alliance organisations (PFCS, CSCG and the Social Platform) have greater similarities in terms of their patterns of relations than with their own members. This suggests that the members of the CSCG and its members, in particular CONCORD and the Social Platform, as well as several members of the Social Platform and EEB, tended to network intensely with the same organisations, which means that European organisations tended to network more intensely with organisations with which they had hierarchical relations.

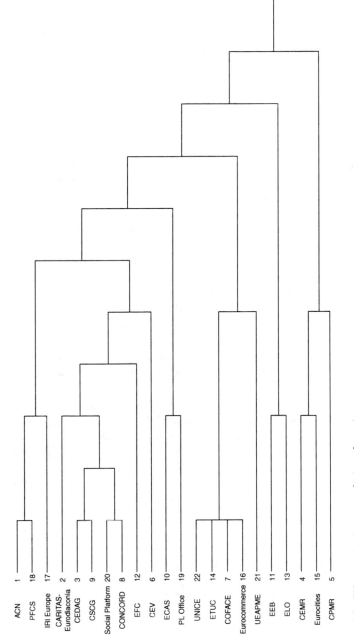

Figure 4.3 EU organisations correlation clustering

Shared activism and communication

So far, the measures have focused on mere contacts and exchanges of points of view between organisations. When collective action by organisations carrying out common actions is considered, a division appears between organisations acting as information or opinion relays and organisations acting together towards the Convention.

Figure 4.4 is very telling, as it shows a central group of EU organisations interacting among themselves beyond exchanges of points of view. It confirms the importance of the Social Platform, in the sense that the most intense flows happen between this organisation and its members, whereas other coalitions such as the CSCG and the PFCS have a minor role in comparison with the centrality in the broader network. This suggests that coalitions such as the PFCS, the CSCG and especially the Social Platform were important for the circulation of information and for favouring common action rather than as substitutes for their own members' activism. In this sense, the network data confirm that these two organisations and their members were frequently communicating and acting together. Interviews suggest that the role of coalitions seems to have been to provide information, access opportunities and coordination for their members. If the agenda-setting process contributed to building a common demand among a substantive number of organisations, their expression of this demand almost unanimously to the Convention (see Chapter 5) was favoured by the existence of these coalitions.

The analysis of communication flows by comparing indegrees and outdegrees (see Annex 7) extends the strong core periphery division to the communication between organisations. It also appears that leaders of the network, the most prestigious actors who advocated more strongly for the recognition of civil dialogue, were not very active in establishing relations with other actors. On the other hand, centrality analysis and prestige measures have somehow unexpectedly highlighted the activism of actors who are relatively distant from this core, such as IRI, PFCS or ETUC. This is explained by stronger communication efforts, which gave them the most significant role in bridging different parts of the network. The implication is that the organisations communicating more actively (those attempting more contacts, outdegree column) were not those that had more actively contributed to create the participatory democracy frame.

The coalition of core organisations does not seem to have tried to extend the frame. This resonates with Mahoney's findings that, unlike

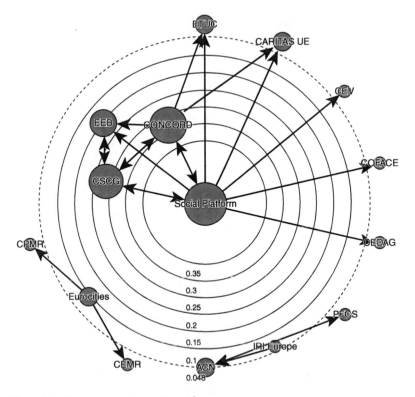

Figure 4.4 Common action network[1]

Note: [1]Organisations' position indicates closeness centrality in the network; the node size indicates their number of contacts.

the USA, the main rationale behind coalitions at EU level is not to anticipate public opinion pressures on political elites (Mahoney 2007, 368;
Hula 1999, 49) but to pool resources efficiently at the EU level, since
the EU's weak democratic structure hinders the ability of civil society
to articulate a strong political pressure (Mahoney 2007, 377). This is a
significant difference from the expectations of social movement literature on frame circulation (Snow et al. 1986, 472; Zald 1996; Muller 2008,
58–61).

In this sense the only claims that one of the reasons for organising
a coalition was to contribute to the diffusion of the Constitution, in
order to promote debate at grassroots level, are from the CSCG and more
particularly its act4europe campaign. As highlighted, this organisation
was relatively active in networking (outdegree 0.2).

Organisations promoting the ECI (IRI, PFCS) and alternative views of the EU (ATTAC, Social Forum) were relatively more active in communicating in comparison with their relatively weak role in the debate. The IRI and PFCS were weak at creating lasting links with other groups and ATTAC and the Social Forum were practically not involved in the Convention (Agrikoliansky 2007). In this sense their involvement in debates seemed to be reduced to individual participation in a few events rather than being a campaign with national organisations:

> During the two referenda campaigns, in France and in Holland, several people from our association went to participate in the debates in France, myself I went to Lille at least twice and once to Paris, and the debate was so feeble. (Interview 22, with a member of the PFCS)

A second relevant dimension of the graph is that it confirms that organisations with similar perceptions of participatory democracy were acting together. In this sense it appears that the Social Platform led the common action on civil dialogue whereas organisations promoting direct democracy, such as ACN, PFCS, IRI or ATTAC, were also acting together. Finding that there is a coincidence between common positions towards participatory democracy and collective action is relevant because it confirms that the convergence of views on participatory democracy was accompanied by common action. This suggests both that the convergence of views was itself a manifestation of collective action and that promoting participation was one of the key elements behind organisations' collective action.

5
Organised Civil Society and the Convention's Agenda

Introduction

Since Article 47 on participatory democracy was essentially a way of raising the profile of an existing mechanism (Pérez Solórzano-Borragán 2007, 281), it has been suggested that it was little more than a way of making the Convention more popular (Lombardo 2007). Furthermore, it has been suggested that civil society had little say in this process, since the EU's focus on participatory democracy is the result of the "continued activism of an elite forum of political, administrative and academic actors" (Saurugger 2010, 471). On the other hand, others have credited civil society with influencing the decision to include the ECI in the Treaty (del Rio Villar 2004, Lamassoure 2004, de Clerck-Sachsse 2012). Chapter 3 highlighted the fact that participatory democracy was used in the consultations that preceded the Convention in order to frame the self-interested demands by civil society organisations. It can thus be asked if this process influenced the Convention's debate on participatory democracy. This chapter analyses how the agenda on participatory democracy made it to the Convention, and through which mechanisms civil society organisations brought it to the Convention's agenda.

The debate about participatory democracy in the Convention

It is important to analyse the mechanisms of linkage between the previous debates and the Convention, and in particular the frame of participatory democracy, for at least two reasons. Firstly, unlike the previous fora, the Convention was not limited to issues of participation, but organisations could express demands relating to the substance of their main field of activism – for instance environment or social questions. It must therefore be asked whether they expressed the same demands regarding participation or whether they prioritised different issues. Secondly, this would allow us to understand how the issue moved from the status of a demand by outside interests to a matter on the Convention's agenda, since it cannot be assumed that being raised previously was a sufficient condition for the issue's inclusion on the institutional agenda (Kingdon 2003; Princen 2009). This section analyses official documents' references to participatory democracy with particular attention to the role of civil society organisations in putting this topic on the agenda.

Civil society organisations wanting to interact regularly with the Convention were divided into eight sectors of different interests. These sectors organised eight meetings chaired by members of the Praesidium that prepared the plenary session hearing of June 2002. It is interesting that about half of the organisations included in this research (ten of them) were designated to speak in the plenary hearing by the 361 organisations that participated in the working groups across all sectors. Despite the high turnout in the preparatory meetings there were no reports of quarrels for representation in the plenary hearing, and the Praesidium paper suggests that this was done by consensus:

> The Chairman asked the attending organisations to inform him of the way in which they would be using their speaking time. Following brief consultations, the following arrangements were adopted. (Secretariat of the European Convention 2002b, 22)

A member of the Convention secretariat confirmed his amazement at this fact:

> And then amazingly, I think amazingly it worked! I mean, they managed to decide amongst themselves and I think it worked reasonably successfully. (Interview 6)

Out of the 37 civil society organisations that took the floor in the plenary session, ten are among the organisations considered in this book. This means that half of the most active organisations in the previous debates took the floor during the Convention. This suggests that the question of civil society participation was high among the issues that civil society organisations wanted to include in the Constitution, given the salience of organisations advocating for this topic at this large meeting. It appears that the issue was an important horizontal topic for organisations from different sectors, as it was discussed in five of the eight sectoral hearings. Among the organisations represented in the main hearing for civil society, 27% had been actively involved in the previous discussions related to participatory democracy. This also suggests that it was a relative minority of organisations with a good reputation who took the lead in advocacy for the topic.

Before the plenary hearing the Convention's Secretariat prepared a digest of the position papers sent by civil society to the online forum, acknowledging the demand for a legal basis for civil society consultation (Secretariat of the European Convention 2002a). This acknowledgement shows that the demand was shared by a noticeable number of civil society organisations as well as indicating a positive attitude from the Praesidium towards this question, probably linked to the Laeken declaration's concern with democracy. Although it has not been possible to identify an individual decision to include participatory democracy in the Treaty, it was supported by members of the Praesidium, as three of them (Hänsch, Dehaene and Amato, who will later be the contact person for the ERC campaign on the ECI) devoted particular attention to this topic in their reports on the hearings (Monaghan 2007, 74). An interview with Mr Hänsch confirmed the fact that the Praesidium took up the issue immediately after the hearing (Interview 37).

This may explain that participatory democracy was placed on the Convention's agenda early. The Secretariat presented a series of articles on the democratic life of the Union on 2 April 2003 (Secretariat of the European Convention 2003), which included an article on participatory democracy (Article 34 in this version of the draft). The Secretariat links this proposal to the ongoing debate on how to bring the EU closer to its citizens in a clear example of a conscious agenda-setting effort to link problem identification and policy proposals:

> The question of how to increase the democratic legitimacy and transparency of the institutions was an essential element of the Laeken Declaration. From the beginning of the Convention's proceedings, it was evident that citizens had high expectations as regards transparency in the Union's legislative process, and wanted the Union to be closer to its citizens, partly through dialogue between institutions and citizens on the Union's activities, through associations and civil society. (Secretariat of the European Convention 2003, 2)

The justification for Article 34 in particular insists that this provides a legal base for current practice (Pérez Solórzano-Borragán 2007), which suggests that preceding agenda-setting work was relevant to this decision:

> Draft Article 34 sets out the main elements of participatory democracy, and is intended to provide a framework and content for the dialogue which is largely already in place between the institutions and civil society. (Secretariat of the European Convention 2003, 2)

This proposal by the Secretariat saw little change in the subsequent months. Since some amendments asked the article to be more concrete, the general recognition of dialogue was supplemented by a particular reference to "broad consultations with concerned parties" in the revision of the article presented on 26 May 2003 (Secretariat of the European Convention 2003b). These changes were debated in a plenary session on 5 June 2003, where, according to the summary by the Secretariat, there were few comments except some calls for the recognition of the ECI (European Convention 2003c, 3), which was not yet in the proposal. This provides interesting information about the Convention's debate on the ECI. On the one hand it was on the agenda of some members from early in the Convention (unnumbered amendment by Spanish socialists Borrell, Carnero and López Garrido, see Borrell et al. 2003). On the other it appears that this mechanism was not seriously considered until later (Lamassoure 2004), suggesting the importance of civil society activism in tipping the balance of internal discussions.

The analysis of the amendments confirms that despite the Convention's acceptance of participatory democracy the topic attracted the attention of many Convention members, who sent 61 amendments to the first draft. That said, this was very far from a heated debate as this is a very small number in comparison with the thousands of amendments received pertaining to the first 16 articles of the Constitution: 1,187 according to Méndez de Vigo (2005, 272). Figure 5.1 summarises the subjects raised by the Convention members, and suggests that discussion on the participatory democracy article (Article 34 in the first draft, Article 46 in the second draft and Article 47 in the text approved by the IGC) was less unanimous when referring to its details than to its principle.

This is confirmed by the analysis of the content. Most of the amendments are reformulations of the wording of the article by the Secretariat, rather than radically different conceptions of participation. The only challenge to the concept of participatory democracy is linked to the fact that the first draft referred only to participatory democracy in the

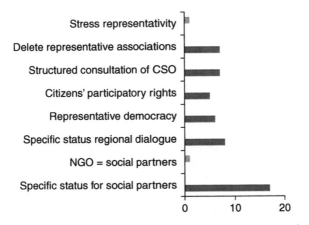

Figure 5.1   Topics of amendments regarding participatory democracy[1]
Note: [1]The lighter grey bars stress amendments diverging from the majority line.

section on the democratic life of the EU, without mentioning representative democracy. Thus six amendments pointed out the need of a distinct article on representative democracy, which was included in the following draft. The rest of the amendments reflect the abovementioned strategies of different sections of civil society to obtain specific recognition.

The first draft did not include a specific recognition of social partners, which created a strong desire for the creation of a differentiated forum, which appeared in the next draft. It is worth mentioning that the EESC itself and in particular the representatives of the social partners within it (Jacobs for UNICE and Gabaglio for ETUC) made calls to make a clear-cut distinction between civil and social dialogue. There was only one call to bring civil society organisations closer to the status of social partners, made by an Irish member of the Convention (de Rossa).

A number of Convention members argued that if civil society was to be recognised, regional and local authorities or their representative organisations should obtain distinct recognition too. There were eight amendments on this point, with particular insistence from the representatives of the British and Spanish governments.

The question of how consultation should be organised and in particular who should be consulted attracted the attention of a number of members. Seven amendments emphasise the need to consult organised civil society and to proceed to structured consultations. In this respect, it seems that the aim was to recognise institutionalised actors rather than to allow for the emergence of new forms of consultation different from those already known. The fact that the notion of civil dialogue was only used by the representatives of the EESC and by Dominique de Villepin (representative of the French government) confirms the decay of this frame in favour of participatory democracy, which the previous chapter has suggested.

The most significant of these attempts to change the wording of the article are the amendments suggesting the deletion of "representative associations" from the reference to civil society in the article. The inclusion of these words despite a majority of contrary amendments (seven against and only one for) is additional evidence that this formulation is intentional. It seems to confirm that the reference to representativeness is a concession to social partners' demands.

The amplification of the participatory frame: the ECI

The Convention clearly saw a blossoming of demands for forms of participation that focused on individual rights rather than on organisations' involvement, the most obvious of which is certainly the ECI.

Civil society organisations' position papers show different demands for a greater focus on the participation of individual citizens, including demands that citizens and civil society organisations be granted access to the European Court of Justice (EEB and PFCS), the creation of a right to access information (EEB, EFC, ECAS and PFCS) or that the Constitution be ratified via referenda (ATTAC Europe, ACN, ETUC and PFCS). Regarding the last aspect, whereas ATTAC's motivation is quite clear, to obtain opportunities for blocking the implementation of the Constitution in national referenda, ETUCs or the PFCS, they risk failing to bring the text closer to public opinions. ETUC and the PFCS consider that the referendum should be at EU level, whereas ATTAC considers that it should take place in as many countries as possible.

Different demands of this nature were put forward in papers by EEB, PFCS, ECAS, EFC, ACN, ATTAC Europe and ETUC. IRI is not in this group because its position papers are not available. Among the organisations demanding the recognition of consultation more actively, only two (the PFCS and EFC) also demanded direct participation mechanisms. Significantly none of these organisations belong to the Social Platform or the CSCG. This suggests that there is clearly a subdivision within the citizens' interests organisations. Firstly, there is a core consisting of organisations involved for a longer time which focus almost exclusively on advancing civil society consultation as a form of participatory democracy. On the margins, there are a number of organisations that amplify demands for participation beyond the institutionalisation of civil society, albeit supporting the core demand.

It is thus less surprising that interviews point out that the ECI is the result of an entirely differentiated mobilisation, as most of the civil society organisations that demanded the recognition of consultation affirm that they were not involved at all in activism for the ECI.

> One example of the openness of the process was the citizens' initiative. It was not our idea, but we were very happy that it was included. (Interview 3, with a representative of the Social Platform)

The literature has credited IRI with this achievement (Lamassoure 2004; del Río Villar 2004, 331–333; de Clerck-Sachsse 2012) pointing out a lobbying campaign that turned the tide after a "a last minute fight" (Interview 4, with Mr Lamassoure; Interview 5, with a member of the Secretariat; Personal Communication 7 and Interview 37 with Mr Hänsch).

However, an interview with a representative of IRI challenges accounts that the ECI was a boldly innovative idea promoted by a bunch of outsiders. The interviewee reports that the organisation convinced Italian and Austrian ministers, who proposed the idea to the Amsterdam intergovernmental conference back in 1996. Furthermore, the interviewee ran an informal working group with Convention members on issues of direct democracy throughout the entire Convention. This suggests that although the principle was accepted only late on, it had undergone an agenda-setting process comparable to the one on civil society consultation, which suggests that it was far from being an action run by outsiders (de Clerck-Sachsse 2012).

Furthermore, the single attribution of the ECI to IRI is not unanimous among interviewees, since ECAS and especially the PFCS claim to be behind the Convention's proposal. The PFCS position papers support the interviewee's claim. Furthermore, as stated above, the idea had already been tabled by Spanish socialist conventioneers. In a different approach, CEDAG asked that civil society organisations rather than a group of individual citizens be granted a right to demand that the Commission should launch initiatives. This demand confirms that the core organisations, such as CEDAG, sought to use the emerging frame on participatory democracy to obtain different routes of access to the EU. It is a further confirmation of the different focuses of organisations advocating citizens' direct involvement and those working for a stronger role for organisations. The fact that different organisations competed to include a similar topic on the agenda explains the lack of cooperation among these organisations, and is highlighted by network analysis in the previous chapter.

The issue of individual citizens' participation made it to the Convention via a number of amendments that addressed the subject. This illustrates the ways in which ideas were formulated in the context of the Convention and the interesting phenomenon of frame amplification (Snow et al. 1986): as soon as the notion of participatory democracy was included in the draft, a number of Convention members submitted different and autonomous amendments relating to different forms of direct democracy, the most significant being different forms of citizens' initiative and citizens' referenda, as well as the right to receive information. In particular, the language of some amendments appears to have been influenced by the language of organisations such as ACN and the PFCS. These amendments were presented by individual members (Bonde, Einem, Voggenhube) or a small group of members (such as the Spanish socialists Borrell, Carnero and López Garrido), although they had very little impact and did not foster further action. However, during the last session of the Convention the successful lobbying by IRI discussed above gave rise to an amendment to the ECI that was proposed by Jürgen Meyer and signed by virtually all members of the Convention. It thus appears that activism in gathering the support of relevant actors or a high number of members was decisive in the promotion of new ideas.

Civil society in the Convention

Several of the organisations, having demanded the inclusion of civil society consultation in the Treaty, are convinced that they influenced the subsequent recognition of this principle. This is noticeable since interviewees do not easily claim success. In fact participatory democracy is one of the rare subjects that they mention as a victory for civil society. As many as six interviewees mentioned that not much was achieved in comparison with other treaties that were negotiated by traditional Intergovernmental Conferences. In particular, little progress was seen in the social domain, and five interviewees mentioned a defensive attitude by environmental organisations which were concerned by the risk of de-communitarisation of the policy.

Regarding the process of inclusion in the Treaty, it seems that differences in arguments and interests notwithstanding, citizens' organisations made an almost unanimous claim for participatory democracy that was easily included in the agenda:

> There was a one day hearing, where you had people coming from NGOs and from different actors at European level to talk to Valéry Giscard d'Estaing and all that. What happened that day is that we had some coordination beforehand and everyone asked things on the content and asked for civil dialogue to be recognised. And it was amazing, because they came the one after the other saying: "We want civil dialogue, we want civil dialogue, we want civil dialogue to be in the Treaty", the Presidium started thinking, "OK we have to do something because they seem to be asking all the same." And I think that's where they started looking at it. (Interview 3, Social Platform)

Although there is no definitive evidence from this author about the rationale behind Article 47 it is noticeable that civil society influence was recognised by five officials and members of the Convention, who admit that the article on participatory democracy was a way to respond to civil society demands:

> Luis Bouza García: I was wondering if this idea came directly from the Presidium, members of the Convention or perhaps directly from hearings with civil society?
>
> Jean-Luc Dehaene: It's hard to say, the technical formulation was certainly made by the Secretariat, but let it be clear that this element of democratic participation, citizens' participation, to be accurate, was widely supported by civil society, this is clear. (Interview 1, with Jean-Luc Dehaene)

At the same time almost all these interviewees point out that this was a low-profile debate for the Convention.

Interviewees consider that the strategy of building a unanimous civil society demand for consultation contributed to setting the Convention's agenda on the issue. Thus it seems that the role of civil society was stronger in building the participatory democracy frame than in influencing concrete decisions about the content or specific wording of aspects of the text. The main reason is the uncertainty about the limits of civil society organisations' influence reported by the interviewees. The Convention was a new venue which included a significant number of new personnel, in particular national MPs, and with a number of very high stakes, as the "prize" for lobbying efforts could be influence in a new Treaty. Interviewees provided several examples of this uncertainty: "we did not know how much we could ask for" (or "we didn't dare to ask for it" (Interviewee 3)); "Everybody who is involved hopes and tries and sees itself as, as, as an important part," (Interviewee 12); "it's difficult to see if we had a clear impact or not." (Interviewee 15). More significantly, there were comments about the relationship between pressure by civil society organisations and the inclusion of the article in the text:

> I think different stories have actually emerged, I mean, it was clearly pushed by the Social Platform, by the Contact Group, by other NGOs as well who thought that NGOs had to be recognised, I think that, you know, if you look to the Laeken declaration which stressed the need to have an inclusive and engaging process, it would have been difficult for the Convention to come up with something that didn't include any way of taking that forward. It was the result just of the way in which the Convention was set up. I think in terms of whether there'd be or not an article on civil dialogue, it's very difficult to say because it came back to the way in which the Praesidium and Giscard worked, which was not the most transparent ... So several stories have emerged but I don't think it is possible to claim credit for a particular group for having added that to the text. (Interview 9, with a representative of the Social Platform)

The significant number of interviewees pointing out common action towards the recognition of civil dialogue tends to deny any possible retrospective explanation by individual actors. The importance of this demand is also confirmed by official reports about civil society consultation during the Convention. Furthermore, the position papers of organisations that supported this demand in the previous process, such as COFACE and CEV, could not be retrieved.

Additionally, references to recognition of civil society other than in terms of consultation were very frequent in contrast with the relatively small number of demands concerning civil dialogue. Eleven out of the 16 available position papers demanded a sort of recognition as relevant partners of the EU. Some demands were not limited to asking for a Treaty article but formulated additional legal demands. The most relevant try was EFC's and the Social Platform's demand to include civil society organisations' right to be consulted in the Charter of Fundamental Rights, whereas the PFCS wanted consultation to be recognised as one of the values of the Union (del Río Villar 2004, 285–286). This could have been a way in which to grant consultation a supra-constitutional status, as a single reference in the Treaty might not have been sufficient to enforce it in court: "The European Court of Justice should in the future determine to what extent the inobservance of these procedural practices could be challenged by civil society organisations as an infringement of the principles of participatory democracy" (Cuesta López 2010, 135). These demands were not exclusive of citizens' organisations, and the content is extremely telling about the importance of the process for interest groups in general. This issue is examined in greater detail in Chapter 6.

It is thus necessary to examine how the demands by civil society were connected to the Convention. Two forms of access are considered, the first being advocacy by the institutions themselves (Saurugger 2010). After all, it has been repeatedly pointed out that the Commission and the EESC were interested in articulating a discourse on civil society, so a Treaty article on this principle could provide a strong justification for participation. The second method is autonomous action by organisations and coalitions to bring the issue to the attention of the Convention.

Access via the Commission, national governments and members of the Convention

The most obvious way in which the issue of participation could have made it to the Convention's agenda is promotion by some of the members of the Convention, as some of them represented institutions which had already been active in the agenda-setting process; examples are the Commission and the EESC.

However, interviews provide strong evidence against the hypothesis that the Commission acted for civil society in the Convention, as none of the interviewees acknowledged support from this institution and five of them actually mentioned that the Commission was not their main interlocutor in the discussion. In particular, two Commission interviewees (13 and 14) present a great distance from civil society:

Luis Bouza García: Contributions asked the Convention that civil dialogue be included in the Treaty.

Interviewee: Yes, but it wasn't. [...] What the [Social] Platform would like is a social dialogue in the civil society field. [...] This is not in the Treaty; this civil dialogue is not there. [...] What is there is a different thing; it is an article saying that there are consultation mechanisms, dialogue mechanisms, but not a civil dialogue in the sense of the social dialogue. (Interview 14, with a member of the Commission's secretariat)

This distance was also perceived by civil society organisations: "I remember we had contacts but difficult contacts" (Interview 11, with a representative of COFACE). This is confirmed by the Commission's staff working documents, which devote almost no attention to the issue of participatory democracy (there is not a single reference to these words) and in general to the mechanisms of consultation with civil society, apart from noting that the "basic principles in the chapter on democratic life" correspond to the Commission's expectations (Secretariat General European Commission 2003). These documents point out that the ECI was an innovation introduced in the last meeting of the Convention and that it was generally welcomed by the members. However, as one of the main items in the Commission's agenda was to safeguard its monopoly of legislative initiative, it may not be surprising that the ECI was not particularly welcomed by the Commission (Interviews 5 and 13).

Although it seems to be far from the norm, it is very noticeable that without a question on this topic being asked five interviewees raised the example of Irish social NGOs' influence via the Irish representative in the Convention. Although this was mainly related to aspects of equality in Part III, it resonated with the question of civil society participation because, as was mentioned in Chapter 4, the Irish member Proinsias De Rossa made the only amendment, suggesting that civil society organisations should be brought closer to the status of social partners:

Strengthen the commitment to dialogue and give civil society organisations similar respect to that guaranteed to the Social Partners in the treaty. (Amendment to Article 46 by Mr Proinsias De Rossa)

At the time this was seen as a strategy for uploading the Irish social dialogue model to the EU:

This idea comes from the Irish tradition where in their social dialogue they have a few NGOs inside and some people said "this must also be important at the European level". (Interview 31, with a representative of ETUC)

In this sense a few national and European officials considered that there were a few attempts to introduce national interests as civil society demands.

This was a way of justifying some contents that were not really demanded by civil society. [...] It should be analysed how national interests were introduced as supposedly civil society interests. (Interview 34, with a representative of the Spanish government)

This seems to suggest that lobbying through the capitals may have been an option for some organisations, although by definition this was limited to sectors where demands by civil society organisations and national governments coincided. This does not seem to have been the case for all governments, as interviews with two Spanish civil servants (interviews 34 and 39)[1] reveal scepticism about national civil society's ability to participate in European affairs.

Finally, as it will appear, several members of the Convention were supportive of civil society demands (IRI 2004). However, in their accounts participatory democracy is frequently equated with the ECI (Borrell Fontelles et al. 2003; Lamassoure 2004; Méndez de Vigo 2005) and there are few references to civil dialogue, which suggests that they were not the first articulators of the demand.

Involvement in formal hearings and networking with Convention members

In accordance with its Laeken mandate, the Convention articulated several ways of access for civil society, from national Conventions to an online forum and hearings with civil society organisations, both regularly in the EESC and the working groups and a plenary session held on 24–25 June 2002 (del Río Villar 2004; Cammaerts 2006; Monaghan 2007, for detailed analyses of these mechanisms).

In the absence of support by the Commission, interviewees report involvement in hearings and direct contact with specific members of the Convention as the two more straightforward ways of access to the Convention. This, together with the fact that a large and influential part of the Convention was composed of well-known European personnel such as MEPs, compensated for the novelty of the Convention (Monaghan 2007). However, the presence of elected politicians as an empowerment factor for civil society organisations seems to have been divisive for interviewees, including members of the Convention themselves. Whereas some consider that the electoral mandate of the members of the Convention made them sensitive to civil society demands, others argue that it is precisely those personnel who are more distrustful of civil society organisations and participatory democracy as a possible competitor for legitimacy. Interviews with officials and MEPs seem to clarify this point: although the Convention did not dispel distrust about civil society's legitimacy among MEPs, they perceived that this institutional setting would make it costly to ignore civil society demands. In this case, institutionalisation of consultation was much easier to accommodate to the Laeken frame than demands regarding substance. Additionally, there seems to have been an expectation that civil society would in exchange contribute to the ratification of the Treaty.

The evaluation of access mechanisms and influence factors adds to the impression that the Convention was business as usual for the organisations (Monaghan 2007; Pérez Solórzano-Borragán 2007). It appears that the plenary hearing in June was a rather formal event which civil society organisations used to strongly frame their unity. That said, calling it a formal event does not diminish its importance (del Río Villar 2004, 295) as it contributed to placing civil society consultation on the Convention's agenda. In terms of influence the interviewees tend to consider the EESC hearings and the working groups as the most effective fora, as 16 interviewees mentioned them as one of the most frequent means of access to the Convention. It is interesting that these mechanisms were used by both the EU and national NGOs, but that neither the social partners nor regional organisations pointed to this aspect as an access mechanism, since these organisations already had more institutionalised access as social partners or via the EESC. The importance of these mechanisms is confirmed by the fact that the five organisations reporting that these hearings were just a formality (IRI, ELO, ACN, Polish Office and PFCS) were clearly at the periphery of the process analysed in the two previous chapters. A similar thing can be said of the Forum website to which civil society organisations submitted their contributions. It seems to have been clear to all the organisations that this was a formality that did not grant any influence (Cammaerts 2006, 241–242), and yet all the organisations invested resources in contributing to it. An interview with a member of the secretariat acknowledges the need for action and presence in order for civil society contribution to be considered:

Interviewee: [...] it would be dishonest on my part to tell you that during drafting and re-drafting the articles, we were looking at the Forum. But there were some probably more organised, I don't know, associations or NGOs, which were much more active than just putting things on the, on the website. (Interview 5)

It seems that civil society organisations perceived that participation in these formal events such as the Forum website or the hearings was not direct influence but rather a way in which they could be perceived as relevant actors. When asked about the conditions for being influential in the Convention, organisations pointed both in position papers and in interviews to the importance of alliances, networking and membership of coalitions as the more important factors of influence, followed by expertise and reputation in EU matters. Therefore expressing demands via formal channels is in itself a form of resource exchange with EU institutions, and at the same time sends a relevant message to decision-makers about the identity of the influential players.

Eleven organisations,[2] nine of which are citizens' interest groups, report direct contacts with members of the Convention. This is another confirmation that alliances were more important for frame convergence than for collective action in the Convention as they did not use their members to voice their demands. These contacts were motivated by the dynamic of continued involvement and trust building rather than by defence of a specific point or amendment. Access via direct contact with members has been more frequent for the organisations in this study than in a broader sample of groups (Monaghan 2007, 152–158). Participation in formal events as a way of ensuring other forms of access does not differ from a broader pattern of consultation processes (Quittkat and Kotzian 2011), already seen in Chapter 2: involvement in formal fora seems to be a way of building trust, obtaining informal access and in general increasing an organisation's visibility.

The presence of civil society consultation in the hearings has been discussed previously. By contrast this topic was not really addressed at the hearings in the EESC. Although the EESC claims to be the appropriate forum for civil dialogue and the institutional representative of civil society in the EU, the minutes of the hearings with civil society organisations during the Convention do not mention any discussion about civil dialogue and do not point to any particular action exercised in this context to influence the Convention's agenda. Although the EESC has refused to disclose the list of organisations that attended these meetings, interviews suggest that these hearings were attended by most of the EU organisations mentioned in this study, but they did not make their main demand in this venue.

The EESC is the institution that first advocated a turn towards civil society and participatory democracy (Smismans 2003). Its documents always associate references to civil society with the EESC, which represents it at EU level. An interview with an EESC official (Interview 20) confirms that this institution intended to use the hearings as a way to frame its role as the most adequate venue for civil dialogue (see also Monaghan

2007, 72). In this sense a strong role for civil society in the EESC hearing would probably have provided the institution with increased grounds to claim a role in civil society consultation. Since most civil society organisations rejected such a role for the EESC because of fears that it would amount to little more than a "talking shop" (see Chapter 2), they seem to have declined the chance to use the Committee hearings as an access door to the Convention.

This chapter has demonstrated that civil society organisations managed to bring their demands of institutionalisation and recognition to the attention of the Convention, and that they did it independently of the Commission. The Convention thus marks a decisive moment in the institutionalisation of the field of civil society participation in the EU. Furthermore, the dynamics of cooperation have been clearly pointed out, given the importance of coalitions. However, there are signs that most organisations also followed their own strategy, although we have yet to evaluate how the recognition given by the Convention influences the positions of actors in the field. Chapter 6 explores how different civil society organisations reacted to the recognition of the principle, and Chapter 7 addresses the way in which the field has been transformed since the Convention.

6
Influence on the Agenda and Field Effects

Civil dialogue institutionalisation: what was at stake

So far it has appeared that policy debates between 1997 and the Convention contributed to the emergence of an agenda of civil society participation strongly shaped by a small number of civil society organisations and the European Commission. Citizens' organisations sought to obtain legal recognition of their access to EU institutions. This demand by civil society does not seem exceptional in the context of EU and civil society relations, as "the degree of institutionalisation of interest groups in the EU political system is what makes it unique" (Greenwood 2011b, 206). However, it has been highlighted that the objective was not the creation of access opportunities but the institutionalisation of existing practices (Pérez Solorzano-Borragan 2007, Lombardo 2007). As this relevant distinction is rarely highlighted, it is important to make sense of its significance.

The strategy of citizens' organisations

The analysis of recognition demands reveals that they are strongly aimed at raising the profile of citizens' organisations and in particular of social NGOs. This is formulated by an interviewee from COFACE as a way of reversing the historical discrimination by institutions and social partners against social NGOs and the Social Platform. CSCG and CONCORD interviewees conclude that institutionalisation is a benefit for weak players, whose contribution to policymaking could be contested by more influential organisations. Furthermore, opponents of this mechanism, such as Eurocommerce and ETUC interviewees, confirm that social NGOs intended civil dialogue to raise their profile. The Social Platform requests the recognition of the autonomy of civil society with the same formula as is used for social partners, as well as use of the notion of organised civil society rather than the finally accepted text, which refers to "representative associations and civil society". In this sense some interviewees perceive institutionalisation as the emergence of an obligation on European institutions to listen. An example is an unusually strong claim about the benefits to be expected from institutionalisation:

> Since the beginning was the idea that by more meetings with the Parliament, by more meetings with the Commission, by more meetings with the Council, get us on an equal footing with the European institutions. (Interview 3, with a representative of the Social Platform)

It is interesting to find two distinct accounts of the emergence and consolidation of a structured field of civil society and interaction with the EU. The first account focuses on the Commission's activism in structuring the civil society field by encouraging and funding the creation of sectoral platforms (Sánchez-Salgado 2007; Greenwood 2011b):

> They [the Commission] hate talking to 50 organisations and they do provide funding to structure. (Interview 10, with a representative of EFC)

The contribution of the institutionalisation of consultation to reducing civil society's disruption potential is probably as important as the motivation of simplifying the field. Although it is frequently argued that EU organisations have a very strong preference for insider registers (Mahoney 2007; Balme and Chabanet 2008), it is also true that these organisations remain able to use protest in some circumstances (Ruzza 2011). In this sense the red card mobilisation of 1998 – when organisations refused dialogue with the Commission until EU funding for organisations was secured (Alhadeff and Wilson 2002) – is an illustration of the benefits that EU institutions would derive from cooperating with rather than opposing organisations. This is acknowledged by an interviewee from Eurocommerce. Despite this organisation's disagreement with a specific legal status for civil dialogue, and with the very notion of "civil dialogue", the interviewee agrees that this mechanism has had several advantages for trade policy:

> I cannot advertise the civil society dialogue enough, because often and we've seen it in Seattle in 1999 at the WTO conference, you allow

me maybe a play on words but in 1999 in Seattle what we have seen was, in French, "la loi de la rue" [the law of the street]. Now civil society discussions and civil society dialogue take place in the "Rue de la Loi" [Law Street, the main street of Brussels' European district].

That's a big change to which civil society dialogue had contributed. (Interview 29, with a representative of Eurocommerce)

This is also related to a frequent expectation made on institutionalisation by citizens' groups: securing access to all the institutions of the EU rather than just to the Commission. The organisations' claims point to two different problems. The first is the Parliament's reluctance to recognise civil society organisations (EFC, PFCS) and the great difficulty of lobbying the Council if this is not done through the capitals. Secondly, claims that practices vary enormously across Commission services are probably the most relevant element. This confirms that the expectation of most civil society organisations, at least those linked to the Social Platform, would be the creation of a horizontal dialogue with Commissioners, in addition to day-to-day consultations with Commission services.

The second account is the argument that civil society organisations themselves took the initiative of creating these platforms, in order to push forward consultation with the Commission (Social Platform, COFACE, CONCORD and EFC interviews). This account is linked to criticisms of the way in which the Commission organises consultation. In this sense the Social Platform, the EFC and COFACE interviewees argued that the Commission has always been reluctant to institutionalise dialogue in order not to be tied to specific partners and to avoid weakening the social dialogue. However, it is clear that the two accounts are not necessarily contradictory. Both sides were interested in structuring the field, so the Commission could expect some legitimacy returns, and European citizens' platforms used this move to try to secure access to the Commission and to outmanoeuvre their competitors.

So we began to fix the Civil Society Contact Group, [...] and we began to push people who said they were civil society but didn't have the credentials, so we said: "I am so and so, I work for this organisation, I'm part of this alliance, which is itself part of this alliance, and I'm mandated to speak on behalf of these organisations". So the other guy would go on to say "I am very important, I have been around Brussels for a hundred years". "Who are you"? (Interview 21, with a representative of CONCORD)

Compared to these accounts, the role of civil dialogue in bringing the EU closer to citizens appears both relatively weaker and much more contested by organisations in the field. The two interviewees from the Social Platform, together with those from COFACE and ETUC, acknowledge that the Commission has turned towards civil society organisations in its search for increased legitimacy. Taking the opposite position the interviewee from ETUC considers this to be a wrong strategy, as he fears that civil dialogue may weaken an already fragile representative EU democracy. Furthermore, the EFC representative argued that legitimacy concerns were only attached to civil dialogue debates at the time of the Convention, and that before this it was never the primary aim (Kohler-Koch and Finke 2007). In this sense EFC and CONCORD interviewees argued that expertise seeking is very much the Commission's primary concern. It thus appears clear that the main driver of the institutionalisation of civil dialogue on the side of civil society organisations was the creation of a recognised and transversal access mechanism to EU institutions (del Río Villar 2004, 282–283).

Differentiation strategies

As seen in Chapter 3, virtually all organisations and not only citizens' interest groups were trying to be recognised as relevant partners of the EU. Until the Convention there was a shared demand by citizens' interest groups for the need to structure consultations and all the organisations used available windows of opportunity to make it. This meant that very different sectors were interested in the consultations preceding the Convention and to some extent fostered cooperation between different organisations. However, a Treaty change was at stake, rather than just raising the issue in the agenda, organisations followed very clearly differentiated strategies. Not only did they seek recognition for civil society in general but they also tried to secure access to institutions for themselves and the constituencies that they represented. Citizens' organisations from at least three sectors (regional organisations, churches and the social partners) followed different paths in order to obtain specific recognition by the Convention. There were also significant attempts made by particular subsectors such as foundations, "third sector" groups or groups experiencing poverty to obtain specific recognition.

Obviously this does not imply that the differentiation that finally took place, Article 47 on "associations and civil society", Article 48 on "social dialogue" and Article 52 on dialogue with "churches and philosophical organisations", and the role of the Committee of the Regions in checking subsidiary, is the result of differentiation strategies on the part of these actors. There are obvious structural differences between the four sectors which are underlined by interviewees: social dialogue has existed at EU level for 20 years; and local and regional authorities are not civil society and could hardly be involved in the same sort of mechanisms. That said, the uncertainty linked to the novelty of the Convention and the fact that the issue at stake was a Treaty change may have made it plausible at some point to reconsider some of these existing practices. In this sense, interviewees from social NGOs (Social Platform, EFC, ACN and CEDAG) admit that they would like civil dialogue to be inspired by social dialogue or to participate themselves in social dialogue (del Río Villar 2004, 277), which is a taboo for social partners. The measure of activism of the latter in order to prevent this (see the next subsection) suggests that at some point this may not have been a foolish possibility.

Local and regional authorities' associations established a strong alliance in order to obtain a legal basis for their EU level cooperation. This should be clearly distinguished from partnerships with civil society (Sloat 2003), as the 2001 governance strategy entailed some risk of confusion as well as some recognition of the importance of the local level in any EU participatory model:

> Eurocities as much as other organisations, organisations with which Eurocities collaborated, wanted that formal recognition of the local or regional authorities and their representatives at different levels as a different sector than civil society. (Interview 35, with a representative of Eurocities)

Churches, with the support of their social action NGOs, sought to obtain a specific recognition of their dialogue with EU institutions (Airiau 2007; Leustean 2007). This seems to have been perceived as a sort of "internal treason" by social NGOs, since church-related NGOs had been strongly involved in demands by social NGOs (Interview 18, with a representative of CSCG).

Interestingly, there were attempts of subsectoral differentiation within citizens' interest groups. The decay of civil dialogue in favour of the participatory democracy frame has been explained as a consequence of the politicisation of the agenda-setting process. However, it appears that this frame was not equally interesting for all citizens' organisations. The fact that actors involved in consultations with DG Trade and DG Environment (CONCORD and EEB), where the standards of consultation are much more developed than in DG Social Affairs, did not make demands on civil dialogue during the Convention is related to concerns that the recognition of a horizontal standard applying to all DGs and EU institutions could downgrade standards where they were already high (interviews with Social Platform, EEB, Eurocommerce and CONCORD representatives). The following quote, even though supportive of the idea that all NGOs shared the same interests in enhanced dialogue, confirms these differences:

> So for the environmental sector the idea of a structured civil dialogue between representative organisations it is less of an issue. Because for them the question was "who's got the best arguments about saving the planet?" And the question whether you have ten behind or a strong structure is less important for them in general than it is for social organisations for example. The same for the development organisations, again, these organisations support...[sigh] development in the south...they are not trying to speak for those voices. So there are different, different approaches, but in general all the organisations agreed that there needed to be enhanced dialogue despite their, their justifications for having that were quite different and in terms of how to do that. (Interview 9, with a member of the Social Platform)

Furthermore EFC, ACN and CEDAG, organisations representing the "third sector" or social economy, asked the Union to recognise the freedom of association (or foundation) on the Charter of Rights, which recalls the mid-1990s discussion on the European association statute (Will and Kendall 2009) and its linkage with economic activity (Interview 22, with a representative of the PFCS). On the other hand the Social Platform interviewee claims the specificity of social NGOs as they stand for the weakest groups of society, otherwise unheard:

> And also because we come from a sector where we are coming from citizens' initiative and where it is hard to be heard. [...] You know, they [member organisations] have access to something that other people, no other expert have, but they are not recognised for that and they are not invited to meet. (Interview 3, with a representative of the Social Platform)

The differentiation strategy of social partners is particularly interesting because it does not build on citizens' organisations but is rather a reaction against them.

The emergence of contestation

A relevant dimension of the process of agenda setting is the emergence, albeit slow and fragmented, of some opposition to the institutionalisation of civil society consultation. It was highlighted that in the agenda-setting process the most significant opposition came from social partners. This is matched by their activism against civil dialogue and in favour of distinct recognition.

It is interesting that the interviewee from ETUC reduces the demand to include civil society consultation in the text to "a few NGOs who are not so happy about the social dialogue article in the Treaty and they wanted to have a counterweight" (Interview 31). In relation to this, social partners were trying to secure a different recognition than civil society consultation, as they already had in the social dialogue scheme. The positions of UNICE and ETUC coincide, in that their role should be distinguished:

> The draft constitutional Treaty contains an article 34 which sets out the general principle of participatory democracy. A clause to the effect that "[...] The EU promotes and support social dialogue between the Social Partners (Management and Labour), respecting their autonomy" should be added. (Gabaglio, Jacobs, and Cravinho 2003)

The frame of this demand goes beyond a particularistic claim, as the point is that the role of social partners is particularly important because they are able to participate in policymaking as "co-regulators" and their representativeness allows them to take decisions for their constituents.

However, ETUC perceived a much stronger threat from social NGOs than UNICE did in that its role as the EU's main social counterpart could be challenged if other non-business organisations acquired a stronger role:

> NGOs would like to come into social dialogue, but business and we, we have experience what happens in the factories, in the offices, and the NGOs are not really inside this business. So we cooperate wherever necessary, let's say on green jobs, or climate change, where they have a lot of experience, on human rights, fundamental rights because there as well they have a lot of experience, but it is already very difficult to get to an agreement with business, and the more people there are in this dialogue, the more difficult it is. (Interview 31, with a representative of ETUC)

The social partners did not try to object to a powerful framing such as participatory democracy. As mentioned in Chapter 3, they were more active in influencing the details of the discussion on participatory democracy, in particular the question of representativeness. On this point they could exploit the internal differences of citizens' organisations on issues of accreditation, representativeness and European status (Ruzza 2004, 46). Although obviously these issues were necessarily marginal in such a broad setting as the Convention, interviews suggest that the wording of the article in relation to "representative associations" may not be the result of a bad translation (Interview 4, with Alain Lamassoure) or of clumsy wording (Greenwood 2007b, 336) but linked to the demands of some civil society actors. Representation is probably the most disputed topic in the first moments of the process and one on which the promoters of civil dialogue appear most divided.

Social partners (business organisations are Business Europe and UEAPME and the European Trade Union Confederation) advocated criteria of representativeness, to the extent that Business Europe (then UNICE) proposed a series of principles tailored to its own structure (Michel 2007). UNICE tried to use its position within the EESC in order to promote its view on representativeness in civil dialogue. Although unsuccessful, this may have contributed to the rejection by citizens' groups of any role for the EESC in civil dialogue. Hence the mention of "representative associations" in Article 47, now Article 11 TUE, is a successful attempt by the social partners to frame civil dialogue according to its more traditional characteristics, including representativeness. The interviewee from UNICE claims influence in the wording of the article:

> Well, we strongly emphasized that we wanted the words representative associations, OK? [...] It is us who called for a real emphasis on representativeness. It was not really a problem because everyone was pretty much on the same line. (Interview 17, with a representative of UNICE)

The evolution towards a more generalised acceptance of representation by citizens' interest groups must be understood as the result of a negotiation between different interests. The promoters of civil dialogue argued that unlike members of trade unions or political parties, NGOs stand for weak groups that cannot cast a mandate, and that in any case groups should be invited according to their capacities and skills rather than their number of members. To put it in the words of ECAS: "There is little point in public authorities dancing with a representative partner who has nothing to say" (ECAS 2002, 3). In this sense several European organisations adopted an approach promoting their representativeness in relation to their expertise in certain domains. The conception of representation by this type of organisations was that their function was not to represent members but to advocate a cause. However, large umbrella organisations such as the Social Platform seemed to be ready to consider criteria of geographical representativeness rather than criteria based on evidence of authorisation by members, which is a form of standing for a group or cause rather than acting for it (Pérez-Solórzano Borragán and Smismans 2012, 405). The Social Platform's turn towards acceptance of representativeness is a reaction to the insistence on this by social partners. The following quote is representative of the different conceptions of representativeness among different organisations:

> If you take an organisation like the European Disability Forum, which is a member of the Social Platform, they can make the case they represent the voices of people with disabilities across Europe. And they are very highly representative, very democratic, voice of people with disabilities. So that's their job. And when they sit in a room the reason you want to listen to them is that they speak with the voices of disabled people, they elect members from different organisations who represent different types of disabilities. So they have a respectable claim in a process deemed to be representative, it's really an important issue. But if you take an organisation like Greenpeace, or Friends of the Earth, they don't sit down and say "you have to listen to us because we have so many members" that may be part of the issue, but the issue for them is really to save the environment and the question of who I am is secondary to that. (Interview 9, with a member of the Social Platform)

This cleavage contains both an organisational and a strategic distinction. As Table 6.1 shows, ETUC, business organisations and three EU citizens' interests umbrella organisations show constant support for this principle, whereas four EU citizens' interests umbrella organisations show constant disagreement. The distinction between a first group containing mostly membership organisations against a second one composed of representatives of causes is substantial (Greenwood and Halpin 2007; Halpin and McLaverty 2010; Kohler-Koch 2010a). That said, it also seems that EU umbrella organisations took a strategic stance on this topic as a number of them adopted opposite positions at different times. In this sense there is an interesting evolution of the discourse of citizens' organisations, where they evolve from claiming to represent minority views and particular causes to represent large numbers of citizens and broad causes.

Table 6.1 shows that the approach to representativeness of organisations (indicated in the third column) is quite volatile, as they adopted very different notions at different times. In addition, statements against representativeness by interviewees of the Social Platform, CSCG and PFCS suggest that the use of the notion in the Convention was highly strategic – see the number of changes in the position of some groups in Table 6.2 below – and that the principle is not yet generally accepted as a criterion for evaluating contributions to consultations. The strategic dimension is thus important in this reframing process. Interestingly it is during the Convention when representation becomes more salient, as only CEDAG and the regional organisations reject it and three organisations assume it for the first time.

Understanding collective action in the emergent field of participatory democracy(1997–2003)

The previous chapters have shown that organisations involved in the debates on participatory democracy before and during the Convention

Table 6.1   Organisations' positions on representativeness criteria

Constant endorsement	Constant rejection	Shifts
1. ETUC	1. Polish NGO office	1. CEDAG
2. ELO	2. PFCS	2. Cittadaninza
3. UEAPME	3. CONCORD	Attiva – ACN
4. UNICE	4. ECAS	3. CSCG
5. Eurocommerce		4. European
6. Caritas – Eurodiaconia		Environment
7. EFC		Bureau – EEB
8. COFACE		5. Social Platform

Table 6.2   Number of position papers making points on representation

	CEDAG	Cittadaninza Attiva – ACN	CSCG	European Environment Bureau – EEB	Social Platform
Alternative ways	2	2	1	0	3
Formal sense	1	1	2	3	6
No representation	3	3	1	1	2

did not simply send their opinions to the EU institutions, but established competition and cooperation relations with them and with other organisations. The emergence and diffusion of the participatory democracy frame implies that organisations involved in the process were engaged in different strategies. It has been found that there is a very strong correlation between discursive references to civil society involvement as a form of participatory democracy and membership of the Social Platform and the CSCG. Furthermore, all the organisations at the core of the network of groups active in civil dialogue shared this emerging frame. It is thus quite clear that civil society organisations perceived that the Commission intended to use existing mechanisms in order to reinforce input legitimacy and that they turned this into an opportunity structure to obtain its recognition. This collided with the interests of other actors in the policymaking process. This strategy met opposition by already institutionalised organisations, in particular from social partners, and there were divergent attitudes from different sectors of the EU's institutions. In this sense the attempt of the EESC to turn itself into the house of civil dialogue or the lead of different DGs and services of the Commission in shaping the civil society consultation agenda is paradigmatic of an inter- and intra-institutional struggle over the rules of civil society consultation (Saurugger 2010). Just like the institutional actors that promoted participatory democracy (Saurugger 2010), civil society organisations were doing so in order to promote their own collective, legal recognition of their right to be consulted, and sector- or organisation-specific goals in terms of recognition. The evolution of the frame and the convergence of different organisations around it tend also to suggest that frame formation and convergence is strongly related to the formation of an organisational field of civil society participation.

It appears that the Convention was sensitive to civil society organisations' demands to include the principle of consultation in the Treaty, as a result of the expression of a common demand and the need to comply with the Laeken mandate on the democratisation of the EU (del Río Villar 2004, 322). The strategy of civil society organisations implied using the participation opportunities provided by the Convention for formal and informal contacts rather than delegating advocacy on this topic to the Commission. Organisations consider that the main reason explaining their success was their involvement and reputation, and especially the fact that organisations produced a unanimous demand for the topic.

Although characterisation of the coalition promoting participatory democracy is not the primary aim of this work, it is important to conceptualise it in order to try to produce general conclusions. In some aspects the creation for a few years of a common frame of ideas about participatory democracy shared by a constituency of civil society organisations and institutions resonates with the advocacy coalition framework (Sabatier and Jenkins-Smith 1993) which has been successfully adapted in the EU context (Sabatier 1998; Engel 2007; Ruzza 2007; Dreger 2008).

However, there are some aspects where the case presented so far differs from the model. Firstly the changes that have been found in the organisations' discourses are difficult to attribute to a learning exercise conducted between different organisations and seem to be directly related to an instrumental framing aimed to better fit the expectations of other partners and EU institutions. In this sense the fact that the enlargement of the frame to include other mechanisms of participatory democracy such as the ECI was undertaken by actors outside the main coalition, such as IRI, suggests that the coalition failed to integrate these sorts of concomitant demands. In the case of an advocacy coalition it could be expected that demands like this would have easily been integrated as policy or as secondary beliefs by the coalition (Sabatier 1998, 103–104).

Secondly, and probably more substantially, there is no evidence that civil society and institutional actors came together under a common coalition for advancing the demand. Although Saurugger attributes a relevant role to the Commission Secretariat General in this achievement (Saurugger 2010, 480), the evidence gathered here (Interviews 13 and 14, with officials of the Commission's Secretariat General and internal staff working documents) is that this institution was not particularly active in promoting civil society consultation during the Convention.

It has rather been found that the actors were interested in the progress of advocacy for different reasons. It is clear that the Commission was interested in framing its exchanges with civil society organisations as a form of participatory democracy and that it was this institution that introduced the issue to the agenda (European Commission 2000, 2001), organisations only assuming this after 2001. Network analysis has confirmed the existence of four different coalitions: social partners, regional organisations, promoters of civil society consultation and direct participants. At no time were all the actors in the discussion, and even the members of a coalition, pursuing exactly the same goals. For instance, within the citizens' interests coalition each actor sought the recognition of its own role besides common advocacy. Furthermore, it is difficult to see a movement advocacy coalition (Ruzza 2004) in that the participants are very diverse, with a combination of actors more or less prone to contestation and with a very weak connection to broader social movements as a coalition, despite the obvious links between some of its members.

This suggests that rather than concentrating on the importance of a network coordinating all the relevant actors it is better to identify a field as a stable and recognisable set of relations where actors deploy autonomous and competing strategies (Bourdieu 1981; Bourdieu 1984; DiMaggio and Powell 1991; Stone Sweet, Fligstein and Sandholtz 2001). The agenda-setting process that culminated in the Convention was a process where some of the most salient actors in each of the civil society areas came to discuss together and with the EU institutions the rules that should generally apply to relations with non-state actors. The actors become aware of each others' strategies to obtain or block each others' routes of access. As has been shown, the field is structured around the frequent presence of actors particularly active on the topic and the development of coalitions and oppositions between them. Institutional theory posits that organisations active in the same field experience institutional isomorphism in the form of the emergence of an organisational ideal type (DiMaggio 1991), common frames and similar forms of collective action (Scott 2008, 185–190). Although this has not yet been the case for organisations active in participatory democracy, participants in this field are rooted in a specifically differentiated EU field, the field's stake being the definition of common norms regarding organisations' access to EU institutions. The fact that the Convention was an open door leading to Treaty change made it a decisive venue in this organisational field. However, the failed ratification of the Constitution, the new agendas from the institutions about transparency (de Castro Asarta 2011; Greenwood 2011a) and the need to develop the secondary norms that were emanating from the Treaty imply that the field is still today immersed in a structuration process, which is discussed in Chapter 7.

The previous chapters have found that a core group of civil society organisations involved in an agenda-setting process from 1997 to the Convention in 2003 played a key role in obtaining the institutionalisation of civil society dialogue under the heading of participatory democracy. The hypothesis that actors were trying to raise their profile under the heading of participatory democracy has been confirmed to a large extent. Whereas civil society organisations clearly endorse the notion of participatory democracy, this belongs to a process of frame bridging (Snow et al. 1986) in which organisations present themselves as key intermediaries for democratic participation in the EU. In this sense, it has been shown that their core demands (recognition under the form of a treaty article) are much more stable than the way in which they are framed. This was achieved by a medium- to long-term activism carried out in specialised fora and venues. In this sense the process has turned bureaucratic justifications of civil society consultation as a way of improving the policymaking process into a politically more ambitious discourse-framing consultation as a mechanism of participatory democracy that will contribute towards making the EU more legitimate.

Although this finding is relevant in itself, it could be pointed out that demands for recognition are not exceptional in the context of EU institutions and civil society because of the already high degree of institutionalisation. However, the process is unique for at least two reasons. The first reason is that the Commission was not the main driver of the institutionalisation of participatory democracy in the Convention. Despite the Commission's attempts to derive input legitimacy from its contacts with civil society, it was not the only actor behind the institutionalisation of this claim, and when it comes to the Convention it was not even the decisive actor. This means that the whole process must be understood by reference to the specific dynamics of competition and cooperation among members of an organisational field. It has thus appeared that the hegemony of the participatory democracy agenda has been overplayed (Saurugger 2010), in that the social partners actively challenged it even though it they later chose to seek differentiation rather than oppose a notion such as 'participatory democracy' that had such positive connotations.

Although the Convention is not a representative enough venue to challenge the general finding that coalitions are relatively rare in the EU (Mahoney 2007), the evidence is that coalitions can be a significant factor in policymaking in the EU, as most recent analysis demonstrates (Klüver 2013). Coalition organisations such as the CSCG or the Social Platform are not only important because of their individual weight but rather because they are able to facilitate the circulation of information, bridging different frames and promoting collective action by the members of the coalition. If the agenda-setting process contributed to building a common demand among a substantive number of organisations, their almost unanimous expression of this demand to the Convention was possible thanks to networking.

Furthermore, it has appeared that citizens' interests organisations were very comfortable within elite fora and managed to achieve their goals therein effectively. This means that civil society organisations are less dependent on the Commission than is traditionally assumed (Lombardo

2007; Michel 2007), that they were able to play "venue shopping" by framing their demands in the most appropriate way for the target they were pursuing (Ruzza 2004) and that they were able to use formal fora to gain informal access to decision-makers (Quittkat and Kotzian 2011).

The agenda-setting process that culminated in the Convention was a process where some of the most salient actors in each of the civil society fields discussed together and with the EU institutions the rules that should apply generally to the EU's relationship with non-state actors. Despite the high institutionalisation of this field with the entry into force of the Lisbon Treaty, it can be expected that the field will remain competitive as different organisations attempt to influence the implementation of the secondary norms that regulate participation. The increased diversity brought to the EU by the discussions over regulation of the ECI (Bouza Garcia and Greenwood 2014) confirms that competition over the definition of participatory norms is likely to remain salient. The study of framing and competition and coalition dynamics over citizens' participation in the EU is thus far from over.

Ruzza suggests that "the crisis of legitimacy of the EU system of governance can be viewed as a political opportunity for movements" (Ruzza 2004, 41). In this sense civil society organisations have been able to use the institutional agenda and needs to legitimate their own demands. Some civil society demands that could be associated with a participatory democracy model were the definition of common, transparent and objective rules of access in contrast to the more or less ad hoc selection of partners that tends to occur in some DGs, as well as the creation of a horizontal and higher profile consultation (Fazi and Smith 2006; Kohler-Koch 2010b).

The whole discussion about the definition of civil society, the characteristics of legitimate actors or issues of representativeness could legitimate the characteristics of some actors and exclude others. The organisations participating more actively in these consultations were thus defining the rules that were going to be applied to all the other sectors, but it is within this field's discussion, rather than in the specific sectors, that these common rules could be modified. This explains why organisations from distinct sectors participated actively in these discussions, and that contrary to expectations there was clear resistance to this agenda.

It is thus clear that the recognition of civil society participation, far from being a commonly accepted democratic progress, had the potential to create winners and losers. With this insight in mind it is less surprising that organisations promoting the institutionalisation of civil dialogue did not try to justify it simply in terms of efficiency, such as the predictability of outcomes for organisations (Ruzza 2004, 45), but rather tried to articulate it as an irresistible cause (Greenwood 2007b, 344). According to Bourdieu fields are characterised by their own *habitus*, a set of interiorised social practices and dispositions that inform the range of possible actions by its participants (Bourdieu 1984, 133–136). In this sense it is clear that the constitution of the field had some visible effects on the actions of the organisations in terms of windows of opportunity, acceptable ways of advocacy and collective action. In the wake of the EU's legitimacy crisis, of the discourse of the Commission and of the Laeken declaration, it would have been impossible for organisations to oppose frontally any proposal framed as a form of participatory democracy and thereafter to be taken seriously within this field. Instead these organisations used democratic arguments to weaken it by arguing that participatory democracy should not endanger the EU's fragile representative democracy. Similarly, they argued that for the sake of democratic accountability sound representativeness criteria should be associated to the article.

In addition to the opposition of social partners, the promoters of civil dialogue had to face distinct attitudes from institutional actors, such as the Parliament's scepticism about participatory democracy, the attempt by the EESC to use it to raise its own profile and the lack of support (if not the reluctance) of the Commission to support civil society demands during the Convention. And yet organisations experienced Article 47 as a victory, which shows that the agenda was not totally set by European institutions and that organisations had a relevant margin of manoeuvre. The very presence of these fragmented interests could have acted as an opportunity structure, as organisations could to some extent engage in some "venue shopping". Furthermore, it may have increased the importance of organisation, coordination and activism as ways to avoid compliance with the institution's colliding expectations.

However, it also appears that "playing by the rules of the game" (or abiding by the habitus of the field), by being providers of expertise, demands and legitimacy, was the most efficient approach, and that recourse to protest, such as the 1998 "red card campaign", was a rare "ultima ratio". As is stated above, the Convention did not produce a change in the methods of collective action of organisations, as organisations did not employ outside lobbying (Mahoney 2008a), let alone protest. On the contrary, it has appeared that the main reaction of the oldest contributors to the increased number of participants (and thus to competition in the Convention) was to foster cooperation between them via the CSCG.

7

The Development of the Participatory Agenda in the Aftermath of the Convention (2003–2011): Consultation and Direct Participation

The stakes of the aftermath of the Convention

The expectation of those organisations that promoted the article on participatory democracy was that recognition of the principle of consultation in the Treaty would grant them secure access to EU institutions. Furthermore, they expected to unify consultation practices across different departments and institutions and to avoid competition with outsiders, because of the recognition of the principle of representativeness that had been elaborated on territorial grounds. In this sense the publication of minimum standards for consultation (European Commission 2002c) could appear as an implementation mechanism of the 2001 White Paper on Governance and of Article 47, in that it defined common rules for all Commission departments and seemed to secure the principle of civil dialogue.

However, there are open questions about the extent to which Lisbon Treaty's Article 11 means a success for civil society and the democratisation of the EU. At the time of writing[1] the Commission has taken no action on civil dialogue since the entry into force of the Lisbon Treaty in November 2009. The review of the legal framework for civil society dialogue on the Commission website refers to the protocol to the Amsterdam Treaty rather than to new Article 11 TUE, which is much more detailed.[2] It is also noticeable that the Lisbon Treaty has not turned participation in civil dialogue into a substantive citizens' right (Cuesta López 2010, 138). The consultation system existing today is thus still shaped by the 2001 White Paper and the 2002 Consultation Standards rather than by the Treaty article negotiated during the Convention. This confirms that in the view of the Commission the Treaty article is a mere recognition of existing practices, rather than an innovation that changes the relations between civil society and institutions.

There has been a clear evolution during the aftermath of the Convention, since 2002, whereby the move towards restricted consultation with insiders in a de facto accreditation system via the CONECCS database (2002–2007) has been replaced by a greater emphasis on non-restrictive forms of interaction with civil society, such as open consultation, transparency and citizens' initiatives. The main landmarks in the subsequent institutional changes were the White Paper on Communication (European Commission 2006a), the European Transparency Initiative and its recent update (European Commission 2006b; European Parliament and European Commission 2011), and the regulation of the European Citizens' Initiative (2011–2012).

Civil society dialogue: from accreditation to openness: communication, transparency and better law making

The Commission defines consultation as "those processes through which the Commission wishes to trigger input from outside interested parties for the shaping of policy prior to decision by the Commission" (European Commission 2002c, 15–16). The Commission website summarises the mechanisms of consultation as follows:

> Interested parties are consulted through different tools, such as Green and White Papers, communications, consultation documents, advisory committees, expert groups and ad-hoc consultations. Consultation via the Internet is common practice. Often, consultation is a combination of different tools and takes place in several phases during the preparation of the proposal.[3]

The Commission emphasises the diversity of procedures and of possible stakeholders (interested parties). Today, despite the recognition of civil society dialogue in the Treaty and the reforms that occurred between 2002 and 2011, mechanisms for dialogue with civil society have still not been unified into a single typology. These mechanisms are basically structured by the Consultation standards (European Commission

2002c) adopted in the aftermath of the White Paper on Governance and by the subsequent transparency devices of 2006 and 2011.

The principle established by these minimal standards is that the Commission must at least carry out consultations on all significant policy proposals, which are understood to be those requiring impact assessments (European Commission 2002c, 15). Nevertheless, the Commission encourages its DGs to apply these rules to any consultation they intend to launch. Furthermore, the 2002 standards contribute to simplify this diversity of procedures by configuring two broad categories, those of open and focused consultations. The Commission's approach in these years, indeed since the early 1990s (European Commission 1992), has been characterised by emphasising the openness of EU institutions to outside interests, and this is also confirmed by the minimal standards for consultation:

> Every individual citizen, enterprise or association will continue to be able to provide the Commission with input. In other words, the Commission does not intend to create new bureaucratic hurdles in order to restrict the number of those that can participate in consultation processes. (Commission 2002c, 11)

The Commission thus establishes open consultation as the guiding principle and rejects the establishment of a system of accreditation that would be characteristic of a corporatist system of interest intermediation.

Nevertheless the same document also foresees that the Commission can organise focused consultations whereby "for practical reasons" access to some consultations such as advisory fora and hearings has to be limited (European Commission 2002c, 11). Focused consultation implies that the Commission chooses the organisations or experts that are going to be invited to provide their views on a particular policy proposal. The Commission acknowledges the need to restrict access to consultation under some circumstances, and in doing so it has discussed the criteria to decide which stakeholders to include and which to exclude; thereby it "underline[s] the importance it attaches to input from representative European organisations" (European Commission 2002c, 11). In fact the Commission endorsed the criteria of representativeness that were established by the EESC in response to the 2001 White Paper on Governance, albeit stressing that they would not be the only criteria taken into consideration. This is completed by the guidelines on target groups, which focus on providing interested parties with an opportunity to be involved.

These criteria were implemented via the CONECCS database (Commission 2002b, 7), replaced later by the Transparency Register. The years between the Convention and the European Transparency Initiative (2002–2007) could be appropriately described as "a niche between accreditation and laissez-faire" (Greenwood and Halpin 2007) because of the use of CONECCS as a way of preselecting accredited and representative consultation partners. However, since the adoption of the White Paper on Communication and the Transparency Initiative the Commission has stressed its openness to a wide range of stakeholders, and sees an open and unrestricted dialogue as an opportunity to communicate about the EU.

That being said, the aftermath of the 2002 principles and the Convention was far from the creation of a corporatist accreditation system based on pre-established criteria. Firstly, some aspects of the consultation standards were applied in a very loose way. Some of the consultative committees have been charged with a lack of transparency over the selection of the members, the way committees are consulted and how their expertise is used (Fazi and Smith 2006). This has led to some successful complaints before the Ombudsman (Friedrich 2011, 102). It remains to be seen whether the inclusion of a Treaty article concerning dialogue with civil society could escalate complaints like this to the European Court of Justice (Cuesta López 2010). Secondly, it has been pointed out that the system has not achieved a balanced representation of interests. Whereas this may not be surprising in relation to the open consultations (Quittkat 2011), as it may be a consequence of openness, it is relatively surprising in relation to corporatist mechanisms. Nevertheless it has been pointed out that some consultative groups are characterised by an lack of balance, favouring representative groups and more particularly business interests (Fazi and Smith 2006; Pohl 2006; Friedrich 2011, 125–169), even though to date there has been no systematic assessment of how balanced representation is across different consultation venues and policy issues (but see Bozzini 2011; Quittkat 2011; Quittkat and Kotzian 2011; and Lindgren and Persson 2012, 67–83 for sectoral assessments).

Making participation more open was a salient issue in the making of the transparency initiatives. Bozzini (2011, 9) mentions the "resistance on the part of 'insiders' to the broadening of consultation to the national and local associations and 'every individual citizen, enterprise or association' in Europe. Consultations in areas like labour law might prove controversial." Bozzini confirms that the competition between social partners and some NGOs did not end even after the Commission started moving the transparency agenda by quoting the following:

For some social partners, primarily trade unions, the consultation should have taken a form of formal consultation of the EU social partners on the basis of Article 138 EC. They perceived the conduct of an open consultation on labour law by means of a Green Paper as a downgrading of the Social Dialogue and of their pivotal role as representatives of employers and workers. The EP and the EESC also expressed reservations about the Commission's recourse to a public consultation. However, a large majority of the Member States and Social NGOs positively welcomed the openness of the consultative process. (European Commission 2007b, 4)

However, corporatist tendencies have been challenged in recent years by the increasing usage of open consultations (Bozzini 2011; Quittkat 2011) and the Barroso Commissions' shift of attention from focused consultation towards an open model aimed at achieving better regulation and transparency, and fostering deliberation on EU policymaking (Greenwood 2011a). The European Transparency Initiative is confirmation of the Commission's move away from the corporatist elements of the consultation standards. The CONECCS database was replaced by the Register of Interest representatives in 2007. The main characteristic of the register is that it removed references to representativeness and that requirements for registration were weaker. However, the register allegedly failed to meet strong transparency standards because of the significant divergences between the Parliament's and the Commission's orientations (de Castro Asarta 2011) and a lack of monitoring, which was evidenced by the registration of two fake organisations (Greenwood 2011a). The latest version of the register maintains a voluntary character but also creates a stronger pressure to sign up to the register (Greenwood 2011a, Castro Asarta 2011), as registration has become a requirement for obtaining a long-term access card to the Parliament premises and because it announces that contributions from unregistered organisations will be treated as coming from individuals.

The insistence on openness can be criticised as creating a "laissez-faire" system that shows the lack of democratic substance to these processes (Smith and Fazi 2006; Cuesta 2010; Kohler Koch 2010), because an openness system does not "guarantee equal inclusion and responsiveness in order to strive for fair and equal justification processes among all concerns" (Friedrich 2011, 93). The Commission prefers to stress that all interests *can* be involved – even if existing open consultation processes remain strongly biased towards business groups and to interest from Northern Europe (Quittkat 2011) – than creating a system that rebalances opportunities of influence at the expense of creating access barriers (Pérez-Solórzano Borragán and Smismans 2012, 418). This may also be explained by its concern about its own legitimacy problems: it can be argued that an accreditation system requires a higher degree of legitimacy from the institution establishing it, which must provide sound arguments about who will be admitted and who will be excluded. The Commission is, however, already portrayed as a distant bureaucratic leviathan, and it simply cannot afford to create further distance from those interests that would have to be excluded through the establishment of a consultation system: "The Commission will avoid consultation processes which could give the impression that 'Brussels is only talking to Brussels'" (European Commission 2002c, 12).

The decisive turning away from the restricted civil dialogue agenda was certainly when the referenda in France and the Netherlands failed, creating a perception that civil dialogue and the participatory democracy agenda had contributed little to increasing the perceived legitimacy of the EU.

> [Speaking about large transnational NGOs such as OXFAM]. And then we have the, you know, the CONCORDs and the Social Platforms. [...] The Convention was where their credibility was smashed. It was smashed because they could not deliver, they made a lot of noise by saying: "Our members are not happy, our members would want this", and they got a lot of what they asked for. And then when the politicians would come and say: "And now your members will be happy and they will be supportive" "Oh! There's no way we can contact them". So anti-poverty networks said no, CONCORD said, "well, no", Women's Lobby said "no, we can't do it". (Interview 20, with a representative of CONCORD)

In this sense, in the aftermath of these referenda the Commission clearly started to move away from the previous agenda. One of the effects of the crisis opened by the rejection of the Constitution was to make EU institutions more concerned about communication, and civil society dialogue was perceived as a contributory solution (European Commission 2005a; del Río Villar 2008). Plan D for dialogue (European Commission 2005a) was a communication plan seeking to decentralise civil dialogue with civil society, in order to engage more with national organisations and make this dialogue visible and far reaching by associating it with communication strategies. This move was followed by the White Paper on Communication elaborated by Commissioner Wallström, which promoted a close association of broad consultations with communication in order to "communicate Europe in partnership" (European Commission 2006a). This strategy depicts consultation as a relevant contribution to a communication strategy, which does not only consist of providing information or "explaining Europe" but also seeks to listen to citizens. The strategy included transforming the Representations of the Commission in the Member States into places for public debate and consultation. This crisis contributed also to promote a change of attitude by the Parliament, from a reluctant attitude (European Commission 2002c, 4–5) to involvement in dialogue with civil society (European Parliament 2008). The targets of open consultation have broadened over time, seeking to involve not only organised civil society but also individual citizens. In doing so the Commission has developed and increasingly uses surveys and questionnaires as a means of obtaining large numbers of individual responses (Quittkat 2011, 661–662). Although there was little follow up to this move (but see Commissioner Margot Wallström Citizens' Dialogues), it clearly indicates a measure of dissatisfaction with the pre-Convention civil society dialogue.

The better lawmaking package and transparency initiatives confirm the move of the agenda away from semi-corporatist arrangements based on de facto accreditation systems towards the increased usage of open consultation and the abandonment of the principle of representation. Since the Convention the politicisation of the agenda (including the need to face the rejection of the constitution and the transparency "scandals") has favoured a neo-pluralist approach which has to some extent marginalised the original movers. This new approach puts less emphasis on participation by civil society in order to bring legitimacy and more on the creation of a transparent regulatory environment, which was carried out in the first years of the Barroso Commissions (Cini 2008, 750). The 2005 Green Paper on the European Transparency Initiative reframes consultation in the context of increasing output legitimacy:

> Wide consultation allows involvement of interested parties in the policy-shaping process. It is an essential tool for improving the quality of the Commission's legislative proposals. The Commission's *minimum standards* form a key part of the *Better Lawmaking* action plan, the primary objective of which is to improve the quality of the EU legislation. (European Commission 2006b, 11)

This is clearly a neo-pluralist approach where civil society organisations are not considered as having specific legitimacy which they can transfer to the policymaking process, as the pre-Convention frame seemed to suggest. Consultation of civil society and business and impact assessment are thus now conceived as helping to create a level playing field for interest representation, contributing to better policy outcomes:

> Such a reinforced application will focus, in particular on providing better feedback, a more coordinated approach to consultation and the need for ensuring plurality of views and interests expressed in consultations. This approach will help improve the quality of the Commission's impact assessments, thereby contributing to the implementation of the Commission's "better regulation" policy. (European Commission 2007b, 6–7)

The rationale now is that all those affected by a decision must be allowed to have a voice, not to make the policymaking process legitimate but to bring about a discussion that considers the issue in a more complex way, allowing all interests to be heard, akin to the discourse conception of democracy. Greenwood (2011a, 332–333) points out the deliberative overtones of the code of conduct included in the most recent evolution towards transparency. Although input and output legitimacy are obviously not necessarily at conflict with each other, the behaviour of the actors and the procedures to be followed to achieve these two forms of legitimacy are different: "there remains a tension between on the one hand ensuring quality and focused contributions and on the other hand opening up the process" (Fazi and Smith 2006, 39).

The question, therefore, is where are we after more than a decade of debate. The review undertaken here suggests that the implementation of the agenda of civil dialogue has failed. Organisations sought to institutionalise access between 1997 and 2003. The EU recognised this claim via a non-binding document setting minimal standards for consultation (European Commission 2002c) and a Treaty article, which is still subject to much legal speculation. This Treaty article mandate has not produced a significant policy development in the direction of institutionalising dialogue with a constituency of organisations representing citizens' interests. On the contrary further policy initiatives have moved the agenda from a civil dialogue aimed at creating a mechanism of participatory democracy in the EU towards a regime of open consultation, which seeks to create a level playing field where all interests can be heard on condition that some procedural rules on transparency are respected.

However, the jury is still out in relation to the EU-civil society agenda. First, the principle of consultation is now in the Treaty and there will be uncertainty until either the European Court of Justice or the Ombudsman is asked to decide whether faults in the consultation process can be used to challenge EU institutions' decisions. Secondly, the prevalence of open consultation does not contribute to a better balance of interests in the policymaking scenario, as open consultations seem to remain balanced in favour of business interests and organisations from Northern Europe (Bozzini 2011; Quittkat 2011). Finally, focused consultation still happens in consultative committees. With the end of the CONECCS database and the lack of revision of the 2002 standards there is no clear guideline about who is invited to participate in consultative committees, and the main criterion for invitation to these fora seems to be reputation (Quittkat and Kotzian 2011). Even though focused consultation now accounts for only 10% of the consultations, these fora remain relevant opportunities for agenda setting. Available research suggests that in real terms it is reputation, trust and membership in coalitions which matter the most, and more importantly, that these factors are relevant determinants of the likelihood of influence via open consultations (Quittkat and Kotzian 2011; Klüver 2013). Hence some suggest that the re-emergence of the question of representativeness and access barriers is not yet to be ruled out (de Castro Asarta 2011; Pérez-Solórzano Borragán and Smismans 2012). Castro Asarta (2011, 14) considers that the disclosure of geographical representativeness in the register still reflects the "long-standing preference for NGOs to be 'representative'".

The next section addresses the impact of the ECI on relations between civil society and EU institutions. As proved in previous chapters, this innovation was introduced to the Convention by a different alliance from the one that promoted civil dialogue. This mechanism has been under discussion between 2009 and 2011 and has entered into force in 2012.

The implementation of the ECI: 2009–2012

The other relevant evolution in this period is the regulation of the ECI (2009–2011) and its entry into force in June 2012. As discussed in Chapter 5, the proposal of a mechanism that would allow citizens to introduce an element on to the EU's agenda was brought to the Convention by a coalition of European organisations led by IRI Europe and Mehr Demokratie (Lamassoure 2004; Clerck-Sachsse 2012). Most of the organisations promoting civil dialogue were not involved in this campaign but this did not make the ECI an outsiders' idea: it was the result of professional lobbying by well-resourced organisations

(Clerck-Sachsse 2012), which had been lobbying the EU on this issue since the Amsterdam ICG (Interview 11).

According to French Convention member Alain Lamassoure the ECI was the least ambitious of the different initiative mechanisms that were discussed during the Convention (Lamassoure 2004). In the wake of the referenda for the ratification – which ultimately failed in France and the Netherlands – one of the central objectives of the proponents of the ECI was to introduce a direct democracy device whereby citizens could call for pan-European debates, akin to those existing in Switzerland or the USA. The more modest ECI was accepted as a compromise, which favoured the creation of complementary participation opportunities that would not demand an in-depth conceptual transformation of EU democratic participation devices.

The ECI survived the redrafting of the symbolically federal elements of the failed Constitution in the making of the Lisbon Treaty in 2009, although the label of 'participatory democracy' disappeared from what is now Article 11. The rapid action by the Commission on the ECI following the entry into force of the Treaty in November 2009 is interesting. Firstly, it means that the concern of EU institutions about their disconnection from European citizens remains high and that participation mechanisms are still considered a viable way of reconnecting with them. On the other hand, it also means that the institutions' focus on participation has changed. Whereas the Commission has taken no new action on civil society dialogue following the entry into force of the Treaty, it was quick to publish a Green Paper on the Citizens' Initiative (European Commission 2009). The fact that the ECI has a potential to engage with citizens directly whereas civil dialogue has hardly spilled over beyond Brussels may be the main reason behind this move.

The implementation of the ECI required a regulation in order to solve some of the questions left open by the Treaty article and to develop the implementation mechanism (regulation 211/2011 of the Parliament and the Council). The regulation had to define first what "a significant number of Member States" is. This also relates to the question of the balanced distribution of signatures among these states, in order to avoid national campaigns being "Europeanised" by collecting a small proportion of signatures in other Member States. In the 2009 Green Paper the Commission defined a significant number of Member States as one third. This was based on what the what the Treaty establishes for enhanced cooperation among Member States, but it was very demanding for ECI promoters. This meant that signatures from nine different Member States would be required in order to carry out an ECI. However, a good number of contributions by civil society organisations to the Green Paper consultation considered this threshold as too demanding for campaigners. It seems unfair to expect organisers to achieve the same degree of representation as Member States, since they lack Member States' resources for cooperating at the European level. The intervention by the European Parliament, which had opposed this demanding threshold since it was first proposed in the Green Paper (Bouza Garcia 2010), was decisive in reducing the threshold to seven Member States (one quarter), which was finally adopted in the regulation. By contrast there was an easier consensus when establishing the proportion of signatures to be gathered in each country. The principle that was adopted was inspired by the allocation of European Parliament election seats but applied in the opposite way. In this case, the smaller the population the larger the number of signatures required.

A critical issue in the negotiation of the implementation mechanism was checking whether the EU had a legal base and the Commission the competence to initiate the legislation that the ECI demands. The risk was that a group of citizens would carry out a campaign and collect one million signatures only to find their proposal rejected because of legal reasons, which was likely to cause frustration rather than allowing reconnection with citizens. In this area the first proposal by the Commission was to carry out an admissibility check only after the collection of 300,000 signatures. The rationale for this proposal was that the Commission wanted to avoid the burden of doing legal checks – with the additional risk of opening avenues for contesting EU competence before the ECJ – for possibly unsuccessful initiatives. However, the idea of having initiatives dismissed after the collection of such a significant number of supports was seen by civil society organisations as still very likely to cause frustration. After the negotiation a decision was made to divide the check in half. The Commission will verify the existence of a legal basis on the moment of registration, but acceptance will depend on a substantial check conducted after the collection of all required signatures (Szeligowska and Mincheva 2012). The Commission has already declined the registration of 18 proposed campaigns after the initial check of competence.[4]

Although Article 11.4 does not mention the promoters of the initiatives, comparative constitutional law tends to consider these as decisive actors and gives them a relevant role in the organisation, and even in the policymaking resulting from their initiative (Cuesta López 2008). The Commission's first scheme recognised the organisers by granting them a right to be auditioned by the Commission and to have an opportunity to introduce their proposal in a hearing at the European Parliament. The recognition of the citizens' committee was an attempt to avoid ECIs being hijacked by lobbies and to ensure that it remained an avenue for the participation of individual citizens. This was secured on the grounds of a proposal by the Parliament that organisers must constitute a citizens' committee consisting of seven persons legally residing in seven different Member States. Additionally, Article 4.1 of the regulation (211/2011) establishes that organisers must disclose the source of the financial support for their campaign, although this provision is far from being implemented systematically.

Two more issues were not raised during the making of the regulation but are likely to remain important in relation to the question of the registers of collective action that are available for civil society in the EU. The first one has to do with the lack of provision for public funding. The cost of organising a signature collection campaign, albeit possibly lowered by the recognition of online signatures, was not discussed during the Green Paper stage nor in the institutional stage. This contrasts strongly with the well-known tendency of the Commission to subsidise the emergence of European civil society platforms (Sanchez Salgado 2007) with the justification that they contribute to make the EU more democratic and to balance the influence of business interests. Using public funding to compensate for the costs incurred by organisers is also a common practice in countries that have this type of agenda-setting mechanism (Cuesta López 2008). Given the significant costs of campaigning and signature collection, and the likely effect of this in communicating EU affairs, it appears surprising that no scheme of support for citizens' initiatives has been designed so far.

The second issue is the mere fact that obtaining one million signatures across seven Member States is a very demanding task. Data on "pilot campaigns" launched before the enforcement of the ECI show that only five out of 21 campaigns attained one million signatures (Bouza García 2012). Salient organisations such as ETUC have been unable to reach the target of one million signatures during the pilot phase. Among the campaigns carried out during the first year of the ECI, only three out of 15 have met the threshold. This means that the cost/benefit relation of organising ECIs is likely to remain suboptimal in relation to other forms of participation. Collecting one million signatures has a significant economic and organisation cost, and yet it does not guarantee success in terms of policy implementation, even though the ECI can have other uses in the agenda-setting process (Bouza García 2012). Other than trying to set the Commission's agenda, the main use for signature collection campaigns is expressing disagreement with the Commission's agenda on a given topic; that is, ECIs may not necessarily target the institutional but also look at the broader public agenda. ECIs can be an effective strategy for building pressure on possible rivals, as a way of "naming and shaming" activities that have an already poor reputation, such as genetically-modified organisms crops or nuclear energy. A third type use is the already mentioned strategy for access to court.[5] Organisations may want to test the limits of EU competence in a given domain by trying to build cases on the grounds of rejected initiatives. The fourth possible use is eventual capture by the Commission itself. In the same way that there is evidence that EU institutions have used civil society organisations to shape the agenda as a way of building irresistible campaigns, it would not be surprising to find out that the Commission could make it known to some organisations that it would take action on a certain proposal if it was to obtain support of at least one million citizens. The fifth possible effect of ECIs is the contribution to the articulation of new coalitions in EU politics. The ECI requires the mobilisation of grassroots citizens, so it is possible that a coalition of national organisations may be articulated at the EU level and then institutionalised in Brussels. The pattern of the ELIANT campaign seems to fit this model. Finally, ECIs may be used to try to block agendas. It may be imagined that groups trying to oppose policy in a given area could try to organise ECIs in order to resist proposals, or more cynically to see them defeated and to discourage further campaigns in a given field.

The contribution by organised civil society to consultation on the Green Paper on ECI regulation is interesting for two reasons. The evidence from this consultation is that the organisations that were most involved in the agenda-setting process analysed above were not interested in the ECI, as only eight out of 22 organisations sent contributions.[6] Furthermore, half of these organisations (EFC, Social Platform, ECAS and CEMR) have as the main purpose of their contribution a demand to the Commission to carry out action in other fields. The following example from the Social Platform reaction stands out as a notable example:

> Social Platform welcomes the Green Paper on the citizens' initiative. As a response, Social Platform calls on the European Commission to launch a public consultation on how to implement the first part of the Lisbon Treaty article 11 on civil dialogue. [...] This would ensure that both parts of the article are properly implemented. Social Platform would like to stress that the right to petition is not the only new instrument related to participatory democracy that the Treaty

of Lisbon introduces into EU decision making processes. (Social Platform 2010: 1)

This paper by the Social Platform is particularly telling, because the abovementioned paragraph is the only reference to the object of the consultation, whereas the rest of it focuses on why the EU needs a new initiative on civil dialogue.

The second relevant evolution is that the consultation attracted a majority of organisations not registered in the transparency register.[7] This is significant because the social pressure existing on organisations active in EU politics to register (Greenwood 2011a) means that unregistered groups are not frequently involved in EU consultations. Even more significantly, it can be anticipated that the ECI can foster the engagement of organisations that were previously not involved in the EU, as the Green Paper encouraged the promoters of the ECI (Initiative and Referendum Institute and Mehr Demokratie) to register (Bouza Garcia 2012).

The origin of unregistered organisations confirms the impression that this constitutes a new constituency becoming interested in EU politics. Only about 20 of the unregistered organisations could be identified as potentially regular contributors to EU policy consultations despite not being registered. These are national sections of the European movement, unregistered European organisations and national members of these organisations. The consultation also attracted a significant number of national and regional political parties and trade unions, such as sections of the French Socialist Party, Germany's CDU and the Basque Nationalist Party, among others. About a third of unregistered organisations are national civil society groups specifically aiming at promoting participatory democracy, such as the Bulgarian Association for the Promotion of Citizens Initiative or the Citizens' Initiative for the Europe of the Citizens. Finally it is interesting that contributions by unregistered organisations represent a higher linguistic diversity, with only 37% of contributions written in English, than registered organisations, which have 57% English contributions.

This does not necessarily make organisations interested in the ECI outsiders to the system of relations between EU institutions and civil society. They have connections to EU level organisations, they may be in the process of engaging with EU institutions and they may end up creating new European organisations. Nevertheless they undoubtedly represent a more diverse and politicised constituency than the one which contributed to influencing the agenda ahead of the European

Convention. The debate on the ECI Green Paper suggests that this mechanism may provide a new institutionalisation opportunity for groups which are not frequently active in EU politics.

Although the organisations that advocated for civil dialogue in order to obtain better access to EU institutions did not show great engagement with the ECI, neither during the Convention nor during the negotiation of the regulation or the first year of its existence. Nevertheless, the first ECI to ever collect in excess of a million signatures is the "Water and sanitation are a human right!" initiative, which has been organised by some of the largest civil society networks in Brussels, including the EEB, ETUC and the Social Platform.[8] In any event it can also be expected that the ECI will bring more diversity and possibly more contestation to the field of EU–civil society relations (see Chapter 8).

Conclusion

In a nutshell, the process following the European Convention has seen the consolidation of the field of participatory democracy. However, the consolidation of the field has been the result of a second round of innovations that has contributed to redistribution of the capitals that resulted from the agenda-setting phase. The promoters of civil dialogue achieved remarkable success in introducing the principle in the Treaty. Their interpretation is that the article was meant to grant them access to all EU institutions rather than just the Commission and to produce a greater homogenisation of consultation practices. They also expected a secure place around the consultation table on an almost equal footing to traditional players such as social partners. If this was to some extent the road travelled from 2002–2006 under the CONECCS database, the Commission has now clearly moved away from this agenda by emphasising openness instead of accreditation via the transparency register and the ECI. This means that capitals in the field have been redistributed. Whereas the promoters of civil dialogue were critically satisfied with the progress achieved in 2002–2006 (Fazi and Smith 2006) and they agree with an increased transparency, the Treaty article has not achieved the degree of recognition they sought. Instead the new participatory mechanisms seem to favour other abilities, such as reputation and the capacity to mobilise supporters. The effect is that the capitals most rewarded today in the field of civil society participation are different from those that mattered when it was established.

8
Assessing the Contribution of Participation to Legitimacy

Citizens and civil dialogue: participation or representation?

As has been previously stated, organisations expect more systematic and uniform consultation practices across Commission services, in particular in the opening up of possibilities in DGs that so far have been rather difficult to access for civil society organisations, as well as the establishment of structured dialogue with more reluctant institutions, such as the European Parliament and the Council. Furthermore, Article 11.2 seems to recognise the demand by civil society organisations for recognition and mandates horizontal or political dialogue with top level officials over the general orientation of Commission policies rather than concrete policy decisions.

1. The institutions shall maintain an open, transparent and regular dialogue with representative associations and civil society.[1]

However, civil dialogue's recognition hardly addresses the issue that this tool remains distant from grassroots civil society. Civil dialogue is certainly a valuable tool from a democratic point of view, in particular when comparing it with traditional lobby strategies (Smismans 2004; Fazi and Smith 2006). The role of the representation of interests in the public space can be grasped with the idea of functional participation in governance as defined by Stijn Smismans (2004,40–41) via a clear distinction between informal lobbying and structured relations. It has a bigger normative assumption than interest groups' participation (Friedrich 2011), as it aims to deal with how participation may complement representative democracy.

Interviews have tended to confirm organisations' weak relations with their members. In this sense four civil society interviewees endorsed the EEB's statement that associating EU level groups does not grant consensus from national members (Ruzza 2011, 461). Officials and members of the Convention share this impression with a critical note:

> But we must be realistic and therefore rather low profile in the way we define relations with civil society, because we may give the impression that we associate all citizens, and that's a utopia that we will never achieve. (Interview 1, with Jean-Luc Dehaene)

> This illustrates one of the large gaps of European civil society which is the insufficient link that they establish with their members at the national level, in particular on what I call horizontal questions. After all what was in the Treaty? What we will do with the European project and what direction and what path it will take. So it was purely a horizontal civil dialogue, that is, outside the traditional scope of civil society organisations from a sector point of view, it was about social questions, not about the environment, there was no trade, no development, no matter what, or culture, on which, I would say, European structures can rarely take a step without consulting their members. However for national organisations, because there is also a part of responsibility of national organisations, you know, these issues, 'the meaning of the European project, we're paid to sell I mean, to lobby on issues of family, culture, education and so on, but we're not paid to discuss the meaning of the European project, we leave that to our European structures.' (Interview 20, with an official of the EESC)

Up to 12 interviewees pointed out civil society organisations' difficulties in getting involved beyond their own field of competence into what the interviewee from the EESC quoted above calls horizontal debates and in particular political or ideological issues.

> We prefer to think of ourselves like constructive activists not engaging on discussions on the big concepts like socialism or liberalism. We prefer to think like this, this and this is useful for our members. (Interview 3, with a representative of the Social Platform)

The only exception to this is the PFCS, which wished to contribute a more horizontal approach. This may have been one of the decisive factors why many CSOs felt that they were not concerned by the national ratification debates.

Interviews also reveal that organisations played a minor role in the diffusion of the debate towards national organisations because they found it extremely difficult to foster the interest of their own members. In this sense some interviewees confirm the opinion of the EESC official quoted above by saying that their members were expecting a debate about the substance of EU policies, whereas the Convention focused almost exclusively on institutional and procedural matters. Pérez Solórzano-Borragán (2007, 280) has argued that this is one of the reasons for the disconnection between European and national organisations. Additionally interviewees tended to say that the Convention chose to focus on these topics, which were not the result of the Laeken mandate. This perception that the Convention tended to ignore most of the substantive demands of civil society may partly explain why members of civil society organisations considered the Convention an issue of indirect concern for them despite its high political profile. This applies in particular to participatory democracy, in that this topic is considered too distant and abstract to make national organisations interested.

The only interviewees who argued that members of their networks very much appreciated these new instruments and were ready to use them are the first interviewee from the Social Platform (Interview 3), COFACE and ACN. It remains that three-quarters of the interviewees did not perceive any interest in the issue among their members. It is noticeable, however, that the organisations outlining the lack of interest among their members were not those at the core of the coalition. It is interesting that references to participation by national organisations and publics did not exclude a lack of interest among their own members, since they most often refer to the ability of national organisations to participate in debates on the EU. Several interviewees explain that a lot of the disconnection has to do with lack of involvement by national publics. Credit for efforts to inform the public goes most often to organisations which rejected the Treaty. The following quotes are representative of these remarks:

> I think it was disappointing but ... I think they [ATTAC] played a role, a really useful role, as they kind of urged a responsible process, they tried really to hold people to account. (Interview 9, with a representative of the Social Platform)

> I've been, I've been myself at the social plat...the social forum. You know this big thing that was started in Porto Alegre and is now everywhere in the world? I was in Paris, there was once one in Paris and it was huge! It was [emphasis] huuuge really, I was impressed about

the size. [...] Many environmental organisations have been outside...a bit outside of this debate. Apart from Spain where the most active and largest member organisation was part of the anti-EU platform, Ecologistas en Acción. (Interview 36, with a representative of the EEB)

Since the entry into force of the Lisbon Treaty, the ECI has been pointed out as "one of the most visible and concrete expressions of the innovations brought by the Lisbon Treaty" (Council of the European Union 2010, 1). Evaluations of the ECI tend to under- or overestimate its significance. For instance, the ECI is sometimes hailed as a method in which EU citizens may deeply transform the EU by introducing a system whereby they can use direct participation to change legislation, as in Switzerland or some USA states (Pichler 2008). On the other hand, sceptical authors argue that as with previous attempts to introduce European participatory mechanisms it will not succeed in bringing citizens closer to the EU because it is still the result of elite civil society mobilisations (de Cleck-Sachsse 2012). It is thus worth considering the eventual contribution of the ECI to the democratisation of the EU in the light of the previous chapters' findings about the evolution of the participatory agenda. This section considers the impact that the ECI may have on the field of civil society involvement in the EU. In particular it addresses whether it can contribute to create a new dimension in terms of participation and representation and whether it can create more diversity in a field so far dominated by tensions between insiders and outsiders. The next section will consider its implications for the evolution and development of a European public sphere.

The EU is not the only polity to have examined participatory mechanisms as a way of rebuilding trust with organised civil society and citizens. The general observation is that participatory mechanisms are conceived as a complement to representative democracy. The consequence is that most of them are as a consequence soft designs whose proceedings cannot bind institutions of representative democracy (Smith 2009, 22–24). The ECI can also be characterised as a weak participation instrument because it does not contest the Commission's monopoly of legislative initiative, which does not allow that the initiative will be discussed by EU legislative decision-makers. The Commission is not bound by the proposal and is entirely free to accept, reject or modify it. Furthermore it is characterised by material limits, as the proposal must fall within the powers of the Commission and must aim to apply the Treaty, which means that it cannot be used to modify existing treaties. Cuesta considers that it is not a direct democracy device since citizens cannot take further action, for example a referendum, if they disagree with the decision finally adopted by the Commission, and that it is thus better conceived as an agenda-setting device, "a mechanism of *participatory democracy* which is fully subordinated to the political will of the representatives that could approve, alter or reject the citizens' proposals" (Cuesta López 2012, 256). Further nuance can be suggested by pointing out that even though the initiative is labelled as a citizens' initiative, it is most likely to be used by organised civil society. As was stated in Chapter 7, the ECI requires a significant measure of organisation – signature collection in at least seven Member States – and knowledge of the EU policymaking process – Commission competences and legal bases – which means it cannot be equated to the simplicity of organising online petitions, for example.

The question about these devices is whether they are something more than an exercise of freedom of expression or whether they can simply be considered "window dressing exercises" (Fazi and Smith 2006, 48–49). It is worth asking if the new mechanism gives citizens a right that they were previously unable to exercise. The ECI appears to provide some apparently soft opportunities which may nevertheless be relevant. The first is feedback on the proposals, as this is significant for the Commission's accountability and so that organisations know how their contribution was used. It is unclear how institutions respond to civil society, since they tend to provide very general evaluations of contributions to consultations (Quittkat 2011, 662–664). However, unlike reports of poor feedback on civil dialogue, the ECI regulation puts a clear requirement on the Commission to justify its decision to take action or not to the promoters of all successful ECIs, and indeed to the public:

> Article 10: Where the Commission receives a citizens' initiative in accordance with Article 9 it shall:
>
> (a) publish the citizens' initiative without delay in the register;
> (b) receive the organisers at an appropriate level to allow them to explain in detail the matters raised by the citizens' initiative;
> (c) within three months, set out in a communication its legal and political conclusions on the citizens' initiative, the action it intends to take, if any, and its reasons for taking.[2]

Representation and diversity

Functional participation remains limited to a narrow constituency of Brussels-based civil society organisations relatively insulated from the general public. Presenting civil dialogue as a form of citizens' participation in the EU policymaking process implies that civil society organisations are a manifestation of the free will of their members to advocate a cause or interest, and as a consequence organisations' involvement in policy consultations provides an opportunity for citizens' participation. However, as legitimate as the consultation of civil society organisations may be, their involvement in policymaking is not a form of citizens' direct participation unless members of the organisations are effectively consulted and involved in the process. Empirical evidence reviewed earlier and the literature suggest that this involvement is relatively weak. Consequently, when organisations participate in policymaking they are not providing a direct participation opportunity for their members but *representing* them.

It has been shown that the Commission has an increasing preference for open over focused consultation. This, however, does not mean that the field of consultation is now characterised by a completely open character. Focused consultation still takes place, and by definition includes some organisations and excludes others. It is unclear which criteria the Commission follows when deciding whether to consider organisations' points of view.

Therefore the question remains why some organisations should obtain the right to be consulted and thus possibly influence policymaking on certain topics. The response that the Commission has traditionally given is that this should be the result of a combination of expertise and representativeness, although representativeness criteria are no longer taken into account in the selection of organisations involved in focused consultations. Representativeness is relevant from a participatory point of view not only from the numerical perspective (number of organisations, members and Member States where the organisation is active) but also from a substantive point of view, since it is assumed that larger organisations are able to "download" Brussels' debates to their members.

However, as has already been said, the main problem is that numerical representativeness does not ensure a fluid relation with grassroots members and that it excludes cause organisations. Organisational complexity, consultation procedures and deadlines, encroachment in the EU's institutional system and members' disinterest make it extremely difficult for organisations to consult their members before taking a decision. In this sense, it is probably necessary to reconsider how EU-level civil society organisations represent their members.

This issue seems to have been addressed by Article 11 TEU, as it commands institutions to conduct dialogue with 'representative associations and civil society', following this several interpretations about whether this might imply dialogue with unorganised civil society or even whether the EU uses a single definition of civil society at all. Although it has been argued that this wording was created more by clumsiness than intentionality (Greenwood 2007b, 336), it has been shown above that this was a real issue for organisations interested in the Convention's discussions (see Chapters 3 and 6).

Several organisations consider that representativeness criteria impose the force of numbers and formal authorisation logic (Buth 2011), both of which are very difficult to adapt to the kind of interests that they advocate, as excluded citizens' or general interest causes can hardly be consulted or authorisation demanded from their constituencies. From a pluralist point of view, participation in consultations does not need any other criterion of justification if anyone interested can participate. However, in an approach where civil society is invited as a representative of citizens' concerns and may potentially influence policy decisions, the problem is that in most situations civil society organisations cannot act as delegates of a group, and they usually act with a high degree of independence. From a democratic perspective this distance between the principals (the citizens) and the agents (the organisations) is a problem. In Pitkin's classical typology (Pitkin 1972), these organisations' representativeness must be considered to the extent that they substantially *stand for* a cause or a group of people.

The move away from representativeness has been inspired by the recognition that organisations do not contribute to the input legitimacy of the EU but to the emergence of public debates (Kohler-Koch 2010a). However, geographical representativeness criteria have never been replaced by substantive assessment of internal democracy (Greenwood and Halpin 2007; Pérez-Solórzano Borragán and Smismans 2012) or of social representativeness in the public sphere. In relation to the claim that representativeness favours some groups over others, it is possible to adapt the criteria to the diversity of relationships between principals and agents (Castiglione and Warren 2006, 10–12). In this sense, the substantive ability to stand for a cause or group is often advocated by civil society organisations. However, if this criterion is to be considered instead of traditional representativeness, the organisations' ability either to consult their members or to mobilise general publics should be assessed too. Additionally, systematic feedback should be a relevant issue in the consultation process in order to allow civil society and citizens to hold the Commission to account with regard to its responsiveness to citizens' organisations' demands.

The most interesting aspect of the ECI is that in the current context its political salience is probably stronger than can be achieved via civil dialogue or is suggested by its weak legal nature. The ECI can be a powerful agenda initiator (Bouza Garcia and Greenwood 2014), in that it can hardly be ignored by the Commission because of the support of one million citizens and because it provides organisations with room for manoeuvre, in the sense that they are not required to wait for the Commission to propose a White or Green Paper to take action. For this reason organisations that may not have been involved in civil dialogue because they do not share the agenda promoted by the Commission or do not find issues of their interest in the consultation agenda may be attracted by this mechanism. As a consequence, the ECI does not appear to be a mechanism of participation in the strict sense but rather a relatively strong agenda-setting device that can serve to express the demands of one million citizens.

On the grounds of the analysis undertaken so far the expected impact of the ECI is that it and civil dialogue will mobilise different constituencies of organisations, thus extending and continuing the competition between insiders and outsiders that has structured the field of civil society relations in the last decades. Furthermore the ECI can increase the diversity of the field of EU policymaking not only in terms of who participates but also regarding the issues on the agenda. Put simply, the ECI may be mostly used by organisations which so far are not involved in European consultation processes but which have an interest in European politics and an ability to mobilise citizens. The tables in Annex 6 show empirical findings about the organisers of signature collection campaigns that were launched before the entry into force of the ECI and those since June 2012. They suggest clearly that signature collection is attracting participation by organisations that were not active in the debate on civil dialogue. Those are national organisations in part, but essentially this statistic suggests that the ECI is favouring the mobilisation of individuals and activists, which may herald the creation of new European organisations.

The conclusion from these tables is that the ECI is already contributing to make civil society relations more diverse. Unlike the "pilot initiatives" of 2003–2011, it seems that the proper ECIs launched since June 2012 do actually originate from beyond the circle of EU organised civil society. That said, the initiatives build on a range of traditional civil society issues, in particular social issues, environment and liberties/

justice. This, together with the abovementioned lack of interest from more established organisations can be used to anticipate that successful ECIs can create a measure of competition in the field of organised civil society. This means that in the near future the Commission will be required to decide whether to follow the demands of an ECI or the proposals received by civil society in a public consultation. To take just one example, the Commission has decided to take action on the initiative *Water and sanitation are a human right*, committing itself to consult stakeholders on a review of the Water Framework Directive (European Commission 2014, 8). Although it is impossible to know what will happen, it is likely that the promoters of the ECI will claim more attention from the Commission in this consultation because of their support by almost two million citizens, in comparison with the usually weak authorisation that EU organisations can claim.

Table (6A.2) in Annex 6 also shows the potential of the ECI as protest device. So far about 44% (19/24) of the ECIs presented to the Commission have been refused registration. Given the nature of the refused registration initiatives, it is hard to imagine that the promoters could have been surprised by such rejections. This rather suggests that one of the possible uses of the ECI is to communicate contentious agendas to the EU and at the same time be used by organisations to stir up discussion with institutions that previously have been unlikely to hear agendas different from their own. This is the nature of the proposal on Greek debt and the nuclear power proposals. Nevertheless agendas such as those coming from movements in favour of secession, against bullfighting or an unconditional basic income seem to be looking for ways in which they can Europeanise policy proposals. They do not so much suggest contention with the EU but a real interest in bringing a genuine cause to the EU's attention. As an example, after a first rejection the proponents of the basic income proposal redrafted their demands, which are now under consideration.

So far it has appeared that the ECI can have a significant effect on the field of participatory democracy in the EU. Although it can hardly be said to promote direct participation by one million citizens, it has the potential to introduce a significant change in the field of EU civil society relations by increasing diversity, competition and contention. Nevertheless it can be debated to what extent the ECI contributes to the function of representation by organised civil society, in particular in relation to already discussed criticisms of traditional representativeness criteria. Involvement in ECI campaigns and other forms of citizen mobilisation provide evidence of the relevance of organisations in the public sphere and could be formulated as one of the criteria to measure the social representativeness of civil society organisations participating in civil dialogue (Bouza Garcia 2010). This would reward organisations able to deliver goods that the Commission is expecting from civil society, namely the ability to engage in debates about the EU with citizens. Furthermore it would contribute to complete the move to representativeness criteria that take into account organisations' involvement in the public sphere, since scepticism about traditional territorial representativeness (Kohler-Koch 2010a) has not yet given place to an alternative measurement.

Article 11 TEU and communication

The structure of this chapter may have suggested that civil dialogue and the ECI are radically opposed mechanisms with different origins and totally different purposes. However, both are democratic innovations that can provide citizens and organisations with a route to access the EU. This section considers their common contribution to the EU and how they could be implemented in a mutually reinforcing way.

Regarding the broader social dimension, the civil dialogue scheme does not seem capable of fostering debate beyond the organisations that are already well established and interested in European policymaking. Scepticism about the contribution of civil dialogue to the emergence of a European public sphere usually builds on the constant assessment of the difficulty of European organisations to communicate with the public. Because of this, their involvement in direct dialogue with the EU or in open consultations can be assessed as contributing little to a broader debate on EU policymaking. There is a risk of a sort of "participatory autopoeisis", where the recognition and inclusion into the treaties of an already existing practice would turn a governance-inspired tool into a participatory mechanism, bringing the EU closer to the citizens by the mere virtue of being included in the treaties.

Eight interviewees related the inclusion of Article 47 to a political calculation of the Convention that these organisations would act as proxies for European publics and contribute to diffuse and support the Convention's work:

> They were happy to see that some expert groups were interested in their work because media did not get interested in this. (Interview 3, with a representative of the Social Platform)

In this sense some interviewees (EFC, IRI, PFCS) explicitly say that one of the reasons why the Convention accepted Article 47 was to make the

Treaty more attractive to public opinion. The Convention would thus have seen civil society participation and participatory democracy as ways in which to address the ratification referenda. Whereas the opinions of the members of the Convention and officials who were interviewed do not coincide on whether it addressed public opinion in general, all these interviewees consider that Article 47 was a way in which to respond to democratic deficit criticisms. On this question, the interviewees from CONCORD and EEB explicitly say that the Convention expected active involvement by civil society organisations in the ratification process in return for its influence in the process:

> Andrew Duff [3] from the UK, we had invited him and two others, at the annual assembly of the EEB. He was really angry with us. Because he felt that all the NGOs, all civil society organisations should actively campaign for it [the Constitution]. And we told him, "look, our role here is to inform everybody and it's at the national level where they have to make up their minds, because there's so many reasons for people in a country to make up their mind that we don't know about and that only national organisations can respond to", of course. It's really up to them. And we are divided, we have groups that are saying "it doesn't go far enough", and some groups like our Swedish member, they look at environment, development and nature, they don't look at the social agenda and at the other international agendas. But for Ecologistas en Accion [Spain], the fact that this Treaty would bring a European army closer is a very important reason for them to say "no, no". [...] And how can we tell them not to take that into account? (Interview 36, with a representative of EEB)

Nevertheless interviews suggest that this strategy was not endorsed by the organisations, which played a modest role in ratification debates. The interviewee from CSCG was particularly critical of it and said that he never tried to give the impression that the organisations would diffuse the text, which raises new doubts about the impact of CSCG's act4Europe campaign:

> Being a promoter of the EU as such, that's not our role. It's not our responsibility, maybe we should have looked to social justice. Did this Convention make any effort to make the life of the people in the EU any better? [...] I think that for environmental NGOs, whether there was a Convention, I mean, a constitution or not a constitution, did it actually matter? (Interview 18, with a representative of CSCG)

Although it could be expected that increasing usage of digital fora as a complement to or replacement for (Bozzini 2011; Quittkat 2011) focused stakeholder consultation could overcome this distance, this does not seem to be happening. This policy seems to be conceived as an information and communication one rather than a participatory one (Michailidou 2010, 79).It rather seems that these instruments suffer from the same problems as "conventional" civil dialogue. Kohler-Koch reports that here too practices are very variable from one DG to another, in particular regarding inclusion of the general public:

> The market-related DGs have been hesitant to use the instrument of online-consultations and when they use it the consultation is mostly addressed to "stakeholders" and not to the "general public". General Directorates with a broader reach such as employment and social affairs or are in charge of a newly established EU policy field such as culture or public health are eager to engage the wider public in their consultations and, accordingly, use online-consultations and open hearings and conferences extensively. (Kohler-Koch 2010b, 9)

On the other hand, though, dialogue with organised civil society can be important for segmented publics. Despite the technical nature of most affairs discussed in Brussels, they appeal to some citizens' primary interests and concerns. In this sense, debates about EU topics within civil society may contribute to the vertical Europeanisation of some sectors of the public space (for instance, citizens concerned by agriculture, health or environment concerns) rather than to a horizontal and politically mediated Europeanisation of the public sphere. Civil society dialogue thus contributes to build relations between EU officials and organisations, conveying expertise and providing transparent access to EU institutions at a relevant moment of the policymaking process, but lacks support and control from grassroots citizens.

On the contrary, the ECI has a potential for building bottom-up campaigns that contribute to raising awareness and build ownership among sections of the general public, even though it may be relatively ineffective as a policymaking device. From this perspective the mechanisms are not mutually exclusive but perfectly complementary. The ECI may contribute to make EU decision-making institutions, the European Parliament and the Council, visible. This will help to hold the democratically elected institutions to account, since it will be clear that the Commission is not taking the final decision on matters submitted by citizens.

The effect on the public sphere if the ECI becomes a frequently used tool would be far from negligible. By arguing that the ECI is "a singular opportunity to bring the Union closer to the citizens and to foster greater cross-border debate about EU policy issues",[4] the Commission's expectation seems to be that, by joining in petitions, citizens will be better informed about what the EU does and will become more knowledgeable in general about the EU. However, citizen initiatives are political participation and interest aggregation mechanisms rather than deliberation mechanisms (Smith 2009, 131–132), and it can be challenged whether signing up to support a campaign will make citizens better informed or encourage them to engage in debates on the EU. Signing a petition can be quite an individual action by which citizens endorse their previously held positions with little or no public deliberation. In terms of cost and benefits, promoters are more likely to look for already convinced citizens than to try to convince new ones. Furthermore, the extent to which signatories will follow an issue after they have endorsed a specific initiative is likely to be dependent on the promoters' activism. Thus this tool will not create a vertical relationship between citizens and EU institutions, as the Commission seems to expect, but a mediated one, where citizens will be informed, mobilised and asked to participate by organisations, including political parties, that are seeking to have an influence on the EU. It may contribute to the fragmented Europeanisation of the public sphere, where citizens concerned by issues addressed by civil society may become involved in EU affairs, whereas large sections of the public remain apart, in particular since the media might have no particular incentive to focus on the ECI.

In addition, competition with outsider organisations using the ECI may give EU civil society organisations a stronger motivation to inform, involve and mobilise their members and public opinion at large than they have had so far, which would in turn contribute to a generalisation of public sphere-oriented participation tools. The consequence may be that Commission–civil society relations would turn from a low-saliency, expertise-oriented and consensus-seeking regime towards a more public opinion-led and contested regime. Thus the expectation is not that the ECI will in itself make citizens better informed, but that it will unleash a degree of mobilisation and competition for attention among different civil society organisations, which may in turn make the public more interested in EU matters.

Granting access to outsider organisations and causes may introduce a controversial approach to a consensus-prone polity. The question about the EU's politicisation is controversial because it deals directly with the transformation of public attitudes towards the EU (Hooghe and Marks 2009): it is incompatible with the permissive consensus approach, but it may on the contrary confirm that the EU is a mature polity that is allowing a space for contestation to emerge (della Porta 2007). In particular, granting a space for contestation and opposition may contribute to fostering citizen ownership through "normalisation" of the EU; that is, the possibility to contest its policies without contesting the polity.

The ECI could clearly increase the impression that the EU does not listen to its citizens. The first and most obvious risk regards initiatives dealing with specifically European or even EU topics on which the Commission cannot act. The best example is the "pilot initiative" seeking to move the European Parliament from Strasbourg to Brussels. The Parliament's seat being established by the treaties, such a proposal would seem unacceptable as a formal ECI. This risk was particularly acute in the first version of the Regulation implementing the ECI, where the Commission suggested checking admissibility after around one-third of the necessary signatures had been gathered, for the sake of fostering European debates. It may be argued that failed initiatives, whether they fail because they do not meet the one million signature threshold or because the Commission does not eventually endorse them, nevertheless contribute to fostering debates on the EU. Whereas this is true, it unleashes a second risk, as the national experience in many countries proves that sustained rejection of successful initiatives, as has been the case in Spain and Italy (Cuesta López 2008), turns citizens' initiatives into irrelevant and unused instruments (Mallaina Garcia 2009). This situation could be worsened at the EU level, since the irrelevance of the instrument would reinforce the view that EU institutions are not accessible to its citizens.

9
A Decade of Debate about Participatory Democracy

This book has reviewed the evolution of the debate about participatory democracy in the EU over the last decade. It has been characterised as a process of frame bridging according to which pre-existing demands and mechanisms were re-oriented towards new goals: the claims from citizens' interest groups to obtain a secure role in the EU are equated with demands by civil society to make the EU more participatory. The decisive moment of this "participatory turn" (Saurugger 2010) are the years from 2000–2003, when the debate about the future of the EU (Habermas 2001) coincided with the administrative reform of the Commission following the collapse of the Santer Commission.

Nevertheless, this does not mean that participatory democracy was an idea "whose time had come" (Kingdon 2003). On the contrary, the changing conditions at the turn of the millennium were favourable for cause entrepreneurs who wanted to set the agenda. Whereas previous research has shown that the transformation of the Commission's relations with interest groups (European Commission 1992) into a legitimacy discourse was the result of intra-institutional advocacy by an epistemic community of academics and civil servants (Saurugger 2010), the role of civil society organisations has been to a large extent neglected. This book has provided evidence that existing civil society organisations in Brussels were not the passive receivers of this discourse but that they actively lobbied the different venues where the agenda was discussed and were able to adapt the frame of their demands to what they expected from EU institutions. Whereas on the ground of the available evidence it cannot be claimed that their involvement was essential to achieve today's Article 11 TUE, it has been found that they had a very strong presence in the Convention and were the main promoters of this agenda in that venue, whereas the Commission was surprisingly inactive or even reluctant.

The analysis of the collective action behind this process has also highlighted that far from being just an internal discussion in the Commission the discussion on participatory mechanisms created strong stakes and collective action dynamics among civil society organisations. It has been highlighted that these discussions created an interorganisational field of rule discussion and creation over the polarised stakes of who should be consulted and how. This is because the principle of participatory democracy and the development of mechanisms of civil society consultation, transparency and agenda initiative have a strong impact on the strategies of influence in Brussels. The institutionalisation of these rules of access together with a justificatory frame meant an important redistribution of the forms of capital in the field, increasing opportunities for some actors and decreasing them for others. The process was characterised by a strong coalition between citizens' interest groups that was opposed by social partners. Organisations sharing the same view about civil society participation tended to act together, with the organisations more strongly involved in the field advocating civil dialogue and more peripheral groups making more frequent references to other mechanisms of participation, such as the ECI. The tension between core and peripheral groups remained strong during the entire process. The internal disagreement of the coalition about the notion of representativeness together with the visible opposition of the social partners and the change of venue that followed the failed ratification of the Constitution meant that the privileged access that core organisations expected has not been realised. On the contrary, the ECI reinforces the tendency towards a more open system, which was launched by the Transparency Initiative and the increasing use of open consultations via the Internet.

Finding that the institutionalisation of mechanisms of participation in the EU is the result of a rather elite-driven process does not mean that these mechanisms do not have a potential for making EU policy-making more legitimate. It has been shown that there is no evidence that the close association of organisations in civil dialogue contributes to making their members more interested. Even in the extraordinary and politically salient context of the European Convention organisations had few incentives to associate their members more closely. Similarly it does not contribute to a stronger communication with the general public. Nevertheless civil dialogue may create a more representative interaction with civil society in comparison with some of the bias that is introduced by open online consultation (Friedrich 2011; Bozzini 2011; Quittkat 2011). The implementation of the ECI may work towards remedying some of the weaknesses of civil dialogue. In particular it may increase the diversity in the field, and thus work towards a more diverse representation of civil society and foster communication with member organisations and citizens. Preliminary data about registered campaigns confirm these hypotheses, although signature collection is proving difficult. At the date of writing only one campaign had obtained one million signatures. It is telling that this campaign was supported by the more established civil society organisations which had been reported as relatively distant from this tool in 2009, and is a further confirmation of the ductility of their collective action repertoire.

The following pages review the main findings of the book in relation to available literature and hypotheses, and discuss to what extent they change our understanding of mechanisms of civil society participation.

Agenda setting and framing

The institutionalisation of participatory mechanisms in the EU is a decade-long process which is characterised by the relative stability of the goals of its participants and the relative flexibility of the justificatory frames. The main stake for involved organisations was the definition of access rules, whereas the Commission sought to obtain legitimacy. That said, Chapter 3 finds evidence that the frame is relatively unstable. From an original demand about a European status for organisations, demands move to the recognition of civil society, only to start elaborating on the notion of consultation as participatory democracy after the 2001 White Paper on Governance. The frame of civil society consultation as participatory democracy was recognised by the Convention, even though the 2002 consultation on minimum standards of consultation moved the focus towards output legitimacy.

The White Paper on Governance and the Laeken declaration convening the European Convention are two politically salient initiatives that decisively shaped the EU's discourse on the need to come closer to civil society in order to make the EU more legitimate (Monaghan 2007), which together with the fact that the Convention was mandated with a revision of the Treaties makes it a privileged occasion for the realisation of the demand to provide civil society organisations with a legal basis for action. That said, the convergence of agendas is not a sufficient condition to include a Treaty article on the topic. The analysis of the agenda-setting process has confirmed the hypothesis that the Convention's debate on participatory democracy was shaped by the activism of organised civil society during the consultations on civil dialogue that preceded the Convention.

Empirical evidence confirms the importance of the preceding consultations. Eleven interviewees from different sectors of civil society acknowledge that the discussion about participation in the Convention was not new but was influenced by the policy dialogues between civil society organisations and the European Commission. This is acknowledged as well by a number of officials and members of the Convention. In particular, interviewees have confirmed the importance of each of the consultations between 1997 and 2002 in the agenda-setting process, with a strong insistence on the 2001 White Paper on Governance, and also including the first Social Policy Forum (1996) and to a lesser extent the First Convention on the Charter of Fundamental Rights (1999–2000). The interviews show the importance of the "red card" mobilisation during the 1998 NGO funding crisis as an important moment for the emergence of a transversal identity for the sector, which realised the fragility of its position and access mechanism (Ruzza 2004, 47).

It appears clear that organisations adapted their demands to what they perceived could be more acceptable in each situation, albeit maintaining stable core demands (Hula 1999). The response of the social Platform to the 2009 Green Paper on the ECI, where it devotes all its attention to dialogue with civil society, is telling about the resilience of the central demands of the core organisations in the network of citizens' interests in Brussels. This is significant because it confirms that civil society is not merely reacting to the Commission's agenda. Organisations tend to adapt to the general frame, but advocacy around their central goals lasts longer, as the abovementioned example regarding the Social Platform shows.

The rationale for civil society activism is clearly the groups' self-interested promotion of institutionalised access to EU institutions. However, advocacy comes with a series of justificatory frames (Schmidt 2010) which were decisive in achieving the inclusion of an article on civil society consultation in the Treaty. Its success is linked to the ability of organisations to use the EU's legitimacy debate at the turn of the century as a political opportunity structure. The Commission sought to use existing structured relations with civil society as a way of obtaining input legitimacy, and the Convention was mandated to provide ways in which the EU could be brought closer to its citizens. This offered two sorts of influence opportunities: an official discourse creating opportunities for frame bridging and a venue for debating treaty reform that provided direct access opportunities for organisations.

Analysis of the debates has shown firstly that the framing of civil society demands evolved over time in response to the expectations of the Commission and then the Convention. The evolution of the frame seeks to adapt an existing system of civil society relations oriented towards the production of output legitimacy (Kohler-Koch and Finke 2007) – which argues that civil society contributes to the quality of policymaking and eventually to communication by the EU – to a more input legitimacy oriented system, which frames the consultation of civil society as an interface for citizens' participation. The most significant evidence of this frame bridging between institutionalisation demands by organisations and the quest of legitimacy by EU institutions is the explicit elaboration of civil society organisations' consultation as a form of participatory democracy. The initiative of formulating civil society consultation as an answer to the recognised problem of democratic legitimacy came from the EU institutions in the 2000 and 2001 consultations by the Commission and the Laeken declaration. Despite the difficulty that some organisations found in assuming the new frame, it has been shown that citizens' organisations used it to formulate a precise policy proposal, civil dialogue, as the remedy to the problem of the EU's distance from citizens. This was done without substantially modifying their demands of access. Furthermore it had two clear effects: it attracted the attention of the Convention because of its congruence with the Laeken declaration and it dissolved the opposition of the social partners because of its irresistible nature.

Stability is also remarkable in the patterns of collective action and influence. Regular involvement, reputation, participation in coalitions and trust of policymakers were the most relevant factors in the agenda-setting process on participatory democracy in the EU. Despite confirming well-known tendencies (Greenwood 2011b; Quittkat and Kotzian 2011) these findings add to the literature on civil society and EU institutions because given the relatively long time frame, the politicisation of the Convention debates and the interests at stake it could have been expected that organisations would use stronger mobilisation of public opinion in the process. Although occasions of dissent and contention exist – such as the 1998 red card campaign – these remain extremely rare even after the rejection of the Constitution in France and the Netherlands.

The ability of civil society organisations to bridge the frame from the Commission consultation venues (1997–2002) to the Convention (2002–2003) is relatively surprising because it was hypothesised that the change of venue would favour diversity of actors and frames. It appears, though, that this was only true for the 2002 consultation, as the proximity of the minimal rules for consultation to the better regulation package favoured a stronger presence of business organisations and a degree of reframing of participation for output legitimacy (Chapter 3). However, the remarkable aspect is that the core organisations and demands remain stable, and that it is only the way in which these are framed that varies. That said, the change of venue and the evolution of the frame are not neutral when it comes to the content of the demands (Princen 2009). The frame-bridging strategy significantly contributed to amplify the frame, which was stretched by newcomers and the Convention to include additional participatory mechanisms such as the ECI. There was a general consolidation of the participatory democracy frame throughout the process as mechanisms of consultation were turned from an emphasis on expertise and to some extent on communication to the idea that these areas are opportunities for citizens' participation and part of a participatory democracy model.

However, it is important to insist that this process is not linear: in other words, it is not because participatory democracy had been discussed before the Convention that it was ready to be included in the Treaty. In understanding this process, it is useful to refer to Kingdon's classical three streams of problem recognition, policy proposals and policy windows (or political opportunities) as distinct phases of the agenda setting (Kingdon 2003, 86–89). It is also important to understand that these streams are not necessarily linear either, as is suggested by the garbage can model where policy solutions search for problems as much as problems seek to be solved.

The change of venue by the Convention is an important moment in the convergence of these streams. It has been highlighted that EU institutions had already very clearly recognised the problem of democratic deficit, and a potential solution, stronger participation, at the turn of the millennium, to be exact between the fall of the Santer Commission and the end of 2001 (Georgakakis 2004). This recognition was made simultaneously by the Commission in the White Paper and the Council in the Laeken declaration. EU institutions therefore play a very prominent role in setting the general agenda. However, it has been shown that civil society organisations played a much more important role than is generally acknowledged in elaborating concrete policy proposals on participation. The key aspect of these proposals is the formulation of civil society participation as citizens' participation and as a way of making the EU more democratic. These proposals frame the answer to the problem: a legal recognition of civil society's right to participate.

This does not mean that the proposals were accepted beforehand. Because of diverse interests in the institutional field, evidenced by the

EESC's attempt to raise its profile, and with civil society's social partners sceptical about dialogue, it is important to add that civil society's demands were difficult to introduce into ordinary policymaking. The best example is the inability of the Commission to include an article on civil dialogue during the Nice IGC. Furthermore, even when issues of detail were at stake, such as in 2002, the Commission had a very limited control of options and decisions. In this sense the incertitude of the Convention was an important change, in that the Commission no longer had such complete control. The Convention therefore bridged the streams, in that it offered a political opportunity to add civil society's demands to a concrete problem, the Laeken mandate.

The stability of the core aspects of the frame is also related to the routes of access to the Convention. Interviewees put great emphasis on the importance of formal access mechanisms such as hearings and working groups. In particular they suggested that it was through these mechanisms and contacts with specific members of the Convention that they expressed their demands. However, most interviews confirm assessments in the literature that these were weak access mechanisms. It appears that organisations advocating for the institutionalisation of civil society consultation acted together as a coalition in order to articulate a strong common voice in these formal fora. The agenda-setting work and the advocacy of this coalition contributed to bring this topic to the Convention. Even though the Commission was far less supportive of these demands than it had been during the agenda-setting process, organisations managed to include the issue in the agenda through alternative channels. These findings must be discussed against what is known about civil society relations with European institutions, since some are clearly divergent from what would be expected. In particular, it is surprising to find that the Commission was relatively unsupportive or at least not engaged with the participatory democracy agenda during the Convention, since the role of this institution as the entrepreneur behind procedural norms regarding civil society consultation is a consistent assessment in the literature (Smismans 2003; Kohler-Koch and Finke 2007; Saurugger 2010). However, these assessments are limited to the analysis of the Commission's civil society relations, where the Commission is in control of the agenda, access opportunities, rule setting and financial resources (Sánchez-Salgado 2007). However, the effect of the change of venue is important, since organisations were confronted with new rules of the game that allowed them to play an independent role from the Commission. It thus appears that the Commission's domination is the normal rule, but that the change of venue provided a relevant opportunity for organisations. Furthermore it has been shown that contrary to assessments pointing out the difficulty of alliances among European organisations because of their strong specialisation and the lack of accountability of policymakers (Mahoney 2007), networking and collective action by the main members of civil society networks in Brussels were decisive factors. Although obviously this is related to the novelty of the Convention's venue, it has also been found that the roots of this alliance were laid in cooperation that has taken place since 1997, showing that civil society organisations have a strong networking potential even in ordinary settings (Klüver 2013), although it is more salient in extraordinary processes such as the Convention.

Given the stability of the forms of collective action and the core demands, how is it possible to explain the remarkable evolution in the agenda? Even though the inclusion of Article 47 in the Constitutional Treaty suggested that the main demands had been institutionalised, the evolution of EU policy in the aftermath of the Convention towards more open consultations rather than privileged access for EU organisations confirms that the influence organisations could have before the Convention was the result of a rather exceptional setting for the White Paper on Governance and the Convention, and organisations' ability to navigate between venues. The agenda between 2006 and 2011 seems to have been more strongly dominated by internal Commission pressures, although it would be beneficial to carry out further research in this field. This suggests that the main evolution in the agenda is the successive changes in the broad political environment leading to successive changes of venues in the discussion of policies. The first two such changes were rather beneficial for civil society organisations. The resignation of the Santer Commission in 1999 gave a higher political ambition to the discussions on administrative reform and framed civil society consultation as a mechanism that was able to make the EU legitimate, via participatory inputs. This happened in the context of the White Paper on Governance, characterised by a long reflection period in multiple consultative venues. The second favourable change of venue was the European Convention. It gathered already known political personnel, institutionalised access opportunities and gave an opportunity to influence primary legislation. Chapter 3 showed that the organisations that had engaged in a strong discussion with the Commission could take up these opportunities to influence the Convention, even in the absence of strong support by the Commission.

That said the rejection of the Constitution clearly meant that the agenda would not be immediately implemented. As has been discussed, even though the content of the Treaty article has been maintained, the substantive agenda moved away from civil dialogue after 2006. The increased usage of online consultation and the abandonment of de facto accreditation criteria based on representativeness go in the opposite direction to the one that organisations were hoping for. Instead of creating common rules about who should be consulted and providing privileged access for EU groups, the substitution of the CONECCS database with the transparency register has not meant that membership of focused consultation groups is more balanced or transparent than before (Friedrich 2011).

The change of the goals associated with the Transparency register was possible because of the change in the agenda. Although the making of the Transparency agenda provided opportunities for civil society influence, and consultation was organised, this was taken up by different organisations such as ALTER-EU (Greenwood 2011a). The new focus on transparency and open consultation clearly emphasised the opportunities of a different constituency. The change in the aims of the institution together with the type of consultation changed the opportunities for influence. Consultations on the ECI in 2009 confirmed the effects of the changes of venue on the agenda-setting process. Only eight of the 22 organisations involved in the making of the Treaty article containing the ECI were involved in the consultation, of which four were there in order to ask for the agenda to focus on civil society dialogue again. On the contrary, this consultation attracted a new constituency of organisations.

This research cannot be generalised to agenda-setting practices in other sectors and policies. Nevertheless the findings are relevant for agenda setting in the EU in general. Firstly it appears that civil society organisations are never entirely dependent on the Commission, and they can follow their own agendas and even achieve success without the clear support of this institution.

Institutionalisation and stakes

The different discussions about which interests should have access to EU institutions are characterised by a set of regularly occurring motifs, such as the stakes, the organisations involved, the patterns of competition and cooperation and strategies of collective action. This is why the process analysed in the book can be conceived as an emerging organisational field (Fligstein and McAdam 2012) of civil society participation. The implication is that actors' behaviour have to be understood in reference to their previous position in the field, to their alliances and to the rest of the "rules" of the game, instead of simply with reference to their individual maximisation strategies. These are relevant, of course, but organisations' activism must be understood to be underpinned by these themes.

Since much of the previous research has focused on EU institutions' perspective on participatory mechanisms, the stakes for civil society organisations have been neglected because of the assumption that civil society is part of the discourse rather than an actor in the process. The evidence provided by this book is that far from reflecting a consensus among the most active European civil society organisations, the institutionalisation of participatory mechanisms created clearly recognisable cleavages and patterns of competition in this field. On the one hand the field is structured through competition for recognition and secure access by different interests. In this sense there was a strong coalition for civil dialogue that met social partners' opposition. Nevertheless, this coalition was diverse and organisations kept trying to improve their individual position even when advocating for the general principle of civil dialogue. In this sense the EEB, CONCORD and the Social Platform wanted to improve "horizontal civil dialogue" albeit without losing their specific role in their policy sector. The second relevant dynamic is competition between established organisations and newcomers. In this sense citizens' interest groups tried to obtain recognised access in order to compete with social partners and at the same time becoming relatively insulated from newcomers. The evolution of the agenda in the aftermath of the Convention shows the opposite tendency. The transparency agenda, the increased usage of open online consultations and the implementation of the ECI are all mechanisms that decrease the role of EU organisations as gate-keepers for access to EU institutions.

That said, this does not mean that EU organisations are about to disappear because of the implementation of the new mechanisms. On the contrary, the first ECI to have reached one million signatures was supported by these organisations. This means that the field is also characterised by the ability of organisations to navigate between competitive pressures by different social institutional actors. The field is thus characterised by its offering of different political opportunity structures where the likelihood of success depends on organisations' ability to meet the expectations of one of the institutions, be it different services or DGs of the Commission, the EESC or the Convention. The evidence is that organisations were able to use different political opportunity structures according to the situation in order to maintain influence.

It appears that the most relevant form of action is repeated involvement in formal consultation fora and in coalitions. The importance of formal venues is related to the neo-pluralist nature of the EU interest intermediation system, where the formalisation of procedures is seen as a way of achieving fairer competition between different interests. All the actors coincide in that the agenda was mostly defined in formalised consultation venues. Even though these fora can also be useful to gain direct access to decision-makers (Quittkat and Kotzian 2011), the pattern which appears from the analysis is that influence was not mainly gained by informal access to decision-makers following participation in one consultation but rather because of the construction of reputation and trust in the field via repeated involvement in several consultation processes. That said, the field seems uncertain in relation to influence: it has not been possible to distinguish a single actor and a decision to institutionalise the civil society agenda because it has been characterised as a typically incremental process. Furthermore most organisations are reluctant to claim or assign influence on concrete decisions to individual organisations, with the exceptions of the social partners regarding the notion of representative associations and IRI and the PFCS on the ECI. On the contrary, they are more prone to explain influence in terms of coordinated collective action via coalitions. Organisations agree that their main strength in the Convention was their ability to present their demands as unanimous within civil society.

Analysis of exchanges of information and coordinated action via network analysis has confirmed to a large extent that the organisations that were involved more often in the field had frequent exchanges between them, and those advocating similar visions of civil dialogue and belonging to the Social Platform and the CSCG actually formed a strong coalition whose members exchanged views much more frequently than typically in the other organisations. The role of coalition organisations (such as CSCG and PFCS) appears stronger in the network analysis than in the assessment of their role in framing and in agenda setting. This means that these organisations were not created and used by their members in order to advocate on their behalf. Their function appears rather to have consisted in facilitating exchanges and coordinating the action of their members.

The field is strutured by competition over well defined and relatively stable stakes. The field is structured by issues that relate to the degree of formalisation of the rules of access (whether they have to be binding or not), whether participation has to be open or focused on accredited organisations (inclusion and exclusion of outsiders) and by the notion of representativeness, which has been found to be the most divisive for citizens' interests organisations. When the frames used by organisations acting together are compared (Table 9.1), it clearly appears that organisations belonging to coalitions tend to share the same framing. The only exception to the finding that strong exchanges came together with a shared frame is ETUC. The role of the trade union confederation in the network is very surprising considering its reluctance to engage in civil dialogue. This has been explained by its membership of the CSCG platform. ETUC distrusts the intention of civil society organisations in relation to civil dialogue and at the same time considers them as potential allies in the construction of a more social Europe. In this sense it decided to engage in a dialogue with them via the CSCG rather than to avoid contact.

The institutionalisation of participation thus appears as competitive process clearly opposing well defined coalitions, which is nevertheless structured by regularities in terms of stakes, the main actors in the field and forms of cooperation and opposition.

Contribution to democratisation

This book has shown the self-interested nature of the claims behind the notion of participatory democracy. European civil society organisations sought and achieved the institutionalisation of their own role between 1997 and the 2003 and they used the EU's legitimacy concerns to frame it in an irresistible way. On the other hand EU institutions themselves, or, according to interviewees, at least the Convention, were also expecting to achieve short-term goals by facilitating the ratification of the constitution via national referenda. That said, the debate on the EU's legitimacy does not seem to have substantially changed ten years after the Convention, making it necessary to ask whether these rules may contribute to change the situation and reconnect citizens with the EU. The findings on the three dimensions of participation, representation and communication are considered in turn to answer this.

The response in relation to participation must be sceptical. The book has provided clear evidence that neither civil society dialogue nor the ECI are mechanisms for direct participation by ordinary citizens in EU policymaking. Regarding civil dialogue, it has been found that most organisations were far from their members and unable to spur their interest in the issues at stake at EU level. Nor were organisations able to mobilise their supporters: the main mechanism of influence for civil society organisations during the entire process was participation and involvement in successive debates and policy consultations. The Convention did not significantly change the organisations' strategy as they did not employ outside lobbying (Mahoney 2008a), let alone protest. The main method of advocacy is exchanges with the institutions, via involvement in formal consultations with the institutions and other organisations and including the submission of written contributions. Unsurprisingly the ability of these mechanisms to associate civil society with the Convention has been evaluated negatively by the literature (Lombardo 2007; Monaghan 2007; Pérez Solórzano-Borragán 2007). Furthermore, the ECI appears as a soft participatory device limited to non-binding policy proposals. Supporting one ECI cannot thus be equated with having a say in policymaking in the EU.

Rather, this book has found that the new participatory mechanisms seem to offer a better opportunity to conceive the role of organised civil society as representing their members, supporters and sympathising citizens. In this sense it has been suggested that representativeness criteria may make sense when evaluating who organisations are representing and whether a balanced policy discussion can be achieved. This should not ignore the bias that representativeness criteria can introduce between membership-based and cause organisations. Nevertheless the opposite seems to be happening: in order not to advantage organisations representing their members over those active in the public sphere, no evaluation of organisations' representativeness is being carried out, not even on evaluating organisations' relevance in the public sphere. The ECI could be one such measure of "social representativeness" in two senses. Firstly it would allow us to visualise how many supporters a given policy proposal has in the public sphere. Secondly it can improve aggregate representativeness of the participatory field by increasing its complexity, and also opening avenues of influence to national organisations and to groups which so far may have avoided taking part in consultations.

Finally, evaluation of the participatory agenda in terms of communication is ambiguous. On the one hand it clearly appears that the institutions have advanced the agenda in order to improve their reputation in the eyes of the public and to the electors in the referenda that were organised to ratify the Constitution and the Lisbon Treaty. The ECI has been typically put forward as one of the key improvements in all the brochures on the new treaties. On the other hand it clearly appears that civil society organisations were unable and unwilling to contribute to the diffusion of this article or the Treaty as a whole. On the other hand, the new mechanisms and in particular the ECI have a clear potential to transform these findings. Firstly the ECI is the first EU participatory mechanism that clearly requires its proponents to communicate with grassroots supporters and citizens in general. Although the deliberative potential of this communication is very limited – supporters are likely already to be convinced citizens rather than those convinced by the campaign itself – its potential to make people aware of the involvement of the EU in an issue of their concern is undeniable. This can be qualified as "vertical communication" or the Europeanisation of segmented publics with a clear concern (for example, protection of the environment, water or political rights). Furthermore, the ECI has the potential to reinvigorate civil society consultation. Since the finding is that most signature collection campaigns have been promoted by an already existing organisation, it must be assumed that the ECI is a tool for civil society. In this sense its development is likely to bring new organisations to try to influence the agenda (see the previous paragraph). Because the emergence of a participatory agenda has been linked to the emergence of an organisational field, this means that those already involved are likely to react to this development. If the perception is that proposals advanced via this tool may be seen positively by the Commission, existing organisations are likely to put it to use, thus compensating for their traditional distance from their members and the public.

Annexes

Annex 1   List of interviews

1. Mr. Jean Luc Dehaene, vice-president of the Convention in charge of civil society relations, 09–02–2009, Brussels
2. Commission civil servant from DG enterprise, 17–02–2009, Brussels
3. Representative of the Social Platform, 06–03–2009, Brussels
4. Mr Alain Lamassoure, member of the Convention, 18–03–2009, Paris
5. Member of the secretariat of the Convention, 03–04–09, Brussels
6. Member of the secretariat of the Convention, 03–04–09, Brussels
7. Personal Communication with a member of the Convention, 17–04–2009, Birmingham
8. Representative of the Social Platform, 04–05–09, Brussels
9. Representative of the European Foundation Centre, 04–05–09, Brussels
10. Representative of COFACE, 04–05–09, Brussels
11. Representative of IRI Europe, 06–04–09, telephone interview
12. Mr David O'Sullivan, deputy member of the Convention for the Commission, 13–05–09, Brussels
13. Official of the General Secretariat of the Commission, 28–05–09, Brussels
14. Two representatives of ELO 02–07–09, Brussels
15. Representative of ACN, 08–07–09, telephone interview
16. Representative of Unice, 08–07–09 telephone interview
17. Representative of the Civil Society Contact Group, 29–07–09, Brussels
18. Representative of the Polish NGO Office, 04–09–09, Brussels
19. Civil servant from the European Economic and Social Comittee, 07–09–09, Brussels
20. Representative of CONCORD, 07–09–09, Brussels
21. Representative of the Pemanent Forum of Civil Society, 26–10–2009, Brussels
22. Representative of ECAS, 29–10–2009, telephone interview
23. Representative of the Permanent Forum of Civil Society, done in Paris, 10–12–09
24. Representative of EUROCOMMERCE, done in Brussels, 05–01–10

25. Mr Carlos Carnero, former MEP and deputy member of the Convention, telephone interview, 07–01–10
26. Representative of ETUC, done in Brussels, 01–02–10
27. Representative of EUROCITIES, 28–05–10, phone interview.
28. Representative of EEB, done in Brussels, 19–07–10
29. Mr Klaus Hänsch, member of the Praesidium of the Convention, telephone interview, 17–11–10

Annex 2   List of EU level organisations and available data

Nombre	Sector	Data	Rationale for inclusion
ACN Cittadaninza Attiva	Citizenship	Interview and position papers	Participation in Convention + 2 consultations
CEMR	Regional	Position papers	Participation in Convention + 2 consultations
CPMR	Regional	Position papers	Participation in Convention + 2 consultations
CEDAG	Third sector	Interview, position papers and networking questionnaire	Participation in Convention + 2 consultations
ELO – European Landwoners Organisation	Business association	Interview and position papers	Participation in Convention + 2 consultations
Eurocommerce	Business association	Interview and position papers	Participation in Convention + 2 consultations
ECAS	Citizenship	Interview and position papers	Participation in Convention + 2 consultations
EFC – European Foundation Centre	Foundations	Interview, position papers and networking questionnaire	Participation in Convention + 2 consultations
UEAPME	Business association	Position papers	Participation in Convention + 2 consultations
UNICE	Business association	Telephone interview and position papers	Participation in Convention + 2 consultations

Continued

Nombre	Sector	Data	Rationale for inclusion
ETUC	Trade Union	Interview and position papers	Relevance in the context of civil society dialogue
Polish NGOs Brussels	Services for Polish organsiations	Interview, position papers and networking questionnaire	Participation in Convention + 2 consultations
Eurocities	Regional	Interview and position papers	Participation in Convention + 2 consultations
Eurodiaconia – Caritas	Social sector	Position papers	Participation in Convention + 2 consultations
EEB	Environment	Interview and position papers	Participation in Convention + 2 consultations
CONCORD	Cooperation and humanitarian aid	Interview, position papers and networking questionnaire	Participation in Convention + 2 consultations
Social Platform	Social Sector	2 interviews, position papers and networking questionnaire	Participation in Convention + 2 consultations
COFACE	Family	Interview and position papers	Participation in Convention + 2 consultations
CEV Centre Européen du Volontariat	Volunteering promotion organisation	Position papers	Participation in Convention + 2 consultations
PFCS – Permanent Forum of Civil Society	Citizenship	2 interviews, position papers and networking questionnaire	Participation in Convention + 2 consultations
CSCG – Civil society contact group	Alliance of different platforms of sectoral NGOs	Interview, position papers and networking questionnaire	Relevance in the Convention
IRI – Initiative and Referendum Institute Europe	Advocacy for participatory democracy	Interview, reports and networking questionnaire	Relevance in the Convention

Annex 3   Coding matrices

The tables below summarise the coding of the written documents by European organisations from 2000 to the Convention. The content of the papers was coded into 19 general frames, divided into three broad themes: conceptions of civil society in the EU, conceptions of participation, and demands in relation to the institutionalisation of civil society consultation. The tables express merely the inclusion of a part of one organisation's demand in one of the codes, not the number of reference or the percentage of the paper that it represents. The result is thus a matrix containing 76 frames vs. 21 organisations, thus resulting in a set of 1596 positions have been used to build the analysis of the frame expressed in the graphs and tables in Chapter 2. These are binary matrices where 1 means that text has been coded in this frame and 0 that none has been coded. In total the matrices contain 330 positive positions (20.68% of all possible positions).

For the sake of smooth presentation, the identification of each consultation phase (2000, 2001, 20002 and Convention) has been replace by 1, 2, 3 and 4 respectively.

Table 3A.1 Coding presence: conceptions of civil society in the EU

	Formal representation				Alternative representation				Against representativeness				CSO link to the public				CSO promote participation and voice demands				Expertise as legitimacy				Definition excludes business groups				Definition includes business groups			
	1	2	3	4	1	2	3	4	1	2	3	4	1	2	3	4	1	2	3	4	1	2	3	4	1	2	3	4	1	2	3	4
Consultation	1	0	0	0	0	0	0	0	0	1	0	0	1	0	0	0	1	1	1	0	0	0	0	0	0	0	0	0	0	0	0	0
ACN	0	0	0	0	0	1	1	0	0	1	0	0	0	0	0	1	1	1	0	1	0	0	0	1	0	0	0	0	0	0	0	0
CEDAG	0	0	0	0	1	1	1	0	1	1	0	0	0	0	1	1	1	1	1	0	1	1	1	0	0	1	1	1	0	0	0	0
CEV	0	0	0	0	0	1	0	1	0	0	0	0	0	0	0	0	0	0	0	0	0	1	1	0	0	0	0	0	0	0	0	0
COFACE	1	1	1	0	0	0	0	0	0	0	0	1	1	1	0	0	0	0	1	0	1	0	0	0	1	1	0	0	0	0	0	0
CONCORD	0	0	1	0	0	1	0	0	0	1	0	0	1	0	0	0	0	1	1	0	0	0	0	0	1	0	0	0	0	0	0	0
CSCG	0	0	0	0	0	0	0	0	0	0	0	0	0	0	0	0	0	1	0	1	0	0	0	0	0	0	0	0	0	0	0	0
ECAS	0	0	0	1	0	0	0	0	0	1	0	0	0	0	0	1	0	0	1	0	0	0	0	0	0	0	0	0	0	0	0	0
ETUC	1	0	0	0	0	0	0	0	0	0	0	0	0	0	0	0	0	0	0	1	1	0	1	0	0	0	0	0	0	0	0	0
EUROCOMMERCE	1	1	0	0	0	0	0	0	0	0	0	0	1	0	0	0	0	0	0	0	0	0	0	0	0	0	0	0	1	1	1	0
CARITAS – EURODIACONIA	0	1	1	0	0	1	0	1	0	0	0	0	0	0	1	1	1	1	1	1	0	0	1	1	1	0	1	0	0	0	0	0
EEB	0	0	1	1	0	0	0	0	0	1	0	0	0	0	0	1	0	0	1	0	0	1	1	0	0	1	1	1	0	0	0	0
EFC	1	1	0	1	0	0	0	0	0	0	0	0	1	1	0	0	0	0	0	1	1	1	0	1	0	0	0	0	0	0	0	0
ELO	1	0	0	1	0	0	0	1	1	0	0	0	0	0	0	0	0	0	0	0	0	0	1	0	0	0	0	0	1	0	1	0
PFCS	0	0	0	1	0	0	0	0	0	1	0	1	1	0	0	1	1	1	0	1	0	0	0	0	0	0	0	0	0	0	0	0
Pol. OFFI.	0	0	0	0	0	0	0	0	0	1	0	0	0	1	1	0	0	1	1	0	0	1	1	0	0	1	0	0	0	0	0	0
Social Platform	0	1	1	1	1	1	0	1	1	1	0	0	0	0	1	1	1	1	1	1	0	1	0	1	0	0	1	0	0	1	1	0
UEAPME	0	1	1	0	0	0	0	0	0	0	0	0	0	0	0	0	1	1	1	0	0	1	1	0	0	0	0	0	0	0	1	0
UNICE	1	1	1	1	0	0	0	0	0	0	1	0	0	0	0	1	0	1	1	0	0	1	1	1	0	0	0	0	0	1	1	0
CEMR	0	1	1	0	0	0	0	0	0	0	0	1	1	1	1	1	0	0	0	0	0	0	1	0	0	0	1	0	0	0	0	0
CPMR	0	0	1	0	0	0	0	0	0	0	0	1	0	0	0	1	1	1	0	0	0	0	1	0	0	0	0	0	0	0	0	0
EUROCITIES	0	0	0	0	0	0	0	0	0	0	0	0	0	0	0	1	0	0	1	0	0	0	1	0	0	1	1	0	0	0	0	0
TOTAL	6	7	9	6	2	5	1	4	0	6	1	4	5	4	3	10	5	7	11	6	4	6	8	4	2	3	6	1	1	3	2	0

Table 3A.2 Coding presence: conception of participation

Organisation	Individual participation rights				Civil dialogue				Participatory democracy				Consultation improves policy-making				CSO consultation as empowerment			
	1	2	3	4	1	2	3	4	1	2	3	4	1	2	3	4	1	2	3	4
Consultation	1	0	0	0	1	0	0	0	1	0	0	0	0	0	0	0	0	0	0	0
ACN	0	0	0	1	0	0	0	0	0	0	0	1	0	0	0	0	0	1	0	1
CEDAG	0	1	1	1	1	1	0	0	0	1	1	1	0	1	1	0	1	0	1	1
CEV	0	0	0	0	0	0	0	1	0	0	0	0	0	0	0	0	0	0	0	0
COFACE	0	0	0	0	0	1	0	0	0	1	0	0	0	1	0	0	0	1	0	0
CONCORD	0	0	0	0	1	1	0	0	0	1	0	1	0	1	0	1	0	1	0	0
CSCG	0	0	0	0	0	0	0	0	0	0	0	0	0	0	1	0	0	0	0	0
ECAS	0	0	1	0	0	0	0	0	0	0	0	0	0	0	0	0	0	0	1	0
ETUC	0	0	0	0	1	0	0	0	0	0	0	0	0	0	1	0	0	0	1	0
EUROCOMMERCE	0	0	0	0	0	0	0	0	0	0	0	0	0	0	1	0	0	0	0	0
CARITAS –	0	0	0	0	0	0	1	0	0	1	1	0	0	1	1	0	0	0	0	0
EURODIACONIA	0	0	0	0	0	0	0	0	0	0	1	1	0	0	0	0	0	0	0	1
EEB	0	0	1	1	0	0	0	0	0	0	1	1	0	0	1	0	0	1	1	0
EFC	0	1	0	1	1	1	0	1	0	0	0	0	0	0	0	1	0	1	0	0
ELO	0	1	0	0	1	0	0	0	0	1	0	0	0	0	0	1	0	0	0	0
PFCS	0	0	0	1	0	0	0	0	0	0	0	1	0	0	0	0	0	0	0	0
Pol. OFFI.	0	0	0	0	0	1	1	0	0	1	0	1	0	1	1	0	0	1	0	0
Social Platform	0	0	0	1	0	1	1	1	0	0	0	0	0	0	1	1	0	1	0	0
UEAPME	0	0	0	0	0	0	0	0	0	0	0	0	0	0	1	0	0	1	0	0
UNICE	0	0	0	0	0	0	0	0	0	0	0	0	0	1	1	0	1	0	0	0
CEMR	0	0	0	0	0	0	0	0	0	0	1	1	0	0	0	0	0	0	0	1
CPMR	0	0	0	0	0	0	0	0	0	0	0	0	0	0	1	0	0	0	0	1
EUROCITIES	0	0	0	0	0	0	0	0	0	0	0	1	0	0	0	0	0	0	0	1
TOTAL	1	3	3	6	6	6	3	3	1	6	5	9	0	6	11	4	2	8	4	6

Table 3A.3 Coding presence: demands in relation to institutionalisation

Organisation	Legal rank 1	2	3	4	Recognise CSO 1	2	3	4	Structure consultation 1	2	3	4	Extend consultation to other institutions 1	2	3	4	Make ECOSOC the place of civil dialogue 1	2	3	4	The EESC does not represent civil society 1	2	3	4
Consultation	1	0	0	0	0	0	0	0	0	0	0	0	0	0	0	0	0	0	0	0	0	0	0	0
ACN	1	0	0	1	0	1	0	1	0	0	0	0	0	0	0	0	0	0	0	0	0	0	0	0
CEDAG	1	1	1	1	0	1	0	0	0	0	1	0	0	0	0	0	0	0	0	0	0	0	0	0
CEV	1	0	0	0	0	0	0	1	0	1	0	0	0	0	0	1	0	0	0	0	0	0	0	0
COFACE	1	1	0	0	0	0	0	0	0	1	0	0	0	1	0	0	0	1	0	0	0	0	0	0
CONCORD	1	1	0	1	0	1	0	0	0	0	1	0	0	0	0	0	0	0	0	0	0	0	0	0
CSCG	0	0	0	0	0	0	0	0	0	1	0	1	0	0	0	0	0	0	0	0	0	0	0	0
ECAS	0	0	1	0	0	0	0	1	0	1	0	1	0	0	0	0	0	0	1	0	0	0	1	0
ETUC	1	0	0	0	0	0	0	0	0	0	1	1	0	0	0	0	0	0	0	0	0	0	0	0
EUROCOMMERCE	0	0	0	0	0	0	0	0	0	1	0	0	0	1	0	0	0	0	0	0	0	0	0	0
CARITAS – EURODIACONIA	0	0	1	1	0	0	0	1	1	0	1	0	0	0	1	0	0	0	1	0	0	0	1	0
EEB	0	0	1	0	0	0	0	1	0	1	1	1	0	0	0	0	0	0	0	0	0	1	1	1
EFC	0	1	0	1	0	1	1	1	0	1	0	0	0	1	0	0	0	0	0	0	0	0	0	0
ELO	0	0	0	0	0	1	0	0	0	0	0	0	0	0	0	0	0	0	0	0	0	0	0	0
PFCS	0	0	0	1	0	0	0	1	0	1	0	0	0	0	0	0	0	0	0	0	0	0	0	0
Pol. OFFI.	0	0	0	0	0	0	0	1	0	0	1	0	0	0	1	0	0	0	0	0	0	0	1	0
Social Platform	1	1	1	0	0	1	0	0	0	1	1	1	0	1	1	0	0	0	0	0	0	0	1	0
UEAPME	0	0	1	0	0	0	0	1	0	0	0	0	0	0	0	1	0	0	0	1	0	0	0	0
UNICE	0	0	0	0	0	0	0	0	0	1	0	0	0	0	0	0	0	0	1	0	0	0	0	0
CEMR	0	0	0	0	0	0	0	0	0	0	0	0	0	0	0	0	0	0	0	0	0	0	0	0
CPMR	0	0	1	0	1	0	0	1	0	0	1	0	0	0	0	0	0	0	1	0	0	0	0	0
EUROCITIES	0	0	0	0	0	0	0	1	0	0	0	0	0	0	0	0	0	0	0	0	0	0	0	0
TOTAL	8	5	7	6	1	6	1	11	1	10	8	5	0	4	3	2	0	1	4	1	0	1	5	1

Annex 4 Networking questionnaire

This questionnaire was circulated among interviewees by email accompanied of the following introduction:

I would be very grateful if you could take some minutes to complete this survey about your contacts regarding *participatory democracy* during the European Convention. I will of course not disclose your name as the provider of this information.

You just need to tick with an X the cases corresponding to the organisations with which you were in touch regarding *participatory democracy* in different forms.

Organisation	Exchange of opinions	Common position	Common activities to promote participatory democracy
ACN – Active Citizenship Network			
Eurodiaconia/CARITAS Europe			
CEDAG – European Council of Voluntary Organisations			
CEMR – Council of European Municipalities and Regions			
CPMR – Conference of Peripheral Maritime Regions of Europe			
COFACE – Confederation of Family Organisations in the European Union			
CONCORD – European NGO Confederation for Relief and Development			
CSCG – Civil Society Contact Group			

ECAS – European Citizen Action Service			
EEB – European Environment Bureau			
EFC – European Foundation Centre			
ELO – European Landowners Organisation			
ERC – European Referendum Campaign			
ETUC – European Trade Union Confederation			
Eurocities			
Eurocommerce			
Eurodiaconia			
European Volunteer Centre– EVC			
IRI Europe: Initiative and Referendum Institute			
Permanent Forum of Civil Society			
Polish NGO Office in Brussels			
Social Platform			
UEAPME – European Association of Craft, Small- and Medium-sized Enterprises			
UNICE – Union of Industrial and Employers' Confederation of Europe			
OTHER EUROPEAN OR NATIONAL ORGANISATIONS – Please indicate their names			

Annex 5   Network analysis method and data sources

The network analysis has been built on three types of data: question-naires, written documents (official ones and organisations' position papers) and interviews. The list below includes the organisations that replied to the questionnaire:

> CEDAG
> CONCORD
> CSCG
> EFC
> IRI – ERC
> PFCS
> Polish Office
> Social Platform

The data from the different sources were introduced into a square EXCEL matrix containing 47 rows per 47 columns (and thus impossible to reproduce here), with each of the organisations as a column and row. This allows introducing information about the relation of every organ-isation with the other 46 members of the network. The entries into the matrix have been valued from 1 to 3 first according to the possible three types of relations identified in the questionnaire: exchanges of opinions, common actions and common opinions. In order to carry out individual actor centralities and structural similarity measures using the UCINET software package these matrices have binarised: as explained in Chapter 4, a separate analysis was carried out for every kind of rela-tion (thus producing three matrices). For similar purposes relations were reciprocated for these analyses even though the matrixes were built on directed data (A contacts B does not mean B contacting A). However, these directed data were used for carrying out the prestige measures indicating the differences between those organisations sending and receiving more ties from the rest of the network.

Table 5A.1 introduces the evidence of networking relations between European organisations derived from position papers and interviews. The table is not square since the matrix only introduces data for the organisations for which evidence was available (those included in the rows) which may refer to other organisations (in columns).

Table 5A.1 Evidence of networking between organisations beyond questionnaires (see code for numbers below)

	PFCS	CEDAG	EFC	ETUC	EEB	CSCG	CEMR	CPMR	Euro cities	COFACE	UNICE	EURO COMMERCE	Social Platform	IRI – ERC	ACN	CONCORD
ACN	4															
CEV		1	1													
ETUC					5	8				7	5, 7	7	5			5
EEB																
CEMR								5	5							
CPMR							5		5							
Eurocities																
UNICE				5, 7						7		7				
Soc Platf					5	5,8										5
EUROCOM.				7						7	7					
COFACE				7							7	7				
CARITAS			6										6			
IRI – ERC					5									5, 9		
CONCORD					5								5			

Type of evidence: the evidence always regards a contact from the organization in the column with the organization in the column:

1. Position paper consultation 2000
2. Position paper consultation 2001
3. Position paper consultation 2002
4. Position paper Convention
5. Common position papers
6. Interview
7. Evidence of contacts in the EESC documents
8. Member of the organisation
9. Website of the organisation
10. Other documentary sources

Annex 6   Evidence of origin pilot and actual ECIs

Table 6A.1   Pilot initiatives

Name and issue	Policy area	Number of signatures	Promoters
Oneseat initiative	Constitutional – treaty change	1.2 million	MEPs
Equality for all!	Constitutional – treaty change		AEDH
Against Nuclear Energy	Environment – treaty change	700000	FoE
European Health Initiative/ European Referendum Initiative	Health – constitutional – treaty change	250000 (claimed)	Dr. Rath Health Foundation
For a political Europe of Freedom, Security and Justice	Home affairs		French politicians
Efficient 112 all over Europe	Internal market		European emergency number association
Help Africa	Cooperation	under 100000	MEPs
Initiative pour un Service Civil Européen	Social – Citizenship		Mouvement Européen France
Save Our Social Europe	Social		Austrian association
1million 4disability	Social	1.65 million	EDF
GMO Initiative I	Environment – Health	1 million	Greenpeace
Initiatives of applied anthroposophy – Eliant	Health	1 million	Anthropophilosophical orgs

Continued

Table 6A.1   Continued

Name and issue	Policy area	Number of signatures	Promoters
High Quality of Public Services	Social	640000	ETUC
For a European Referendum on the EU Constitution	Constitutional – treaty change		Union of European federalists
Initiative for the Initiative	Democratisation – civil society	under 1 million	AEGEE, ECAS, King Baudouin, Madariaga
Emergency Initiative for Darfur	EFSP	340 000	French orgs.
Referendum on the next EU Treaty	Constitutional – treaty change		MEPs
Cancer Unite	Health		Stakeholders on cancer care
GMO Initiative II	Health – environment	1 million	Avaaz Greenpeave
Free Sunday Initiative	Social		German catholic orgs.
European Obesity Day Charter Initiative	Health		Pharma. Industry

Source: Fischer and Lichtbau (2008) and Kaufmann (2010).

Table 6A.2 Registered European citizens' initiatives since the entry into force (June 2012)

Initiative and signatures (when figure available)	Citizens' Committee characterisation	Policy area
Act 4 Growth	Women in female entrepreneurship associations	Internal market/equality
Do not count Education as part of deficit	Youth and student activists mainly from Greece	Social rights
European Free Vaping Initiative	Association of e-cigarette manufacturers	Health
European Initiative for Media Pluralism	*European Alternatives*, London, Paris, Rome & Cluj Napoca	Liberties/Justice/Constitutional
New Deal 4 Europe – For a European Special Plan for Sustainable Development and Employment	Italian trade union Confederazione Generale Italiana del Lavoro and the Union of European Federalists	Economic policy
Teach4Youth – Upgrade to Erasmus 2.0	Science-Po students	Education
Turn me Off!	French students and activists	Environment
Weed Like to Talk	Science Po students	Health
30km/h	Road safety organisations from Germany & the UK, with diverse supporting organisations (cycling, environment, car sharing) from 8 member states and 2 EU NGOs	Transport
ECI online collection platform	*Open House/Democracy and Human Rights* (Berlin)	Participatory democracy
End Ecocide in Europe 135.693signatures	Private individuals	Environment

Continued

Table 6A.2 Continued

Initiative and signatures (when figure available)	Citizens' Committee characterisation	Policy area
Let me Vote	An initiative of the *'European Without Borders'* foundation, led by Euronews director Philippe Cayla	Liberties/Justice
Fraternité2020 71,000 signatures	Activists and organisations for student mobility in the EU level	Education
High quality European Education for All	*MEET European Education Trust*	Education
Responsible waste incineration	Private individuals	Environment
Single Communication Tariff 145,000 signatures	2 individuals	Information society/ communication
Suspension of the EU Climate & Energy Package	Committee members emphasise their status as a group of volunteer individuals	Environment
Unconditional Basic Income 285,042 signatures	*European Alternatives &Basic Income Earth Network* (ATTAC). Less demanding version of the rejected registration initiative under same title	Social rights
One of Us 1,897,588 signatures (pending verification)	Against EU funding for stem cell research. Italian based. Financial contribution from the Italian anti-abortion group *Fondazione Vita Nova*	Liberties/Justice
Stop Vivisection 1,326,807 signatures (pending verification)	*Equivita*	Animal welfare

Continued

Table 6A.2 Continued

Initiative and signatures (when figure available)	Citizens' Committee characterisation	Policy area
Water and Sanitation are a Human Right! 1,884,790 signatures verified	*European Federation of Public Sector Unions EFPSU/ETUC). Social Platform, European Environmental Bureau, European Public Health Alliance*	Public services
Dairy Cow Welfare 293,511 signatures	Ben & Jerry's, World Society for the Protection of Animals and Compassion in World Farming	Animal welfare
End EU-Switzerland No collection campaign	Two London-based individuals.	Migration/internal market
MOVEUROPE CARD	Sciences-Po students	Social rights/ Constitutional symbols (celebrate the European Union day

Table 6A.3 Initiatives rejected at registration

Proposed ECI	Citizens' Committee characterisation
Abolish the European Parliament	Bavarian Eurosceptic party Gesunder Menschenverstand Deutschland (GMD)
Confidence vote on EU government	Bavarian Eurosceptic party Gesunder Menschenverstand Deutschland (GMD)
EU decision making by referenda	Bavarian Eurosceptic party Gesunder Menschenverstand Deutschland (GMD)
A Europe of Solidarity (cancel Greek debt)	Self-description as 'Greece's debt relief social movement'*
A European public bank for social development, ecology and solidarity	*Party of European Left* (GUE at the European Parliament)
Abolition of bull fighting	Different Catalan anti-bullfighting organisations, *Veterinary Association for the Abolition of Bullfighting*, and PACMA (single issue political party)
Against legalized prostitution	Citizen activists, claims of no links to the Europan Women Lobby
Harmonise member state protection of pets & strays	Swedish NGOs and*European Stray Dogs and Animal Welfare* (ESDAW)
Minority Safe Pack	*Federal Union of European Nationalities*. South Tyrolean People's Party
Cohesion Policy for regional Minorities	Romanian NGO seeking right of Szeckler people in Romania to self-determination
My Voice Against Nuclear Power	Friends of the Earth Austria (*Global 2000*)
Right to Lifelong care	Brussels based FERPA – *European Federation of Retired & Older Persons* (ETUC affiliate)
Self Determination a Human Right	Catalan; Flemish and Scottish independence campaigners
Recommend singing the European Anthem in Esperanto	Brussels based NGO *European Esperanto Union*
Stop Cruelty for Animals	Mainly Italian and German organisations

Continued

Table 6A.3 Continued

Proposed ECI	Citizens' Committee characterisation
Strengthening citizens participation in decisions on collective sovereignty	*Reagrupament Independentista* (RCAT): Catalana pro-independence movement, with support from Catalan municipal authorities
Unconditional Basic Income	*European Alternatives* &*Basic Income Earth Network* (ATTAC)

Note: * http://www.1millionsignatures.eu/?a=en

Annex 7   In- and out degrees

id	indegree (std)	id	outdegree (std)
ETUC	0.26	PFCS	0.26
Social Platform	0.22	CEDAG	0.24
CSCG	0.2	CONCORD	0.2
PFCS	0.18	CSCG	0.2
CEDAG	0.16	RCE ES	0.2
COFACE	0.16	Social Platform	0.2
CARITAS UE	0.14	CCOO	0.14
ECAS	0.12	ETUC	0.14
World social forum	0.12	IRI Europe	0.12
CCOO	0.1	ATTAC Spain	0.1
EEB	0.1	ONCE – CEPES	0.1
IRI Europe	0.1	ATTAC EUROPE	0.08
ACN	0.08	CARITAS España	0.08
CONCORD	0.08	CCDF – LDH	0.08
Eurocommerce	0.08	EFC	0.08
UNICE	0.08	UNICE	0.08
ATTAC Spain	0.06	ACSUR	0.06
CEP-CMAF	0.06	CGT	0.06
CEV	0.06	CJvtdEs	0.06
Ecologistas	0.06	COFACE	0.06
EFC	0.06	Eurocommerce	0.06
Eurodiaconia	0.06	FCCE	0.06
FONDA – CAFECS	0.06	Ecologistas	0.04
ACSUR	0.04	EEB	0.04
CGT	0.04	Eurocities	0.04
CJvtdEs	0.04	MEDEF	0.04
ERC	0.04	PL Office	0.04
F. Copernic	0.04	ACN	0.02
ONCE – CEPES	0.04	ADICAE	0.02
RCE ES	0.04	ELO	0.02
UEAPME	0.04	F. Copernic	0.02
AFEM	0.02	F. Schuman	0.02
CEMR	0.02	FONDA – CAFECS	0.02
Conv. Cat.	0.02	AFEM	0.0
CPMR	0.02	CARITAS UE	0.0
Demopunk	0.02	CEMR	0.0
Eurocities	0.02	CEP-CMAF	0.0

Continued

id	indegree (std)	id	outdegree (std)
F. Luis Vives	0.02	CEV	0.0
Maison d'Europe	0.02	Conv. Cat.	0.0
MIC	0.02	CPMR	0.0
PL Office	0.02	Demopunk	0.0
ADICAE	0.0	ECAS	0.0
ATTAC EUROPE	0.0	ERC	0.0
CARITAS España	0.0	Eurodiaconia	0.0
CCDF – LDH	0.0	F. Luis Vives	0.0
ELO	0.0	Maison d'Europe	0.0
F. Schuman	0.0	MIC	0.0
FCCE	0.0	UEAPME	0.0

Notes

1   The Contribution of Civil Society to Bridging the Gap with EU Citizens: Reviewing a Decade of Debate

1. http://europa.eu/lisbon_treaty/glance/democracy/.
2. This notion will be preferred here to that of NGOs, since social partners are non-governmental organisations "strictu senso". See Ruzza (2004) and Greenwood (2007a) for explanation of this term. It is used in order to avoid the exclusion of social partners and in particular business interests, while acknowledging differences between organisations that defend particular interests and those acting on behalf of visions of the general interest.
3. UNICE, created in 1956 to represent employers and business organisations, changed its name to Business Europe in 2007. However, since most of the documents used in this research relate to the period predating this change, the name of UNICE will be used throughout this book.
4. Interview with a Commission official in Brussels, 17 February 2009.
5. Declaration 11 of the Amsterdam Treaty is sometimes presented as the first recognition of civil society in the Treaty. Nevertheless this non-binding declaration simply declares the EU's respect for "the status under national law of churches and religious associations or communities in the Member States".

2   From the Regulation of Lobbies to Participatory Democracy: Agenda Setting and Civil Society in the EU

1. http://ec.europa.eu/civil_society/coneccs/question.cfm?CL=en; CONECCS website, 4 April 2007. The website no longer exists, having been replaced by the register of interest groups and then by the transparency register.

3   Interpretive Frames in the Agenda-Setting Process, 1997–2003

1. The platform started systematically using the shorter name "Social Platform" in 2002.
2. http://ec.europa.eu/civil_society/apgen_En.htm#5, consulted 16 January 2011.
3. Up to nine different organisations in different consultations.

5   Organised Civil Society and the Convention's Agenda

1. An advisor to the Spanish government during the Convention (Interview 34) and a member of the Secretariat of the Catalan Convention (Interview 39).

2. Social Platform, COFACE, ACN, IRI, ELO, CSCG, Polish Office, PFCS, ECAS, CEDAG and Eurocities.

7 The Development of the Participatory Agenda in the Aftermath of the Convention (2003–2011): Consultation and Direct Participation

1. March 2014.
2. http://ec.europa.eu/transparency/civil_society/general_overview_En.htm#6 (consulted 12 February 2013).
3. http://ec.europa.eu/transparency/civil_society/general_overview_En.htm#6 (consulted 12 February 2013).
4. List available from the Commission's ECI portal: http://ec.europa.eu/citizens-initiative/public/initiatives/non-registered (consulted 1 April 2014).
5. The promoters of the campaign ONE MILLION SIGNATURES FOR A EUROPE OF SOLIDARITY filed a complaint to the ECJ following the rejected registration of the initiative: http://curia.europa.eu/juris/document/document.jsf?d oclang=EN&text=&pageIndex=0&part=1&mode=DOC&docid=132107&occ=f irst&dir=&cid=288544 (consulted 1 April 2014).
6. ACN, Forum of European Civil Society, CSCG, ETUC, EFC, Social Platform, ECAS and CEMR.
7. Seventy unregistered organisations against 62 registered ones according to the Consultation website: http://ec.europa.eu/dgs/secretariat_general/citizens_ initiative/contrib_cit_En.htm#noregorg (consulted 16 March 2013).
8. http://www.right2water.eu/ (consulted 24 March 2013.

8 Assessing the Contribution of Participation to Legitimacy

1. Article 11.2, Consolidated version of the Treaty on European Union, Official Journal of the European Union, C 83, 30 March 2010
2. Article 10. Regulation (EU) No. 211/2011 of the European Parliament and of the Council of 16 February 2011 on the citizens' initiative [11 March 2011] Official Journal of the European Union L 65/1.
3. British Liberal Democrat MEP, member of the Convention, well known for his federal position.
4. European Commission, 'Proposal for a regulation of the European Parliament and of the Council on the citizens' initiative' (31 March 2010), 3.

References

Agrikoliansky, Eric. 2007. "Une autre Europe est-elle possible? Les altermondial-istes Français et la constitution: les conditions d'une mobilisation ambigüe." In *La Constitution européenne. Elites, mobilisations et votes*, ed. Antonin Cohen and Antoine Vauchez, 209–236. Bruxelles: Editions de l'Université de Bruxelles.

Airiau, Paul. 2007. "Disputatio Dei', L'action Politique Des Catholiques Français Partisans De 'L'héritage Chrétien." In *La Constitution européenne. Elites, mobilisations et votes*, ed. Antonin Cohen and Antoine Vauchez. Bruxelles: Editions de l'Université de Bruxelles.

Alhadeff, Giampiero and Simon Wilson. 2002. "Civil Society Coming of Age." http://www.globalpolicy.org/ngos/int/eu/2002/05civsoc.htm.

Armstrong, Kenneth A. 2002. "Rediscovering Civil Society: The European Union and the White Paper on Governance." *European Law Journal* 8 (1).

Baisnée, Olivier. 2007. "En être ou pas. Les logiques de l'entre-soi à Bruxelles." *Actes de la recherche en sciences sociales* 166–167: 110–121.

Balme, Richard and Didier Chabanet. 2008. *European Governance and Democracy.* Lanham: Rowman & Littlefield.

Barber, Benjamin. 2003. *Strong Democracy. Participatory Politics for a New Age.* Berkeley and Los Angeles: University of California Press.

Bastin, Gilles. 2002. "Les journalistes accrédités auprès des institutions européennes à Bruxelles." In *Les métiers de l'Europe politique: acteurs et profes-sionnalisations de l'Union européenne*, ed. Didier Georgakakis. Strasbourg: Presses Universitaires de Strasbourg.

Baumgartner, Frank R, Jeffrey M. Berry, Marie Hojnacki, David C. Kimball and Beth L. Leech. 2009. *Lobbying and Policy Change: Who Wins, Who Loses, and Why.* Chicago: University Of Chicago Press.

Bee, Cristiano. 2010. "Understanding the EU's Institutional Communication." In Bee, Cristiano and Bozzini Emanuela (eds) *Mapping the European Public Sphere: Institutions, Media and Civil Society.* Farnham: Ashgate. pp. 83–98.

Bee, Cristiano and Emanuela Bozzini. 2010. *Mapping the European Public Sphere: Institutions, Media and Civil Society.* Farnham: Ashgate.

Bertoncini, Yves and Thierry Chopin. 2010. *Politique européenne. États, pouvoirs et citoyens de l'Union européenne.* Paris: Presses de Sciences Po and Dalloz.

Bindenkrantz, Anne. 2005. "Interest Group Strategies: Navigating between Privileged Access and Strategies of Pressure." *Political Studies* 53: 694–715.

Borrell Fontelles, José Borrell, Carlos Carnero, Diego López Garrido and Ramón Suárez Vázquez. 2003. *Construyendo la constitución europea: crónica política de la Convención.* Madrid: Real Instituto Elcano de Estudios Internacionales y Estratégicos.

Boucher, S. 2007. "Possible to Get Citizens Interested in EU." EurActiv, October 26. http://www.euractiv.com/en/opinion/boucher-possible-get-citizens-interestedeu/article-167912.

Bourdieu, Pierre. 1981. "La représentation politique. Éléments pour une théorie du champ politique." *Actes de la recherche en sciences sociales* 36–37: 3–24. doi:10.3406/arss.1981.2105.
————. 1984. "Quelques propriétés des champs." *Questions de sociologie* 113–121.
Bourdieu, P and Loïc Wacquant. 1992. *An Invitation to Reflexive Sociology* Chicago: University of Chicago Press.
Bouwen, P. 2002 "Corporate Lobbying in the European Union: The Logic of Access." *Journal of European Public Policy* 9 (3): 365–390.
Bouza Garcia, L. 2010. "Democracia participativa, sociedad civil y espacio público en la Unión Europea." Estudios de Progreso. Madrid: Fundación Alternativas.
————. 2012. "How Could Article 11 TEU Contribute to Reduce the EU's Democratic Malaise?" In Dougan, Michael Shuibhne, Niamh Nic and Spaventa Eleanor (eds) *Empowerment and Disempowerment of the European Citizen*, Oxford: Hart Publishing.
Bouza Garcia, L. and Justin Greenwood. 2014. "The European Citizens' Initiative: a new sphere of EU politics?" Forthcoming in *Interest Groups & Advocacy*.
Bozzini, E. 2010. "Framing Anti-discrimination Policy at the EU Level: The Role of Civil Society Organisations." In Bee, Cristiano and Bozzini,Emanuela (eds) *Mapping the European Public Sphere. Institutions, Media and Civil Society.*– Farnham: Ashgate. pp. 195–208.
————. 2011. "The Potential for EU Participatory Engineering. An Empirical Assessment." Paper presented at the ECPR Joint Sessions 2011, University of St Gallen.
Buth, Vanessa. 2011. "Professionalization of NGOs: Friend or Foe of Grassroots Representation?" Paper presented at the 6th ECPR general conference, University of Iceland.
Cammaerts, Bart. 2006. "The eConvention on the Future of Europe: Civil Society and the Use of the Internet in European Decision-making Processes." *Journal of European Integration* 28 (3): 225–245.
Caritas – Eurodiaconia. 2000. *Joint position on the "Consultation Document: Towards a reinforced culture of consultation and dialogue.".*
Castiglione, Dario and Mark E. Warren. 2006. "Rethinking Representation: Eight Theoretical Issues." Paper presented at the conference Rethinking Representation, University of British Columbia, Vancouver.
Castiglione, Dario, ed. 2007. *Constitutional Politics in the European Union: The Convention Moment and Its Aftermath.* Houndmills: Palgrave Macmillan.
de Castro Asarta, Isabel. 2011. "Transparency Register: The Negotiation between Three Different Views of Lobbyists' Legitimacy." Paper presented at the conference New Frontiers in European Studies University of Surrey.
CEDAG. 2003. "'Memorandum on Governance and Civil Dialogue', Position Paper Submitted to the Convention's Forum by CEDAG, 17 January 2003."
Chalmers, Damian. 2003. "The Reconstitution of European Public Spheres." *European Law Journal* 9 (2): 127–189.
Chopin, Thierry. 2008. *Le bal des hypocrites. France – Europe.* Paris: Saint Simon – Lignes de repères.
————. 2010. "Le désarroi Européen." Commentaire 129.
Cini, Michelle. 2008. "European Commission Reform and the Origins of the European Transparency Initiative." *Journal of European Public Policy* 15 (5): 743–760.

de Clerck-Sachsse, Julia. 2012. "Civil Society and Democracy in the EU: The Paradox of the European Citizens' Initiative." *Perspectives on European Politics and Society* 13 (3).

Coen, D. 1997. "The Evolution of the Large Firm as a Political Actor in the European Union." *Journal of European Public Policy* 4 (1): 91–108.

Cohen, Antonin and Antoine Vauchez, eds. 2007. *La Constitution Européenne: Elites, Mobilisations, Votes.* Bruxelles: Editions de l'Université de Bruxelles.

Cohen, Jean and Andrew Arato. 1992. *Civil Society and Political Theory.* Cambridge MA: The MIT Press.

Cook, Deborah. 2008. "Bringing the Citizens Closer to the EU? The Role of Civil Society in Wales in the European Convention." In *Civil Society and Governance in Europe,* ed. William Maloney and Jan van Deth, 91–108. Cheltenham: Edward Elgar.

Costa, Olivier. 2009. "Le Parlement européen dans le système décisionnel de l'Union européenne: la puissance au prix de l'illisibilité." *Politique Européenne* 28 (2): 129–155.

Cuesta López, Víctor. 2008. *Participación directa e iniciativa legislativa del ciudadano en democracia constitucional,* Pamplona: Aranzadi.

——. 2010. "The Lisbon Treaty's Provisions on Democratic Principles: A Legal Framework for Participatory Democracy." *European Public Law Review* 16 (1): 123–138.

——. 2012. "A Comparative Approach to the Regulation on the European Citizens' Initiative." *Perspectives on European Politics and Society* 13 (3): 257–269.

Curtin, Deirdre. 2003. "Private Interest: Representation or Civil Society Deliberation? A Contemporary Dilemma for European Union Governance." *Social and Legal Studies* 12 (1): 55–75.

Delanty, Gerard and Rumford, Chris. 2005. *Rethinking Europe: Social Theory and the Implications of Europeanization.* London and New York: Routledge.

Della Porta, Donatella. 2007. "The Europeanization of Protest: A Typology and Empirical Evidence." In *Debating the Democratic Legitimacy of the European Union,* ed. Beate Kohler-Koch and Bertold Rittberger, 189–208. Lanham: Rowman & Littlefield.

Diedrichs, Ulrich and Wolfgang Wessels. 2006. "The Commission and the Council." In D. Spence and G. Edwards (eds) *The European Commission.* London: John Harper. pp. 209–234.

DiMaggio, Paul J. 1991. "Constructing an Organizational Field as a Professional Project: U.S. Art Museums, 1920–1940." In *The New Institutionalism in Organizational Analysis,* ed. Walter W. Powell and Paul J. DiMaggio, 267–292. Chicago: The University of Chicago Press.

DiMaggio, Paul J. and Walter W. Powell. 1991. "The Iron Cage Revisited: Institutional Isomorphism and Collective Rationality." In *The New Institutionalism in Organizational Analysis,* ed. Paul J. DiMaggio and Walter W. Powell, 63–82. Chicago: The University of Chicago Press.

Dreger, Jonas. 2008. "The Influence of Environmental NGOs on the Design of the Emissions Trading Scheme of the EU: An Application of the Advocacy Coalition Framework." *Bruges Political Research Papers* (9). http://www.coleurope.eu/template.asp?pagename=polresearch.

Dufour, Pascale. 2010. "The Mobilization Against the 2005 Treaty Establishing a Constitution for Europe: A French Mobilization for Another Europe." *Social Movement Studies* 9 (4): 425–441.

ECAS. 2002. "ECAS Contribution to the Commission's Consultation Document 'Towards a Reinforced Culture of Consultation and Dialogue'."

Eder, Klaus and Hans-Jörg Trenz. 2007. "Prerequisites of Transnational Democracy and Mechanisms for Sustaining It: The Case of the European Union." In *Debating the Democratic Legitimacy of the European Union*, ed. Beate Kohler-Koch and Bertold Rittberger. Lanham: Rowman & Littlefield.

Eising, R. 2007. "The Access of Business Interests to EU Institutions: Towards Elite Pluralism?" *Journal of European Public Policy* 14(3): 384–403.

Eliasoph, Nina. 1998. *Avoiding Politics: How Americans Produce Apathy in Everyday Life*. Cambridge MA: Cambridge University Press.

Engel, Filip. 2007. "Analyzing Policy Learning in European Union Policy Formulation: The Advocacy Coalition Framework Meets New-Institutional Theory." *Bruges Political Research Papers.* http://www.coleurope.eu/template. asp?pagename=polresearch.

Eriksen, Erik Oddvar. 2000. "Deliberative Supranationalism in the EU." In *Democracy in the European Union: Integration Through Deliberation?* ed. Erik Oddvar Eriksen and John Erik Fossum. London and New York: Routledge.

———. 2007. "Conceptualising European Public Spheres. General, Segmented and Strong Publics." In *The European Union and the Public Sphere. A Communicative Space in the Making?* ed. John Erik Fossum and Philip Schlesinger. London: Routledge.

Eriksen, Erik Oddvar and John Erik Fossum. 2000. *Democracy in the European Union: Integration through Deliberation?* London and New York: Routledge.

Eurocommerce. 2000. "Commission Discussion Paper: 'The Commission and NGOs: Building a Stronger Partnership'."

European Commission. 1992. *An open and structured dialogue between the Commission and special interest groups*. Brussels: European Commission.

———. 1997. *Communication from the Commission on Promoting the Role of Voluntary Organisations and Foundations in Europe*. Brussels: European Commission.

———. 2000. The Commission and Non-governmental Organizations: Building a Stronger Partnership. Brussels: European Commission.

———. 2001. *European Governance. A White Paper*. COM (2001) 428 final. Brussels: European Commission.

———. 2002a. *Communication from the Commission on Impact Assessment*. COM(2002) 276 final. Brussels: European Commission.

———. 2002b. *Communication from the Commission. Action Plan "Simplifying and Improving the Regulatory Environment"*. COM (2002) 278 final. Brussels: European Commission.

———. 2002c. *Towards a Reinforced Culture of Consultation and Dialogue – General Principles and Minimum Standards for Consultation of Interested Parties by the Commission*. COM (2002) 704 final. Brussels: European Commission.

———. 2005a. *The Commission's Contribution to the Period of Reflection and Beyond: Plan D for Democracy, Dialogue and Debate*. COM (2005) 494 final. Brussels: European Commission.

————. 2005b. *Report from the Commission "Better Lawmaking 2004" pursuant to Protocol 9 on the application of the Principles of subsidiarity and proportionality.*COM (2005) 98 final. Brussels: European Commission.

————.2006a. *White Paper on European Communication Policy.*COM (2006) 35 final. Brussels: European Commission.

————.2006b. *Green Paper European Transparency Initiative.*COM (2006) 194 final. Brussels: European Commission.

————. 2007a. *Communication from the Commission – Follow-up to the Green Paper 'European Transparency Initiative'.* COM (2007) 127 final. Brussels: European Commission.

————. 2007b. *Communication from the Commission – Outcome of the Public Consultation on the Commission's Green Paper "Modernising labour law to meet the of the 21st century"* COM (2007) 627 final. Brussels: European Commission.

————. 2009. *Green Paper on a European Citizens' Initiative* COM(2009) 622 final. Brussels: European Commission.————. 2014. *Communication from the Commission on the European Citizens' Initiative "Water and sanitation are a human right! Water is Water is a public good, not a commodity!"* COM(2014) 177 final, provisional final version. Brussels: European Commission.

ECAS (undated) "Comments on the paper 'Towards a reinforced culture of consultation and dialogue – proposal for general principles and minimum standards for consultation of interested parties by the Commission'".

European Council. 2001. *Presidency Conclusions of the Laeken European Council (14 and 15 December 2001): Annex I: Laeken Declaration on the Future of the European Union.* Brussels: European Council.

European Foundation Centre 2002. "European Commission White Paper European Governance (Com 2001 – 428 final). EFC Position" Brussels, 18 March 2002.

European Parliament. 1998 *Report on the Communication from the Commission on promoting the role of voluntaryorganizations and foundations in Europe* (COM(97)0241 – C4–0546/97), May, PE 226.444/fin.

————. 2008. *Report on the Perspectives for Developing Civil Dialogue Under the Treaty of Lisbon.* Brussels: European Parliament.

European Parliament and European Commission. 2011. *Agreement between the European Parliament and the European Commission on the establishment of a transparency register for organisations and self-employed individuals engaged in EU policy-making and policy implementation. Official Journal of the European Union* 22.7.2011. L191/29.

Fairclough, Norman. 2003. *Analysing Discourse: Textual Analysis for Social Research.* London: Routledge.

————. 2005. "Discourse Analysis in Organization Studies: The Case for Critical Realism" *Organization Studies* 26: 915–939.

Fazi, Elodie and Jeremy Smith. 2006. "Civil Dialogue: Making It Work Better. Civil Society Contact Group." http://act4europe.horus.be/module/FileLib/Civil%20 dialogue,%20making%20it%20work%20better.pdf.

Fligstein, Neil and Doug McAdam. 2012. *A Theory of Fields.* New York: Oxford University Press.

Follesdal, Andreas and Simon Hix. 2006. "Why There Is a Democratic Deficit in the EU: A Response to Majone and Moravcsik." *Journal of Common Market Studies* 44 (3): 533–562.

Font Fábregas, Joan and Elisa Rodríguez Ortiz. 2007. "Contenidos, estrategias y consignas: factores de voto en el referéndum español sobre la Constitución Europea." *Revista de Estudios Políticos* (138): 95–127.

Fossum, John Erik and Philip Schlesinger (eds). 2007. *The European Union and the Public Sphere: A Communicative Space in the Making?* London: Routledge.

François, Bastien and Erik Neveu. 1999. *Les espaces publics mosaïques : acteurs, arènes et rhétoriques des débats publics contemporains.* Rennes: Presses universitaires de Rennes.

Friedrich, Dawid. 2011. *Democratic Participation and Civil Society in the European Union.* Manchester: Manchester University Press.

Gabaglio, Emilio, Georges Jacobs and Joao Cravinho. 2003. "Joint Contribution by the Social Partners' Representatives in the Convention Working Group on Social Europe. Question 7: Role of the Social Partners."

Georgakakis, Didier. 2004. "Was It Really Just 'poor Communication'? Lessons from the Santer Commission's Resignation." In Andy Smith (ed.) *Politics and the European Commission. Actors, Interdependence, Legitimacy.* London: Routledge. pp. 119–133.

Giorgi, Liana and John Crowley. 2006. "The Political Sociology of the European Public Sphere." In Giorgi, Liana, Ingmar Von Homeyer and Wayne Parsons (eds) *Democracy in the European Union: Towards the Emergence of a Public Sphere.* London and New York: Routledge. pp 1–23

Giorgi, Liana, Ingmar Von Homeyer and Wayne Parsons. 2006. *Democracy in the European Union. Towards the Emergence of a Public Sphere.* London: Routledge.

Glencross, Andrew and Alexander Trechsel. 2011. "First or Second Order Referendums? Understanding the Votes on the EU Constitutional Treaty in Four EU Member States." *West European Politics* 34 (4): 755–772.

Goffman, Erving. 2006. *Frame Analysis.* Madrid: Centro de Investigaciones Sociológicas.

Grant, David, Cynthia Hardy and Linda Putnam. 2004. *The Sage Handbook of Organizational Discourse.* London: Sage.

Grant, Wyn. 2000. *Pressure Groups and British Politics.* Basingstoke: Palgrave Macmillan.

Green 8. 2002. "The future of the European Union. Environment and sustainable development. Initial Contribution to the Convention on the Future of Europe" 18 April 2002.

Greenwood, Justin. 2007a. "Governance and Organised Civil Society at the European Union Level: The Search for 'Input Legitimacy' Through Elite Groups." In Della Sala, Vincent and Carlo Ruzza (eds) *Governance and Civil Society: Policy Perspectives.* Manchester: Manchester University Press.

———. 2007b. "Review Article: Organized Civil Society and Democratic Legitimacy in the European Union." *British Journal of Political Science* 37: 333–357.

———. 2011a. "The Lobby Regulation Element of the European Transparency Initiative: Between Liberal and Deliberative Models of Democracy." *Comparative European Politics* 9 (3): 317–343.

———. 2011b. *Interest Representation in the European Union.* 3rd ed. Houndmills: Palgrave Macmillan.

———. 2011c. "Actors of the Common Interest? The Brussels Offices of the Regions" *Journal of European Integration* 33 (July): 437–451.

————. 2011d. "The European Commission's Relations with Interest Organisations: Master of the Information Universe?" In *The Politics of Information in the EU*. University of Maastricht.

Greenwood, Justin and Darren Halpin. 2007. "The European Commission and the Public Governance of Interest Groups in the European Union: Seeking a Niche between Accreditation and Laissez-Faire." *Perspectives on European Politics and Society* 7 (2): 189–210.

Haas, Peter. 1992. "Introduction: Epistemic Communities and International Policy Coordination." *International Organization* 46 (1).

Habermas, Jürgen. 1989. *The Structural Transformation of the Public Sphere*. Cambridge: Polity Press.

————. 2000. La *Constelación Postnacional*. Barcelona: Paidòs.

————. 2001. "Why Europe Needs a Constitution." *New Left Review* 11 (September–October): 5–26.

Halpin, Darren and Peter McLaverty. 2010. "Legitimating INGO Advocacy: The Case of Internal Democracies." In *Evaluating Transnational NGOs: Legitimacy, Accountability, Representation*, ed. Steffek, Jens and Kristina Hahn. Basingstoke: Palgrave Macmillan.

Hix, Simon. 2005. *The Political System of the European Union*. 2nd ed. Houndmills: Palgrave.

Hooghe, Liesbet and Gary Marks. 2009. "A Postfunctionalist Theory of European Integration: From Permissive Consensus to Constraining Dissensus." *British Journal of Political Science* 39 (1): 1–23.

Howarth, D. 2000. *Discourse*. Buckingham: Open University Press.

Hula, Kevin W. 1999. *Lobbying Together. Interest Group Coalitions in Legislative Politics*. Washington, DC: Georgetown University Press.

Imig, Doug and Sidney Tarrow. 2001. *Contentious Europeans: Protest and Politics in an Emerging Polity*. Lanham: Rowman & Littlefield.

IRI. 2004. *Transnational Democracy in the Making*. IRI Handbook. Amsterdam: Initiative and Referendum Institute Europe.

Joerges, Christian. 2002. "Deliberative Supranationalism-Two Defences." *European Law Journal* 8 (1).

Johansson, Håkan and Lee Jayeon. 2014. "The European Social Platform as a Strategic Action Field." Paper presented at the workshop *Towards a Relational Approach to EU Civil Society Networks* 17–18 February 2014 Lund, Sweden.

Jorgensen, M.W. and L.J. Phillips. 2002. *Discourse Analysis as Theory and Method*. London: SAGE.

Kaelble, Hartmut. 2002. "The Historical Rise of a European Public Sphere?" *Journal of European Integration History* 8 (2): 9–22.

Kaldor, Mary. 1995. "European Institutions, Nation-States and Nationalism." In *Cosmopolitan Democracy. An Agenda for a New World Order*, ed. Daniele Archibugi and David Held. Cambridge: Polity Press.

Kingdon, John W. 2003. *Agendas, Alternatives, and Public Policies*. 2nd ed. New York: Longman.

Klüver, Heike. 2013. *Lobbying in the European Union: Interest Groups, Lobbying Coalitions, and Policy Change*. Oxford: Oxford University Press.

Knoke, David and Song Yang. 2008. Social Network Analysis: Quantitative Applications in the Social Sciences. 2nd ed. Thousand Oaks: SAGE.

Kohler-Koch, Beate. 2007. "The Organization of Interests and Democracy in the European Union" In *Debating the Democratic Legitimacy of the European Union*, ed. Beate Kohler-Koch and Bertold Rittberger, 255–271. Lanham: Rowman & Littlefield.

———. 2010a. "Civil Society and EU Democracy: 'Astroturf' Representation?" *Journal of European Public Policy* 17 (1): 100–116.

———. 2010b. "Is There an EU Model for Participatory Governance and Does It Hold Its Promises?." Paper prepared for the conference "What Can Canada and the European Union Learn from Each Other?" University of Victoria.

Kohler-Koch, Beate and Barbara Finke. 2007. "The Institutional Shaping of EU-Society Relation: a Contribution to Democracy via Participation?" *Journal of Civil Society* 3 (3): 205–221.

Kohler-Koch, Beate and Christine Quittkat. 2011. "What Is 'Civil Society' and Who Represents It in the European Union?" In *The New Politics of European Civil Society*, ed. Ulrike Liebert and Hans-Jörg Trenz, 19–39. London; New York: Routledge.

———. (2013). *De-mystification of Participatory Democracy: EU-governance and Civil Society*. Oxford: Oxford University Press.

Kohler-Koch, Beate and Bertold Rittberger, eds. 2007. *Debating the Democratic Legitimacy of the European Union*. Lanham: Rowman & Littlefield.

Kriesi, Hanspeter. 2007. "Going Public in the European Union: Action Repertoires of Western European Collective Political Actors." *Comparative Political Studies* 40 (1): 48–73.

Kværk, Geir. 2007. "Organised Civil Society in the EU Constitution-making Process." In *Public Sphere and Civil Society?* ed. John Erik Fossum, Erik Oddvar Eriksen and Geir Kvaerk, 141–224. ARENA Report Series. http://www.arena.uio.no/cidel.

Lamassoure, Alain. 2004. *Histoire secrète de la convention européenne*. Paris: Albin Michel.

Leustean, Lucian. 2007. "The Place of God: Religious Terms in the Debate on the European Constitution." In *La Constitution européenne. Élites, mobilisations et votes*, ed. Antoine Vauchez and Antonin Cohen. Bruxelles: Editions de l'Université de Bruxelles.

Liaison Committee of Development NGOs to the European Union. 2000. "European Commission Discussion Document on 'NGO-Commission relations: Building Stronger Partnerships.' Response from the NGDO-EU Liaison Committee." Brussels, April 2000.

Lijphart, A. 1999. *Patterns of Democracy: Government Forms and Performance in Thirty-six Countries*. New Haven and London: Yale University Press.

Lindblom, Charles E. 1977. *Politics and Markets: The World's Political-Economic Systems*. New York: Basic Books.

Lindberg, L. and S. Scheingold. 1970. *Europe's Would Be Polity*. Englewood Cliffs, NJ: Prentice Hall.

Lindgren, Karl-Oskar and Thomas Persson. 2011. *Participatory Governance in the EU*. Houndmills: Palgrave Macmillan.

Lombardo, Emanuela. 2007. "The Participation of Civil Society." In *Constitutional Politics in the European Union: The Convention Moment and Its Aftermath*, ed. Dario Castiglione. Houndmills: Palgrave Macmillan.

Magnette, Paul. 2004. "La Convention Européenne: argumenter et négocier dans une assemblée constituante multinationale." *Revue Française de Science Politique* 54 (1): 5–42.

———. 2006. "Democracy in the European Union: Why and How to Combine Representation and Participation." In *Civil Society And Legitimate European Governance*, ed. Stijn Smismans, 23–41. Cheltenham: Edward Elgar.

Mahoney, Christine. 2007. "Networking vs. Allying: The Decision of Interest Groups to Join Coalitions in the US and the EU." *Journal of European Public Policy* 14 (3): 363–383.

———. 2008a. "The Role of Interest Groups in Fostering Citizen Engagement: The Determinants of Outside Lobbying." In *Civil Society and Governance in Europe. From National to International Linkages*, ed. William Maloney and Jan van Deth. Cheltenham: Edward Elgar.

———. 2008b. *Brussels versus the Beltway: Advocacy in the United States and the European Union*. American Governance and Public Policy Series. Washington, DC: Georgetown University Press.

Mahoney, Christine and Michael Beckstrand. 2011. "Following the Money: European Union Funding of Civil Society Organizations." *Journal of Common Market Studies* 49 (6): 1339–1361.

Majone, Giandomenico. 2002. "The European Commission: The Limits of Centralization and the Perils of Parliamentarization." *Governance* 15 (3): 375–392.

Mallaina García, C. 2009. *Nuevos desafíos democráticos: hacia una iniciativa legislativa popular efectiva*. Madrid: Fundación Alternativas.

Maloney, William and Jan van Deth, eds. 2008. "Introduction." In *Civil Society and Governance in Europe: From National to International Linkages*. Cheltenham: Edward Elgar.

Mazey, S. and J. Richardson. 2006. "Interest groups and EU policy-making: organizational logic and venue shopping". In J. Richardson (ed.) *European Union:Power and Policy-Making*, London and New York: Routledge. pp. 247–265.

McLaverty, Peter. 2002. "Civil Society and Democracy." *Contemporary Politics* 8 (4): 303–318.

Méndez de Vigo, Íñigo. 2005. *El rompecabezas. Así redactamos la Constitución Europea*. Madrid: Biblioteca Nueva – Real Instituto Elcano.

Michailidou, Asimina. 2010. "Vertical Europeanisation of Online Public Dialogue: EU Public Communication Policy and Online Implementation." In *Mapping the European Public Sphere. Institutions, Media and Civil Society*, ed. Cristiano Bee and Emanuela Bozzini, 65–82. Farnham: Ashgate.

Michel, Hélène. 2007. "Les groupes d'intérêt et la consultation sur le Livre blanc: objectivation et institutionnalisation de la 'société civile' " In *La nouvelle gouvernance européenne. Genèses et usages d'un Livre blanc*, ed. Didier Georgakakis and Marine de Lasalle. Strasbourg: Presses Universitaires de Strasbourg.

Milton, Guy and Jacques Keller-Noëllet. 2005. The European Constitution: Its Origins, Negotiation and Meaning. London: John Harper Publishing.

Monaghan, Elizabeth. 2007. "Civil Society, Democratic Legitimacy and the European Union: Democratic Linkage and the Debate on the Future of the EU". PhD thesis, Nottingham: University of Nottingham.

———. 2012. "Assessing Participation and Democracy in the EU: The Case of the European Citizens' Initiative." *Perspectives on European Politics and Society* 13 (3): 285–298.

Moravcsik, Andrew. 2006. "What Can We Learn from the Collapse of the European Constitutional Project?" *Politische Vierteljahresschrift* 47 (2): 219–241.

Muller, Pierre. 2008. *Les politiques publiques*. 17th ed. Paris: Presses Universitaires de France.

Naurin, Daniel. 2007. *Deliberation behind Closed Doors: Transparency and Lobbying in the European Union*. ECPR Monographs. Hampshire: ECPR Press.

Nicolaïdis, Kalypso. 2003. "Our European Demoi-cracy: Is This Constitution a Third Way for Europe?" In *Whose Europe? National Models and the Constitution of the European Union*, ed. Kalypso Nicolaïdis and Stephen Weatherill. Oxford: Oxford University Press.

Norman, Peter. 2005. *The Accidental Constitution: The Making of Europe's Constitutional Treaty*. 2nd ed. Brussels: EuroComment.

Papadopoulos, Yannis and Paul Magnette. 2010. "On the Politicisation of the European Union: Lessons from Consociational National Polities." *West European Politics* 33 (4): 711–729.

Parés, Marc, ed. 2009. *Participación y calidad democrática. Evaluando las nuevas formas de democracia participativa*. Barcelona: Ariel.

Pérez Díaz, Víctor. 1994a. "Le défi de l'espace public européen." *Transeuropéennes* 3: 39–48.

———. 1994b. La primacía de la sociedad civil: el proceso de formación de la España democrática. Madrid: Alianza.

Pérez Solórzano-Borragán, Nieves. 2007. "The Convention Experience: Between Rhetoric and Participation." *Journal of Civil Society* 3 (3): 271–286.

Pérez-Solórzano Borragán, Nieves and Stijn Smismans. 2012. "Representativeness: A Tool to Structure Interest Intermediation in the European Union?" *Journal of Common Market Studies* 50 (3): 403–421.

Pichler, Johannes W. 2008 (ed.) *We change Europe! The European initiative – Art 8b(4) Treaty of Lisbon*. Wien: Neuer Wissenschaftlicher Verlag.

Pitkin, Hanna F. 1972. *The Concept of Representation*. Berkeley and Los Angeles: University of California Press.

Pohl, Christine. 2006. *Transparency in the EU decision making: reality or myth?* Brussels: Friends of Earth Europe. http://www.foeeurope.org/publications/2006/ Transparency_in_EU_decision_making_May2006.pdf.

Polish NGO Office in Brussels (Undated document) "European Governance White Paper".

Princen, Sebastiaan. 2009. *Agenda-setting in the European Union*. Houndmills: Palgrave Macmillan.

Princen, Sebastiaan and Bart Kerremans. 2010. "Opportunity Structures in the EU Multi-Level System." In Beyers, Jan, Rainer Eising and William A. Maloney, ed. *Interest Group Politics in Europe: Lessons from EU Studies and Comparative Politics*, London and New York: Routledge.

Quittkat, Christine. 2011. "The European Commission's Online Consultations: A Success Story?" *Journal of Common Market Studies* 49 (3): 653–674.

Quittkat, Christine and Peter Kotzian. 2011. "Lobbying via Consultation — Territorial and Functional Interests in the Commission's Consultation Regime." *Journal of European Integration* 33 (4): 401–418.

del Río Villar, Susana. 2004. "La Sociedad Civil y Su Progresiva Participación En La Construcción Europea: De La Conferencia Intergubernamental De 1996 a La Convención Constitucional. Un Proceso Constituyente Para La Unión, Un Referéndum Para El Demos Europeo." Tesis doctoral, Universidad del País Vasco.

———. 2006 "La creación de un modelo europeo de debate participativo, comunicativo y solidario." In del Río Villar et al. *Europa: el estado de la Unión*, Pamplona: Arazandi.

———. 2008. *Ciudadanía Activa En Europa: Proceso Participativo y Nuevos Espacios Para La Comunicación*. 2nd ed. Madrid: Grupo Difusión.

Ruzza, Carlo. 2004. *Europe and Civil Society: Movement Coalitions and European Governance*. Manchester: Manchester University Press.

———. 2007. "Advocacy Coalitions and the Participation of Organised Civil Society in the European Union." In *Governance and Civil Society: Policy Perspectives*, ed. Vincent della Sala and Carlo Ruzza, 47–71. Manchester: Manchester University Press.

———. 2011. "Social Movements and the European Interest Intermediation of Public Interest Groups." *Journal of European Integration* 33 (4): 453–469.

Sabatier, Paul A. 1998. "The Advocacy Coalition Framework: Revisions and Relevance for Europe." *Journal of European Public Policy* 5 (1): 8–130.

Sabatier, Paul A. and Hank C. Jenkins-Smith, eds. 1993. *Policy Change and Learning: An Advocacy Coalition Approach*. Boulder, CO: Westview Press.

Sánchez-Salgado, Rosa. 2007 *Comment l'Europe construit la société civile*. Paris: Dalloz.

———. 2007b. "Civil Society Mapping Study: The Case of Spain." Civil Society Mapping Study, Notre Europe.

Saurugger, Sabine. 2007. "Démocratiser l'Union européenne par le bas? Des 'groupes d'intérêt' à la 'société civile organisée '." In *La Constitution européenne. Elites, mobilisations et votes*, ed. Antonin Cohen and Antoine Vauchez. Bruxelles: Editions de l'Université de Bruxelles.

———. 2010. "The Social Construction of the Participatory Turn: The Emergence of a Norm in the European Union." *European Journal of Political Research* 49: 471–495.

Scharpf, Fritz W. 1999. *Governing in Europe: Effective and Democratic?* Oxford: Oxford University Press.

Schlesinger, Philip and Kevin Deirdre. 2000. "Can the European Union Become a Public Sphere of Politics?" In *Democracy in the European Union: Integration Through Deliberation?* ed. Erik Oddvar Eriksen and John Erik Fossum, 206–229. London and New York: Routledge.

Schmidt, Vivien. 2010. "Taking Ideas and Discourse Seriously: Explaining Change through Discursive Institutionalism as the Fourth 'New Institutionalism'." *European Political Science Review* 2 (1): 1–25.

Schmidt, Vivien A. 2009. "Re-Envisioning the European Union: Identity, Democracy, Economy." *JCMS: Journal of Common Market Studies* 47 (Annual Review): 17–42.

De Schutter, Olivier. 2002. "Europe in Search of Its Civil Society." *European Law Journal* 8 (2): 198–217.

Scott, Richard. 2008. *Institutions and Organizations. Ideas and Interests*. 3rd ed. Thousand Oaks: Sage Publications.

Secretariat General of the European Commission. 2003. "Memo to the Members of the Commission. Subject: Update on the Work of the European Convention SEC (2003) 614. Agenda 1613 — Item 6."

Secretariat of the European Convention. 2002a. "Digest of Contributions to the Forum CONV 112/02." Brussels, 17 June 2002

——. 2002b. "Information Note: Contact Groups (Civil Society) CONV 120/02." Brussels 19 June 2002.

——. 2003a. "Note from Praesidium to Convention. Subject: The Democratic Life of the Union." CONV 650/03."

——. 2003b. "Draft Constitution, Volume I. Revised text of Part One" CONV 724/03 Brussels, 26 May 2003

Sloat, Amanda. 2003. "The Preparation of the Governance White Paper." *Politics* 23 (2): 128–136.

Smismans, Stijn. 2003. "European Civil Society: Shaped by Discourses and Institutional Interests." *European Law Journal* 9 (4).

——. 2004 (ed.) *Law, Legitimacy, and European Governance: Functional Participation in Social Regulation.* Oxford Studies in European Law. Oxford: Oxford University Press.

——. 2006. *Civil Society and Legitimate European Governance.* Edgar Elgar.

Social Platform (2000) "Response of the Platform of European Social NGOs. 'The Commission and NGOs: Building a Stronger Partnership'." Brussels, 27 April 2000. Available online at: http://cms.horus.be/site/99907/PolicyStatement.asp?Policy=8104

——. 2001. "Democracy, Governance and European NGOs. Building a Stronger Structured Civil Dialogue", Brussels, March 2001. Available online at: http://cms.horus.be/site/99907/PolicyStatement.asp?Policy=8104

——. 2002a. "Letter to Commission's President, Romano Prodi. Contribution of the Social Platform to the 2002 Consultation on the minimal standards of consultation." Available online at: http://cms.horus.be/site/99907/News.asp?news=9431

——. 2002b "*(un)CONVENTIONAL EUROPE. Position paper submitted to the Convention's Forum by the Social Platform.*" Available online at: http://cms.horus.be/site/99907/Page_Generale.asp?DocID=11617

——. 2010 "Re: Green Paper on citizens' initiative – complement it with a consultation on how to organise the dialogue with civil society organisations, as provided by article 11 of the Lisbon Treaty, contribution of the Platform of European Social NGOs to the consultation on the Green Paper on a European Citizens Initiative" Brussels, 27 January 2010. Available online at: http://ec.europa.eu/dgs/secretariat_general/citizens_initiative/docs/social_platform_En.pdf

Smith, Graham. 2009. *Democratic Innovations.* Cambridge: Cambridge Univerity Press.

Snow, David E, Burke Rochford, Steven Worden and Robert Benford. 1986. "Frame Alignment Processes, Micromobilization and Movement Participation." *American Sociological Review* 51 (4): 464–486.

van de Steeg, Marianne. 2010. "Theoretical Reflections on the Public Sphere in the European Union: a Network of Communication or a Political Community?" In *Mapping the European Public Sphere. Institutions, Media and Civil Society*, ed. Cristiano Bee and Emanuela Bozzini, 31–49. Farnham: Ashgate.

Steffek, Jens and Kristina Hahn, eds. 2010. *Evaluating Transnational NGOs: Legitimacy, Accountability, Representation.* Houndmills: Palgrave Macmillan.

Steffek, Jens and Patrizia Nanz, eds. 2008. *Civil Society Participation in European and Global Governance: A Cure for the Democratic Deficit?* Transformations of the State Series. Houndmills: Palgrave Macmillan.

Stone Sweet, Alec, Neil Fligstein and Wayne Sandholtz. 2001. "The Institutionalization of European Space." In *The Institutionalization of Europe*, ed. Alec Stone Sweet, Neil Fligstein, and Wayne Sandholtz, 1–28. Oxford: Oxford University Press.

Sudbery, Imogen. 2003. "Bridging the Legitimacy Gap in the EU: Can Civil Society Help to Bring the Union Closer to Its Citizens?" *Collegium* (26): 75–97.

de Swaan, Abram. 2007. "The European Void: The Democratic Deficit as a Cultural Deficiency." In *The European Union and the Public Sphere. A Communicative Space in the Making?* ed. John Erik Fossum, and Philip Schlesinger. London: Routledge.

Szeligowska, Dorota and Elitsa Mincheva. 2012. "The European Citizens' Initiative – Empowering European Citizens within the Institutional Triangle: A Political and Legal Analysis." *Perspectives on European Politics and Society* 13 (3): 270–284.

Tarrow, Sidney. 2004. *El Poder En Movimiento*. 2nd ed. Madrid: Alianza.

Trenz, Hans-Jörg. 2007. "A Transnational Space of Contention? Patterns of Europeanisation of Civil Society in Germany." In *Governance and Civil Society in the European Union: Normative Perspectives*, ed. Carlo Ruzza and Vincent della Sala, 89–112. Manchester: Manchester University Press.

———. 2010. "The Europeanisation of Political Communication: Conceptual Clarifications and Empirical Measurements." In *Mapping the European Public Sphere. Institutions, Media and Civil Society*, ed. Cristiano Bee and Emanuela Bozzini, 15–30. Farnham: Ashgate.

Trenz, Hans-Jörg and Klaus Eder. 2004. "The Democratising Dynamics of a European Public Sphere: Towards a Theory of Democratic Functionalism." *European Journal of Social Theory* (6): 5–25.

UNICE. 2002. "UNICE position on the EU Convention". 17–06–2002.

———. 2002. "Communication from the Commission: Towards a Reinforced Culture of Consultation and Dialogue. UNICE Comments."

Warleigh, Alex. 2001. "Europeanizing' Civil Society: NGOs as Agents of Political Socialization." *Journal of Common Market Studies* 39 (4): 619–639.

———. 2003. *Democracy and the European Union. Theory, Practice and Reform.* London: Thousand Oaks: SAGE.

Warren, Mark E. 2001. Democracy and Association. Princeton: Princeton University Press.

Weiler, J. H. H. (2003) "In defence of the status quo: Europe's constitutional Sonderweg." In Weiler, J. H. H. and M. Wind eds. *European Constitutionalism beyond the State*. Cambridge: Cambridge University Press.

Wessels, Bridgette. 2010. "The Public Sphere and the European Information Society." In *Mapping the European Public Sphere. Institutions, Media and Civil Society*, ed. Cristiano Bee and Emanuela Bozzini, 47–62. Farnham: Ashgate.

De Wilde, Pieter. 2011. "No Polity for Old Politics? A Framework for Analyzing the Politicization of European Integration." *Journal of European Integration* 33: 559–575.

Will, Catherine, Isabel Crowhurst, Ola Larsson, Jeremy Kendall, Lars-Erik Olsson and Marie Nordfeldt. 2005. "The Challenges of Translation: The Convention and Debates on the Future of Europe from the Perspective of European Third Sectors." *Third Sector European Policy Working Papers* (12).

Will, Catherine and Jeremy Kendall. 2009. "A New Settlement for Europe: Towards 'open, Transparent and Dialogue with Representative Associations and Civil Society'?" In *Handbook on Third Sector Policy in Europe: Multi-Level Processes and Organized Civil Society*, ed. Jeremy Kendall, 293–316. Cheltenham: Edward Elgar.

Zald, Mayer. 1996. "Culture, Ideology and Strategic Framing." In *Comparative Perspectives on Social Movements*, ed. Doug McAdam, Mayer Zald and John McCarthy, 261–274. Cambridge: Cambridge University Press.

Zimmer, A. and M. Freise 2008. "Bringing Society Back In: Civil Society, Social Capital and the Third Sector." In Maloney, W. and J. Van Deth (eds) *Civil Society and Governance in Europe: From National to International Linkages*Cheltenham: Edward Elgar.

Zito, Anthony R. 2001. "Epistemic Communities, Collective Entrepreneurship and European Integration." *Journal of European Public Policy* 8 (4): 585–603.

Index

CPSIA information can be obtained at www.ICGtesting.com
Printed in the USA
LVOW07*2310270315

432297LV00002B/18/P